MD

3+

D0085172

WITHDRAWN

Responses to
Christa Wolf

838.91
W 831zf

Responses to Christa Wolf
Critical Essays

Edited by
Marilyn Sibley Fries

WAYNE STATE UNIVERSITY PRESS   DETROIT   1989

Copyright © 1989 by Wayne State University Press, Detroit, Michigan 48202.
All rights are reserved. No part of this book may be reproduced without
formal permission.
93 92 91 90 89   5 4 3 2 1

Library of Congress Cataloging-in-Publication Data

Responses to Christa Wolf : critical essays / edited by Marilyn Sibley
Fries.
    p. cm.
    "Conceived around the response to a special session on Christa
Wolf at the annual convention of the Modern Language Association of
America, held in Los Angeles in December 1982"—Pref.
    Includes bibliographical references.
    ISBN 0–8143–2130–5
    1. Wolf, Christa—Criticism and interpretation.   I. Fries,
Marilyn Sibley, 1945–
PT2685.O36Z86   1989
838'.91409—dc20
                                        89–36490
                                              CIP

Contents

CAT Mar 12 '90

5

ALLEGHENY COLLEGE LIBRARY

89 - 6317

Contents

Acknowledgments

This volume was conceived around the response to a special session on Christa Wolf at the annual convention of the Modern Language Association of America, held in Los Angeles in December 1982. In 1981, when the session was being organized and the proposal submitted for inclusion at the annual conference, several colleagues expressed reservations about the appropriateness of such a topic and cautioned that the proposal might face opposition; this was an East German author, the translation of whose *Quest for Christa T.*, published in 1970, had been out of print for several intervening years. Fortunately, this was not the case; not only was the session accepted, but the call for papers elicited more excellent responses than I could include there, and the audience in Los Angeles overflowed its space to listen to papers by Helen Fehervary, Anne Herrmann, Karin McPherson, and Rainer Nägele, all of which are presented here in revised form.

What might have been regarded as a groundswell then has become unremarkable in the interim. Christa Wolf's works are no longer known only to the initiated few, taught only in German departments, or the concern only of people interested in the literary developments of a divided postwar Germany. As Joyce Crick correctly (and reluctantly) notes in her essay, Christa Wolf has become something of a "cult figure"; Crick is seconded explicitly by Rainer Nägele and implicitly by many of the other contributors to this book.

It is not my intention to embellish that cultish image with this volume. I want, rather, to provide to readers whose acquaintance with Wolf is limited mainly to the English translations of her works a spectrum of critical opinions and approaches. For, if the overwhelming production and variety of critical literature on Wolf attests to nothing else, it demonstrates that Christa Wolf's project as a writer is fulfilled —in part, at least—by its evident ability to engage in fruitful dialogue readers whose language and discourse differ widely. She touches the (critical) consciousness of her readers; her works strike chords, not always tonic, in socialists and nonsocialists, in feminists and nonfeminists, in Germanists and non-Germanists alike.

These essays demonstrate such diverse responses to Christa Wolf and present ways in which these responses are suggested by the interpretative communities in which we live and work. Although the collection focuses on readings by scholars in the United States and Great Britain, it also includes translations of three seminal articles by East German and West German critics Hans-Georg Werner, Hans Kaufmann, and Heinrich Mohr. These latter articles predate the others by several years; they constitute a point of departure for much ensuing literature on Wolf in both East and West, and they are forceful illustrations of the sociopolitical and literary-critical contexts in which Wolf is and was read in the two Germanies.

The preparation of a critical volume on an author still actively engaged in literary production runs obvious risks. Particularly in the case of Christa Wolf, whose later works always seem to alter the way in which we regard the earlier ones, we face—as she does—a constant need to revise our readings. Some authors represented here wrote their pieces before the publication of *Cassandra* (1983), thus their interpretations and references represent the scholarly status quo of the early 1980s. Others, in contrast, have written their papers more recently and are able to take that major work and the relevant critical literature into account. Wolf's two most recent publications, *Störfall. Nachrichten eines Tages* [*Accident/A Day's News*, 1987] and *Die Dimension des Autors* [The Dimension of the Author, 1986], appeared after this volume had been submitted to the Press.

In seeking to provide some critical approaches to Wolf in English for the reader whose familiarity with the author and her works derives chiefly from perusal of translations, I have relied as fully as possible on those translations. I am grateful for permission granted by their various publishers to quote liberally from them: by Seven Seas Books (Berlin/East), for *Divided Heaven* and *The Reader and the Writer*; by Farrar, Straus & Giroux (New York) and Virago (London) for *The Quest for Christa T.* and *Patterns of Childhood* (*A Model Childhood*); by Farrar, Straus & Giroux for *No Place on Earth* and *Cassandra*; by *New German Critique* (formerly at the University of Wisconsin Milwaukee, now at Cornell University) for "Self-Experiment: Appendix to a Report" and "'Shall I Garnish a Metaphor with an Almond Blossom?': Büchner-

Acknowledgments

Prize Acceptance Speech." I also thank Luchterhand Verlag (Darmstadt) for permission to translate excerpts from *Lesen und Schreiben: Neue Sammlung* that are not yet available in English.

I wish, finally, to thank Christa Wolf for her encouraging support of several contributors to this volume and of the project in general. Thanks are also due to all the authors, not only for providing manuscripts and helpful information, but also for their cooperation, patience, and understanding during the long period of preparation. Much appreciated are the help and suggestions of Brigitte Peucker, Helene Scher, Ingo Seidler, and Susan Winnett, who read portions of the manuscript; the ready assistance of Jeffrey Sammons; the inspiration of Ernestine Schlant, who introduced me to Christa Wolf's works; Walburga Zahn's patient assistance with bibliographical sources and proofreading; the beneficial advice of Lee Ann Schreiner and a meticulous anonymous reader for the Press; superb copyediting by Lisa Novak Jerry and Anne Adamus; the support of Brant and the distraction of Kyra and Lorin. Yale University provided a leave of absence, the University of Michigan a research grant and a generous publication subsidy, and the American Council of Learned Societies a stipend to support an enterprise of which this book represents a part.

Contributors

Ute Brandes teaches at Amherst College, Amherst, Massachusetts. She studied American and German literatures in Münster, at the University of New Hampshire, and at Harvard University, where she received her Ph.D. in 1982. Publications include *Zitat und Montage in der neueren DDR-Prosa* (Frankfurt: Lang, 1984), as well as articles on Plenzdorf, Volker Braun, German women of the baroque period, eighteenth-century utopias, and language pedagogy.

Joyce Crick was educated at University College, the University of London, where she currently teaches. She also studied at Freiburg im Breisgau and Vienna, has taught at the University of Erlangen, and has lived in Germany and the United States. She received her M.A. with a thesis on Thomas Mann and psychoanalysis and has published articles on translation and translation theory, on Thomas and Heinrich Mann, Kafka, Grass, and Christa Wolf. Her most recent project is an edition of Coleridge's translation of Schiller's *Wallenstein* for the *Collected Coleridge*. She also occasionally broadcasts for the BBC on topics of current German literary interest and frequently reviews for the *Times Literary Supplement*.

Helen Fehervary was born in Budapest, Hungary, and raised and educated for the most part in the United States. She studied at Smith College, Brown University, the universities of Hamburg and (West) Berlin, and received her Ph.D. in 1975 from the University of Wisconsin. Fehervary is associate professor of German at Ohio State University and an editor of *New German Critique*. She is author of *Hölderlin and the Left* and numerous articles devoted to modern German literature, especially GDR literature, theater, women's studies, and critical theory. Currently she is completing a book on documentary fiction.

Sandra Frieden studied and has taught German, women's literature, and film at the University of Houston. She completed her doctoral work at the Universität-Gesamthochschule Siegen in the fields of contemporary German literature and film, comparative literature, and English. She has published articles on Christa Wolf, Ingeborg Bachmann, Peter Handke, Elisabeth Plessen, on contemporary German-language autobiographical writings, and on German film. Her *Autobiography: Self into Form. German Language Autobiographical Writings of the 1970's* appeared in 1983.

Marilyn Sibley Fries teaches at the University of Michigan. She was educated at Bennington College, Middlebury College, in Mainz and Berlin, and at Cornell University, where she received her Ph.D. in 1975. She is author of a book on the image of Berlin in the German novel between 1848 and 1933, and of articles on Döblin, Kaiser, Christa Wolf, Siegfried Lenz, the Daedalus legend in contemporary GDR literature, German women writers from 1875 to 1975, and the city in literature. An investigation of the problems of narrating the *Heimat* in recent German fiction is her chief enterprise at present.

Heidi Gilpin is a Ph.D. candidate in comparative literature at Harvard University. She is editor of *Copyright*, a new journal of cultural criticism. A longer version of the article included in this volume formed part of her B.A. thesis (1984) at Amherst College. "The Quest for a Female Voice: Three Writers of the German Democratic Republic" traces the development of a female voice in the works of Maxie Wander, Irmtraud Morgner, and Christa Wolf, with reference to the social and political conditions of women in the GDR.

Anne Herrmann studied at Stanford University and at the University of Zurich, where she received her Liz. Phil. She completed her Ph.D. at Yale University in 1984 and currently teaches in the English department and Women's Studies Program at the University of Michigan. She has written a book forthcoming from Columbia University Press in the Gender and Culture series, *The Dialogic and Difference: An/Other Woman in Virginia Woolf and Christa Wolf.*

Andreas Huyssen is chair of the German department at Columbia University. He received his Ph.D. from the University of Zurich in 1969; he then joined the faculty of the University of Wisconsin, from 1969 to 1971 at Parkside and from 1971 to 1986 at Milwaukee. He has published widely on subjects ranging from eighteenth-century drama and poetry to pop art and postmodernism. He is author of books on *Sturm und Drang*, on the early German Romantics' utopian dream of a world literature, and most recently of *After the Great Divide: Modernism, Mass Culture, Postmodernism* (1986). He is also editor of the critical and theoretical writings of Friedrich Schlegel and coeditor of *New German Critique*, of *The Technological Imagination: Theories and Fictions*, and of *Postmoderne: Zeichen eines kulturellen Wandels.*

Hans Kaufmann, one of the GDR's strongest proponents and scholars of contemporary literature, works at the Central Institute for Literary History of the East German Academy of Sciences in Berlin. He is coeditor of the multivolume *Geschichte der deutschen Literatur* and

11

has headed the author-collectives responsible for several of its volumes. From 1948 to 1961 he studied history and German literature and held several teaching positions at the Humboldt University in Berlin. He was professor at the Friedrich Schiller University in Jena from 1962 to 1968. He has published books (on Brecht and Heine, among others), essays, and reviews of post-eighteenth-century German literature and theory and has produced a ten-volume edition of Heinrich Heine's works for the Aufbau-Verlag.

Sara Lennox teaches German and directs the Social Thought and Political Economy Program at the University of Massachusetts, Amherst. She is editor of *Auf der Suche nach den Gärten unserer Mütter: Feministische Kulturkritik aus Amerika* and the author of articles on Christa Wolf, Bachmann, Brecht, Plenzdorf, Johnson, GDR literary theory, feminist teaching and research, and recent writing by women in the Federal Republic of Germany and the German Democratic Republic. She received her Ph.D. from the University of Wisconsin in 1973. Her current work deals with the intersection of gender, race, and history in Ingeborg Bachmann's work and within feminist practice and theory in general.

Myra N. Love received her Ph.D. from the University of California at Berkeley in 1983 with a dissertation on Christa Wolf. She teaches in the German department of Bryn Mawr College. Her publications include articles on Christa Wolf, who remains the focus of her current research.

Karin McPherson teaches at the University of Edinburgh, Scotland. She studied in Edinburgh, Freiburg, and Kiel, where she received her Ph.D. in 1962. Her areas of special interest include poetry of the twentieth century, radio plays, and German literature since 1945. She has published on Brigitte Reimann and Christa Wolf and is currently preparing a monograph on Wolf.

Heinrich Mohr is professor of literature and the social history of literature at the University of Osnabrück. He cofounded the coalition "Literatur und Germanistik in der DDR" (Literature and Germanistics in the GDR) and now coedits (with Paul Gerhard) that group's yearbooks. He studied Germanic languages and literature, history, philosophy, and political science in Berlin, Munich, and Freiburg and has taught at the universities of Bochum and Besancon (France). Mohr's publications include articles on Hermann Kant, Christa Wolf, Sarah Kirsch, Volker Braun as well as more general analyses of literary developments in the GDR.

Rainer Nägele teaches at Johns Hopkins University. He received his Ph.D. from the University of California in 1971. He has published books on Freud, Hölderlin, Böll, and Handke, and articles on Goethe, Hölderlin, Kafka, Freud, Handke, Lacan, and others as well as on general problems of literary theory and hermeneutics.

Brigitte Peucker received her Ph.D. in 1977 from Yale University, where she currently teaches German literature and film. She is author of books on preromantic modes in eighteenth-century poetry and lyric theory, most recently *Lyric Descent in the German Romantic Tradition* (1987). She has published articles on the theory of lyric, Klopstock, Goethe, Eichendorff, Droste-Hülshoff, Fassbinder, and Herzog, and she continues to pursue her dual interest in theories of lyric and film.

James I. Porter studied at Swarthmore College and the University of California at Berkeley, where he received his Ph.D. in comparative literature in 1986. He currently teaches Greek, Latin, and comparative literature at the University of Michigan. His widely divergent publications include articles on Grillparzer, Aristotle, Saussure, Derrida, and Philo as well as forthcoming essays on Philodemus, Aeschylus, and Nietzsche. In preparation are three book-length works: aesthetic discourse in antiquity, figuration theory, and a critical edition, with translation and commentary, of *PHerc. 994.*

Christiane Zehl Romero teaches at Tufts University. She was educated at the University of Vienna, where she received her Ph.D. in 1963, la Sorbonne, and Yale University. She has written a book on Simone de Beauvoir and Anna Seghers, and articles on Bahr and Stifter, Goethe, Musil, Monk Lewis and E. T. A. Hoffmann, Helen Lowe-Porter, women writers of the GDR, Anna Seghers, and Christa Wolf.

Judith Ryan studied at the University of Sydney and the University of Münster, where she received her Dr. phil. in 1970. She teaches German and comparative literature at Harvard University and is the author of books on Rilke and the postwar German novel. Her publications also include numerous articles on twentieth-century poetry and the modern novel.

Laurie Melissa Vogelsang received her B.A. from Bryn Mawr College in 1981. She is currently a graduate student at Yale University, where she is completing a dissertation on canon formation in the eighteenth century.

Hans-Georg Werner studied German literature, history, and philosophy from 1950 to 1954, taught German literature at the University of Bukarest (Roumania) from 1955 to 1958, received his doctorate in 1960, and has been professor of German literature at the Martin Luther University in Halle (GDR) since 1969. His publications include books on Heine, E. T. A. Hoffmann, the history of German literature, the political poem between 1815 and 1840, GDR literature, Lessing, methodology of literary analysis, and Büchner. He has also edited the works of Herwegh, Clemens Brentano, Achim von Arnim, and Christian Dietrich Grabbe.

Chronology

(including Wolf's major publications; fuller information is found at Section I.A of Bibliography)

1929 (March 18)	Born in Landsberg/Warthe
1939–1945	High school in Landsberg
1945	Flees with family to Mecklenburg
1949	Completion of high school (Abitur) in Bad Frankenhausen Joins SED (Socialist Unity Party)
1949–1953	Studies Germanic Languages and Literature in Jena and Leipzig, Thesis (Diplomarbeit) under Hans Mayer on "Problems of Realism in the Works of Hans Fallada"
1951	Marries Gerhard Wolf
1952	Birth of first daughter, Annette
1953–1959	Research assistant for German Writers' Union, after 1954 on staff of *Neue deutsche Literatur*, chief editor for publishing company, "Neues Leben" (specializes in publications for young people)
1955	First of several trips to Soviet Union
1955–1976	Member, executive committee of the Writers' Union, GDR

14

Chronology

1956	Birth of second daughter, Katrin
1958–1959	Editor for *Neue deutsche Literatur*
1959–1962	Moves to Halle; factory work under influence of Bitterfeld Movement; involvement in "Association of Writing Workers"; freelance editor in Mitteldeutscher Verlag (Halle); editor of several anthologies of contemporary GDR literature
1961	*Moskauer Novelle*
1962	Artists' Prize of the City of Halle
since 1962	Freelance author, lives in Berlin
1963	*Der geteilte Himmel* (*Divided Heaven*, 1965) Heinrich Mann Prize of the Academy of Arts of the GDR
1963–1967	Candidate of the Central Committee of the SED from the sixth to the eighth party congress of the SED
1964	DEFA-Film *Der geteilte Himmel* (directed by Konrad Wolf) National Prize Third Class of the Academy of Arts of the GDR Speech at the Second Bitterfeld Conference
1965	Membership in PEN-Center, GDR
1967	"Juninachmittag" ("An Afternoon in June," 1970)
1968	*Nachdenken über Christa T.* (*The Quest for Christa T.*, 1970)
1971	*Lesen und Schreiben. Aufsätze und Betrachtungen* (*The Reader and the Writer: Essays, Sketches, Memories*, 1977)
1972	*Till Eulenspiegel. Erzählung für den Film* (with Gerhard Wolf) Wilhelm-Raabe Prize of the City of Braunschweig (refused)

15

ALLEGHENY COLLEGE LIBRARY

Chronology

1973	Theodor Fontane Prize for Art and Literature

1974   *Unter den Linden. Drei unwahrscheinliche Geschichten*
Gesammelte Erzählungen
Membership in the Academy of the Arts, GDR
Seventh Max Kade German Writer-in-Residence at Oberlin College, Oberlin, Ohio

1975   DEFA-Film *Till Eulenspiegel* (directed by Rainer Simon)

1976   *Kindheitsmuster* (*A Model Childhood/Patterns of Childhood*, 1980/84)
Signs "Open Letter" in Biermann affair
Dismissal from the executive committee of the Berlin Section of the Writers' Union of the GDR

1977   Literature Prize of the City of Bremen

1979   *Kein Ort. Nirgends* (*No Place on Earth*, 1982)
Fortgesetzter Versuch: Aufsätze, Gespräche, Essays

1980   *Lesen und Schreiben. Neue Sammlung* (expanded edition, 1981)
Georg Büchner Prize

1981   Travels to Athens and Crete

1982   Guest professorship in Poetics, University of Frankfurt am Main

1983   *Kassandra. Vier Vorlesungen. Eine Erzählung* (GDR)
Kassandra: Erzählung (FRG)
Voraussetzungen einer Erzählung: Kassandra (FRG)
(*Cassandra. A Novel and Four Essays*, 1984)
Guest professor at Ohio State University, Columbus, Ohio
Schiller Prize

1985   *Erzählungen*
Austrian National Prize for Literature
Honorary Doctorate, University of Hamburg (FRG)

1986   *Die Dimension des Autors. Essays und Aufsätze, Reden und Gespräche 1959-1985*

16

Chronology

1987	*Störfall. Nachrichten eines Tages (Accident/A Day's News*, 1989) Geschwister-Scholl Prize, Munich
1988	Ansprachen

Abbreviations

The volume employs essentially two categories of abbreviations: works cited throughout the articles (chiefly by Christa Wolf, but also by Virginia Woolf and Ingeborg Bachmann) are given in the first list; the second supplements the first to include abbreviations for materials cited frequently in notes and bibliography.

I. The following will be found in parenthetical notation throughout this volume. The reader is referred to the bibliography of primary works at the end of the volume for complete information. (Titles given in parentheses are not available in English translation.)

AJ   "An Afternoon in June" / "Juninachmittag" (quotations from this work found in the essays are translated by the editor or the authors from the German original [in *Gesammelte Erzählungen*, 41–64]; citations refer to that publication)

AS   "A Visit to Anna Seghers" / "Bei Anna Seghers" [in *The Reader and the Writer*, 138–143]

BL   (Yes indeed! But the next life starts today. A Letter about Bettina) / "Nun ja! Das nächste Leben geht aber heute an. Ein Brief über die Bettine" [in *Lesen und Schreiben. Neue Sammlung*, 284–318]

BO   "Brecht and Others" / "Brecht und andere" [in *The Reader and the Writer*, 57–59]

BP   "'Shall I Garnish a Metaphor with an Almond Blossom?': Büchner-Prize Acceptance Speech" / "Büchner-Preis-Rede" [in *NGC*, no. 23 (Spring/Summer 1981): 3–11]

Abbreviations

C   *Cassandra* (translation includes both the story and the four "Lectures on Poetics": "Conditions of a Narrative" / (*Kassandra. Erzählung* and *Voraussetzungen einer Erzählung. Kassandra* are listed separately below)

CA   (Continued Attempt) / "Fortgesetzter Versuch" [in *Lesen und Schreiben. Neue Sammlung*, 151–157]

CE   *Collected Essays* (of Virginia Woolf)

CI   "Culture Is What You Experience" / "Kultur ist, was erlebt wird" [in *NGC*, no. 27 (Fall 1982): 89–100]

CP   "Change of Perspective" / "Blickwechsel" [in *Gesammelte Erzählungen*, 5–23]

CT   *The Quest for Christa T.* / *Nachdenken über Christa T.*

D   "Diary—Aid to Work and Memory" / "Tagebuch—Arbeitsmittel und Gedächtnis" [in *The Reader and the Writer*, 63–75]

DA   (The Dimension of the Author) / *Die Dimension des Autors*, Luchterhand edition

DH   *Divided Heaven* / *Der geteilte Himmel*

DO   "Documentation : Christa Wolf" [in *GQ* 57, no. 1 (Winter 1984): 91–115]

DW   (Discussion with Christa Wolf) / "Diskussion mit Christa Wolf" [in *SuF* 4 (1976): 861–888, rpt. in *CWM*, 33–48]

FT   "Faith in the Terrestrial" / "Glauben an Irdisches" [in *The Reader and the Writer*, 111–137]

IB   "Truth that Can Be Faced—Ingeborg Bachmann's Prose" / "Die zumutbare Wahrheit (Ingeborg Bachmann)" [in *The Reader and the Writer*, 83–96]

IM   "Interview with Myself" / "Selbstinterview" [in *The Reader and the Writer*, 76–80]

IT   "In Touch (Maxie Wander)" / "Berührung (Maxie Wander)" [in *German Feminism. Readings in Politics and Literature*, 161–169]

K   *Kassandra. Erzählung*

L   (A Letter) / "Ein Brief" [in *Mut zur Angst. Schriftsteller für den Frieden*, 153–54]

MN   (Moscow Novella) / *Moskauer Novelle*

NA   (Necessary Argument) / "Notwendiges Streitgespräch" [in *NdL* 3 (March 1965): 100–101]

NP   *No Place on Earth / Kein Ort. Nirgends*

PC   *Patterns of Childhood / Kindheitsmuster*

RW   "The Reader and the Writer" / "Lesen und Schreiben" [in *The Reader and the Writer*, 177–212]

S   "A Speech" / "Eine Rede" [in *The Reader and the Writer*, 23–26]

SA   "Subjective Authenticity: A Conversation with Hans Kaufmann" / "Subjektive Authentizität. Gespräch mit Hans Kaufmann" (also published as "Gespräch mit Christa Wolf" [*WB* 6 (1974)] and as "Die Dimension des Autors. Gespräch mit Hans Kaufmann" [*Lesen und Schreiben. Neue Sammlung*]). English translation in this volume taken from *The Fourth Dimension* (London: Verso, 1988)

SE   "Self-Experiment: Appendix to a Report" / "Selbstversuch. Traktat zu einem Protokoll" [in *NGC*, no. 13 (Winter 1978): 109–131]

SD   (The Shadow of a Dream. Karoline von Günderrode—a Sketch) / "Der Schatten eines Traumes. Karoline von Günderrode— ein Entwurf" [in *Lesen und Schreiben. Neue Sammlung*, 225–283]

SN   (On the Sense and Senselessness of Naiveté) / "Über Sinn und Unsinn von Naivität" [in *Lesen und Schreiben. Neue Sammlung*, [56–67]

TS   (Tuesday, September 27, 1960) / "Dienstag, der 27. September 1960" [in *Gesammelte Erzählungen*, 24–40]

TY   *The Thirtieth Year* (by Ingeborg Bachmann)

UE   (Unusable Example. Speech at the PEN-Conference in Stockholm, 1977) / "Beispiel ohne Nutzanwendung. Beitrag zum PEN-Kongress Stockholm 1977" [in *Lesen und Schreiben. Neue Sammlung*, 106–112]

UL   Unter den Linden: Drei unwahrscheinliche Geschichten, includes "Unter den Linden," 7–75, and "Neue Lebensansichten eines Katers" (New Life and Opinions of a Tomcat), 77–121.

V   Voraussetzungen einer Erzählung. Kassandra

VI   "The Meaning of a New Thing—Vera Inber" / "Der Sinn einer neuen Sache (Vera Inber)" [in The Reader and the Writer, 60–62]

WS   (I'm in favor of a certain immoderation—Christa Wolf in Conversation with Wilfried F. Schoeller) / "Ich bin schon für eine gewisse Masslosigkeit—Christa Wolf im Gespräch mit Wilfried F. Schoeller" [in CWM, 53–63]

II. Abbreviations used in notes and bibliography:

CWM	Christa Wolf Materialienbuch
DVjs	Deutsche Vierteljahresschrift
FAZ	Frankfurter Allgemeine Zeitung
GE	Gesammelte Erzählungen (Wolf)
GLL	German Life and Letters
GQ	German Quarterly
GR	The Germanic Review
LS.NS	Lesen und Schreiben. Neue Sammlung (Wolf)
MLN	Modern Language Notes
ND	Neues Deutschland
NdH	Neue deutsche Hefte
NdL	Neue deutsche Literatur
NGC	New German Critique
NGS	New German Studies
NR	Neue Rundschau
NYRB	New York Review of Books
NYTBR	New York Times Book Review
PMLA	Publications of the Modern Language Association
SuF	Sinn und Form
SR	Saturday Review
STCL	Studies in Twentieth Century Literature
SZ	Süddeutsche Zeitung
TuK	Text und Kritik
TLS	Times Literary Supplement
WB	Weimarer Beiträge
ZfdPh	Zeitschrift für deutsche Philologie

Editor's Note

For the sake of readers not entirely familiar with German, most references and quotations here are provided in English. With the exception of "An Afternoon in June," the translation of which was not accessible, quotations are taken from the published English translations of Christa Wolf's works. For translations from that story, I have relied on those provided by Helen Fehervary in her essay. It is gratifying to note that further translations of Wolf's works are in process as this volume goes to press: *Sommerstück* and a volume of essays are scheduled for publication within the next several months.

Quotations in these articles not taken from existing translations have been rendered by me and approved and revised by the several authors. In a few cases, it has been necessary to modify the published translation and/or include the German words in order to illuminate an argument based on the original text. References to such modifications will be found in the notes to the respective essays.

I have used English titles throughout, whether the works referred to exist in translation or not. The abbreviations used in notations are all derived from these English titles. The lists of abbreviations, together with the bibliography, should provide clarity on the status of these various works.

The reader may note inconsistencies in the spelling of the names Bettina (Bettine) and Günderrode (Günderode). These differences, determined by the usage of various contemporary writers in referring to these two figures, are not meant to confuse.

Translations of the contributions by Brandes, Huyssen, Kaufmann, McPherson, Mohr, and Werner are mine; they have been amended and approved by the authors, but the final responsibility lies, of course, with me.

Locating Christa Wolf:
An Introduction

Marilyn Sibley Fries

*The ingenuous open heart preserves one's ability to say "I"
to a stranger, until a moment comes when this strange "I"
returns and enters into "me" again.*

—Christa Wolf, The Quest for Christa T.

Christa Wolf's prose is demonstratively insistent. Rooted in the dialectic, it lays stubborn claim to the socially redemptive power of the logos and seeks to realize the integration of reader and writer in a dialogue initiated by, and ultimately surpassing, the text. Wolf's writing displays the searching tentativeness of its own creative process, engages its readers as interlocutory participants in this procedure, vacillates between question and assertion, requires a response. It may enthrall us, but its emancipatory gesture would release us (as it has its author) to our own subjective space.[1] We are enjoined to discover a discourse in which to formulate our response without ending the dialogue Wolf's works engender; to treat them as art objects and attempt "interpretation" with traditional tools and methods of literary criticism is to misunderstand the value of reading as Wolf comprehends and demonstrates it. For reading involves, above all, a reinscription filtered through the complexities of the individual reading consciousness; approaching an understanding of the text is correlative to increased self-understanding. Our responses to Wolf should thus be as "subjectively authentic" as the author's own position toward her project: ideally, we should create our own discourse and speak in our own voices, ceasing to rely on the unsuitable language of "objective criticism." Such a charge posits a self-confrontational activity paralleling Wolf's project and inventing the language in which to record it. Searching, we write.

The several essays in this collection demonstrate this searching activity and—sometimes more, sometimes less—the way in which literary scholars appropriate various discourses (of literary criticism and theory, politics, and psychoanalysis, for example). Wolf's highly allusive and ideologically motivated writings allow ready access via these discourses: her own erudition and knowledge of major works of literature, literary movements, theoretical and philosophical developments, and history are everywhere evident, as constitutive elements of the "fabric" (C 142) of her (anti)poetics. Our experiential, ideological, and intellectual idiosyncracies determine our critical attention to one or another strand in this fabric in order to speak with/about Wolf; but if we are honest interlocutors, we will not deny the existence of the whole, and we will resist the claim to closure.

Wolf's complexly woven fabric is integral; this volume wants also to be seen as a many-threaded construct—less as a tapestry, perhaps, than as a patchwork quilt, in which many pieces intersect and occasionally overlap with each other. Leaving the analysis of that quilt and its pieces to the reader, this introduction aims to expose some strands from which Wolf's fabric has been woven. If my procedure appears at times nonlinear, this results from my desire to avoid damaging the cloth. I want to locate Wolf in the context of her individual experience, within her own society and literary tradition as well as in the larger scope of modern and contemporary writing. Finally, I will outline briefly the changes in her angle of vision as these are revealed in her work and suggest some ways in which she tries to realize the elimination of dualistic perception by abolishing the opposition between the reader and the writer.

Without indulging in crass proscriptive categories, we might nonetheless mark a delineation of "the widening of [Wolf's] visual angle" (C 278), of the shifts in her ideological perspective that permit concomitant changes in the nature of her narrative. From an early anchoring in Marxist/Leninist theory (1949 to approximately 1965), the "readjustment to [her] depth of focus" (C 278) has led to necessarily including the subjective element of experience and a fundamentally humanistic and all embracing concern for the moral predicament of the world (from the mid-sixties to the late seventies). To this she adds, in the eighties, certain tenets of contemporary feminist thought as offering some possible alternatives for our society. While the later positions do not replace the earlier ones—she speaks of "readjustment," "widening," "increased depth"—these shifts have enlarged the space of her narrative metalanguage to permit greater resonance in her prose.

Her appeal has not always been quite so global. She has universalized her message as she has come to realize that Western civilization, as we know it today, is the creator as well as the victim of its own potential end. In *Cassandra* and the lectures on poetics (*Conditions of a Narrative: Cassandra*) that accompany and counterpoint the story (both 1983), she focuses on an analysis of the patriarchal system that has

24

brought our civilization to that impasse. Her deep-rooted moral commitment, the convincing honesty of her articulation, and the interactive gesture of her prose make Wolf an important—and often irresistible—author.

I. Historical and Personal Background

Honored with major literary awards in both Germanies, widely translated and read, Christa Wolf is beyond a doubt the best known German woman writer of this century. She was born in Landsberg on the Warthe (now the Polish town of Gorzów Wielkopolski) on March 18, 1929; her father, Otto Ihlenfeld, ran a small grocery business; her mother raised their daughter and son and helped in the shop. Wolf spent her first sixteen years (twelve of them under Hitler) in that town but fled to Mecklenburg with her family at the approach of the Red Army in 1945. Converted to socialism through her reading of Marx and Engels, Wolf joined the SED (German Socialist Unity Party)[2] in 1949, the founding year of the German Democratic Republic (GDR). Although she still adheres to the tenets of socialism, she has indicated some disillusionment with the way it is practiced by the system under which she lives, most pronouncedly in her participation, with eleven other important GDR writers, in petitioning her government on behalf of their expatriated colleague, Wolf Biermann.[3] But her life and work since 1949 must be seen always in light of her commitment to socialism and to a society that regards its writers and intellectuals seriously, as affective and effective participants in the common socialist cause. This mutual commitment is a major precondition of Wolf's narrative.

While actively engaged in both theory and practice of socialist reconstruction, Wolf studied Germanic languages and literature in Jena and Leipzig from 1949 to 1953; parts of *The Quest for Christa T.* (1968) convey a sense of both the collective efforts of that period and the dominant role of politics in all lives. From 1953 to 1962 she worked as a research assistant for the League of German Writers and an editor for a major journal and for two publishing houses. Her writing during these years—chiefly book reviews that betray a doctrinaire appropriation of socialist realist and Lukácsian discourse—has been understandably overshadowed by the creative effort that began in the late fifties and is seldom treated as an integral part of her oeuvre. As exemplary programmatic criticism, it demonstrates the self-alienating barriers erected by the "false objectivity" of dogmatic reading. In 1973, Wolf would complain that her university courses in literature had obstructed her access to literary works: "I had almost begun to forget how well I had learned my lessons in the Germanistics seminars and from many . . . articles: on useful and harmful effects, on realism and formalism, progress and decadence in literature and art—so well that I unconsciously allowed my vision to be colored by these articles, thus distancing myself greatly from a realistic manner of seeing and writing" (SN 60). Seeing and writing "realistically" does not involve measurement against an infallible and unalterable external "reality"; the real (the truth) must emerge from and return to the innermost depths of individual consciousness.

The cited remarks appear in Wolf's retrospective commentary on her first fictional work, *Moskauer Novelle* (Moscow Novella, 1961). Like most of her following works, this short narrative is transitional, signaling her move from critical to creative writing, although the demarcation of these two categories is particularly questionable in Wolf's case. *Moskauer Novelle* adheres somewhat too stridently to the prescribed formulas of socialist realism (Wolf calls the work "traktatenhaft" [like a (political) treatise] [SN 60]),[4] but it is delivered in that forceful voice that Wolf would continue to modulate and define as a freelance writer after 1961.

Wolf has been married since 1951 to Gerhard Wolf, also a respected literary critic, with whom she is coeditor of several literary anthologies (most dating from the fifties) and coauthor of *Till Eulenspiegel* (a "narrative for a film," 1972). They continue to reside in Berlin and, during the summer months, in Kleinmachow (near Berlin). They have two daughters.[5]

Although Wolf would deceive her readers—usually by means of qualifying prefatory notes—of the notion that her works and their figures are grounded in historical reality, she paradoxically insists that they all emerge from her own personal experience. This is contradictory only if we ignore Wolf's premise that the self-transforming value of experience occurs when that experience is *read*, i.e., understood, analyzed, integrated. The (narrative) record of that reading makes its author important—as exemplary reader. The autobiographical aspect of Wolf's work is thus paradigmatic; her "subjective authenticity" is grounded in a broad appeal. Wolf's disclaimers testify to her recognition that the coherent articulation of personal experience inevitably fictionalizes it; that her figures, although modeled on existing individuals, are inventions rather than copies. This insight belongs to the crux of Wolf's artistic and theoretical enterprise, and I intend less to ignore than to suspend it in briefly tracing Wolf's biography through her fiction.

If we are willing to subscribe momentarily to a reductive reading that permits isolating the (auto)biographical moments, we may wonder about the valuative hierarchy of her record. What leads her to give fictional permanence to certain moments in her life, while looking past other ones? Her fiction and the essays, articles, speeches, and interviews that Wolf has selected for inclusion in the several collections of such materials give us a full, if somewhat skewed, outline of the course of her life—or, perhaps more correctly (and in keeping with the approach Wolf's narrator takes toward Christa T.), they re-collect the significant moments of that life. The narrator telling of Christa T. isolates those moments in her subject's life that together constitute Christa T.'s essence and importance for *her*. Christa Wolf the author, who has provided us with no conventional autobiographical statement, assumes an analogous role of narrator toward Christa Wolf the person, presenting her reading audience with moments of singular significance while overlooking others. Her readers can construct a certain continuity, can view an (as yet incomplete) fabric. It is, however, a continuity of Wolf's making: individualized, to be sure, stressing moments of crisis and stress; but sketching a *Lebenslauf* (life-course) that demonstratively locates its author in a larger society than the one in which she lives and works. This implies a departure from the binary thinking of East-West politics (although not a capitulatory or conciliatory gesture) coincidental with a perception of the self as member of a society whose political division seems today less threatening than the unity imposed by the common danger of nuclear catastrophe. Impelled by her profound concern for the future of humanity, Wolf has stressed the more generally demonstrative moments of her life and understated those more particularly circumscribed by the politics and progress of the GDR. Literature cannot be "peace-research" (BP 10) if it continues to promulgate divisive ideological notions.

The lacunae in the "life-course" we trace in her works can be filled only by speculation. Wolf is notably reticent, for instance, about her activities during the period between 1949 and 1959. These have probably been the most historically and politically turbulent years since World War II ended in 1945: the reconstruction that followed the founding of the two German states in 1949 (the Federal Republic of [West] Germany and the [East] German Democratic Republic) was accompanied by the desperate defensiveness of cold war mentality and the sustained notion of an inimical other. The Germans who had been taught to hate and fear the non-German were now, under the aegis of the two superpowers, being taught to despise each other. The East Germans were busy constructing their interwoven governmental system with the help of the Soviet Union—a system that, among other things, regarded members of the intelligentsia as servants of the state; they erected massive organizations for controlling cultural policy and, in the process, forced thinkers like Hans Mayer and Ernst Bloch[6] into exile. But in both Germanies it was also, at the beginning at least, a time of euphoria prompted by a sense of liberation and a faith in the possibility of total renewal—a renaissance from the ruins. Wolf's commitment to socialism as the necessary foundation for such renewal was evidently complete. She demonstrates this by her active participation in several organizations formed to promote socialist reconstruction, from student collectives to governmental cultural policy committees. The nature and intensity of her commitment are critically refracted through the narrative perspective in *Christa T.*, whose main character's resistance to certainty made the lives of others—including the narrator's— "questionable" (48).

We know that Wolf spent the first four of these years as a student, subsequently working as editor and book reviewer. Her critical articles can still be located in the journals and newspapers, although they have not, like much of her later critical work, been anthologized. Her stature in the world of East German literary criticism and cultural policy was significant; as a highly visible member of the first postwar generation of East German intelligentsia, she served on the executive board of the League of Writers (1955–1976), was a candidate of the Central Committee of the SED (1963–1967), was named to the membership of the PEN-Center of the GDR, and was speaker at such important meetings as the second Bitterfeld Conference in 1964.[7]

Wolf's attention in her fiction is directed, however, not at this period in which ends and means, individual activity, and social goals seemed to correspond; she does not stress the activities that might "prove" her commitment to "real existing socialism" or to "socialist reconstruction." She turns instead to the breaks and ruptures, not to criticize her society as much as to question her self and the viability of existing language for what emerges as her purpose. Her university training and her careful conformity to regulated doctrine, she suggests, produce an unauthentic echo. Such implication may be found as the negative imprint, as it were, of those moments recorded in the positive: her several essays on Anna Seghers,[8] or her pieces on Ingeborg Bachmann,[9] Bettina von Arnim,[10] Karoline von Günderrode,[11] and Maxie Wander,[12] for instance; her interviews with Hans Kaufmann,[13] Joachim Walther,[14] Wilfried Schoeller,[15] Frauke Meyer-Gosau,[16] and others; and, of course, in her fictional works. At one point, Wolf speaks of the public's terrible addiction to trivial literature—a condition she wants to help correct. It is possible that, as a reader reading her own life, she regards most activities and writings of that ten-year span as trivial literature, insignificant—perhaps even harmful—because formulaic. The narrator in Christa T. confirms this: what she finds remarkable in Christa T.'s thesis on the nineteenth-century author Theodor Storm is precisely not Christa T.'s facility with the accepted terminology of socialist literary criticism; it is, rather, her daring willingness to assert and insert herself as reader, to respond to the works she reads in her own voice.

The chronological direction of the fictional works written between 1963 and 1983 goes against the historical grain: each successive major prose work moves the temporal locus further back in history. The autobiographical revelations from one work to the next occupy an analogously remote position in the text. Reaching into historical depths (in her chronological reversal) parallels a profounder self-comprehension, in turn expressed in multiple narrative levels; such activity suggests an archaeological and psychoanalytic digging effort.

The first work that brought her immediate recognition, Divided Heaven (1963), takes place in the GDR of the early 1960s. The Quest for Christa T. (1968), Wolf's next novel and perhaps the best known, begins at the end of World War II and spans the crucial first fifteen years of the

GDR, while *Patterns of Childhood* (1976) presents Wolf's most obviously autobiographical attempt at reconciliation with the realities of a childhood in the Third Reich. Still further removed historically is *No Place on Earth* (1979), set among the German Romantic writers in 1806 and positing a fictional meeting between two historical characters, Heinrich von Kleist and Karoline von Günderrode. Finally, *Cassandra* (1983) makes a leap back to the putative beginning of Western civilization and presents the end of the Trojan War as narrated by Cassandra. The fears articulated by Cassandra seem uncannily and frighteningly realized three years later in the nuclear catastrophe at Chernobyl, the stimulus for Wolf's most recent narrative work, *Störfall. Nachrichten eines Tages* (*Accident/A Day's News*, 1987).

Wolf's style is fundamentally lyrical, her structure open and multilayered, her didactic message often coined in aphoristic phrases. She elucidates her prose in theoretical essays that often serve as a counterpoint to the novels. "Interview with Myself," for example, explains and justifies the "subjective authenticity" of *Christa T.*; other essays to be found in *The Reader and the Writer* (1972) and in the *Cassandra*-lectures[17] exemplify her comprehension of the reading and writing process as a "working-through." "For without books [i.e., literature—Ed.] I am not I," Wolf claims in "The Reader and the Writer" (190). And later she writes, "the author is an important person" (206). The reader and the writer are equally important; Wolf's theoretical essays and her fiction confirm this and demonstrate her idiosyncratic manner of reading.

II. Social and Cultural Contexts

In an era of literary theories of reader response and reception, Wolf's work seems crafted for the critic who has been instructed in these schools. And yet she writes in—and, at least at the outset, predominantly for—a society whose concern with reader response is equally strong, if differently motivated. Western critical theory of the last twenty to thirty years has discovered what has always been assumed by politically committed literature: the reader can be changed in the act of reading; the narrative posits its receiver. A great distinction must be made, however, between a didactic literature that announces itself as such and is produced in accord with prescribed expectations and one where these features are invisible if not absent. Christa Wolf has moved in her writing from one level to the other, always directing herself toward a reader but redefining the contours of that reader as she has redefined herself in the process of reading.

The critical reception of her work is complicated by both these redefinitions and the critical tools available to her readers in East and West. Socialist critics, while upholding the importance of writer-reader interaction, seem generally inclined to view this only within limited ideological parameters, and Wolf appears to be eluding their grasp as

29

her perception coincides less and less with those circumspect lines. Although the publication of *Divided Heaven*, for instance, resulted in an extended debate,[18] its point of departure—Wolf's sincere attempt to realize the goals of Bitterfeld, to integrate "brain workers" *(Kopfarbeiter)* with "hand workers" *(Handarbeiter)*—was acknowledged and praised by her compatriots. A common effort was still evident. But critical recognition of shared goals and purpose has given way to some bafflement and considerable silence in the face of her more recent production. *The Quest for Christa T.* led to lengthy critical discussion and partial censorship of the work,[19] and *No Place on Earth* and *Cassandra* have elicited relatively sparse critical comment in comparison to the earlier works. Western criticism, in contrast, has been more and more receptive to Wolf as her reading has become more emancipated— which is to say: subjective, authentic, realistic, nonconventional, "modern." Her later works, having suppressed the ideological superstructure in favor of self-revelation determined by more private norms, permits an easier identification of moral and humanistic purpose.

Wolf's development is marked equally by an increasing awareness of the ineradicability of the past and by her belief in the human capacity to change. Her quintessential historical development and status cannot be strongly enough stressed. Childhood and youth under the self-blinding Nazi banner; radical ideological and geographic displacement at the age of sixteen, followed by a series of "lens-widening" experiences: the reading of Marx and Engels, active commitment to the physical and ideological restoration of the socialist Germany, the first of several encounters with Anna Seghers, increased access to literature and critical theories earlier banned or unknown, self-confrontation during the composition of *Christa T.*, censure, criticism, and self-criticism, the government's action against Biermann and the concomitant or subsequent departure from the GDR of many other prominent colleagues, dismissal from the League of Writers executive and the Central Committee's candidates' list, immersion in feminist theory and ancient literature, nuclear catastrophe.

Wolf's emergence from the immediate realm of East German literature onto the international arena has far less to do with any "dissident" thrust in her work (although she has been accused more than once in the GDR of "providing ammunition to the enemy")[20] than with two factors quite independent of ideological drum banging. First, the undeniable moral impulse of her work aims at the "very inmost part [of the reader of prose]" (RW 201) to call that reader's thinking and life into question and stimulate self-reflection; second is the "modern" sophistication of her style. The two aspects are inseparable, to be sure: a critical reader's interaction with a text is enabled more successfully by a nondogmatic, open prose than by writing that adheres to a conventional, closed narrative scheme. Wolf's understanding of the interdependence of form and purpose and the underlying faith in the intelligence of the reader mark her project.

Part of the postwar effort in Germany involved "catching up" on literary developments: "The isolation from all contemporary literature could not have been more complete than it was up to my sixteenth year" (RW 187), Wolf remarks. Her avid reading results in an increased awareness of modernist and postmodernist literary trends and techniques, and the nature of this always dialectical reading is reflected in her works after *Divided Heaven*. The synthesis of text and reader is dually manifest in these writings: an appropriation of modernist devices and a focal shift from ideological to ontological and epistemological questions relocate this author on the map of contemporary literature. In exceeding the limitations of convention, she extends the potential of her readership.

In *Christa T.* and thereafter, Wolf employs devices and themes typically associated with Western European modernism (and anathema to the concept of socialist realism): montage, direct appellation to a reader/narratee/interlocutor, employment of interior monologue and shifting use of personal pronouns, intentional confusion of narrative voice, multiple temporal levels, avoidance of absolute statement, and language skepticism. The stylistic shifts correspond to a perceptual redefinition, attest to the self-consciousness of the artist, and echo questions about art's purpose that have dominated artistic activity in the twentieth century. In essays and conversations, Wolf demonstrates her growing acquaintance with and reception of the major literary movements of this century, especially of modernism, the *nouveau roman*, and the problematic committed literature of her West German colleagues.[21]

But we should have to probe the motivation for the use of these techniques before setting Wolf firmly into the modernist or postmodernist tradition. For their employment is primarily an act of subjective emancipation; such devices permit a formal correspondence to the way in which Wolf has come to perceive the "network" of reality. Wolf's language skepticism seems rooted less in the philosophical inquiries of thinkers like Wittgenstein and Heidegger than in the brutal realities of Nazi propaganda; her forms of address to an other ultimately underscore her dialectically based central premise concerning the necessary dialogue of writer and reader rather than functioning as a literary device; her use of multiple time levels suggests a dialectical or synchronous integration of past into present and future and refers as well to the conflation of subject/object dualism in the reading process.

The desire to obviate dualistic, antagonistic thinking also prompts Wolf's search for linguistic and social alternatives among female precursors. This leads her, via various foremothers, finally back to the legendary matriarchy of "Persephone and her daughter" (*C* 159), to the primordial mother Gaea (*C* 286), to Cassandra. Her form anticipates the contextual thrust of her most recent works, which tempt us to locate her among feminist writers of West and East.

31

But the socialist consciousness, marked by the hopeful principle of the dialectic, is not abandoned. There emerges, in Wolf's case, a certain tension whose resolution constitutes one of the strongest elements of her enterprise. I mean the tension between aesthetics and ideology, on which so many politically committed writers have floundered. It is precisely the subjective moment that allows Wolf to avoid many of this tension's dangers; by "taking responsibility," by demonstratively revealing the processes of her own search and asking her readers to "take [her] problematic for [themselves]" (CI 89), she resists the alienation of didacticism.

Wolf cannot, therefore, be simply aligned with the authors of postwar West German literature, modernism, or feminism. Her position in the German literary tradition is better understood, initially, at least, in respect to a particular literary heritage and aesthetic theory as they are fostered in a specific political atmosphere. Wolf's acceptance of socialism endows her early works with positive vision and remains the foundation for her narrative structure, now much refined; her training in German literature and socialist literary theory prescribes conventions and critical judgments from which she frees herself only gradually, while her familiarity with the canon of the eighteenth and the nineteenth century is always referentially present in her work. Later she is less convinced that systematic politics can offer solutions to the individual, but she never reveals the cynicism or resignation that often mark the works of her Western colleagues, for she retains the conviction that the dialectics of history affect society and the individual primarily by sustaining movement and change. She pushes aside the traditional masters of German literature—the accepted great men of the "cultural heritage"—and dominant socialist theories (particularly those of Lukács) in the process of discovering and delineating her own literary lineage and personal aesthetic. She takes cues from Bertolt Brecht, arguing for an "epic prose" that parallels his epic theater.[22] She listens receptively to Anna Seghers, sympathizing with her position in the famous debates with Lukács concerning expressionism and realism,[23] and follows Seghers's lead to the German Romantic poets. The skepticism of GDR colleagues such as Günter Kunert and Wolf Biermann may have influenced her thinking as much as Franz Fühmann's insistence on the dialectical perspective of fairy tales. Thomas Mann provides lessons in composition, while Johannes Bobrowski, finally, looms as a major influence on the reflective/reflexive style that leads ultimately to Wolf's insistence on "subjective authenticity." In the later stages of her development, she (re)reads Ingeborg Bachmann, the Grimms' fairy tales, the writers (especially the women) of the German Romantic era. Seeking new direction, she turns to other women writers (her predecessors Annette von Droste-Hülshoff, Marie Luise Kaschnitz, and Marieluise Fleisser; her contemporaries in the GDR, especially Maxie Wander, Irmtraud Morgner, and Sarah Kirsch; her English precursor Virginia Woolf),[24] and feminist theoreticians.[25] She locates herself, finally, in respect to those works whose value is revealed by her understanding of them as she comes increasingly to identify self understanding as a process of reading. Wolf internalizes the dialectic to conform to this personal experience, in which it denotes the confrontation of the "reader" with the "text," both terms understood in their broadest sense. Her readjustment of this oppositional stance involves a move away from its implicit polarity in the suggestion that reader and writer operate synchronously and that the text is re-formed in the reading/writing process. But the dialectical underpinning keeps her narrative perspective, as sophisticated as it might become, always in the realm of social interaction; her "subjectivity" and her internalization do not signify a withdrawal from society.

The notion of self-understanding as an act of reading is present already in *Divided Heaven*, where the protagonist "reads" her past during her physical and psychological recuperation in the hospital, and in *Christa T.*, in which the narrator bases her story partly on the posthumous writings of Christa T. and partly on her own recollection of her. The idea is further substantiated in Wolf's later works: in *Patterns of Childhood* we might overlook the narrator's references to the many hours spent in libraries verifying her recollection of past events, and we may not know, unless we read the accompanying theoretical essays, that *No Place on Earth* emerges from and is constructed around Wolf's reading of the works of her protagonists; the essays that accompany *Cassandra*, finally, are clear evidence both of the function of the reading process in the development of the narrative *and* of the manner in which the subject/author is merged with the object/textual material. To trace Wolf's references to her reading—of actual written texts or the less concrete record and recollection of personal experience—is to recognize that reading (which is to say: interpreting, seeing, evaluating, recognizing patterns) provides for her the network for the self's identity.

Her repeated epistemological question—articulated most succinctly in the motto to *The Quest for Christa T.*: "This coming-to-oneself —what is it?" (*CT* n.p.)—gives thematic unity to her oeuvre as it progresses through its several phases. Wolf's unrelenting penetration into her own truth (her "reality") leads toward profound self-recognition; the resistant aesthetics of her oeuvre are anything but arbitrary. Rather, they manifest the rigorous adherence to the logic of her personal quest, taking her from ideologically motivated confession to humanistic revelation, from manifesto to epic prose.

In fiction and nonfiction, Wolf demonstrates the difficult nature of her own movement toward a clearer view of what constitutes truth for her. In her earliest works, such as *Moskauer Novelle* and *Divided Heaven*, the truths she transmits are not (only) her own; they belong to an impersonal ideological superstructure and require participation in *its* discourse, which thus defines the meeting point of reader and writer. With *The Quest for Christa T.*, Wolf turns her view inward and backward. Allowing her narrator to look at herself and Christa T. in the historical context of their friendship, she outlines the struggle of the person who tries to "cope with things" and to arrive at self-understanding through a reflective self-confrontation recorded in writing. To define the "search for a new method of writing which does justice" to the "different reality" generated by such self-confrontational writing, Christa Wolf coined the term "subjective authenticity." It is necessary, she explains, in order to reveal "new structures of human relations in the present" (SA). "Subjective authenticity" keeps the text in motion and engages the reader, by virtue of its confessional nature, in an intimate dialogue; it admits to the dubiousness of "facts," the lie of language, and the honesty of relativity and engenders a narrative style of conjecture, the conditional, and insistent alternatives to the status quo.

Although Wolf confesses, even in her recent "Büchner-Prize Acceptance Speech" (1980), to an indulgence in utopian notions, she admits that the word "utopia" has itself been radically redefined. Once connoting the foreseeable realization of the new socialist society, it now signals the questionable hope that some means exist by which humanity can save itself from extinction. In Wolf's latest statements, faith in the improved future promised by "visionary socialism" has turned to doubt, for she now suspects that existing political systems offer people few alternatives to live their lives.

Recognizing that the location of alternatives requires revision— an analysis of history and society according to new perceptual structures not defined in terms of familiar (male) convention and tradition— Wolf suggests that it is time attention be paid to the voice and vision of the "other," of woman. Women, she urges, can and must alter the course of Western civilization by changing its "viewing lens" (C 278), by finding voices strong enough to overcome the tyranny of a two-thousand-year-old tradition. This exhortation issues from Wolf's recognition that experience is gendered—an insight that must have startled her[26] and preoccupied her explicitly for the past decade. The shock of this perception precipitates the radical alteration of her own assumptions: no longer can she posit a common denominator in her reader; women and men will read differently, unless they admit (as Günderrode does, while Kleist does not) to their androgyny. Ways of seeing, writing, relating to others need revision. The reappraisal of humanity must be launched without the intervention of long-established patterns of thought and behavior.

Early on, at least as early as *Divided Heaven*, Wolf articulates the insight that individual identity is established and defined in relation to others (or an other). Whether their lives are historically synchronous with that of the author/protagonist/narrator is irrelevant; their importance lies in their (positive) antithetical function, the provocation of self-questioning. The identificatory/alienating process that occurs is the theme of *Christa T.*, summarized in this passage: "losing one another and ourselves. The ingenuous open heart preserves one's ability to say 'I' to a stranger, until a moment comes when this strange 'I' returns and enters into 'me' again. Then at one blow one is captive, one is prepossessed; that much can be foretold" (*CT* 14).

After admitting that her self-definition is determined by books—a confession that intentionally blurs the boundary between "art" and "life" and suggests that proclivity for crossing borders that will come more and more to dominate the structure of her works—Wolf increasingly locates her authorial persona in reference to a female literary tradition, while her subject matter alludes to literary-historical moments that she recognizes as analogous to her own. These are defined in *No Place on Earth* as the era of German Romanticism (circa 1800 to 1830) and in *Cassandra* as the time of the Trojan War (around the thirteenth century B.C.).[27] The first embraces the Romantic poets who rebelled against enlightened German classical literature, represented by Goethe and Schiller, by insisting on the inclusion in art of a subjective element resistant to rational explanation; it also includes concerted efforts at collecting and recording materials from the German oral tradition, of which the most important, for Wolf's purposes, are the famous fairy tales of the Brothers Grimm. Recent analysis of these stories has demonstrated the profundity of both their psychological and their sociological content.[28] Wolf is especially aware of what they convey about the human subconscious, but she also suspects a sociological motivation for their emergence. The legendary Trojan War, on the other hand, marks for Wolf the beginning of Western civilization's glorification of patriarchy, whose legacy was encoded and ensured by the great heroic sagas of classical antiquity. Although she relies in her evocation of the Romantic era on the actual writings of the figures she designates as protagonists, her readings of the Cassandra-legend merely provide a path to the imagined narrative of the seer. Her story is simultaneously invented and "rescued" by Wolf; some three thousand years later, she responds to Cassandra's plea to Clytemnestra: "Send me a scribe, or better yet a young slave woman with a keen memory and a powerful voice. Ordain that she may repeat to her daughter what she hears from me. That the daughter in turn may pass it on to her daughter, and so on. So that alongside the river of heroic songs this tiny rivulet, too, may reach those faraway, perhaps happier people who will live in times to come" (*C* 81). For "[t]heir singers will pass on none of all this" (*C* 107).

Common to the two historical ages and Wolf's present time is the quality of rupture, of temporal hiatus: they are "gaps in time" that "we cannot let . . . pass without taking advantage of [them]" (*C* 124). "There at last," says Cassandra, "I had my 'we'" (*C* 124). The "we" embraces the text's author as well as its reader.

It may serve us here to recall three illuminating instances in Wolf's career; always the outcome of her questioning of self through text, these moments broaden her perspective and compound the metaphoric fabric that constitutes her aesthetic essence and essential aesthetic.

Wolf identifies two of these revelatory experiences in the fourth lecture of the *Cassandra*-series. This lecture takes the form of "A Letter, About Unequivocal and Ambiguous Meaning, Definiteness and Indefiniteness; About Ancient Conditions and New View-Scopes; About Objectivity" (C 272–305). Wolf describes how her reading of feminist theory has radically altered the lens through which she subsequently views Cassandra. This realignment of her perceptive angle parallels the moment of rupture experienced thirty years before, when the encounter with Marx and Engels at the beginning of her adult life molded her understanding of history and led toward socialism. That was in the late forties, just after the Second World War. Her immersion in feminist thought occurs in the early eighties. These two definitive experiences bracket the thirty years of Wolf's development as a writer. The third instance of revelation lies in this interim; as a durative and progressive moment, its temporal location is unfixable; it is defined by Wolf's reading of her self and her ultimate insistence on the "subjective authenticity" of the writer.

The "Interview with Myself" (1968), written during her work on *Christa T.* and constructed as a self-critical appraisal of that work and the path determined by its logic, can be read as articulating this procedural moment of transition. The "interview" comments on and justifies the fictional topic and the necessary idiosyncracy of Wolf's approach; it demonstrates an abolition of the author/material hierarchy, showing how she as author endows her thematic object with subjective force. The emergent fictional totality presents itself as a synthesis of the subject author and the object material:

> I noticed that the object of my story was not at all, or did not remain so clearly herself, Christa T. I suddenly faced myself. I had not foreseen this. The relations between "us"—Christa T. and the narrator "I" —shifted of themselves into the center; the differences in character and the points at which they touched, the tensions between "us" and the way they dissolved or failed to dissolve. (IM 76–77)

The forms of the self are realized as that self integrates aspects of the object/other. As part of experience, of both history and the experience of reading, such integration enables Christa Wolf (or one of her narrators) to posit an identity with (and in) a historical figure. In her works, Wolf successively probes ever more deeply into the past to understand and express the contemporary human condition and to speculate about the future. Historical confluence and temporal displacement govern this enterprise; by denying conventional categories —historical novel, for instance, or (socialist) realism—it operates by analogy grounded in its author's reality.

III. Changing Perspective: The Major Works

Our priorities are wrong; our world is "awry" (BP 5). Wolf's increasing engagement of history as allegory to voice her intensified concern about present and future determines the counterchronology of her works and the changes in her perspective.

Both narrated and historical time correspond in *Moskauer Novelle*. A rekindled love between the East German physician, Vera Brauer, and the Russian interpreter, Pavel Koschkin, provides the plot line and a model for dialectically resolving personal contradictions in a social frame. The two had known each other at the end of the war; each has since married and established a career. They meet by chance fifteen years later, when Vera participates in a Moscow medical technology conference, at which Pavel is the interpreter for the German group. The story is simple, its presentation straightforward. Wolf herself was later to consign it to relative oblivion by noting its too-rigid ideological conformity. In her essay "On the Sense and Senselessness of Naiveté" (1973), she asks: "How can someone who's nearly thirty years old write something so incredibly dogmatic *(traktatenhaft)*, nine years after the middle of this century and anything but untouched and unmoved by its momentous and moving events? (Dogmatic in the sense of propagating pious views . . .)" (SN 60).

Pavel and Vera must renounce their love for personal and political reasons. The conjunction of these realms marks the story as a model of socialist realism; the exemplary characters act in the spirit of party-mindedness; historical sins are forgiven; life on a farmer's collective is simply idyllic, and so on. The text's lessons are encoded in a central conversation inspired by the question, What will the human being of the future look like? The conversants endow the human being of the envisioned socialist utopia with characteristics such as "brotherliness," "truth," "spontaneity," "naiveté," "tenderness," "lack of hypocrisy," "thirst for knowledge," "courage," "modesty," "strength of character," and "the power to overcome the self" (MN 53).

Vera, whose perspective guides the narrative, indeed struggles with the dilemma posed by her love for Pavel. She is overcome by collective and personal guilt: she is German, and Pavel, who intended to study medicine after the war, suffered severe eye injury while saving her brother from a burning munitions store. Vision lost in 1944 is figuratively restored in 1959 as the dilemma of emotional entanglement is resolved with the aid and for the sake of socialist society.

Wolf's move to Halle in 1959 to work in a factory underscores her acceptance of the Bitterfeld Program. The doctrine and Wolf's participation in factory life found their literary expression in *Divided Heaven*. Continued dogmatism is tempered here by gradations in character presentation. The central plot is again the love crisis of a woman, Rita Seidel, and her growth in self-awareness as she overcomes the crisis. Rita is younger than her author and the fictional Vera of the earlier work:

37

she is unspoiled by the preconditioning of earlier (i.e., fascist) ideologies, a ready recipient of socialist ideas.

Shortly after her lover, Manfred, flees to West Berlin (in August 1961), the GDR erects the Berlin Wall in response to many difficulties—a two-year period of economic crisis, widespread discontent, and depletion of the work force, especially the skilled and professional workers. This "stop-gap measure" which "most people hoped . . . would lead to greater cultural freedom by making the population assume more responsibility for the socialist experiment"[29] signals the absoluteness of the lovers' separation and estrangement. The Wall's actuality is the implicit inducement for Rita's apparent suicide attempt; at the factory she falls between two train cars moving toward each other at a switch.

The love story is related retrospectively, as Rita lies in the hospital recovering from her "accident." The framed narrative permits Rita's recollection and evaluation of past events while creating two temporal levels whose interweaving demonstrates a notable sophistication of style. Rita's reflections and her gradually increasing self-understanding add a depth to her character (and to the others in the story) missing in Wolf's earlier work. The norms—both public and private, or "objective (social) reality" and "subjective authenticity"—that operate in this novel signal its transitional nature and propel the heated discussion around it. For Wolf, while supporting the Bitterfeld Program, is also in the process of "defining her face," as Günter de Bruyn puts it.[30] She—with Rita, perhaps, and certainly with Christa T.—is struggling with her recognition of the inauthenticity of heroic models; she doubts the "reality" of the correspondence between individual and abstract concept implied in Vera's name (truth). *Divided Heaven* confronts the catch-phrase criteria set forth by socialist realism. "Positive hero," "party-mindedness," "class struggle," or "social contradictions" imply the unanimous acceptance of certain meaning: they belong to the unquestioned and unquestionable language of the political cultural machine. Such monolithic discourse was certain to become problematic for as skeptical a writer as Wolf. The "party-minded" author, for instance, will act and write always in the interests and service of the socialist state. Sanctioned with professional status by governmental policy, he/she is normally a member of the League of Writers, in some cases also of the German Academy of the Arts, in every case subject to censorship, self-censorship, approbation, and applause accorded on the basis of fixed standards of acceptability. Socialist realist literature employs an omniscient narrative perspective (the reader must be secure, his/her confidence must not be shaken); its structure is contiguous; the heroes positive (i.e., exemplary, providing possibilities for identification and emulation). Western imperialism's class struggle operates as a foil for depicting the East's classless society; society is presented in its "revolutionary development," and "social contradictions" are solved through socialism.

Such criteria still prevail in *Divided Heaven;* the West is negatively portrayed, Rita's recuperation signifies a socialist resolution of the "social contradiction" of her love for the egocentric and disillusioned son of fascist parents, and so on. But the novel also harbors the germs of Wolf's emancipatory process in her increasing recognition that the text is inscribed by the reader who must be free to interpret and to evaluate. Rita's story narrates the character's reading of her own text, and the blending of different narrative voices as well as judgmental statements that redefine both narrator and narratee facilitate the reader's participation in the narrative. The beginnings of Wolf's gradual departure from socialist realism, although not from socialism, are signaled by her differentiated understanding of the materiality of experience as defining the individual or subjective truth of each person. Because she suspects the notions of historical determinism, which suggest a mechanical determination of individual lives—a supraindividual process of cause and effect that is universally legible—she destabilizes the idea of a common language. Such questioning of shared and inviolable meaning is fundamental to her work; it is also the main source for the contradictions that exist within and around it. Ultimately, in her efforts to avoid imagistic (finalizing) portrayal, she forfeits description for the sake of vision; her truths, won at such expense and so strongly felt, so articulately transmitted, ask for—and receive—approval or rejection. The lyrical power of her epigrammatic language is at once her strength —and her danger. For it runs the risk of countering its own intention by imprisoning its reader; it pulls us in, but it also wants to let us go. Wolf's privileging of "subjective authenticity," of a truth constituted by the "traces left in us by events," is an act of self-exposure that leaves her and her enterprise in a vulnerable position. It asks to be read by critical analogy. This truth's irrevocable logic should lead us to our own "traces," which include the "event" of reading Christa Wolf; we misread if we (mis)appropriate Wolf's truths for ourselves.

Wolf has not yet discovered her narrative balance in *Divided Heaven.* Although we might appreciate her sensitive and differentiated treatment of the complexities and transitoriness of love, we may be alienated, in comparative retrospect, by the resolution that transpires more in an ideological than in a private realm. The exclusive and positive description of socialist society limits the text's accessibility. The adulation of technological advances—both in the small world of Rita's factory brigade and in the larger world, where the Russian, Yuri Gagarin, makes the first manned trip into space, is qualified by subsequent historical developments. The chronicle of healthy self-evaluation that finally allows Rita to call things by their right names (*DH* 202) and to see everything in the correct perspective seems too simple. Ideological alienation would, however, bar our recognition of this text's transitional nature. Its emancipatory gesture is more clearly visible in the context of Wolf's later works, but it is also signaled by the storm of critical controversy that washed over it in the East and the West German press. The lengthy and fascinating debate demonstrates two central points: the language of this work is polyvalent, not entirely correspondent to conventional meanings; and the character portrayal, in resisting caricature, is sensitive to the irreducibility of the individual. Herein lie the roots of that tension I referred to earlier; it will define and endanger Wolf's enterprise between aesthetics and ideology. The aesthetics of *Divided Heaven* unleashed the critical debate in the GDR; the ideology engenders criticism in a larger critical community.

Structurally, *Divided Heaven* moves toward that agreement of form and content that Wolf would refine in *The Quest for Christa T.*: it presents a dialectically determined interaction of the present self with the historical self that projects an envisioned future self. At the end of her lengthy hospitalization, Rita has overcome her past in the recollection of her story and emerges at once finished and unfinished: she has assimilated and interpreted her experience, has changed because of it, and is now prepared to "live [her life] to the full" (*DH* 212).

The affirmation of socialism, of the collective as a life-style, of technology as progress—all still possible for the visionary Marxist of the early sixties—was to dim as Wolf's view of self and world became more acute. The formal indicator of her increasing reluctance to embrace a political system as a guiding principle is suggested by the difficulty of saying "I." When she wants to shift from third- to first-person narrative, she finds that the "I" is not definitive, lacking clear contour in relation to its external surroundings. The positive perspective, the vision, in her next novel, *The Quest for Christa T.*, is thus much more difficult to locate than in Wolf's earlier works.

Wolf's redefinition of self as author that occupied her in the years following *Divided Heaven* would determine the fundamental differences between the earlier works and her seminal *Quest*. It is articulated in the short narrative, "An Afternoon in June," written in 1965—the same year in which Wolf completed a first draft of *Christa T.* Anticipating the published version of that work in many aspects of style and content, this story manifests the decisive bending of her angle of vision that was to alter radically her narrative presentation and her authorial identity. The earlier works affirmed and sought to practice socialist ideology; they focused on the locales where this ideology is government policy, thereby implicitly or explicitly excluding as radically "other" the capitalist societies to the west. "An Afternoon in June" posits a nonspecific locus and permits thereby a universality not obtaining in the previous works. At the same time as it stresses those humanistic values that underlie Wolf's socialism (and deemphasizes—indeed, seems to abandon—the didactic criteria outlined above), however, it also withdraws itself from the immediate grasp by virtue of its ambiguous stylistic simplicity.

It is hardly coincidental that the woman in this story spends the afternoon reading in a garden, while her husband and two daughters are involved with various kind of chores and amusements, or that the story itself is addressed to an invisible narratee referred to by the narrator as "you." The interruption of the idyll by the noise of airplanes overhead, gruesome newspaper headlines, and the news of a fatal train collision in which a neighbor has died makes the story into an allegory (another taboo of socialist realism) of lost paradise. Indeed, the garden is described as "the original concept of a garden" (AJ 41), which realizes its potential independent of all human effort. In the complex allusions to (threatened) utopia and primeval natural abundance and perfection, the story tempts to various interpretations: it could be read as a statement of Wolf's disillusionment with "real existing socialism," with the policies in her country that demand conformity and deny individuality; but it may serve equally as a more general statement on the conditions of contemporary civilization (a reading made even more plausible by Wolf's later utterances in her "Büchner-Prize Acceptance Speech" and *Cassandra*).

The temporal and spatial enclosure of "An Afternoon in June" paradoxically abolishes the story's limits. As the woman reads about Italy and the Mediterranean, she transcends her actual location; by inventing new words out of components of existing ones in a private word game, the family members release themselves from the thrall of established language. In the references to the garden's condition in earlier years, the rose that shows it particular beauty only for a day, the dandelion seeds that invade the neighbor's lawn, the deliberately slow movement of a snail, and so on, time is made fluid, and spatial boundaries become flexible; the importance and function of the human beings within this fluidity become more a matter of reference to self and others than to time and place. For all its intimacy, and despite the increasing formal complexity of her works, this perspective facilitates our access to Wolf's conviction that people, not ideological systems, may yet locate alternatives to permit the survival of humanity.

In *The Quest for Christa T.*, Wolf addresses directly these issues of alternatives and survival (or lack of alternatives and death). *Christa T.* tells the story of the friendship between Wolf's anonymous narrator and Christa T., and of Christa T.'s death from leukemia at the age of thirty-five. It is a recollection, preserving, in the conditional uncertainty of self questioning prose, Christa T.'s resistance to conformity, to labels, to verbal finalization, to enclosure. The narration allows the narrator to understand the person she has become in the process of integrating the "otherness" of Christa T. into her own being. She enters into dialogue with her, by both consulting her own memory and reading Christa T.'s writings; she reflects on those experiences of interchange and reformulates them into a narrative which, like the character it commemorates, has beginning and end but invites dialogue and resists closure. The book containing the thoughts about Christa T. thus expresses its intention in its structure, as it enables the reader to assume a reflective posture similar to that of the narrator. The book becomes an intimate interchange between the writer and the reader, who thus reenact the relation between Christa T. and her narrator.

Christa T., in notable distinction to the recuperated Rita, "didn't trust . . . names . . . she didn't trust herself . . . She shrank from stamping any name on herself" (CT 35). Perhaps if she had succeeded in her project of writing and managed to express the alternatives in this way, her attempt to "*dichten*," to make herself secure against the intrusion of the "barbarism of the modern age" (C 159), might have functioned much in the way the garden idyll does—permitting (en)closure and the freedom of alternatives at the same time. Christa Wolf succeeds at this where Christa T. does not; but she succeeds partly at the expense of the character whose life she narrates, only to demonstrate the inherent dangers in narrating a life, for to do so is to impress upon it that imagistic stamp of finality Christa T. so anxiously sought to avoid.

There are in *Christa T.*, as many critics have noted, hints of disenchantment with systems that demand conformity as a price for individual "health." Indeed, it has been suggested that Christa T.'s resistance to definition, her abhorrence of labels and dislike for those "up-and-doing people" without imagination (CT 51), her inability to fit herself into the collective society, her distrust of language, her role playing, and her self-doubt are symptoms of the illness that really kills her: reductive ideological normalization, not leukemia, is the cause of her death.[31] Because she is "out of date" (CT 62), she is destroyed by the time in which she lives. The work that meditates about her and presents these disturbing meditations through a complex narrative structure, appears—at least in the East German literary context—also to be "out of date," although it, like Christa T., who sensed that she was "born too soon" (CT 182), would be accommodated by a time belonging to the future rather than to the past.

The subjective stance Christa Wolf assumes through her narrator in *Christa T.* was anathema to the norms of socialist realism and represents a radical formal break with her earlier published works. Wolf's questioning leads to a positive restlessness about the self and its expression that is formally and linguistically reflected in *Christa T.* Here we witness the full employment of those modernist devices developed in earlier times by other writers as an aesthetic response to the loss of certainty—absolutely constituted by natural law, religion, or governmental system—and the concomitant recognition of the relativity of truth and the individual's responsibility for self definition.[32] *Christa T.* signals for Christa Wolf a forfeiture of the absolute as it questions the concept of "facts" and privileges the singularity of individual truths. Her personal frame of reference will henceforth be more directly filtered through the lens of her own reading.

Wolf's ensuing use of a mixture of literary devices and generic styles is reminiscent of her narrator's definition of Christa T.'s "vision of herself" (117): she is trying all the possibilities, exploring the alternatives of expression, all the while insisting on the reader's partnership.

With similar insistence, she demonstrates the imprisoning dangers of figuration; she avoids that imagistic language that fixes author, reader, and subject matter, abolishes their dialectic potential, and thereby diminishes their "reality." Her subsequent experimentation with "mixed form," a term she uses to describe and praise the eclectic writings of Bettina von Arnim, denotes primarily her attempt to communicate her own truth by casting off conventional formal categories. The conscious avoidance of generic convention wants to liberate writer as well as reader and suggests a simultaneous interaction of both with the material. This interaction undermines the traditional subject/object dichotomy between reader/author and text, for all are discovered in the process of reading.

Wolf realizes, with Bettina, that "the structures of the aesthetic known to her must be related in whatever sort of mediated manner to the hierarchical structures of society. It is an insoluble contradiction— that literature is dependent on the systems which it must nonetheless transcend in order to become literature" (BL, 316). Thus, in adopting the notion of "mixed form," Wolf seeks aesthetic as well as social emancipation from imposed structures. The more pronounced this endeavor has become in the past two decades, the more Wolf's writing eludes generic categorization: one form complements or functions as metatext or interpretation of another, so that a full reading demands considering the essays, speeches, interviews, reviews, forewords, and afterwords *together* with the fictional attempts around which these other forms appear. Her most recent works, especially *Cassandra*, include all the components of these several forms (*Cassandra* consists of two "records of a trip," one "work diary," one "letter," and one "story") and thus become formally representative of the whole of Wolf's literary project.

The short fictional pieces published between *Christa T.* and *Patterns of Childhood* evince a new level of assurance in her continued search for self while voicing a growing distrust of scientific-technological thinking. "Instrumental thinking" (also inevitably a component of political ideology) strives to classify everything according to measures of utility, thereby eliminating from consideration (and from view) those noncategorizable elements of human existence not subsumed under the Enlightenment concept of *ratio*. These are increasingly seen to belong to the realm of woman: sensitivity, sensuality, the yearning for happiness, love. Wolf's critical position parallels the German Romantics' rebellion against Enlightenment thinking and feminism's encounter with patriarchy; the allusions in *Unter den Linden: Drei unwahrscheinliche Geschichten* (Unter den Linden: three improbable stories, 1974) confirm these connections. The title story (1969) displays manifold references to several romantic works; disenchantment with "instrumental thinking" is most evident in the other two: "Self-Experiment: Appendix to a Report" (1972) and "Neue Lebensansichten eines Katers" (New Life and Opinions of a Tomcat, 1970). The same doubts and fears are articulated differently in her later "Büchner-Prize Acceptance Speech" (1980).

"Unter den Linden" narrates a dream. This device suspends the organizing tendencies of the conscious mind of those "traces left in us by events" that comprise personal reality. The story's title is resonant: Unter den Linden was the Prussian military's parade street in the undivided Berlin of earlier times; it is now the most important street in East Berlin, flanked by old and new monumental architecture and ending at the famous symbol of old Berlin, the Brandenburg Gate, as well as new Berlin's Wall. The street connects the dreamer's private inner world with the external world of history, politics, and culture.

The narrative integration here of elements that will expand the intertextuality of Wolf's subsequent writing betrays her reconsideration of works from the German Romantic period. A historical context is implied in the preface, a quotation from the nineteenth-century Berlin saloniere, Rahel Varnhagen;[33] the dream-persona encounters a fairy tale figure, a "golden fish"; her pretext is, in part, the fabulous water spirit, Undine.[34] Allusions abound to the formulaic language of fairy tale and to its representation of the simultaneous existence of everyday reality and wondrous elements (Christa Wolf would point to the folk-etymological relationship of *wound* and *wonder*).

The speaking subject in "Unter den Linden" again reaches beyond itself, and beyond purely self-referential narrative, by addressing an other and simultaneously asks that that other become the subject in the dialogic process of reading. Theory and practice converge once more; but the theory is now more epistemological than ideological, and the practice seems intentionally abstruse. Wolf has moved through levels of consciousness, from the primary and naive upper level to subconscious depths. In the process, she has abandoned the conventional portrayal of exemplary characters intended to prompt in the reader identification and self-correcting emulation.

The narrator's direct address in "An Afternoon in June" and in "Unter den Linden"—to an unspecified "you"—is one means of generating the dialogue that defines the experience of literature. Another entails mediation through intimate documents. Already in *Christa T.*, letters, diary entries, and other materials written by the protagonist constitute part of the book about her. The other two stories in *Unter den Linden* are also conceived as reports or letters addressed to others. In "New Life and Opinions of a Tomcat," the feline narrator describes to an obviously sympathetic narratee how he undermines the scientific attempts of his master and his colleagues, who plan to use cybernetic programming to rid humanity of all those questionable manifestations of the "soul" that stand in the way of man's attainment of total happiness. The tomcat Max sabotages the professor's system by clandestinely rearranging the cards in his well-organized files. This satire of extreme human behavior, conceived as a latter-day revision of the musings of a character from the late Romantic period, E. T. A. Hoffmann's famous Kater Murr,[35] also obliquely questions the "rational" authority of Hoffmann's contemporary, Goethe: the scientists' omnipotent and infallible servant, the computer named "Heinrich," evokes associations with Goethe's Dr. Faust.[36]

Hoffmann discovered new ways of depicting the human soul, appealing in his tales to subrational processes and insisting that some elements of human existence cannot be dismissed by the concept of *ratio*. The self-discoveries to which Wolf's literature takes her parallel Hoffmann's in many ways. She does not forsake the notion of *ratio* but implies that it must be accompanied by nonquantifiable concepts recognized nonetheless as part of total human experience. More recently, she has suggested that *ratio* is a male conception, a "logic whose ultimate manifestation is the rocket" (L 153). Rationality, she claims, has become equated with utility; our unilateral focus on instrumentality excludes any and all other processes of the human mind and undermines humanity itself.

The association of *ratio* with the male sphere—and the concomitant exclusion from that sphere of all elements not embraced by *ratio*, notably love—is the radical basis for "Self Experiment: Appendix to a Report." The "Appendix" to which the title refers again takes the form of a letter, here with a specified addressee. The reader must imagine the report that precedes it and details in scientific language a thirty-day period of drug-induced manhood in the life of the female writer. The letter, addressed to the director of the institute in which the experiment was performed and in which the writer/experimental subject is also part of the scientific research team, imposes an idiosyncratic interpretation on the objective report as the writer explains why she chose to reverse the experiment after thirty days. Her inability to conform (in a male body with a female "mentality") to the role expected of her by men and women alike, and her recognition that the director, whom she had loved as a woman, is himself incapable of love, contribute to her disillusioning discovery that the male world excludes subrational emotion. The writer concludes that the very values of male tradition demand suppressing or eliminating much that is precious to humanity and that she must invent for herself the object of her affection: "Now my experiment lies ahead: the attempt to love. Which incidentally can also lead to fantastic inventions—to the creation of the person one can love" (SE 131). (Karoline von Günderrode echoes this conclusion in *No Place on Earth* [117].) Woman's "creation of the person one can love" suggests the necessary rewriting of history to circumvent the dominance of *ratio*-based tradition.

Wolf implies neither that male domination is equivalent to rational thought and behavior nor that reason and rationality should be forsworn for the sake of some alternative mode of thinking and acting. Indeed, it has been necessary here to insert the notion of the subrational as a category separate from the irrational, which has often disastrously dominated the historical actions of man. In *Patterns of Childhood*, Wolf excoriates the tyranny of the irrational, the Germany of the Third Reich. The subrational, in contrast, is a positive and necessary element of humanity that has too often been suppressed. The antagonism between reason and the subrational is portrayed in the violently torn consciousness of Heinrich von Kleist in *No Place on Earth* and is behind Wolf's appeal to move beyond "the citadel of reason" in her "Büchner-Prize Acceptance Speech" (BP 6). Finally, in *Cassandra*, Wolf herself rejects categorization according to traditional aesthetic norms by declaring that she does "*not* have a poetics" (C 141), continues her development of a "mixed form," and identifies with and integrates into her own consciousness her version of the Cassandra figure.

Patterns of Childhood, Wolf's autobiographical novel of 1976, renews her quest for the synthesis of first person and third person, here presented as two distinct parts of one indistinct self. The adult rereads her childhood—a reading much burdened by the realities of Germany in the thirties and the forties—in a project of personal and aesthetic reintegration. The writing, in which the narrator addresses herself as "you" and the child as "she," constitutes "[a] game in and with the second person and the third person, for the purpose of their fusion" (PC 158) into a newly-defined "I." Despite the complexity of its organization, *Patterns of Childhood* demonstrates clearly Wolf's understanding of the reading process. For whether we seek insight and sight by means of a printed text with a named author (a key author in this work, as in the "Büchner-Prize Acceptance Speech," is Ingeborg Bachmann, for instance) or by deciphering a text authored mainly by historical vicissitudes, it is evident that the text is reinscribed by the reading individual. The narrator in this novel—unlike Wolf in her readings of authors with whom she senses an "elective affinity," whose works reach out to her own sensibilities—could not be more alienated from the text her memory thrusts upon her. The reading is an obligatory and severely taxing exercise; its result is dubious: "the past, which can still split the first person into the second and the third—has its hegemony been broken? Will the voices be still? I don't know" (PC 406).

Patterns of Childhood entails the verbalization of nightmares and the admission of particular guilt. But the attempt to locate the child, echoing the Neruda-poem that prefaces the narrative,[37] poses universal ontological and aesthetic questions; although Wolf's patterns may not be ours, we share her moral and narrative predicament. Marxism projects the abolition of self-alienation through work. *Trauerarbeit* (the work of mourning) is Wolf's word for the recuperation of her alienated former self in this book: "The adult left the child behind, pushed her aside, forgot her, suppressed her, denied her, remade, falsified, spoiled and neglected her, was ashamed and proud of her, loved her with the wrong kind of love, and hated her with the wrong kind of hate. Now, in spite of all impossibility, the adult wishes to make the child's acquaintance" (PC 7).

"The Difficulty of Saying 'I'" (*CT* 169) originates here in at least two separate realms. One is the specific historical situation of the author/narrator—her admitted identity with the child of another historical period, another Germany than the one in which the adult lives. Wolf explores here with relentless honesty, essentially for the first time, the self she was before 1945 and the experiences described in *Christa T.* and *Moskauer Novelle*.

Patterns of Childhood functions as both summary and new beginning. Viewed in the context of Wolf's oeuvre, it appears as a necessary confessional effort, a task required by the unavoidable logic of the dialectical base established in earlier works and by her repeated ontological questions. I suspect that Wolf was compelled to this narrative confrontation with her entire personal history (rather than beginning with the "change of perspective" at the war's end) in order to free herself from the restricting bonds of that past and to move her vision beyond the temporal borders of her own life-span.

Wolf's excruciating reinscription of suppressed childhood required four years; it was followed by an event of similarly disturbing consequence. In 1976, the GDR government expatriated the popular and talented singer and composer, Wolf Biermann. Christa Wolf found herself—and this is, in her case, an extraordinary lament—"utterly cast back on literature." Explaining the motivation for her ensuing work on the Romantic figures Kleist and Günderrode, Wolf also makes it quite clear that an enforced distinction between "life" and "art" (a rift that preoccupies the characters in *No Place on Earth*) results for her in an artificial and alienating position:

> 1976 was a caesura in cultural policy development in our country, outwardly indicated by Wolf Biermann's expatriation. . . . A group of authors became aware that their direct collaboration, the kind that they themselves could answer for and thought was right, was no longer needed. We are socialists after all; we lived as socialists in the GDR because that's where we wanted to be involved, to collaborate. To be utterly cast back on literature brought about a crisis for the individual, an existential crisis. It was the origin, for me among others, of working with the material of such lives as Günderrode's and Kleist's. . . .
>
> I took these two figures in order to rehearse their problematic for myself. (CI 89)

"Their problematic," now recognized as Wolf's own and intensified by her questioning of the correspondence between her goals for a humane and moral society and her government's practice, denotes an acute sense of being "out of step" or of existing in a "gap in time."

Wolf's sense of crisis and displacement is reflected in the title, *No Place on Earth* (1979). Synchronous narrative voices, multiple perspective, and temporal overlay demonstrate Wolf's integral reading of literary artists whose era mirrors the social discrepancies of her own time and place. Displacement of subject and object is evident at every level, from the work's narrative strategy, to the interaction between the central figures, to the author's literal appropriation of their own words, presented as hers through her particular compositional devices. In previous works, Wolf's material had come mainly from her own experience; the products of her interaction (her reading) of that experience are her (fictional) texts. In *No Place on Earth*, while she again admits to an autobiographical impulse, she deals with material that is the already existing product of her two authentic figures' self-confrontation. The work demonstrates the dialectical process in which she hopes to engage her own readers; like many of her essays on other writers, it manifests a revision that constitutes a portion of the reader's private truth. To criticize Wolf for misrepresenting Kleist or Günderrode is to misunderstand the project of her reading *and* her writing, or to refuse to participate in this enterprise; it is to insist on adherence to a theoretical, preexistent truth.

The narrative's primary level reclaims the ill-fated poets of the Romantic era who, as Anna Seghers described them, "wrote hymns to their country, against the walls of whose society they beat their brows" (FT 116). Wolf's abundant use of authentic materials from the lives of these poets underscores the validity of their representation. Her additional essays, on Günderrode and on Bettina von Arnim, contribute to and verify the historical authenticity of the speech, gestures, and interrelationships of the characters in the fictional work.[38]

Filtered through Wolf's revisionary lens, the authentic documents effectively reinforce the subjectivity of her statements. "Rehearsing their problematic," Wolf masters the narrative representation of dialectical synthesis, demonstrates the abolition of binary hierarchies. As the object-other is integrated to constitute an element of personal experience, she develops the communicative method that allows that other to emerge simultaneously as autonomous entity and as part of the author/narrator. The authentic sources in the fictional presentation of *No Place on Earth* substantiate the independence of their authors; Wolf's particular method of integrating them simultaneously defines her creative act and her statement.

The work's structure reflects this synthesizing process. The distinct narrative voice of the opening passages soon merges with the speakers, whose voices merge with each other in turn. Such confluence prompts the repeated rhetorical question: Who is speaking? (*NP* 4 et passim). But the question merely draws the reader's attention to the impossibility of an answer; it confirms simultaneity in the integration of multiple voices: Kleist and Günderrode, narrator—and narratee.

Such a narrative position is now familiar; new is the introduction of voices belonging to historically recognizable others to sound the different aspects of the self.[39] The doomed characters figure in their reader's subjective narrative fabric; they complicate the pattern and reinforce the design. As we have seen, Wolf had been moving gradually toward delineating male and female spheres in her earlier works, and she had celebrated the independent thinking of women in her laudatory essay on Maxie Wander, "In Touch" (1978).[40] The appropriated language of the coequal protagonists of *No Place on Earth* articulates what Wolf increasingly recognizes as a primary source of Western civilization's ominous dilemma. Convention requires Kleist, whom Günderrode accuses of not acknowledging the "feminine" in himself (*NP* 104), to submit to the patriarchal military bureaucracy of nineteenth-century Prussia; he must conform despite himself and ultimately at the cost of his life. Günderrode, whose writings are dictated by her inner being while her aesthetics are determined by the dominant tradition of German letters, is destroyed by her inherent inability to meet that tradition's norms.[41] Both are torn by an internal male-female dichotomy, by the discrepancy between art and reality to which only they seem attuned, by the threat of literary precursors and traditions they despair of matching. It is hardly coincidental that their discussion reverts so often to that dominating genius in Weimar, Goethe. Wolf finds a contemporary parallel to the Romantics' obsession with Goethe when, in her *Cassandra*-lectures, she notes the assumption in her *Classical Antiquity Lexicon* that anyone who proclaims a "poetics" must measure himself or herself against Brecht.[42]

The "precursors" are figures for the predicament of the woman writer in the GDR. Kleist's resistance to Prussian bureaucracy and Günderrode's simultaneous defiance and acceptance of canonical tradition combine to delineate Wolf's unhappy position in 1979. But having once committed herself to the concept of socially redemptive art, Wolf cannot succumb to pressures brought upon her by an unseeing and an unhearing world or by the apparent ineffectiveness of words. In her important "Büchner-Prize Acceptance Speech," she insists that we must alter our way of seeing and listen to the seers—the poets: "literature ought to be taken at its word and applied to the preservation of human affairs" (BP 11). She pleads for the invention of a new language, for "words that do not merely negate the old sense of values but that might express a different, contemporary sense" (BP 5), allowing "literature . . . to confront [the] map of death with its own map" (BP 11).

The central figure of Wolf's confrontational map is Cassandra, a legendary name evoking complex associations. The seer Cassandra told the truth to which no one listened. In Wolf's revision, she is defined by the "stories told in the inner courts" (*C* 33) and equally at home in the world of the temple (read: literature) and the world of daily affairs. Despite her warnings, her city is destroyed by the Greeks who henceforth determine the course of Western civilization. She understands the actions of Penthesilea and Clytemnestra in her terms and theirs, in contrast to the accusatory categories of the male world. Cassandra's perspective offers, in Wolf's interpretation, the revised way of seeing necessary for reevaluating the terms by which we live today. Cassandra speaks finally, for Christa Wolf, in the first person.

"I have arrived," Wolf says in the first of her *Cassandra*-lectures (C 159). The moment of self-recognition asserted here corresponds to her literal and figurative arrival in Athens. The mandatory rereading of history must begin at the beginning; revision and the language necessary for its articulation must redefine that early moment. Cassandra's words must be (re)created, (re)interpreted, and, perhaps, heard and understood for the first time.

Cassandra goes to her death having recited her (hi)story and Troy's destruction as she sits, slave to the victorious Agamemnon, before the gates of the Greek's residence. Past, present, and future are synchronized in the interior dialogue of which the entire narrative is constituted; recalling the past, she foretells Agamemnon's death at the hands of Clytemnestra. Her story's narrative spans a few hours in the present moment preceding her death; the narrated time includes her personal history and extends forward, by implication, several thousand years into our present time. Cassandra's recollection is paradigmatic for the history of woman and for literature: it describes her/their brutal exploitation, suggesting that the "barbarism of the modern age" derives from the celebration of warfare and heroism. Image making alienates human from human; Cassandra cannot love Aeneas after he becomes a hero. Does this not echo the personal fears of Christa T.'s narrator-friend, here writ large on the scene of ancient history? Repeatedly Wolf refers to Cassandra's fated inability to use her prophetic insight to save her people. It was, notably, the male god Apollo who placed the curse of ineffectiveness on Cassandra: because he could not ravish her as a love object, he caused the impotence of her subjective visionary powers. Such, implies Wolf, is the historic fate of woman; and she hopes that her resurrection of Cassandra will lead to the recognition of this exploitative denial of woman and to the revision of the norms that permit it. The other, having recognized herself and begun to take herself seriously, must now be recognized and taken seriously by the world whose condition is "awry."

The cipher Cassandra is deciphered anew by Wolf. Against all odds, Wolf associates herself with the prophet doomed not to be understood and pleads for understanding. Such identification admits the implicit fear that her words will have no effect; but it also warns that denial of her words (i.e., of literature) may have a corresponding parallel: the destruction of the world as we know it. It is a paradoxical identification, then, in which hope and despair are joined in a message that demands our attention and participation. With this narrative, Wolf wants to realize her hope that "one might again be able to speak and tell a story to another without feeling ashamed" (BP 5). For to eliminate the sense of shame from the act of storytelling is tantamount to abolishing the dualism that distinguishes narrator from narratee. Shame derives only from an awareness of otherness, of different standards of judgment held by writer and reader. Their fusion, realized formally in Wolf's recent writing through the use of the all-inclusive "we," should permit us to read ourselves through a new lens.

Notes

1. Hans Kaufmann compares this gesture to a highly individualized variant of the poetic principle of catharsis, noting that Wolf's works represent a "working through" of periods of crisis (see his article in this volume). The procedural complexities of Wolf's writing indeed represent an attempt to "cope with things by writing" (CT), and their confessional nature suggests an act of cleansing. But the matter is complicated. The Aristotelian notion of catharsis, even if qualified, locates Wolf in opposition to Brecht (in ways that she would resist—see, for example, her comments in the prefatory remarks to *Conditions of a Narrative: Cassandra*, C 141). And it suppresses the aspect of labor, the *Trauerarbeit* to which Wolf refers, not the labor of the writing, but the mental and spiritual effort demanded by remembrance. The "work" is part of Wolf's Marxian premise and remains a constant in her oeuvre. The cathartic function of narration is questioned, however, by the implicit opposition of two assertions that hover over her project: she doubts (in her later writing, at least) Anna Seghers' idea that a problem can be solved in the telling ("what has become narratable is already mastered" [SA]) and confronts with similar challenge the Wittgensteinian proposition that there are things of which we cannot speak: "Wovon man nicht sprechen kann, darüber muss man schweigen" (what we cannot talk about we must consign to silence). (See Ludwig Wittgenstein, *Tractatus Logico-Philosophicus*, in *Werkausgabe*, vol. 1 [Frankfurt/Main: Suhrkamp, 1984], 85.)

2. The SED is the Communist Party of the German Democratic Republic.

3. Wolf Biermann, an extremely popular and controversial singer and composer of satirical songs and ballads in which he often took the actions of his government to task, was refused permission to reenter the GDR in November, 1976, after a concert tour in West Germany. The letter questioning the government's action was signed by Sarah Kirsch, Christa Wolf, Volker Braun, Franz Fühmann, Stephan Hermlin, Stefan Heym, Günter Kunert, Heiner Müller, Rolf Schneider, Gerhard Wolf, Jurek Becker, Erich Arendt, and Fritz Cremer, and submitted, as an open letter to the Central Committee of the SED, on November 17, 1976, to *Neues Deutschland*, Reuters, and France Presse. The protest burgeoned when more than 150 individuals, mostly artists and writers, signed the letter or wrote their own statements. As a direct result of her signing of the letter, Christa Wolf (among others) was first censored by the League of Writers on November 26 and then removed from the leadership of the League on December 20. For more information on this incident and on Wolf Biermann, see *NGC*, no. 10 (Winter 1977): 9–11, and Karl-Heinz Jakobs, "'Wir werden ihre Schnauzen nicht vergessen,'" *Der Spiegel* 48 (1981): 86–108.

4. Two principal decrees dominated literary production during the years of socialist reconstruction in the GDR: the denunciation of "modernist" or "formalist" art, and the espousal of the doctrine of socialist realism. The cutting-off from nonsocialist literature was launched by Georg Lukács and his followers in the late 1920s and early 1930s, when they denounced what they termed "avantgardism," "aestheticism," and "formalism." The introduction of socialist realism is credited to Gorky (1934); it was refined by Zhdanov into the dogma accepted as official policy by the GDR in 1951. Its basic principles require that the author must study exactly the life of the workers and the social and technological conditions of their work; that literature has the task of educating the public toward socialism—the writer must follow Stalin's call to become "an engineer of the soul"; and that literature should not represent the reality of work and society as "objective reality" but rather "reality in its revolutionary development." In Lukács's definition, "socialist realism examines human traits and abilities according to the extent to which they contain the will and capacity for the creation of a positive new reality." Quoted in Werner Brettschneider, *Zwischen literarischer Autonomie und Staatsdienst. Die Literatur der DDR* (1972; 3d ed. Berlin: Erich Schmidt, 1980), 24. For the texts of the speeches given by Gorky

and Zhdanov at the First Conference of the Union of Soviet Writers in 1934, see *Marxismus und Literatur. Eine Dokumentation in drei Bänden*, ed. Fritz J. Raddatz (Reinbek: Rowohlt, 1969), vol. 1, 335–353. For a fuller discussion of socialist realism, see *Marxism, Communism and Western Society: A Comparative Encylopedia*, ed. C. D. Kerring (New York: Herder and Herder, 1972–), vol. 8.

5. For more information on Wolf's biography, see Alexander Stephan, *Christa Wolf* (Munich: Beck, 1979). See also the Chronology in this volume.

6. Mayer, a major literary scholar and critic, and Bloch, an important Marxist philosopher, were among several others whose interpretation of Marxism did not conform to officially imposed ideology. Both professors at Leipzig in the early fifties (when Wolf studied there), they were dismissed from their university positions and virtually forced to seek a forum in exile. Mayer— in the words of Wolfgang Emmerich "a wanderer between two worlds"—spent World War II in exile, the years from 1945 to 1947 in Frankfurt am Main and 1947 to 1963 in Leipzig, and has lived in West Germany since 1963. Bloch moved to West Germany in 1961. Emmerich sketches the alarming drain of artists and intellectuals from the GDR in his *Kleine Literaturgeschichte der DDR* (Darmstadt/Neuwied: Luchterhand, 1981), especially 189ff.

7. For more detail on this biographical history, see Jack Zipes, "Introduction," in *Divided Heaven* (rpt. New York: Adler, 1979–1981), xi–xviii. The Bitterfeld Movement was named after the great electrical-industrial complex of Bitterfeld, site of the first conference in April 1959. The movement was an organized attempt on the part of the government's cultural policy makers, here represented by the Mitteldeutscher Verlag (a major publishing company), to bring about a cultural revolution by involving the worker in writing, the writer in the world of the simple worker. Its slogan was: "Greif zur Feder, Kumpel, die sozialistische Nationalkultur braucht dich!" (Buddy, grab your pen—the socialist national culture needs you!). The practical result of the movement was the organization of a number of "Associations of Writing Workers," out of which there emerged several publications that sustained the tradition of "workers' literature" begun at the inception of the socialist movement in Germany in the late nineteenth century and strongly established during the period of the Weimar Republic. Several of Wolf's literary colleagues participated directly, as she did, and based literary works on their experiences in industrial and agricultural settings. Examples are Brigitte Reimann's *Ankunft im Alltag* (1961), Hermann Kant's *Die Aula* (1965), Franz Fühmann's *Kabelkran* (1961), and Erik Neutsch's *Bitterfelder Geschichten* (1961). See Emmerich, *Kleine Literaturgeschichte der DDR*, especially 86–104.

8. Wolf's most important essays on Seghers are collected in *Lesen und Schreiben: Neue Sammlung* and in *Die Dimension des Autors: Essays und Aufsätze, Reden und Gespräche, 1959–1985*. These include "Glauben an Irdisches" ("Faith in the Terrestrial," 1969), "Bei Anna Seghers" ("A Visit to Anna Seghers," 1972), and "Fortgesetzter Versuch" (Continued attempt, untranslated, 1975).

9. "Truth that Can Be Faced—Ingeborg Bachmann's Prose" (1972), in *The Reader and the Writer*, 83–96.

10. "Nun ja! Das nächste Leben geht aber heute an: Ein Brief über die Bettine" (Yes indeed! But the next life starts today: A letter about Bettina, 1980).

11. "Der Schatten eines Traumes: Karoline von Günderrode—Ein Entwurf" (The shadow of a dream: Karoline von Günderrode—a sketch, 1979).

12. "In Touch" ("Berührung," 1978).

13. "Gespräch mit Christa Wolf," (1974). Also published as "Die Dimension des Autors" (in *Lesen und Schreiben. Neue Sammlung*) and as "Subjektive Authentizität" (in *Die Dimension des Autors*); and included in translation in this volume: "Subjective Authenticity: A Conversation with Hans Kaufmann."

14. "Unruhe und Betroffenheit: Gespräch mit Joachim Walther" (1973).

15. "Ich bin für eine gewisse Masslosigkeit: Gespräch mit Wilfried F. Schoeller" (1979).

16. "Kultur ist, was gelebt wird: Ein Interview mit Christa Wolf" ("Culture is What You Experience—An Interview with Christa Wolf," 1982).

17. Published separately in German as *Voraussetzungen einer Erzählung: Kassandra. Frankfurter Poetik-Vorlesungen (Conditions of a Narrative: Cassandra. Frankfurt Lectures on Poetics)*.

18. The heated and lengthy discussion of this work in East Germany and West Germany is collected in *"Der geteilte Himmel" und seine Kritiker*, ed. Martin Reso (Halle: Mitteldeutscher Verlag, 1965).

19. For the complicated publication history of this work in the GDR (first excerpted in *Sinn und Form* in 1968, then published in May 1969 in a limited run of disputed number [disagreeing critics put it at anywhere between 400 and 15,000 copies], the number of printed copies in the GDR alone had reached approximately 80,000 by 1973–1974), see *Wirkungsgeschichte von Christa Wolfs "Nachdenken über Christa T."*, ed. Manfred Behn (Königstein: Athenäum, 1978), 1–24 et passim. Behn's book, which provides excerpts from articles that constituted the early critical discussion of *Christa T.*, gives a good synopsis of the problematic reactions in both East and West. Heinrich Mohr, too, devotes the second part of his article (included in this volume) to an intense analysis of the publication and early reception of *Christa T.*

20. See Heinrich Mohr, "Productive Longing," in this volume.

21. See Peter Beicken and Rolf J. Goebel, "Erzählerische Selbstverständigung: Christa Wolf zwischen Moderne und Tradition," *Monatshefte* 74, no. 1 (Spring 1982): 59–71.

22. See "The Reader and the Writer," 201.

23. See "Faith in the Terrestrial," 118–121.

24. Annette von Droste-Hülshoff, 1797–1848; Marie Luise Kaschnitz, 1901–1974; Marieluise Fleisser, 1901–1974; Maxie Wander, 1933–1977; Irmtraud Morgner, b. 1933; Sarah Kirsch, b. 1935; Virginia Woolf, 1882–1941.

25. In the fourth *Cassandra*-lecture, Wolf mentions the following titles: *The First Sex. Mothers and Amazons. Goddesses. Patriarchy. Amazons, Warrior Women, and He-Women. Women—the Mad Sex? Women in Art. God-Symbols, Love-Magic, Satanic Cult. Male Fantasies. Female Utopias—Male Casualties. Women and Power. The Sex Which Is Not One. The Secret of the Oracle. Utopian Past. Outsiders. Cultural-Historical Traces of Repressed Womanhood. Mother Right. Origin of the Family, Private Property, and the State. Woman's Wild Harvest. The White Goddess. Woman as Image. A Room of One's Own. Womanhood in Letters (C 273).*

26. Women's equality is constitutionally guaranteed in the GDR; superficial sexism and biases are thus eliminated. Only recently have women writers begun to recognize and respond to the more deeply rooted prejudices and patterns of patriarchal thinking. On this, see especially the essays by Karin McPherson and Christiane Zehl Romero in this volume.

27. See Michael Wood, *In Search of the Trojan War* (New York and Oxford: Facts on File Publications, 1985).

28. See Bruno Bettelheim, *The Uses of Enchantment: The Meaning and Importance of Fairy Tales* (New York: Knopf, 1976); Jack Zipes, *Breaking the Magic Spell: Radical Theories of Folk and Fairy Tales* (London: Heinemann, 1979); John M. Ellis, *One Fairy Story Too Many* (Chicago: University of Chicago Press, 1983); Ruth B. Bottigheimer, *Fairy Tales and Society: Illusion, Allusion and Paradigm* (Philadelphia: University of Pennsylvania Press, 1986), for example.

29. Jack Zipes, "Introduction" in *Divided Heaven* (New York: Adler, 1981), xxxii–xxxiii.

30. "Fragment eines Frauenporträts," in *Liebes-und andere Erklärungen*, ed. Annie Voigtländer (Berlin/Weimar: Aufbau, 1972), 410–416.

31. See, among others, Marcel Reich-Ranicki, "Christa Wolfs unruhige Elegie," *Die Zeit*, May 23, 1969; Fritz J. Raddatz, "Mein Name sei Tonio K.," *Der Spiegel*, June 2, 1969; Manfred Durzak, "Ein exemplarisches Gegenbeispiel. Die Romane

von Christa Wolf," *Der deutsche Roman der Gegenwart*, 2d ed. (Stuttgart: Kohlhammer, 1973), 270–293; Heinz Sachs, "Verleger sein, heisst ideologisch kämpfen," *ND*, May 14, 1969; Jörg B. Bilke, "Die Wirklichkeit ist anders. Kritik und Pessimismus in drei neuen DDR- Romanen," *Der Rheinische Merkur*, October 10, 1969; Manfred Jäger, "Auf dem langen Weg zur Wahrheit: Fragen, Antworten und neue Fragen in den Erzählungen, Aufsätzen und Reden Christa Wolfs," *Sozialliteraten. Funktion und Selbstverständnis der Schriftsteller der DDR* (Düsseldorf: Bertelsmann, 1973), 11–101; Hermann Kähler, "Christa Wolfs Elegie," *SuF* 1 (1969): 251–261.

32. Wolf speaks of "celestial mechanics," referring to Newtonian physics and suggesting that his laws of motion had been transferred to the sociohistorical (and literary) realm as explanation for historical (mechanical) determinism. In suggesting that Einstein's relativity theory and Heisenberg's uncertainty principle are better suited as "models" for the literary enterprise, she is articulating a recognition of (social) fragmentation—against all official socialist stances but very much in common with the insights that propelled modernism in the early twentieth century. See "The Reader and the Writer," especially 193–197.

33. Rahel Varnhagen kept a remarkably lively literary salon in Berlin during the first half of the nineteenth century and corresponded with many of the important writers of her time. She lived from 1771 to 1883; her life and influence have been explored by such writers as Ellen Key (*Rahel Varnhagen: A Portrait*, 1907), Hannah Arendt (*Rahel Varnhagen: The Life of a Jewess*, 1958), and Ingeborg Drewitz (*Berliner Salons*, 1965).

34. The mythological nature spirit, Undine, figures centrally in many German Romantic works, most notably in Fouqué's *Undine* (1811). As Hans-Georg Werner shows, however, the Romantic pretext is filtered for Wolf through Ingeborg Bachmann's "Undine geht" ("Undine goes," 1961) (see his article in this volume).

35. The tomcat Murr is the narrator in Hoffmann's story (1820–1822), *Lebensansichten des Katers Murr nebst fragmentarischer Biographie des Kapellmeisters Johannes Kreisler in zufälligen Makulaturblättern* (Life and Opinions of the Tomcat Murr, with a Fragmentary Biography of the Conductor Johannes Kreisler from Miscellaneous Papers).

36. I am indebted to Helene Scher for this insight.

37 From Pablo Neruda's *Book of Questions*.

38. The essay on Günderrode was originally published as the foreword to Wolf 's edition of Günderrode's writings, *Der Schatten eines Traumes*; the Bettina-letter appeared as the afterword to the reissued book by Bettina on Karoline, *Die Günderode*.

39. While Kleist and Günderrode are clearly drawn after figures whose historical reality is documented by their own works and other materials, the question of whether or not Christa T. actually existed has concerned many critics. I find the question irrelevant because the figure that emerges there and those portrayed in *No Place on Earth* are clearly reinterpretations issuing from Wolf 's reading. Their reality lies in her investment; it is not essentially inherent.

40. The essay on Wander, "Berührung," appeared as the foreword to the West German edition of Wander's book, *Guten Morgen, du Schöne* (1978). This slightly abridged version has been translated by Jeannett Clausen: "In Touch," in *German Feminism. Readings in Politics and Literature*, ed. Edith Hoshino Altbach et al. (Albany: SUNY Press, 1984), 161–169.

41. Günderrode committed suicide in 1806, Kleist in 1811.

42. "New aesthetic positions are reached . . . via confrontation with these norms (in parentheses, Brecht)" (*C* 141).

Subjective Authenticity:
A Conversation with
Hans Kaufmann

Christa Wolf

Hans Kaufmann: In the section entitled 'Tabula Rasa' in your essay 'The Reader and the Writer' (Lesen und Schreiben), you try to arrive at a clear understanding of the role books, or rather 'prose'—something I'd like to come back to—play, by imagining what your life would have been like if there had been none and you had not even known of the existence of the Grimms' fairy tales, Gulliver's Travels, Wilhelm Meister or Anna Karenina. 'Without books,' you conclude, 'I am not me.' By examining your own experiences, you try to present a kind of empirical argument to counter the fear—which you express in the section of the essay entitled 'Lament'—that as the sciences, communications technology, film, radio and television increasingly enter our lives, contemporary literature, and especially prose, might lose its purpose. I'd also like to mention the part of the essay you call 'Rough Outline for a Writer', where you discuss the social status of 'literary artisans' in the GDR, compare their situation with that of writers living under capitalism, and at the same time highlight the moral risks run by those who make their living from writing. I believe, by the way, that too little attention is given to this subject in public literary debate.

Yes, but as you know that is beginning to change, because in recent years authors like Günter de Bruyn, Jurek Becker, Erwin Strittmatter and Anna Seghers, for example, have begun to debate the ethical issues raised by their professional activity.

55

Hans Kaufmann: *Leaving aside the other, equally significant, points the essay makes about history, literary theory and epistemology, would this be a more or less fair summary of what you say there: in order to firm up the conviction that writing prose was worthwhile, you had to subject that conviction to doubt, and in so doing, you were also able to show the sense—and necessity—of writing a specific kind of literature which you felt at the time—and which you perhaps still feel—to be relevant?*

I can only write about things that disturb me. I wrote 'The Reader and the Writer' in 1968. I had finished *The Quest for Christa T.* a year before, but it had not yet been published, though the first critical reactions to it had given me a good idea of what the tone of public criticism would be. So at the time I wasn't so bothered about anything as pompous and general as 'the fate of the novel.' The book would run its own course, irrespective of what I thought about it. Nor did I see any reason to justify myself in any way. But I did feel a need to re-appraise my experience of writing the book, and so I set out to articulate my feelings, at the same time asking myself what was uniquely significant about a book, and which aspects of it could be used again in future works. To that extent, there is not a fundamental difference between the prose and the essay aspects of my work—the one follows on from the other, they are intertwined. The root they share is that of an experience which needs to be assimilated: experience of 'life', by which I mean experience of the tangible reality of a particular time in a particular society; experience of myself, of writing—which is an important part of my life, of other literatures and art. Prose and the essay are two different tools used to tackle different types of material for different, though not opposed or mutually exclusive ends.

In any case, in both genres you start completely from scratch; it isn't like the hedgehog entering the race with the hare, secure in the knowledge that his wife will be waiting at the finishing post to squeak 'I'm already here'. Having defined prose for myself and recognising it as the form most suitable for me, I was not sure whether I would become more convinced of the point of writing it when I began to inquire whether it was—or at least could be—really appropriate for modern times. I must admit, by the way, that in the long run there was no question of my not carrying on writing, whatever the result of my inquiry, though I might have started to write differently. This kind of soul-searching has, in some way, to be ruthless, even with axioms that you take for granted and hold dear. An example of one such axiom is that socialist authors do not need to worry about the state of the novel; that they can quite comfortably leave that to those writers who are embroiled in the capitalist literary business, who are forced to grapple with the bourgeois novel in its terminal state.

But why should I be asking these questions? Because as a reader I rarely come across a novel written here that concerns me? Because I fear that our prose writing fails to express the problems that many people—even entire social strata—face in their lives? Even though I am increasingly coming across work that is well-written, polished and has artistic merit. But show me a book that sears into you as life itself does. That you can't find.

Any debate about the life and death of the novel starts and finishes there. If it can no longer excite me, then it deserves to die! Now, the parts of the essay you mentioned deal with the conditions in which prose as a genre can survive, and in doing so, they refer to the domains that prose has 'lost' during its historical development. Yet the history of art is not a history of wars; its gains and losses can't be described in the language of the General Staff; its territory can't be measured in square miles; there are no devices for assessing its effects. Strangely enough, writers of my own and younger generations react to these simple and indisputable facts with uneasy consciences. This comes out—if it isn't already apparent—in the way they seek to defend themselves (a way I am very used to, may I add) by themselves adopting their critics' misguided notions, protesting that they simply want the same as everyone else (which is not true), and ending up merely trying to prove their worth in areas where literature has never lost anything, and hence has nothing to gain either. So, when I wrote the essay, I wanted to express my opinion of what prose can and should do.

Hans Kaufmann: Can we insert a snippet of biography here? From a letter Louis Fürnberg wrote to you in 1956, a year before he died, I deduce that you had told him of your intention to work as a writer, at the same time expressing your doubts and reservations. Fürnberg encouraged you with great passion. Could you say something about the motives behind your decision to enter the world of literary production?

I had been 'writing' for ages—mainly diaries in the early days, but also folk-tales, 'short stories', even drafts of 'plays'. Looking back, I was irritated by my German studies, and moved into criticism and theory—I wrote literary criticism. Perhaps I had lost a degree of immediacy in my contact with reality, as well as the carefree spirit that is necessarily part of the decision to throw caution to the winds and add one's own two penny-worth to the mountain of words already written. Anyway, I was faced with serious obstacles which needed a great deal of shaking before they could be overcome and before the urge to write could be released. Louis Fürnberg was wonderfully good at encouraging people, even when he didn't have much to be encouraged by. I think of him when someone who is just beginning to write gives me a manuscript to read. These days, by the way, young people don't seem to be writing prose . . . .

Hans Kaufmann: Let's talk about 'prose'. Allow me to indulge in a little crude philology. Citing Thomas Mann, you call the 'prose author' the one who 'murmurs the spell of the imperfect'. Yet that was how Thomas

Christa Wolf

Mann described the Erzähler—*the story writer*—*whom he understood in the more or less 'traditionalist' sense. Is the distinction meaningless in your eyes? If it is, we can drop the subject, but I do suspect that your essay deliberately avoids terms like 'narrative literature' or 'epic', preferring 'the prose genre'. Its generic features, you say, are that it is written by individuals (a fate it shares with the major part of poetry and most drama) and read by individuals (which is indeed especially true of prose literature). Now, in 1961 your 'Moscow Novella' was published, a short work whose very title puts it in a particular category; Divided Heaven (1963) is called an Erzählung, a short story. You didn't assign The Quest for Christa T. (1968) to any particular genre. Is it true to say that on the one hand the word 'prose'—as far as critical considerations of a general kind are concerned—refers to more or less any type of narrative literature, but that, on the other—insofar as it suggests an idea of a particular objective—it means a very special type of style which you are loath to connect with any idea of 'story-telling', because—taking Quest for Christa T. for instance—it is a combination of biographical and autobiographical details, critical observations and documentation, and is, in essence, built of reflections?*

You're right. When I wrote the essay I noticed that the distinction between 'story-teller' and 'prose writer' was not insignificant. It was not by chance that I took up this idea of a writer who 'murmurs the spell of the imperfect', a formulation I find wonderful; and I had reason to question a remark—made by Anna Seghers—to which I subscribed, and which seemed to be confirmed by my earlier experience of writing: what has become narratable is already mastered. You see, I had learned —and I must say I learned to my surprise, and despite my own considerable unwillingness to accept it—what it really meant to have to tell the story of something in order to master it. I had found that story-writers—or perhaps I should say prose writers—can be compelled to abandon the strict sequence of first living through something, then digesting and 'mastering' it and, lastly, writing about it. In order to achieve the inner authenticity for which they are striving, they can be forced to express the living and thinking processes they are embroiled in directly in their work process, in an almost unmitigated way (though form always does tone things down, that is one of its functions). They can be forced to drop all artificial categories, empty moulds into which, almost always with the unconscious help of the author, the raw material pours with alarming inevitability.

Am I making myself clear? I would be so delighted if, when I expressed my thoughts on these questions, I were not seen as relapsing into some kind of ecstacy or taking refuge in the inaccessible recesses of the so-called artistic labour-process. Yet this new spontaneity, which I believed had almost been lost forever, had burst to the surface in such a tangible, liberating way that I would have been ill-advised to underestimate its value or to recoil from it in fear. (And this also meant I could very quickly recognise what was worthy of criticism in the product of this labour-process.)

In saying this, I am well aware that 'inner authenticity' is not a literary category that means something to everyone, like 'positive hero', 'conflict', 'the comic' or even 'plot' (by the way, the German word for 'plot', *Fabel*, used to mean a made-up story, as opposed to 'true account'). In this sense, the plot can on occasion be an obstacle to creating precisely that inner authenticity (genuineness, credibility) which you can immediately spot—though you may find it hard to define—in a piece of prose writing. This, however you look at it, is the opposite of the positivist approach that separates author and subject-matter and counterposes the one to the other. In that approach, authors have to proceed as though they were using a kind of lasso, with which they must haul in their poor subject-matter and then interpret it. They can either be on foot or on horseback, clumsy cowboys or expert ones, casual or hard-working. However they go about it, when they show us their catch, they are still the same people as when they started out. And then they make so bold as to hope their readers will have been 'changed' by reading the book!

Recently a friend advised me not to get bogged down in a polemic against 'plot'. That, he said, could become as dogmatic as glorifying it. He's right: this is not the crux of the argument. Let me quote Erasmus here, as a precaution: 'Everything I say is merely conversation. None of it is advice. I would not speak so boldly, were people supposed to act upon what I said.' What I mean is that I am only speaking for myself when I confess that in writing of that kind, I was struck by an element of dishonesty that increasingly worried me: namely, the unfortunate possibility authors have of sheltering behind their 'material', 'subject', 'work' or whatever; of turning that work into something they can play around with at will (and of thus treating readers as objects too); of ending up with a piece of work which took x number of hours to write, which can be reproduced by technical means, and then sold as a commodity. (A developed socialist society will have to question the commodity character of intellectual work.)

To my mind, it is much more useful to look at writing, not as an end product but as a process which continuously runs alongside life, helping to shape and interpret it: writing can be seen as a way of being more intensely involved in the world, as the concentration and focusing of thought, word and deed. It is also a process that gives rise to certain printable by-products (from which, last but not least, the writer can earn a living). These represent the material evidence of a productivity that is mainly oriented towards the creation of new structures of human relations in the present, in other words towards something that is not material, and yet intensely real and meaningful.

This mode of writing is not 'subjectivist', but 'interventionist'. It does require subjectivity, and a subject who is prepared to undergo unrelenting exposure—that is easy to say, of course, but I really do mean as unrelenting as possible—to the material at hand, to accept the burden of the tensions that inexorably arise, and to be curious about the changes that both the material and the author undergo. The new reality you see is different from the one you saw before. Suddenly, everything is interconnected and fluid. Things formerly taken as 'given' start to dissolve, revealing the reified social relations they contain and no longer that hierarchically arranged social cosmos in which the human particle travels along the paths pre-ordained by sociology or ideology, or deviates from them. It becomes more and more difficult to say 'I', and yet at the same time often imperative to do so. I would like to give the provisional name 'subjective authenticity' to the search for a new method of writing which does justice to this reality. I can only hope I have made it clear that this method not only does not dispute the existence of objective reality, but is precisely an attempt to engage with 'objective reality' in a productive manner.

One more thing. When I say 'authenticity', I don't mean 'truthfulness'; I'm not moralising. Truthfulness must be taken for granted; it is absolutely undeniable that literature cannot exist without it. This is also true in a wider sense, because the unfortunate outcome of remaining in artistic blindness and ignorance and attempting to be 'truthful' from only a restricted point of view, is provincialism. Similarly, that form of retreat which seeks to keep one's own inner passions apart from the burning issues of the day causes your creativity to wane and you're left with the kind of artistic activity about which nothing bad can be said apart from the fact that nobody—particularly its producer —feels it to be necessary.

Hans Kaufmann: *I would like to return to the idea of experience. I realise, of course, that the artist cannot give shape to any object or process that takes his fancy, which has no bearing on him. His work expresses the personal relationship he, as an individual human being, has with the world; he cannot present a world devoid of subjects. You're aiming at something similar by insisting adamantly on experience. On the other hand, the idea is undeniably elastic and amorphous, and hence has little philosophical value. There is always the great danger that 'experience' is, rightly or wrongly, understood in the empiricist sense that an individual can only relate to what he or she receives from the sensible environment. For this reason, I would like us to remember that around the turn of the century literature began to discover that (empirical) experience was not, or was no longer, adequate for portraying the determining factors in individuals' lives, and that these were to be found 'in the invisible', as a despairing Rilke put it. Later on, Brecht put the debate on a decisively more realist course, by rejecting the notion of 'milieu' and arguing that it should be replaced by that of the 'causal social nexus'. In order to make conscious the dialectic between determination and individual freedom of action, factors relating to society in its entirety have to be considered, which, while they are beyond sensory experience, are very real. (It is precisely for this reason that the break with nineteenth-century realism is both justified and necessary.) It is still true today, is it not, that the only way of comprehending the reality and scope of individuality is through the causal nexus, which, though it has in some respects undergone change, is far from inoperative?*

You're touching on such a fundamental point that we must get to the bottom of it, even if we have in the end to agree to differ. You are clearly afraid that my 'adamant insistence on experience' might let idealism slip in through the back door—'Here I am, I can't do anything about it, God help me, Amen'. So for the sake of clarity, I'd like to repeat something I've often said before (including in 'The Reader and the Writer'). Marxist philosophy is one of my fundamental experiences, and plays a decisive role in the selection and evaluation of new experiences; writers living in an age when they can choose the way they wish to write, are responsible for the content of their experience; finally, writing from experience is not the same as always describing oneself (although self-depiction often does and will come into it). In other words, none of this has anything to do with what might be called 'unfettered subjectivism', which may obscure rather than illuminate reality (of which the writer is part).

Yet have you ever realised how steeped in unfettered subjectivism are those who urge authors to write in accordance with idealised images and theoretical constructs rather than from experience? No, it is still, and always will be, a question of realism and the fight for it. And this fight, which led Brecht (for a time) to place emphasis—and it is an emphasis I cannot quibble with—on the social ties in which individuals are embedded, and the interplay between social and individual factors, part of this fight is that today we—for I am not the only one—take a certain pleasure in insisting on a category, 'experience', that has so long been ignored, underestimated and regarded as suspect, and which appears to give you some cause for alarm. We cannot deny the plain fact that the writer of 'good' literature cannot depict 'the world', or 'reality' or anything so intangible. Writers are not natural scientists, and literature is not a branch of philosophy. As Anna Seghers said, 'The writer is the curious crossing point where object becomes subject and turns back into object.' The reservoir writers draw on in their writing is experience, which mediates between objective reality and the authorial subject. And it is highly desirable that this should be socially meaningful experience, the determinants of which do not reside in 'the invisible'.

Even if 'experience' really were so suspect a philosophical term as you assume, I wouldn't put it any differently, for there still wouldn't be a good case against using the term in a sphere that is distinguished from science and philosophy *precisely* by the importance of the subjective dimension. (This is one of the crucial issues in the argument between Marxist authors and their Marxist critics that has been going on for more than forty years now.) In any case, natural scientists and Marxist philosophers who are concerned with science are now taking the category of 'experience' seriously again. In molecular biology, for example, debate is focusing on whether a molecular system can acquire 'experience', in other words whether it can learn.

Don't worry, I'm not going to overdo the comparison between the regulatory mechanisms of an insensate cell bound by the constraints of biology and an individual consciously living in a set of historical and social relations. But the very fact of historical determination, with which present-day writers should be familiar, ought to prompt them to ask how much scope individuals have for freely-determined action—how far, for example, they are responsible and culpable for inaction in an age of extreme terror. Brecht himself spoke of the 'testing ground of social causality', an arena where various forces are at work. One of these forces is the individual whom we must not paralyse by presenting his or her fate as being exclusively determined by objective, economic factors. If, for a time, Brecht tended to lay emphasis on the social determinants, while the current trend among Marxist writers is to examine the role of the individual in this 'causal nexus', isn't this something we can also explain with the aid of a historical materialist approach?

Hans Kaufmann: For obvious reasons, the whole of GDR literature has paid a great deal of attention to the analysis of fascism. It isn't only writers of the older and middle generations who write about it; those who were not more than children when liberation came do so too. What might be the reasons for this, and what significance does it have for today's reader? Which major new elements of this subject still have potential for literature?

The question is closely tied in with what I said before, because I do tackle, well, how can I put it, 'the subject of fascism'. We only have to look at ourselves. A past like fascism envelops us like a wave, unless we put up an internal barrier against it (which is a defence mechanism that is commonly employed). But nobody can evade the effect, or seal themselves off from influences that penetrate from childhood and youth into later life, even when—indeed, especially when—they would prefer to forget and deny (first and foremost deny to themselves) the influences to which they were exposed as children, and the behaviour they acquired. Tracing the maturation process my generation went through, seeing where that process came to a halt, is an enormous subject. Those who grew up under fascism cannot say they had 'got over' it by such and such a date. It is a matter of working through this monstrous—in the true sense of the word—occurrence at ever deeper, and hence ever more personal levels; a process that literature has to pursue, which can also mean 'get at the causes of', perhaps even 'help to resolve'.

It is, moreover, a very difficult thing to do, and the resistance one encounters indicates how radioactive the material still is, even today (another sign is that certain themes related to our childhood never come up in conversation). Perhaps that is why we have become accustomed to describing fascism as a 'phenomenon' which existed outside us and which ceased to be as soon as its centres of power and organizational forms had been destroyed. Have we not for some time now ascribed it to the past of 'the other Germany', so that we can simply regard anti-fascism and resistance as our own traditions? (This, I believe, has also clearly been present throughout the various stages of literary treatment of fascism, particularly if film and television dramas are included.) And yet young people are constantly asking why, 'in spite of everything', people like us, their parents, could live through those days without being oppressed by a constant sense of calamity. More importantly, how we were able to carry on living afterwards. In this 'in spite of everything' they are referring to all the films they've seen, all the history they were taught at school about the circumstances surrounding Hitler's take-over. But they have a right to understand it, and we have a duty to answer their questions as best we can.

Apart from the more psychological difficulties involved, which seem to have remained insurmountable for so many years, I would also like just to mention that problems of method also arise. Again, it's a question of finding a style of writing that allows this undertaking a great degree of realism—or even better, imposes that realism upon it—so that past and present can be seen not only to 'meet' on the paper, but, as they constantly do in every one of us, to interact and be endlessly rubbing up against each other. In other words, you have to find writing techniques (and make it known that you are looking for such techniques, and why) that manage to free up those almost indissoluble bonds and constrictions that hold us in their grip, to unravel that vast range of elements that have become entwined during our development, so that patterns of behaviour in which we thought we were firmly entrenched can be explained, and, where possible (and where necessary), still be changed. It's a rather demanding task.

Hans Kaufmann: *I've been struck recently by the way a number of books dealing with the past—the years before or around 1945 for instance— are written with great talent, but the same authors clearly find it hard to portray the dialectical relation in our present day between the opportunities real people have for action and the conditions in which that action takes place. While theory has noisily proclaimed the greater significance of the individual, in practice we are left with really insipid, shallow figures. Alongside this, I have noticed elements of idealist philosophising appearing when writers attempt, in literary theory, aphorisms and other forms of writing, to conceptualise their own present situation and work —and this is true of writers whose socialist convictions cannot be doubted. I even think there is something of this in your writings. I won-*

der whether these two features—involving, as they often do, conflicts, disappointments and crises—are not connected with the difficulties one has in putting one's own experiences in the context of the overall state of things, of the way things are developing generally. Of course, this is not only an individual concern; it also has to do with the image our society as a whole has of itself—and I shall come back to that in a moment. But how and to what extent the individual becomes aware of this; whether he sets out to recognise the concrete historical, true nature of these moments of crisis; whether he is incapable of or even uninterested in doing so: none of this is inconsequential. Where he fails—for whatever reason —the result is partly that curious emptiness we have seen over the last few years, partly the kind of self-interpretation tinged with idealism that I have just mentioned. (I am talking, by the way, about a few exceptional publications, not about anything like a general trend in modern GDR literature.)

I'm very glad to hear you speak of 'experience' and the significance of individual assimilation of experience . . . . I also agree with what you have just said—avoiding contradiction inevitably creates emptiness in literature, because real, concrete movement drops out of the picture and only apparent motion is left.

Hans Kaufmann: What I'm getting at is that experience has to be supplemented before it can be assimilated. Following Marx and Lenin's indications on the phases of communism, an important contribution was made at the 8th Party Congress[1] and in the subsequent period, to the definition of developed socialist society and its historical status. It seems to me that we have not given enough thought to what realism in literature can gain from this 'realism' in scientific self-understanding and political praxis, which Erich Honecker spoke of there. For example, the developmental stage we consider ourselves to be living in is important—indeed it is crucial—for the form the relationship between the ideal and the real takes in a work of art. If our conceptions and our practice treated socialism as a complete and isolated social formation, things that appear to need criticising—and such things inevitably come to the surface as writers and others observe and get to grips with the lives we lead—would have no historical status; such things would be regarded as merely chance phenomena, abnormal and untypical. Or, alternatively, one would spontaneously be tempted to regard every source of discord as 'evidence' refuting the definition society had given of itself. Either way, we would be lacking a dialectic of contemporary development, and the ideal and reality would be rigidly cast in an irresolvable antinomy, with an emotional, moral and aesthetic overlay.

If, however, bearing in mind the developmental level of the forces and relations of production, we perceive society in terms of the features that cast the last shadows of class antagonism, which still exist even though that antagonism has largely been eradicated, and, more impor-

tantly, in terms of its readiness for communism, then we arrive at a quite different way of viewing and evaluating the general significance of individual phenomena. This does not of course mean that the tensions between the ideal and reality dissolve into a harmonious relation; yet they do help us to understand the historical dynamic and thereby to become a subjective force and hence an element in that dynamic itself. Furthermore, any phenomenon that appears undesirable from the point of view of socialist goals does not simply fall out of the 'system'; it loses it abnormal, monstrous and ultimately inexplicable character and is put into historical perspective, which in turn reveals how it might successfully be tackled. The relative and general significance of any source of discontent can then be understood without its acquiring the character of abstract generality, or of a 'bad reality' standing over against a subjective 'good will'. Would this not also do away with the need—which can be problematic—to attribute general validity to one's own, sometimes complex, experiences in intimation, antitheses, allusions and similes? Perhaps we could quote Heinrich Heine here, who said:

> *Don't bother with your holy parables,*
> *Nor with your pious theories,*
> *Try and answer our damned questions,*
> *Without beating about the bush.*

> (Lass die heil'gen Parabolen,
> Lass die frommen Hypothesen
> Suche die verdammten Fragen
> Ohne Umschweif uns zu lösen.)

That was a long digression on my part, there won't be any more.

Let me express my respect for Heine. Though I must say I'd like to see the look on his face if I showed him some of our 'damned questions'. . . . But that's by the by. I don't deny the problem you have been broaching exists; indeed I have been aware of it for a long time, occasionally to the point of despair. Anna Seghers was right when she wrote to Georg Lukács thirty-five years ago, in the course of their still very relevant correspondence, that 'fear of deviation has the effect of rendering unreal'. It is indeed the case that if, over a long period of time, you are prevented from doing things openly, you can even forget how to avoid beating around the bush when you ask important—though not always answerable—questions (damned or otherwise), even if you only ask them of yourself. This is true in many fields, but it lies at the very heart of literature. Mechanisms of self-censorship are even more dangerous than the censorship from which they develop, for they internalize the kinds of demands that can prevent literature from being created, and bog writers down in a sterile and hopeless web of incompatible codes ordaining, for example, that they should write realistically and yet disregard conflict, that they should faithfully depict the truth and yet disbelieve what they see because what they see is 'untypical'. A writer who is not acutely aware of this process, who fails to monitor his or her own work implacably, will start to give in, make excuses and produce 'pulp'. And you will do so whether you are writing a period novel, a parable or an utopian work—the genre is immaterial.

There is still some point in talking about this today. Ingrained mechanisms go on producing effects. It wasn't for nothing that Volker Braun recently asked where our 'reserves of realism' were. . . . What is it you had in mind when you mentioned elements of idealist philosophising in my work?

Hans Kaufmann: Is it not possible—and I beg you to treat what I say as a question rather than an assertion—that the unresolved problems of the last few years, which I hinted at, are at the roots of these flashbacks to fascism and to its effects upon our generation? I also suspect that an element of 'intellectual history' is creeping in. But perhaps we should pass over this question, because it really concerns a book that's still being written, and with which I am therefore not fully acquainted.[2]

Why pass it over? Let's try and get to the bottom of your worries and reservations. Perhaps by formulating my thoughts in a more exact way, I can put your mind at rest a little without having to say too much about my current project. The questions have been put in a sufficiently general manner.

You suspect that my treatment of the fascism theme could involve 'intellectual history', in other words reference merely to the psychological and moral processes in the development of consciousness, and you wish to warn me that the actual reality that lies behind these processes may be left out of account. I agree with you that this shouldn't be allowed to happen. But contemporary authors writing about fascism find themselves in a different environment from anti-fascist writers in exile or just after the war. As time passes, and in this case as our lifetime passes, each period of history is constantly acquiring a new dimension, and this is particularly true of the age of fascism. As a result, the reality that provides me with my material is no longer fascism—its socio-economic roots, the property relations from which it evolved, and so on—but the structure of the relations my generation has with the past; in other words, the way people in the present come to terms with the past. This is something quite different from a procedure of working by analogy; that really would be quite inadmissible. I have no intention of finding an ersatz 'solution' to the difficulties facing literature when it tries to come to terms with the present by turning real contradictions that issue from a concrete social situation into general psychological categories, and thereby concealing them.

In fact, I set out to do just the opposite. I hope to gain access to the present by treating the past in a concrete, historical fashion. As Brecht wrote in 1953: 'We have been all too keen to turn our backs on the immediate past and, hungry with curiosity, to look to the future. But the

future will depend on whether we can come to terms with the past.'
Perhaps you will agree that Brecht's point about the dialectical relationship between the past and the future is equally valid today.

Hans Kaufmann: *In terms of attitudes to German fascism, things are not
exactly as they were in 1953. But the last sentence is undoubtedly still
significant.*

Well, quite independently of what Brecht said of course, the
deficiencies in this 'coming to terms with the past' became very apparent to me each day as I dealt with and reflected upon the problems and,
in particular, as I dealt with and thought about the people who created
them—and I include myself here. No other generation will ever go
through what we did: growing up in and being educated and shaped by
one society and then having the opportunity, in the GDR, to express a
form of criticism and self-criticism that went right to the very roots of
society; being given the chance to think, understand and act, and, as a
result, coming up against new, far from simple conflicts and contradictions; and, what is even more important, being involved in creating and
resolving those contradictions, while at the same time being unable to
disown the model of behaviour that had shaped our childhood and
youth. Now try telling me that isn't a contradictory continuum! And of
course it is a continuum, because the person who experiences all that is
one and the same—or are they the same at the end of it all? Whatever
the case, there was no 'zero hour' when they were changed from one
person into another. . . .

This is probably what we mean by 'the subject of fascism'.
Shouldn't we be permitted, indeed required to get to grips with it? And
shouldn't we also be able to take for granted what has been written
about it in other types of literature, which, though they adopted a
different approach, are still important and valid? What I am asking is,
can't we start out from the achievements of earlier generations, the best
of which we can call classics, without having to repeat what they did?
And start out from the economic and historical analyses our children
are taught at school, which were like revelations to us when we first
heard them?

I do not believe my attitude to this issue simply reflects my own
private feelings, or even my resentment. It seems to me, rather, that it is
in society's fundamental interest to see re-established the connection
between this part of our lives and the present, which seemed almost to
have been lost forever. We will have to talk about property relations;
but we should not be wary of enquiring into psychological mechanisms
as well. We will have to go through the history that we seem to 'know
so well' again and again, without ceasing to be astonished and, I can assure you, horrified at what we find. We will have to resurrect what appeared to be dead and open up that which has become ossified and intractable to abstract analysis. Surprisingly enough, in this case 'to

historicize' will not mean 'to alienate', but to draw closer to us a historical period that we had distanced from ourselves and turned into a battlefield of impersonal social forces; it will mean making individuals —in their actions or inaction—visible once again, to inquire into their —our—motives and responsibilities. . . .

Can you call all this intellectual history? Not at all. Rather, it is a self-assured affirmation of the kind of 'interventionist thinking' that Brecht called for as early as 1933. 'The need to criticise fascism as a complex body of modes of behavior by means of interventionist thinking. To criticise also ideas when they represent interventionist behaviour.' Moreover, it means to attempt to answer new types of questions posed by an audience living in a new and different concrete historical environment.

Hans Kaufmann: *Together with Gerhard Wolf, you wrote the script for a film about Till Eulenspiegel. You set his story among the various struggles that preceded the German Peasant Wars. In the traditional version of the Till Eulenspiegel story, things are, of course, quite different: feudal society is stable, and the hero appears as a bourgeois individual ahead of his time, because he is set off against the rest of society as the only radical in both practical and intellectual terms—for Eulenspiegel, God, the idea of a 'beyond' and redemption, are meaningless. It would also have been possible to cast a contemporary eye on the famous rascal from this point of view. What you focus on, however, is his relation to the Peasant Wars, a relation which, as the plot develops, follows a twisting and contradictory course. Now, Marx called the Wars the 'most radical fact of German history'; bearing in mind that today we can call the establishment of a socialist society on German soil the 'most radical fact of German history', we gain some idea of the fundamental ties between the two ages.*

It is indeed the case that the character of Till Eulenspiegel can be set in various ages. Brecht, for instance, had the idea of setting an elderly Eulenspiegel in the period after the Peasant Wars, as a figure gathering together the downtrodden and the despairing and giving them encouragement. You could also see him as a timeless figure—the fool, in terms of both his role and function, in the Great Machine of History. . . . Right from the outset, we were interested in a character who, by dint of his experience of life, started out naive and credulous, and ended up seeing right through the power relations and convention of his day, and at length—thoroughly without illusions, but by no means resigned to his fate—acquired the ability to cope with, indeed manipulate them. A forerunner, in other words, but not a revolutionary. As Friedrich Engels says when writing about the Peasant Wars: 'Before existing social relations could even be called into question, they had to be divested of their holy aura.' And debunking is exactly the job of the fool. The pillars of authority at the time—the Church, the feudal order, guilds, etc.—had begun to totter, giving the outsider (for the fool is an outsider) ample scope for adventure. And we did not, by the way, seek to be faithful to history in a pernickety manner, for both the Eulenspiegel character and his circumstances contain elements of legend. . . .

I would be bored if the historical material I was working on did not have some relation to the present. As soon as we looked at Eulenspiegel, we realised that here was a man who meant something to us. I imagined a face that became harder yet more human as generations passed; I could imagine the attitudes of a man who, under great pressure, learned with supreme skill how best to use the means at his disposal, not simply in order to defend himself, but to extend the scope of real freedom both for himself and for the other commoners like him. We were attracted to this folk hero, this intelligent, cunning chap who dares to walk the tightrope. Moreover, the Renaissance is the age that gave birth to modern humanity; in it we find certain attitudes we immediately understand and with which we can empathise. It is also, however, an age we can keep at arm's length; our view of it is not prejudiced by direct involvement in the events of the time. What we have, in other words, is a kind of distanciation (*Verfremdung*), which permits us to deal with certain problems and conflicts which, for a variety of reasons, we do not or cannot yet say have concrete historical pertinence for the present. This is because the most radical fact of German history, i.e., the redirecting of society towards socialism from the roots up, does not always match the radicalism of our (historical, economic, sociological, moral and artistic) questioning of this society. But now we're getting into very big questions . . .

Hans Kaufmann: *Is it just coincidence, or is it, as I suspect, in the logic of your subject-matter, that there is more of the traditional epic in the plot of the film-script, than you recommend in your essay on 'The Reader and the Writer'? In your version, Eulenspiegel often gets involved in the struggles of the rising peasant and plebeian movement of the early sixteenth century. He is shaped by his actions and his sufferings; his experiences change and develop him. A causal connection is established between the various events; even the famous tricks he gets up to, some of which you include, acquire meaning only in the light of other episodes. In short, it is illuminating that the structure of character and plot that is produced by combining Eulenspiegel with an emerging revolutionary movement is quite different from the one we find in the traditional folk tale. But doesn't that structure contradict the theory you expounded in 'The Reader and the Writer', which holds that the 'traditional', epic fable corresponds to a mechanistic view of the world? Precisely by trying to arrive at a dialectic of individuality and historical movement, don't you in fact end up here with an epic fable? I realise, of course, that a film script is not a piece of prose writing. And yet your argument confronts the relationship between world-view and structure in such a general manner that it is impossible, taking the theory as it stands, to see why it should not also apply to film scripts. Or would you explain the difference by saying that the subject is set in a distant epoch that has come to an end, and that it is easier to see what that period led to than it is to survey the present? Is it to do with the fact that in this case you do not have to conceive or perceive yourself as an element in the action, so that ways of knowing and objectifying do not become problematic? If this were the case, Eulenspiegel would lead us back to the questions we have already been discussing.*

I could choose to get out of this one easily by saying that in 'The Reader and the Writer' you find me arguing that prose—at least, prose as I imagine it—is impossible to film. And in actual fact, this 'short story for a film' did emerge from a genuine scenario, and is in that sense not prose, which expresses precisely those invisible aspects of reality that the camera cannot capture. But this doesn't mean that historical dialectics can't be captured in a story, and I've never claimed otherwise. Leaving aside the obvious need, where any film is concerned, to make the development of the cast of characters visible, it's true that specific creative methods might be necessary when we take a step back into history, into a time about which we need to convey information. But as you've indicated, the main thing is that film necessarily lacks the fourth dimension of modern prose—what I call the dimension of the author, which I've described here as subjective authenticity. (This also gives me the chance to point out that personal *engagement* is not, and does not have to be, any less great where this kind of historical material is concerned.) I can't yet tell whether my current preoccupations with prose represent a transitional phase or whether they indicate any particular difficulties concerning knowledge and objectivity. At any rate it's unlikely that I'll 'change tack' in the future to forms of—how can I put it—conventional writing (though I don't like using pejorative terms), for these forms are now quite alien to me.

Above all, however, this film scenario's fourth dimension is left to the director and the actors. They have to be given scope to adopt their own approach to the substance of the work. And here lies the difference between writing for film and writing a prose text. The same material would look quite different in prose form—though it wouldn't really be the 'same' material, of course.

Hans Kaufmann: *From the point of view of material, your short story 'Selbstversuch' ('Self-Experiment'), which appeared in* Sinn und Form *in 1973, is 'hyper-modern', one might say, for the action presupposes that medical science can turn a woman into a man. How did you hit upon the idea?*

You're going to find this funny: 'Selbstversuch' was commissioned. One day Edith Anderson came up with the idea of producing an anthology. Five female and five male writers would each do a piece on the topic of

'When I was a man/woman'. I liked the thing, even though I cursed it a few times when I was actually writing. You see, the subject offered an opportunity for utopian mimicry—I like reading utopian books anyway, I just wish most of them were better! I immediately thought of a scientist who would be forced to help transform her own body for the sake of scientific progress. I am, in any case, interested in psychology, medicine, and the collective work of teams of scientists. I knew a thing or two about it, and could find out whatever else I needed to. But finding the right imaginative vehicle for this, putting the flesh on the bones of the idea, getting round the treatise-like nature of the question —that was difficult, and it remains problematic. I tried to make my job easier by highlighting the difficulties. The form, and indeed the whole thing, has an ironic feel to it: a report about a piece of scientific work that increasingly acquires the character of a subjective confession. . . .

Hans Kaufmann: *The story uses some of the paraphernalia of utopian science, though it only uses a little because you're clearly not concerned with expressing a utopian vision. The science fiction elements are, rather, merely instruments for analyzing a very contemporary problem: relations between the sexes. If I have understood correctly, your findings are not very encouraging. Humans are creating a more and more significant material built environment, and have even managed to change their biological nature, but they have neglected to change their social and human nature. This is brought out in relations between the sexes, the norms of which are still dictated by men and, as you rather clearly point out, uncritically accepted by women who interiorize those norms. 'Selbstversuch' ('Self Experiment') was published along with Günter de Bruyn's' Geschlechtertausch' ('Changing Sex'), which takes a similar line. There is probably no fundamental difference between you, in terms of your theoretical appraisal of the problem, but there is in the execution a difference in emotional quality. De Bruyn largely treats the subject with a sense of satire and comedy—at times his tone is downright comic, though this is not to say he doesn't take the issue seriously. You, by contrast, betray unmistakable unease, even bitterness. Leaving aside the inevitable stylistic differences between two writers, could one conclude that she is less inclined to joke about this matter than he is?*

I'll have to keep a tight rein on myself here. We're getting on to one of those subjects where my blood tends to boil, because the danger is that our radical starting-point—the emancipation of women—gets obscured by our complacency about having battled our way through to what are really only preliminary stages, whereas in fact what we need are new radical ways of posing questions that can advance us further. The kind of questions I attempted to provoke through my story might be: should the aim of women's emancipation be for them to 'become like men'?; would it even be desirable if they could do the same things, enjoy the same rights, so that men themselves would soon badly need emancipating?

71

I have deliberately tried this story out on the audience at many readings and watched for their reactions, especially their non-verbal reactions. Women laughing incredulously; young girls giggling as if you were telling them a dirty joke; men's down turned mouths and stiff shoulders. Then suddenly their expressions—both men's and women's—change, they get agitated, they make excited gestures as they try and formulate their own experiences. How earnestly they grasp the opportunity to question a set of circumstances they had previously taken for granted. As the material conditions allowing the sexes an equal start improve—and this must necessarily be the first step towards emancipation—so we face more acutely the problem of giving the sexes opportunity to be different from each other, to acknowledge that they have different needs, and that men and women, not just men, are the models for human beings. This doesn't even occur to most men, and really very few women try and get to the root of why it is that their consciences are permanently troubled (because they can't do what's expected of them). If they got to the bottom of it, they'd find it was their own identification with an idealised masculinity that is in itself obsolete.

There you are, I've lost my sense of humour again. Although in fact my story does have a comic side to it, if you can call it comic, for the woman transforms herself into a man for the sake of the man she loves. . . . It's simply a matter of overcoming alienation, no more, no less. And we should be careful not to think we've already done that. I do feel we should pay more attention to such things as the use of scientific research, which is also questioned in the story, or to certain types of positivist thought that barricade themselves in behind so-called natural scientific method and ignore the human aspects. There is an interesting debate going on among scientists about these things; the very fact that they are being debated means I feel no need to be bitter about them.

It would also be worth considering whether, in a society which differs from bourgeois society in that it has a genuine sense of historical perspective, utopian features to some degree lend literature greater validity and perhaps even a sharper focus. This would simply mean that our society was in a position to render its own contradictions more productive, and regard the conflicts that authors create as tools which can be usefully employed. That too is a process, of course.

Hans Kaufmann: 'Selbstversuch' *will also be included in the forthcoming volume subtitled* Drei unwahrscheinliche Geschichten *(Three Improbable Tales). The first of these, 'Unter den Linden', which also gives the book its title, relates a fictitious dream; the second the observations of a tom-cat, of all things; and the third we've already discussed. Apart from the 'improbability' of the stories, what the three pieces also have in common is that in them the unreal becomes a vehicle for analysing current problems. At the same time, there are differences between them, in terms not only of subject-matter but also of emotional tone. 'Unter den*

Linden' might be seen as expressing the inner struggle between depression and a new surge of enthusiasm for life; the 'New View on Life of a Tom-Cat' is a biting satire drawing on caricature and the grotesque. All three stories debate problems from contemporary life, and make out a case for change. Both their themes and the unusual way in which those themes are treated somehow challenge the reader. Now, I know that we literary critics like to categorize and classify, but are you embarking on a new phase in your work?

I wrote the three stories between 1969 and 1972, and they are representative of that phase of my work (I was also writing other things, and had started the larger project). It is not a coincidence that two of them are deeply satirical, nor that I come up with one or two provocative arguments. I hope that their 'improbability', their dreamlike, utopian and grotesque character will produce an alienation-effect towards certain processes, circumstances and modes of thought which have become so very familiar that we no longer notice them, are no longer disturbed by them. And yet we should be disturbed by them—and I say this in the confident belief that we can change what disturbs us.

A 'new' phase? No, I don't think so. Little experiments with new tools, perhaps, testing out methods that appeal to me. Whether I'll use them again later, I can't tell.

Hans Kaufmann: You've already hinted at an answer to the question a journalist would be bound to ask you—what are you working on at the moment? I would like to slant the other inevitable question, about your plans for the future, in a more problematizing, more provocative way, if you like. Since 'The Divided Heaven', the image of the writer Christa Wolf has been based in considerable measure on the seriousness you bring to the great moral questions of our time. This has continued through Christa T. to the Improbable Tales. The advancement of socialism demands that humanist principles of behaviour take firm root within human beings and become the subjective motives behind their actions. Such an attitude serves as the necessary starting point for fictions which communicate socialist-humanist impulses. This for me is beyond all doubt, even though I should perhaps add that the problem of humanism is here posed in a one-sided fashion—merely theoretically, as a matter of thought and feeling alone. Artistic activity can 'sublate' [aufheben] this one-sidedness by bringing it to consciousness. Satire, for instance, implies one-sidedness, imbalance; reading a work as a satire means mentally 'redressing' the imbalances portrayed. Something similar holds for works such as your Improbable Tales, that are based on the unreal and the fantastic. So far, so good. But we can't overlook the fact that the establishment of humanism is not only a matter of thought and feeling, but also—or rather primarily—of practical, material, social activity. If 'making humans human' is seen merely as having to do with the acquisition of moral values and not also (perhaps even primarily) as the bringing to *fruition of skills, capacities and dispositions, does this not rather limit the possibilities of art's impact (just to take one aspect of the question)? Is there not a danger that a human being's thoughts and actions might be regarded as being opposed to one another, rather than being seen as standing in a vital contradiction whose inner unity and motion distinguishes the 'whole person'? To get back to my original question about your future plans, do these or similar considerations play a part in your thinking? Might they affect what you choose to write about in the future, and how you will tackle your subject matter?*

I'm afraid I haven't perhaps grasped your meaning, because I don't see such a gulf between the 'acquisition of moral values' and the way in which humans become human through their active involvement in the process of historical change.

Hans Kaufmann: *My question—and it is a question, not a demand—concerns whether in the future you as a writer will be interested in those changes in the human psyche that are engendered by practical activity.*

You mean, whether I would find the subject of material production interesting?

Hans Kaufmann: *That would be one example, yes.*

I might cite 'The Divided Heaven', though I realise you may think it belongs too much in the past to be relevant to your question. But even there I was of course interested not only in material production—material production in the sense of the labour process itself, operating mechanical equipment, the endlessly repetitive motions of a production line, being shackled to the instrument panel of a machine. The only kind of 'praxis' that literature can use creatively is social praxis. The relationships that producers establish with each other and with other institutions and social strata as they go about their production; how and to what extent—I must come back to this—their practical activity enables them to take part in the historical process of change: these are the interesting points. This is, of course, an enormous subject, and it is one that I may possibly come back to dealing with directly.

On the other hand I don't think my work has ever appealed to an abstract morality, to an authority soaring above the raging sea of the class struggle from which a socialist author could take guidance.

Hans Kaufmann: *I wasn't implying that either.*

I reject moral voyeurism by any author, and this is a major reason why I attempt to write in a certain fashion. I insist writers should expose themselves to contradictions. . . .

At the same time I don't share the contempt some Marxists show for the little word 'morality', for the very reason I have already mentioned. I cannot, will not be swayed by the kind of crude historical determinism that regards individuals, groups, class and peoples as nothing but the objects of relentless laws of historical development, and which amounts to a fatalistic philosophy of history. Nor will I be convinced by any soulless pragmatism that sees the morality of classes and individuals as nothing but a means to an end to be manipulated or ignored at will, as a vehicle to be used or discarded as they wish. Which of us is not touched by the pain and tragedy of Brecht's words: 'We who wished to lay the ground for friendliness could not ourselves be friendly'?

'How must this world be constituted for a moral human being?' Bobrowski's question is still provocative, for it urges that the world be adapted to a morality of human dignity, not that human morality be adapted to a world that still abuses human dignity. To do the latter would be to invite the physical death of humanity. . . .

None of this has anything to do with Christian antinomies of good and evil, with a rigid contradistinction between thought and deed, nor with an abstract, fruitless and ultimately paralyzing demand for integrity. Indeed, our errors can be 'moral' if they continually allow us productively to resolve our contradictions. By contrast, everything that prevents us, that prevents the masses from becoming the subject rather than the object of history, is immoral. So, proceeding from this argument, why can't socialist writers be 'moralists' too?

My feeling is that the issues that arise within this whole area of problems, including the potential it contains for personal conflict, provide more than enough material for the things I would still like to write: indeed, they could keep literature busy for an age. I do have short-term and long-term plans, but it's much too early to talk about them.

1973

Notes

Originally published in *Weimarer Beiträge*, no. 6 (1974): 90–112. [Also in *Lesen und Schreiben. Neue Sammlung* and *Die Dimension des Autors*. The translation appears in *The Fourth Dimension: Interviews with Christa Wolf*, trans. Hilary Pilkington, intro. Karin McPherson (London: Verso, 1988), and is reprinted here with the permission of the publisher.—Ed.]

1. This was the Congress of 1971, the year in which Honecker took over.—Trans.
2. Kaufmann is referring, here and elsewhere in the conversation, to *Kindheitsmuster (Patterns of Childhood)*, on which Wolf was working at the time.—Ed.

On Christa Wolf's Principle of Poetics

Hans Kaufmann

I cannot postpone love. I can't wait
for a new century. Not for next year.
Not for one single day.
                    —Christa Wolf, Unter den Linden

As though it were nothing. As though it
all had no meaning.
                    —Günter de Bruyn, parody of C. Wolf[1]

C hrista Wolf's slim collection of "three im-probable stories" includes the story "Unter den Linden" that gives the volume its title. In that story, the author transcribes things seen and remembered into dream-visions. Yet her aim is not to suggest a continuous dream-atmosphere to the reader—one that would leave him/her entirely enmeshed in a dream. On the contrary, a first-person narrator tells her dream to a close friend; she has achieved a temporal distance from it, reflects on it, and thus also makes room for the reader's reflection. The narrative stance is meant to create an intimate and trusting atmosphere that stimulates the narrator "to tell the truth freely" (*UL* 7) and allows the reader to participate in the process. This intention is soon realized in the way in which a famil-iar cityscape—the title names it—is introduced. The dreaming woman looks through the external, tourist-populated picture at internal things, things hidden and personal. Granite facades provide the occasions to recall much that went on and goes on behind them. The dream enables this; it permits free rein with space and time, permits the montage of impressions, memories, visions, events, and reflections.

The motto, a quotation from Rahel Varnhagen, announces the theme: to be told is the story of overcoming an individual crisis. The dreamer summons people to whom she was once close; they are people in whose potential for social and human renewal she had believed, but they had not fulfilled her expectations. The narrator's personal entanglement in the fortunes of these people is hinted at rather than demonstrated and can sometimes only be assumed; the identity of the figures that come and go in fragments of memory cannot, as might be expected in a dream, always be absolutely determined. All the more intense is the emotional perplexity with which the narrator notes how conformity to convention, the preference for the more comfortable route, and indifference toward others have harmed their human character. These have caused the erasure of their former personal uniqueness, their individuality. This is made clear especially by the repeated motif, intensified by the dream-situation, of the "role," from which the figures cannot or do not want to escape and which they perform for each other. The narrator confesses her complicity in this regard: She, too, plays her "role"; she behaves, for instance, as though she had met an acquaintance by chance when she had schemed to bring about the encounter. She also frequently behaves in exactly the way one expects a woman to behave in relation to a man. This "complicity" leads to the connection with themes related to the court of law: guilt, hearings, interrogations, punishment or acquittal at the hands of strict or charitable judges— these play an important role in conversations, visions, and parallel plots. The crisis peaks in the image of a dreamlike suicide or suicide equivalent: submerged below the water surface of a fountain, the narrator is removed from all the horrors she sees.[2]

Events of this kind intersect, to be sure, with others that function as counterbalance. People appear, especially young people, who are or seem to be free of horror, disappointment, role-playing, and guilt (a school class with its teacher, couples in love). There are lovely, desirable things, and the sight of innumerable people on their way home from work, in whom dwells "the secret longing for the true flesh, for the succulent, red flesh" (*UL* 73), ultimately provides a turning point. At the end, the narrator recognizes herself in the image of an attractive and vivacious woman. In her review of the many contradictory visions, she has cleansed and freed herself and takes her place in that organization mentioned at the beginning of the narrative—that "league whose austerity is surpassed only by its generosity—the league of the happy ones" (*UL* 7). This occurs with her renewed claim to a full life—with the words we used above as motto: "I cannot postpone love." She can "connect to the world" only through love (*UL* 72).

It is not difficult to recognize that Christa Wolf continues to deal in "Unter den Linden" with problems that had concerned her already in *Christa T.* There, too, the human personality appeared endangered by conformity to convention; that work also suggests the dubiousness of role-playing. The thrust in *Christa T.* is different, to be sure—the concept of "role" in *Christa T.* refers only coincidentally to the notion of a conventional mask; it has much more do with integration into a working society, that is, into a necessarily particular activity. The position the narrator assumes in regard to the contradictions posed is differentiated in the two works especially by the ending: death in the one, reintegration in the other case. Although its formulation is emphatically utopian, even fabulous (the "league of the happy ones"), the ending theme in "Unter den Linden" is exceptionally significant as a decisive announcement of the will to participate actively in life. This theme reminds us, incidentally, of important aspects of *Divided Heaven*: Did not Rita's previously naive and unbroken relationship to the world suffer a serious setback when she discovered that love, too, is finite? Did she not also achieve reintegration following a crisis that led to a suicide attempt from which she recovered only by summoning all her moral strength? It is clearly a matter here not of passing similarities but rather of thoughts and formulations of utmost significance in this author's creative process. The story "Unter den Linden" is a pure and mature demonstration of the poetic principle that has dominated Christa Wolf's work to date: it is the principle of catharsis or, more precisely, a thoroughly individual variant of the catharsis principle. Based on a certain concept of the human being, it is realized in the interaction of three factors: in the selection and treatment of the narrative topic, in the intended function ('effective strategy') of the work, and in the manner in which the hypothetical purpose is manifest (individual artistic method, the writing style).

The succession of events and impressions in "Unter den Linden" does not demonstrate objective movement and development but rather activity and, finally, a sudden change in the thoughts and feelings of the first-person narrator. Although the turn of events at the end is stimulated by an external cause, its roots lie not in this or that outside force; it results, rather, from an inner decision, made by a free will enabled by the dream. By mobilizing her will, her mental energies, the dreamer rescues herself from a situation in which she—following bad conventions, playing roles—was object of the events. The dream permits a particularly clear presentation of such an intention. But the author of *Christa T.* had already pursued a similar aim when she followed the traces of her protagonist. That allowed her to realize that Christa T.'s inner essence did not correspond to her social role and that she occasionally sought to find the courage to "be herself" and to express this self in artistic creation. Exhaustion, sickness, and death admittedly prevented Christa T. from experiencing the kind of breakthrough achieved by the dream narrator in "Unter den Linden." We have already noted that the personal crisis and its conquest in *Divided Heaven* also belong to this constellation.

This release of emotional energies to gain self-assertion and development determines not only the theme but—and this is the second component of the cathartic principle in Christa Wolf—also the pathos of the presentation. Intended to be transmitted to and reenacted by the reader is primarily the author's intellectual and emotional attitude toward the events portrayed. Through her presence and participation, the author enables the limited individual's connection to great and significant things, to human potential and possibility; she wants to pass on that personally experienced shock (the feeling and awareness of an incongruity that must be overcome), which in her case produces the liberating cleansing. Christa Wolf's prose style is cut to these intentions. Information about conditions, events, and things are embedded in passages or expressions—either coherent commentaries and reflections or merely a "but" or an "indeed" thrown into the description —in which the author makes it clear that the story has passed through her consciousness, been evaluated, and given significance by her; it is irrelevant here whether we are dealing with authentic information or the author's inventions. Günter de Bruyn's friendly parody, from which we quoted above, takes aim at this characteristic, among others. (In a different place, de Bruyn has publicly declared his respect for Christa Wolf.)[3] In *Christa T.* and "Unter den Linden," this detracts variously from the reader's imaginative potential, which receives very little nourishment. The reader largely depends on the power of persuasion at the disposal of the commenting narrator. It is said that reflection in a literary work is cold. The reflection that dominates in *Christa T.*, however, is warmed by the author's participation. Christa Wolf interprets the concept of communication expressly in the sense of participation, of being-amidst: "Im-part, to be part in . . . Intensely subjective, but not capricious," she writes in her postscript to stories by Ingeborg Bachmann.[4] With this we have arrived at the third factor. The literary aesthetic that Christa Wolf avows demands authorial presence in the work. It is not, we must note, the simple matter of a fictional narrator who functions as the "I" in the text but from whom the author keeps his/her distance under certain circumstances (see Serenus Zeitblom in Thomas Mann's *Doktor Faustus*, for instance). It has to do, rather, with the true subjectivity of the author, who transmits his/her attitude toward the events in the sense outlined above. Christa Wolf calls this the "fourth dimension . . . the dimension of the author" (SA), which must necessarily be present in modern prose. In his analysis of *Divided Heaven*, Dieter Schlenstedt noted that the aspect of subjective lyric appraisal—in "emotionally heavy images," in the interaction of "prologue, epilogue, and the spheres of experience and reflection"—already plays an intrinsic role in that work, even though it contains, formally speaking, no narrative "I."[5] The title of *Christa T.* (Thinking about Christa T.) already formulates the "communicative" role of the author, and in the work itself the narrator discusses repeatedly and extensively how she approaches her object through thought and feeling in order to achieve unity with her. The narrator in "Self-Experiment," a woman scientist who, in the year 1992, is temporarily transformed into a man, is obviously a fictional figure; and yet her inner attitudes and appraisals—

and this is by no means meant to remain hidden to the reader—are very much those of Christa Wolf.

This so-called "fourth dimension" is no interchangeable formal device; the formal application is different in each work, as we have seen. It belongs, rather, at the center of Wolf's poetics. This may be made clear with a counterexample, an exception in Christa Wolf's production to date. The volume of stories, *Unter den Linden*, also contains the story, "Neue Lebensansichten eines Katers" (New Life and Opinions of a Tomcat). As the title already implies, this "improbable" story is imparted by a first-person narrator whose opinions, attitudes, and emotions are obviously not to be identified with those of the author, although the author slyly puts in to his mouth some things that she has to say. The narrator is a tomcat in the house of the psychology professor Barzel; there he witnesses the attempt to produce a universal psychological-cybernetic model for the complete happiness—in fact for the manipulation and depersonalization—of the human being. The attendant difficulties are admittedly considerable, for they lie in the nature of the human being. Since this creature must first be shoved into the correct position of the "normal human being" (abbreviated "NH"), more and more "disturbing" human attributes must be amputated. And although, or rather because Barzel and his assistants go to the utmost extremes in the process, the experiment fails.

The satirical thrust is initially directed at a rationalistic scientific attitude that exhausts itself with its vain efforts to categorize the corporeality and diversity of the real human being. Beyond this, it aims at a notion about the management of social processes that regards human beings as mere objects of superior control systems—whereby the "formation of the personality" reverses to manipulation. The means are confused with the ends: the human in the human being becomes the disruptive factor in a "system" that is supposed to be concerned with the human being. The narrative perspective is naturally not a multilateral observation of the problem. On the contrary, as satire, the story proceeds in a consciously one-sided manner; the crude devices employed make this clear. The figures are caricatures: the academician who wants to lead mankind to perfection is mentally and physically crippled (inimical to art, impotent); his wife is an unfulfilled, sex-hungry little woman who consoles herself with liqueurs; the author uses speaking names, and so on.

Educated, cultured, and proud of his lineage, the tomcat Max summons his literary predecessors: Puss in Boots, E. T. A. Hoffmann's Kater Murr, but especially that devil's accomplice in *The Master and Margarita*, Bulgakov's Behemoth. The Bulgakov allusion on Christa Wolf's mind moves the story into the realm of the Faust tradition. The most important scene of this parodistic adaptation is the study; the lead character is no new Faust but rather a new Wagner, distilling Homunculus in his alembic.

This satire, based on fantastic assumptions and bordering on the grotesque, may be accorded more or less value than the remaining stories of the volume. Its artistic effect is, in any event, of a different, comical, nature. The introduction of a first-person narrator, regarded with ironic humor and distanced from the narrative events, alters the system of evaluation entirely. The result is not empathy but rather a feeling and consciousness of superiority caused by the comic element. This makes one thing clear: the poetic enterprise favored by Christa Wolf in practice and defended in theoretical statements (in her essay "The Reader and the Writer," for example, or in her conversation with the author of these lines) excludes the comical as an aesthetic principle. We refer to the comical that is seriously treated and logically examined in theoretical formulations—the comical in its broadest sense of creating a distance to the portrayed events. The protestation that Christa Wolf could not possibly have meant it that way would help as little in regard to this conclusion as would the reminder that she likes to hear funny stories and laughs at them. It is a matter here of the logic of her poetics—a logic that has been worked out with remarkable consistency. What we tried to describe briefly at the outset as an individual variant of a cathartic principle is the position whose negative expression constitutes the theoretical polemics so repeatedly and vehemently presented by the author. The majority of her efforts and thoughts, her confessions of likes and dislikes are discharged into this principle, and it permits the resolution of many contradictions in her statements. We should add, however, that—as is the case with many writers who make theoretical statements—the actual artistic achievement does not correspond completely to that which the author describes as her creative principle in essays, interviews, and the like. A writer's poetics generalizes an admittedly significant tendency of personal creation. Artistic activity is not stimulated primarily by a literary-theoretical construct, however, but rather by the relationship of the writer to his/her environment. Thus works can emerge from a variety of causes, motives and claims that cannot be grasped by the theoretically formulated central notion of artistic creation. This is demonstrated by the "Neue Lebensansichten eines Katers" as well as by *Till Eulenspiegel*; and *Divided Heaven* implies a cathartic principle in some ways but is not entirely absorbed by it.

The elements for a systematization of this principle evolve in connection with *Christa T.*[6] And the more Christa Wolf has succeeded in generally expressing the creative direction undertaken here, the more pointedly we must ask just what such a concept can achieve in our literature as a whole. Although it remains an assumption, one can assume that the choice and treatment of the theme for *Christa T.* were oppositional, that they were determined in part to contrast with the once-preferred artistic treatment of "planners and leaders," directing attention instead to those whose qualities and value are not conspicuously evident, who have no success and do not move upward. This far-reaching problem is not the concern only of literature. When, on the one hand, our society creates entirely new expectations that thrust the active workers who manage great social developments and grow in this activity into the foreground of events, one runs the risk, on the other hand, of precarious moral and actual results if one exaggerates the aspect of upward movement. A presentation that has too one-sided a development, in which the person who is good moves up into leading positions, necessarily provokes the question concerning the value or worthlessness of those who remain "simple" workers, teachers, and so on for their entire lives. The plea for sensitivity, the urge to think in a new and deeper way about human qualities and to search for them in those places where their manifestation is limited, has not only a general moral justification but also ultimately a practical social significance. When she fulfills such a desire, Christa Wolf can refer to democratic literary traditions. Her repeated enthusiastic remarks about Büchner's Lenz cause us to suspect that Büchner's statement served her as a guiding concept: "One should try once to lower oneself into the meanest life and to represent it in the twitches, the intimations, the whole delicate and hardly noticeable play of the features."[7]

The author of Christa T. does not only want intensely to elucidate an individual, however, but also simultaneously to validate some general aspects of such an elucidation. The polemic aim carries her away, allowing her to formulate antitheses that become all the more contestable, the more the author gives them a separate theoretical articulation. Beginning with the Büchnerian-Lenzian project to see the entire and worthy fellow human being even in the person who is denied the realization of his abilities and powers, she strides tendentiously forth considering whether precisely this nonrealization does not define the truly human. She asks whether what happens to a person determines the quality of the "human" and is less concerned with what a person might actively achieve. The stigma of Christa T., who is inhibited and marked by a fatal disease, borders on becoming a sign of special selection. According to everything we learn about her, incidentally, the protagonist of the book makes no claim to such a thing; the "secret superiority" contained in her "weakness" belongs solely to the author's commentary (CT 140).

Seen in the broader perspective of philosophy of history, Christa Wolf's polemic against compliancy and grasping for success—although real and in a certain sense justified—leads her to treat every individual's necessarily limited exercise of these things in a fundamentally disdainful manner and to look for humanity beyond it, in the area of the unrealized. Temptations that can and must be resisted, to which it is reprehensible to succumb, appear in her moral judgment on the same level with objective givens of social development which, to quote Marx, can only be conquered by submitting to them. This "submission" appears suspect, "objective givens" begin to sound like lazy excuses for lack of conscience. Now it might be frivolous to maintain that we are dealing here with insignificant or easily soluble problems. Even in those places where she provokes contradiction, Christa Wolf articulates complicated and important matters of concern to us. The objective determinants that our activity must take into account if it is to have any meaning are mixed with things that do not need to be, not primarily in the book, but in life. Still, decisions assume the ability to make distinctions. The notion that the liberty to behave morally can be reached by the divestiture of "constraints" does not recognize that our behavior is, in fact, always conditioned. It delegates dubious value to such behavior; it even goes so far as to relegate it entirely to the obscurity of the forgotten.

Philosophical considerations like Christa Wolf's poetic conception turn on this fulcrum. The cathartic principle, whose description we attempted above, is the aesthetically practiced equivalent—also formulated in part as theoretical confession—to the briefly described historical-philosophical moral problem and its attempted solution. Clearly this principle can be most purely developed and most convincingly maintained when the author deals with topics whose concern is the kind of individual decision that is not thwarted by any "must" (this "curse" that is central to the Büchnerian heritage). These are topics in which the dimensions of the work are no greater than the latitude within which its possibilities of plot can be freely selected. There are such aspects of life, naturally, and the representation of such situations and developments, in which only "the heart counts," is therefore justified and meaningful.[8] It is inadequate to object that the stories that come to mind here, "Unter den Linden" and "Self-Experiment," are based on fantastic assumptions. The fantastic and the utopian, when made artistically recognizable for what they are, can intensify the sense of reality; they can also permit a clearer representation of the really existent and possible. This latter transpires in "Self-Experiment." This story raises current and universally important questions, emphatically and with psychological power of conviction; the questions are of the kind in which things depend to a great extent on whether men and women employ the already existing possibilities in order to achieve the kind of behavior appropriate for our epoch. (The utopian disguise permits as a given the unspoken imputation of the material preconditions of the possibility of behaving one way or another.) Her transformation into a man—to be thought of as a genetic experiment—permits the woman scientist to comprehend fully just how strongly her behavior was and remains determined by her existence as a woman in a world that receives its standards of evaluation silently and unquestioningly from and in relation to men—in which, for instance, a woman scientist's worth is measured by the recognition that she is as good as a man. The first-person narrator is secretly driven to undertake the self-experiment by the unscientific goal of wanting to prove her "value as a woman," both to herself and to her always coolly superior boss. Her behavior, like his, is revealed at the end to be role-playing ("like at the movies" [SE 130]). But the winner is the loser. The boss has purchased his professional superiority at the price of the inability to love, of inhumanity. The woman, who interrupts the experiment of trying to equal him on his own turf, gains the chance to begin again in a way humane and appropriate to her. The search for the person "one can love" (SE 131)[9] stands at the end, thus corresponding closely to the ending of "Unter den Linden."

Some may hold different opinions or may find the whole thing too theoretical. The device Wolf chooses in presenting the work as a "protocol," as a "piece of scientific work that increasingly acquires the character of a subjective confession" (SA), seems convincing nonetheless. And one cannot deny that the story proves the potential power of Christa Wolf's poetic principle. By abolishing exploitation and the inimical positions of the classes toward each other, socialism creates new conditions for the real possibilities of realizing humane behavior ("I cannot postpone love"); it proves such behavior is more than an empty hope. Christa Wolf thus regards and defends her project correctly as an effective and necessary element in developing socialist society. The programmatic sentence from "The Reader and the Writer": "Prose must try to maintain man's contact with his roots" (RW 211), becomes meaningful in the context of the liberation of humane abilities and forces buried in the individual. The notion of "contact" with "roots" admittedly comprehends the humane as an abstract element inherent in the individual—how it gets there is not considered. The works that have appeared since *Divided Heaven* do not demonstrate convincingly whether such an ideological-poetic project also permits the representations of the individual in the true multiplicity of his social relationships. Such representations would have to portray the individual in the true dialectic of the existing—not optional and interchangeable—conditions of his behavior and possible decisions in accordance with his conscience, which is, in turn, socially conditioned. And Christa Wolf's theoretical efforts raise strong doubts in this regard.

Now, such statements by writers should be seen primarily in the context of their creative process; they are intended to solidify and clarify the writers' own artistic position—to work it out more definitively. The most interesting thing about Brecht's malicious statements about Thomas Mann, for instance, is not to what extent they present a correct picture of the novelist. More important is Brecht's need for a specific polemical foil to make his own creative principles more precise. Even unjust and false judgments can play a productive role in this process. This applies in principle to Christa Wolf as well. On the one hand, therefore, one must demonstrate the connection that exists between the writer's poetics and artistic practice; on the other, the artistic achievement should not be derived from the author's ideas about this connection. Finally, one must consider the fact that such ideas, once spoken, do indeed have an influence on creative activity—on both the author's own and that of others. For this reason they must be discussed

like any other theoretical text, although admittedly not with the aim—
à la Georg Lukács—of canonizing certain writing methods and con-
demning others. We want to question, rather, whether the connection
between the human figure, the poetic principle, and certain procedures
in the structuring of a prose work is as inevitable, necessary, and indispensable as Christa Wolf perceives it to be.

When Christa Wolf objects to "closed" narrative works, with
which a nonapparent and unmoved author wants nonetheless to move
his/her reader, she is presumably aiming at certain books or tendencies in our literature that displease her because she holds them to
be untrue; this would have to be discussed case by case. For her part,
she undertook in *Christa T.* to show how she, remembering, followed
the life-traces of her protagonist (she describes a few invented episodes
expressly as speculations). Rejection on the one hand and personal approach on the other combine to produce the notion that the untruth of
certain prose works has its roots in the structure of this prose ("closed"
story, absence of the author). But she couches her polemic in general
terms, so that, if one takes her at her word, even Anna Seghers and
Tschingis Aitmatow—to stick with the contemporaries—are subject to
rejection.[10] In "The Reader and the Writer" she extends her argument
with literary-historical excursuses that one could euphemistically describe as daring or, more skeptically considered, reckless.

She subsumes what has heretofore been generally termed "epic,"
"narrative literature" or something similar, under the concept of
"prose" ("the prose genre," "modern prose," etc.).[11] In spite of certain
reservations, in spite of her display of respect for a few older narrative
works, this concept summarizes the tendency to reject a literary tradition thus far thought important. Now this can be absolutely necessary if
one wants to create something new. A philosophical argument joins a
political one in justifying this rejection. "Conventional narrative" with
its "established plot" is for Christa Wolf a kind of clockwork that is
wound up according to external regulations—corresponding to Newton's celestial mechanics (she even speaks of a "Newtonian
dramaturgy" (RW 195). Such stories were appropriate earlier, she
claims, "to tame a pretty turbulent world" (RW 194); it was "gradually"
found "natural for the mechanism of society to function in the same
way" as Newton's celestial mechanics (RW 194). This illusion of objective motion thus confirmed precisely the way the world was. The task
today is to develop a prose art that occupies heights analogous to Ein-
steinian and Heisenbergian thinking.

The polemic thrust of these remarks—in which I recognize very
little real history of narrative literature—is aimed at the objectivity of
movement. What disturbs her about the "mechanics" of the heavens
and the earth is materialism, to be precise, and she tries to get past the
objective reality, which she places in quotation marks, by referring to
dialectics and relativity. It is the same philosophical misfortune that
befell Gorky when he declared, in the argument against Lenin regard-

85

ing materialism and empiriocriticism, that Lenin and Plechanov were "of different opinions on the question of tactics, although they both believe in and propagate historical fatalism; the opposing side, on the other hand, embraces the philosophy of activity. On which side the greater truth lies is clear to me."[12] Christa Wolf believes that "conventional narrative," which adheres to the principles of Newtonian mechanics, already "departed a long way from the rules of conduct to which people were accustomed in their day" (RW 195); still, it cradled people in comfortable illusion and sanctioned the status quo: "I perish, but it [the 'mechanics' of social movement—H. K.] remains and moves" (RW 195). A narrative literature that corresponds to this model of the world is thus suited to create an illusion and to manipulate. For this reason, art needs the "mediation of the artist"; for this reason a literature should be created in which the author stands "with his destiny and his life's struggle, . . . between 'reality' and the empty page and has no choice but to fill that page, to project the controversy between himself and the world upon it" (RW 197). This is noted in response to Robbe-Grillet's description of a world of things "in minute detail" (RW 196)—which minimizes the role of the human being—but it is also meant to have general significance. While the "closed plot" prohibits verification, the author who is present in the work vouches for what he/she tells. Christa Wolf calls this "subjective authenticity" (SA).[13]

There is yet a further basis (she alludes to it in our conversation) for her clearly profound dislike for literary prose in which the author is not present. Her desire to make her own subjectivity evident in her prose constitutes a reaction to that situation in which the work is passed on, as a printed and purchased book, to an impersonal public. The "closed work," from which the author has withdrawn, as it were, appears in this regard to represent the analog to the anonymity of the recipient. This must be countered; hence the desires to maintain intact the umbilical cord between author and work and to construct as well a personal contact from the work to the reader—as author-individual to seek the reader-individual in the anonymous public—emerge. Personal speech is intended to anchor such a function structurally in the work; consider the situation presented as frame and starting point of "Unter den Linden"—a conversation with a trusted friend. We are dealing here with a far-reaching problem not only of but also especially of narrative literature; it deserves further exploration in regard to its relevance for different social formations and their stages of development.

Not only Christa Wolf, we would suggest, feels herself struck by this problem. Hermann Kant should be mentioned, for instance. His prose style is clearly organized with reference to oral narrative and speech, and he is present as author in his work especially because of this; we leave the question aside here concerning the degree of his identification with the central characters of his novels. In this respect his procedure is thoroughly comparable to that of Christa Wolf. This does not mean, however, that Kant therefore practices a poetic principle overwhelmingly based on empathetic "communication." The connections between the contemporary artist's desire to locate truth's traces, his/her efforts to establish vital contact with the reader, and the empathetic mediating role of the author in the work are hardly as constraining—thus the example of Kant—as they seem to be for Christa Wolf.

On the one hand, there are significant epic traditions in which the presence and the interruptions of the author do not serve empathetic-subjective communication, but rather precisely opposite purposes, that is, rationalistic-ironic "alienation"; consider Diderot, for instance. On the other hand, literary history provides us with curious examples of the way in which authors with whom Christa Wolf has absolutely nothing to do employed procedures that have a striking formal similarity to those she affirms. Cäsar Flaischlen, for example (it can be useful to read him for analytical purposes, but only for these), developed and practiced the concept of a prose "animated" by the author's presence seventy years ago in opposition to those "closed" narratives that, in his opinion, were written only to achieve cheap effects and financial gain. In his eyes, contemporary realism was the expression of the dominant literary condition; he wanted to shield himself from the latter; in the process he levied his polemic thrust at the former. And this "animated" prose was loaded onto the market in hundreds of thousands of copies and fit excellently into the literary industry of imperialism.[14] This example can clarify precisely because it arises from entirely different conditions of production and from a world view and aesthetic perspective with which Christa Wolf, as we have noted, has nothing in common. It is not possible to ascertain how a work of art functions under certain literary conditions; this function does not derive in a straight and unilateral way from a certain writing style or from a group of literary procedures and techniques. No writing style, taken alone, could not also be made to serve other hypothetical purposes or could be protected a priori from misuse.

An author obviously has to find and perfect the creative method appropriate to him/her. But it can lead to one-sidedness when he/she allows the manifestation of his/her image of society and the human being to be too strictly bound by certain procedures and techniques. The difference between a developed artistic method and a mannerism consists not least in the author's ability to allow himself/herself to be corrected by life and to react to the manifold aspects of social development in appropriate ways—that is to say, in every case differently—and in connection with his/her personal set of values, to which he/she adheres and which therefore return. Christa Wolf's creative production to date is richer than her concept of "modern prose." Why shouldn't this continue?

Notes

This essay first appeared in *WB* 6 (1974): 113–125, where it was published back-to-back with Kaufmann's "Conversation" with Christa Wolf, as it is in this volume. The version from which this translation was taken was revised by Kaufmann for publication in Eva and Hans Kaufmann, *Erwartung und Angebot. Studien zum gegenwärtigen Verhältnis von Literatur und Gesellschaft in der DDR* (Berlin: Akademie-Verlag, 1976), 45–61 (notes 220–223). It is printed here with the permission of the author and the publisher.

1. "Rita und die Freiheit. Nach Christa Wolf," in *Das Lasterkabinett: Deutsche Literatur von Auerbach bis Zweig in der Parodie* (Leipzig: Reclam, 1970), 198.
2. Compare the similar image in Ingeborg Bachmann's "Undine geht": "I love the water, its dense transparency, the green in the water and the dumb creatures (I too shall soon be equally dumb), my hair among them, in it, the just water, the indifferent mirror that forbids me to see you differently. The wet frontier between me and me. . . ." (TY 172).
3. Günter de Bruyn, "Fragment eines Frauenporträts," in *Liebes- und andere Erklärungen: Schriftsteller über Schriftsteller*, ed. Annie Voigtländer, 2d ed. (Berlin/Weimar: Aufbau, 1974), 410–416.
4. Christa Wolf, "Nachwort" [Afterword] to Ingeborg Bachmann, *Undine geht* (Leipzig: Reclam, 1973), 140.
5. Dieter Schlenstedt, "Motive und Symbole in Christa Wolfs Erzählung *Der geteilte Himmel*," *WB* 10, no. 1 (1964): 77–78.
6. Cf. SA.
7. "Man versuch es einmal und senke sich in das Leben des Geringsten und gebe es wieder in den Zuckungen, den Andeutungen, dem ganzen feinen, kaum bemerkten Mienenspiel." Georg Büchner, *Lenz*, in *Werke und Briefe* (Leipzig: Insel, 1952), 92.
8. I stress and justify this also in my conversation with Christa Wolf.
9. Compare also Christa Wolf's statements in our conversation.
10. In our conversation, Christa Wolf stresses that her attitude toward Anna Seghers's creative principles were transformed during her involvement with CT: "I had reason to question a remark—made by Anna Seghers—to which I subscribed, and which seemed to be confirmed by my earlier experience of writing: what has become narratable is already mastered. You see, I had learned . . . what it really meant to have to tell the story of something in order to master it. I had found that story-writers—or perhaps I should say prose-writers—can be compelled to abandon the strict sequence of first living through something, then digesting and 'mastering' it and, lastly, writing about it."
11. Cf., for example, SA. A similar use of words can be found in Irmtraud Morgner when she writes that she does not regret that Annemarie Auer did not become a "prosaist," but rather the author of "critical essays": "I read her essays like prose." "Sündhafte Beteuerungen," in *Liebes- und andere Erklärungen*, 14. According to this, essays are not prose; that word ("prose") is reserved for a certain kind of narrative literature that doesn't want to call itself *that* because it wants to avoid being confused with literary traditions from which it distinguishes itself.
12. Maxim Gorky, letter to Pjatnitzki, quoted without a date in Marietta Schaginjan, *Weihnachten in Sorrent* (Berlin, 1974), 114. Cf. also Christa Wolf's objection to "pure historical determinism," etc. in SA. Once again it turns out that, as stated above, the relationship between determination and possibility of action forms the philosophical background of the poetic principle.
13. Cf. also SA, where "inner authenticity" is mentioned. Heinz Plavius, in his review of *Unter den Linden* ("Mutmassungsmut," *NdL* 22, no. 10 [1974]: 154–

158), comes to Christa Wolf's aid by grasping at nothing less than Marx's "Theses on Feuerbach," the first fundamental laws of historical materialism, in order to justify a writing method in which "the story does not derive from a given unrolling of events, but rather from the sense, from the intentions, from the hypothetical aim that are manifest in the figures, in the narrator." This is "the way in which to conceive the thing, reality, subjectively as *human sensuous activity, practice*" (155). There is much confusion here in a few sentences. First, the question of chronology or nonchronology, with which Plavius begins, is in no way identical with the question of the "closed" story, and the question concerning the presence of the author in the work must in turn be distinguished from the former. Second, what Christa Wolf is attempting is not distinguished alone by the fact that there is a first-person narrator, let alone by the manifestation of meaning via the figures. Third, Plavius reverses the argumentation of the first thesis on Feuerbach: Marx identifies as the "chief defect of all hitherto existing materialism—that of Feuerbach included . . . that the thing, reality, sensuousness, is conceived only in the form of the *object* or of *contemplation*, but not as *human sensuous activity, practice*, not subjectively." (Karl Marx and Friedrich Engels, *Basic Works on Politics and Philosophy*, ed. Lewis S. Feuer [Garden City: Doubleday, 1959], 243.) Plavius's logic assumes a connection between subjective and active practice. With this, he eliminates the materialist basis that Marx does not deny but rather describes as inadequate in its mechanistic form for comprehending sociohistorical processes. Because Plavius evidently anticipates the far-reaching consequences that could result from this questionable appeal to the authority of Marx ("The evaluation of the two writing methods is undoubtedly connected to these speculations."), his own courage to speculate recedes quickly, and he abandons the prickly topic. He neither attempts to demonstrate the particular description—so massively put forth—of "writing methods" and "practice" in Christa Wolf's stories, nor does he ask further about what the "evaluation of the two writing methods" might signify. He is possibly repelled by the equation he establishes in his argument between "traditional" narrative and mechanical materialism and by the establishment of a "mechanistic-materialistic" and a "dialectical-materialist" writing method as the fundamental mark of distinction of modern narrative literature.

And he would be right in being so repelled.

Seduced by his idea, Plavius maltreats the multidimensionality of the concepts "subjective" and "subjectivity." For instance, one frequently refers to the special way in which the individuality of the author makes itself known in a lyric poem as "subjective." That is not an assessment; this "subjectivity" can turn up in good poems as well as bad. (The "subjectivity" that Christa Wolf defends in her prose is related to that of lyric poetry. This is also not a valuative statement.) However, every literary work of art, whether or not an "I" appears in it, formally speaking, contains a personal attitude toward the events presented and is, in this respect, "subjective." Neither of these need have anything to do with subjectivism as an element of a world view for which the objective world is only a subjective setting. But such a view could also refer to Marx, according to Plavius's argumentation!

If one wanted to talk seriously about "modern prose"—in a way, in other words, that would admit some general conclusions—one would first have to examine an enormous amount of literary material for its ability to make significant statements about today's world. Second, the sociopolitical background for the current opinions about "modern prose" would have to be studied. Just as Christa Wolf speaks of "Newtonian dramaturgy," in "What is literature?" Jean-Paul Sartre refers similarly to "the novelistic technique of Newtonian mechanics"; he declares as anachronistic that narrator of earlier times who stands "outside (the) (hi)story" (quoted in Manfred Naumann et al., *Gesellschaft - Literatur - Lesen: Literaturrezeption in theoretischer Sicht* [Berlin/Weimar: Aufbau, 1973], 72; cf. also the authors' discussion of this quotation). The evident context for Sartre and others views the traditional novel against the backdrop of the stabilized materialist society of the postwar era, regarding it as an embodiment of bourgeois culture that has the power to affirm and to stabilize the system. A separate investigation would be necessary to examine how this affects artistic practice and to what extent such a process can be instructive for a literature that originates and affects under the conditions in our country.

All this lies beyond the aim of this essay, however. Nor am I raising "objections"—as Plavius imputes—to the concept of "modern prose" (154). But I am merely examining an author's artistic method on the basis of what, in my opinion, it can and cannot achieve. This is an attempt to understand an author's poetics, in which I air my doubts about a few arguments that seem to me to be faulty and to detract from the development of the manifold possibilities of expression in socialist realist prose art.

14. Cf. *Geschichte der deutschen Literatur*, vol. 9: *Vom Ausgang des 19. Jahrhunderts bis 1917*, Autorenkollektive headed by Hans Kaufmann and Silvia Schlenstedt (Berlin: Volk und Wissen, 1974), 105.

Christa Wolf and Virginia Woolf: Selective Affinities

Joyce Crick

What a discovery that would be—a system that did not shut out.
                    —Virginia Woolf, A Writer's Diary, October 2, 1932

Assigned to perform a work which remains open, open like a wound.
                    —Christa Wolf, No Place on Earth

hrista Wolf and Virginia Woolf? An implausible coupling. Name magic—and both writers were susceptible to it—may cast its poetic spell, but it will not carry us very far analytically. Besides, compare-and-contrast exercises are notoriously full of pitfalls. An inductive approach risks forcing both writers to fit whatever grid there may be; proceeding suggestively and empirically, as I propose, can be random. But both approaches aim at a greater discrimination in placing and characterizing; the presence of the one illuminates aspects of the other, which might otherwise remain in shadow. Moreover, its built-in insecurity and tendency to relativization make this approach particularly appropriate to these two novelists, who move on such shifting epistemological grounds themselves. For there are a number of startling general similarities, which may repay further exploration, between the novels and essays of the daughter of the high English Edwardian bourgeoisie on the one hand and the prose of the uneasy and distinguished member of the East German literary élite on the other. They both developed their distinctive internalized and poetic literary styles against the grain of prevailing realist orthodoxy: the one abandoned plot and externality, that earthenware pot,[1] for lyricism; the other turned from story, that pot with two handles (AJ

41),[2] to vision and to a prose halfway between fiction and essay. Their finest works have been elegiac in tone and cathartic in function; I am thinking here mainly of *To the Lighthouse* and *The Quest for Christa T.* For both, epistemology, and with it the act of memory, the relation of subject to object, self to world, is problematic;[3] both celebrate the moment of vision. Both present living as process and flux; consequently the novels of both tend to be open-ended. Both maintain a conversational tone, although Virginia Woolf's conversation is more brilliant, because both conceive their writing as an encounter with the reader. Moreover, both write as readers themselves: the one collected her essays under the title *The Common Reader*, the other as *The Reader and the Writer*; and both make literature part of the fabric of their own fictions (*Orlando; Between the Acts; The Quest for Christa T.; Patterns of Childhood; No Place on Earth*). For both, imaginative literature is a means of self-discovery and of extending the possibility of this awareness of self to the reader; both care deeply about the fragility of that self, particularly in their fellow women, and both have rethought women's imaginative possibilities in their respective social and literary worlds. Both have become models. Both, alas, have become cult objects.

But are such generalities enough for us to assume a meaningful affinity?[4] One might object that such a catalogue treats two developing and changing oeuvres as uniform, that it has filtered out all those immediately obvious differences in the writers' respective worlds locating them in place and time and history and determining what Virginia Woolf would call their angle of vision.[5] The years of the aging novelist and the days of the schoolchild coincided only as the Nazis came to power and into the first years of the Second World War. But even then, what the older woman promptly perceived as the larger psychological issue, blurring the specifics of history as she did so ("Let us try to drag up into consciousness the subconscious Hitlerism that holds us down. It is the desire for aggression; the desire to dominate and enslave."),[6] became the painful and far more differentiated task of exorcism of the later writer who had lived through those social and historical specifics and had them offered to her as childhood patterns. A long novel (*Patterns of Childhood*, 1976), which did full justice to both the historical substance and the psychological pattern, functioned precisely to drag up into consciousness that latent fascism. Not only her Marxism, but also what she had lived through, made the later writer take account of history more urgently. The one woman had her roots in the seeming securities of the late nineteenth century; she wrote during the sheltered and vulnerable span between two wars; she knew madness; she chose suicide. Her freedom as a writer and publisher was far greater than she knew, for she was much occupied with her unfreedom as a woman. The years of the later writer have been unimaginably more disturbed: her beginnings lay in the illusory, corrupting securities of

National Socialist Germany; her maturity coincided with the life-time of the GDR, with which she identified closely; she writes exposed to multiple pressures toward ideological conformity, not least from her own internal censorship; she has made a space for the imagination against far greater odds of external and internal unfreedom than Virginia Woolf lived to see.

A wide range of common ground is undeniable nonetheless, and this essay proposes to concentrate on, always in the light of that difference in generation and the fact that they are differently placed in European history and in European literary history—which is not entirely the same thing—three related areas of mutually illuminating problems: first, their innovatory responses to the prevailing aesthetic orthodoxies; second, the place and function of the authorial self in their fictions; third, writing as a means to self-realization. Because these are central issues, the discussion radiates outward. In Virginia Woolf's case, current practice was the tired and trivial realism that she mocked in Arnold Bennett's novels,[7] while the prevailing theoretical attitude, more deeply internalized, was the exclusive Flaubertian aesthetic that insisted on the autonomy of the work of art, the impersonality of the author, and the distinction between discursive and poetic language and hence between fiction and essay. In Christa Wolf's case, the orthodoxy was that of Zhdanov's socialist realism, particularly as adapted to create a new German national and socialist literature, with its conventional expectations of the exemplary hero and the realist mode and its assumption of the ideological instrumentality of literature. Each also had her own deeply assimilated prior assumptions that, however they quarrel with them, give their novels an ultimate moral bedrock: for the older writer, there was the characteristic Victorian combination of moralism and imagination of her father, Leslie Stephen;[8] for Christa Wolf the humanism of the early Marx and Ernst Bloch.[9]

Both began by writing well within convention. Virginia Woolf's first novels, unlike her short stories, remain caught in the customs of the polite social novel. Not until she needed elegy to mourn her dead brother and the young dead of the First World War did she develop a questing, questioning approach in *Jacob's Room* (1922). Guided by the unguiding principle that "nobody sees any one as he is—they see a whole—they see themselves,"[10] the narrator goes in quest of Jacob F., partially recapturing him from his habitations, the perceptions of the people in his life. Under the same conditions of uncertainty of knowing and the need to mourn, Lily Briscoe in *To the Lighthouse* (1927) goes in search of the dead Mrs. Ramsay: "Who knows what we are, what we feel? Who knows even at moments of intimacy, This is knowledge?"[11] "She must try to get hold of something that evaded her. It evaded her when she thought of Mrs. Ramsay; it evaded her now when she thought of her picture."[12] "Such is the manner of our seeing. Such the conditions of our love."[13] Given the presence in English of an oeuvre so strongly marked by elegiac search, by losing and finding through the prismatic uncertainties of individual perceptions, I wonder whether this did not prompt Christopher Middleton, the translator of *Nachdenken über Christa T.*, to render Wolf's title as *The Quest for Christa T.*[14] It is fully in keeping with the spirit of a title such as *To the Lighthouse*. It also does rather less justice to the distinctive characteristic of the novel, its constant foregrounding of the narrator's thoughts, than a more literal version would have done. And that, after all, is the novel's great innovation. For Christa Wolf too had begun conventionally. Her first fictions, *Moskauer Novelle* (Moscow Novella, 1961) and *Divided Heaven* (1963) were couched in an unexceptionable Bitterfeld style. But the very change in form to the reflective exploration of the private spaces of conscience and imagination was itself a departure from official literary expectations.

But when Virginia Woolf triumphantly announced in "Mr. Bennett and Mrs. Brown" (1924) that "in or about December, 1910, human character changed,"[15] it was as a manifesto for the new novels she was to write. Gaily she ranged herself among the new writers, Messrs. Lawrence, Forster, Strachey, Joyce, Eliot, whom we have come to regard as representative of the modern movement. Life itself—the elusive Mrs. Brown—alone was important to the novelist, not the manipulations of plot, not the solid reality of fact that was the prime literary assumption of the second-rate realists who had dominated the literary scene. Reality was unstable; perceptions were relative; social and moral values had shifted. To convey the myriad fragmentary sensations of human life one needed imagination, not tired descriptive convention. Entreating the reader to collaborate in understanding human nature in terms of its bewildering complexity, not its falsified simplicity, she ends by prophesying one of the great ages of English literature.

And so it was. And not only in England. The changed imaginative perception of human nature was part of a major European shift and gave rise to a rich literature that has since become classic. Bloomsbury looked to Paris for its painters, and they found their writers in Proust, the explorer of memory, and in Gide, the diarist-novelist. If Virginia Woolf's critical tool of "angle of vision" has an outside origin, it may have derived from Roger Fry and his first Post-Impressionist exhibition of 1910 (about December). Rilke, too, was bound for Paris and Rodin and set his *Notebooks of Malte Laurids Brigge* there (1910!); that lyrical novel's reflective mode and epistemological uncertainty make it more surely the ancestor of Christa Wolf's *Quest for Christa T.* (1968) than anything of Virginia Woolf's. Dostoevsky was translated, and among the translators was Virginia Woolf.[16] Bloomsbury's connections with Germany on the whole were negligible, but the Woolfs' Hogarth Press became Freud's English publisher.[17] In the 1920s, the German novel became European, as it had not been since Goethe: it, too, shared the fragmentary perception of personality (Hesse), the enigmatic symbol

(Kafka), the relativized perception of time (Thomas Mann). Above all, these writers shared a tremendous literary self-consciousness: literature is their subject matter as well as their medium. More darkly, they share a sense of historical ill ease, of a late time and an impending doom not to be met in Virginia Woolf's high spirited essay at the outset of her career, but it can be heard in her last novels, *The Years* (1937) and *Between the Acts* (1941).

My point is this: many characteristics I first enumerated as common to Virginia Woolf and Christa Wolf are in fact, allowing for their personal modulations, characteristic of the modern novel. They are modes of insight and expression available to the European tradition in the first quarter of this century.

But literary history, like private lives, was interrupted by cataclysmic political history. Nazi cultural policy drove the modern novel from Germany. German authors retreated into exile, withdrawal, or death, and the public memory of foreign modernists was wiped out. Christa Wolf declares, "The isolation from all contemporary literature could not have been more complete" (RW 187), and she sees this as a possible cause for her generation's late development. How poignantly this contrasts with the free run the Edwardian daughter had of her father's library! Moreover, the Germany that began to pick up threads again at the end of the war was divided. The need for catching up on lost literature was conceived differently in West and East, as was the very nature and function of literature. The wide-ranging possibilities of the nonrealist novel were seized upon by writers in the West; publishers were as eager. Virginia Woolf was among the first foreign novelists to be republished. But in the East, the communist writers and cultural functionaries who returned from Stalin's Russia brought back Zdhanov's prescription of socialist realism and Lukács's view of literary history as culminating in the great realists of the nineteenth century, creators of representative types who, whether they knew it or not, held up the mirror to the embodiment of the Marxist theory of history. The modern novel returned in the representative forms of Heinrich and Thomas Mann, but they were conceived as the last of the bourgeois realists. The literature of the past had to satisfy the first greedy need to catch up. The literary conventions the eager beginner encountered were not those of Arnold Bennett's freehold villas and copyhold estates but the positive heroes and "New Men" Christa Wolf later satirized in "Short Trip to H." (1971).[18] Above all there was the massive convention of a stable external reality, whose only latent pattern was Marxist-Leninist. These were conventions that were as falsifying to "real [true] life" (RW 181) as Mr. Bennett's had been to "the spirit we live by, life itself."[19] So "The Reader and the Writer" (1968), Christa Wolf's manifesto, also announces a change in perceiving the world—though she does not date it as confidently. Nor is "manifesto" the right word for a tentative, questioning, disturbed essay. In the very first paragraph she questions the nature of the perceived world: "A change has occurred in one's perception of the world that even casts doubts on the unimpeachable memory; we see 'the world' once more—but what do we mean by the world?—in a different light" (RW 177). There is none of Virginia Woolf's gleeful iconoclasm here, rather the suggestion of a crisis of silence. Nevertheless, against the grain of the prevailing orthodoxy and a generation late Wolf has not only virtually introduced the modern novel to East Germany, but she has even gone beyond it in the openness and apparent tentativeness of her structures and the combination, peculiarly her own, of an (almost) immediate subjectivity and an extreme novelistic self-reflectiveness and "literariness" of texture. And she has recovered memory, the repressed memory of complicity, on behalf of the larger world of her readers.

So, as liberating pioneers in finding new lyrical forms of the novel appropriate to more elusive perceptions of reality, Virginia Woolf and Christa Wolf can be seen as playing a comparable role in their respective literary traditions. The older writer joyfully saw herself as one of many peers in a great, exhilarating movement. The later novelist comes almost alone, catching up on the great risk.

But "what do we mean by the world?" It must be said that however elusive that social and physical world the sensuous and linguistic responses of the Englishwoman are far more vivid than her German counterpart's. Event and externality retreat in Christa Wolf's work into thoughtfulness, not into sense-impression. Do we ever learn what any of her figures *look* like? In "An Afternoon in June," a rare enough instance, the child's helmet of hair bleached in the sun is primarily the occasion of a reflection on the loss of memory and passing of time (AJ 42).

These differences must be kept in view, not just of the cultural and moral deprivations and resilience of the later writer, but of differences of place and class, of social and political allegiance—the one was a skeptical, detached socialist, the other is a communist convert who learned disappointment. There are differences of personal history, of assumptions about the nature of reality; one began close to mysticism, the other set out toward it from materialism. Differences exist in language, literary tradition, choice of theme, and appropriate novelistic form. What strikes one above all is Virginia Woolf's greater freedom—of wit and fantasy and imaginative play, her comic sense, the confidence that enabled her to refuse honors, the ease of literary and moral judgment. The defiance. Antigone speaks, not Cassandra.

This enumeration of historical and biographical factors is—intentionally—continuous with the catalogue of literary ones. It blurs the distinction between art and life, aesthetics and history, fiction and the life that feeds it, and in doing so will clear some theoretical ground. Such continuity is axiomatic for the later novelist: the writer is not outside history; the social self is not separate from the writing self: "No one, least of all the writer, can seek freedom beyond the co-ordinates of space and time, beyond or outside history" (RW 208). Moreover, such an assumption of continuity has important consequences for her choice of open, procedural narrative forms, the reflective mode she prefers to call "prose," rather than by the clear genre terms of essay or fiction: "To my mind, it is much more useful to look at writing, not as an end product, but as a process which continuously runs alongside life, helping to shape and interpret it: writing can be seen as a way of being more intensely involved in the world, as the concentration and focusing of thought, word and deed" (SA).

A similar continuity is implicit in the critical essays of her older namesake, as she characterizes a writer's work by way of her or his "perspective," or "angle of vision," especially when she dwells on the particular limitations under which women writers have written in the past: the Brontë sisters, Jane Austen, Elizabeth Barrett Browning. It is not declared as theory—that is not her way—but is part of the flexibility her fine eclectic approach allows her. However, such continuity is not the case when she takes up her pen as novelist herself. She takes the liberty to imagine "beyond the coordinates of time and space," in her celebration of the absolute moment of being. And in *Orlando*, she turns history into fantasy. On the other hand, time and place reassert themselves in the chronicle of *The Years*, once called *Here and Now*; and history provides a stable frame for the fragmented present in *Between the Acts*. But as a practicing novelist she does regard writing from its end product.

Virginia Woolf assumes the autonomy of the work of art, the impersonality of the controlling consciousness, and the separation of the personal self from the artist is the legacy of an older, Flaubertian aesthetic, and this compels indirect narrative strategies.[20] She distinguishes between discursive essay and poetic novel in a way Christa Wolf's "prose" does not. She did once toy with the idea of writing something in the reflective mode but rejects it as a *pis aller*: "Not exactly diary. Reflections. That's the fashionable dodge. Peter Lucas and Gide both at it. Neither can settle to creative art. . . . It's the comment—the daily intercourse—that comes in handy in times like these. I too feel it." The temptation lies in the pressures of the times: the date of this diary entry is August 7, 1939. War was about to break out. It was no time for stillness and concentration. The seismographic entry from the brink of disaster continues: "I have been thinking about Censors. How visionary figures admonish us. . . . If I say this, So-and-so will think me sentimental. If that . . . will think me bourgeois. All books now seem to me surrounded by a circle of invisible censors. Hence their selfconsciousness, their restlessness."[21] Here across the years is a psychological and historical intuition into Christa Wolf's thematic concern with "pretense" (*Verstellung*), relating it to her choice of reflective mode. How deep the insight, how slight, in comparison, the occasion!

Christa Wolf's first, partial, venture into the reflective mode, in "An Afternoon in June" (1965) even makes the disturbance thematic; the attempt to establish a closed idyll in the garden of gardens is broken and threatened by every slightest incident, even by threatening nonincident: "You can believe me that it is unsettling when our peaceful surroundings are really peaceful" (AJ 43–44). The concentrated moment of insight is rare in her works: Christa T. recognizing herself in the rare, late-blooming flower; Nelly Jordan escaping to the moment of the lizard in the sun. In "An Afternoon in June" the moment of vision is a vision of death, a moment of panic:

> The entire feather-light afternoon hung on the weight of this minute. One hundred years are like a day. A day is like a hundred years. The sinking day, one says. Why should one not be able to feel how it sinks —past the sun, which is already submerged in the lilac bushes, past the little apricot tree, past the loud cries of the children, also past the rose, which will be yellow on the outside and pink within only until tomorrow. But one is afraid if there is still no ground in sight; one throws off ballast, this and that, just so as to float up again . . . (AJ 64)

Reflections and restlessness go together. The times are not propitious to the full, rounded work. In their different ways, of course, both *Christa T.* and *Patterns of Childhood* are personal meditations of the kind of which Virginia Woolf was suspicious. But the procedural reflections of a biographer-author reconstructing the life of a friend-alter ego of the one text and the multilayered self-reflective autobiography of the other contrast with the more elusive narrative strategies of the older modernist; reflections were a "fashionable dodge" in 1939. Erich Auerbach's question, "Who is speaking?"[22] arises at every turn. Christa Wolf herself does not significantly attempt the paradox of the impersonal-lyrical narrative that the older novelist had made her own until *No Place on Earth.*

However, the posthumous publication of Virginia Woolf's diaries, *A Writer's Diary* (1953, 1954), selected by her husband Leonard Woolf, has altered our perspective on the autonomy of her novels, throwing light on the intensity and procedural nature of her life in literature, quite in the spirit of Christa Wolf's view of literature "as a possibility of being more intensely in the world." So has the publication of early drafts of her work, which encourage a reading in terms of work-in-progress and of work as masquerade.[23] In this light, readers are now tempted into reconstructing a kind of running metanovel out of Virginia Woolf's works, on similar, though less purposeful lines, to that interweaving of the present life of the author with the composition of the book that is fundamental to the structure of *Patterns of Childhood.* This is the frame-within-frame perspective, to change the dynamic metaphor for a static one, that Christa Wolf's Kleist regards as an interesting possibility (NP 15–16). It is doubtful whether Virginia Woolf would have given her entire assent to this reading of her life and work. Not only did she value her privacy, but she also acknowledged the device of narrator-as-author as just that: a strategy to create the illusion of authenticity. There is a difference between her method of distributing the author's self into themes and characters and maintaining an impersonal narrator, or virtually no narrator at all, and Christa Wolf's strategies in *Christa T.* and *Patterns of Childhood* of using the barely veiled author as narrator; in the former, however, Christa T. is never to be thought of as a figure entirely separate from the author-narrator.[24]

Virginia Woolf seems neither to have envisaged that one day she too would be read historically, as she had read the Brontës, Jane Austen, Elizabeth Barrett, and the rest nor that her work too would be understood functionally and psychologically in the way that she had presented, say, Lily Briscoe's painting in *To the Lighthouse:* Lily's finally achieved form in her painting is indicator and agent of a finally achieved understanding of an important part of her life, the part played by Mrs. Ramsay. How many times has that novel been interpreted as Virginia Woolf's own coming to terms with the lives and deaths of her parents—and that, after all, was how she understood it herself; how often has Lily's painting been seen as a figure for the novel itself. Where Christa Wolf can demonstrate the working-out of such a catharsis in the barely fictionalized figure of the author herself, Virginia Woolf delegates it to the fictional figure. She composed within a tension between her Flaubertian sense of the finished work and the hidden author on the one hand and her private wound on the other, healed in the process of writing. But now the modern reader has the frame of her *Writer's Diary*—the "novel of a novel," as Thomas Mann might put it—and reads her novels against the grain of the claimed completion and impersonality, as one reads Christa Wolf, whose use of the author-as-narrator has been the main strategy of her mode of "subjective authenticity," untrammelled by any aesthetic of autonomy of the finished work. Curiously, Virginia Woolf has caught up with her successor. On the brink of a new writing project she observed in her diary: "I want to . . . see how the idea at first occurs. I want to trace my own process."[25] Exactly. The title of Leonard Woolf's last volume of (classic) autobiography sums up a fundamental impulse in both novelists: *The Journey, Not the Arrival, Matters.*

A passage from Christa Wolf's important essay "The Reader and the Writer" illuminates the necessary, even compulsive nature and purpose of that journey for the writer: "One of the most important conditions for producing literature is a desire for self-fulfillment: this is what produces the urge to write things down, as perhaps the only possibility for the author not to fail of his purpose (and it explains the persistency with which a writer holds on to his profession even under unfavorable conditions)" (RW 208). Self-fulfillment, even under unfavorable conditions. This is a connection that Virginia Woolf makes mainly when she speaks of women's writing, not only in *A Room of One's Own,* where it provides the main theme, but in essay after essay on women writers in the English tradition.

These essays on both minor and major writers, on Sara Coleridge as well as on George Eliot, form an important part of her critical work. Christa Wolf's essays on Günderrode and Bettina von Brentano[26] are in some sort an equivalent to these, not least, given the far greater paucity of women writers in the German literary past, in order to strengthen that tradition retrospectively. But it is important to note that neither of them is exclusively concerned with the restrictions and inhibitions of women writers only. Being English, Virginia Woolf is aware of the restrictions of both class and gender and couples Robert Burns's amazing emergence from peasant obscurity with Emily Brontë's from her father's parsonage.[27] Being German, Christa Wolf is aware of the pressures toward political conformity, and her catalogue of the maimed writing for their lives and with their lives includes Büchner and Kleist (RW 198). This is also to be seen in the two women's novels, though less directly. In *The Waves*, for example, Virginia Woolf distributes her own resentment of the privileges of the cultural establishment to a man, the gifted, excluded Louis, with his Australian background and bad accent, and he is made to express his defiant will to write against the grain of his mean, clerk's world in markedly masculine terms: "'To translate that poem so that it is easily read is to be my endeavour. I, the companion of Plato, of Virgil, will knock at the grained oak door. I oppose to what is passing this ramrod of beaten steel. I will not submit to this aimless passing of billycock hats and Homburg hats and all the plumed and variegated head-dresses of women.'"[28] This complex refusal, defying the exclusions of class and culture ("the grained oak door") in the name of a kind of eternal, hard "Parnassien" art, is more fixed than Virginia Woolf's own, which delighted in the passing show. But the author's experience of sex-determined exclusion found its objective correlative in the class-determined exclusion of her figure.

The pattern of exclusion and defiance is common to both. In Virginia Woolf's social tradition, class was the more available and universal issue and offered a readily accessible equivalent for the more buried issue. The comparative "more buried" is important. I am not suggesting that feminism was not an issue in literary England in the 1930s—the author of *Three Guineas* was certainly not writing alone[29]—but class certainly was an issue, endemically and overridingly, particularly in the circle of a literary lady who once headed a talk, "am I a snob?"[30] and who recognized very scrupulously her separation from the working women's movement.[31] The older Bloomsberries combined high bourgeois bohemianism with an active socialism (Maynard Keynes, Leonard Woolf); their children, in a decade of economic depression and rising fascism, discovered Marxism (Julian Bell). The more accessible was offered as a means of understanding the less available: class exclusion acts as an allegory for sex exclusion.

Christa Wolf on the other hand writes a generation later in a country whose public ideology and whose public arrangements at any rate have gone a long way toward removing social constraints on women, leaving only—only—the private stresses,[32] so that emancipation is not the more buried issue, but available, accessible, and, I would suggest, ready to be used as an allegorical equivalent for less speakable issues in the GDR. It may be rewarding to look at "Self-Experiment" in this functional context of the availability of metaphorical language, rather than make the more immediately obvious contrast with the fancy-free *Orlando*. *Orlando* is after all an extended figure for the creative imagination, and its sexual inclusiveness is as appropriate to this theme as its wit and lavish playfulness. Orlando is bisexual. Contrariwise, it is important for the allegorical system of "Self-Experiment" that the characteristics of the two sexes should be kept distinct. In this fantasy, the woman scientist who undergoes an experimental sex-change —out of love for her boss—enters the world of men, perceives the deep discrepancy between her feminine sensibility and sense of self and her new public role, sees the further danger of internalizing its manipulative, careerist values, and, glimpsing the ultimate lovelessness of this role, finally rejects it and returns to her original sex and true self, conceiving at the end the project of inventing the kind of human being for whom love is again possible. It can be read as a humanistic fable only apparently concerned with a change of sex.

Masculine figures in Christa Wolf's later work have been increasingly identified with political and technological manipulation. Brother Lutz in *Patterns of Childhood* is the technologist without memory or imagination; the smart young neighbor in "An Afternoon in June" has a language that does not extend beyond the jargon of administration; Professor Barzel, the long-suffering owner of the tomcat Max in "New Life and Opinions of a Tomcat" (1970), proposes to remake the human constitution into a satisfied creature without conflict or imagination, courage, altruism, or mercy.[33] The playfulness ceases in Christa Wolf's "Büchner-Prize Acceptance Speech," in which men—not Man, and certainly not women—threaten the very existence of the world with that triumph of technology, the nuclear bomb. Administration and technology, authority and manipulation have cooperated in an antihumanistic practice, and in Christa Wolf's writing masculinity has become the figure for this unholy combination.[34] It was, I believe, already the *figure* for it before—in the "Büchner-Prize Acceptance Speech" and the powerful *Cassandra*-project—she perceived it as a *cause*.

She has subsequently taken her metaphor literally. Seen thus, the pattern of "Self-Experiment"—entry into the world of authority, insight into its distortions, and the decision to leave it in favor of imagining a richer humanity, and by imagining it to bring it into being, offers a reading that has less to do with sex-change than with the temptation to compromise with the corruptions of power, specifically with those to which imaginative writers are exposed in a state that wishes to make of them administrative and ideological instruments. Virginia Woolf's urging of what she calls "mental chastity" sounds simple, even priggish, in such a context, but she has understood the moral dilemma.[35] What little we know of Christa Wolf's own career would seem to have found its objective correlative (or "allegorical disguise"), as she would put it[36] in "Self Experiment": the early entry, out of conviction, into the functionary world of official editing and reviewing, of literary prizes and the Central Committee; the humane departure from it most importantly signaled by *Christa T.* At a more general level the pattern of commitment, danger of corruption, saving decision to leave, could perhaps also match the much younger Christa Wolf's departure from National Socialism. To resume, where Virginia Woolf had used the experience of class exclusion easily available to the English imagination as an equivalent for the more buried issue of sex exclusion, Christa Wolf has used the distortions imposed by sex-role, more readily available to the modern East German imagination, as a correlative for the more buried issue: the unhumane deformations of power. Virginia Woolf, who proposed a society of outsiders, would have cheered.[37]

Neither writer, of course, is as wholly culture-bound as these very specific readings would suggest. Writing out of their experience and the dispositions of their time, each has found patterns we can read and use in another time, another place: the one a pattern of creativity in defiance of rejection; the other a pattern of the return to creative humanity after voluntary exposure to the temptations of power. As Susan, the reader, says of Bernard, the novelist: "Thus he directed me to that which is beyond and outside my own predicament; to that which is symbolic, and thus perhaps permanent, if there is any permanence in our sleeping, eating, breathing, so animal, so spiritual and tumultuous lives."[38]

Bibliographical Excursus

I do not at this stage propose to raise the question of Christa Wolf's possible reception of Virginia Woolf. One can merely speculate here, but I guess that her acquaintance is of a fairly recent date, at a stage when her own literary identity was firmly established, and when she could more easily recognize a fellow than submit or reject. But "firmly established" is a relative term, especially for a writer who has developed so late and so far. We should recall Virginia Woolf's observation on Jane Austen at the height of her powers: "She was still subject to those changes which often make the final period of a writer's career the most interesting of all." (CE I, 151) Reception has to do with the availability of texts, receptivity with Christa Wolf's own readiness.

There have been three waves of translations and commentary on Virginia Woolf in Germany and the earlier ones may have survived into Christa Wolf's youth. (See B. J. Kirkpatrick, *A Bibliography of Virginia Woolf* [Oxford: Clarendon, 1980].) First there was the contemporary wave in the late 1920s and early 1930s when the literary life of the Weimar Republic was generously open to new experiments from abroad. The novels of these years were translated and published by Insel Verlag, Leipzig, soon after their first appearance in England: *Eine Frau von fünfzig Jahren.* Mrs. *Dalloway,* translated by Therese Mutzenbacher in 1928; *Orlando,* translated by Karl Lerbs in 1929; and *Die Fahrt zum Leuchtturm,* also by Karl Lerbs in 1931. S. Fischer Verlag's "Die neue Rundschau" carried a small number of her essays during these years. A number of good, pioneering critical works of a similar openness date from this time, for example, Ruth Gruber, *Virginia Woolf* (Leipzig: Tauchnitz, 1935), and Gertrud Lohmüller, *Die Frau im Werk von Virginia Woolf* (Leipzig: Nocke, 1937).

With the coming of the Nazi ideology and the Second World War, links with the experimental novel and England were broken. When it was all over, the second wave of interest came in West Germany as part of the tremendous urge to catch up with lost time and lost reading after twelve years of isolation. Immediately there came a small flood of essays and short stories in the many postwar little magazines, West and East: in *Karrusell, Prisma, die Literarische Revue.* More important, the new Soviet-zone journal *Aufbau* carried "Der geneigte Leser und der Krokus" (3, no. 10, [1947]), and *Die neue Rundschau* published not only "Herr Bennett und Frau Brown" (61, no. 2, [1950]) as part of a rich year catching up on Yeats, Eliot, Malraux, Thomas Mann, but also extensive extracts from *A Writer's Diary* from the years 1932 to 1937 in 1955 (65, nos. 1, 2). Their particular combination of sense of history and sense of process would make them congenial reading to a later Christa Wolf.

S. Fischer Verlag (Frankfurt am Main) began to republish the novels, bringing the list up to date and in some cases having them retranslated. This continued into the 1960s. Mrs. *Dalloway* was retranslated by Herbert and Marlys Herlitschka in 1955, likewise *Die Fahrt zum Leuchtturm* in 1956 and *Orlando* in 1961. Fischer's earlier version of *Flush* was republished in 1954; *Die Wellen* followed in 1959 and *Zwischen den Akten* in 1963. So Virginia Woolf became known primarily as a novelist. The only volume of essays to be translated (by Herbert Herlitschka) was the posthumous compilation *Granit und Regenbogen* (Berlin and Frankfurt: Suhrkamp, 1960). These publications were followed by wide interest in the seminars, which produced a full and varied range of critical comment, such as the typological study by Magdalene Brandt, *Realismus und Realität im modernen Roman. Untersuchungen zu Virginia Woolfs "The Waves"* (Bad Homburg: Gehlen, 1968); Emilia Dölle's study of linguistic self-reflectiveness in *Experiment und Tradition in der Prosa Virginia Woolfs* (Munich: Fink, 1971); and Ingeborg Weber Brandies's neo-Marxist *Virginia Woolf: "The Waves": Emanzipation als Möglichkeit des Bewusstseinsromans* (Frankfurt: Lang, 1974).

The last titles are some indication of the most recent wave, when she has been very widely read indeed. It came partly as a reflection of renewed English interest in Bloomsbury with the publication of Quentin Bell's biography *Virginia Woolf* (London: Hogarth, 1972) and a mass of related material, such as Spater and Parsons's *Marriage of True Minds* (London: Chatto, 1977); these were translated in 1978 and 1980 respectively. More important, the interest has been stimulated by the feminist movement. Fischer responded by reprinting the major novels (also—as a mark of respectability—in an elegant boxed edition) between 1977 and 1979 and completing their list with *Jacobs Raum* (1981), *Nacht und Tag* (1982), and *Zwischen den Akten* (4th ed., 1982). The Deutsche Verlagsanstalt of Stuttgart brought out *Augenblicke, skizzierte Erinnerungen* in 1981, and it was left to fringe publishers to bring out her two most important feminist essays: *Ein Zimmer für sich allein* (Berlin: Gebhardt Verlag, 1979) and *Drei Guineen* (Munich: Verlag Frauenoffensive, 1978). Virginia Woolf was no longer only a novelist in Germany but also a feminist. Still missing is a sense of the literary critic.

103

Joyce Crick

High on this wave came what appears to be the one East German publication: Insel Verlag of Leipzig disinterred their old Mutzenbach translation of Mrs. *Dalloway* and reissued it in 1977 with notes and afterword by Wolfgang Wicht. Of all her novels, this one is most vulnerable to the conventional Marxist judgment of bourgeois decadence. And even if the imagination of the East German reader is not prematurely closed by such labels, Mrs. Dalloway's social world would still be remote. What the GDR reader might respond to rather is the exposure of Septimus's frailty and madness to thick-skinned authority. But even so this is not the best of introductions to her work.

But what of Christa Wolf's response as possible reader? It seems she owns the Fischer boxed edition. And earlier editions would have been available to the employee of a State publishing house. But during the "catching-up" phase, her interests were focused on the Socialist literary tradition, and at that time its critical categories would have dismissed the English writer's novels as decadent. It appears in fact to have taken little account of her. Lukács's not very discriminating judgment on James Joyce will have to serve. Not surprisingly, he regards the separation of "the inner life of man" from "social and historical factors" as a sign of decline, declaring that "the transformation of human beings into a chaotic flow of ideas destroy[s] . . . every possibility of a literary presentation of the complete human personality." ("Preface," in *Studies in European Realism* [New York: Grosset & Dunlap, 1964], 8.)

The same critical attitude could well have blocked any receptivity to Erich Auerbach's influential use of a passage from *To the Lighthouse* as his culminating example in his study of occidental realism: "The Brown Stocking," in *Mimesis: The Representation of Reality in Western Literature* (Garden City, N.Y.: Doubleday Anchor Books, 1957), 463–488 (German original published in 1946 by A. Francke, Bern.) His description of Virginia Woolf's style in terms of the dissolution of event into experience and above all his analysis of how the characters' reflections merge with the narrator's read like an anticipation of how Christa Wolf was to learn to write. He actually raises the question, Who is speaking? in so many words. And so does Christa Wolf in the course of that last duet—or is it a trio?—between Kleist and Günderrode in *No Place on Earth*, 4. But Auerbach's revelation came too early. Or perhaps it had a very long fuse.

The only conclusion of this excursus is the speculation with which we began. Christa Wolf would probably have been ready to receive Virginia Woolf's novels only from about the time of "Juninachmittag" [An Afternoon in June]. Indeed, it is not unlikely that "Juninachmittag," which marks the real new departure in her style, was a response to Virginia Woolf's argument in "Modern Fiction" against the falsifying tyrannies of outmoded literary conventions:

> look within and life, it seems, is very far from being 'like this.' Examine for a moment an ordinary mind on an ordinary day. The mind receives a myriad impressions—trivial, fantastic, evanescent, or engraved with the sharpness of steel. From all sides they come, an incessant show of innumerable atoms; and as they fall, as they shape themselves into the life of Monday or Tuesday, the accent falls differently from of old. . . . (CE II, 106)

However, most editions she is likely to have read probably date from the late seventies. In her polemic in the *Frankfurt Lectures* against the forward linear march of the heroic epic she offers the alternative form of Virginia Woolf's web-like structures (C 262), and includes a collection of Woolf's essays in her list of feminist reading (C, 273): in the German version *Ein Zimmer für mich allein,* which translates to "A Room of My Own." For a writer whose use of the personal pronouns is poetically so important, the misquotation is, to say the least, curious. There may be a buried comment in the slip, perhaps discerning a certain self-centeredness in Virginia Woolf's plea for the emancipation of the woman writer. But she has spoken warmly of rereading *To the Lighthouse* "with delight." (See "Das starke Gefühl, gebraucht zu werden. Gespräch mit Christa Wolf zum Erscheinen ihres Buches *Kassandra*," *Wochenpost* 31 (February 10, 1984), 15; reprinted in *Die Dimension des Autors* [Darmstadt/Neuwied: Luchterhand, 1987], 939.) So it may be better to pursue the question of affinity rather than of reception. Perhaps there are some traces of the impersonal lyrical style of *To the Lighthouse* in *No Place on Earth*. Perhaps *Orlando* reinforced an interest in the theme of the androgyne imagination, but, if so, how sadly transformed it has been from a celebration of wholeness to a lament for imbalance. Contrast the joyful chiasmus:

> "You're a woman, Shel!" she cried.
> "You're a man, Orlando!" he cried.
> (*Orlando* [New York; Harcourt Brace, 1928], 252.)

with this unhappy exchange:

> Sometimes I find it unendurable that nature has split the human being into man and woman.
> You don't mean that, Kleist. What you mean is that man and woman have a hostile relationship inside you. As they do in me. (*NP* 104)

As a late postscript to this excursus, a selection of Virginia Woolf's literary essays should be mentioned, edited, again, by Wolfgang Wicht: *Die schmale Brücke der Kunst* (Leipzig: Insel, 1986). It includes "Mr. Bennet and Mrs. Brown," "Die schmale Brücke der Kunst," "Frauen und Romanliteratur," and "Moderne Literatur." Its appearance is a token of a changed literary climate, itself created to a large extent by the presence of Christa Wolf's writing.

Notes

1. Virginia Wolf, "Robinson Crusoe" (1919), in *CE* (London: Hogarth, 1966), I, 72.

2. Translations from this work rely on those by Helen Fehervary in her "Christa Wolf's Prose: A Landscape of Masks," in this volume. The page numbers refer to the original German version in *Gesammelte Erzählungen* (1974, 1980). —Ed.

3. "We do not know our own souls, let alone the souls of others," in "On being ill," *CE*, IV, 196.

4. The reader is referred here to the bibliographical excursus at the end of this essay.

5. Woolf, *CE*, I, 70–71.

6. "Thoughts on peace in an air raid" (1940), in *The Death of the Moth* (New York: Harcourt Brace, 1942), 245. For Christa Wolf's comment, laden with the burden of the intervening years, see SA: "You suspect that my treatment of the fascism theme [in *Patterns of Childhood*] could involve . . . reference merely to the psychological and moral processes in the development of consciousness." Prompted by Kaufmann, she repudiates "general psychological categories" alone but differentiates and avoids the total rejection he wants to hear: her purpose has been the cathartic one of "coming to terms with the past," a function both psychological and historical.

7. See Woolf, "Mr. Bennett and Mrs. Brown" (1924), in *The Captain's Death-bed* (New York: Harcourt Brace Jovanovich, 1950). Translated as "Herr Bennett und Frau Brown" in *NR* 61, no. 2, 1950.

8. See Noel Annan, *Leslie Stephen: His Thought and Character in Relation to his Time* (London: McGibbon and Kee, 1951), esp. 228–261.

9. See Andreas Huyssen, "Traces of Ernst Bloch: Reflections on Christa Wolf," in this volume.

10. Woolf, *Jacob's Room* (London: Hogarth, 1965), 28–29.

11. Woolf, *To the Lighthouse* (New York and London: Harcourt Brace Jovanovich, 1981), 171.

12. Ibid., 193.

13. Woolf, *Jacob's Room*, 69.

14. The model also lies in the title of A. J. A. Symon's pioneering, procedural biography, *The Quest for Corvo: An Experiment in Biography* (New York: The Macmillan Company, 1934), of course.

15. Woolf, *The Captain's Deathbed*, 96.

16. *Stavrogin's Confession*, trans. Virginia Woolf and S. S. Koteliansky (London: Hogarth, 1922).

17. See Leonard Woolf, *An Autobiography*, vol. 2, 1911–1969 (Oxford: Oxford University Press, 1980), 307ff.

18. Wolf, "Kleiner Ausflug nach H.," in *Gesammelte Erzählungen*, 151–191.

19. Woolf, *The Captain's Deathbed*, 119.

20. See Ruth Z. Temple, "Never Say 'I': *To the Lighthouse* as Vision and Confession," in *Virginia Woolf*, ed. Claire Sprague (Englewood Cliffs, N.J.: Prentice Hall, 1971). Claire Sprague herself also comments (see "Introduction," 4) that Virginia Woolf was unusually insistent on separating the self from the artist. This is a just observation as far as the novels are concerned: the self is there not directly but as the diffused, distributed presence of the masquerading fiction. However, when it comes to that procedural metanovel, the (diarized) life of the artist, the remark needs qualifying. Virginia Woolf acknowledged the division postulated by fin-de-siècle aesthetics within the artist between the feeling human being and the detached observer. She quotes Maupassant on the subject (and could just as well have quoted the young Thomas Mann) as she recollects a poignant occasion at her mother's deathbed when she found herself all too shrewdly observing the nurse's tears: "She's pretending, I said, aged 13, and was afraid of not feeling enough." (*A Writer's Diary*, ed. Leonard Woolf [New York: Harcourt Brace, 1953, 1954], September 12, 1934.) And it is also true that there were times when she perceived her social identity and her writing function as different in kind. Claire Sprague quotes: "Sydney [Webb] comes in and I'm Virginia; when I write, I am merely a sensibility" (4). But with all respect for Maupassant's elegant formulation of the topos and for the unexpected humanizing powers of Sydney Webb, such perceptions need to be relativized in the light of other observations where her patron seems to be Coleridge the unifier rather than Maupassant the divider. Even after the intrusion of the outside world on the work in the person of Mr. Frank, the other member of the Rodmell Labour Party, she can remark: "Odd, how the creative power at once brings the whole universe to order," (*Writer's Diary*, July 27, 1934), and "the difficulty is the usual one—how to adjust the two worlds. . . . one must combine" (*Writer's Diary*, February 18, 1934). (I select these passages particularly because they were among the entries translated in *NR*, 66, no. 2, 1950, and so might have been available to Christa Wolf.) And even observation, far from dividing us from ourselves, can also unite us with the outer world, sometimes—in light of the date—heroically: "No: I intend no introspection. I mark Henry James' sentence: observe perpetually. Observe the oncome of age. Observe greed. Observe my own despondency. By that means it becomes serviceable. Or so I hope" (*Writer's Diary*, March 8, 1941).

21. Woolf, *Writer's Diary*, August 7, 1939.

22. Erich Auerbach, "The Brown Stocking," in *Mimesis: The Representation of Reality in Western Literature* (New York: Doubleday, 1953), 469.

23. See Louise A. De Salvo, *Virginia Woolf's First Voyage: a Novel in the Making* (London: Macmillan, 1980).

24. The situation is complex. The narrator's confrontation with her friend sharpens the narrator's awareness of herself ("I suddenly faced myself" [IM 77]); on the other hand, the narrator has given her dead friend sharper definition, existence. As she so often does, Virginia Woolf provides the illumination but *within* the self-reflecting fiction, not from its frame. Christa T. might well say of Christa Wolf what Virginia Woolf's Neville says ironically of Bernard, the novelist in *The Waves*: "'How useful an office one's friends perform when they recall us. Yet how painful to be recalled, to be mitigated, to have one's self adulterated, mixed up, become part of another. As he approaches I become not myself but Neville mixed up with somebody—with whom?—with Bernard? Yet, it is Bernard, and it is to Bernard that I shall put the question, Who am I?'" ([New York: Harcourt Brace, 1931], 83). And when Bernard, the novelist, in turn asks "Who am I?" he has to ask also "Am I one and distinct?" (288).

25. Woolf, *Writer's Diary*, September 30, 1926.

26. See Wolf, "The Shadow of a Dream. Karoline von Günderrode—A Sketch," and "Yes indeed! But the next life begins today. A letter about Bettina."

27. Woolf, *A Room of One's Own* (1929; New York and London: Harcourt Brace Jovanovich, 1981), 99.

28. Woolf, *The Waves*, 95.

29. See Woolf's own "Notes and References" to *Three Guineas* (1938), (New York: Harcourt, Brace and World/Harbinger, 1938, 1966), 145–188. See also Herbert Marder, *Feminism and Art: A Study of Virginia Woolf* (Chicago and London: University of Chicago Press, 1968), chap. 1.

30. In J. Schulkind, ed., *Moments of Being* (London: University of Sussex Press, 1976), 181–198.

31. Woolf, "Memories of a Working Women's Guild," *Captain's Deathbed*, 214–17.

32. But see Michael Dennis, "Women and Work in the GDR," in Ian Wallace, ed., *The GDR under Honecker, 1971–81* (GDR Monitor, Special Series, No. 1). See also David Childs, *The GDR, Moscow's German Ally* (London: Allen and Unwin, 1983). Chapter 10: "The New Woman . . . with some old Problems," 250–269.

33. Wolf, "Neue Lebensansichten eines Katers," in *GE*, 118–150.

34. Since her changed "view-scope" ["perceptual grid"] of *Cassandra*, she also perceives it as its historical cause.

35. See Woolf, *Three Guineas*, 93–99.

36. Wolf, UE, 111.

37. Woolf, *Three Guineas*, 122.

38. Woolf, *The Waves*, 248–249.

"Remembrance of Things Future": On Establishing a Female Tradition

Christiane Zehl Romero

*The son of many fathers, today's male writer feels
hopelessly belated; the daughter of too few mothers,
today's female writer feels that she is helping to create a
viable tradition which is at last definitively emerging.*[1]

Whatever the validity of this general statement—made in the context of Western feminist criticism—for male authors from socialist countries, it holds true for the women from the GDR and, above all, for Christa Wolf. Her development and her reputation as the most important woman writer from the German speaking countries hinge upon it. As I will try to show, Christa Wolf found her own voice—in large part at least—through the search, unconscious at first, for such a tradition and through her contributions toward its emergence. And we as readers, women as well as men, are drawn to her writings because we recognize the authenticity[2] and authority that her halting, probing voice has assumed in the process.

As is well known, Christa Wolf is one of the few authors who has successfully made the difficult transition from critic to creative writer.[3] In retrospect, she has spoken disparagingly of her academic studies and of her work as editor and critic: "Looking back, I was irritated by my German studies, and moved into criticism and theory—I wrote literary criticism. Perhaps I had lost a degree of immediacy in my contact with reality, as well as the carefree spirit that is necessarily a part of the decision to throw caution to the winds and add one's own two-penny-worth to the mountain of words already written" (SA). Did her literary studies alone make her modest, or did her doubts have to do with the fact that she was a woman and that "women have historically hesitated to attempt the pen"[4]—in spite of her society's official commitment to emancipation? Certainly Christa Wolf never did gain "immediacy" or a "carefree attitude," yet she eventually found the courage to try creative writing and, more important, to make her uncertainties and misgivings part of that endeavor.

Usually Louis Fürnberg is credited with giving Christa Wolf the support she needed when she was asking herself if she could write more than reviews. He did so in a kind, hortative letter written in 1956.[5] But for real, continued inspiration, Christa Wolf turned to a woman—the famous Anna Seghers. She was the one role model Wolf's society offered, the only outstanding woman writer among the great names of the time. Scholars have duly recognized the great importance that Seghers has had for Wolf,[6] but thus far only Peter Beicken in his article on the relationship between Anna Seghers and Christa Wolf[7] has dealt with its complexities in some detail. However, nobody has as yet discussed this in the context of women writers, of a female tradition.[8]

Christa Wolf has of course "always" known Seghers, that is, since her own postwar days in the Bad Frankenhausen school where she completed her *Abitur* and where the *Seventh Cross* was required reading. Nor could the student and editor of German literature go without "knowing" the doyenne of GDR letters, the classic of socialist realism: "I had read her books, had seen her at conferences, heard her speak, admired the aura which surrounded her" (CA 151). But the real contact, the moment of "touching,"[9] came when Wolf attempted to write herself.

The first meeting was routine, in line with Wolf's duties as editor and critic: "I was told—it was 1958, I worked in the editorial offices of *Neue Deutsche Literatur*: go see Anna and do an interview" (CA 151). Seghers's novel *Die Entscheidung* (The Decision), which, if Wolf's date is correct,[10] was to be published the following year, provided the occasion. Thus, the interview concentrates on that novel, but, as Beicken has pointed out, Wolf does not appear to be in tune with her subject.[11] This woman who asks such incessant and for the most part pedestrian questions seems to have little in common with the later Wolf and her sensitive appreciation of Seghers: "Are there prototypes for your characters?" "Have you familiarized yourself with the technical problems of steel production?" "What materials did you use in preparing your novel?" "How can one, in your opinion, correctly represent a part of life which is still very close?"[12]

Yet there is a common thread. From the very beginning the person speaking is not really a critic trying to bring an author closer to her readers—even if that may very well be the result. It is the fellow writer attempting to understand a common craft and to learn from an experienced, established author. At this point Wolf is a novice grasping for direction. She has accepted the new cultural policies of the Bitterfeld

Movement[13] and is attempting to absorb them into her own writing, which will lead to her breakthrough, *Divided Heaven* (1963). In its light Wolf's questions to Seghers assume a special significance: we realize that she is trying to see the other in terms of categories and demands set by the cultural politics of the time and that she seeks instructions on how to deal with *the* contemporary subject: work in and life around the factory.

Seghers's responses go deeper than the questions. Maybe she sensed—or knew—that her interviewer came more as a writer than a critic. As always, she firmly protests against too mechanistic, too representational an interpretation of her art, any art. Christa Wolf does not really pick up on these answers. It is as if she were racing through prepared questions, which may well have been the case. Still, the interview made a profound impression on her.

Consequently Wolf undertook a close reading of *The Decision* and developed a much more sensitive understanding. It resulted in her first essay on Seghers, "The Land in Which we Live. The German Question in the Novel *The Decision* by Anna Seghers," published in 1961.[14] Wolf was now deeply affected by the older woman's subject and art and speaks in a voice resonant with the intense positive provocation that the novel and its author had become for her: "This book does not only explain, it does not only instruct. It awakens desires and yearnings, hopes and dreams which will, perhaps, continue to smolder even after one has forgotten what ignited them in the first place."[15] Here Wolf is, perhaps unconsciously, alluding to her own unique reaction: for her, the wishes and hopes raised by Seghers and her achievement were above all those of following in her footsteps, of becoming a major woman writer representative of the next generation. More specifically, at this point, she wanted to deal with the question of divided Germany in a way that would express that generation's perceptions.

From the very beginning—and throughout—Christa Wolf's relationship to the famous older writer has been determined by a refraction of themes, subjects, and undeveloped strands from Seghers's work in light of her own time and personal experience. There could never be imitation because, from the onset of the association, Wolf was aware of what she would later call Seghers's "fundamentally different life-pattern" (CA 155). As Wolf explored it more fully, this awareness would help her design her own pattern of life and work.

However, neither was there anything similar to the father-son combat that, according to Harold Bloom, defines literature (i.e., male literature) and that, as he describes in his "theory of influence," has made writers (i.e., "male" writers) "feel increasingly exhausted by the need for revisionism."[16] Such Freudian interpretations are of course alien to the GDR's concept of tradition, but that does not necessarily invalidate them as a possible approach to its writers. Wolf certainly emphasized the nurturing, loving aspects of her connection with Seghers and, albeit indirectly, contrasted them with what would become an important theme to her, namely man's (including the male writer's) inability to love, as exemplified, for instance, by Kleist.[17]

It is equally significant though that, as a "role model," Seghers communicated none of the "infection in the sentence"—to use a phrase from the American poet Emily Dickinson—the debilitating sense of anxiety and self-doubt that female authors seeking "motherly precursors" have so often absorbed from them.[18] Seghers considered it inconsequential to art whether it was produced by a man or a woman and matter-of-factly took her place in the mostly male world of communist letters. In her writings she adopted what has been characterized and questioned as "the masculine perspective of Anna Seghers."[19] Emancipation and self-realization occur within the larger scope of revolutionary action and socialist reconstruction. Women can and do join this "men's realm of action." But "self-discovery bears no feminine characteristics."[20] Thus, Seghers communicated to Wolf as a starting point a sense of assurance of what women in general, and women writers in particular, could do alongside men in their world—an assurance that eventually carried the younger writer on into asking whether that was indeed enough.

Divided Heaven (1963) is Wolf's first major work and the first to reflect her creative dialogue with Seghers. It picks up and transforms elements from *The Decision* that had struck a responsive chord in the reader turning author. In her interview Wolf had already shown interest in the tragic love story between Katharina and Riedl. With seeming naiveté she had asked: "Katharina, for instance: Did she *have* to die just when she had made the decision to join us?"[21] In *Divided Heaven* she now tells a different, ultimately more positive love story but one in which she—like Seghers and unlike many of her contemporaries—takes the love between two people on opposite sides as seriously as she does the political realities of a divided Germany that separate them. However, in *The Decision*, Katharina and Riedl represent only one small strand in a complex plot, for in Seghers's work, love between man and woman hardly ever takes center stage. Wolf was well aware of that and later remarked: "The novels . . . deal only incidentally with the longing for love and fulfillment. What is passionately longed for is not a woman but freedom, what is desperately missed is not the love of a loved one but social justice, what is believed in is not personal happiness but the day-to-day happiness of mankind which at last appears attainable" (FT 136). Wolf knows, though, that she no longer belongs to such heroic times and attitudes of struggle and exile. Thus, she concentrates on one love story, between Rita and Manfred, and on one individual's expectations of private happiness. Significantly, this individual is a woman, and Wolf tells her story from a female perspective, a point of view Seghers very rarely used. She did employ it to great effect, however, in "The Excursion of the Dead Girls," a novella that Wolf would come to appreciate highly and would call "one of the most beautiful stories in modern German literature" (FT 125). "The masculine perspective of Anna Seghers" and its exceptions helped Wolf realize that she wanted to explore something different, "a female perspective."

In the interview, Seghers had described what she considered the main purpose of *The Decision*: "For me the most important thing was to show how in our times the break which divides the world into two camps affects all parts of our lives, even the most private, the most intimate: love, marriage, profession."[22] As the title indicates, this is also the focus of *Divided Heaven*. But Seghers speaks of the world, Christa Wolf only of Germany. In her essay on *The Decision*, she had recognized that this novel, with its global perspective, continued Seghers's *Heimatbeschwörung*—her longing for and evocation of a reconstructed and of course undivided homeland—which she had begun so eloquently during her exile. In spite of the clarity with which Seghers portrayed the choices of postwar Germans, of the postwar world ("For whom are you, against whom?") she never, at least not at that time, totally relinquished the vision of a renewed and whole Germany that had sustained her during many difficult years. Christa Wolf saw that, in *The Decision*, "unity cannot be proclaimed; it exists—contradictory, interrupted, but not destroyed, and not destroyable."[23] Against the background of this reading and of the contemporary political situation—the building of the Berlin Wall in 1961, which is alluded to in the foreword of *Divided Heaven*—Wolf begins her own more complex task, not of *Heimatbeschwörung*, but of *Heimatfindung*—of realizing where she belongs and then later (in *Patterns of Childhood*) where she comes from. The dream of German unity that was still alive in *The Decision* must be given up, certainly for now. In the dialogue between the parting lovers of *Divided Heaven* this point is clearly made:

> "They can't divide the sky, anyway," said Manfred.
> The sky? This whole arch of hope and longing, love and grief?
> "Oh yes," she murmured. "The sky divides first." (*DH* 198)

For the young Rita, as well as her creator, only the small territory between the wall and the eastern border on the Oder/Neisse will be home.

While working on *Divided Heaven*, Wolf also studied Seghers's *Seventh Cross*. In its structure as well as in its emphasis on the strength and continuity of everyday decency and courage Wolf's novel reflects this close reading. Shortly after *Divided Heaven* was published, a new edition of Seghers's classic came out with a thoughtful afterword by Wolf.[24]

In the following years her fascination and preoccupation with Seghers grew. The newly successful author continued to question the older, long-established woman—about her life, her work, her views on art and society—in a manner that became more and more probing and personal. She reflects herself in the other to gain insights into herself. In the process, her published remarks on Seghers assume a special incisiveness. These pieces are so stimulating because we as readers get a sense of a vital connection being established, vital for Wolf and her generation as well as for still younger writers, particularly women. Wolf uses Seghers to discover and often to legitimize new directions she will pursue, directions that then open the path for others.[25]

Her next interview with Seghers in 1965[26] is a case in point. It begins with questions on "The Excursion of the Dead Girls," a story that, as Wolf points out, had not been accepted into the canon of Seghers's masterpieces:

> I notice that your story, "Excursion of the Dead Girls," is not mentioned at all in a lexicon of socialist literature recently published here. I don't know if this has to do with the fact that this piece of literature is so difficult to categorize—as long as one judges by the contents. It is in any case remarkable that this story is the only one of your works which bears directly biographical traits. Does the biographical play no role otherwise in your work, or merely an indirect role?[27]

Seghers's response is legendary to all those who have studied her:

> Concerning the biographical questions: I believe that the experiences and views of a writer become clearest through his work, even without specific biography.[28]

It was a gentle rebuff to Wolf who at that point might have intended to write a biographical essay on the admired writer, a project she then abandoned. But as Wolf's response to Seghers indicates, there was a much more important reason for her interest in Seghers's use of autobiographical material: "That's right: I am interested in the biographical. But not for its own sake, rather insofar as it is transformed into the artistic work; this very involved process—just how the individual biographical experience is manifest in books, for instance in your books."[29]

Wolf had already begun her second novel, *The Quest for Christa T.*,[30] a work whose closeness to "Excursion of the Dead Girls" in structure and theme is striking, even though the differences are obvious. Seghers's story, its first-person narrator, that narrator's imaginary resurrection of the dead (girls) in order to understand and communicate the meaning of their lives, discontinuous narration and a complex treatment of the dimension of time, provided Wolf with a model and gave her courage to pursue a writing project that was at best controversial. It also furnished a foil against which Wolf could better realize her own artistic identity.

One of the most important differences between Seghers's tale and Wolf's novel is the way in which the process of "resurrection" is presented: for Seghers's narrator, recollection of her dead classmates comes in a trancelike vision; upon awakening she decides to record her experience. She considers this to be a serious obligation but in no way

113

difficult or problematic. On the contrary, it gives purpose to her own life and meaning to the passage of time. Seghers had absolute confidence in the powers of the tale and ultimately derived her ideas about storytelling from old, oral traditions of narrative, where the author is anonymous and the teller emphasizes his story. For Wolf in *The Quest for Christa T.*, however, remembering and recording have become difficult and laborious tasks. She has begun her struggle for "subjective authenticity"[31] in order to write not only, as Seghers had done, against forgetting but also against "*Vergessenmachen*" (making forgotten).[32] Thus as problems of perception, memory, and expression gain importance over the tale, they become the tale. "For the author is an important person" (RW 206), says Wolf, not only about the author's prominence in society but also about his prominence in the text. And she expresses her admiration for Seghers by exclaiming, "She charms. Enchants. How is it possible to charm in these sober times?" (AS 138); but she also voices her sense of difference. Magic, as she sees it effected by Seghers, "by not letting herself know what she is doing" (AS 138), is not for her. Wolf must constantly reflect on what she is doing and incorporate those reflections into her work. "I write searching," she notes.

In this second interview Wolf tries generally to steer the conversation toward works by Seghers that reveal and thus support openness in artistic matters. She has obviously studied Seghers's essays[33] as well as her fiction and has found ideas and suggestions that will occupy her for years to come. They all point away from the narrow definitions of realism and the standard Seghers interpretations prevalent at the time, toward closer ties with Romantic and post-Romantic figures and traditions. Wolf specifically refers to Seghers's championship of the "losers" of German literature, talented writers who died "young and in despair":[34]

> I have the impression that you have a special love for a certain group of names from German literature, or that you refer to them frequently for other reasons; for instance you name them quite expressly at the Paris Convention on the Defense of Culture in 1935. In your speech there on "love of fatherland," and later in your essays in Mexican exile, you talk about the following German writers: Hölderlin, Büchner, Günderode, Kleist, Lenz, Bürger.[35]

Not only had Wolf already embarked upon writing the story of a gifted "loser" in her own society, she would later return to the two names that Seghers had brought together more than once: the relatively obscure poetess Günderrode and the more famous poet Kleist. The well-read Seghers, a native of the Rhine area where Günderrode is buried, knew her tragic fate as well as Kleist's. In her essays Seghers also recalled another woman from that generation whom she wanted her fellow exiles to rediscover, Bettina Brentano/Arnim: "Read Bettina Brentano, read Günderode! Read what they write about education, faith, the Jewish question!"[36] That Bettina and Karoline von Günder-

rode were indeed friends, that Bettina years later published their correspondence as well as many other often derided but important books—
these connections Wolf would eventually explore at length.

Seghers's essays impressed Wolf so much that she edited the first
major collection, *Faith in the Terrestrial* (1969),[37] and provided an important afterword. She comments on this "late publication of important
essays, lectures, and articles" (FT 111) and sees it as proof that "we"
recognize Seghers's life as "a model," her work as "classical," "but without fully knowing, let alone understanding her" (FT 111). The reading
she then proposes continues the direction begun by her second interview. She looks beyond the "classic" Seghers to the woman who indeed
showed little interest in *the* classic, Goethe, but a great deal of understanding for "all those who died young during Goethe's time."[38] This
sympathy in Seghers is particularly strong in the essays from the late
thirties and in the 1938–1939 letters to Georg Lukács, a contribution to
the long- standing Expressionism/Realism debate:

> Here Anna Seghers asks what price must be paid for a classical work
> under conditions inimical to art. What price must be paid for a round-
> ing-off, for complete fulfillment? . . . Nowhere else during that time
> does she express her own problems more directly. With an extraordi-
> narily sure insight into the terrible, frustrated efforts of those long-
> dead writers, she interprets facts in the history of literature psycho-
> logically. . . . Nevertheless, one senses in her letters a more than
> historical link with the doubts and despair that lie more than a cen-
> tury in the past. An inkling that it is possible to fail, that a decision
> may have to be made between revolt and unconditional participation
> in the contemporary struggle and the rounded-off, perfect work in
> which it must no longer be possible to detect the disruption of the
> times and its effect on the artist. The urgency of this question can still
> be felt after thirty years: one can try to wrest fragments from reality,
> as directly and honestly as possible, without venturing to hope to say
> something valid, finally valid. (FT 119)[39]

Wolf too has much more than a historical or critical relationship to
what she says about Seghers. By this time she has finished *The Quest
for Christa T.* It expresses profound sympathy with failure because in
difficult, changing times failure may indicate deeper commitment to
life and society than any healthy adaptation. And it uses a structure
and a style that do not purport to give anything but the "splinters of
reality" of which Seghers had spoken in characterizing the style of
those writers from transition periods. "An inkling that it is possible to
fail"—Seghers may never, or only very fleetingly, have felt it.[40] Christa
Wolf did have such premonitions, and in *Christa T.* she expressed them
through, among other things, the complex relationship between narrator, character, and author of which she speaks in her "Interview with
Myself": "I suddenly faced myself. The relations between 'us'—Christa
T. and the narrator 'I'—shifted of themselves into the center" (IM 77).

From then on, "failure" becomes a major theme. In *Patterns of
Childhood* Wolf reveals that social conformity may, given sociopolitical

conditions such as existed under Hitler, result in real failure. On the other hand, in *No Place on Earth*, in many of her stories, her essays on Günderrode and Bettina von Arnim, the "Büchner-Prize Acceptance Speech," and *Cassandra*, she will treat the refusal or inability to adapt, failure in terms of a given society, as potentially valuable, because its origin is "our ineradicable faith that man is destined for self-perfection, a faith which runs counter to the spirit of this and every age. Is it an illusion?" (NP 119). In her pursuit of the theme, Wolf goes far beyond what Seghers ever wrote, but it is important to note that she first found suggestion and confirmation in Seghers's work.

In her afterword Wolf also notes the closeness of Seghers's essays to her fiction: "Experience is mastered in these essays as well. The voice that speaks here is the same [as in the novels and stories]. Things are not claimed here, but meditated upon. Before she tries to convince others she comes to an understanding with herself" (FT 113). Again reflecting on the other helps Wolf come to terms with herself and her direction. In 1971 she published her own collection of essays, *The Reader and the Writer*, from which she excluded her early critical pieces that tended toward the ideologically doctrinaire.[41] Most essays in the volume, what Wolf herself will later call an "attempt at self-understanding" (D 65), begin to show the kind of formal and thematic interrelationship with her fiction that will become characteristic of her later work. The fact that Seghers could be claimed as a precursor and model provided inspiration and reassurance.

Beyond that, Wolf recognizes a deep bond between herself and the other woman, which has to do with their profound concern for the continuation and dignity of human life on earth. In the afterword to *Faith in the Terrestrial* Wolf writes: "This century has done more than any other to undermine belief in the continuity of the terrestrial . . . especially since August 1945 faith and lack of faith affect not only man's moral but also his physical existence. To put it more exactly: under the conditions of the atomic age the moral existence of humanity has become the condition for its physical existence" (FT 136). She would elaborate on these shared concerns only much later in her "Büchner-Prize Acceptance Speech" (1980). In that speech there is no mention of Seghers; it concentrates rather on one of Seghers's favorites among the writers of the "lost generation," Büchner. But Wolf will make the connection between her anxieties—by now much stronger than Seghers's—and the female tradition she is seeking to establish. We shall return to this point later.

Along with rediscovering an Anna Seghers that had long ago rebelled against too narrow a definition of art, tradition, and realism, Wolf also tried to make the "classic" of the social novels more accessible to a broad public. Thus she worked on the script for the filming of *Die Toten bleiben jung* (The dead stay young).[42] But in the process she may already have decided that Seghers's vision of recent German history did not correspond to her own experiences. Eventually she would write her own "historical novel," *Patterns of Childhood* (1976), in direct contrast to the heroic communist and antifascist past evoked by the older author and considered the norm. Not only the *Heimat* Wolf presents but also the past she tries to uncover involve a world about which Seghers, the exile, knew little. It was time this dimension be added and the view of recent history that had emerged from GDR literature be "corrected."

In subsequent essays on Seghers, Wolf reflects more on these differences while at the same time analyzing the relationship and defining how much it has meant to her. The most personal among them are "A Visit to Anna Seghers" and "Continued Attempt." Here Wolf's explicit "attempt at self-understanding" via Seghers reached its final stages. "A Visit to Anna Seghers"[43] (1972) begins and ends with questions suggesting, rather than clearly expressing, the intense but also complex attachment Wolf has formed. She has come to know Seghers quite well as a person and can lovingly draw on some of her private mannerisms and idiosyncrasies. But she also knows that by doing this she is contributing toward the myths around the other that have removed her somewhat from those struggling in the present: "Does she need to be loved?" she asks. And immediately she answers: "She certainly sees that we need to love her" (AS 138). On Wolf's part the need to love and admire is great. It is also a kind of protection, for in her next essay Wolf refers to Goethe's "'defense' . . . against 'the superiority of another person.' . . . He called it love" (CA 155). Ultimately Seghers's great achievements are perceived not with envy or discouragement but as a powerful stimulus: "What do we need more than the hope that we could be the way we secretly wish to be—if only we really wanted to?" (CA 150), Wolf asks at the end of her essay. Although she speaks very generally and so somewhat cryptically, in their context the words gain more specific meaning: the hope she needed was the hope that she too could become a major writer if she kept asking questions rather than listening to answers.

"A Visit to Anna Seghers" is sketchy and interspersed with anecdotal material. In "Continued Attempt" (1974)[44] Wolf gives a more complete account, her own summation, of what the connection with Seghers has meant to her: "It is a rare stroke of luck that I have been able to learn more precisely about myself through an enduring, intense interest in a life pattern which is fundamentally different [from my own]" (CA 155). Wolf speaks of her relationship as involving "feeling and understanding in equal amounts," but she also, and for the first time openly, acknowledges the ache of the other's remoteness: "Whether one admits it or not—in any case there exists a necessary pain of alienation in the sphere of desired nearness; one must expose oneself to this, along with so many unnecessary pains which we inflict upon each other" (CA 155). That distance has to do with the fact "that people of different generations are in certain respects incomprehensible to each other, one should not deny this" (CA 155). But above all it has to do with art and achievement: "To be moderate—who wouldn't desire this for himself?—She has, perhaps surprising even herself, found her measure. . . . At its base lie indubitable and undoubted certainties" (CA 156).

Wolf is a little wistful, she knows she shares in what she calls "the huge amount of uncertainty, from which successors . . . believe they again must draw" (CA 156). Yet in Seghers, the woman she knew, and even more in her work, she found understanding for such needs, such situations:

> She is, however, inwardly aware not only of the conditions under which a "classic national author" comes into being, but also of the desperate, usually vain attempts of those generations for whom their time does not want to form itself into a conclusive image. And since she herself is vital, uneasy, and curious, she is able not only to admit but joyfully to welcome that which she considers to be talented, and she can, when necessary, defend it. Who, if not she, should realize the significance of the meeting of certain generations with certain periods of history? (CA 156–157)

Wolf's essays on Seghers—there are four more, all introductions to unknown or lesser-known works by the author[45]—are unusually perceptive analyses of what an older writer has been to a younger one, as model, mentor, foil. Wolf clearly "claims" Seghers for herself and her generation, for a literary tradition where innovation, experiment, search would have their place and where the impatience for "classical national authors" would be put in perspective. In return, Seghers said much in support of a more open attitude toward tradition, as she had done in exile, but relatively little directly and publicly about Wolf.[46] The connection clearly meant much more to the younger woman. Still, Wolf felt the association to be overwhelmingly supportive. In this context it may be useful to recall that other very different and very destructive relationship between two writers, namely between Kleist and Goethe, mostly because Wolf and Anna Seghers were well aware of its nature. Did Wolf reflect on the contrast? She does not do so explicitly, but in *No Place on Earth* she has Kleist discuss his love/hatred for Goethe with a woman, Günderrode, who responds with a feeling of "alienation," of difference (*NP* 83ff.).

Here we reach a point in the Wolf-Seghers association that to my mind is very important but on which Wolf does not comment openly, probably because she herself only realized its significance after her period of most intense dialogue with Seghers (through interviews with and more personal essays on her) had ended around 1975: that the person and writer who plays such an important role for her is a woman. It seems as if it were a matter of course for Wolf that only a woman—and one who in work and life also valued traditionally female qualities, such as caring, supporting, enduring—[47]could give her what she felt Seghers had. But if Wolf did not reflect on this aspect of her experience openly, its implications, its "lesson," so to speak, became all the more important to her further work, continuing the dialogue with Seghers, albeit more indirectly and obliquely. In *No Place on Earth* (1979) we find the crucial lines: "For things have reached such a pass that women —even women who are far removed from each other in many respects —must lend each other support, since men were no longer capable of doing so" (*NP* 93). They express the idea of "sisterhood," which will become more and more central to Wolf's writing. Implicitly, the notion of women supporting each other, with the woman writer a vital link, has informed theme and structure in much of Wolf's work. In *The Quest for Christa T.* and in *Patterns of Childhood* the narrators are clearly identified as women writing caringly about women. But in her 1977 essay, "In Touch,"[48] her novel *No Place on Earth*, her essays on and editions of Karoline von Günderrode and Bettina von Brentano (1979 and 1980), the "Büchner-Prize Acceptance Speech" (1980), and *Cassandra* (1983), Wolf turns to fully developing her idea of "sisterliness" in its social and cultural implications. In "In Touch" she explains:

> Virtually every one of the conversations [in Wander's book] extends out beyond itself through longing, challenge, life expectations. Collectively—if one sees the book as a coming together of some of the most diverse people in matters of greatest importance—they give an intimation of a community where the rules would be sympathy, self-respect, trust and friendship. Marks of sisterliness, which, it seems to me, appears more frequently than brotherliness. (IT 161)

"Sisterliness" among women, and women writers in particular, is the perspective under which Wolf now comes to see past, present, and future. Thus in *No Place on Earth* and in "The Shadow of a Dream" she reaches across the ages to bring to life the poetess Günderrode, who had been a friend to some Romantics and had committed suicide at the age of twenty-six. Wolf's interest had begun with Seghers's intriguing references. She recounts: "Once I went to Winkel on the Rhine and sought out the cemetery and the grave of Günderrode: I had encountered her name repeatedly in the essays and letters of Anna Seghers" (CA 154).

In *No Place on Earth* Wolf juxtaposes Günderrode's "failure" with that of her male contemporary, Heinrich von Kleist, to suggest why "sisterliness" and the establishment of a female tradition have become so important to her: both Günderrode and Kleist are destroyed by their time, which has split the world into "doers and thinkers" and given neither man nor woman a chance to realize the dream "to become active and still remain oneself." But while Kleist suffers from his inability to fulfill his "masculine duty to act" and knows "that we can only act wrongly or not at all" (*NP* 112), Günderrode never even has the choice, not to mention the obligation, to join the world of action. Thus, she has avoided Kleist's wrenching conflict as well as his male contemporaries' self-mutilating adaptation and has preserved a sense for wholeness which she can only share with other women: "because the men for whom we might care are themselves entangled in inextricable dilemmas. The constant round of responsibilities you men must deal with cut you into pieces which scarcely bear any relation to each other. We women are looking for a whole human being, and we cannot find him" (NP 93).

In the essay on Günderrode and, shortly thereafter, in the "letter" on Günderrode's friend, her "sister" Bettina von Brentano, Wolf pursues this theme further, explaining why that friendship has become so important to her: "The world is sick, and she doesn't notice it. Women in these few years, a gap between the historic ages, who have suddenly discarded their old molds—including the molds regarding their sex—strike a kind of agreement to make it well. Only now can the signals they give be noticed, taken up, and interpreted again" (SD 254). The reasons why these and other "signals" from different ages[49] can and indeed must be read now will become more and more explicit as Christa Wolf continues her exploration.

For the moment let us return to the two women, Günderrode and Bettina, and the contrast between them, which is, I believe, a major point of the "letter about Bettina." In No Place on Earth Wolf had concentrated on the juxtaposition of man and woman and suggested that the split that destroyed both was also, and most important, a split into male and female spheres. "What you mean is that man and woman have a hostile relationship inside you. As they do in me" (NP 104), Günderrode had remarked to Kleist. Now Wolf elaborates in more detail how ultimately this division affected Günderrode negatively and shows how Bettina managed in some ways to benefit from it. Günderrode wants to be a poet and accepts the only norms she knows, "male" norms she as a woman cannot really fully adhere to:

> Thus she subjects herself to a canon of law which, since its orientation is that of the masculine concept of "work" and "genius," demands of her that which she cannot achieve: the division of her work from her person, the creation of art at the cost of life; the generation in herself of the distance and coldness which sires "the work," but which kills the immediate relationship to other people because it makes them into objects . . . . There is no doubt that she wears herself out with the aesthetic concepts behind masterworks which she cannot hope to create (have you ever heard the expression "mistressworks?"). She renounces them for the sake of truth, but with a feeling of failure . . . (BL 316–317)

Bettina, on the other hand, accepts "insignificance" and can therefore refuse to "subject herself to an aesthetic canon" (BL 310). Thus she survives as both a person and an authentic female voice: In her youth she was "androgynous, mysterious, contradictory, doomed to an early death." But Bettina "succeeds at the difficult trick of destroying her own myth, the deceptively finished portrait of her youth, and exposes herself to the usual routines of an 'ordinary' life" (BL 289). "This distinguishes her from Günderrode" (BL 285). Christa Wolf significantly speaks of Bettina's "retreating" into marriage, raising children. As a wife and mother, without ambition or office in the male world, she can hold on to the dream of her youth and "apply" it much later in her stance toward the Prussian state and in her books. Precisely because Bettina's *Die Günderode* is what Wolf calls "mixed form," it can communicate women's thoughts and experiences "without having to deform them" (BL 310) and thus become a timely reminder of an important friendship, "an experiment in which two women agreed to participate, mutually supporting, strengthening, and teaching each other. 'Utopian,' certainly" (BL 313). It is, Christa Wolf suggests, more radical and more promising than anything their male contemporaries produced, precisely because it came from women who were excluded from what she later calls the "citadel of [male] reason" (BP 6).

> Here you find a form of enlightened thinking which wants to unite sharpened *ratio* and greater sensitivity in one and the same person; it fears—only now can we fully comprehend with what justification— the onesidedness of instrumental, thing-oriented reasoning (of another irrationalism); to the soulless mechanisms of philosophies that "kill the spirit" it opposes another, personal way to get close to nature —including one's own. (BL 314)

As Christa Wolf sees them, Karoline and Bettina both exemplify "the positive, even utopian potential of female experience within patriarchy,"[50] but it is Bettina, who, refusing to accept traditional, that is, male standards for achievement, fully represents in her writing and her actions that "utopian potential of a historically female subjectivity."[51] Approvingly Wolf comments on Bettina's role in the Prussia of the 1830s and 1840s: "It is not without a secret sense of satisfaction that one observes the way she knows how to exploit the advantage which in male societies is occasionally concealed in the disadvantage of being a woman—that is if the person concerned and affected can endure being considered slightly insane" (BL 294).

With increasing urgency Wolf appeals to this "utopian potential" in women's experiences and associations. Only if we realize it can we save the world from narrow "utilitarian thinking" and its last consequences—aggression, war, nuclear holocaust. Christa Wolf develops these ideas more and more clearly in her recent works, her "Büchner-Prize Acceptance Speech," the *Frankfurt Lectures on Poetics,* and *Cassandra* (1983). Precisely because Wolf believes that women, in her society at least, have achieved a measure of equality and emancipation, they can for the first time fully and consciously explore this potential. In her enthusiastic review of Maxie Wander's *Guten Morgen, du Schöne* (Good Morning, Thou Pretty One), Wolf says:

Conditions in our country have enabled women to develop a self-awareness which does not simultaneously imply the will to control, to dominate, or to subjugate, but rather the ability to cooperate. For the first time in their history they are defining their *differentness*—an immense step forward; for the first time they are not only developing creative imagination: They have also developed that clear-headed vision which men believe to be a typically masculine quality.

I am not claiming that women are by nature more immune than men to political delusions or flights from reality. Only this: A specific historical phase has given them the bases for a voice in shaping life-expectations for men. Of course aggression and fear are loosed when one must shatter old images—especially of oneself. But we will have to become accustomed to the fact that women are no longer just seeking equality, but new ways to live. They are countering mere pragmatism and utilitarianism—that self-deceptive "Ratio"—with rational thinking, sensuality, longing for happiness. (IT 167–168)

What Wolf expresses here appears to be more of a program than an observation. A little later, in her "Büchner-Prize Acceptance Speech," she no longer speaks of allowing such changes to happen, but of needing them very urgently. They are civilization's only hope. In the allusive language of that speech, in which Rosetta represents woman through literature and time, Wolf says that after two world wars woman has finally won "the ultimate compliment: she is like him [man]" (BP 8). It is a crucial point because woman now clearly realizes that history has always been male: "Never, she now admits to herself, never has time passed to the beat of her feet. Yet in a strangely insistent, at times already uncanny way, she is now prepared to take herself seriously" (BP 8). Because of her present ambivalent and difficult position in two traditionally separate spheres, her old "female" one and the newly accessible "male" one, she has been given a unique and decisive choice:

Has Rosetta under her many names only the choice between being driven back into the dead space or becoming like him? Does not every step she takes toward liberation intensify his fear and thus his defensiveness? Should she now erect barricades and fire from the citadel of her reason "with the cannon of truth"? Consider him her enemy, who ought to be "crushed"? And: to help each other see the light —would that not be possible? Welded to the same paradox, would they both be unable to take a single positive step toward each other? Should this historic moment go to waste as well? (BP 9)

Christa Wolf clearly is not a feminist in some Western senses of the word. She neither wants contemporary women and women writers to establish their separate and often hostile spheres, nor does she wish to join the male world as it is and accept its standards, its traditions. She speaks to men *and* women but leaves no doubt that at this point in history woman must make herself an important, if not for a while the most important, voice in her culture because she is not yet totally trained to the "structures of thought and observation he [man] established" (BP 8). Woman must make use of her past outside the "citadel" of male reasoning, "instrumental thinking," to save both men and women.

If Christa Wolf speaks of "the memory of the future" (RW 212) (for this essay I prefer to render it "remembrance of things future") as the task of writing, of prose, then this task assumes a special significance in the context of her concern with women as writers and participants in history. For women there is the need to reflect back and to realize as well as express the radical utopian nature of a traditionally female existence of "mutual recognition and nurturant activity which may guide us in our struggle against instrumental rationality."[52] Such activity, Christa Wolf suggests again in *Cassandra*, is not necessarily only women's domain (in that story men like Aeneas and Anchises share in it). But it has been assigned to them by the split that has divided the world into male and female, aggression, high achievement, instrumental rationality on the one hand, and subjugation, ordinary everyday living, and sensitive thinking ("fühlendes Denken") on the other. And unless women in general and women writers in particular can heal that split by recalling, reexamining, and applying what values the female experience has given them, their fate at best will parallel that of Cassandra, the woman and seer who could foretell the fate of Troy but could not prevent it.

The burden Wolf places upon women, women writers, and particularly herself, is a heavy one. But for Wolf this burden has also been an energizing force. With new self-assurance she confesses to the madness which has traditionally been a means of asserting—but also of betraying—female otherness and proclaims it to be vitally important to all of mankind: "Sheer madness, you say. Fine. I therefore lack—in the language of psychiatry—insight into my illness, and I surrender myself to this sheer madness, so as not to fall victim to the dark side of reason" (BP 11). (Crazy and mad, we remember, were also attributes applied to Bettina von Arnim and Cassandra.) Ultimately Christa Wolf marshals the female tradition against the threat of extinction. No wonder she became fascinated by the fates of Cassandra, Penthesilea, and Clytemnestra and their roles in the events surrounding the extinction of Troy. Yet, although Wolf in *Cassandra* seems to merge with Western feminists' interest in matriarchy, her concern, it seems to me, lies not with matriarchy. It takes the form, rather, of a search—imaginative for the most part, as it is in *Cassandra*—for "prepatriarchal" structures, for an equal partnership between man and woman such as exists between Priam and Hecuba (before the Trojan War and what Wolf calls "prewar"), and between Aeneas and Cassandra before he leaves Troy. In fact, Cassandra, in Wolf's reinterpretation, refuses to leave with Aeneas precisely because the fall of Troy signals the fatal split into "male" and "female," a new era in which their kind of equality and mutual recognition can no longer exist:

The new masters would dictate their law to all the survivors. The earth was not large enough to escape them. You, Aeneas, had no choice: You had to snatch a couple of hundred people from death. You were their leader. "Soon, very soon, you will have to become a hero." . . . I cannot love a hero. I do not want to see you being transformed into a statue. . . . You knew as well as I did that we have no chance against a time that needs heroes. (C 138)

Aeneas will of course become the founder of Rome, and its patriarchal civilization, the model of ours, will continue that of the victorious Greeks. But it was not a matriarchy in which the earlier relationship between Aeneas and Cassandra flourished; it was the Trojan society in transition. In it, their love became part of a larger experiment of living in caves, in a subculture of sisterly and brotherly association—an experiment carried on during the Trojan War under the threat of extinction:

It amazed me to see that different though we all were, the women by the Scamander felt without exception that we were testing something, and that it was not a question of how much time we had. Nor of whether we could convince the majority of Trojans, who of course remained in the dismal city. We did not see ourselves as an example. We were grateful that we were the ones granted the highest privilege there is: to slip a narrow strip of future into the grim present, which occupies all of time. (C 134)

These are dark words, especially if one draws the parallels between the story and the present that Christa Wolf wants us to draw—not necessarily in order to say that such experiments will always be doomed, but to warn that, should they be doomed again, the fall will involve a whole world, not just one city.

With *Cassandra*, Wolf has come a long way from her early attachment to Seghers as model and foil, yet her development shows striking continuity and inner consequence toward a more and more pronounced sense of the need for a female tradition in writing and in history and toward defining the nature and purpose of that tradition. She has faced and tried to overcome that "difficulty of saying 'I,'" which has plagued women writers, the voices of women in general, throughout civilization. "To say 'I,' as a woman" (C 298)—what has it meant in the past, what can it mean now and for the future? These are the questions she asks with more and more temerity because she hopes—and the hope is utopian—that women for the first time have a choice other than the two equally destructive ones offered them in the past: "to adapt or disappear" (C 299–300). They can now become makers of literary history (and of history) by exploring and expressing themselves as women, as part of a female tradition. They must find their voices and be heard in the interest, however, not of dividing the world, but of healing it.

There can be no doubt that the surge and direction of recent woman's writing in the GDR owes a great deal to Wolf. First, Christa Wolf herself has shown "sisterhood" and reached out to other women writers in support, thus in a way continuing what had gone on between her and Seghers. There is, for example, the exchange of letters with Gerti Tetzner,[53] author of *Karen W.* (1974), a story very much in line with the explorations begun by *The Quest for Christa T.*: A woman's failure (to stay with a career and a husband that demand adaptation) is presented in positive terms as a search for authentic ways of being and of contributing to society. There is also the supportive interview with Elke Erb in *Der Faden der Geduld* (The Thread of Patience, 1978), an interview that attempts to make a difficult and experimental writer accessible and acceptable. And there is of course Christa Wolf's enthusiasm for Maxie Wander and her *Guten Morgen, du Schöne*. Wolf's review, "In Touch," which became the foreword of the West German edition of Wander's book, beautifully underscores the book's significance to the female tradition as Wolf sees and defines it.

In addition, a long list of novels and story collections by and on women has appeared in the wake of *The Quest for Christa T.* These include, for example, Brigitte Reimann's *Franziska Linkerhand* (1974), Christine Wolter's *Wie ich meine Unschuld verlor* (How I Lost My Innocence, 1976) and *Die Hintergrundsperson. Versuche zu lieben* (The Background Person. Attempts to Love, 1979), Helga Königsdorf's *Meine ungehörigen Träume* (My Unseemly Dreams, 1978), Christa Müller's *Das verlorene Paradies* (Paradise Lost, 1979), and Rosemarie Zeplin's *Schattenriss eines Liebhabers* (Silhouette of a Lover, 1980).[54]

In all of these, female authors and heroines look beyond the emancipation and equality granted to them by their society. They try to refuse those "structures of thought and observation which he [man] has established" and to find their own.[55] That this must be done if the earth is to continue, and that women writers are in a unique position to do so, is precisely Christa Wolf's message to all, the force behind the female tradition she has established.

Notes

1. Sandra M. Gilbert and Susan Gubar, *The Madwoman in the Attic* (New Haven and London: Yale University Press, 1979), 50.

2. Alexander Stephan, *Christa Wolf* (Munich: Beck, 1976), 7–22.

3. Manfred Jäger, "Die Literaturkritikerin Christa Wolf," in *Christa Wolf, Text und Kritik*, 46 (June 1980), 48f.

4. Gilbert and Gubar, 15, and the entire first chapter.

5. Cf. Louis Fürnberg, *Ein Leben für unsere Zeit*, ed. Hans Böhm (Berlin and Weimar: Aufbau, 1963), 420.

6. Cf. Frank Trommler, *Sozialistische Literatur in Deutschland* (Stuttgart: Kröner, 1976), 703; Alexander Stephan, *Christa Wolf*, 34, 120; Peter Beicken, "Nachfolge nicht Nachahmung: Zur Beziehung Anna Seghers—Christa Wolf," in *Deutsche Exilliteratur*, ed. Wolfgang Elfe et al. (Bern, Frankfurt, Las Vegas: Lang, 1981), 114–132.

7. Beicken, "Nachfolge nicht Nachahmung."

8. Peter Beicken, especially at the end of his article, appears to point in this direction.

9. Cf. Wolf's essay, "In Touch."

10. *Die Entscheidung* and Wolf's interview appeared in 1959. The interview originally was entitled "Anna Seghers über ihre Schaffensmethode. Ein Gespräch (No. 8)." It is most accessible in Anna Seghers, *Aufsätze, Ansprachen, Essays 1954–1979* (Berlin and Weimar: Aufbau, 1980), 399–406, and in *DA*, 255–262.

11. Beicken, 122.

12. Seghers, *Aufsätze, Ansprachen, Essays 1954–1979*, 399f.

13. This movement was first proclaimed in 1957 and then fully articulated at the Bitterfeld conference in 1959. In that very year Wolf moved to Halle and followed the "call" of the movement: to take a job in a factory and to participate in circles of writing workers.

14. *NdL* 9, 5 (1961): 49–65; cf. also Beicken.

15. Christa Wolf, "Land in dem wir leben. Die deutsche Frage in dem Roman 'Die Entscheidung' von Anna Seghers," *NdL* 9, 5 (1961): 51.

16. Cf. Harold Bloom, *The Anxiety of Influence* (New York: Oxford University Press, 1973), 11, 26.

17. Cf. Christa Wolf, BP and NP.

18. Gilbert and Gubar, 52f.

19. Erika Haas, "Der männliche Blick der Anna Seghers," *Notizbuch 2*, ed. Friederike J. Hassauer and Peter Roos (Berlin: Wölk und Schmid, 1980), 134–149.

20. Haas, 136.

21. Seghers, *Essays*, 402.

22. Ibid., 400.

23. Wolf, "Land in dem wir leben," 65.

24. Anna Seghers, *Das siebte Kreuz* (Berlin/Weimar: Aufbau, 1964).

25. Cf. my essay, "The Rediscovery of Romanticism in the GDR: A Note on Anna Seghers' Role," in *Studies in GDR Culture and Society 2*, ed. Margy Gerber et al. (Washington: University Press of America, 1982), 19-29. [Seghers referred consistently to Bettina Brentano/Arnim and Günderrode and to other Romantic writers such as Lenz, Kleist, and Büchner who were misunderstood or not appreciated in their times. But German Romanticism in the GDR needs to be seen in the light of efforts by cultural politics, literary history, and criticism to define that country's "appropriation of the (literary) heritage" *(Erbeaneignung)* and its "national literature" *(Nationalliteratur)*. Although Seghers's sensitivity to individuals whose society constituted an impenetrable and unyielding wall against which they battered themselves was articulated early on (in a speech in 1935), East Germany's cultural policy makers have only gradually begun to accept the German Romantics as part of the official "cultural heritage." This process of acceptance has been treated at length in recent literature, some of which is referred to elsewhere in this volume (see especially the essays by Peucker and Ryan). Wolf's allusions to German Romanticism are carefully explored within the larger context of GDR cultural politics by Hans-Georg Werner in his article, "Unter den Linden," in this volume. —Ed.]

26. "Christa Wolf spricht mit Anna Seghers," in Seghers, *Essays*, 410–423 (first published in *NdL*, June 1965; also in Wolf, *DA*, 279–292).

27. Seghers, *Essays*, 410.

28. Ibid., 411.

29. Ibid.

30. Cf. Stephan, 77.

31. Cf. Stephan, 7–22.

32. Jäger, 50.

33. Many had not been collected and were not easily accessible other than in Seghers's manuscripts.

34. Seghers, *Essays*, 414.

35. Ibid., 413f.

36. Anna Seghers, *Aufsätze, Ansprachen, Essays 1927–1953* (Berlin and Weimar: Aufbau, 1980), 69.

37. Anna Seghers, *Glauben an Irdisches*, ed. Christa Wolf (Leipzig: Reclam, 1969).

38. Seghers, *Essays, 1927–1953*, 70.

39. Translation modified by author.

40. Anna Seghers herself said: "In meiner Arbeit gab es keine Krisenzeiten" (There have been no periods of crisis in my work). *Anna Seghers: Materialienbuch*, ed. Peter Roos and Friederike Hassauer-Roos (Darmstadt and Neuwied: Luchterhand, 1977), 158. However, some of her letters from the last months of her exile in France and the novel *Transit* from that period suggest that Seghers certainly came close to the fear of failure and futility.

41. Jäger, 50.

42. *Die Toten bleiben jung* (Film Script), 1968. Director: Joachim Kunert; Script: Christa Wolf, Joachim Kunert, Gerhard Helwig, Günter Haubold, Ree von Dahlen.

43. In *Liebes-und andere Erklärungen: Schriftsteller über Schriftsteller*, ed. Annie Voigtländer (Berlin/Weimar: Aufbau, 1972). Also in *Fortgesetzter Versuch*, 323–331.

44. First in *Über Anna Seghers. Almanach zum 75. Geburtstag*, ed. Kurt Batt (Berlin/Weimar: Aufbau, 1975). Most accessible in *Fortgesetzter Versuch*, 151–157 or *DA*, 339–345.

45. Wolf's additional work on Seghers includes her essay on Seghers's dissertation ("Die Dissertation der Nelly Reiling") and three postscripts: "Anmerkungen zu Geschichten" (afterword to Anna Seghers, *Aufstellung eines Maschinengewehrs im Wohnzimmer der Frau Kamptschik* [Neuwied and Berlin: Luchterhand, 1970]); "Zeitschichten" (afterword to Anna Seghers, *Ausgewählte Erzählungen*, ed. Christa Wolf [Darmstadt and Neuwied: Luchterhand, 1983]); and "Transit: Ortschaften" (afterword to Anna Seghers, *Transit* [Rome, 1986]). All are reprinted in *DA*.

46. Anna Seghers, "Für Christa Wolf," in *Aufsätze 1954–1979*, 393–395 (first published in *SuF*, March/April 1979). The personal friendship between the two women continued until Seghers's death. One of the last entries in Seghers's calendar before she died was "visit by C.W."

47. In spite or because of Seghers's "male perspective," she did value these traditionally female qualities, especially in the works she wrote in exile and afterwards.

48. On Maxie Wander's collection of women's voices from the GDR, *Guten Morgen, du Schöne*.

49. In *Cassandra* Wolf turns to antiquity.

50. Myra Love, "Christa Wolf and Feminism: Breaking the Patriarchal Connection," *NGC*, no. 16 (Winter 1979): 51.

51. Love, 42.

52. Jessica Benjamin, "Authority and the Family Revisited: or A World without Fathers," *NGC*, no. 13 (Winter 1978): 57.

53. Gerti Tetzner—Christa Wolf, correspondence. In *Was zählt die Wahrheit. Briefe von Schriftstellern der DDR* (Halle: Mitteldeutscher Verlag, 1975), 9–33.

54. Cf. my paper, "Vertreibung aus dem Paradies. Zur neuen Frauenliteratur aus der DDR." In *Studies in GDR Culture and Society 3*, ed. Margy Gerber et al. (Washington: University Press of America, 1983), 71–85.

55. In the words of Wolfgang Emmerich in his *Kleine Literaturgeschichte der DDR* (Brief History of GDR Literature, 1981): They are women from the GDR who have been the most likely in recent years to succeed in taking a look at the "objectified dreams" of "instrumental thought" (Christa Wolf), a look which has brought this objectification into renewed motion, even if it has not made it disappear . . . (Darmstadt/Neuwied: Luchterhand, 1981), 203.

Christa Wolf and Ingeborg Bachmann: Difficulties of Writing the Truth

Sara Lennox

In the West German edition of Christa Wolf's essays, *The Reader and the Writer* (1980), the two oldest essays, dating from 1966, deal with the works of Bertolt Brecht and Ingeborg Bachmann. Along with Anna Seghers, Brecht and Bachmann count among authors whose writing Wolf respects most, and the presence of those essays in *The Reader and the Writer* provides a useful metaphor for understanding Wolf's own work: one might maintain that it exists in a tension between those two poles, Brecht and Bachmann. For all the differences between Wolf and Brecht, they evidently share certain convictions and concerns: Wolf too is a socialist, deeply committed to social change and to creating a literature that promotes it. Brecht's example encouraged Wolf to develop other literary forms appropriate to the problems of her own age, as she explained in her 1966 essay: "The possibility of applying Brecht's art and his theory of art lay not in simple imitation . . . , but in encouraging people to make their own discoveries" (BO 58). Yet if in this sense Wolf's project continues Brecht's own, one can sometimes also detect in Wolf's remarks on Brecht a hint of impatience, as if the model provided by this now classic GDR literary figure could also have a retarding effect on the literary discoveries Wolf wishes to undertake—might even, one suspects, share some complicity in the problems Wolf's work has increasingly sought to critique. Pursuing in detail Brecht's influence on Wolf and her growing distance from him would be a fascinating enterprise; however, it is one that I will explore here only indirectly, as I investigate instead Wolf's attraction toward that other pole, the writing of Ingeborg Bachmann.

The nature of Bachmann's influence on Wolf is less easy to grasp and, though Bachmann's name recurs again and again particularly in Wolf's writing of the seventies and eighties, scholars with some rare exceptions[1] have not addressed the relationship of these two major women writers, no doubt in some part because Bachmann's own work has proven so difficult to comprehend. With the elaboration of feminist theory and a methodology for feminist literary scholarship, Bachmann's work has become more transparent for us, though it may be that we still do not possess a conceptual apparatus capable completely of understanding what connects Wolf to Bachmann. That is an investigation I would like to begin here. In this essay I want first to outline the qualities of Bachmann's work that Wolf identifies and admires in the 1966 essay, relating them to themes in Wolf's work from the mid-sixties onward. Then I would like to trace some parallels between Wolf's work and Bachmann's which might be regarded as conscious allusions or even as homages to Bachmann on Wolf's part. Finally I want to look closely at Wolf's most recent writing, examining her work on the women Romantics, her "Büchner-Prize Acceptance Speech," the *Frankfurt Lectures*, and *Cassandra* to show that in the late seventies Wolf, encouraged by Bachmann as well as by events of recent history, arrived at a standpoint very similar to Bachmann's in her last writing, the novels of the *Todesarten* (Types of death) cycle. I maintain that the seventies saw a movement in Wolf's writing away from Brecht and toward Bachmann, as Wolf increasingly challenged the received truths of Marxism and, from the perspective of a woman within European society, both insider and outsider, grappled with the difficulties of expressing another truth that would question some of the most basic assumptions on which European culture rests and on which Marxism itself also relies.

Certainly this critique was not fully elaborated in 1966, when Wolf wrote her Brecht and Bachmann essays; yet already the title of the Bachmann essay, "Truth That Can Be Faced—Ingeborg Bachmann's Prose" deriving from an essay of 1959 by Bachmann, "Man Can Face the Truth,"[2] shows that Wolf had grasped something of Bachmann's philosophical project, her struggle to formulate a different epistemology, to articulate a different model for truth. More impressionistic than analytic, Wolf's early essay does not provide, probably could not have provided, handy categories for understanding Bachmann's prose. But two themes in the essay are striking. First, Wolf emphasizes that Bachmann aimed to provide her readers access to a truth they had not seen before: "To become seeing, to make people see: a fundamental motif in the work of Ingeborg Bachmann" (IB 85). Bachmann seemed to suggest that humans might not even successfully grasp the nature of their own suffering, might lack the categories enabling them to recognize it at all. "For it is time," Bachmann had written, "to understand the voice of man, the voice of a chained creature not quite able to say what it suffers from" (IB 85). And, on the other hand, failing to challenge conventional truths might mean not only individual pain but complicity in the world's evils altogether: "the haunting temptation to join hands—through conformity, blindness, acceptance, habit, illusion or treachery—with the deadly dangers to which the world is exposed" (IB 84). As Wolf viewed it, Bachmann's endeavor was to hold fast to the legitimacy of her own experience and to find a language that could accurately express it: "It is her cause to have the courage to create her experience anew in herself and to assert it in the face of the truly overwhelming mass and discouraging dominance of empty, meaningless, ineffectual phrases" (IB 85). And this explained Bachmann's concern with a new language, which critics had too often understood as only aestheticism. Quoting Bachmann herself, Wolf emphasized what Bachmann sought in her quest: "To seek 'a new language,' 'a thinking that desires knowledge and wants to achieve with and through language. Let us call it, for the time being, reality'" (IB 94).

As its second structuring theme, Wolf's essay insists—remarkably enough for a Bachmann study written at this time—that Bachmann intended her writing to be deeply and directly political. In the fifties and sixties, Bachmann's lyric poetry was generally thought to be the beautiful, if somewhat obscure, expression of the personal experiences of the poetess, timeless and generally applicable to the human condition, while her prose in contrast was regarded as unsuccessful, weak, and confused by some, although enthusiastically and positively received by others. But Wolf had read carefully Bachmann's essays, particularly her "Frankfurt Lectures" of 1959–1960, observing there the centrality of Bachmann's insistence that literature should promote social change, and Wolf was able to use those essays to illuminate qualities of Bachmann's imaginative writing other readers had not grasped. Epigraphs from Bachmann's essays begin each section of Wolf's own essay and document her emphasis on the connectedness of Bachmann's concern with language and consciousness to a society she wishes to transform. Thus, for instance, the third section of Wolf's essay begins with a quote from the "Frankfurt Lectures": "But what in fact is possible is change. And the changing effect of new works educates us to new perception, new feeling, new awareness" (IB 89). Wolf emphasizes, too, that Bachmann understood literature to derive from a particular historical period and to address historically specific problems, as she had again maintained in her lectures: "'writing does not take place outside the historical situation'" (IB 89). If this is the case (as Wolf obviously also believes it to be), Bachmann's works need to be read as both written from the perspective of her own historically specific experiences and as addressed to quite specific, if far-reaching, problems of her society. The categories of perception she wants to encourage in her readers would be ones that would enable them both to understand and to change the world. Simultaneously, the insufficiencies and weaknesses of her works—as well as the difficulties of her own life—can be understood as having historical causes, too. For Christa Wolf, then as now, "the historical situation is such that the question of the possibility of man's moral existence must be at the center of all writing. This approach is one of the main drives in [Bachmann's] prose—often in curious disguises, not immediately recognizable, as a subjective reflex, as fear, doubt, a feeling of menace: 'Hanging on to the high-voltage current of the present'" (IB 89).

But if social change is the central emphasis of Bachmann's prose, the literary strategies she chooses could scarcely be more different from those of Brecht, who exemplified the engaged experimental writer: neither the arena she identifies as crucial for change nor the techniques she employs resemble Brecht's at all. Instead, Wolf emphasizes, Bachmann's stress is on the human subject, its "self-assertion," even its "spreading" of itself (IB 85–86). For this author, as later for Christa T., it is important to be able to say "I," "without arrogance but with head high" (IB 87). But this is a subject that also finds itself deeply imperilled, and its salvation might come through reasserting human power to comprehend the object world. "To regain a sovereignty lost through submission. To master it by designation" (IB 86). "It may stimulate her," writes Wolf, "to conquer banality in the course of writing" (IB 89). "Banality," a noun that could not be used carelessly after Hannah Arendt's 1963 book on Adolf Eichmann,[3] suggests even in this early essay some connection between the crisis of the subject and National Socialism, a theme that Wolf's and Bachmann's later works would pursue in great detail. For Wolf, most important in Bachmann's work is her defense of that subject itself against the many forces that threaten it: "She defends no outlying regions but 'regions of the heart.' Man's right to self-realization. His right to individuality and to unfold his own personality. His longing for freedom" (IB 91). Defending those human capacities, Bachmann's work begins to make it possible for new subjects to be created: "brave, deeply moving picture[s] of a new man" (IB 95).

Bachmann's concentration on the subject rather than on events in the external world is, for Wolf, not a quality to be understood only, or even primarily, negatively. From the perspective of Wolf's later work clearly her description of Bachmann's prose is not really intended as criticism: "One will often seek in vain for concrete situations or for a realistic presentation of social processes. What we have here are stories of feelings" (IB 89). Bachmann's prose reveals the movements of subjectivity: "taking up her own position, showing her own weaknesses, being hit, rising again, attacking the enemy at its center, constantly in danger at the very heart of life . . . self-assertion as a process" (IB 86). When Bachmann portrays the external world, it is a world made luminous and transparent by the subject's comprehension of it, a vision of its hopes and its dangers.

Another frame of reference produces another reality: "This, subordinated to a surprising system of references, is the irrepressible and

Sara Lennox

insatiable longing to penetrate into the natural and social environment with the help of human standards" (IB 86). What "system of references?" "Unnamed," says Wolf, "probably not thought out. Literature as utopia" (IB 95). The pursuit of that "system of references," or "viewing lens," as Wolf termed it most recently in her own "Frankfurt Lectures," is what draws Wolf back repeatedly to Bachmann's work.

To be sure, Wolf's response to Bachmann in this essay is not solely positive. She perceives obscurities and inadequacies in Bachmann's writing, but those often derive from Bachmann's real situation: she felt she lacked an audience who could understand her and was deeply pained by that. And she also could not foresee any mediation between her fantastic visions and their realization in the world, so that the resolutions her stories achieve also seem sometimes abrupt and unmotivated:

> If it accords with no social movement the radical claim to freedom becomes a ravaging longing for absolute, unlimited and unreal freedom, complete despair about what steps to take next turns into illusionary demands "to set up a new world" by "abolishing all that exists." And the departure from this radicality, a return to normal activities and attitudes to life is either regarded as capitulation or remains unmotivated and without foundation, as in The Thirtieth Year: "I say to you: Stand up and walk! No bones are broken!" (IB 92)

In 1966, Wolf seemed still able to distinguish her position as a socialist writer in the GDR clearly from Bachmann's. Bachmann stood for the furthest extreme of integrity and resolution one could reach in a capitalist society. Wolf wanted to hope that socialist writers, learning new lessons from Bachmann, could also provide the setting to bring them to concretion: "Only then," says Wolf, "on a new social foundation, can the 'defence of poesy' begin" (IB 95).

Yet one of Wolf's observations in the Bachmann essay also points beyond her confidence in GDR socialism toward a position she herself would come close to assuming in the coming decades. The fourth section of her essay begins with the quotation from The Thirtieth Year: "But a few drank the cup of hemlock unconditionally" (IB 94). Without access to a social movement radical enough to realize the social changes her works had envisioned, Bachmann is inclined to withdraw her characters from society altogether instead of making them pay the price necessary to survive in it. In this gesture, she joins others in the history of German literature: "Some refused to be bought, to be won over by temptation or forced by blackmail; they preferred death to self-surrender, in order to remain alive in their own time and to have an effect on the future. Ingeborg Bachmann appears to be trying to hold on to these, to their moral example" (IB 94–95). In Bachmann's prose of this period, the most striking example of non-conformity is the Undine in the last story of The Thirtieth Year, "Undine Goes."[4] Wolf understands fully how radically Bachmann had rejected the achievements of an entire culture: "Weariness of civilization and doubts about progress are most strongly marked in 'Undine goes': total alienation of man from himself and his like and romantic protest against it" (IB 92). She grasps as well that this is a protest advanced against a male world from the standpoint of a female figure who stands outside it, "accusing a man's world in the barely disguised voice of the author" (IB 93). Given Wolf's recognition of the extremity of the positions Bachmann assumes in this story, it is all the more startling to observe how closely Wolf's description of Undine corresponds to figures in her own work, particularly Christa T. and Karoline von Günderrode: "also romantic in attitude, the comparison of commonplace utility thinking with 'a spirit that is destined to no use.' . . . Since [Undine] sees no possible way to take up the struggle, she retreats before the unacceptable demands of society in the hope that she can thus preserve herself. But this retreat always ends in surrender of self, since separation from the practices of society also wears away the individual's inner powers of resistance" (IB 92–93). "The acceptable truth" that the (woman) writer can provide, should she withstand "the unacceptable demands of society"[5]—this dilemma threads its way through Wolf's work to the present.

Though Wolf did not really explicitly acknowledge Bachmann as a mentor until the late seventies, a careful reader of Wolf's work can clearly perceive her indebtedness to and acknowledgment of Bachmann much earlier. Her own literary-theoretical essay of 1968, "The Reader and the Writer," reveals great debts to Bachmann's writing in general and more specifically to the concerns in Bachmann's work on which Wolf had commented in the earlier essay. Remarkable in this essay is its attempt to pose its concerns in Brechtian terms while moving at least in some respects ever further from Brechtian literary models. Though Wolf, like Brecht, places her considerations "in the scientific age," the science she stresses is that of Einstein and Heisenberg, where scientific regularity and reliability have given way to relativity and imprecision. In the wake of these scientific changes and given the continuation of Brecht's project, she calls for a new "epic prose." But in contrast to epic theater, Wolf's epic prose is produced and consumed by single individuals; indeed, Wolf expressly criticizes here Walter Benjamin's assertion that the individual author as producer was as inevitably fated to disappear as the individual entrepreneur, "crushed between mass-producing institutions" (RW 207).[6] Moreover, epic prose does not undertake to show its readers a world "changing and changeable" into which they—cool, critical, and dispassionate—can intervene, but instead it offers to address and transform those readers' very subjectivity itself: "Epic prose should be a genre which undertakes to penetrate along paths not yet traveled into the inner regions of this individual, the reader of prose. Into the innermost interior, where the nucleus of the personality develops and takes root" (RW 201).[7] As Wolf had argued in her "Interview with Myself," published in the same year as "The Reader and the Writer," the achievement of the real basis for socialism

133

in the GDR meant that socialist literature could, indeed should, now concern itself with human subjectivity, comprised of emotions as well as reason. As a socialist writer, Wolf thus turns to the elaboration of precisely those dimensions of human experience virtually excluded in Brecht's work.

Wolf's shift reveals the influence not just of Bachmann but also of Ernst Bloch—the thinker whom *Bachmann* in the "Frankfurt Lectures" had proposed, along with Wittgenstein, as a central impulse for contemporary writing. The last of Bachmann's Frankfurt lectures was entitled "Literature as Utopia"; from "The Reader and the Writer" and *The Quest for Christa T.* onward, Wolf also places her own work, as Andreas Huyssen has shown, in the service of the Blochian principle of hope.[8] Her writing, like Bachmann's, projects an unrealized vision and reveals the desires and disappointments beneath the surface of the present, employing epic prose to project, as she maintained in "The Reader and the Writer," "the future into the present" (RW 201). Wolf argued eloquently in that essay that formulating utopias should be the most important function of socialist prose, indispensable in a socialist society:

> [Prose] can keep awake in us the memory of the future that we must not abandon on pain of destruction.
> It helps mankind to become conscious subjects.
> It is revolutionary and realistic; it entices and encourages people to achieve the impossible. (RW 212)

In 1968, what still distinguished Wolf's utopias from Bachmann's was of course Wolf's ability to imagine a society in which they might be realized—a hope she still, against mounting evidence to the contrary, tries doggedly to maintain. One might suggest that Wolf's use of Bachmann is what Benjamin would have termed redemptive: rescuing the most radical in her work from misunderstanding and oblivion, making it accessible to the present, in order to bring her visions about in reality. "Her part," Wolf had promised in 1980, "will not vanish" (BP 10).

In Wolf's writing until the late seventies one can detect a series of parallels with and allusions to Bachmann's writing too obvious, particularly in the case of the names Wolf chooses, to be anything but deliberate. To readers familiar with Wolf's Bachmann essay, the words with which Wolf's narrator introduces her short story, "An Afternoon in June," for instance, recall the description of Bachmann's prose. The last two clauses ("A vision perhaps, if you know what I mean" [AJ 41]) reveal the narrator's expectation that, as was the case with Bachmann's work, the vision that comprises this difficult story is not immediately evident. What the story reveals, beneath an exterior that could not be more banal—a family afternoon in a weekend garden plot outside Berlin—is the fantastic texture of subjectivity underlying it. On the one hand, the garden itself, not unlike other literary gardens, stands as a container for "the immoderate desires, always held in check" of the

Bachmann essay. This very real garden, says the narrator, also contains within it the dream of its own perfectibility. "Since we've known it, . . . it has never been allowed to show what it contains. Now it turns out that it was no more and no less than the dream of being a green, verdant, wild, and bountiful garden. The original idea of a garden. The garden of gardens" (AJ 34). Simultaneously, the banal everyday is filled with vague and ominous threats—"Corpse of Husband in Bed" (AJ 39) reported in the newspaper, the lost ropes needed to tie up the roses, the dismembered dead in a train wreck, the fear of death itself: "Who says that already the arm has been irrevocably raised to deliver that blow which tears one's hands away from everything?" (AJ 52–53). Although the story, drawing conventional conceptions of reality into question, never moves altogether into the realm of the fantastic or the surreal, it succeeds in undertaking nonetheless the epistemological experiment Wolf began to describe in "The Reader and the Writer," questioning the immutability of a physical and a social world exterior to human subjects. Readers, recalling Wolf's comments there on Newtonian "celestial mechanics" (as well as *Divided Heaven*), will apply them to the narrator's remark in "An Afternoon in June": "We became vaguely uncertain about the dependability of celestial landscapes" (AJ 37–38). Instead, in this vision, reality is often constituted through the creative use of language; the family engages in spontaneous play with words that brings into being that which has never existed before: "*Wurmgespenst und Mauseregen und Nachtloch und Pilzwurm und Lochglück und Nachtregen und Pilzmaus*" (Earthmare and mushhole and wormroom and nightmouse and mushworm and holemouse and housemare) (AJ 43).[9] But to their creativity is contrasted the attitude of their neighbor, the engineer, of whom the narrator remarks: "His thinking is generally determined by what exists in print" (AJ 41). The danger the engineer represents is his attractiveness for the thirteen-year-old daughter, who regards him as "modern," "confident." On this ordinary afternoon, two models for the future compete for the allegiance of the next GDR generation.

Such themes evidently continue into Wolf's next creative work, *The Quest for Christa T.* Critics have remarked on some similarities between Christa T. and Bachmann herself, or at least Bachmann as Wolf describes her.[10] Christa T. too formulates fantastic visions, longs to be useful, and laments "that I can only cope with things by writing!" (*CT* 34). For Christa T. also, "seeing" is a key term: "*Sehnsucht* comes from *sehen*, to see, and *Sucht* craving. This craving to see, and this was her discovery, accorded with actual things in a simple but irrefutable way" (*CT* 88). But the most striking concrete parallel between this work and Bachmann's can be found in the single extended narrative written by Christa T. in Wolf's novel, which bears the same title as Bachmann's longest prose work—"Malina." Assuming that even the deep affinities between these two writers could not have caused them to arrive independently at this same and unusual title for a prose work, I will risk here the assertion that Wolf meant the title as an acknowledgment of Bachmann's work and her influence on *The Quest for Christa T.*[11] Christa T.'s "Malina" presents puzzles similar to those of Bachmann's writings: an apparently realistic narrative whose purpose is unclear but which touches on the themes of National Socialism, a mother who encourages her young daughter to accede to the assertions of a dominant order, a journey over a border to a destination simultaneously foreign and not foreign (recalling Bachmann's metaphoric use of the both real and Wittgensteinian language *Grenze* from which she derived), and a text a female narrator fails for unknown reasons to conclude. "Now one ought to know why she stopped at this point" (*CT* 90), writes Wolf's narrator. But we can assume that Christa T.'s inability to continue, despite the vital importance of writing for her, is deeply connected to the larger dilemma of women (and particularly women writers) in this time, the dilemma that both this work and Bachmann's writing are devoted to exploring.

The complex eighth chapter of *Patterns of Childhood* then pursues explicitly the connection of the most important themes of Wolf's writing to Bachmann's work. In this novel again the somewhat unusual name, Jordan, had already revealed affinities between *Patterns of Childhood* and Bachmann's work. The family whom Wolf chooses to illustrate the functioning of "everyday fascism" shares its name with the central figures of "Das Gebell" ("The Barking") from *Simultan* (*Simultaneous*) and the novel *Der Fall Franza* (*The Franza Case*), published first in 1978 but from which Bachmann had given readings in the late sixties. Chapter 8, which, Wolf's narrator tells us, had long been intended to deal with the topic of war, becomes explicitly structured around references to Bachmann's work when the narrator learns through a radio broadcast on October 19, 1973, that Bachmann had died from burns. "With my burned hand I write about the nature of fire" (*PC* 163) is the epigraph from Bachmann that heads the chapter, and, like the "I" of *Malina*, the narrator broods over all-pervasive war; but war here is not just metaphorical, as it sometimes seems in Bachmann, but real—in Poland, Vietnam, the Middle East, and in Chile, where in 1973 Allende had just been murdered. The connections to Bachmann's female "Types of Death" are underlined also in the links the narrator establishes between Goebbels's declaration: "At last the Teutonic Empire of the German Nation has come into being" (*PC* 164), and young Nelly Jordan's mournful assertion to her mirror image: "Nobody loves me" (*PC* 165). "How can anyone be made to understand," the narrator asks of her character, "that these two completely unrelated sentences are, in your opinion, somehow connected?" (*PC* 165). In this dark chapter the despair that led Bachmann to her death is comprehensible, though staggering to the narrator:

The military junta in Chile has forbidden the use of the word "compañero." There is, then, no reason to doubt the effectiveness of words. Even when someone on whose serious relationship to words you have counted for a long time can no longer make any use of them, who lets go of herself and records these days with the sentence: With my burned hand I write about the nature of fire. Undine goes. Make with the hand—with the burned hand—the sign for finality. Go, Death, and stand still, Time. A solitude into which no one follows me. It is necessary, with the echo still in the mouth, to go on and to keep silent.

Be prepared? For what, then? And not overcome by sadness? Explain nothing to me. I saw the salamander go through every fire. No fear threatens him, and he is pained by nothing.[12]

But the temperamental and/or historical differences between Wolf's narrator and Bachmann reassert themselves: "To regain oneself after a brief stumble, caused by the increased burden on one's shoulders. It is necessary to talk."[13] Bachmann's 1953 script for a radio broadcast on Wittgenstein, "Sagbares und Unsagbares" (The Speakable and the Unspeakable) very early had maintained that it was altogether impossible to speak about that which was most important. For Wolf, however, this position is not at all sufficient, and her narrator responds to Bachmann's death by maintaining: "One must eventually break the silence about difficult things" (*PC* 178). And this narrator also recognizes the small concrete utopias of everyday life, as Bachmann sometimes recognized, too; consider, for example, the Bachmann citation with which this dark chapter ends: "The most beautiful thing under the sun is being under the sun" (*PC* 197).

Wolf's writing since *Patterns of Childhood* can be regarded as centrally concerned with the dilemma posed by Bachmann's death: whether the (woman) writer can have faith enough in the hope of remedying the evils she details, of realizing the visions she projects, to preserve her from despair. In Chapter 8 of *Patterns of Childhood*, Nelly's mother had already been described as the figure with whom Wolf's more recent work is concerned, the prophet whose words are not heeded: "Always expecting the worst. Cassandra, behind the counter in her store; Cassandra aligning loaves of bread; Cassandra weighing potatoes" (*PC* 165). For instance, in an interview published in 1982, Wolf explained that this problem informed *No Place on Earth*—written after Biermann's expulsion from the GDR:

I wrote *No Place on Earth* in 1977. That was a time when I found myself obliged to examine the preconditions for failure, the connection between social desperation and failure in literature. At the time, I was living with the intense feeling of standing with my back to the wall, unable to take a proper step. I had to get beyond a certain time when there seemed to be absolutely no possibility left for effective action. (CI 89)

In "The Shadow of a Dream," the foreword to her edition of Karoline von Günderrode's writing, Wolf uses Bachmann's term to describe the generation of young Romantics to whom history offered no hope: "Deutsche Lebensläufe. Deutsche Todesarten" (German life spans. German death types) (SD 231). The metaphor of the injured hand also threads its way through the story of Günderrode's ill-fated love for a married man not her equal. But Wolf's clearest response to the dilemmas posed by Bachmann's life and death is found in her "Büchner-Prize Acceptance Speech," which circles the issues posed in Bachmann's last published poem, "Keine Delikatessen" ("No Delicacies"). In that poem, published in the 1968 issue of *Kursbuch* that proclaimed the death of literature, Bachmann declared her unwillingness henceforth to seek beautiful words to adorn her writing at this time of grave social crisis. In yet more dire times, Wolf also expresses great doubts about the efficacy of writing, in which she continues to believe nonetheless. Bachmann's writing, even in its despair, gives precise expression to the extremity of a state of consciousness that we would not have known so well without her description of it, showing us more clearly what conditions unworthy of human beings we need to combat. In this time, Wolf explains, "all, nearly all products of our age must bear within them, or at least within their invented opposites, the seed of self-destruction. Art cannot transcend itself as art, literature not as literature" (BP 10). Bachmann had concluded "Keine Delikatessen" by renouncing her vocation: "As for my part, let it vanish" (BP 9). In the "Büchner-Prize Acceptance Speech," Wolf will not accept that resignation: "One who expresses herself completely does not cancel herself out: the wish for obliteration remains as a witness. Her part will not vanish" (BP 10). In the 1982 interview Wolf, herself unresigned, seemed also to promise that she would not choose Bachmann's way out: "But many readers also see that by probing deeper and deeper into the wounds of our times, which are also my wounds, I don't intend to give up" (CI 96).

It remains still to be asked what these wounds of our times are that occasion responses so dark from these writers and in what senses they, women writers in central Europe in the last third of the twentieth century, arrived at a corresponding understanding of themselves and their culture. Now, looking back on Bachmann's writing, we can see that she sought from the beginning, in her prose writing at least, to understand the causes for the troubles of her time. Although her explanations seem now too vague, too imprecise, or too restricted to the realm of ideas, those defects may derive from Bachmann's lack then of an appropriate theoretical vocabulary or framework—a lack that theory writing of the last twenty years, including that of feminism, has helped to address. Elsewhere I have argued that it is possible to observe in Bachmann's essays insights into the structures of Western thought akin to those of contemporary French poststructuralism:[14] she discerns both the limitations of Western discourse and the connections between Western thought and Western history. In her essay on Wittgenstein, for instance, Bachmann emphasizes that Western thought is unable to speak, to formulate meaningful propositions, about precisely what is most important to human beings, which nonetheless is available to us as *"das Mystische"* (the mystical), about which nothing can be said. This "negative" dimension of Wittgenstein's philosophy, as she terms it, interests Bachmann most and makes Wittgenstein represent for her the insoluble dilemmas at which Western thought, indeed Western culture altogether, has arrived. "These efforts may permit us to call Wittgenstein *the* great representative thinker of our time, since in him are expressed the two extreme tendencies of the intellectual trends of the West. He occupies the pinnacle of scientific thought of the age—that thought which accompanies and precedes the development of technology and the natural sciences; and yet it is precisely he who reminds us of the Nestroy quotation: 'The altogether unique aspect of progress is that it appears to be much greater than it really is.'"[15] An Austrian writer in the late twentieth century, Bachmann obviously understood the danger of challenges posed to reason, particularly within a German context. But simultaneously she insisted on the necessity of questioning a destructive form of reason that could not transcend the limitations of scientism and positivism. Moreover, even Bachmann's early essays indicate her clear awareness that the problems she was addressing were not merely those of the realm of thought but were, on the contrary, expressions in thought of the real cul-de-sac at which our culture seemed to have arrived. Her radio essay on Simone Weil pursues the deep connection in Weil's work between structures of Western thought and the misery of the proletariat—a misery against which a Marxism that fails to repudiate its roots in the Western philosophies from which it derives is also powerless. In Bachmann's essays on Musil she also stresses that *The Man Without Qualities* addresses the same cultural problematic, showing, as Bachmann herself also wants to maintain, that its logical outcome is war: "It is not the Kakanian situation alone that has shown that the thought-processes of rigid ideologies lead directly to war."[16]

Read from this perspective, Bachmann's creative writing and particularly her prose reveal themselves as concerned from the beginning, if sometimes somewhat obliquely, with the destructiveness at the heart of our culture, flawed at its fundament. "The Thirtieth Year" attempts a far-reaching critique of all hitherto existing cultural structures: "The rejection of every traditional view and every traditional condition, of states, churches, organizations, tools of power, money, weapons, education. The great strike, the momentary pause of the old world. The cessation of labor and of thinking for this old world. The rejection of history, not for the sake of anarchy, but for the sake of a new start."[17] "Ein Wildermuth" ("A Wildermuth"), recalling Wittgenstein's *Tractatus* and Hofmannsthal's "A Letter,"[18] deals with the impossibility of talking about a truth that is more than facts. As Wolf had recognized, the last story of the collection makes Bachmann's point with the greatest clarity and finality: Undine goes, repudiating the monstrous male world, that is incapable, for all its achievements, of grasping human happiness. As Bernd Witte has perceptively observed, Bachmann's writing from the mid-sixties onward pursues the insights first expressed in "Undine goes": "Ingeborg Bachmann hints already in this anti-fairy tale at the central motif of her later prose works by attempting to combine in thought the catastrophic course of world history and her own self-alienation as a woman. She locates their common cause—she blames the thoughts and actions of men."[19]

In those late works Bachmann shows us her "death types" directly: women mentally or physically destroyed, often themselves unaware of how their own condition is connected to a social order that makes a happy and autonomous female subjectivity impossible. In *Malina*, the female "I" disappears into a crack in the wall, leaving her male alter ego to tell her story. "It was murder," says the narrator.[20] In "Gier" (Greed) the central female figure is literally murdered by her husband; in *Requiem für Fanny Goldmann* (Requiem for Fanny Goldmann) Fanny dies mysteriously after a man betrays her, and the women in the stories of *Simultan* suffer all manner of psychic and physical distress. Bachmann's argument is made most decisively and completely in the unfinished novel *Der Fall Franza*: here the causes for Franza's madness are linked explicitly to both National Socialism and European imperialism; they aim to extend their totalitarian grasp over the entire world, colonizing minds they cannot control through physical violence. Like the other *Todesarten* women, Franza is destroyed, but this time she recognizes she is a victim of the white culture to which she belongs, and she dies resisting, cursing the whites: "The whites be damned."[21] Given these far-reaching and devastating recognitions, then, it must be no surprise that there is no way out for Bachmann's characters. If white history culminates in fascism and imperialism, in murder and destruction, then how can a white woman, excluded from that history but part of no other, find another place to stand? By the time of her death, Bachmann was thus left with an increasingly more radical and more clearly formulated analysis of the major failures of our culture—a critique so far-reaching that only that culture's abolition could have seemed adequate response to the abuses she detailed. But virtually nowhere in Bachmann's work do we find expressed even the hope for her culture's transformation, scarcely even the hope that that to which she gives expression will be understood.

Wolf's *Frankfurt Lectures on Poetics* make it possible to maintain that the position toward which her writing of the seventies moved increasingly resembles Bachmann's both in the radicality of her cultural analysis and to some degree in its pessimism as well. As early as the stories in *Unter den Linden*, published in 1973, the critique of scientific positivism and instrumental rationality, to which GDR functionaries were only too clearly also not immune, became a central theme of Wolf's work. However, although Wolf reveals the deep-reaching consequences of technocratic thought, a reading of her stories generous to the GDR might still understand them as attacking social *abuses* there, not the fundamental orientation of her country or even of Marxism altogether.[22] But in Wolf's essays on the Romantics, written after the expulsion of Biermann as a thinly-veiled examination of conditions in her own country, the varieties of ways in which she takes issue even with Marxism are scarcely concealed; Marxism continues rather than breaks with structures of thought and action that had led civilization to its present pass. In the letters of Bettina Brentano and Karoline von Günderrode Wolf finds, for instance, an alternative to the instrumental reason about to conquer all of Europe, triumphant, Wolf clearly believes, to this day: "An alternative, yes. Thought out and offered in a time when the switches had just been irrevocably set on the exploitation of nature, on the reversal of means and ends, and on the suppression of every 'female' element in the new civilization" (BL 314). Contrasting Bettina's sympathy with and tenderness toward nature with Faust's attempt to subdue the Earth Spirit, Wolf shows herself willing to reverse an entire orthodox Marxist tradition of the appropriation of the cultural heritage (*Erbeaneignung*) within which Faust, unbounded in his energy and ambition, is a paradigmatic figure, a culture hero:

> What a different scene! Not the challenge to the death, not the unconditional subjugation of nature; not the hubris of the "Faustian" human who only gains knowledge by taking nature to the den of torture and forcing her to false confessions by the use of screws and levers. A different kind of progress. A different sort of magic from the satanic being to whom Faust commits himself and who, when Faust has become a stranger to himself, brings about his destruction. (BL 314–315)[23]

Wolf obstinately rejects a model she also identifies as male, and Bettina joins Undine in the female opposition: "God the Father created Mephisto in order to prod man to schismatic creation. What a different adversary from that of Mother Nature, with her army of witches, nymphs, and spirits—a force now suppressed, cursed, taboo, but whose ranks Bettina, as a late successor, joins with a pounding heart" (BL 315). Wolf's "Büchner-Prize Acceptance Speech" only makes completely explicit and pursues to its final, most contemporary consequence what had been clear already in these essays: committed in East and West to its destructive course, a culture based on principles that alienate human beings from nature, each other, and themselves, now stands poised to destroy itself altogether.

What is not, however, so clear in the essays on the Romantics is the exact object of Wolf's attack; there it might still be possible to regard that attack as limited to residues of bourgeois thought—the Romantics, after all, produced their counterproposals at the moment when bourgeois industriousness and utilitarianism triumphed. Yet even in these essays there are indications that Wolf's analysis of the flaws of Western civilization might reach as far as Bachmann's imprecations against "the whites." In "The Shadow of a Dream," for instance, Wolf praises Bettina and Karoline for their discovery of models other than those of classical Greece, other than those of Europe:

> Forces that were born from the mother's "womb" and not, like Pallas Athena, from the father's mind, that is, the head of Zeus—an alternative to the origins of classicism, a leaning toward archaic, partially matriarchal models. Myth is read anew, and added to that myth which has thus far been singularly dominant are prehistory and the teaching of India, Asia, the Orient. Eurocentrism has been pierced through, and with that the total domination of consciousness." (SD 258)

With the "Büchner-Prize Acceptance Speech" Wolf aligns herself more clearly with the analysis of Horkheimer and Adorno's *Dialectic of the Enlightenment*, tracing the destructive tendencies of the present back to the Greek beginnings of Western culture; and Wolf's recently published narrative, *Cassandra*, reveals in its fullness, often with virtually explicit allusions to Bachmann, the extent of her critique. Here Wolf returns to the roots of our culture to tell of its origins from the perspective of a woman who, like the figures of *Todesarten*, is simultaneously inside and outside that culture, destroyed because of her complicity in it. Surely, as in *The Franza Case*, one must understand the real events of this story to be internal to the female psyche, an illustration, perhaps, of Freud's remark that Greek culture, that is, the Oedipus complex, stood in the way of the analytic discovery of an earlier layer of civilization, the Minoan-Mycenean preoedipal phase so crucial for femininity.[24] For Cassandra, a "seer," as for Bachmann, seeing is primary, and her own insights deepen as the narrative progresses, but, like Bachmann, she is fated not to be understood. Indeed, Cassandra laments "that they did not even understand the questions to which I was seeking an answer" (C 48), and she will perish as a consequence of what she recognizes—"to give birth to what slays me," as Karoline von Günderrode had written. Cassandra, also, writing with her burned hand: "I was noted for my endurance of pain. For my ability to hold my hand over the flame longer than anyone else" (C 31).

What does Cassandra see, and how does that correspond to Bachmann's visions? Wolf has explained the new position at which she has arrived and explicitly acknowledged her indebtedness to Bachmann in her Frankfurt Lectures, held in May and June 1982 at the University of Frankfurt and entitled *Conditions of a Narrative: Cassandra*. Her lectures begin by explaining, with some irony, why she herself has no poetics of her own, a new poetics according to her *Classical Antiquity Lexicon* coming into being via an oedipal struggle with one's fatherly precursors: "'Poetics' (the definition reads): theory of the art of poetry, which at an advanced stage—Aristotle, Horace—takes on a systematic form, and whose norms have been accorded 'wide validity' in numerous countries since the age of humanism. New aesthetic positions are reached (the book says) via confrontation with these norms (in parentheses, Brecht)" (*C* 141). From that warlike patriarchal lineage that ends with Brecht, from that entire literary-theoretical tradition, Wolf here distances herself altogether: "I have never felt the raging desire for confrontation with the poetics, or the model, of a great writer (in parentheses, Brecht). This has only struck me in the last couple of years, and so it may be that, incidentally, these essays will also treat a question that I have not been asked: the question of why I do *not* have a poetics" (*C* 141). Advancing another model, "a fabric [that] . . . is an aesthetic structure, and . . . would lie at the center of my poetics *if* I had one" (*C* 142), Wolf attempts in the lectures to explicate the complicated and subjective process whereby she arrived at the Cassandra narrative. Her first and second lectures deal with her trip to Greece; her third, a "Work Diary," records "the vise grip between life and subject matter" (*C* 142). The fourth lecture explores, with explicit and detailed reference to Bachmann, the "historical reality of the Cassandra figure" and the "conditions for the woman writer past and present" (*C* 142). The fifth lecture is *Cassandra* itself.

In the fourth lecture Wolf declares that the discoveries she has made in writing *Cassandra*, the epistemological changes forced upon her, still difficult even to describe, are comparable only to the transformation of her vision to which her discovery of Marx had compelled her thirty years before:

> With the widening of my visual angle and the readjustment to my depth of focus, my viewing lens (through which I perceive our time, all of us, you, myself) has undergone a decisive change. It is comparable to that decisive change that occurred more than thirty years ago, when I first became acquainted with Marxist theory and attitudes; a liberating and illuminating experience which altered my thinking, my view, what I felt about and demanded of myself. When I try to realize what is happening, what *has* happened, I find that (to bring it down to the lowest common denominator) there has been an expansion of what for me is "real." Moreover, the nature, the inner structure, the movement of this reality has also changed and continues to change almost daily. It is indescribable; my professional interest is wide-awake and aims precisely at description, but it must hold back, withdraw, and it has had to learn to want and to bring about its own defeat. (*C* 278)

The title of this lecture draws our attention to those epistemological concerns that had already served as the basis of Wolf's original essay on Bachmann: "A Letter, About Unequivocal and Ambiguous Meaning, Definiteness and Indefiniteness; About Ancient Conditions and New View-Scopes; About Objectivity" (*C* 272). And the essay's epigraph comes from Bachmann's *The Franza Case*: "For the facts that make up the world need the non-factual as a vantage point from which to be perceived" (*C* 272)—the same sort of vision, that is, that Wolf had detected in Bachmann's early prose.

And indeed, insights learned from Bachmann, the epistemological changes forced upon her by her reading of Bachmann, form the structuring principle of this lecture. As Wolf began to think about Cassandra, she explains, as she began to pose herself the question: "Who was Cassandra before anyone wrote about her?" (C 273), she began also to meditate upon the meaning of the Bachmann poem she had also cited in the eighth chapter of *Patterns of Childhood*, "Erklär mir, Liebe" ("Enlighten me, love").[25] Wolf devotes several pages of the essay to explicating the poem, stressing the concern of the poem's speaker with her status as thinker, which might preclude her from love. Says Wolf, "'Must someone think' may perhaps mean: must a man—or a woman—think like *that*? So—exclusively? In a way that excludes love, and what is lovely" (C 274). But the poem simultaneously offers another model of thought and feeling: "Reflecting on this, regretting it, even lamenting it, the poem itself gives an example of the most precise indefiniteness, the clearest ambiguity. Things are this way and no other way, it says; and at the same time (this cannot be thought logically) things are that way, a different way. You are I, I am he, it cannot be explained. The grammar of manifold simultaneous relations" (C 276).

Wolf had begun this lecture/letter by telling her friend A., the addressee of the letter, about the "mountain of books" she had taken to the country with her, listing almost half a page of works of mostly feminist scholarship from Europe and the United States. From feminism, from Euroamerican women's conscious refusal to accede to the structures of men's reality, she begins to derive her explanation of that new model, as she had often hinted in earlier works and stated clearly in her third essay:

> To what extent is there really such a thing as "women's writing"? To the extent that women, for historical and biological reasons, experience a different reality than men. Experience reality differently than men and express it. . . . To the extent that they stop wearing themselves out in trying to integrate themselves into the prevailing delusional systems. (C 259)

In the fourth essay Wolf pursues women's status in classical works, especially in Aristotle and Goethe, tracing women's loss of the authority they had possessed in European prehistory and linking it to the triumph of a mode of thought that was to culminate in the technological nightmare of the present. "To put it in simplified terms," Wolf tells us, "this one-track-minded route is the one that has been followed by Western thought: the route of segregation, of the renunciation of the manifoldness of phenomena, in favor of dualism and monism, in favor of closed systems and pictures of the world; of the renunciation of subjectivity in favor of a sealed 'objectivity'" (C 287). But thinking men still need women to preserve them from the limitations of their own rarified thought: "They need cunning little devices to avoid dying of the cold. One of these devices is to develop women as a power resource. In other words, to fit them into their patterns of life and thought. To put it more simply, to exploit them" (C 294). Leaping unabashedly 2500 years to show in what that thinking culminates, Wolf quotes a few sentences of dialogue from Marie-Luise Fleisser's "Tiefseefisch" (Deep Sea Fish). The setting is Berlin in the twenties; the speakers are Wollank, a former bicycle racer, and Tütü, head of a literary clique, obviously modeled on B.B.—Brecht. Wollank maintains, "These women are dreadful, the way they swarm around you and each one dies to perform a different service." But Tütü asserts in reply, "I don't see why I shouldn't take what I can get. I have turned it into a system. Everything that is able to stimulate me is brought to me without my having to lift a finger." "My energies," he continues, "are freed for what is essential" (C 295). How, asks Wolf, can *this* be an aesthetic that women writers could use to free us from the West's destructive thinking?

And the woman who starts to speak in her own voice, to say "I," faces enormous obstacles. "I claim," Wolf asserts, "that every woman in this century and in our cultural sphere who has ventured into male-dominated institutions—'literature' and 'aesthetics' are such institutions—must have experienced the desire for self-destruction" (C 299). Her example is the unnamed female "I" of Bachmann's *Malina*. Bachmann, Wolf maintains, had succeeded in naming what had happened to women in the course of the development of Western civilization, their "death types," and had also consciously chosen another aesthetic from that of "Goethe, Stendhal, Tolstoy, Fontane, Proust, and Joyce" (C 300) to do so. But Bachmann found also that her experience as a woman scarcely allowed itself to be pressed into form at all:

> Whichever direction you look, whichever page you open the book to, you see the cave-in of the alternatives which until now have held together and torn apart our world, as well as the theory of the beautiful and of art. A new kind of tension seems to be struggling for expression, in horror and fear and tottering consternation. There is not even the consolation that this is still capable of being given form; not in the traditional sense. (C 301)

What is the "this" of this sentence? Wolf asks, and she looks for an answer in *The Franza Case*, where Franza's brother asks a similar question: "What could have destroyed her in this way?" (C 302). Concluding her lecture, Wolf offers a reading of that unfinished novel, quoting passage upon passage to underline her own argument that women, like Franza, have been colonized by a culture culminating in National Socialism that destroys them and itself. Franza dies cursing the whites; Wolf's final words in this lecture come from *The Franza Case*, and they are, she says, what Cassandra would say today,

> mocked, of course, not heard, declared abnormal, ejected, turned over to Death. She says:

*The whites are coming. The whites are landing. And if they are re-
pulsed again, they will return again once more. No revolution and no
resolution and no foreign currency statute will help; they will come in
spirit if they can no longer come in any other way. And they will be
resurrected in a brown and a black brain, it will still always be the
whites, even then. They will continue to own the world in this rounda-
bout way.* (C 305)

The Cassandra metaphor is almost as bleak as those of Bachmann's novels, and one stands sobered and aghast before so devastating
an assessment of our contemporary condition. In the third lecture Wolf
had asked herself, "How can you teach younger people the technique of
living without alternatives, and yet living?" (C 251). In the Cassandra
image Wolf gives with one hand the possibility of Euroamerican wom-
en's providing that alternative, only to take that hope back with the
other hand—like Bachmann in that respect, whose late works offer almost only "types of death." It might be, of course, as a male East German writer, Heiner Müller, suggested in a recent interview, that there
is no answer for Euroamericans because the proletariat on whom Marx
and Brecht counted can no longer be relied upon to redeem the system
that created it.[26] If one has really grasped what Bachmann and Wolf
have said in its materiality and historicity, it is hard not to come as
close to despair as they. Quotations from Wolf, however, spring to
mind. In *No Place on Earth* she had written, "If we cease to hope, then
that which we fear will surely come" (NP 117). Or her words on Bachmann in the "Büchner-Prize Acceptance Speech": in describing clearly
the historical dilemma at which we have arrived, in advancing, at least
as vision, an alternative, these women writers may, we can hope, help
to forestall the worst. Or perhaps they may not. Wolf's third lecture began with that fear: "The literature of the West (I read) is the white
man's reflection on himself. So should it be supplemented by the white
woman's reflection on herself? And nothing more?" (C 225).

To these depressing notes let me add, however, a coda, drawing
on a recent essay on Brecht and Bachmann by Gerhard Wolf, Christa
Wolf's husband. Käthe Reichel, one of Brecht's female collaborators,
had preserved a copy of *Die gestundete Zeit* ([The] Marked Time), Bachmann's first poetry volume, that she had brought from West Germany
to give to Brecht. (One recalls the comment in Fleisser's dialogue:
"Everything that can excite me is brought to me.") Reading the volume
"an einem kleinen Nachmittag" (on a short afternoon)—the title of Gerhard Wolf's essay—Brecht had undertaken to make corrections in
Bachmann's poems, so that they became linear, pointed, didactic, political, like his. A "we"—Gerhard Wolf fails to specify to whom, apart
from himself, that pronoun refers—travels to visit Reichel and record
her impressions of that arrogant Brechtian undertaking, so illustrative
of his aesthetic, political, and human failings. But Reichel's judgment
of Brecht is more differentiated. His commitment to those ordering
principles was, she maintains, also a way of managing his own pain at

the world he saw around him, a poetry written with tightly pressed lips. Bachmann's advantage as a woman, though it brought her greater pain, was to pursue that suffering to its depths, with open mouth. In this she joins another lineage, another tradition: "It will be written on a new page that here speaks a woman whom one regards today in a line of tradition: Else Lasker-Schüler—Nelly Sachs—Bachmann—Sarah Kirsch—the open mouth!"[27] Into which sisterhood, Christa Wolf, though not a poet, may also be admitted, to write upon that new, unwritten page.

Notes

1. Most notably Klemens Renolder, "Im ungeistigen Raum unserer traurigen Länder: Zu Utopie und Geschichte bei Christa Wolf und Ingeborg Bachmann," in *Der dunkle Schatten, dem ich schon seit Anfang folge: Ingeborg Bachmann— Vorschläge zu einer neuen Lektüre des Werks*, ed. Hans Höller (Vienna: Löcker Verlag, 1982), 185–198.

2. [While we use the title as rendered by Joan Becker in her translation of Wolf's essays (*The Reader and the Writer*), we wish to remind the reader that "man" is used generically here and elsewhere—that, indeed, Wolf uses the all-encompassing *Menschen* to refer to "people" or "human beings."—Ed.]

3. Cf. Arendt, *Eichmann in Jerusalem* (New York: Viking, 1963).

4. In Ingeborg Bachmann, *Werke*, ed. Christine Koschel, Inge von Weiden-baum, and Clemens Mönster (Munich: R. Piper, 1978), 4, 426, the following information is given about this edition: "*Undine geht*. Stories. Afterword by Christa Wolf. 148 pp. (after 2nd edition 239 pp.) Phillip Reclam jun., Leipzig (=Reclams Universal-Bibliothek Nr. 530). 1st edition 1973, 2nd, expanded edition 1976, 3rd edition 1978." The only copy in this country seems to be in the Library of Congress, and as yet I have not been able to consult it.

5. Translation altered by editor.

6. Translation altered by editor.

7. Translation altered by editor.

8. See Andreas Huyssen, "Traces of Ernst Bloch: Reflections on Christa Wolf," in this volume.

9. [The word game described in the story cannot, of course, be rendered in any way literally. The parenthetical English is included to give some idea of how the "game" is played.—Ed.]

10. See Alexander Stephan, *Christa Wolf* (Munich: Beck, and edition text + kritik, 1976), 122.

11. Obviously I am expressing myself so cautiously because the publication dates of the two novels make my assertion somewhat problematic. Bachmann's novel was not of course published until 1971, while *The Quest for Christa T.* appeared in 1968. However, Bachmann's plans for the *Todesarten* cycle date from 1963; her work on the novel *Malina* began in 1967, if not earlier, and she repeatedly made her intentions for the Malina figure clear in her interviews. The editors of her works tell us: "The 'Sketches for the Character Malina,' which appear in the appendix, hint at Bachmann's intention, voiced repeatedly in interviews, to have Malina function as the superior character in all books of the novel-cycle which narrates the different types of death." (*Werke*, 3, 558). Of course, it could conceivably be the case that Bachmann found the name in *Christa T.* or even that the two authors arrived at the name "Malina" independently.

12. *Kindheitsmuster* (Berlin/DDR: Aufbau, 1976), 233–234. Passage omitted from English translation.

13. *Kindheitsmuster*, 234. Passage omitted from English translation.

14. See Sara Lennox, "In the Cemetery of the Murdered Daughters: Ingeborg Bachmann's *Malina*," *STCL* 1 (Fall 1980): 75–105.

15. Bachmann, *Werke*, 4, 116–117.

16. Bachmann, *Werke*, 4, 27. [Musil coined the term "Kakania" to refer to the Austro-Hungarian empire on the eve of World War I. —Ed.]

17. Bachmann, *Werke*, 2, 131–132.

18. [The reference is to Wittgenstein's *Tractatus logico-philosophicus. Logisch-philosophische Abhandlung* (1921) and Hugo von Hofmannsthal's "Ein Brief" (1902).—Ed.]

19. Bernd Witte, "Ingeborg Bachmann," in *Neue Literatur der Frauen: Deutschsprachige Autorinnen der Gegenwart*, ed. Heinz Puknus (Munich: Beck, 1980), 37.

20. Bachmann, *Werke*, 3, 337.

21. Bachmann, *Werke*, 3, 469.

22. In his essay in this volume, for instance, the GDR scholar Hans-Georg Werner suggests that the protagonist of "Unter den Linden" immerses herself in the fountain in front of the municipal library in imitation of Bachmann's Undine. But because her historical circumstances are different, Wolf's figure, unlike Undine, is willing and able to reemerge: "In contrast to the writer surrounded by the 'Bastille walls' of capitalist reality, Christa Wolf recognizes that it is possible, in her country, to achieve the conditions that should exist." I am grateful to Katharina von Ankum for drawing my attention to Werner's essay.

23. When Wolf's essay was published in *Sinn und Form*, it was this assertion to which the editor of the journal, Wilhelm Girnus, objected in a note (unusual for *Sinn und Form*) at the end of the volume: "Christa Wolf's assertion that Faust (she apparently means Goethe's figure) was destroyed is untenable. It contradicts Goethe's presentation." After citing textual evidence to show that Goethe had not intended Faust to perish, Girnus concludes with a remarkable celebration of the Faustian impulse that Wolf had condemned: "Precisely this radical reversal of the old Faust legend into its opposite, into the ultimate victory of Faust in his wager with the devil, is Goethe's greatest literary act—not only in the context of his own works, but for all German literature, indeed, for world literature" (*SuF* 32, no. 2 [1980]: 498–499).

24. Sigmund Freud, "Female Sexuality" (1931), *Standard Edition of the Complete Psychological Works of Sigmund Freud*, ed. James Strachey (London: The Hogarth Press and the Institute of Psycho-Analysis, 1964), 21, 226.

25. See Francis Golffing's recent translation of this poem in *Translation* 10 (Spring 1983): 45–46.

26. Heiner Müller, "The Walls of History," *Semiotexte* 4, no. 2 (1982): 38–76.

27. Gerhard Wolf, "An einem kleinen Nachmittag: Brecht liest Bachmann," in Höller, *Der dunkle Schatten*, 180.

Female Subjectivity as an Impulse for Renewal in Literature

Karin McPherson

By the beginning of the 1970s at the latest, Christa Wolf was discussing her methods and intentions as a prose writer in public with critics and reviewers. The most important document in this discussion is her 1973 "Conversation" with Hans Kaufmann, "Subjective Authenticity," which first appeared in 1974. In addition to this relatively polemical document, it is useful to examine the more personal interview with Joachim Walther of 1972, which was printed in 1973, and also the self-critical essay, "Über Sinn und Unsinn von Naivität" (On the Sense and Senselessness of Naiveté), written on commission in 1973.[1] The common factor in these three documents is that Christa Wolf openly acknowledges the individuality of her prose based on her particular concept of experience. At the same time she clearly distinguishes between the cultural-political norms of a dogmatic socialist-realist conception of literature and her own work.

Proceeding from the demands made on the writer by modern prose, as she outlines them in the essay "The Reader and the Writer" of 1968, Christa Wolf develops her concept of "inner" or "subjective authenticity"[2] and makes it her concern to discuss the large questions of humanity and reality, of thinking and acting. She uses the concept of "subjective authenticity" only "provisionally" (SA). Since then the term has been applied widely to literary tendencies in the GDR in the 1970s, without its origins always being appropriately acknowledged. For Wolf it is the result of an unconditional demand for truth in dealing with one's own experiences. That requires a new relationship to reality: instead of trying to create an objective reproduction of facts in which the subjective element is submerged and which, at its most negative, becomes a mere reflection of reality, Wolf includes the subjective element, which involves the thinking, judgment, and experience of the individual in the writing process. From this position she rejects the idea that she, as the author, is sheltering behind her "material," her "theme," her "subject," or her "work" to make out of it "something they can play around with at will (and of thus treating readers as objects too)" (SA). Against this stance she sets the interaction of work and author in a process that "accompanies" life itself.

In her poetic confession there lies a departure from the concept of genius and art as established in classical literature, an anticipation of Christa Wolf's attempt to come to terms with Classicism in her "Letter about Bettina," as will be shown. With her insight into the connection between living and writing, Wolf distances herself from the model of her otherwise respected teacher Anna Seghers, already a "classic" of GDR literature, who was an important influence in Christa Wolf's early development as a writer. Wolf here questions Seghers's concept that "what has become narratable is already mastered" (SA). There is also a tacit reaction contained in this against the great representative of Classicism, Goethe, who described his works as "fragments of a great confession."[3] For Christa Wolf, by contrast, writing now becomes an actual confrontation with the problems of life, out of which there develops for her (following in Büchner's footsteps) a new concept of prose and the prose writer:

> I had found that story-writers—or perhaps I should say prose writers —can be compelled to abandon the strict sequence of first living through something, then digesting and 'mastering' it and, lastly, writing about it. In order to achieve the inner authenticity for which they are striving, they can be forced to express the living and thinking processes they are embroiled in directly in their work process, in an almost unmitigated way (though form always does tone things down, that is one of its functions). They can be forced to drop all artificial categories, empty moulds into which, almost always with the unconscious help of the author, the raw material pours with alarming inevitability. (SA)

How Wolf gradually overcame a somewhat dogmatic conception of literature between the 1950s and 1960s has been amply demonstrated, especially by Western critics.[4] In her essay "On the Sense and Senselessness of Naiveté," she herself assumes a critical position in regard to her earliest works.

Christa Wolf ascribes considerable importance to the question of the development in the relationship of the sexes on the basis of newly-won equal rights. She defends most zealously this aspect of her humanistic concept against Kaufmann's reproach of an all-too-introspective perspective.[5] Proceeding from the utopian narrative "Self-Experiment," which had appeared a year earlier in *Sinn und Form* and which, like "Unter den Linden" and "New Life and Opinions of a Tomcat," explores new possibilities of expression not only thematically, but also formally —as dream, grotesque, and utopia—she presents here the tension between conduct based on purely scientific principles and that determined by moral criteria.

In "Self-Experiment" the science-fictional transformation of the woman into a man is used to reveal the failure of the human relationship between man and woman. The prevailing perspective is that of the woman, who as narrator is also simultaneously object of the research and researcher. In her function as researcher she provides the proof that the pure imitation of male existence robs the woman of those significant qualities on which her "happiness" depends: language and feelings. As the research object she fulfills the scientist's expectations: the transformation is biologically a complete success. In her scientific stance as well she meets the standards set by the male. But she can offer only disappointment to her fellow females: those women for whom equality has brought a conflict between profession and family and from which they promise themselves a liberation as they become the same as men: as "man" she lacks the language to communicate her experiences. Only when she voluntarily reverts to her womanhood does she find self-fulfillment; not, at first, in love but rather in the regained spontaneous relationship to language and to feelings. A vision at the end implies the resolution of the conflict in Wolf's terms: the self-realization of the woman in her individual state of being different from the man and, correspondingly, that of the man in his different state, is the "utopian" element of the story.

In the "Conversation" Wolf makes it clear that she regards the "liberation of woman" in her society to be stuck in the initial stages, at a preliminary level (of equal rights as equal roles). For her part, she insists that "we need . . . new radical ways of posing questions that can advance us further" (SA). Questions of this nature are asked tentatively in "Self-Experiment" and expressed more categorically in the "Conversation": "should the aim of women's emancipation be for them to 'become like men'?; would it even be desirable if they could do the same things, enjoy the same rights, so that men themselves would soon badly need emancipating?" (SA).

The great thematic issue underlying the prose narrative "Self-Experiment," and indeed the development of her prose concept as a whole at least since *The Quest for Christa T.*, is emphatically stated by Wolf in the "Conversation": "It's simply a matter of overcoming alienation, no more, no less" (SA).

She responds to Kaufmann's critical objection that her restriction to the inner, subjective inclinations of human behavior leads to a one-sided presentation of "the problem of humanism . . . , i.e., that it is viewed only theoretically, as a matter of thinking and feeling," and to his point that "the establishment of humanism is . . . a matter primarily

151

. . . of practical, material social activity" (SA), by insisting that feeling, thinking, and acting for the whole human being may no longer contradict or be separated from each other. For her, this is the only way to safeguard the continuation of the "moral" and the "physical" existence of mankind. On this issue she concurs with Bobrowski, who asked Schiller's question anew: "How must this world be constituted for a moral human being?" This appears to her as the basis for a future-oriented social development because "it urges that the world be adapted to a morality of human dignity, not that human morality be adapted to a world that still abuses human dignity" (SA). (Later, in her essay on Günderrode, Wolf sees in this question the key to the relationship between the young Hölderlin and Günderrode: "They place the question of all questions at the beginning [Johannes Bobrowski will take it up, since it has remained unanswered]" [SD 240].)

In the period from 1975 to 1978, between the completion of *Patterns of Childhood* and the appearance of the essay on Karoline von Günderrode, Wolf's most important work is the essay "In Touch" of 1977. This is her interpretation of nineteen reports by women in the GDR, protocols that had been gathered and published in book form as *Guten Morgen, Du Schöne* (Good Morning, Thou Pretty One) by Maxie Wander,[6] who died before Wolf wrote her essay. Christa Wolf sees the greatest contribution of these reports from women of all ages and from all walks of life in the fact that the historical development of equal rights has given women a new self-awareness and, with it, the ability to articulate their own demands on life. Historically viewed, the tragedy in the fate of all women lies for Wolf in the fact that they have been, "for a long time . . . virtually speechless" and, regardless of their class, "robbed of adult status [entmündigt]" (IT 164).

Wolf reports of the author Maxie Wander that she searched "for a long time, restlessly, for her language, her means of expression." The book allows Wolf to recognize "her talent was establishing open friendly relations with people; her gift was letting others find out that they are not sentenced to a lifetime of silence" (IT 162). Here, and elsewhere, Wolf does not address herself purely to questions of equal rights for their own sake, but rather she examines the relationship to creative language, which concerns her, as author, too. The particular character of the reports, which cannot be defined by any established literary genre and therefore "defies all normative standards of literary criticism," brings, according to Wolf's interpretation, entirely new impulses to literature: "The texts, . . . antecedents of literature, not subject to its laws and not open to the temptations to self-censure—are particularly well-suited to document new realities" (IT 163). The innovative and valuable aspects rest precisely in the fact that they "did not come about as evidence for preconceived opinions; they support no thesis, the familiar 'look how emancipated we are' included" (IT 162). Christa Wolf reads these reports as evidence of a "historical situation" (the development of women under socialism), "which gives women from various strata this sovereignty with respect to their personal experiences which, until very recently, they concealed from themselves and others" (IT 162). "It's becoming clear: unrestrained subjectivity can become a criterion for what we call (inaccurately, I believe) 'objective reality'—though only when the subject is not restricted to empty self-observation, but is actively involved in social processes" (IT 163). In Christa Wolf's interpretation of these reports one recognizes—with near verbatim correspondence of certain phrases—the demands she makes of her own prose in the "Conversation" with Hans Kaufmann. The reports are "authentic" in their expression, and they meet the basic requirement that Christa Wolf asks of the prose author (thereby following Anna Seghers), in the "Conversation": "The reservoir writers draw on in their writing is experience, which mediates between objective reality and the authorial subject. And it is highly desirable that this should be socially meaningful experience" (SA).

The social component is provided through establishing equal rights, on the basis of which these women's reports now proceed to ask what they themselves are and what they want. With that, Wolf's fear that the "liberation of woman" could remain stuck in its inception is refuted; the "radical" questions she demands in the "Conversation" are posed by the women: "Women, who have matured by coming to terms with real and consequential experiences, are signaling a radical expectation: to be able to live as a whole person, to make use of all their senses and abilities" (IT 167).

The claim of women to the right of self-realization for all human beings as a means to overcome alienation from oneself cannot, however, be fully realized as long as society upholds its patriarchal thought patterns, setting duty, profession, and public activities as norms to which the individual subordinates himself. Women who assume public office experience the conflict "between authoritarian thinking and being oneself" (IT 167).

In *The Quest for Christa T.*, the narrator had perceived one conflict for her central character as arising from her opposition to unimaginative, solely pragmatic people. In "Self-Experiment," the woman pits her imagination against the male *ratio*. In Maxie Wander's reports, Christa Wolf discovers the possibility, in women, of a synthesis of rational understanding (*Verstand* in the sense of *Vernunft*) and imagination as the basis of self-discovery. The new values women introduce into a view of the world determined up to this point by male norms assume a prominent position in Christa Wolf's poetic language. We must regard them as those factors from which, in the battle with institutions and external restrictions, she promises herself and literature new impulses that could promote profound changes. The emancipation of women to define their own identity points the way toward the emancipation of mankind at large; they are, on the basis of their new historical situation and the development they have undergone under socialism, in a position to have a "voice in shaping life-expectations for men" (IT

168). It is significant that Wolf includes herself in her concluding question: "How can *we* women be 'liberated' as long as all people are not?" (IT 168, italics mine).

The more recent phase in Wolf's creative work is marked by her concern for female characters from the past, whereby the presence of the author herself serves to create formal and contextual links between past and present. The two female figures from the first decades of the nineteenth century, Karoline von Günderrode and Bettina Brentano, can only, from Wolf's standpoint, be understood anew and more deeply after historical changes have taken place (with which Wolf means her own history). In the essays "The Shadow of a Dream. Karoline von Günderrode—A Sketch" of 1979 and "Yes indeed. But the next life begins today. A Letter about Bettina" of 1980, Wolf provides her individual contribution to the contemporary understanding of the cultural heritage, in which she distances herself from the "worn-out formula of the 'fostering of the heritage'" (BL 309). In conscious opposition to the official tendency, she adopts the cause of those figures from literature who, as she establishes in her Günderrode essay, have fallen victim to the coldness, rationality, and narrow-mindedness of literary criticism up to and into the present time. Her criticism of the "literary history of the Germans . . . which is organized around the monumental cultural icons of their classical writers and which, up to very recently—when Georg Lukács pronounced his weighty verdict against Kleist, against the Romantics—light-heartedly and light-headedly dismissed those figures, branded as 'incomplete'" (SD 226), must certainly also be seen as a reassessment of her own critical stance as young reviewer and author in the 1950s. On the basis of insights won in the 1960s and 1970s regarding the relationship of the writer to his material and the significance of women in overcoming a social position determined by the male *ratio*, she develops her new perspective that comprehends heritage as a vital, continually effective, tension-rich point of reference. For the relationship to certain figures of the past she coins in the Bettina letter the profound statement: "Those who have gone before us do not detract from our lives. They add to it." (*"Die Früheren nehmen uns nichts ab. Sie fügen uns etwas zu"* [BL 309]). *"Abnehmen"* as well as *"zufügen"* is ambiguous. The former means "to detract [from our lives]" *and* "to relieve us from anything," while the latter must be read both in the sense of "inflicting a sorrow or pain" as well as in the sense of "giving us something that we do not have." Both meanings are present in Christa Wolf's discussion of Bettina von Arnim's book, *Die Günderode*, and of the relationship presented there of the two young women from the circle of the Romantics—a discussion innovative with regard to both form and approach.

In the Günderrode essay, which establishes a vital connection between the life and work of Wolf's own time and the life and work of a "peripheral figure" underestimated by society and by literary critics, Wolf selects a formal and thematic approach that is open to the present and that traces the struggle of women to combine life and thought (writing) from the past right up to the present: "Before one can write, one must live. That is banal and concerns both sexes. Women lived for years without writing; then they wrote—if the expression is permitted —with their lives and for their lives. They're doing that still—or again —in our time" (SD 225).

A more profound and implicitly tragic presentation of the connection of the past to the present is contained in the introduction to the novella *No Place on Earth* of 1979. This work originated in a time in which Wolf's own existence as human being and writer was subjected to the strongest pressures on the part of her own society.

> The wicked spoor left in time's wake as it flees us.
> You precursors, feet bleeding. Gazes without eyes, words that
> stem from no mouth. . . .
> And we, still greedy for the ashen taste of words.
> Not yet mute as is suitable. (*NP* 3)

Tone and language of these lines contain the ring of poems by Paul Celan and Nelly Sachs from the early postwar years, bemoaning man's fate. They also recall the language of that poet so honored by Christa Wolf, Ingeborg Bachmann, who herself died a death by fire. The "we" indicates the fateful connection to those who have gone before, including Günderrode and Kleist, which the writer of today must recognize. The warning of a potential (necessary or possible?) loss of speech contrasts radically with her optimistic vision of overcoming speechlessness, as it is expressed in the essay "In Touch." The last line of *No Place on Earth*, "We know what is coming" (*NP* 119), also bridges the distance from past to present and future, and it is tragic in tone—half prophecy, half resignation. An examination of Christa Wolf's treatment of literary models, inappropriate here, would have above all to take into account the language and tone of the novella in which she re-creates (*nachdichtet*) the figures of the past, whereby she strives not for imitation or documentary faithfulness but for what might be termed inner authenticity, embracing her own experiences.[7]

With Karoline von Günderrode Wolf presents to us, in essay and novella, the fate of a woman who cannot expand within the narrow boundaries of a role prescribed by society and tradition. More strongly than all limitations imposed by family, origin, and material pressures, Wolf stresses in Günderrode's case her obligation "to her talent"; the question, "When did this exist for women heretofore?" (SD 235), indicates that Wolf sees in her the beginning of a new development. In the novella, attention is focused on the (fictitious) relationship to Kleist and the schismatic bond to the *Realpolitiker* Savigny (the Tasso-conflict is never very far away), but in her essay Christa Wolf permits Günderrode to emerge on her own, from her life and work. More important than the connection with the Romantics, to whose circle, as the novella shows us, she belonged loosely, seems a sense of communion with the

155

young Hölderlin, whom she never met: "Between Hölderlin and her there is a relationship which goes to the roots, and which opens up surprising possibilities of comparison" (SD 239). The "question of all questions"—"how must the world be constituted for a moral being?"— is posed by the young poets and philosophers in the wake of the French Revolution and then, as shown above, taken up again in Wolf's own time by the poet Bobrowski and by Wolf herself. "Sensuality," "beauty," "poesy," "reason" are correspondences between not only Hölderlin and Günderrode but also these figures and Wolf's own conception of human spirituality (SD 240).

At the beginning of her essay Christa Wolf places an authentic document, the letter of the young Karoline, in which Günderrode expresses the deep split in her nature and in her sense of self, manifest in the desire to be a man: "Often I have had the unfeminine desire to throw myself into the tumult of a wild battle, to die. Why was I not born a man? There is an unhappy disproportion in my soul; and it will and must remain so, for I am a woman and have desires like a man, without a man's strength. That is why I am . . . so at odds with myself" (SD 225). A similar feeling of inner disunion is expressed in the dream-vision of death that precedes the novella as motto.[8] In the essay Wolf sees the deep basis for this inner conflict in Günderrode's alienation from her time, of which she herself is "as yet" unaware: "The dissonance of her soul . . . is, but she does not know it yet, the inconsistency of the times" (SD 225). In this way, the reader is shown the link to the present and also is confronted with the question of how to make a character and fate such as Karoline's accessible to the modern reader. In her own exposition Wolf shows us a figure with a strong will to life, limited on all sides, who seeks to express herself in a series of different "roles." Only in comparing the essay with the novella does it become evident that the "desires like a man" are not only the expression of another role but also a basic characteristic of Günderrode that separates her from her female contemporaries (especially from Bettina, as will be shown), and in which Wolf perceives the inner relationship to the poet Kleist. Only in Wolf's own time can the "untimely" aspects of the character and disposition of Günderrode be recognized; the Maxie Wander reports break new ground in this kind of self-expression.

Christa Wolf sees the short life of Günderrode up to her suicide in 1806 as the attempt "to work on that perfection toward which she strives," which is "a kind of self-experiment, she knows it" (SD 237). (Here, of course, one notes the verbatim correspondence with the title of Wolf's earlier narrative.) Günderrode's strength becomes, in Wolf's interpretation, the reason for her tragic failure: she fails not because of an unfulfilled love, but because of the unfulfillable demand for the absolute, with which she wants to emerge as woman and as poet. At the same time, Wolf sees in this self-imposed demand this figure's signal toward the future. Günderrode overtaxes herself as human being and as poet in the attempt to produce new "patterns of life": "Poetry is related to the essence of utopia, which is to say, it possesses a painful-pleasurable inclination to embrace absolute values" (SD 282).

As at the beginning, so at the end of her essay Wolf establishes the connection with the present. But her prognosis for the future of humanity now sounds ominous when she asserts that the separation of thinking and acting, of art and science will continue: "The rigorous division of labor effects its results. The producers of material values and those of spiritual values oppose each other, alienated on separate shores, and are prevented from creating conditions under which they can live together" (SD 283). The consequences from this situation of mankind's self-alienation are pronounced for the poet by Wolf in a prophetic tone, in timeless dimensions, with echoes of Hölderlin and Greek tragedy, without self-pity and, significantly, without reference to the difference between man and woman: "*poets* are, this is not a lament, predestined to sacrifice and self-sacrifice" (SD 283, emphasis mine).

The image of Günderrode only becomes complete when we consider Bettina's view and juxtapose the two women in Wolf's "letter" about Bettina. These two women, bound together in their attempt to overcome the alienation of art and life, release, each in her own way, creative impulses whose consequences for the present age Wolf reveals to the future readers of Bettina's book on Günderrode. Again a field of tension emerges between historical past and present, inviting a critical comparison as well as the establishment of points of reference. Above all, however, and as in the Günderrode essay, Christa Wolf's own position in the field of tension between past and present is also reflected. She herself provokes this through her choice of form: she addresses her observations in the style of a letter to a woman, "D." The letter form, through which she not only consciously evades formal requirements and rules but probably also associates with a genre suitable to women writers of the nineteenth century, is relativized in the first sentence: "Dear D., in place of the letter you are expecting I want to write to you about Bettina" (BL 284).

In explaining her choice of form and subject, Wolf refers to a continuing dialogue with her addressee, who must also be a writer, and involves Bettina, as "precursor," in the dialogue as well. In the course of the letter the form of address, "you," alternates with the personal pronoun "we." This assumes the involvement of the reader, that is, of Wolf's contemporaries. Altogether the form of address within the letter narrows the distance between past and present; thus Wolf introduces the final section of the letter, the most revealing one with regard to creative impulses from past to present, with a question directed to both the addressee and the reader: "Do you wish to see the spiritual—not just temporal—connection . . . with the Günderrode book?" (BL 308). She mitigates her own doubts as to whether she will succeed in arousing in the reader of today an understanding for the historical references and the unusual linguistic expression by appealing to a—still undiscovered—need on D.'s part, which can be satisfied through involvement with the Bettina book: "When I reread these texts . . . I think of you and your unfulfilled greed for history as well as of your urgent attempts to remove, with the help of unrestrained language, layers of unlived life which separate your spirit, your consciousness, your feelings, your body from yourself" (BL 309). Here again is articulated the desire to overcome the sense of being alienated from oneself, to liberate the "I" from the limitations and formal rules of art, as expressed also in the "Conversation" with Kaufmann; in the "women's reports" of Maxie Wander this self-alienation has been—at least partially—conquered. In the Bettina letter, on the other hand, Christa Wolf comes to the resigned conclusion: "We ought to change our lives. But we are not doing that" (BL 309).

For Christa Wolf as writer, the most important insights and impulses derived from Bettina's book on Günderrode have to do with language and form: "That which should be most noticeable in this book is also that which is most easily overseen, because it is not formulated: the statement which lies in the structure of the book—namely its refusal to conform to an aesthetic canon" (BL 309–310). This aspect is due solely to the influence of Bettina, whose actual significance for her successors rests in the fact that she rose above the rules of artistic form and aesthetics determined by the Classical era, and—reverting to the Romantics, to whose circle she, as a nonpoet, belonged just as much as the poet Karoline—rediscovered a "mixed form" as the only suitable means of expression for her material (BL 310). Only in this way can she resolve the conflict between life and art and express herself and her relationship to Günderrode spontaneously (BL 310).

Christa Wolf makes it clear that she is strongly drawn to the creative alternative embodied by Bettina, but for the achievement of which mankind, especially in her own time, has not yet shown itself to be mature enough: "Gently Bettina draws Günderrode over to the side of her counter-proposal, her female philosophy, her "suspended religion" which, had it only had the slightest chance of being realized, would not have been forced by the male culture of aggression to the edge of self-destruction" (BL 312). The impulses that enter literature from the dialogue of these two women are called "joy of life," "pleasure in the senses," "humanity"; they are released by the spontaneity and carefree attitude with which Bettina expresses her love for Karoline. Thus there emerges from this testimony an ideal symbiosis of art and life which, however, must remain a dream, a utopia for literature: "To use love and longing as means of gaining insight, to think and gain insight without having to deny one's own personality" (BL 313).

One rich consequence of this kind of literature that emerges from self-utterance is a new, uninhibited, creative relationship to language. Wolf ascertains with "sadness" that this intimacy with language has been lost in her time: "For poetry, the essentially human phenomenon, flourishes only with the innocent; they had it; we have verse, but poetry as a form of intercourse is inaccessible to us" (BL 309). The creative aspect of this language is expressed in a sense for play and imagination (BL 313) not dissimilar to the word-games in the narrative "An Afternoon in June." There these games express the individual claims of the family's private world and a way of avoiding having to adapt to official language. In the narrative "Self-Experiment" as well there is a joy in "playing" with words.[9]

In the Bettina letter Wolf invites the addressee and her contemporary readers to remember their own dreams. In doing so, she presents to them the prospect of access to the unconscious, the irrational, as a potential for the discovery of new creative possibilities: "That, and even more, you will discover for yourself. You and many others will, I believe, understand this language as though you had dreamt of it" (BL 313). The language itself contains evidence that those women who concern themselves with art and literature, with aesthetics and science by "submitting" to them are rejecting their own nature: "I must smile at the cunning of our language, which makes 'literature' and 'aesthetics' —institutions to which we secretly submit—words of the feminine gender, although the participation of women in them is meager, and although, as you have experienced painfully in yourself, a woman who takes it upon herself to establish her own identity through writing does not move freely within its great regulatory system" (BL 310). There is no doubt that Wolf counts not only her addressee, "D." but also herself among those women who seek access to great literature at the cost of their own lives, who make sacrifices of the kind that are illuminated most vividly in Wolf's view of Günderrode.

As alternative to this possibility, she presents Bettina's stance vis-à-vis art and aesthetics. She did not set as her goal the production of great literature: "The letters which Bettina and Karoline exchange do not claim to be 'art' and, as a book, are in their formlessness just that form which permits them to transmit their experiences without having to deform them" (BL 310). But Wolf shows that even this position involves sacrifice. Bettina renounces fulfillment, in art as well as in love. She does not wish to be a poet, is perhaps incapable of it, as she herself would admit to Karoline. "A dark, meaningful connection exists between these testimonies to a forced renunciation of love and Bettina's refusal to write poetry" (BL 316). Through the contrast of the two figures and their antithesis, Wolf poignantly shows us the conflict between art and life into which those creatively active women are inevitably drawn: "It is an insoluble contradiction that literature is dependent upon that order which, however, it must continually supersede in order to become literature. Bettina tries to avoid this trap. She submits neither to love nor to art. This strategy is not available to Günderrode. . . . She can only submit entirely or refuse entirely, wants to be lover and poet" (BL 316). Christa Wolf's own judgment of each of these two positions expresses her own situation as woman and as writer. Bettina's stance must appear to her as the more worthy of emulation because

Bettina disregards and rises above the canons of form, censorship, and self-censorship. But this stance is not available to Christa Wolf when she follows the claim to the absolute Günderrode makes of herself. Wolf ultimately gives two reasons for the failure of this figure: "Günderrode is led to death by the experience of not being able fully to live her individuality, neither in love nor in art. The common voice, which set a norm for her which was not hers, killed Günderrode" (BL 318).

In the closing remarks of the letter, this ambiguous complex of problems is connected—abruptly and with ominous interpretability—to the present. These remarks are directed simultaneously at the addressee, at Wolf herself as writer, and at her readers and contemporaries, and thus they induce us to continue the thoughts presented through the alternatives embodied by Bettina and Karoline.

It is said of Günderrode that she "wears herself out with the aesthetics of the masterworks which she cannot hope to create" (BL 317), but Wolf intimates that the emulation of this aesthetic concept is not the only creative possibility for a woman, indeed, that perhaps precisely this claim to male norms is misguided. Thus she asks the reader: "Have you ever heard the expression 'mistressworks' (Meisterinnen-Werke)?" (BL 317). Günderrode submits unwillingly to the formal canon "as yardstick" because "to become important as a poet means to submit to it." (Wolf adds the suggestive question: "As woman poet too?" [Auch als Dichterin?] [BL 317].) She discovers in a personal testimony of Günderrode, which she presents at the end, "the beginnings of a different aesthetic code, whose fragments we ought to collect. We will hear Georg Büchner speak similarly" (BL 318). Christa Wolf draws this conclusion from a passage in a letter in which Karoline laments the "poverty of the images with which I apprehended my poetic moods," but where she nonetheless confesses to that which "was genuine emotion in me" and refuses to make use of "more abundant forms or a more 'significant' material" which she knows to be nearby, because they "did not emerge as the first mood from the soul" (BL 317–318).

In the final analysis, Christa Wolf demands that the writer be genuine, true to the self. In Günderrode she shows us a character whose deep inclinations, whose passion for philosophy and love for myth and drama, together with the absolute demands she made of herself and of others, forced her into an unavoidable conflict with a time and a society that faced these attitudes without understanding. Here lies, certainly, a correspondence to Wolf. Günderrode emerges from the three available sources—the essay, the novella, and the Bettina letter—as a figure who defies definition determined by gender. She is no "typical" woman, nor, indeed, a typical woman writer; she may be understood only in her individuality of character, perhaps even in her one-sidedness of talent.[10]

Notes

1. In Joachim Walther, ed., *"Meinetwegen Schmetterlinge." Gespräche mit Schriftstellern* (Berlin: Buchverlag Der Morgen, 1973), 114–134. Also as "Unruhe und Betroffenheit (Gespräch mit J. Walther, 1972)" in Christa Wolf, *Fortgesetzter Versuch. Aufsätze Gespräche Essays* (Leipzig: Reclam, 1979), 59–76. The conversation with Hans Kaufmann, included in translation in this volume, is reprinted under the title "Subjektive Authentizität" in *DA*, 773–805; that collection also contains "Unruhe und Betroffenheit," 751–772, and "Über Sinn und Unsinn von Naivität," 42–53.

2. On the role of this concept in the context of Christa Wolf's prose style, see Alexander Stephan, "Die 'subjektive Authentizität' des Autors. Zur ästhetischen Position von Christa Wolf," in *Christa Wolf, Text und Kritik* 46, ed. Heinz Ludwig Arnold (April 1975), 33–41. Also see Alexander Stephan, *Christa Wolf* (Munich: Verlag C.H. Beck, 1976), especially chapter 1: "Subjektive Authentizität: Biographie und Zeitgenossenschaft," 7–22. Also see Karin McPherson, "In search of the new prose: Christa Wolf's Reflections on Writing and the Writer in the 1960s and 1970s," *NGS* 9, no. 1 (Spring 1981): 1–13.

3. J. W. von Goethe, *Dichtung und Wahrheit* II, 7 (Hamburg: Christian Wegner Verlag, 1955), vol. 9, 283. ("Alles, was daher von uns bekannt geworden, sind nur Bruchstücke einer grossen Konfession. . . .")

4. For a comprehensive analysis of these developments, see Manfred Jäger, "Auf dem langen Weg zur Wahrheit. Fragen, Antworten und neue Fragen in den Erzählungen, Aufsätzen und Reden Christa Wolfs," in *Sozialliteraten. Funktion und Selbstverständnis der Schriftsteller in der DDR* (Düsseldorf: Bertelsmann, 1973). See also A. Stephan, *Christa Wolf*, chapter 3 "Privater Anspruch und öffentlicher Auftrag: Literaturkritik, Herausgebertätigkeit, Essayistik," 117–129.

5. In the final stages of the "Conversation," Christa Wolf sets her ideas of a humanity based on moral responsibility against a narrow concept of social commitment that her own conception embraces by its very definition in terms of human experience.

6. First published Berlin/GDR: Buchverlag Der Morgen, 1977. In the West German edition with Christa Wolf's preface: "Berührung. Maxie Wander" ("In Touch"), preface to Maxie Wander, *Guten Morgen, du Schöne. Frauen in der DDR. Protokolle* (Darmstadt/Neuwied: Luchterhand, 1978). Now also in *DA*, 196–209.

7. For a discussion of such treatment, see Ute Brandes, "Quotation as Authentication: *No Place on Earth*" in this volume.

8. "But for this reason I fancy that I am seeing myself lying in the coffin, and my two selves stare at each other in wonderment" (*NP* n.p.).

9. In "Self-Experiment," the narrator's identity as a woman is reflected in a spontaneous relationship to language that leaves room for creativity and phantasy. A comparison with the word games in "An Afternoon in June" shows Christa Wolf's increasing insistence on the need to follow the dictates of her own language in her creative style.

10. I am grateful to Professor Marilyn Sibley Fries for her initiative in inviting me to contribute the present paper and for her most helpful undertaking to translate the paper from German into English. I am also greatly indebted to Professor Peter Liddell and to Dr. Linda Dowling and Professor W. C. Dowling for their helpful advice with regard to my own translation queries. I accept responsibility for the translation in its present form.

Christa Wolf's Prose:
A Landscape of Masks

Helen Fehervary

Authorship and Uneven Development

Whether we consider her within the context of GDR literature or literary discussions in the West, Christa Wolf remains idiosyncratic within the development of contemporary German literature. Wolf began writing as a committed socialist in the GDR, whose membership in the SED went as far as her candidacy for the party's Central Committee in the 1960s. Yet she has always been at odds with the presuppositions of socialist realism and authoritarian notions of Party hegemony. She is closer to the traditions of critical Marxism and dissidence, yet she has never shared with Brecht and most representatives of the avant-garde the ideas that modernist abstraction be put into the service of political and aesthetic functionalism or that materialistic forms or "technique," coupled with the historical consciousness of the author as producer, could be effective media for cultural praxis in modern industrial societies. Wolf's skepticism toward contemporary avantgardism also sets her apart from more recent critical theories as embodied by Adorno and French poststructuralism. She is at home in neither the inherited totalities of realism nor the open-ended experimental projects of modernism and the avant-garde. Without an established tradition to account for the radicalism of her work, Wolf's writing appears to some to be conservative, eclectic, and moralistic. Others more positively inclined defend her within ideological categories and ascribe to her work the historically and aesthetically obscure regions of *Lebenshilfe*: "subjectivity," "authenticity," "utopian vision"—i.e., moral support.

If there is a possibility of delineating an alternative "third" tradition, we would have to begin by acknowledging the literary quality of "retarded" or "uneven" development. Unlike most writers of her generation, Wolf did not write fiction for publication until she was thirty years old. In the intervening twenty years, her literary productivity has been relatively modest, the pace increasingly accelerated, and the quality uneven. Most reputable writers begin with at least one stroke of genius before their thirtieth year, then either come to a crashing halt or develop an organic, mature work.[1] By contrast, Wolf's literary beginnings were halting and tedious; her writing has become thematically more erratic and formally more radical. We can find an underlying development in the body of her work, but the changes from one work to the next are more suggestive of incongruous and often contradictory aesthetic attitudes than of the usual progressive development. The transition from *Divided Heaven* (1963) to *The Quest for Christa T.* (1968), for example, was not simply a step, or even a leap, from one kind of literary form to another. It involved the author's (much like her character Rita's) eclipse between the "trains" of literary history before finding the next "vehicle" in which to move on. It necessitated not only the transformation of form but also the collapse and regeneration of authorial identity.[2] The same can be said of the transition from *Patterns of Childhood* (1976) to *No Place on Earth* (1979), where she propels herself backward into history, from the aesthetic questions raised by the experience of fascist culture to the failure of early Romanticism and the demise of the German salon. The subsequent journey backward from Romanticism to early Greek mythology in *Cassandra* (1983) is even more precipitous.

The project of Wolf's writing does not demonstrate the concepts of literary production and progress, but rather, regressing into history, it seems to retard progressive development and brush history against the grain. At the same time, this project seeks the promise of subjective agency and historical self-realization: "The difficulty of saying 'I'" (CT 169). Wolf's literary creation of self (and history), however, rests in neither the teleological development of the bourgeois individual nor the decentering or deconstruction of this very same individual. In each of her works, the authorial identity and the narrative voice seem entirely redefined, different, and "other": There are many selves and many histories at work here. Rather than demonstrating the unified and progressive developmental career of the writer, Christa Wolf's work exhibits both a retrogressive and expansive unfolding of many *different* authorial lives.[3]

Wolf's relationship to literature and history seems to corroborate the ideas put forth by Ernst Bloch in his essay "Nonsynchronism and the Obligation to Its Dialectics" (1932):

Not all people exist in the same Now. They do so externally, by virtue of the fact that they may all be seen today. But that does not mean that they are living at the same time with others. Rather, they carry earlier things with them, things which are intricately involved. . . . Moreover, they do not emerge in a hidden way as previously but rather, they contradict the Now in a very peculiar way, awry, from the rear. The strength of this untimely course has become evident; it promised nothing less than new life, despite its looking to the old.[4]

The philosopher Bloch attempted to explain heterogeneous social interests during the 1930s by conceptualizing a perspective of subjectivity based on nonsynchronist development. This perspective can also apply to literary developments that seem reactionary, retarded, or subjectivistic according to the prevailing critical theories.

Christa Wolf has devoted her entire prose work to creating a dialogue with the voices that articulate the historical subjectivity and uneven development of which Bloch speaks. However, there is a crucial difference between the referential framework of Bloch's theory and the implications of Wolf's development as a writer. Bloch developed a theory of nonsynchronism in order to explain the retarded historical development of *Others*. His theory leaves his own historical position unaccounted for because it is assumed synonymous with the standpoint of a progressive historical Now. As the voice of the historical vanguard, Bloch's theory of nonsynchronism continues the privileging of the present over the past. From this position of the Now his voice is radical and generous enough to understand the distortions and silences of other voices but too firmly self-identified as *the progressive* discourse of history to identify with them. By contrast, Wolf's theory of uneven development is synonymous with her own historical experience. Nonsynchronism is not a description of Otherness, as it is for Bloch, but a statement of self in one's own language. In her "Büchner-Prize Acceptance Speech," for example, Wolf speaks not of "they" but as "we":

The condition of the world is awry, we say as a test, and we realize, it is true. We could defend this sentence. The word is not pretty, merely correct, and it is thus a balm for our ears, lacerated by the clamor of great words, a small relief also for our conscience, deranged by too many false, wrongly-used words. Could it perhaps be the first word of a different, accurate language that we have in our ear but not yet on our tongue? . . .

Whoever wants to search for this language would probably have to endure a nearly complete loss of self-esteem, of self-consciousness, for all the accustomed patterns of speech, narration, thought, and literary composition would no longer be available. Most likely, one would experience what it really means: to lose control. (BP 5)

The loss of control, then, as compared to the linear perpetuation of production and tradition, is essential to the production of literature, history, and self. Such loss of control would not apply, of course, to the conscious writing of the literary work but to the quality of silence that exists within the work and between one work and the next. These lapses of language—and the historical lapses they echo—belong to the writer, not to the work. Given a literary quality, they question the authority of literary history and assert the preeminence of the author—as experimental person as well as producer. When Wolf says "the author is an important person" (RW 206), she recalls Benjamin's concept of the "author as producer"[5] but shifts the quality of authorship by foregrounding the individual. Thus, literary history would be not only the history of its production (the work) but also the history of authorial experience (the silences as well as the products of the creative process.)[6]

Myth and Gender

The invocation of authorial presence—"When if not now?" (CT 185)—is a leitmotif in Christa Wolf's entire work. Wolf belongs to the generation of German authors who grew up under fascism and survived it at great personal cost: the loss of fantasy and mythic storytelling; the suppression of the creative immediacy of play; the lack of reliance on one's legitimacy as historical subject, as author. Fascism succeeded by political force and, more permanently, by colonizing the human imagination. It created a spectacle of barbarism that gave mythic proportions to the most banal historical events and, conversely, transformed the irrational parameters of myth into real history. Its legacy to the writers of the future who survived was a sense of mythic deformation and historical arrest. During his exile in the 1930s Brecht was still able to name the five difficulties he experienced while trying to write the truth, or to lament in a poem about the impossibility of writing in lyrical form about nature.[7] Ten years later Theodor W. Adorno uttered the words: "To write poetry after Auschwitz would be barbaric."[8] Wolf's writing responds to this problematic by returning again and again to the contradictory paradigm of fascism and utopian thinking. However, unlike so many of her contemporaries who stress the burden of German history and its deformation of ideology and myth, Wolf points to the absence of subjective agency that could respond authentically to the present before imagining the future. Her approach to *Vergangenheitsbewältigung* (coming to terms with the past) does not posit the individual in relation to history and myth but attempts to examine the history of the self in relation to others. Thus collective guilt would stem from the inability of the individual to experience fully the present within collective relationships. Wolf's writing seeks the human faces of subjective agency that have been obscured by the inherited myths of collective barbarism and collective guilt.[9]

Writing his "Theses on the Philosophy of History" shortly before his suicide in France in 1940, Walter Benjamin described "Angelus Novus" as a mythic archetype emerging from a confrontation with the "wreckage" of fascism, yet allowing for the moment of mediation between past and future:

A Klee painting named "Angelus Novus" shows an angel looking as though he is about to move away from something he is fixedly
contemplating. His eyes are staring, his mouth is open, his wings are
spread. This is how one pictures the angel of history. His face is
turned toward the past. Where we perceive a chain of events, he sees
one single catastrophe which keeps piling wreckage upon wreckage
and hurls it in front of his feet. The angel would like to say, awaken
the dead, and make whole what has been smashed. But a storm is
blowing from Paradise; it has got caught in his wings with such violence that the angel can no longer close them. This storm irresistibly
propels him into the future to which his back is turned, while the pile
of debris before him grows skyward. This storm is what we call progress.[10]

The image of history in Benjamin's "Theses" is neither dialectical
nor teleological, but it is one "filled by the presence of the now."[11] It is
"the notion of a present which is not a transition, but in which time
stands still and has come to a stop. For this notion defines the present in
which he himself [the historical materialist, i.e., the author, H. F.] is
writing history."[12] For Benjamin, historical impasse is synonymous
with subjective impasse. Breaks, silences, and lapses would thus be
part of historical agency, not deviation. Productivity and progress
would depend not on the rationality of an historical continuum but on
the "shock" of recognition that takes cognizance of the "debris" accumulated in its wake: "Thinking involves not only the flow of thoughts,
but their arrest as well. Where thinking suddenly stops in a
configuration pregnant with tensions, it gives that configuration a
shock, by which it crystallizes into a monad. A historical materialist . . .
recognizes the sign of a Messianic cessation of happening, or, put
differently, a revolutionary chance in the fight for the oppressed past.
He takes cognizance of it in order to blast a specific era out of the homogenous course of history."[13]

Benjamin's own cultural heritage—messianic Judaism and philosophical Marxism—allowed him to merge myth and history within a
radical concept of subjective authorship, and thus he has left an indeli-
ble mark on contemporary theories of history.[14] The similarities to
Christa Wolf's insistence on authorial presence are self-evident. But
Christa Wolf is also a woman writer who lacks a philosophical or theo-
logical tradition that specifically accounts for her. As a female author
she has been absent—as Other—within messianic time as well as
within the territories of historical materialism. Moreover, the tradition
of women's writing to which she might be assigned (pejoratively called
Frauenliteratur in German) hardly possesses the metaphoric powers
that could "blast" an era out of the course of history.[15] What, then, does
such a revised myth of historical consciousness mean for her?

Shortly before her suicide in 1943, which, like Benjamin's, was
historically linked to fascism, Virginia Woolf reflected on another archetypal angel—"the Angel in the House":

The shadow of her wings fell on my page; I heard the rustling of her skirts in the room. Directly, that is to say, I took my pen in hand to review that novel by a famous man, she slipped behind me and whispered: "My dear, you are a young woman. You are writing about a book that has been written by a man. Be sympathetic; be tender; flatter; deceive; use all the arts and wiles of our sex. Never let anybody guess that you have a mind of your own. Above all, be pure." And she made as if to guide my pen. . . . I turned upon her and caught her by the throat. I did my best to kill her. . . . Had I not killed her she would have killed me. She would have plucked the heart out of my writing. . . .

Thus, whenever I felt the shadow of her wing or the radiance of her halo upon my page, I took up the inkpot and flung it at her. She died hard. Her fictitious nature was of great assistance to her.[16]

The texts by Benjamin and Woolf both address the discrepancy between accumulated historical consciousness and subjective presence. Yet their respective archetypal "Angels" signify two very different relationships between authorship and myth. On one level, Woolf's and Benjamin's "Angels" can be seen as one and the same: He the "Angel of History" simply reappears as domesticated She in the house. But the respective author's relationship to the mythic archetype reveals a crucial difference. Whereas Benjamin is still able to rely on a mythological apparatus in order to formulate a creative experiential relationship to history, in Woolf's model the myth itself is the killer. Historically, male authorship has perpetuated itself through myths, while women's literary quality has largely been restricted to being the myth itself. Woman has not been the author of literature but its abstraction and muse.[17] Female authorship has essentially impacted on history as a reflective mirror, not as a primary creative art. Precisely the mythic inspiration that has guided male authorship has been the inhibition of women's authorship: When the muse nears the desk of the woman writer she becomes the "Angel in the House."

Like Benjamin, for whom "thinking suddenly stops in a configuration pregnant [sic!] with tensions" and "gives that configuration a shock,"[18] Woolf invokes unconsciousness as a "state of trance"[19] in which writing is possible. Thus, she can kill the "Angel in the House," just as for Benjamin the human subject can "blast a specific era out of the homogenous course of history."[20] For Benjamin this moment signifies the renewal of historical consciousness and authorship: The universal human subject remains intact. For Woolf, the woman writer, this moment culminates in paralysis. Woolf describes the girl with her pen in hand as the

fisherman lying sunk in dreams on the verge of a deep lake with a rod held out over the water. She was letting her imagination sweep unchecked round every rock and cranny of the world that lies submerged in the depths of our unconscious being. Now came the experience, the experience that I believe to be far commoner with women writers than with men. The line raced through the girl's fingers. Her imagination had rushed away. It had sought the pools, the depths, the dark place where the largest fish slumber. And then there was a smash. There was an explosion. There was foam and confusion. The imagination had dashed itself against something hard. . . . To speak without figure she had thought of something, something about the body, about the passions which it was unfitting for her as a woman to say.[21]

The myth of the "Angel in the House" is not replaced by the female body, the subject, but by the unknown: at best a persona, a mask. In Woolf's words: "The Angel was dead; what then remained? You may say that what remained was a simple and common object—a young woman in a bedroom with an inkpot. In other words, now that she had rid herself of falsehood, that young woman had only to be herself. Ah, but what is 'herself'? I mean, what is a woman? I assure you, I do not know."[22] Woolf summarizes "two very genuine experiences" of her writing career: "The first—killing the Angel in the House—I think I solved. She died. But the second, telling the truth about my experiences as a body, I do not think I solved."[23]

Christa Wolf's uneven development as a writer can be explained satisfactorily by neither the historical experience of fascism nor the fluctuations of cultural policy and socialist development in the GDR. The problems of her first work of fiction, *Moskauer Novelle* (Moscow Novella, 1961), for example, are generally dismissed as a youthful error of socialist realism. Indeed, the characters are stereotypical, the plot schematic, the dialogues contrived, the narration awkward, and the entire fictional framework placed in the service of an overriding idea. Christa Wolf herself has described this early work as a "treatise for the propagation of pious views" (SN 60). But the tenets of socialist realism were not the only prescriptive categories that informed the literary landscape of her first fictional work. Commenting on *Moskauer Novelle* in 1973, Wolf continued: "This is what probably must have happened in that text: From the head, arm, pen, typewriter to the paper, there was not only a transformation of energy, as required by literature, but a loss of energy. For fear of losing control of what might explode inside me, I apparently tried to invent dams, building blocks that could hold a story together" (SN 61). The metaphoric similarity to Virginia Woolf's description of the woman sitting at her desk, facing an empty page with pen in hand, is striking: The author of *Moskauer Novelle* had also been writing in the shadow of the "Angel in the House." The first attempt to tell the truth about her "own experiences as a body" would have to be postponed for several years: until the writing of *The Quest for Christa T.* (1968).

The literary conventions of *Moskauer Novelle* seem at least as embedded in the tradition of *Frauenliteratur* as they are in the tradition of socialist realism. Written in 1959, at the juncture between the reconstruction literature of the 1950s and the Bitterfeld Movement that addressed the relationship between production and everyday life, *Mos-*

kauer Novelle barely touches the thematic concerns that constitute the literature of this time: industrial and agricultural production, class conflicts, and the development of the positive hero as an allegorical representation of the state. In this work, production relates to the labor of friendship, intimacy, and love; class conflicts are replaced by the relationships between the sexes; self-realization is situated in the notion of human interdependence rather than in the self as embodiment of the state. The sociopolitical structure of her own GDR society is strikingly absent in Wolf's first work of fiction. The plot is set in far-off Moscow, yet the city of Moscow itself—sketched hurriedly, almost as an obligatory gesture—is hardly conveyed as a social entity, or even as a national symbol. The main character Vera's trip to Moscow is rather the topos for a state of being: a narrative journey into another space, another time. The journey to Moscow is a thematic detour for a process of narrative reflection that takes shape in a much more authentic historical manner in *The Quest for Christa T.* (1968) and *Patterns of Childhood* (1976).

The least contrived passages of *Moskauer Novelle* dwell on Vera's memories of the past: the end of the war, the defeat of fascism, and her first meeting with the Russian soldier Pavel. The first of these passages reveals a mixing of tenses and the use of the pronoun "I," which never recur in the text and, in retrospect, almost appear to be an involuntary lapse. This "lapse" anticipates Christa Wolf's later theoretical reflections on "losing control" in order to find a new language (BP 5), and it allows the brief glimpse of a narrative style that can tell a story without the self-censorship permeating the rest of the text:

> Who cares if it's raining. The first time I met him it was raining, too. To say we met is a good one. . . . I panicked at the sight of his gray-brown uniform and bolted out the door. Once I was in the backyard, I made a beeline for the parsonage, running like mad across the fields and climbing over the fences—all this while it was raining cats and dogs. And as I'm standing muddy and breathless in the open door of the parish kitchen, where a group of women would usually be sitting arguing around the fire, there he sits utterly alone in the middle of the room. (*MN* 11)

But this release of narrative spontaneity soon comes to an abrupt end, and in the next paragraph the author imposes once more the stylistic and thematic constraints of her narrative "line." Reminiscent of Virginia Woolf's description of the young woman writer, the imagination of the author "had dashed itself against something hard": "Vera laughed quietly to herself. The wet asphalt glistened in the circles of light from the streetlamps. A soft rain moistened her face. She turned her collar up, put her hands deep into her pockets and moved slowly down the street that was still full of people" (*MN* 12).

Wolf's comments in 1973 on *Moskauer Novelle* shed light not only on her own history as an author but also on the process by which she gradually transformed her character Vera into an abstract principle, a teacher:

> But a childhood that stretches between private trivialities and public fanaticism can possibly find no other outcome than a surreptitious eccentricity and the attempt to counteract this with an obvious occupation: the vocation of a teacher, for example, which I wrote on all questionnaires up to my twenty-first year. For years thereafter I moved on the edge of an endeavor that I never even presumed to think myself capable of. This cannot simply be explained by the fact that very young people are rarely able to write prose. There was an inhibition at work here that could only be overcome by the experience of severe concussions, and by no means all at once. (SN 57)

Just as the creative ambitions of women have been channeled since the nineteenth century into the socially permissible vocations of teacher and nurse, Wolf's heroine Vera is rarely seen at work in her actual profession of medical doctor. Transcending her difficulties by assuming the characteristics of the "eternally feminine," she nurses Pavel out of his lovesickness for her, even patches up his relationship to his wife, and teaches him the benefits of sublimation for the larger cause of humanity. All this, in fact, keeps her from reflecting sufficiently about her own past and her own history. Like Vera, who at the end cuts short her journey to return to her other life in the GDR, the author of Wolf's literary project remains truncated in this first work. In *Die imaginierte Weiblichkeit* Silvia Bovenschen reminds us of the "detours the female imagination must take in order to come into its own."[24]

Or, the initial detour of *Moskauer Novelle* may have been the path of least resistance toward being able to write at all. Rooted in nineteenth-century realism, the prose tradition of *Frauenliteratur* provides an authorial voice, however borrowed or foreign it may be, to the woman writer whose personal literary heritage is largely absent or at best obscured.[25] Wolf's first work, in the modest and conservative form of the nineteenth-century novella, is an attempt to preserve the notion of a unique, significant (hi)story and thereby to rationalize the vulnerability of female authorship. The two available prose alternatives would have been the abstractionism of the modernist novel or, more likely, the teleological gesture of the socialist *Bildungsroman*: either the further dismantling of an already fragile literary ego or the increasing collectivization of an already anonymous authorial self. Seen in this light, *Moskauer Novelle* validates the historically authentic quality of Wolf's early literary "immaturity" and "naiveté." "A certain measure of self-deception—naiveté—, which is continuously drained and continuously replenished, seems to be necessary for our lives," Christa Wolf writes in her 1973 essay, entitled "On the Sense and Senselessness of Naiveté" (SN 63). Thus she is able to end her reflection "in praise of folly":

The folly that has many faces, among them those that go hand in hand with insight and knowledge. The folly on whose soil the great experiments flourish and frivolity, cynicism, and resignation cannot bear fruit. The folly that enables us to build houses, plant trees, bring children into the world, write books—to act, as vulnerably, awkwardly and incompletely as we know how. Which is always more reasonable than to capitulate in the face of the many perfect but sometimes inscrutable techniques of destruction. (SN 67)

A Landscape of Masks

The literary folly of naiveté that has "many faces" emerges metaphorically in Christa Wolf's writing as a landscape of masks. "Faces" and "masks" appear throughout her work and function as alternatives to the mythological topography that has supported the development of modern literature. Even the mythic structures of the Enlightenment that inhabit GDR literature are strikingly absent from her work. There are no Herculean feats of labor, there is no Promethean revolt, no Odyssean cunning, no Faustian striving for perfection and truth. The specter of myth does not even function as a point of reference for Marxist deconstruction, as it does for most avant-garde writing in the GDR since Brecht.[26] Yet Wolf does not turn the dialectic of Enlightenment on its head. History is not displaced by subjectivity, political discourse by individualism, nor the public sphere by the personal. The radicalism of her work lies neither in a transcendent nor a private quality but in an immanent historicity. Christa Wolf conveys this historicity in the form of masks.

The mask is not an idea or story, as is myth, but the premonition or memory of a face, a gesture, a person, a historical identity. It belongs not to the tradition of a progressive literary history but to the tradition of the historical persona. The mask is the persona of authorship that hangs suspended between female subjectivity absorbed by myth and the absence of another system of language. In contrast to the literary avant-garde's perpetual construction, deconstruction, and reconstruction of myth, the literary quality of the mask allows for the expansion and multiplication of one literary self into many: literature as reproduction, not production.

The history of theater illustrates the difference between the archetypes of myth and mask. Traditionally, myth has informed the objective dramatization of life on the stage: through concept, story, and meaning. The mask, or the persona of the actor, has mediated the subjective agency of this dramatization: in the physicalization of concepts, in affective suggestion, and in the individual experience of meaning. The significance of myth belongs to the theater director; the body of the mask belongs to its actor. In the course of her work, Christa Wolf gradually hands over the "theater" of literature to the "actor." She initiates this process at the end of *Moskauer Novelle*: "Vera spent the day alone with her travel preparations and journal entries. Whatever it was that she did, at the same time she worked at drawing a mask over her face. She was unable to be sure about her thoughts and feelings and so she had to learn to hide them. A layer of indifferent friendliness had to grow over her face which seemed naked to her ever since this night" (MN 43).

Wolf describes the inner conflicts of her character in the tradition of psychological realism. However, drawing the mask is not only a psychological solution for the character Vera. It is also an aesthetic solution for the author in attempting to create an authentic literary character. Between the suffocation of femaleness in myth and, according to Virginia Woolf, the virtual impossibility of "telling the truth about the [female] body,"[27] there is the possibility of survival through the mask. The mask provides a face to keep the character Vera from succumbing to the stereotypical heroine of *Frauenliteratur* who loses herself in endless "travel preparations" and "journal entries." It also defends her against the pitfalls of exposing her naked face—the impossibility to write at all.

In the autobiographical reportage "Tuesday, September 27," written between *Moskauer Novelle* and *Divided Heaven*, the mask is directly linked to the problem of writing. At the end of the text the narrator struggles with her manuscript of *Divided Heaven*: "I know that neither the written pages nor the sentences I write today will stay—not one syllable. I write something, then cross it out again: As always, Rita bolted like lightning from her sleep and was awake, with no memory of a dream. Only a face must have been there. She tried to hold onto it, it faded. Robert lay beside her" (TS 40). The tentative written words are likened to the face that is fleeting. In this reportage Christa Wolf uses the first-person narrator for the first time. In so doing she is able to envision a literary presence besides her character Rita: a third presence in the form of a face, a mask. In *The Quest for Christa T.* this mask becomes the "secret of the third person":

> Her secret, which I'd been looking for all the time we'd known one another, was a secret no longer. . . . Among her papers are various fragments written in the third person: *she*, with whom she associated herself, whom she was careful not to name, for what name could she have given her? *She*, who knows she must always be new, and see anew, over and over again. . . . I understand the secret of the third person, who is there without being tangible and who, when circumstances favor her, can bring down more reality upon herself than the first person: I. The difficulty of saying "I." (CT 169–170)

The anonymity of the third person does not constrict; it allows for a pluralization of entities. The quoted passage is followed by the lines: "Was I really asleep? I saw her go by, in all her forms; saw suddenly behind all her transformations the meaning; understood that it's inept to wish for her to arrive and stay anywhere" (CT 170). The literary character Christa T.—the name implies a personal yet collective identity—is thus herself a composite of masks. She signifies the accumulation of authorial presence, of a collective tradition, of literary history. One of her many forms, or masks, is given a name in the novel: Sophie La Roche, the first acknowledged woman novelist of the German Enlightenment. While "playing" her at a costume party, Christa T. need not wear a mask because, like Sophie La Roche in her day, she *is* the mask: "For one is always involuntarily grasping for definitions. But then came the fancy-dress ball, at which Christa T. arrived as Sophie La Roche, though she hadn't dressed up at all, she wore only her goldish-brown dress with the exotic pattern, telling everyone who she was supposed to be" (CT 117–118).

In "Self-Experiment" (1972), the female narrator undergoes an experimental scientific sex change and, as a man, is called Anders (Other). The real name of her "I" is never divulged. Both the "I" and Anders are only partial forms of what might be called a gender, a person, an identity. On the way to this realization, which culminates in a new form of authorship—"the invention of the person one can love"—, the narrator/Anders experiences the silence of language and the conscious inability either to self-identify or to name:

> Do you know what "person" means? Mask. Role. Real Self. A prerequisite for language, it seems to me after all this, must be the existence of at least one of these three conditions. The fact that all of them were lost to me had to mean virtually total silence. You can't write down anything about nobody. This explains the three-day gap in my report. (SE 127)

At the end of *Patterns of Childhood* (1976) the narrator affirms the insufficiency of language and the fluidity of voices and masks. She imagines a human being who is more than a person and less than an identifiable body or definable shape. This human being does not assert himself by his "upright posture" (Bloch: "der aufrechte Gang")[28] but abandons the self to the experience of a world that we know (and fear) as the limitless Other:

> The closer you are to a person, the harder it seems to say something conclusive about him; it's a known fact. The child who was hidden in me—has she come forth? Or has she been scared into looking for a deeper, more inaccessible hiding place? . . .
> And the past, which can still split the first person into the second and the third—has its hegemony been broken? Will the voices be still?
> I don't know.
> At night I shall see—whether waking, whether dreaming—the outline of a human being who [in fluid transitions will change perpetually], through whom other persons, adults, children, will pass without hindrance. I will hardly be surprised if this outline may also be that of an animal, a tree, even a house, in which anyone who wishes may go in and out at will. Half-conscious, I shall experience the beautiful waking image drifting ever deeper into the dream, into ever new shapes no longer accessible to words, shapes which I be-

lieve I recognize. Sure of finding myself once again in the world of solid bodies upon awakening, I shall abandon myself to the experience of dreaming. I shall not revolt against the limits of the expressible. (PC 406–407)[29]

Examples such as these abound in Christa Wolf's later work, where the appearance of the mask often coincides with the use of the second person, as well as the third. The story "Unter den Linden" (1969) bears a motto derived from Rahel Varnhagen; inspired by Rahel's written accounts of her dreams, the story begins with the intimate appellation "Du" (you): "Under the linden trees is where I always like to go. Most of all, as you know, alone" (UL 7). We find a similar relationship in the essay on Bettina von Arnim (1980), written in the personal form of a letter. The title of the essay on Karoline von Günderrode, "The Shadow of a Dream" (1978), suggests that the brevity of this Romantic writer's creative life was only the mask of a larger historical presence. In *No Place on Earth* (1979) the main characters, Günderrode and Heinrich von Kleist, are positioned like actors—with many roles, many faces, and many masks—on the stage set of the early nineteenth-century salon. Most recently, the figure of *Cassandra* (1983) suggests the archetypal origins of the literary mask: The mythical voice that speaks but is not heard can only be perceived as an image, a face frozen by history, a mask.

In Wolf's "Büchner-Prize Acceptance Speech" of 1980 the mask multiplies as "Rosetta under her many names" (BP 7). She first becomes Georg Büchner's other women characters: Marie, Marion, Lena, Julie, Lucile; then Gerhart Hauptmann's Rose Bernd and Ibsen's Nora; later she is the revolutionary Rosa Luxemburg and the radical vamp Marlene Dietrich; finally she emerges as Ingeborg Bachmann, the author. Within the development of Christa Wolf's work, each appearance of a mask anticipates its proliferation as it becomes historically objectified: in the form of the third person, the second, and finally a literary name —Sophie La Roche, Rahel Varnhagen, Karoline von Günderrode, Heinrich von Kleist, Bettina von Arnim, Georg Büchner, Rosetta under her many names, Ingeborg Bachmann, Cassandra. All these masks, personas, and names are facets of Christa Wolf's gradual accumulation of literary history, and at the same time they expand her authorial self. The "difficulty of saying 'I'" is ultimately the desire *not* to say "I."

For it is the desire to say more than "I." The mask, a form of relational being, enables the stripping away of an isolated individual identity. It is the wish to participate in a body of affinities and not to become the summation of an individual or collective teleology. In this sense the mask is the subversive underside of myth, an alternative to mankind's progressive journey toward perfection. It is the prophetic answer to the Odyssey of Enlightened Man and outlines a human face beyond the dialectic of the Enlightenment. The mask is the voice that survives consolidating the state and the myth of Odysseus: "Cassandra must have loved Troy more than herself when she dared to prophesy to her compatriots the downfall of the city" (BP 11).

Christa Wolf closes her Büchner-Prize essay by suggesting that her literary identity, like Rosetta "under her many names," is also a mask: "this skin too will be stripped away and hang in shreds" (BP 11). Traditionally, the myth of the satyr Marsyas, follower of the goddess Cybele and defeated by Apollo in a competition, has defined the historical limitations of the creative voice as mask. In the words of Robert Graves, Marsyas

> stumbled upon the flute [made by Athena] and he went about Phrygia in Cybele's train, delighting the ignorant peasants. They cried out that Apollo himself could not have made better music, even on his lyre, and Marsyas was foolish enough not to contradict them. This, of course, provoked the anger of Apollo, who invited him to a contest, the winner of which should inflict whatever punishment he pleased on the loser. . . . The contest proved an equal one, the Muses being charmed by both instruments, until Apollo cried out to Marsyas: I challenge you to do with your instrument as much as I can do with mine. Turn it upside down, and both play and sing at the same time. This, with a flute, was manifestly impossible, and Marsyas failed to meet the challenge. But Apollo reversed his lyre, and sang such delightful hymns in honour of the Olympian gods that the Muses could not do less than give the verdict in his favour. Then, for all his pretended sweetness, Apollo took a most cruel revenge on Marsyas: flaying him alive and nailing his skin to a pine (or, some say, to a plane tree), near the source of the river which now bears his name. . . . Becoming the acknowledged god of Music, [Apollo] has ever since played on his seven-stringed lyre while the gods banquet.[30]

The myth of Apollo and Marsyas represents the victimization of the creative popular voice by cultural dogmatism and power. This interpretation, for example, underlies Thomas Brasch's rendering of the myth in "Der Zweikampf" (The Duel), one of the prose texts in the volume he appropriately entitled: Vor den Vätern sterben die Söhne (The Sons Die Before the Fathers, 1976). In much of the West German women's literature of the 1970s, exemplified by Verena Stefan's Shedding of 1976, the concept of stripped skin or shedding has the opposite function: The narrator sheds a false, superimposed persona and language on the way to an authentic identity and a true voice. In Brasch's and Stefan's texts, the metaphor of stripped skin or shedding has to do with the oppression or absence of literary identity. For Christa Wolf, the mask itself is a form of identity and, as such, only one aspect of multiple literary identities. The final words of the "Büchner-Prize Acceptance Speech"—"This skin too will be stripped away and hang in shreds"—do not simply negate or affirm Christa Wolf's narrative persona, they also echo the masked personas of other literary voices and other literary lives.

One of them is Ingeborg Bachmann, who affirmed the vulnerable literary ego as an "I without guarantees" and whose writing reveals the many variations of the "yet hardly used, hardly exhausted 'I': What we consider to be its face appears here as an ideal image, elsewhere as a mask, and then again all at once as its true face."[31] Another is Ulrike Meinhof, author and political activist, whose language on death row in 1972–1973 is a formidable antecedent to Christa Wolf's phrasing in her "Büchner-Prize Acceptance Speech" eight years later:

> A strain to speak in a normal tone of voice,
> as if speaking loudly, almost roaring—
> the feeling of losing speech—
> one can no longer identify the meanings of words, only guess them—
> the use of hissing sounds—s, ss, tz, sch—
> is absolutely unbearable—
> guards, visitors, the courtyard seem to be out
> of celluloid—
> headaches—
> flashes—
> sentence formation, grammar, syntax—out of control—
> While writing: two lines—at the end of the second line one cannot
> retain the beginning of the first—
> the feeling of extinguishing internally—. . .
> The feeling that time and space
> are interlocked—
> the feeling of being in a room of distorted mirrors—
> reeling—
> Afterwards: a terrible euphoria, hearing something—
> the acoustic difference between
> night and day—
> The feeling that time is running out now, the brain expands once
> more,
> over the weeks the spinal cord gives way again—
> The feeling that one's skin has been stripped away.[32]

Inadvertently, it seems, the last line of Christa Wolf's Büchner-Prize essay cites the last line of the above text by Ulrike Meinhof. In her evoking language, the essay affirms Ulrike Meinhof's subjective agency and creates a dialogue with the invisible and hence unfinished potential of her historical authorship. She is not the "new myth" of progress that "could incite passion but not love" (BP 6). Like Cassandra, the voice of the person behind the myth, she "must have loved Troy more than herself" (BP 11). As one aspect of Rosetta "under her many names," she is not the heroic victim but a masked persona "definable by what she is not" (BP 7). The unnamed Ulrike Meinhof emerges inadvertently in our reading of the Büchner-Prize essay as an author of "a different, accurate language that we have in our ear but not yet on our tongue," a contemporary example of one who has actively "search[ed] for this language" and has experienced "what it really means: to lose control" (BP 5).

Just as Christa Wolf's writing extends beyond the traditional confines of Frauenliteratur, symbolized by the "Angel in the House," her literary project supersedes patriarchal myths perpetuated by the "citadel of reason" (BP 6) and its teleology of myth. By acknowledging the "fear [that] leaps into the vacant spaces" (BP 5) of history, Wolf's language creates associations and affinities that defy the "mortician literature . . . no longer offering euphoria but only euthanasia" (BP 4). "Today," she writes, "literature must be peace-research" (BP 10). This literary project of peace begins by uncovering an obscured past, mediated historically by a landscape of masks. It involves the participation of the reader as well as the writer and thus relinquishes the traditional boundaries between the language of literature and the creative agencies of historical experience. "This is language on the other side of belief, but language nevertheless," Christa Wolf writes about Ingeborg Bachmann's last poem. "One who expresses herself completely does not cancel herself out: the wish for obliteration remains as a witness. Her part will not vanish" (BP 10).

The Reader and the Writer: Narrative Bonding and Friendship

In her essay on Bettina von Arnim, Christa Wolf quotes Bettina in a letter to Karoline von Günderrode: "I can write no fragments, I can only write to you" (BL 315). As an alternative to the many fragments in the history of German literature since the Romantics and Büchner, Wolf's prose incorporates, either explicitly or implicitly, the "you" of the reader into its narrative structure. The "you" is not an abstract, anonymous addressee, as suggested, for example, by Max Frisch's "The Public as Partner" (1967). It is not a partner constructed by the aesthetic or social imagination but a known historical agent whose impact directly affects the formation of the literary work.

The German salon of the late eighteenth and the early nineteenth century provides a historical model for Wolf's aesthetic of the reader and the writer. In her book on Rahel Varnhagen, Hannah Arendt writes: "The salons were the meeting places of those who had learned to represent themselves through conversation. The actor can always be the 'seeming' of himself."[33] In the salon, women took the art of letter writing one step further and came face to face in order to speak and simultaneously listen to each other. For German women writers, the salon, not the theater, provided the most viable forum for public discourse. It was a new kind of "moral institution" in which there was no need for an audience, for this "stage" was not the representation of life but its verbal enactment. In the salon there was also no third literary category which, as narrator, abstractly guided conversation or, as reader, passively observed and absorbed it. The form of the salon demanded subjectivity—as intersubjectivity—on everyone's part. In the salon, subjectivity and Otherness were two sides of the same persona because no one was able to speak alone or for others. The art of conversation assumed the human presence of a literary partner, an active listener, a real "reader." Like the epistolary form, the salon can be seen as

Helen Fehervary

belonging to a genre: women's conception of the drama perhaps, which, incidentally, would answer the tedious question as to why women don't often write plays. Yet unlike the epistolary form, written in domestic isolation, the salon was a public institution that established domesticity and conversation as the center of literary life. The salon imagined no literary authenticity or authorship without reciprocity. It was a literary utopia whose participants might have transformed the genres of the novel and the drama had it not been for the ensuing Restoration and its cultural conservatism. The rest is literary history: the myths of the femininity in domestic tragedy and the monumental social novel.

Christa Wolf's writing can be seen as incorporating the public sphere of the salon in prose form. The literary tradition of the salon is based on the social relations of affective perception and communication between Others, on the pattern of human interaction called friendship. As an aesthetic category, this pattern of interaction can be distinguished from the system of kinship, based on male bonding, that permeates the dominant myths of literary history and comprises what we call tradition.[34] Agnes Heller's distinction between her personal history and the heritage of her philosophical discipline exemplifies this discrepancy:

> I was three years old when my father first told me the parable of the three rings. . . . Since then my relationship to Lessing has always been an intimate one. The word "intimacy" is completely applicable here. The philosophical structures of Aristotle, Kant, or Marx have influenced my thought profoundly, but I would not have been able to deal on a personal level with the people who created these structures: I never would have chosen them for my friends. Lessing, however, was and still is my friend. He extends his hand to us, he imparts no uneasiness in us with his greatness: he is on our level.[35]

The friendship between reader and writer that Heller shares with Lessing corresponds to the relational form between Christa Wolf's narrator and the many names, voices, and masks that emerge in her work. The narrative voice is simultaneously a reader who listens, reflects, cites, and thereby invites others to participate in the creative process. Wolf's recent essay on the question of peace, for example, supports her theoretical speculations.[36] Written in the form of a letter, it presents a narrative voice that is at once a reader and a writer of letters, a hesitant promulgator of ideas and answers, a critical observer of world politics, a vulnerable historical witness to the nuclear threat, an individual in crisis, and, finally, an essayist, a peacemaker. Significantly, she invokes the Hölderlin elegy "Komm! ins Offene, Freund!" Her language invites intimacy, the generosity of friendship, and the relinquishment of the authorial ego in favor of reciprocal involvement. It is an alternative to the open-endedness of epic theater that, in Brecht's view, assumes the attitude of friendliness (a one-sided process) but that nevertheless teaches with craft and cunning while others learn.[37] It is a theater of actors, not directors. The dramatic dialogue of Wolf's prose does not offer the instructive challenge of change but the experience of interdependent Otherness and friendship. As a structural category, friendship is synonymous with the politics of peace.

The relationship between the reader and the writer is more complex in Wolf's fiction. The first and paradigmatic example is her short story "An Afternoon in June," written in 1965, during her authorial transformation from the writing of *Divided Heaven* to *The Quest for Christa T.* The story begins with a question: "A story? Something solid and tangible, like a vessel with two handles, to hold and drink from?" And it continues with a rejoinder: "A vision perhaps, if you know what I mean" (AJ 41). In this, her first short story, Christa Wolf uses the second-person pronoun for the first time in the narrative structure of her prose. In German it is the formal "Sie," and it reoccurs throughout the story: "You can imagine how disquieting it is" (AJ 43–44); "How can I explain to you in plain terms" (AJ 51); "If you ask me" (AJ 52); "Forgive me. But it's difficult not to be swept away. Maybe there are better words" (AJ 53); "Do you know what he said? You won't be able to guess" (AJ 53); "Do you know the feeling when a question strikes at your inner core?" (AJ 55). Clearly, the narrator is addressing someone with whom she is on familiar, though not intimate terms, and with whom she talks about language and communication. The "Sie" she addresses is distinct from the familiar "Du" with which the narrative "I" within the story addresses her husband and children, as well as from the formal "Sie" she uses with the other characters in the story. The "Sie" with whom the narrator is in dialogue is absent from the plot line of the story but present on the level of narration. Conversation with this "Sie" takes place in the present tense of the narrator's time frame, while the conversations with the characters of the story take place in the past.

The narrator is a reader as well as a writer. In fact, the act of reading is the pivotal point around which the events, conversations, and reflections of the story unfold. The storyline is simple: A woman, the narrative "I," is reclining in a chair in her garden, reading a book. Meanwhile, her husband prunes the hedges, her two daughters chatter and play, and neighbors drop in to exchange news. The topos of the woman reading in the drawing room or the garden has been a familiar device since the Enlightenment. The sentimental heroine reads frivolous, even dangerous novels. In the works of Jane Austen her efforts are misunderstood, chastised, or perceived as trivial; in Flaubert's *Madame Bovary* she pays for this preoccupation with her life. The traditional cultural image of the woman reading is shrouded in mystery. Not the content of the book but the very act of reading provides the framework of significance. As typically portrayed in nineteenth-century paintings, the woman is not directly involved with the spectator but engrossed in a third presence. Her involvement in the life of the book takes her out of the control of the spectator and hence makes her aesthetically intriguing and mysterious. By contrast, a nineteenth-century merchant reading a book is aesthetically uninteresting. If involved with a book at all, he holds it in his hand as a sign of his person and wealth. For the hero of the eighteenth-century novel, the book also has symbolic value. The title of the book is worthy of mention, not the act of reading itself. Werther cites *Ossian*, and *Emilia Galotti* is found on his night-table after his suicide. In the tradition of the nineteenth-century novel, Thomas Mann's hero Thomas Buddenbrooks reads (Schopenhauer and Nietzsche) for philosophical contemplation. As a cynical contemporary comment on the hero's accumulated wealth of literary associations, Max Frisch lists the chaotic array of titles on his main character's bookshelf in *Homo Faber*. With its ready body of meanings, the book usually serves the literary hero as an affirmation or aggrandizement of his identity. It is a container of ideas that belongs to him and feeds his development. It is a mirror, not a mystery.

Nor is it a vision. The traditional function of the literary work in literature is akin to the narrator's first tentative definition of a story in "An Afternoon in June": "Something solid and tangible, like a vessel with two handles, to hold and drink from?" Wolf's second attempt at definition—"a vision perhaps"—comes closer to the topos of the woman reading and hence shrouded in mystery. However, from the perspective of the woman reading the book, as opposed to the perspective of the spectator, this relationship not only allows mystery but also provides another way of seeing—a vision. Wolf's initial reflections on the nature of a story comment not only on the writing of her story, but they also pertain to the stories in the book she reads as a character in her own story. Neither the title nor the author of the book contributes to her sense of authorship; indeed, the book and its author are never named. Rather, the process of perceiving and experiencing the metaphoric landscape of the book allows her to write her own story and to exist as its author. The book does not legitimate but rather demands that she extend herself beyond her previous narrative identity. It is not a symbol but part of an interdependent narrative process, a literary partnership. The "vision" of the stories being read and the story being written is a way of seeing and a possibility for growth through communicative interaction.

It is significant that the narrator has not directly inherited the book she reads from its author but that it was recommended to her by her husband. She is in fact reluctant to merge her own experience as reader and writer with the literary tradition to which her husband has greater historical access and for which he possesses sharper critical tools:

> You know, I said to my husband a little later—I couldn't see him but I could hear his pruning shears . . . . Dear, I said, you were right after all.

Of course, he said. I don't know why you never wanted to read it before!

She can write, I said.

Although it's not all good, he said, so that I wouldn't run the danger of overshooting the mark once again.

Clever! But the way she comes to terms with that country . . .

Yes! he said in a superior tone. Italy!

And the sea? I challenged.

Ah yes! he cried, as though that were irrefutable proof.

The Mediterranean!

But that's not it at all. One very precise word next to another. That's what it is.

Although the Mediterranean is not to be dismissed entirely either, he said.

You with your foreign words all the time, the child said reproachfully. (AJ 42)

Because she has indirect access to the products of the literary heritage, when she does read she reads differently. Or she discovers a different landscape within this heritage. Although her husband is interested in the description of a historical place (Italy and the Mediterranean are familiar topoi within German literature), she is concerned with the landscape that emerges from an unfamiliar arrangement of words. Increasingly absorbed in her book, the narrator is interrupted repeatedly by her children's questions, her husband's rejoinders, the sound of jets breaking the sound barrier overhead, the gossip of neighbors. Nevertheless, her relationship to the book and its author creates a dialogue that emerges from beneath the scattered comments and fragmented conversations surrounding her. The book acts as the centering device for the story and thus provides a third presence, an alternative Other to the "I"/"you" relationship between the narrator and the other characters: "The book for example, that I still held in my hands and that had the advantage of not interfering with the contemplation of apricot trees . . . in all modesty it contributed its own, as the third person should" (AJ 49).

The third person or presence is as threatening as it seems familiar, for it articulates many fears and premonitions that slip by unnoticed in the fragmented conversations of the lazy afternoon. The book reveals the strangeness of foreign territories and "too many hermits, prophets, and hexes" (AJ 49). At one point the narrator is engrossed in a "somewhat sad dialogue" (AJ 47); at another she allows herself to skip a story that describes "a horrible mob revenge against a traitor" (AJ 49). She admits that she is incapable of enduring "all these mutilations and murders of men before the eyes of their wives held in bondage" (AJ 50). At the end of the story the garden idyll appropriately fades with the setting sun, and the narrator rises from her chair to stand upright. But the Marxist paradigm of base-superstructure has been turned on its head. The earth that should provide a firm foundation is fluid, and the narrator is not grounded but at sea: "One is afraid if there is still no ground in sight; one throws ballast overboard, this or that, only to float up again"

(AJ 64). The closing line of the story, ironically phrased as a question, brings the reading experience of a faded afternoon into sharp focus: "When was that with the Mediterranean, asked the child. Today?" (AJ 64). The child's vague question leaves us with the final indirect reference to the book and encourages us to reflect as readers on the masked presence of the "third person."[38]

One year after "An Afternoon in June," Wolf wrote her well-known essay on Bachmann: "Truth That Can Be Faced—Ingeborg Bachmann's Prose" (1966). Once again Christa Wolf is a reader as well as a writer. She begins the essay: "When preparing to read this prose one should not expect stories, descriptive action. Information about events or characters in the accepted sense is no more to be expected than harsh assertions. A voice audacious and lamenting. A voice speaking honestly about its own experience of things certain and uncertain. And, when the voice fails, an honest silence" (IB 83). At the end of the essay Wolf speaks in the "we"-form about the interrelationship between reader and writer demanded by Bachmann's prose: "We read Ingeborg Bachmann's prose through the filter of this experience. Thus, it may indeed gain a further dimension, a dimension that the author herself could not foresee, for every reader works with the author on the book he reads. And Ingeborg Bachmann is one of the writers who expressly depends on the cooperation of her readers. She raises and fulfills the claim to be contemporary" (IB 95–96).

Wolf writes her essay in a language that cites Bachmann, is metaphorically prefigured in "An Afternoon in June," and forms the basis of her later prose fiction. The most explicit parallel to her earlier story is her reference to the notion of "vision":

> Vision! people say casually. What is it—vision? When one suddenly sees what cannot be seen but must be there because it has effects. The past in the present, for example. Or the immoderate desires, always held in check, that can arise in anyone at any time, who knows from whence . . . . But, above all else, relationship and meaning behind apparently unrelated and insignificant things. The discovery of what they all live on and, no matter what they try to pretend, what they are really dying of. (IB 88)

The transition from *Divided Heaven* to *The Quest for Christa T.* reveals a critical period in Wolf's literary development as she formulated her subsequent relationship to prose. Her description of Bachmann's authorial vulnerability suggests her own vulnerability as author between the writing of her first two major prose works:

> Ingeborg Bachmann, fully aware of the tradition of which she is a part, of the group of problems on which she can draw and to which she is bound, is affected by her experience so convincingly, so fundamentally and so much in her own individual way that the idea of imitation cannot arise. She does not play with despair, the sense of menace and bewilderment—she is in despair, she is menaced and

bewildered, and therefore genuinely desires to be rescued. The signs she makes—the tapping, the attempts to break out—are real. She is ruthless to herself, too, in her efforts. (IB 90)

Wolf's phrasing in this passage directly anticipates the language of her narrator's reflections in The Quest for Christa T. Indeed, her story "An Afternoon in June" and her essay on Bachmann are the prolegomena to her subsequent novel. Written during this period but not published until 1968, The Quest for Christa T. ends, like her story, by invoking "the past in the present": "When, if not now?" It pursues in greater depth the literary project first evident in Wolf's story and essay: the articulated presence of the authorial self as both reader and writer —the author Christa Wolf as both self and Other, as both narrator and Christa T. Whereas in her story the author is the anonymous third person and in the essay she is the historical persona of Bachmann, in her novel Wolf finds the mask of authorship in terms of her own first name: Christa T.

Notes

This article first appeared in NGC, no. 27 (Fall 1982): 57–87. The text has been slightly revised and updated.

1. This pattern evidently applies to all the German classics: Goethe, Schiller, Hölderlin, Kleist, Büchner, Kafka, Thomas Mann, Brecht, etc.

2. Rita's breakdown in The Divided Heaven is synonymous with the author Wolf's literary crisis during this time. By comparison, Anna Karenina's suicide by throwing herself under a train is largely a symbolic gesture and has little to do with the author Tolstoy's literary life.

3. Cf. the expansion of authorial identity in Gertrude Stein's The Autobiography of Alice T. Toklas and the narrative relationship to identity and difference in her Three Lives.

4. Bloch, "Nonsynchronism and the Obligation to Its Dialectics," NGC, no. 11 (Spring 1977): 22.

5. Cf. Benjamin, "The Author as Producer," in Reflections: Essays, Aphorisms, Autobiographical Writings, ed. Peter Demetz; trans. Edmond Jephcott (New York: Harcourt Brace Jovanovich, 1978), 220–238.

6. In her correspondence with Lukács during the realism debate of the 1930s, Anna Seghers argued on behalf of those writers (Kleist, Hölderlin, Günderrode, et al.) who for historical and personal reasons did not exhibit the totality of literary production as exemplified by Goethe, and she suggested that the notion of realism be expanded to account for these writers' authorial experiences and the ensuing literary quality of their works. Christa Wolf, who has often acknowledged her literary debt to Seghers, frequently refers to these letters in her essays. Cf. for example her three essays on Seghers in Lesen und Schreiben. Neue Sammlung, 115–157. The Reader and the Writer contains only the first two essays on Seghers: "Faith in the Terrestriial" and "A Visit to Anna Seghers," 111–143.

7. Brecht, "Writing the Truth: Five Difficulties," trans. Richard Winston, in Brecht, Galileo, trans. Charles Laughton (New York: Grove, 1966), 149 ff.; Brecht, "To Posterity," in German Poetry, 1910–1975, ed. and trans. Michael Hamburger (New York: Urizen, n.d.), 169–173.

8. Adorno, Prismen: Kulturkritik und Gesellschaft (Berlin and Frankfurt/M.: Suhrkamp, 1955), 31. Unless otherwise indicated, translations from German are by the author.

9. Cf. Alexander and Margarete Mitscherlich, *The Inability to Mourn: Principles of Collective Behavior*, trans. Beverly R. Placzek (New York: Grove, 1975); Margarete Mitscherlich, "Die Frage der Selbstdarstellung: Überlegungen zu den Autobiographien von Helene Deutsch, Margaret Mead und Christa Wolf," NR 91 (1980): 291–316.

10. Benjamin, "Theses on the Philosophy of History," in *Illuminations*, ed. Hannah Arendt, trans. Harry Zohn (New York: Schocken, 1969), 257–258.

11. Ibid., 261.

12. Ibid., 262.

13. Ibid., 262–63.

14. Regarding contemporary German literature, cf. Heiner Müller's "Der glücklose Engel" (The Hapless Angel), in *Theater-Arbeit* (West Berlin: Rotbuch, 1975), 18. Cf. also my analysis of Benjamin's and Müller's texts in "History and Aesthetics in Bertolt Brecht and Heiner Müller," *NGC*, no. 8 (Spring 1976): 80–109.

15. Cf., in this spirit, the phallic associations Klaus Theweleit finds in Ernst Bloch's formulation of "der aufrechte Gang" (standing upright or the upright posture) as a utopian model within critical theory: Theweleit, *Männerphantasien* (Male Fantasies), Vol. 2: *Männerkörper: Zur Psychoanalyse des Weissen Terrors* (Frankfurt/Main: Roter Stern, 1978), 68; for Theweleit's comments regarding Bloch on women, cf. vol. 1: *Frauen, Fluten, Körper, Geschichte* (Women, Floods, Bodies, History), (Frankfurt/Main: Roter Stern, 1977), 212–213.

16. Woolf, "Professions for Women," in *The Death of the Moth and Other Essays* (New York: Harcourt Brace Jovanovich, 1974), 237–238.

17. Cf. Simone de Beauvoir, *The Second Sex*, trans. and ed. H. M. Parshley (New York: Vintage, 1974), 205–206: "Women being the very substance of man's poetic work, it is understandable that she should appear as his inspiration: the Muses are women. . . . A Muse creates nothing by herself; she is a calm, wise Sibyl, putting herself with docility at the service of a master."

18. Benjamin, "Theses," 262.

19. Woolf, "Professions," 240.

20. Benjamin, "Theses," 263.

21. Woolf, Professions," 240.

22. Ibid., 238.

23. Ibid., 241.

24. Bovenschen, *Die imaginierte Weiblichkeit: Exemplarische Untersuchungen zu kulturgeschichtlichen und literarischen Präsentationsformen des Weiblichen* (Frankfurt/Main: Suhrkamp, 1979), 43.

25. The modernist's battle against the omniscient narrator is one more example of the literary revolts of sons against fathers that do not take into account the absence of women's narrative omniscience. From this perspective it might seem more plausible that Anna Seghers, generally criticized in the West for the "dogmatism" of her later work, has increasingly exerted her narrative omniscience in her writing—perhaps as an inadvertent attempt to make up for the previous lack of narrative control by her own sex in her own language. Luise Rinser exhibits a similar tendency toward narrative omniscience and "dogmatism" (in her case Catholicism, not Marxism). It is surely significant that the two most prolific German women writers of the twentieth century, Seghers and Rinser, have succeeded in the public forum of literary history in the tradition of realism, whereas the foremost women writers in the modernist tradition, Else Lasker-Schüler and Ingeborg Bachmann, barely survived in the shadows of their more successful male counterparts. The difference between Seghers/Rinser and Lasker-Schüler/Bachmann applies no less to the lives of these writers than it does to their works. Christa Wolf's literary development demonstrates the struggle to overcome the limitations that both of these traditions present for women writers.

26. Cf. my articles "Prometheus Rebound: Technology and the Dialectic of Myth," in *The Technological Imagination: Theories and Fictions*, ed. Teresa de Lauretis, Andreas Huyssen, and Kathleen Woodward (Madison: Coda Press, 1980), 95–105; and "Die erzählerische Kolonisierung des weiblichen Schweigens: Frau und Arbeit in der DDR-Literatur," in *Arbeit als Thema in der deutschen Literatur vom Mittelalter bis zur Gegenwart*, ed. Reinhold Grimm and Jost Hermand (Königstein/Ts.: Athenäum, 1979), 171–195.

27. Woolf, "Professions," 241.

28. Cf. Bloch, *Das Prinzip Hoffnung* (Frankfurt/Main: Suhrkamp, 1959).

29. The words in brackets are left out in the American edition.

30. Robert Graves, *The Greek Myths*, vol. 1 (Harmondsworth: Penguin, 1960), 77.

31. Ingeborg Bachmann, "Das schreibende Ich" (The I That Writes), (Third Frankfurt Lecture), in *Werke*, vol. 4 (Munich: R. Piper, 1978), 229.

32. Quoted in Peter Brückner, *Ulrike Meinhof und die deutschen Verhältnisse* (West Berlin: Verlag Klaus Wagenbach, 1976), 157.

33. Hannah Arendt, *Rahel Varnhagen: The Life of a Jewish Woman*, trans. Richard and Clara Winston (New York: Harcourt Brace Jovanovich, 1974), 38.

34. Cf. the countless variations of Oedipus, Odysseus, and Faust, invocations of Orestes and Hamlet, and the ensuing revolts of literary sons against literary fathers, fictional brothers against brothers, in order to perpetuate the inherited lineage and produce future kin. The primary others within the system of kinship are women, existing in isolation as idealized or castrating projections of the central characters.

35. Agnes Heller, "Enlightenment Against Fundamentalism: The Example of Lessing," *NGC*, no. 23 (Spring/Summer 1981): 13.

36. Wolf, " 'Komm! ins Offene, Freund!' Können wir den Frieden retten?" *SZ* 42 (February 20/21, 1982): 100.

37. Cf. BO 57–59.

38. Shortly after the publication of the original version of this article, I learned from Christa Wolf that her fictional account in "An Afternoon in June" was based on her actual reading of Marie-Luise Kaschnitz's *Lange Schatten* (Long Shadows, 1960), not Ingeborg Bachmann's *Das dreissigste Jahr* (*The Thirtieth Year*, 1961) as I had conjectured in my article. Although this fact clearly proves my original hypothesis to be erroneous—namely, that Bachmann's *Das dreissigste Jahr* had provided the referential literary framework for Wolf's first short story—it hardly affects my basic argument regarding the narrative relationship between reading and writing and its significance for the development of Wolf's work at that time. Consequently, aside from occasional editorial revisions having to do with a more critical eye toward one's work after the passing of almost two years, I have found it necessary to make only one substantive change in the present version: the deletion of one paragraph devoted to a discussion of Bachmann's *Das dreissigste Jahr* (pp. 84–85 of the original printed text). My pursuant discussion of Bachmann's influence on Wolf seems no less pertinent than it was, and, except for slight stylistic changes and the deletion of four tedious concluding sentences, I have let it stand in its original form. After all is said and done, I would venture to say that the information concerning Wolf's reading of Kaschnitz does less to diminish the crucial influence of Bachmann, which stands uncontested in any case, than to further support the notion of literary interdependence and "friendship" and to broaden the context of contemporary women writers influencing Christa Wolf's early work.

"To render the blind spot of this culture visible": Prose Beyond the "Citadel of Reason"

Myra N. Love

You began musing about the vicissitudes to which reason can be subjected; reason and irrationality changing places suddenly, in times of upheaval; the enormous spreading of insecurity before each has been reestablished and defined" (PC 92). These lines from the fifth chapter of Christa Wolf's *Patterns of Childhood* emphasize the insecurity produced by the vicissitudes of reason in times of transition—a theme taken up again four years later in her 1980 "Büchner-Prize Acceptance Speech"—but are marked by an optimism that more recent publications and utterances lack: a trust that reason and unreason do eventually assume their proper places again.

"The condition of the world is awry" (BP 5), Christa Wolf announced quietly yet with conviction in her "Büchner-Prize Acceptance Speech." "A new cycle of historical contradictions is imminent—will it, under the sign of 'overkill,' be granted enough time to develop?" (BP 4). The frightening possibility that reason and unreason may never again assume their proper places and that the disruption of their relationship may have fatal consequences for the human species haunts both that speech and the short prose piece originally broadcast over the *Südwestfunk* (December 31, 1981) and first published in the collection *Mut zur Angst. Schriftsteller für den Frieden* (Courage to Fear. Writers for Peace) under the title "A Letter":

When I observe myself, I catch myself daily, nightly in a continual inner monologue which rarely ceases—can Europe, can we be saved? When I think clearly and rationally, when I consider all the information available to me about the armament of both sides, when I contemplate above all the thought structures which support this armament, then my answer is no—or probably not.

. . . If they dare to consider the destruction of this Europe in their military calculations, then we—numbered deaths in the statistics of the nuclear planning staffs—may indeed be permitted to venture a few things ourselves; then our subordination to the logic whose ultimate manifestation is the rocket has become senseless. That is to say, we cannot be radical enough in our questions about the causes of this radical threat; in the face of the "situation," militarily speaking, in which we find ourselves—shouldn't we think, suggest, and attempt that which "is actually impossible?" (L 153–154)

In *The Quest for Christa T.*, Christa Wolf had written of her protagonist: "she said we had a right to invent, to think out inventions that should be audacious but never careless. Because nothing can become reality unless it has been thought out beforehand" (CT 169). The possibility of thought that escapes and overthrows the logic "whose ultimate manifestation is the rocket" has increasingly been a major concern of Christa Wolf and a central focus for her writing.

One can trace this concern back quite far, at least to the utopian aura[1] of *Divided Heaven* (1963), where Ernst Wendland and Manfred Herrfurth argue about the role of reason in history. Wendland's faith in reason as a constitutive factor in history, like Rita Seidel's belief that life has meaning, contrasts with Manfred's rejection of reason as a historical force and his reduction of it to technical rationality. Manfred's resignation and surrender to indifference reproduce his mother's fascistoid, petit bourgeois world-view despite his rejection of her. His choice, manifest in his move to West Germany, of the society with the more rationalized productive and technological capability is not the choice of a more rational society, and he knows it. It is instead a decision against the struggle for a society in which reason could be realized in the structure of its social relations.

In 1964, a year after the publication of *Divided Heaven*, Christa Wolf was still optimistic that the GDR could become such a society: "Reason, we call it socialism, has penetrated into everyday life. It is the measure, the ideal, by which we judge how praise or blame is to be meted out" (S 26). The belief in the eventual triumph of reason in the form of socialism in the GDR would be the ultimate justification of Rita's decision not to stay with Manfred in the West, for to do so would then implicate her in his betrayal of reason. But Rita's decision itself is not based in reason but in faith that the world can be judged according to an absolute moral standard. This becomes obvious in her last conversation with Schwarzenbach:

187

"I sometimes wonder whether we ought really to judge the world by our standards—of good and evil, I mean," Rita went on. "Shouldn't we just take it as it is?"

But if that were really true, she thought, it would have been silly not to have stayed with Manfred; any sacrifice would be silly. (*DH* 196)

Here a major contradiction emerges in *Divided Heaven*.

The meaninglessness that Rita finds in life in the West derives from reducing reason in capitalist society to a formal logic incapable of addressing social and moral questions other than as problems of efficient organization. Christa Wolf based Rita's trust in the future of socialism in the GDR on her own hope that the redistribution of the means of production (thematized in the text as the introduction of collective farming) would result in a radical transformation of social relations and human personality in the GDR. Hence Wolf's positive thematization of the development of the productive sphere in the text. She did not investigate the dangers posed by the expansion of the realm governed by instrumental rationality because its primacy was understood to be provisional, a temporary state of development on the way to the realization of reason in social life. In her "Büchner-Prize Acceptance Speech" and later, however, Wolf was to acknowledge the continuing predominance of this sort of (destructive) thinking that gives precedence to *ratio* at the cost of what might be "reasonable" in human terms; it describes a mode of (anti-)social behavior that is strictly utilitarian. "Sober to the marrow," she says, "we stand aghast before the dreams made real by instrumental thinking that still calls itself reason, although it has long since lost its enlightened impulse toward emancipation, toward maturity, and has entered the Industrial Age as barefaced utiliarian mania" (BP 4).

The redistribution of the means of production in the GDR did not lead to the revolutionary transformation of social life. On the contrary, it extended such instrumental rationality beyond the productive sphere into the organization of society in the GDR. GDR socialism thus failed to break out of the historical continuum in which progress is identical with the reduction of reason to a formal logic similar to that in the West—lacking social and ethical content and relegating questions of social morality to the realm of ideology.

In *Divided Heaven*, Rita's coupling of the possibility of "sense" to an abstract and ahistorical moral standard introduces a timeless element that contrasts markedly with the emphasis on the transitoriness of the present in the rest of the work. In Rita's insistence on the necessary correspondence between the world and static moral categories, as in her supposed recovery of the power to call things by their correct names (*DH* 202), there is an implicit identification of utopia with a retrogression to a fixed world order and with a prescientific world-view that excludes change. But the separation of rationality from morality that accompanied the breakdown of that world-view in the period of the Enlightenment cannot be abolished retroactively without recourse to some nonrational authority. The attempt to do this leads to the degeneration of reason, whose emancipatory potential always involved rejecting irrational authority, into an agency for the affirmative reflection of what exists.

Divided Heaven minimizes the distance and the radical difference between an imperfect present and utopian perfection in an attempt to insure the preservation of the social and moral dimensions of reason in the face of reason's reduction to the regulatory mechanism of industrial society that occurred under capitalism. Rita's admission that "sense" depended on a moral standard that could be derived not from reason but only from faith in the future revealed the chasm across which formalized rationality and abstract morality confront each other in modern industrial societies—a gulf most familiar, perhaps, in the epistemological designation: fact-value dichotomy.

Rita's faith could not convert a skeptical Manfred whose disillusionment with a real present could not be compensated by a possible future, and whose disbelief in reason as a historical force led him to dismiss the possibility of social morality as a mere illusion: "'I'm only sorry that such quantities of illusions and energy are wasted in trying to do the impossible—to make people good'" (*DH* 153). For those determining the direction of social and economic development in the GDR, whose belief in reason does not take into account its historical evolution into instrumental rationality and therefore takes the form of an identification of the progress of reason with scientific-technological progress, the positive evolution of social relations follows "logically" and inevitably the industrial development of a society that has abolished private ownership of the means of production. Hence a concern with social morality is ultimately the same as legitimation of the system which results "logically" in the realization of reason in social life. This is one definition of socialist "party-mindedness" (*Parteilichkeit*), a dominant concept of socialist theory that, most generally, denotes the expected commitment of all people engaged in intellectual activity to the ideological welfare of the state.[2]

"It is not that I would deny the eminent connections between literature and social morality," Christa Wolf wrote in "On the Sense and Senselessness of Naiveté" (1973), "but the social morality of an author should not exhaust itself in withholding from his society what he knows about it" (*SN* 61). Already in 1965, in her contribution to "Necessary Argument," Christa Wolf had questioned the sort of "partisanship" that could be equated with "blind support of the party" and is therefore irreconcilable with the tasks of literature, which lie "in the realm of the discovery of truth and in the attempt ... to express this truth literarily" (*NA* 100–101). "The discovery of truth," the antithesis of "the justification of that which is (a justification that is equal to a renunciation of knowledge)" (*NA* 103), is the link that Christa Wolf establishes between art and reason. Such a link is essential, facing the inability of advancing technical rationality to reflect upon its own ends:

> In this land we have worked and are working hard. And the question is now acute: what are we working for? To what end do we practice this socialism at all? For it can happen that concentration on the means—politics, economy—can cause the end to be forgotten: the human being. Here, I believe, is the point to which literature must attend and at which it must defend its position. (NA 102–103)

The main theme in this passage is familiar: the danger implicit in the confusion of means and ends. It reappears fifteen years later in the statement: "The condition of the world is awry." "The discovery of truth," generated by a need "to think together about the meaning of our efforts and our struggles" (NA 102), can occur only through the development of structures for communication that allow a shared participation in the very processes of reflection that technical reason excludes.

"To think together about the meaning"—precisely what Rita and Manfred could not do: "There had been too many things left undiscussed between them, Rita thought" (DH 115). The very idea only occurs to Rita after Manfred has left, when she is on her way to Berlin to see him for the last time. In that context it emphasizes the disjunction rather than the relationship between them: "It would be good if he didn't think that everything is decided when he sees me coming. He ought to let me think about things, together with him" (DH 171).[3] The obstacles to communication that lie at the heart of the conflict in *Divided Heaven* do not affect only Manfred and Rita. They are built into a society in which authorities didactically distribute praise and blame in the name of reason but where reason has yet been unrealized in society in the form of "a rational coexistence of human beings"; thus, judgment actually relies not on reason, but on the opposition of good and evil as understood from the perspective of authority. In the GDR this translates into the equation of "party-mindedness" with uncritical "justification of that which is."

The establishment of a context for communication free of domination[4] will prove to be a much more serious problem. The condescending didacticism of those in power does little more than reinforce Manfred's tendency to "disinterestedness," a tendency that is a product of his personal history (and the history of his generation).

The problem is not and cannot be resolved in *Divided Heaven*. Rita, who allowed time to do its work, recovers from her crisis by learning "exact thinking" (DH 120), "to call things by their correct names" (DH 202), and "to avoid touching the wound—that too" (DH 120). "But," Christa Wolf wrote in *The Quest for Christa T.* only a few years after this, "there are scars which only give pain when one has to go on growing. Should one keep quiet because one's afraid of the pain?" (CT 71). The regression to "the naive belief that one can exact total correspondence between word and thing,"[5] that characterized *Divided Heaven* is superseded in *The Quest for Christa T.* by the liberation of language from the impossible (and ultimately unproductive) task of reproducing or simply reflecting a reified reality.

In a situation where the effective penetration of everyday life by science occurs without establishing communication free of domination, literature becomes a tool in the attempt to make such communication possible:

> It seems absurd to try to achieve an "epic prose." And yet one has the feeling that there ought to be such a thing; a genre that has the courage to think of itself as an instrument, sharp, accurate, attacking, changing, to be used as a means, not as an end in itself. As a means to shift the future into the present, and in detail; for prose is read by individuals who withdraw alone with a book, paying no attention to all the temptations of modern technology. (RW 201)

Insofar as language refuses simply to reflect the reified reality, "the inevitability of things in the world" (CT 71) that Christa T. feared, it breaks through the passive human subject by revealing how apparently unrelated facts are constituted and connected by relations. Christa Wolf insisted on the importance of art in her essay "Diary—Aid to Work and Memory" (1964): "The great questions with which art confronts us cannot be abandoned. What else but art is to find a synthesis between all those contemporary human attitudes that are often so hard to explain? What else but art can bring some reasonable order, suitable for us, into the flood of so-called facts?" (D 64). An order that is both "reasonable" and "suitable for us" seems almost a contradiction in a world where rationality is identical with "utility," the efficient functioning of larger systems in which human beings are generally interchangeable parts.

Prose is constituted, according to Christa Wolf, by a language that refuses to subordinate the human subject to its ends; instead, it insists on its own instrumentality by revealing its functions in the course of revealing the relations and processes that underlie "reality":

> The new reality you see is different from the one you saw before. Suddenly, everything is interconnected and fluid. Things formerly taken as "given" start to dissolve, revealing the reified social relations they contain and no longer that hierarchically arranged social cosmos in which the human particle travels along the paths pre-ordained by sociology or ideology, or deviates from them. It becomes more and more difficult to say "I," and yet at the same time often imperative to do so. (SA)

The language of literature differs radically from the language of science and of politics because it refuses to participate in the scientistic subordination of human beings to the progress of efficient systematization and thereby falsely to equate the utopian realization of reason in social life with the triumph of instrumental rationality in an administered society. As Christa Wolf explains in her "Büchner-Prize Acceptance Speech":

> But ... if the three languages of politics, science, and literature
> —which Büchner managed to unite in his person through physical
> and intellectual overexertion—have diverged irrevocably from one
> another: the language of literature, strangely enough, seems to come
> closest today to human reality, to know human beings best, however
> many objections may arise from statistics, data charts, standardiza-
> tion and performance tabulations. Perhaps because an author's cour-
> age—courage for self-knowledge—always enters into literature.
> (BP 10)

The moral courage of the author has nothing "to do with Christian antinomies of good and evil, with a rigid contradistinction between thought
and deed" (SA), but it consists rather in an ongoing attempt to constitute a world of discourse aimed at making possible the discovery and
communication of generalizable human interests suppressed or distorted in the course of history.[6]

Literature reconstitutes the link between reason and morality
and the connection between reality and utopia by basing the possibility
for realizing reason in society's relations on the human capacity for reciprocal communication rather than on an abstract antithesis of good
and evil. Reason, no longer understood as an abstract standard for
praise and blame, becomes active: "earthly good sense, thinking, sympathizing, understanding" (FT 133). Its activity, understood as social
communication—"to help each other see the light" (BP 9)—not only
prefigures a social utopia but helps to bring it closer by shifting attention too often focused on technique to the question of purpose.

That shift in focus, however, does not occur easily: "That we are
afraid to peer into the 'dark, unrevealed depths of language' of which
Humboldt speaks, and to participate in their fates does not surprise, especially since we find it so difficult to confront ourselves."[7] The self-interest that requires self-knowledge, "without which, however, reason
cannot exist, according to Kant" (BP 6), has long since been superseded
by another sort of self-interest, whose most striking characteristic is its
adaptability to even the most self-destructive situations. Reason, initially an instrument of human self-emancipation, is no longer, in its reduction to formal logic, even adequate to self-preservation:

> We are producing that which kills us; the absurd is true, the fantastic
> is realistic, and the formal-logical thought of the "healthy human
> mind" is an insane notion. The prognoses of art are coming true, the
> progress-obsessed predictions of science now take aim at their inven-
> tors. The needs they served, which they aroused, which they are in
> service to—too many of them "perverted"—have broken loose and
> whip them on. To where, they hardly dare to ask any more. (L 155–
> 156)

When the claim that reason is more than a regulatory mechanism
oriented toward expedient and adaptive behavior is declared irrational,
the temptation to reject reason becomes very strong. The artist who refuses either to accept that current definition of reason or to embrace ir-

rationality risks being considered naive and unrealistic at the very least. When the artist's advocacy of reason, like her devotion to her society and to humanity, questions the understanding that reason, her society, and humanity have of themselves, she may be dismissed as overwrought, oversensitive, a little hysterical, even insane.[8] In any case, her concerns are not, as Lutz quite correctly points out in *Patterns of Childhood*, taken into account where decisions about the organization and aims of society are made: "It's the domain of the experts. The suffering soul doesn't enter into the picture" (PC 339).

Even though the issue for the narrator was not really "the suffering soul" but rather the fear that the direction taken by her society may end "in self-destruction" (PC 339), she admits: "When Lutz was right, he was right" (PC 339). In a discussion following a reading from *Patterns of Childhood* in 1975, Christa Wolf pointed out that the members of her generation now occupying positions of responsibility and power in the GDR might very well not even read her book and would therefore not be moved to the sort of reflection at which it aims: "You know, those people . . . probably won't read the book. Not out of ill will; they don't have the time for it, their lives take place outside of literature" (DW 873). She is by no means convinced of the capacity of literature to influence larger social, political, or economic developments:

> I do not believe that books directly effect anything in the political realm. It is a misunderstanding to believe that they should do this at all. . . .
>   Sometimes I am tempted to claim that literature effects nothing at all. But then I resist this false standard myself—for literature . . . gives me—and I know I'm not an exception—a depth, an additional dimension in life which makes its possible for me to look forward to the next day. This seems to me a kind of effect which cannot be overestimated—nor can it, however, be measured. (WS 57)

The sense of reality institutionalized in advanced industrial societies excludes the unquantifiable: "That which cannot be measured, weighed, counted, verified, is as good as nonexistent. It does not count" (L 154). This sense of reality is shared by bureaucratic capitalist and socialist societies alike, appearing and being experienced, according to Christa Wolf, in both German states as a "harsh current of unqualified realism, in the sense that the only thing officially valued as 'real' is what's institutionalized in one form or another." She continues: "Both states are institutionalized; very tangible expectations that must be met by institutions have become institutionalized. This has become highly developed in both countries. . . . Basically, everything that institutions can imagine is covered. However, the fact is that institutions cannot imagine the essential things; they slip through the perfect structures" (CI 98). Whatever escapes institutionalization is also officially excluded as irrational and unreal: "needs for communication" that do not contribute to the smooth functioning of the system and to the facilitation of impersonal but socially adaptive interaction and are therefore more often perceived as eccentricities than needs. These include chiefly the complex of emotions, attitudes, and habits of behavior once designated as "sensibility" but now more often viewed as a weakened condition of the nerves common to artists and women, and any and all other experiences whose censorship is part of civilized behavior: "everything that we are not and have not been permitted to see, hear, smell, taste, feel, and say" (L 156).

Only factual or formulaic knowledge can officially be known. The question raised in *Patterns of Childhood*, "why the conviction that man should be guided by his knowledge, rather than by his faith, has thus far produced so little beauty," is, so the narrator thinks, "posed wrongly" because it excludes from consideration "the type, the extent, the direction, and the goal of this knowledge" (PC 338).

Certainly the modes of knowledge that have arisen in the course of "progress" of Western civilization have been implicated in the barbarism that accompanied that progress:

> I am plagued by the thought that our culture, which can achieve that which it calls "progress" only through force, through internal suppression and the destruction and desolation of foreign cultures; which has reduced its sense of reality in the pursuit of material interests; which has become instrumental and effective—that such a culture had to come to the stage at which it is. (L 157)

A civilization "that with insane shortsightedness focuses solely on products, that turns its most loved and valued possessions—money and technological perfection—toward self-destruction" (BP 4) has simply rationalized that barbarism rather than overcome it. The possibilities for intersubjective knowledge and communication offered by such a civilization are limited by the distortions introduced through the structures of domination that facilitate that civilization's exploitation of the material world. The division of labor, which makes efficiency and control possible, reduces the human subject to a function of larger systems and offers protection and power only at the price of fragmentation and self-estrangement that make self-knowledge and open communication almost unachievable.

Christa Wolf's writing cannot and does not claim ability to reverse the process through which the means of production are transformed into the agencies of destruction. "Poetry," she wrote in her essay on Karoline von Günderrode, "is related to the essence of utopia, which is to say, it possesses a painful-pleasurable inclination to embrace absolute values. Most human beings cannot endure the verbalization of dissatisfaction with that reduced life with which they must be content" (SD 282).

The expression of dissatisfaction with a reduced life is, however, essential in the face of the intensifying contradictions whose resolution appears unlikely. But her writing points beyond false consolation and pointless and paralyzing despair to what is necessary for a human life whether or not hope remains a possibility: "We must create that which is ignored or denied: friendliness, dignity, trust, spontaneity, grace, fragrance, sound, poesy. Unrestrained life . . . the fundamentally human" (L 158), for the attempt to do so is the greatest source of hope. Christa Wolf's writing is invaluable because it generates the communicative context for this shared creation.

Notes

1. WS 54–55.
2. See *Marxism, Communism and Western Society: A Comparative Encyclopedia*, ed. C. D. Kernig (New York: Herder and Herder, 1972-), vol. 8, 3: Partymindedness in literature was interpreted by theorists of socialist realism as "active support of party policy, expressed in the production of literary works imbued with a proper ideological content."
3. Translation altered by editor.
4. See translator's introduction in Jürgen Habermas, *Legitimation Crisis* (Boston: Beacon Press, 1975), xvi-xvii.
5. Manfred Jäger, "Die Grenzen des Sagbaren," in *Christa Wolf Materialienbuch*, ed. Klaus Sauer (Darmstadt/Neuwied: Luchterhand, 1979), 136.
6. Horkheimer and Adorno summarize: "Men had to do fearful things to themselves before the self, the identical, purposive and virile nature of man, was formed." See Max Horkheimer and Theodor Adorno, "The Concept of Enlightenment," in their *Dialectic of Enlightenment*, trans. John Cumming (New York: Seabury Press, 1972), 33. Horkheimer and Adorno emphasize the difficulties specifically attendant on masculine identity formation. Compare with Christa Wolf's comments on difficulties resulting from male internalization of values imposed by industrial society in WS (62).
7. "Ein Satz," in *Lesen und Schreiben. Neue Sammlung*, 104.
8. See CI 99; DW 883.

Productive Longing: Structure, Theme, and Political Relevance in Christa Wolf's *The Quest for Christa T.*

Heinrich Mohr

I

"A literary work that is easy to attack and difficult to grasp . . . a novel that demands and resists interpretation at the same time."[1] Thus reads a description of *Nachdenken über Christa T.* (*The Quest for Christa T.*), the German novel of recent years that has been reviewed and discussed perhaps more than any other. And the description is right: this novel is tantalizingly multileveled and polyvalent. It cannot be explained in an interpretation; it remains a puzzling thing—enticing or annoying.

The structure of the narrative is already problematic, even though *Christa T.* seems at first to adhere to a traditional scheme. A figure, the narrator, thinks, just as the title promises, about a second figure—Christa T. Her goal is to recreate the image of the dead friend or, perhaps, to get to know this friend only after her death, to extract and set forth her essence ["*Gestalt*"], her "truth" from the cast-off reality of her interrupted life. "So that the doubts may be silenced, so that she may be seen."[2]

The process of thinking about her is as important theoretically as the always only partial results of the thinking. In contrast, the thinking agent is neglected. The figure of the narrator remains without face, without (hi)story; she has no name and exists almost only in relation to

Christa T.—and then usually only referentially, when, for instance, she says "I" or "we." What little the reader knows about her is learned only in connection with Christa T. She is somewhat younger than the other: at the time of writing, shortly after Christa T.'s death in the spring of 1963, she is a little more than thirty-five years old.[3] Like her friend, she studied German literature in Leipzig; like her, she married and had children; she is what Christa T. wanted to be—an author.

The noticeable neglect of the narrator-figure, together with the stress on correspondences between that figure and the object of her narrative, lead to the suspicion that it is not at all a question of two figures, that, in fact, Christa T. and her remembering friend are one and the same—the author Christa Wolf. The identity of names already seems to point in this direction. The division of the author into two literary figures—into the dead woman and the living one who concerns herself with remembering the deceased—would be an artistic device, then, whose purpose is to conceal the autobiographical substance of the novel and to make possible the thus concealed autobiography.

Hans Mayer has provided just such a model of interpretation.[4] He speaks of the "representative significance" of the life and death of Christa T. for Christa Wolf and refers to *The Sufferings of Young Werther* as an example. Christa T., he maintains, also dies "paradigmatically," so that her author can continue to live and to work as a writer in the GDR.[5]

I intend to take the narrative situation in *Christa T.* at its word, to "believe in" two separate and juxtaposed characters. The structure is dialogical rather than monological. The author's cautionary note at the text's outset is also to be understood literally: "Christa T. is a fictional character. Several of the quotations from diaries, sketches, and letters come from real-life sources. I did not consider myself bound by fidelity to external details." There was, then, a real person who is transformed in the book into the character, Christa T.[6] But the book does not present itself as the result of this transformation; it demonstrates the creative process. This process has a demanding goal. It aims to retrieve the "actual" from the coincidences of history; to distill the "truth" from reality, and to present this all in the literary figure of Christa T. The real friend is meant to be "preserved" (*aufgehoben*) in the literary figure. Once present, the figure is expected to have an effect. We can suggest a new explanation for the paleness of the narrator-figure, who appears only to probe and to question—as the creative intelligence. The subject and object of the narrative are not identical; the novel's narrator and author, however, are the same. The narrator is not transformed into a literary figure—or, perhaps, only on occasion; for this reason she must remain faceless and nameless. The anonymity of the narrator is the price Christa Wolf pays for her own presence in the novel, suggesting a direct commitment of the author.

This results in a new perspective. Christa Wolf is undertaking a serious project of moral and political relevance: she wants to establish truth by means of fiction. The task is circumscribed in a prefatory chapter of the book; indeed, it is given already in the book's first sentence: "The quest for her: in the thought of her" (3). Thinking and remembering are the two poles of the "work" the narrator does in regard to her dead friend; the goal is that she might "stand and be recognized" (5). "So that people may see her" (124): this is repeated like a leitmotif, often and with pathos. It functions as a kind of watchword that spurs one on and, at the book's end, recapitulates the narrative situation of the beginning, appeals to the present time: "So that the doubts may be silenced, so that she may be seen. When, if not now?" (185).

The goal determines the structure of the book. To label *Christa T.* as a "novel of remembrance," as some have done, says little and is partially misleading. We remember something we have had and that we want to keep. The remembering person has a defensive relationship to time. But that is only one aspect of *Christa T.* The narrator is not satisfied with a literary recapitulation and preservation of the reality of the dead woman's life; she wants to find and establish her "truth," to elicit her essence and make it present; thus, she may have an effect. In the process of "re-collection" (*Nachdenken*), remembering becomes productive and points toward the future.

Time is an important subject of the "thinking"; for the narrative process itself it is largely irrelevant. Narrated time is not conceived in its actual temporal dimension but rather as a "time of memory," in which all past events are simultaneously present and at the disposal of the narrator. Christa T.'s life is not sequential; it consists of stages, often only seconds, images of the moment. "Significance," not chronology, is the ordering principle of the novel; this is expressly stated: "Chronology is disturbing" (110).[7] But there is sufficient temporal reference, apparently coincidental and unintended, to allow the reader to reconstruct Christa T.'s life from the given stages with little effort. That is intended. The reader's persistent mental questioning should not be directed backward to illuminate obscure events or to decipher a biography; the inquisitive faculty should point "ahead," at the present and to the future. For this reason—and probably also to avoid shocking those with conservative reading habits—a coarse outline of her *vita* is provided, as it were, in passing, although it is not free of empty spaces and dark spots.[8]

Several means are available to the narrator for her enterprise of establishing the truth, the essence of Christa T.: her own memory of the years mutually shared; demonstrable, "objective" facts; stories and information from friends and acquaintances—primarily from Christa T.'s husband; Christa T.'s creative and critical writings, and her diaries.

The narrator controls this rich and manifold material and thereby risks controlling her dead friend as well: "I can do what I like with her" (4). This power frightens her. To "do what I like" with the deceased means to do away with her, to "rid oneself" of her. The awareness of this danger is an important ingredient of the narrator's contemplations and remains so until the end.

It is, first, a danger of memory, a selfish, possessive memory that wants, after the fact, to "have" the friend, who withdrew so easily. That is the opposite of "knowing." But also the kind of memory that is disciplined, prepared to work, insistently concentrated on the other—this memory, too, repeatedly turns out to be unreliable. "Memory puts a deceptive color on things" (3), she notes. What really happened seems concealed and distorted, standing too often for a missed "actuality," which would be the important thing. Reality is confused, not to say falsified; and even if it were possible for memory simply to reproduce it, the result would have little value. Criteria that could direct the recollective faculty and assure security do not surface. When the narrator compares her friend's diaries and other writings to her own recollections, she is completely overcome by helplessness. Things taken for granted crumble; memory joins with the language of the dead friend only with difficulty; and even the unison of these two engenders nothing.

The specific difficulties that attend the thinking about Christa T. generalize into doubts about the literary craft. Narratability seems anathema to what is important, what really elicits a reaction. Only what is finished can be narrated. "Because [the story] has become tellable it now seems like a thing of the past" (65). Telling is a form of disposing of something. The process of narration seems of necessity to run counter to one's own intentions.

The narrator trusts the "facts" least of all. What matters to her is to be found in or behind the facts, hidden in a strangely vexatious way that we shall have yet to determine. Whoever holds to the facts as such seems to her to be flippant. "Flippancy" is a negative keyword; it would "finally kill a dead person. . . . Therefore, one cannot, unfortunately, cling to the facts, which are too mixed up with chance and don't tell much" (23).[9] Facts as such are not interesting. In the narrative perspective, therefore, they become abstract—strangely devoid of reality. Interesting reality is, for her, the effect these facts have on the people they concern. It is difficult, if not absolutely impossible, to provide "objective" proof of such reality. Christa T. notes, *"But what are facts ?"* And the meditative narrator answers in the dead woman's place: "Facts are the traces left in us by events" (172). This is precisely the reality level of Christa Wolf's book and the level of its intended effect. "Recollection" should lead to the creation of facts.

The narrator makes little use of the reports and opinions of others who had contact with Christa T.—little, too, of her husband's, although she is in touch with him and he knows of and supports her project. He, too, seems uncertain about the figure that will emerge from this undertaking—he's more someone who "expects" and wants to receive something than someone who gives. Usually the narrator believes she already knows what one or another of these people who occupy her thoughts could have seen in Christa T. She knows this on the basis of his/her character and circumstances. She is, in fact, so well informed about this that she is able, for example, to imagine a conversation with a mutual university friend; it is not at all necessary that it actually take place (46–50).

The narrator is intelligent and full of scruples; she is entirely aware of the questionability and unreliability of her means and materials. She demonstrates her difficulties repeatedly; the novel about Christa T. is, in fact, essentially demonstrative; it depicts also and especially the aesthetic mind in the creative process. In a most comprehensive sense, the whole is a book of demonstration. The narrator is repeatedly tempted to abandon the undertaking as being infeasible. She is overcome by resignation: "let sadness do as it pleased" (75) seems the only possible response to the dead friend.

A moral upswing is necessary to master such despondency. The narrator repeatedly encourages the reader and herself. She urges us on and demands that we not give up—with expressions such as: "but we must shake off the sadness and take her and place her before us" (75) or: "pulling ourselves together, let's see her writ large" (174). These are challenges addressed to the power of the imagination or, more precisely, challenges to entrust that power with something, to place one's trust in it. The possibility of succeeding in the undertaking, of "inventing" the "essence" of Christa T. with the means provided by the available materials can only exist when the narrator has courage, when she places her faith in the faculty of creative imaginative power. She is expected, and—reluctantly—also trusted, to make visible and effective the "truth" of a life.

We need to investigate this process of the creative imagination. The narrator begins with an image: Christa T. as teenager, who releases her shout, who suddenly holds a rolled newspaper to her mouth and calls or blows through it. That happened on an afternoon toward the end of the war, on the way to the movies. The narrator "knew" Christa T. for the first time in this gesture, and her "essence," still contained in this image, is now even more clearly represented by it. "I can see her now, today, but it's only today that I can see her aright" (10). Just what could be "seen" can be expressed only with difficulty and insufficiently; in any event, effect and significance must be figuratively transcribed, as the "shout which erased everything and for a fraction of a second lifted the sky up higher" (10). This "true" moment of the beginning is a kind of sign of identity. It is quoted repeatedly: in the narrator's last letter to her dying friend (5), in a significant conversation between the two of them (169). It constitutes the point of crystallization in composing the first chapter, around which everything else is organized.

While plumbing her memory, turning a wealth of material this way and that, the narrator recognizes that "one has to invent, for the truth's sake: the truth of that being who does now appear to me at times, and whom I approach with caution" (23). "Invent"—this creates the distance that makes it possible to step out of the realm of the helpless and always insufficient rewriting of presumed reality, to become "productive," to translate remembered reality into "truth," into a "figure." *Christa T.* lives on the courage of the freedom released only by imaginative power as the specific faculty of the literary artist.

The work demands and uses a "sense of the possible." Certainties of reality, at times even decisive ones (i.e., the death of the friend, 5, 124), are abandoned for the sake of knowledge. The relationship to reality changes; the priorities are constantly shifting. Reality can force the narrator to push inclinations and wishes aside. There is, for example, the rough draft of a letter written by Christa T. that the narrator would "have liked to suppress" (69); she repeats this three times in two pages, pleads for understanding—"I must unfortunately include this letter" (70)—and stresses that she is not responsible for it. "I'm not inventing it" (70). She has to give in here to the stronger force of reality. She speaks with similar deprecation of an "ordinary summer," about which she has to talk nonetheless; for "she won't have many more summers, we have no right to deprive her of this one" (74).

The attitude of the narrator in her encounter with her "material" is sometimes imperious, sometimes modest—but it is always an "encounter." Her reunion with her friend seems to her, in retrospect, not quite satisfying. After she has provided a faithfully "realistic" description of the scene (25–27), she wants to supply a literary correction to the unsatisfactory reality, that is, she wants to tell the scene again— the way it really ought to have been. She wants to make a piece of literature in which reality comes into its own.

Reality is frequently helped on by the creative imagination, whereby the reader always receives glimpses of the play with the poles of reality and fiction. The narrator seems to feel most comfortable when she does not know too many facts, although she does not neglect to refer to them. She is not creating "nice" stories. About the summer love of her friend, for instance: "A difficult story. But not tellable at all under the disheartening pressure of facts we are fortunately ignorant of. . . . An evening toward the end of June. She was standing, if we so choose, by the fence among the cherry trees in the school garden—which, as we do know, are authentic; likewise the duck pond on which her back was turned" (37). After the story has been told, the narrator steps forth, admits that she is author of the scene and stresses its fictive character. "It was like that, or maybe it was different. In that year or the next. That man or another." Immediately thereafter she attributes the story to the deceased with a definitive gesture—as something rightfully hers: "That's what she had of it; it's how I want it. She must have learned what she had to know; and then she must have left" (41).

From "summer love" it is a mere step to the kind of stories that we would like to call "variations on a given theme." These are sketches with which the narrator counters her distress, the "old mistrustful-ness," doubts reawakened during the writing down of verified events— "because every statement is doubly authenticated and stands up to the scrutiny of review" (117)—that her net is worthless. These sketches

201

offer the purest fulfillment of the intention to invent "for the truth's sake" (23). The topic is Christa T.'s love for the man she will marry: Justus, the Just. The important moment of the decision is invented. Very precisely, with date and attention to historical detail, the narrator describes a costume party at which she and the two of them are present. Previous to that she had spoken of her difficulty "to create" (117) a room for the couple's love. After narrating the party scene, she forgoes the invention of the room. Her invention, it seems—and this is clearly stated—has been made superfluous by what really happened; the narrator does well simply to record reality. "That evening he took her home with him. I've given up the idea of inventing the room, it's not important. And now she doesn't need time any more. The playing was over, the role lapsed into irrelevancy, he loved her" (120).

What has here been so definitively established as real is, in the following chapter, drawn back into the realm of the possible. It again becomes "an attempt," fiction that circles around truth and is overshadowed by doubts concerning its adequacy. "We can make another attempt: it wasn't the fancy dress ball, which was an invention in any case, but a simple arrival, an arrival, what's more, in a small country town" (121). And there follows, as a second variation on the same theme, another precise and richly detailed story. Christa T. going to visit Justus, her train trip, his reception of her (121–123).

Thus the narrator appeals to the imagination and intelligence of the reader, makes him/her a partner—almost, in fact, an accomplice. Before this double love story she had made a single reference—absent from the remaining narrative—to "the person to whom I tell the story, whom I need and whose support I solicit" (117). Her relationship to the reader is elsewhere more progressively pedagogical. She deprives him/her of security, lets him/her make discoveries and experience the serious game with reality and possibility in her relationship to the truth.

The narrator reports on a visit to Christa T. in the hospital (130–132) and stresses how clearly she remembers the "whole afternoon." That would be simple. A kind of prologue, however, sets the report under the sign of the paradoxical. "So I shall visit her in the hospital again, that Sunday in autumn, after her wedding day, in search of what I've overlooked. I have a reason for repeating the visit: it's because I was never with her when she was really sick" (130). The paradox is introduced here as a particular way of gaining proximity to a truth that cannot be "possessed."

The same blurring of fiction and report dominates the narrator's conversation with a mutual former friend. It begins in the subjunctive ("I would"), changes into the future tense, and occasionally moves into the present indicative. Initially presented as a mere possibility, its becomes ever more "real," until, at the end, a decision of the narrator's reestablishes the fiction. "I shan't go to her. . . . The conversation won't take place, we'll save ourselves the emotions" (50). A similar ambiguity is maintained as well in Christa T.'s conversation with the director of her school. At its end, the narrator is emphatically clear: "Their conversation might have been like this, but I won't insist that it was" (106). Even in those places where the narrator depends closely on her memories, that is, really reports, her presence remains evident. The matter is not, as it were, automatically reproducible; it is neither self-generated nor transferred through a neutral medium; it remains a dialogical situation in which the narrator is present and her intentions are obvious. "If everything was as I now wish it to have been . . . If we had all behaved that evening as I now wish we had . . . All that evening . . . Christa T. was setting us . . . an example—setting it for the infinite possibilities still in us" (165–166).

The narrator proceeds in two ways with the creative and critical writings of Christa T. that she has at her disposal. She quotes a poem and interprets it (59–60), as she does as well with the beginning of a story (88–90) and other fragments, even mere titles (87). Where the deceased has given literary form to events from her life that belong to the realm of "re-collection," however, she does not undertake this sort of thing: she insists on telling her own story in every case. Christa T. once went to see a soothsayer and had fixed the experience as a literary scene, with the ironically distancing title *Wat de Generool seggt hett* (78–83).[10] She hadn't invented him in the traditional sense; there really was a séance, and she had attempted to retain those aspects of it that were important to her and seemed potentially significant. For the narrator, however, this is already "inventing," and she maintains her position and her task even in the face of this testimony. "I take the liberty of correcting her and invent my own general for myself. To do justice, as anyone would. What else?" (80).[11] When she adheres to Christa T.'s story, she does this quite noticeably, thus preserving her narrative position and distance. She remains master of the story: "I take the whole story from her now with a clear conscience. . . . Let's begin, as she does. . . . Let's move on to the following day" (107–108).

Christa T. is a complexly structured book, but it is not confused; the artistic design is visible. Christa Wolf's formal modernity even has a pedagogic aspect. Her evident creative finesse, which works away, as it were, under the eyes of her reader, demonstrates modern narrative for a public that needs to "catch up" on such things. *Christa T.* is also, like many a modern novel, simultaneously the "novel of a novel"—in an unusual way, to be sure. There is no directionless and abstract pondering, but rather a narrator who works beset by scruples and with great effort, whose goal is established and known to the reader. It is the production of the "truth," the "essence," and their significance for present and future. The structure of *Christa T.* results from the difficulties of thinking about Christa T. These are demonstrated to the reader, who thus "understands" the various attempts to overcome them.

The narrator assures us repeatedly that she did not choose Christa T. There was no choice; the deceased "forced herself" onto her, couldn't be repulsed, "pulled" the narrator into the undertaking. "Ah, if

I could freely and happily choose to invent without being ambiguous. . . . It would never have occurred to me . . . to think of her" (45). Yet it is not a matter of an obsession from which the living woman seeks to free herself through narrating; nor is it a case of an attempt somehow to "redeem" the deceased by transforming her into a lasting literary figure and thus preserving her. Nor is the narrative motivated by a devout and melancholy self-satisfying piety that conjures up the figure of the dead friend only for itself and is content when the remembered person is thus at the disposal of private sorrow and love. The narration comprehends itself, rather, as a process of "making public." Christa T. becomes a public figure. She is "pointed to," she is "introduced": "So that people may see her" (124). The dialogue between the narrator and the deceased takes place before and for a public.

The reader, "the person to whom I tell the story" (117), is regarded as a compatriot and contemporary. "Compatriot" means citizen of the GDR; "contemporary" has several meanings. In the narrowest sense, the concept refers to the generation of those who, in the year zero— 1945—were young but no longer children; in the broader sense it means all those who have consciously lived through the epoch that includes the collapse of the fascist and the reconstruction of the socialist state in Germany; in the broadest sense, the meaning of "contemporary" corresponds to that of "compatriot," thus referring to all who now live in the GDR and who regard the period from 1945 to the present as "their" time.

The personas of the novel, the reader, and the narrator are closely connected to each other. Shared experiences and knowledge, typical for the times and the generation, are assumed. All have the same "home." Christa T. is introduced as "one of us." The stations of her life are typical for her generation and her times: childhood in a village to the east of the Oder River, flight in 1945, school teacher, study, profession, marriage, children. As "special" as is her person, her life—except for her early death—is normal and in many regards representative.

The specific proximity of all to all is expressed in the frequent and sudden switch from "I" to "we" and from "she" to "we." This "we" can signify three things: the alliance of narrator and reader vis-à-vis the protagonist; narrator and Christa T. as a pair; and a group surrounding the narrator (or possibly surrounding both her and Christa T.). "I" denotes the subject of the narration, the remembering friend, the narrator identical with the author. But it can also designate the contemporaneous friend, Christa T.'s complementary figure. The narrative subject is simultaneously an object of the narrative and is, as such, like Christa T. subject to a transformation of the real "I" into an artistic figure. What Christa Wolf discovers with such astonishment is entirely consistent, that is, that in the process of writing she suddenly confronted herself as an other (IM). The problems of such transformation are not played out in the novel; rather they are suppressed because the narrator remains, as complementary figure to Christa T., pale and without contour. This has an important result that is, to be sure, difficult to demonstrate. The suppressed complementary figure is somehow incorporated into the artistic figure, Christa T. The life material from which this figure is constructed is evidently that of not only the deceased but also the narrator who, while thinking about Christa T., unexpectedly confronted herself. I would like to speak of an osmosis that has taken place here. The choice of identical first names could be a sort of subsequent admission of such a process.

Regarding the relation to reality, there is an unusual correspondence between Christa T.'s characteristics and the book's qualities. To Christa T. is attributed the trait of seeming "to be at home everywhere and a stranger everywhere, at home and a stranger in the same instant" (13). She is distinguished by the primary philosophical trait: she is capable of amazement; she cannot avoid being amazed. She is restless— not due to nervous weakness but because she knows herself to be always in process, because she has a feeling for the manifold layers of reality. She is fascinated and frightened by life. This woman has a very intimate, strained, and respectful relationship to all reality and finds it therefore difficult to conform to conventions. For this reason, some people "said she had no sense of reality" (57), she has been called "out of date" (62) and "naive" (65). But the sharpness and alertness of her consciousness also enable her to "penetrate": "she saw things as they were" (12). Her "precise" relationship to reality is based on a strong sensuality. She calls herself "a creature who lives by her eyes" (73). It can happen that her senses react more quickly than her consciousness, which then has to work things through after the fact. From the beginning she is concerned with "certainties"—like someone for whom objects and relationships are not taken for granted, who wants to know their exact nature. Such certainties ask to be held on to, to be "written up." She hopes to gain certainty in the act of writing. From writing she expects assistance—"*To think that I can only cope with things by writing!*" (34); in writing she believes she can keep herself "intact" and achieve "self-discovery" (57). The narrator maintains that she was "extremely averse to anything formless" (16). Christa T. reacts by writing. In the terms of trivial etymology: "'dichten,' *condensare*, make dense, tighten; language helps" (16). The "unformed" has to do with "the world's darker half" (22), which does not cease to be there as a threat, as a negation of life, as an arsenal of evil possibilities that are possible even for the own "I." This threat is presented in a few images and scenes that are concretely specific and yet, since they are repeatedly quoted, of general significance. These are variations on evil: the cat that is thrown against the wall (20, 31, 109), the departure of the persecuted gypsies (22), the eggs that have been thrown out of the bird's nest (31, 39, 109), the beheaded toad (108f), the frozen boy (22, 31), the stages of flight (19f.). Schwab's "Der Reiter und der Bodensee" (The rider and Lake Constance) is quoted several times (29, 31, 73).[12] It stands for an important aspect of Christa T.'s sense of life and of that of the person who thinks about her. "*How thin it is, the surface I'm walking on*" (73).

The "precise" relationship to reality is a poetic force. The "desire for reality" is revealed as a trait that molds the style and structure of *Christa T.*, also a search action that discloses realities. Like Christa T., the narrator defies convention, established norms. Thus she writes, for instance: "Just for once, for this once, I want to discover how it is and to tell it like it is: the unexemplary life, a life that can't be used as a model" (45). The most important level of reality for the novel, *Christa T.*, could be called "inner reality." The goal of Christa T.'s literary attempts, this reality is precisely defined as constituted by those "experiences into which the facts of real life had crystallized in her" (174).

Fascination with life is a basic quality of Christa Wolf's literature. The last paragraph in *Divided Heaven*, confident and once again sure of itself, had made mention of "this strange substance." It is expressly stated that the protagonist is no longer afraid.[13] The mental landscape in *Christa T.* is gloomier, to be sure, but the fascination with this "strange substance" remains. In contrast to Rita Seidel, however, Christa T. is afraid. She writes to her sister of "coldness in everything. It comes from a long way off; it gets into everything" (70). And "fear" is one of the narrator's key words, to which she opposes the project of "recollection," just as Christa T., too, wanted to write ["*dichten*"]. "Why else her inclination to 'write poems,' to tighten the structures, make resistant the beautiful, bright, and firm world that should be for her? Press your hands, both hands, against the rifts through which it keeps pouring, cold and dark . . . " (20).

Christa Wolf had prefaced *Christa T.* with a motto with which she anticipated the theme of her friend's life as well as her own book: " 'This coming-to-oneself—what is it'? Johannes R. Becher." Below the text from which this quotation is taken, Becher notes: "From the life of a citizen of our age." Here's a fuller version of the passage: " 'For this profound restlessness of the human soul is nothing but the premonition and the ability to sense that man has not yet come to himself. This coming-to-oneself—what is it?' " (IM 77). Christa T. evokes Becher—without mentioning the name—in a similar connection when she varies the title of his literary journal *Auf andere Art so grosse Hoffnung* (To hope so greatly—in a different way) as a formula for her life: "The Big Hope, or The Difficulty of Saying 'I' " (169).

"Coming to oneself," "saying 'I'"—that is the theme. It has an historical dimension. Expressionist pathos of humanity—"become essential, oh man!"—in turn reaches back to broad traditions; this is alive in Christa Wolf's book, unencumbered by the "modern" refraction of skepticism. Literary tradition encounters political ideology. For in Marxist terminology, "coming to oneself" means the "abolishment of self-alienation." Thus we have a threefold identity: communist ideology, the life of Christa T., and the theme of the book by Christa Wolf. And Johannes R. Becher, author and cultural minister of the GDR, stands paradigmatically for the correspondence between literature and politics.

In three scenes Christa T.'s "coming to herself" seems momentarily successful. First, a teenager, who plays the trumpet on a rolled newspaper, releases a shout that "erased everything and for a fraction of a second lifted the sky up higher" (10). That is a promise of Christa T.'s in which she promises nothing other than herself. It is a moment of truth and the beginning of the quest. The narrator fixes this image: "I wanted to share in a life that produced such shouts" (11). She quotes the scene several times; she even refers to it in her last letter to the dying woman (5).

The second image is not future-oriented but present; it makes no promise but rather expresses a condition of happiness—a powerful, sensually warm happiness. It shows Christa T. at the beach: "How she runs, Christa T., after the huge white and red ball that the wind is driving across the beach, how she reaches it, laughs aloud, grabs it, brings it back to her small daughter" (74). This image, too, is repeatedly evoked. The narrator uses it as a kind of documentation of happiness with which she proves to herself that Christa T. was completely there, that she "lived her life to the full."[14]

The third image, finally, is significantly suspended between real scene, dream, and poetic invention. Dressed in a worn-out red bathrobe, Christa T. sits in the twilight of a New Year's morning and writes. She notes that key sentence: "The Big Hope, or The Difficulty of Saying 'I'" (169). She has "the same" face as she had eighteen years ago, when she blew the trumpet. The narrator "recognizes" her again, but this time much more explicitly. She believes she comprehends her "secret": it is the secret of authorship. The self-realization of Christa T.—"this long and never-ending journey toward oneself" (174)—is meant to be achieved through the production of literature. The theme of Christa Wolf's book can therefore be defined more precisely as "thinking about the journey of an author in the GDR to herself."

Christa T. realized the politically and ideologically new beginning after 1945 very personally as the new beginning of her own existence. The turning point is marked by a mental breakdown. Her collapse occurs in the summer of 1945 when she acknowledges the eclipse of her own consciousness during the Hitler era—"her old diaries . . . vows . . . enthusiasms . . . songs" (29)—an enormous terror of the awful things that were also possible for her. The whole is captured in an allusion to the "rider and Lake Constance" (29).

The "new world" takes quick possession of her. Among other things, it comes to her via literature: "the new names on the covers, Gorky, Makarenko, the new pamphlets which everyone was given, as important as one's daily bread, unless one's hand was shut" (30). Christa T. comprehends very quickly because "this rational clarity" corresponds exactly to an obscure and confused "longing" of which she is aware in herself. "Yes, that's how it will be, this is the way to ourselves" (30). She experiences the thrill of the beginning, the "pain of self-expansion, also the pleasure, which is unforgettable and by which

207

one will measure all future pleasures" (31) Such a beginning has the gleam of utopia; what becomes problematic later, in the course of the novel, is here still simple. The awakening of the individual is simultaneously that of a new community moving toward a just society: a celebration of togetherness that—fortunately and advantageously—corresponds for Christa T. to her own youth. Toward the end of her work, the narrator sums up this epoch: "It gives one a good feeling to be at the beginning of things. One loves that feeling, and one's only anxiety comes with the fear that one might fail to live up to the passion at large in society. Like ourselves, Christa T. had the luck to be forced to create her identity at an age when one is passionate. With that as the standard, all other attractions are shallow" (132–133).

Christa T. remained faithful to this beginning. She never stopped believing in the "new world," not even when she despaired of the future—and of herself. When the narrator speaks of herself and her contemporaries from the perspective of her narrative present, her deceased friend is always included in the "we" of her political confession of faith. "For the new world . . . really did exist. It exists, and not only in our heads; and that period was for us the beginning of it. But whatever happened or will happen to that new world is and remains our affair. Among the alternatives offered there isn't a single one that's worth a nod in its direction . . . What she wished for more intensely than anything, and I'm speaking now of Christa T., was the coming of our world; and she had precisely the kind of imagination one needs for a real understanding of it" (51). She had the "faith," but it was no blind faith. She had lost the ability to deceive herself about realities, lost as well that confused confidence that hides and excuses everything in the present by evoking a very distant future. She even recognizes that one cheats oneself out of a dimension of the future when one misuses it as an alibi —and how in this way one also bypasses the present (101).

Sensitivity, that "precise relationship" to reality, is maintained in a manner that is often difficult and painful for the individual in question. It isolates her. Despite all the agreement in principle, it necessarily places her—without her striving for it at all—in the position of a person who also always stands on the outside; it creates the distance of the experiencing observer who questions—who must call into question —herself and her world. She observes uncanny things: how the behavior of people becomes "untrue," determined by prescribed norms and molds to which individuals conform unthinkingly, as it were; how human beings withdraw themselves and leave only their names behind.

> She couldn't do that. But she also lost the capacity to live in a state of rapture. The vehement overplayed words, the waving banners, the deafening songs, the hands clapping rhythms over our heads. She felt how words begin to change when they aren't being tossed out any more by belief and ineptitude and excessive zeal but by calculation, craftiness, the urge to adapt and conform. Our words, not even false ones—how easy it would be if they were!—but the person speaking

them has become a different person. Does that change everything? (55–56)

Christa T. mistrusts the speaker but also the language that seldom names things without deforming them, altering them according to prescribed convention, falsifying them. And even when words and things correspond and the named object seems truly to reside in the name—it's still nothing definitive. Word and thing separate quickly: "She didn't trust these names, oh no. She didn't trust herself. She was doubtful, amid our toxic swirl of new name-giving; what she doubted was the reality of names, though she had to deal with them; she certainly felt that naming is seldom accurate, and that, even if it is accurate, name and thing coincide only for a short time. She shrank from stamping any name on herself" (35). Her world begins to appear spooky to her. Human beings disappear "behind the gigantic cardboard placards they carried around" (56). The reference is to the exemplary individuals, "the frightful beaming heroes of newspapers, films, and books" (56), whose task it is to enable all those whose delegates they are to recognize their own nullity. Such recognition promises to eradicate joy, to eliminate "the puny ego" (173), to dissolve individuality into pure function. This is an oddly pleasurable sacrificial action by which one becomes a "small screw" in the large "apparatus." Recalling this, the narrator thinks:

> So there emerged around us, or in us too, it is the same thing, a hermetic space which had its own internal laws, with its stars and suns, revolving with apparent effortlessness around a center which was subject to no laws, to no change, and least of all to doubt. The machinery which made it all move—or did it move?—the cogs, chains, and rods, were submerged in darkness; one rejoiced in the absolute perfection and purposiveness of the apparatus, and to keep it going smoothly seemed worth any sacrifice, even the sacrifice achieved by self-extinction. And only today do we feel any proper surprise: feelings have to travel a long way. (56)

Christa T. reacted more quickly and with greater sensitivity. And what is unusual, she even—after much restlessness and pondering—dared to criticize and explained to her friend that "there must be some misunderstanding" (173). The path to the goal contradicts the goal itself; to encourage the full potential of the individual, she thinks, is precisely the idea of the new world. But the individual, on the path to that new world, is suffocated by a false conception of collectivity (55f.) Christa T. looks for the "mistake" almost always within herself. "She wasn't able to doubt the world, so all that was left was to doubt herself" (71). She defines as a contemptible weakness her inability to keep "apart things that didn't belong together: the person and the cause he supports, nocturnal unlimited dreams and limited daylight actions, thoughts and feelings" (64–65). She considers herself profoundly inferior to the "factual people," the "up-and-doing people" who appear to

her, and to the narrator, to be nonetheless despicable and very dangerous (51). Those who know how to play every role, whether because
they lack "conscience" and "imagination" (172) or because they are disciplined; the optimists who do not sense the urge to think for themselves, or who repress it—she finds these people suspicious, although
they still impress her as the industrious ones "who'll carry on, who are
right, because they're stronger, who can't look back, because they
haven't got the time" (71).

Her doubts lead to despair. It seems to Christa T. as though this
age, which she has unflinchingly and faithfully accepted as "her" age,
doesn't know what to begin with her; that she fits in nowhere, can fit
herself in nowhere without abandoning herself, that she is therefore
alone and fated to go under: "too soft; all the fruitless ponderings; a
scrupulous *petite bourgeoise* . . ." (70). She wrote this in the unfinished
and unsent letter to her sister, in which she spoke of suicide. It describes Christa T.'s situation exactly. "This breathlessness, or this inability to draw a deep breath. As if whole areas of the lungs have been
out of action for an eternity. When that is so, can one go on living?" (70).
The letter-writer is not kind to herself, she is strict and precise; she
sees herself clearly in her age and comes to a negative conclusion: "The
whole world like a wall facing me. I fumble over the stone: no gaps.
Why should I go on deluding myself: there's no gap for me to live in"
(70).

In a departure from her common practice, the narrator assigns a
date to this partially shared letter: "in summer 1953" (70). The revolution of June 17 is not mentioned in the book, to be sure. But I would
read the brief description of an early summer night on the boulevard,
Unter den Linden, as a reference to it: "The order of things is finally
falling apart" (173).[15] The choice of the date for the suicide-letter is naturally not accidental, the congruence not to be overlooked. Christa T.'s
"reduced vitality" (81) is, after all, of a social, political nature. A certain
individual no longer knows how she is supposed to live in a society that
is working its way toward socialism; she continues, nevertheless, to
write: "All of which makes no difference; the contradiction can't be resolved—none of this makes any difference to my deep sense of concurring with these times of ours and of belonging in them" (71). The doctor's diagnosis, couched in the technical jargon of the psychiatrist,
confirms the social character of her illness: "The death wish as a sickness. Neurosis as deficient capacity to adapt oneself to existing circumstances." Offering help and advice, he recommends social-political behavior. "You'd have to realize what's involved. . . . You'll learn to
adapt" (72).

"Adaptation" and the corresponding binary pair, "sickness" and
"health," are key concepts of the book. Late in her life Christa T. will be
instructed—ironically by one of her former students: "conformity is the
means of survival: adaptation, conformity at any price" (112). But by
then she has already become secure in rejecting this adaptation and the

survival it promises. By then she is aware of her choice that, if it has to, also accepts unhappiness as "a reasonable price to pay for refusing assent" (157). To adaptation she opposes responsibility (114), or, in a different place, her central concepts of "conscience" and "imagination." She no longer regards these as egocentric ideas of petit bourgeois ideology, but rather as socially necessary virtues, "indispensable for the survival of mankind" (172). She has become secure in her position "against the grain"; precisely with this position she wants to maintain her "deep sense of concurring with these times" (71). She wants to serve society, less—we might pointedly observe—as a part than as its counterpart.

The external biography of Christa T. remains undramatic and common. The drama is shifted inward; the intended reality of the book is "the experiences into which the facts of real life had crystallized in her" (174). These are applied to the present in the reflections of the remembering narrator. Noisy situations of conflict or dramatic confrontations hardly exist. There is no actually tangible opponent. There is "evil" but no "villain" in the entire book.

As a teacher, reading her class's essays on "one of the regulation topics of those years: Am I too young to contribute to the development of the Socialist society?" (102), Christa T. encounters the phenomenon of the collective lie. She opposes it. Her pupils are simply amazed, just as they find it "a riot" when the new teacher takes Goethe-lines like "*Edel sei der Mensch*" ("let man be noble") seriously and demands that they do the same. It comes to a kind of pedagogical reversal of roles. "Almost wordlessly the students taught her about certain rules of the game in practical life" (103). They are the superior ones who share their experiences in a somewhat surprised but friendly way. They understand "the teacher's anger but saw it as the anger of inexperience, the sort of feeling they'd got over long ago" (103). The school's director to whom she turns in this matter is not the blinkered dogmatician and bureaucrat whom a more traditional work would introduce here. He is an old and highly respectable man who observes the young woman with a rather melancholy sympathy. What he has to say—"learn to keep your own thoughts to yourself" (104)—admittedly solves nothing, but it does incline to thoughtfulness. "You want to have everything at once: power and goodness and I don't know what else besides" (105).

All in all, Christa T. is treated in a friendly manner by those people with whom she deals. With her doubts and questions she exercises an unusual power of attraction on the "iron believers," those who say "completely" frequently and with pleasure; she is like a problem that must be solved or a terrain that must be conquered. To others she appears "unbalanced" by "her imagination," "eccentric" (47). They want to help her, to facilitate her "integration," although and perhaps also because they feel that she makes their lives "questionable" (48). Even the one cynic of the book—also a writer, an antipode to Christa T.—has a curious, almost tender affection for her, as he might for someone in need of protection whose "purity" fascinates him (147–48).

Seen in respect to the facts of her life and her professional development, Christa T. is neither a "social failure" nor a real success. Despite making it difficult for herself and others, she finally completed her university education successfully; she practiced her profession with analogous difficulties; she married after rather long—but not too long—groping and hesitation, had children, built a country house in Mecklenburg, was a mother and a housewife, chose not to avoid the temptation of adultery, and finally died, early and very much against her will. Her death is the book's fulcrum and its point of departure. The narrator resists this death by writing; she wants to abolish it with her thoughts of Christa T.[16] Her first action is to surround the death with ambiguity. On the one hand we have the concrete illness, leukemia, and a concrete, demonstrable medical history. Simultaneously, however, there are doubts about this illness, a reluctance to accept it as a sufficient and finite explanation. In her thinking, the narrator transforms the death of her friend, gives it a "different" significance; she moves it into a sociopolitical dimension. Sickness and death are suggested as the price that must finally be paid after all for "refusing assent" (157), for nonconformity, for the consistent attempt, that is never willing to compromise, to say "I." An attempt to which belong, to be sure, the theory and—as Christa T. unshakably believes—the future of the society in which she lives but not its current practice. Her friends occasionally called her "out of date" in the sense of old-fashioned (62). But the narrator lets the outdatedness of her protagonist refer to the future. Christa T. is for her, insofar as such a thing is possible, "our person of tomorrow." That does not reduce the difficulties of living "today," and it makes dying more bitter. Emphatically we are assured that "she hadn't got much time" (60). And she herself responds to the doctor who wants to assist her in preparing for death: "For me the most important things are still to come" (179). This gives Christa T.'s strong battle with death a second meaning, as is generally the case with the words and sentences in which there is mention of sickness and death. The narrator is aware of this when she says: "Lived too soon, she perhaps thought" (183). This refers concretely to a not-yet-existing medicine for leukemia, but the same sentence alludes to time in general. Two levels of meaning are artistically entwined in the thoughts about the death of Christa T., and this entwining is consciously demonstrated: "At last! she writes . . . and this is as much as to say: now there is no death. It's beginning, the thing she so painfully missed: we are beginning to see ourselves. Distinctly she feels that time is on her side, and yet she can't help saying: I was born too soon. For she knows that before long people won't still be dying of this disease" (182).

What is this disease? Leukemia, naturally. But the disease of the blood also stands for the—curable—disease of society in which the "attempt to say 'I'" cannot yet be undertaken. The most noticeable symptom of Christa T.'s sickness was tiredness. "Today one can ask, to be sure, what this tiredness meant. . . . This much is certain: what one does can never make one so tired as what one doesn't do or cannot do. That was the case with her" (140).

Our project here is to elucidate. The novel *Christa T.* resists clarification; it provides only hints meant to spur us on to our own recollection and continued thinking. That is the structure of the book. It confronts the reader with open questions, especially with the question concerning the death of Christa T. This death is presented as just such a question to the reader early on and very emphatically in an imaginary conversation:

> Or do you think she died of this sickness?
> No.
> . . . the question, what Christa T. died of, I shall ask on my own account, in due course, without doubting that the sickness, leukemia, was the thing she couldn't deal with or bring to a stop. (50)

The question of Christa T.'s "success" is open as well. "They'll force me to talk about success," we read, "that's for sure" (86). Christa T. was extremely severe. "The obligation is to end tragically, or to achieve a life task fully. Thus to be happy" (97). That was the alternative she had given herself. But it is not suitable for grasping her life and death. Her death is sad rather than tragic. This is why she doesn't want to die. Always thinking of "the full achievement of a life task," she resisted conformity and brought to society what she was able to bring under the given circumstances, by bravely and steadfastly trying to say "I." But a "positive achievement," something that can be separated from her, something lasting, is admittedly not demonstrable. She is represented as an "unrepeatable and unfulfilled" promise (15), not as a failure. The narrator insists on this, as does the author in her "Interview with Myself."[17] "Nothing could be more inappropriate than pity or regret. She did live. She was all there. She was always scared of getting stuck; her shyness and her timidity were the reverse side of her passion for wishing. Now out she came, calm even in the unfulfillment of her wishes, for she had the strength to say: Not yet" (174).

An important and strange position is assumed by "idylls" in these contemplations about Christa T.'s restless journey, undertaken to achieve "self-discovery" and to keep "oneself intact" (57). They are the sort of idylls with which one is familiar from nineteenth-century literature: pictures of the simple, beautifully blessed life that are saturated with illustrative power. The father's house—the thatched cottage of the village teacher—already has idyllic traits. This house is repeated—a malicious reader might note that it's on a socially higher plane—in the house on the lake with poplar trees and swans that Christa T. builds with so much effort. Idyllic as well are many of the narrator's scenes on themes from Christa T.'s life. She stands at the fence under the cherry trees and hands cherries to her admirer (37); the two of them run across the meadow, the hay gives off its fragrance, the sun goes down, and so on (39).

The narrator herself stresses the cliché elements of these scenes; she notes how they conform to familiar literary expectations and ready-made material. With this she intends to abolish triviality and forbid the reader any vague sentimentality. "Her mother," we read, "sent them into the jasmine arbor and brought some cider; later, also, the moon rose" (90). By means of this "also," the narrator reaches an understanding with the reader about the scene, about the pretexts equally familiar to both of them. "Now the sun has sunk into the hedgerows. Best thing would be for them to run across the fields and for the spread hay to give off its fragrance. So they run, and there's the fragrance of hay, everything's just as it should be" (39). The purpose of the intrusion of this reproachful and distancing consciousness is not the ironic destruction of the scene. On the contrary, it wants to make such a scene possible again, wants to rehabilitate it. Wolf attempts here to abolish the insincere effect that results from the arbitrary availability of the moveable scenery of the idyll; she wants to make the significance of the idyll effective once more. Writers like Christa T. love nineteenth-century literature: Raabe, Keller, and especially Storm. Christa Wolf's attempt to rehabilitate the idyll in *Christa T.* stems not least from this affection.

In her thesis on "the writer, Theodor Storm" (94–98)[18] Christa T. speaks of the "quiet places" of childhood in Storm's writing, which remind her of "similar experiences in my own childhood." She lists them, "*Stalking red deer . . . in the woods . . . grandfather's tree nursery. . . . bee house . . . Grandfather on the bench telling stories; Grandmother's beloved and beautiful face among the confusion of leaves at the gate in the hedge*" (98). Christa T. discovers that she shares with Storm the same kinds of memories. The narrator makes it clear that her way of remembering is also similar to his. In her interpretation of Storm, Christa T. recognizes and justifies her own way of evoking "quiet places" in memory and fantasy. She interprets the idyll as interesting and thought-provoking when applied to Theodor Storm but pointing more significantly to the function of the idyll in Christa T.'s life and Christa Wolf's novel. The "*quiet places*," we read, have become " *landscape[s] of longing*" (97) for the person remembering them; and through this they are elevated to "*image[s] of human beauty created by longing*" (98).

Memory transforms itself into longing. Longing implies a dissatisfaction with the present; it directs the human being toward past and future. Longing usually takes its material from memory, but it remains bound to the past only in borderline cases of extreme weariness with life. Its true characteristic is ambivalence. The stronger one's will to life, the more that person's longing is directed toward the future. It projects into the future a past remembered and transfigured by that memory. It becomes something that one awaits the opportunity to experience. Longing is also, and above all, anticipation.

What interests us is the fact of the transformation. Transfigured past becomes an element of anticipation of the future. This clarifies the function of the "old-fashioned" idylls that call attention to themselves in *Christa T.* They are evoked by the narrator as a kind of "proof of happiness" and are, at the same time, "promises of happiness." The "idylls of recollection," that Christa T. would like to write and that her remembering friend sketches for her are also and above all "utopian."

This is especially the case with those images in which Christa T.'s "essence" is really visible: Christa T. blowing the trumpet, with the ball on the beach, at the desk in the early morning. These are perfect idylls, poetic-philosophical images of happiness that represent a person who has become identical with herself, in which the motto's question seems answered. The motto and the leitmotif of the book refer to the utopian idyll, the endless goal, the great utopia toward which Christa T. wants to set things in motion.

Christa T. builds herself the kind of house one might well find described in one of Storm's stories—in the country, on a large lake; far away, on the other shore, are the red roofs of the village. She constructs a shelter for living whose traditional idyllic traits are emphasized. In her remembrance, Christa T.'s friend understands the house "as a sort of instrument that she meant to use to link herself more intimately with life" (153), as a place that would provide her with protection and security and "on whose territory she could take her stand against anything alien" (153). "I'm digging my way out" (151); thus Christa T. comments on the building of the house—this attempt of hers to materialize the idyll.

In the paper on the writer with whom she feels kinship, Theodor Storm, Christa T. had written that *"he had rescued poetry from the destruction threatening human personality when it becomes merely marginal to events"* (96). *"The conflict between willing something and the inability to do it thrust [Storm] into a corner of life"* (97). Is Christa T. also speaking about herself here? Is she, especially, anticipating her final activity? Is the house on the lake "marginal to events," "a corner of life"? Christa T. is also familiar with the "conflict between willing something and the inability to do it." Her project of unconditional self-realization is opposed by a society that demands alignment and conformity. The house indeed suggests withdrawal but not resignation. It functions instead as a place of preservation where one can pass the winter and cross over into another time, into the hoped-for age of possible effectiveness: "she hadn't got much time" (60). The house, erected with so much energy as a refuge, was also there for the sake of future activity. It demonstrates Christa T.'s will toward the future, it is protective space and a sign of hope. She created for herself a place in which she believed she would be able to find her own answer to the question posed early on: "how, if at all, and under what circumstances, can one realize oneself in a work of art" (95).

Christa T.'s "authorship" is a problem for the reader. It is difficult to read *Christa T.* as a novel about the artist. The person Christa T., with her own rare qualities, her "latent possibilities" (136), her uncon-

215

ditionality and her great restlessness, is shown clearly in her tension with the society of the GDR that she affirms and under which she suffers. The artist, on the other hand, remains oddly alien. The little bit of her literary attempts that is shared is not very imposing; it is naively amateurish, sooner "well-meant" than good, hard to take seriously even as a sign of "potential." This is all much too obvious to be unintentional. But the other possibility, that is, to read *Christa T.* as the novel of a mistake—a sensitive and talented person mistakenly sees herself as a poet and is destroyed by this error—doesn't work either. The "authorship" is the point of role reversal between Christa T. and Christa Wolf. A process of unusual, partial identification has taken place.[19] Christa Wolf is what Christa T. wanted to be. In thinking of and about her Christa Wolf realizes the longing of the deceased: to pay her dues to society in "her own currency" (87), that is, in literary currency. She transforms Christa T. into an artifact that presents itself to the society of the GDR as a great question. Christa T.'s "essence" is created in *Christa T.*; her "truth" is grasped. This conforms to the intended effect of the novel. Questioning the past, it challenges the present and future socialist German state to enable this "coming-to-oneself." Christa Wolf transforms the deceased into a question and an appeal to the present and future of her country. *Christa T.* is skeptical and active at once, it demonstrates a sort of angry hope. It denies the satisfied pride in things actually or allegedly achieved, and it warns of the error in the notion that economical and technical developments in a socialist country will lead automatically and as if independently to abolishing alienation. But it believes in the possibility of the individual to achieve self-identity; it believes in the great humane utopia. And it is based on the conviction that this utopia can be concrete only for a socialist society.

II

Christa Wolf's novel has become a political *cause célèbre*. Desirable or not, there is a Christa Wolf "case" that needs to be carefully examined, for it provides some insight into the current conception of literature in the GDR—at least insofar as this conception is manifest in political and administrative actions, in reviews and theoretical articles appearing in the cultural and literary journals, and in various words spoken during the Sixth German Writers' Convention in 1969.[20] Among the "measures taken" at this convention was the virtual suppression of Wolf's novel. This caused a scandal because the reading public in the GDR had been alerted to the very popular author's new novel by previews in *Sinn und Form* and *Sonntag* and selected readings on GDR radio. Twenty thousand copies are supposed to have been preordered from the publisher. *Christa T.*, announced for 1968, was published by the Mitteldeutscher Verlag in Halle early in 1969 (1968 is given as the year of publication), but only a few copies arrived in select bookstores, and these were sold immediately. Since then the book has been unavailable in the GDR.[21] The number of copies printed in the Federal Republic by Luchterhand rose quickly to 200,000, and the novel was widely praised in critical reviews. The Mitteldeutscher Verlag plans no new printings "for the time being."[22] The novel was not exhibited at the Leipzig Book Fair in fall 1969, nor was it announced in any book catalog or publisher's list.[23]

In the place of the book, the reading public in the GDR was treated to criticism and self-criticism. The "political aesthetics" or "aesthetic politics" of the book were condemned; the publisher was scolded at the very highest level—at the tenth plenary session of the Central Committee of the SED.[24] This was followed by *Mitteldeutscher Verlag's* Director Heinz Sachs's publication of a self-criticism under the title "Verleger sein heisst ideologisch kämpfen" (To be a publisher is to wage an ideological battle).[25] About *Christa T.* he writes:

> It was ascertained that the aesthetic concepts of some members of the publishing company are not sufficiently considered. . . . This book indisputably presents the author's attempt to seek answers to the question of how one ought to live. But it cannot be overlooked that the protagonist of this novel is developed in such a way that it is difficult to answer this question in a socialist manner; the portrayal seems to make it *a priori* impossible for the girl Christa T. to become an example. In addition [to this choice of protagonist] we note that Christa Wolf does not sufficiently stress the possibilities made available to the individual by socialist society. Christa Wolf finds no distance to her protagonist. Pessimism becomes the basic mood of the book's aesthetic. The answer that Christa Wolf ultimately finds remains generally humanistic. But if socialist literature is to fulfill its function and find world-wide recognition, it can achieve this only if it provides specific socialist answers to universally important problems. It is precisely in this that we can locate the publishing company's decisive failure in its interaction with the author Christa Wolf.

Reviews and judgments of *Christa T.* in a broader context differentiate and concretize what has been said here; in so far as they reprove, they are surprisingly unanimous.[26] Heading the list is the reproach that the dialectical relationship between the individual and society is reduced to a false inwardness.[27] The conceptualization of reality as one's inner world was perceived by the critics as ominous subjectivism. They criticized the way in which this world is defined by the structure of the narrated world in *Christa T.* and theoretically articulated as Christa T.'s tenet: "Facts! . . . But what are facts? Facts are the traces left in us by events" (172).[28]

We are told that the novel's leitmotif—individual self-discovery —is presented in a process of failure. Christa T. is understood as a necessary failure because her journey moves consistently inward, into a "poetic enclave of the self" (Kähler 258) rather than in the direction of "communal change" (Simons 201).[29] The author, it is maintained, pursues this journey through the figure of the narrator with sensitive and loving compassion where only a critically judgmental distance can lead to fruitful insight. This insight would exist in noting the necessity of such failure. The artistic "harmony" of the novel (Haase 180) emerges from a "submissive empathetic lyricism" (Kähler 260) and is purchased at the price of knowledge—or worse, with the suggestion of false knowledge. What should be shown to be the result of incorrect behavior is made to appear as fate.[30]

The figures in the novel—so runs the judgment—do just about everything wrong. This is, however, never admitted. Christa T. abandons herself entirely to her sensitivity and a personal "ethical rigor" (Kähler 257); alarmed by her confrontation with the external world, she withdraws into herself and her small circle of friends instead of fighting in and with the new society to alter what is possible and to recognize the impossible or not yet possible for what it is.[31] She lacks an objective view of the social and world political situation; her "ideals," positive in themselves, become "dubiously pretentious," offer a "world of beautiful appearances" in view of the constant threat of the "U.S. aggressors" and "West German imperialism" (Haase 181). The narrative "I," Christa T.'s friend, limits her friendship—and her memory—to the always renewed attempt at understanding. Despite the "poetic warmth" (Kähler 260) generated by her loving respect for the novel's protagonist, the friendship remains irresponsible: she never really "confronts" Christa T., never tries energetically to change her friend's life.[32] The book, molded by the recollections of such a friend, remains similarly irresponsible because it is socially uncommitted. Even after Christa T.'s death the remembering friend learns nothing of any relevance—neither about the deceased nor about herself. The author disappears entirely into or behind the sketchily drawn narrator. One looks in vain for the decisive demonstration of the "correct" view of things: the author dispenses with evaluation; she does not take a position; she avoids the duties of party-mindedness.[33]

Just as problematic for the critics is the function of Christa T. as an account of the postwar period, of the development of the GDR. Here, too, they find much fault and many ambiguities. Although the author's personal good intentions are not doubted, the book is regarded objectively as harmful and dangerous. It makes the GDR reader insecure; it serves the class enemy from elsewhere as a weapon.[34] Confusion is caused by Wolf's method of arbitrarily distorting correct perceptions, placing these into the mouths of dubious characters and thus dismissing them.[35] And finally, doubt is expressed concerning the decisive force of progress, science, and technology in assisting in the process of "coming-to-oneself." This undermines the confidence of people living in a socialist society in the continual humanization of reality.[36]

At the representative forum of socialist writers in the GDR, the Sixth German Writers' Convention, Max Walter Schulz summarized the discomfort and criticism generated by Christa T. in his axiomatic speech and passed this summary on to Christa Wolf as a warning:

> Here we must make room for an open word about Christa Wolf's *Christa T.* We all know Christa Wolf as a talented companion in our cause. Precisely for this reason we cannot hide our disappointment about her new book. However party-minded the subjectively honest intention of the book is meant to be—as the story is told, it is designed to cast our sense of life into doubt, to dislodge a past that has been mastered, to produce a broken relationship to the here and now and tomorrow. — What good is that?

Schulz justifies these comments by calling on "openness and mutual willingness to engage in fundamentally comradely criticism." In this spirit he addresses Christa Wolf: "Think about your origins, think about our progress if with your clever pen you would serve the German working class, its party and the cause of socialism."[37]

The criticism of *Christa T.* is basic; in the comments to which we refer there is no aggression toward the author, no suspicion of her personal political attitude, her good socialist intentions.[38]

Christa Wolf belongs to that generation of GDR authors who experienced Hitler's rule and the war and who, after the collapse, consciously accepted communism as the great hope and the work needed to see it realized in the GDR as their task. Her communist conviction is steadfast; it cannot be shaken, nor is it doubted by her critics in the GDR. Christa Wolf is a successful author. Her 1963 novel *Divided Heaven* very rapidly became a bestseller in the GDR; 300,000 copies have been sold. The novel was filmed by Konrad Wolf. Christa Wolf received the Heinrich-Mann Prize and the National Prize, was even placed in 1963 on the list of Candidates for the Central Committee of the SED. She never became a full member of the Central Committee. In 1967 her name was no longer on the candidates' list. There is a perceptible opposition between Christa Wolf's position and the SED's cultural politics; these have become dogmatically narrower and more intense since 1965. At the Party Congress she spoke of "the right to make mistakes" and was the only one to defend Robert Havemann and Wolf Biermann before this body.[39]

"I believe that literature, like science, has productive potential."[40] This creed is the foundation of the socialist conception of literature.[41] Literature affects—always; the questions are only in what direction and to what degree. This determines its "value." The value is the "true social value of our work as writers" (Schulz 24). "The standard of literary achievement is derived from our standard of progress and from the perspective of our universal social development." There are "standard-setting achievements": these are the "classics" of socialist realism; the most recent one is Anna Seghers's novel *Das Vertrauen.* The common denominator for literary evaluation is established by those works "that document their faith in the German working class, in its revolutionary party and in the cause of socialism most recognizably, most vitally in their characters, most effectively and broadly" (Schulz 25).

219

Roughly sketched, three tasks are to be undertaken by a literature that wants to see itself as potentially powerful.[42] First, there is the treatment of the past, of history, preferably of the construction of the new socialist society in the GDR. An example for this would be Hermann Kant's successful novel, *Die Aula*. That work strives to balance assessing and presenting an important phase in the development of the GDR from the perspective of a member of the "new class," a former student of the workers' and farmers' institute. For the narrator and for the author the past is preserved in a present that represents a "higher" level. Progress is retrospectively ascertained; the finished journey is revealed as a progression. This does not imply a rose-colored falsification of the past. On the contrary, contradictions are manifest; there are structural faults, false and malicious behavior of individuals, irreparable personal misfortune. The reader is enjoined to become involved in critically reworking the past and to take a personal position vis-à-vis history. The "positive aspect" of such a confrontation is provided by the "upward-directed" perspective that is unquestioningly established and maintained throughout without a moment of hesitant doubt. The "true social value" of literary works of this sort resides in the raising of "socialist historical consciousness" and thereby in a deepening of socialist self-understanding. Kant's motto, taken from Heine, expresses this intention precisely: "Today is a result of yesterday. We must explore what the latter expected if we wish to know what the former demands."[43]

Second, literature must demonstrate that its productive potential deals with representing problems and conflicts of an amplified present. It presents possible contradictions in the current phase of socialist development and illustrates varieties of correct and incorrect behavior; it should then either demonstrate the ultimate solution or point to the direction in which it may be found. The presentation is not innocuous; it is quite possible to show human frailty, to show destruction or death. Consider, for instance, Erik Neutsch's *Spur der Steine* or Erwin Strittmatter's *Ole Bienkopf*. It is important that failure and destruction not appear as "necessary" but rather as the result of an incorrect attitude or wrong behavior; it is essential that contradictions be understood and revealed to be basically soluble rather than antagonistic. Reference is often made, in this context, to the "new hero's" "awareness of solutions".[44] Desired are "monuments . . . of human size and beauty." Literature is supposed to provide a "pace-setter function,"[45] for "we need lessons for living" (Schulz 25, 36, 40). Christa Wolf's first novel, *Divided Heaven*, belongs to this group. It shows failure and perseverance in confronting the problem of "illegal departure from the GDR." It does this without creating villains and heroes, with understanding and humane warmth, but still in a way that permits a clear perception of "right" and "wrong" behavior. The "social value" of this kind of literature may be defined as "the raising of socialist crisis-consciousness," as a lesson in the new socialist "awareness of solutions."

Third, literature must make the envisioned future present and tangible: not the future as utopia—this is decisively rejected (cf. Selbmann)—but the future as progress and plan. It is recognizable and accessible from the vantage point of the present because it is designed in the present. The designs for this future that is understood as progress, envisioning a purified and intensified present, should be a part of socialist consciousness, as conscience and knowledge of that which will come and toward which one is moving. The writer is expected to cooperate in providing these designs for the future; he/she is supposed to incorporate them in literature, make them "probable," accord them suggestive power. And the writer is fully expected in the process to be more than and different from a mere versifier of the plan. "The problem of production lies in the creative appropriation of the methods and knowledge of forecasting science" (Schulz 33). It is an important element of literature's "duty to contribute." Literature is expected to be able to make socialist conceptions of the future into a part of the sense of life and self-consciousness of those who live in the present. "Prose" must "be understood and written as part and expression of scientific social forecasts" (Simons 201).

The Sixth Writers' Convention insisted on just this task and proclaimed it as a goal still to be reached. Two things were suggested: first, the writer should have a connection to the science of social forecasting —this connection should be realized in an "institutionalized system of continuing education . . . , a personal educational system for the collective entity literature," a "Johannes R. Becher University for Literature" (Schulz 35). Cooperative work with the literary institute in Leipzig, with "universities, research institutes and industry" should facilitate the integration of writers into the plans for the future of the GDR.[46] Second, in connection with social and cultural forecasting, consideration is being given to collective production of literary works; short of this, a work's genesis might include a preliminary stage of collective discussion, a period of "collective work on the material." The research industry has altered the position and working methods of the scientist, "the German professor"; perhaps the position of "the German writer" should also be seen "in a different connection," ought to be "put into a different context" (Neutsch 55): the production of literature as socialist teamwork, then, the writer as an engineer of literature.

> Our socialist human community develops its way of thinking, its awareness of the solutions to its own problems collectively; collectively it ascertains the tasks necessary to reach these solutions and turns them over to responsible individuals. This applies for the government official, for the factory head, for the worker as well as for the writer. In this process, scientific social forecasting is unalterable. We have entered the phase of the established cooperative system of socialism. The major historical task we have before us is to increase our material and intellectual productivity in complete harmony with each other, with reciprocal and constant interaction, such that the whole progresses ever higher as a system of established socialist con-

ditions of life, in order finally to achieve superiority over capitalism and its material and intellectual production. (Schulz 29)

The current phase of development in the GDR is thus defined as a period of an "established cooperative system of socialism." It demands of the author a "pace-setting attitude" (Schulz 28). We have attempted here to outline crudely what is meant by this. Our sketch also intends to illustrate how the fuller integration of the producer of literature into the total system of social production is envisioned. A new position has been created in the publishing houses—that of "social editor." This editor is especially responsible for such integration.[47] The rejection of "negative" phenomena in literature conforms to its accepted responsibility. All forms of "subjective idealism," such as "inflexibility, wishful thinking, leftist radicalism," are devalued (Schulz 28). "Subjectivism" forswears an orientation toward social development, rejects the duty "to derive our literature's tasks as demands of the day from the needs of the battle" (Schulz 32). In the current phase of "the intensification of the ideological class struggle" (Schulz 27), "subjectivism" in all its variations serves only the enemy. In particular, it raises and perpetuates the strongly embattled thesis of the "third way" (Schulz 46), which supposedly provides an arena in which the literature under capitalism and that under socialism might meet. Anything that produces, or seems to produce, commonality between the GDR and the FRG is therefore sharply rejected. This applies to the "new left," whose radical socialist criticism is aimed at both German states, and to everything that has anything to do with "convergence theory."[48] Subjectivism, it is maintained, leads to an objectively false opposition of attitudinal ethics and socially political behavior; it creates a false freedom that signifies "loss of reality" and "loss of knowledge," which the formal acrobatics currently fashionable in literature attempt to conceal. Such freedom results in "false inwardness." And with this we return once again to the condemnation of *Christa T.*

This condemnation is no cultural-political "accident" rooted in dogmatism, in individual persons' incompetence or maliciousness. It follows, rather, quite logically from the conception that held sway at the time in the GDR. The notion has to do with the "position and function of literature in the established cooperative system of socialism," and we have attempted to represent it, if somewhat briefly, still, we hope, justly. This representation alone ought already to have made it clear that *Christa T.* does not correspond to the official conception. Christa Wolf's novel is not effectively "productive" in any of the three prescribed realms of literature's tasks. Its effect is different. Thus the "case" of Christa Wolf is not of "accidental" origin; it has come about "of necessity."

Christa Wolf cannot be regarded as a naive author, as "ignorant of the world." Her biography alone demonstrates her familiarity with the GDR, especially with those authorities and organizations relevant to cultural politics. She wrote *Christa T.* knowingly and intentionally "against the grain" and certainly also intended to stir up "annoyance" with its publication. She was clearly aware of her potential for becoming a "case." She made allowances for that: not for the sake of negative publicity because she didn't need that; nor for the pleasure of opposition and contentiousness because that contradicts her rather timid temperament and her strong and emotional connection to the state and the party; and certainly not in order to please the much-referred-to class enemy. But rather because she thought it her duty as a communist writer in the GDR to write, not the expected integrated literature, but rather committed literature.

Her book is a creative manifestation of a conception of the essence and social function of literature that opposes the officially valid notion. This is true already of the structure. The serious game of speculation is not intended to bring about assurance; it evokes questions. In such a narrative, truth has more to do with possibilities than with things definitive and manipulatable. The poetic mind at work here, whose creative process is demonstrated, regards itself and its functions as unsettling forces. As memory, the "re-collection" constitutes a search that knows moments of certainty but achieves no total result. As a reflection it is a reminder of an open future.[49] Christa Wolf also speaks theoretically about what she realizes in her literary project—in "Interview with Myself," for instance. In addition, various reflections of the narrator often lead to discursive theoretical discussion in the novel itself. These make reference to cultural-political postulates and defend the narrative undertaking that has no intention of conforming to them. Writing, we read, "means . . . to furnish examples." But Christa T. "isn't an exemplary case at all. I won't say the same could be presumed of every real and living person; and I profess the freedom and responsibility of invention. Just for once, for this once, I want to discover how it is and to tell it like it is: the unexemplary life, a life that can't be used as a model" (45). The literary project presents itself here as an "exploration of reality," not as an illustration or "figurative transformation" of prescribed theorems. Such things are not condemned, nor are the value and profit of "invent[ing] without being ambiguous" (45) discussed. But the narrator insists on a different poetic principle for *Christa T.*: that of experiencing reality by writing—followed, we might add, by reading—literature that is limited by no authority. Christa T. speaks of "coping with things by writing," and Christa Wolf, in her "Interview with Myself," describes her literary project similarly. "Searching, I write" (IM 76). She answers with "yes" the question she poses to herself: "So you wanted to discover in writing something you did not know before?" (IM 78).

The literary figure Christa T., the product of this kind of literary exploration of reality, is understood and presented emphatically as a socially and politically relevant character. This occurs already at the beginning of the book, in the narrator's prefatory thoughts: "So we should be certain of one thing: that it's for our sake. Because it seems that we need her" (5). Later she writes: "You haven't understood a thing if you shrug your shoulders, turn away, turn from her, Christa T., and attend to grander and more useful lives. My concern is to attend to her" (136). The "attention" to Christa T.—"that people may see her" (124)— determines Christa T., whose last sentence constitutes a challenging question to the present: "When, if not now?"

When Christa T. encounters a former student during her vacation, he reminds her of a phrase from Gorky about which she had spoken and he had frequently thought: "about the half-real and half-imaginary existence of human beings." Christa T. listens carefully and then asks, "So it unsettled you?" (111). This seems to me an apt formula for Christa Wolf's understanding of the essence and the social function of literature. She thinks remarkably highly of such a function, even daring to use the word "vital" (IM). But she does not regard literature as "confirmation," not as a "lesson in proper behavior" and also not as the "transformation of social forecasting into image and attitude." She comprehends literature as an unsettling force. The writer should purposely "ask the great questions" whose answers cannot automatically be serenely offered with the other hand, as it were. The writer should disclose what has not yet been seen—or has been overlooked by unspoken mutual agreement, should "refuse to be distracted" from intended "appeals" to the individual and society. Wolf wants to see literature as a force of movement and change, aimed toward an "open" future, prepared and inciting others to "transcend," "to break through and go beyond" (IM 80).[50] Christa Wolf stresses "the deep roots of conformity between genuine literature and socialist society: both have the purpose of helping man to realize himself" (IM 77).

The motto and the leitmotif of the novel, "this coming-to-oneself," thus have a double aspect. They suggest both the goal toward which socialism is moving and the great unknown, "utopia," in the creation of which literature plays its own unique role. This is most certainly a "social" responsibility that neither can nor should be taken from literature by some other authority—not even by scientific social forecasters. Literature should "activate."[51] For Christa Wolf this means, among other things, establishing forces that can oppose the self-sufficient laws of scientific and technological development that cause her considerable concern. She expresses her fear of the world of the technocrats quite clearly in "Interview with Myself"; in Christa T. it is present as the horror of "the new world of the people without imagination . . . Factual people. Up-and-doing people" (51). She means with this the world of those people who are responsible for nothing, who are thoroughly healthy because they are so perfectly adapted. In the New Year's game, which puts the question, "what is indispensable for the survival of mankind?" Christa T. suggests those counterforces that Christa Wolf wants to "activate" with literature. Her key words are "conscience" and "imagination" (172). In the phase of the "established cooperative system of socialism" to which she refers just as much as do her critics, Christa Wolf perceives the social position of literature to reside not in integration, but rather in a critical and warning opposition. Christa T.'s meaning for the life of one of her friends is put like this: "she made it questionable" (48). The novel, *Christa T.*, is intended to have an analogous social function.

Through memory and reflection—*nach-denkend und nachdenkend*—the attempt is made "to break through and go beyond the circle of what we know, or think we know, about ourselves" (IM 80). The past positions itself in relationship to an unknown or only anticipated future. The "productive longing" works for the "believed-in" future, for the future as the "other" dimension. It is present as hope, as hope that can be disappointed. The restlessness that the book evokes and the movement it stimulates are directed at this future. For this reason, I regard *Christa T.* as a utopian book. The utopian content is given in the Becher-motto, in the form of the question: "What is it—this coming-to-oneself?" *Christa T.*, which succeeds in evoking the deceased woman in portraying, in a few vicariously livable images, the "truth" and its "essence" as a great promise, is a future addicted novel of remembrance, a utopian book. I know nothing comparable in the literature of the GDR. It is an extraordinary accomplishment by a great socialist writer.

Notes

This article was first published as "Produktive Sehnsucht. Struktur, Thematik und politische Relevanz von Christa Wolfs *Nachdenken über Christa T.*," in *Basis 2*, ed. Reinhold Grimm and Jost Hermand (Frankfurt/Main: Athenäum, 1971), 191-233. It is reprinted in translation here with the permission of the author.

"Es gibt kein Vergangenes, das man zurücksehnen dürfte, es gibt nur ein ewig Neues, das sich aus den erweiterten Elementen des Vergangenen gestaltet, und die echte Sehnsucht muss stets produktiv sein, ein neues Besseres erschaffen" (There is no past for whose return one should long, there is only the eternally new, which forms itself from expanded elements of the past; and genuine longing must always be productive in order to create something new and better). Kanzler von Müller, *Unterhaltungen mit Goethe*, Diary entry of 4 November 1823.

1. Marcel Reich-Ranicki, "Christa Wolfs unruhige Elegie," *Die Zeit* 21 (23 May 1969): 21.
2. *The Quest for Christa T.*, 185; henceforth cited parenthentically.
3. For references to time and age, see CT 4, 95, 166.
4. Hans Mayer, "Christa Wolf: Nachdenken über Christa T.," NR 81, 1 (1970): 180–186.
5. Mayer stresses that Christa T. reads Dostoevsky. He speaks of a "Dostoevsky-motif" that permits "possibly the clearest identification of the autobiographical substance of the book." From Christa Wolf's essay on Dostoevsky he quotes her thoughts on the genesis of *Crime and Punishment*. In these, Christa Wolf imagines a Dostoevsky oppressed by poverty and hate, how he creates a character—Raskolnikov—who carries out the murder so that the author doesn't need to do the deed. *Christa T.* is, Mayer suggests, organized according to this "work principle," and Christa T. is thus connected to Christa Wolf. Wolf's

Heinrich Mohr

essay on Dostoevsky is indeed apt as an illustration of Mayer's interpretative model. But the connection between essay and novel seems to me too weak. After all, there is only one mention of Dostoevsky in *Christa T.* (47); that's not sufficient for a "Dostoevsky-motif."

6. Mayer informs us in a footnote that there was a "real" Christa T. with a similar life-story. She was a friend of Christa Wolf. They studied German language and literature together in Leipzig. Mayer, who was a professor in Leipzig at that time, also remembers the thesis on Theodor Storm that is quoted in the novel and plays an important role. These are welcome supports for our interpretative approach. For Mayer, this "life material" has approximately the same function here as Jerusalem's actual suicide for *The Sufferings of Young Werther.*

7. Translation altered by editor. Middleton has "disturbing our chronology" (110). The original reads: "Die Chronologie stört" (111).

8. Christa T. was born in 1928 in a village east of the Oder River. She has an older sister. Her father is a social-democratic village schoolteacher: westward flight from the Red Army in winter of 1945; then agricultural work, teacher training, three years working as teacher, then university study. Her first subject of study is not clearly defined. In Leipzig, 1954, she completes her exams in German language and literature with a thesis on Theodor Storm and then works at a school. A second profession remains undefined. Friendships and love affairs with a teacher-colleague and a fellow student. Marriage to a veterinarian. Three children. Housewife-existence. Construction of own, self-designed home in Mecklenburg on a lake. Illicit love affair. Incurable disease of the blood. Death after stubborn resistance.—Since childhood, the desire to be a "poet." "I would like to write poems and I like stories too" (16). Fragmentary attempts at writing, which she keeps secret. Also diaries. After her death in 1963, her husband turns this "material" over to the narrator. She begins with the work of writing her thoughts about Christa T. a short time after the death of her friend. A first version of Christa Wolf's novel was completed around 1965, was then revised and printed in 1968.

9. See also 37, 67.

10. [Note: The title is retained—in low-German dialect—in the English translation. It can be rendered approximately: What the General said.—Ed.]

11. Translation altered by editor.

12. [This ballad by Gustav Schwab, 1792–1850, a minor Swabian poet, is also a pretext for Peter Handke's play, "Der Ritt über den Bodensee," as well as a central metaphorical allusion in his *Sorrow Beyond Dreams* (*Wunschloses Unglück*). The ballad tells the story of a horseman determined to reach Lake Constance and take a boat across it before nightfall. Lost and isolated in a barren wintry wilderness, he seeks a person who can give him directions. When, finally, he finds a small village and asks a young woman how far it is to the lake, she tells him that it is far behind him. To her amazement and his frightened astonishment, he has ridden over the bottomless abyss of the frozen lake; she calls together the people of the village—the old men and women bless him—but the rider, glimpsing the awful depths in his imagination, falls dead with horror from his horse.—Ed.].

13. "And she was not afraid that she would miss her share of kindliness. She knew that she would sometimes be tired, sometimes angry. But she was not afraid. And what made up for everything was the feeling that people could learn to sleep soundly again and live their lives to the full, as if there were an abundance of this strange substance—life—as if it could never be used up" (*DH* 212).

14. Here is Christa Wolf's answer to the suspicion that Christa T. should be understood as a failed person: "You mean because she died so young? Because it is not easy to count the results of her life or point them out? No. I have discovered that she lived fully in the time vouchsafed her" (IM 78).

15. The Hungarian revolution in 1956 was extremely significant for Christa T. and the narrator. They had regarded it spontaneously as a "darkening of the

world," subsequently understood as a lasting sobriety and a brutal lesson in reality. But both Christa T. and the narrator forbade themselves "to retreat into the roles of dupes. But the role of the iron believer was now defunct as well; the stage on which such roles had been played was plunged in darkness. Yes, there had been a sudden change in the lighting" (133).

16. Christa Wolf on the origin of her book: "I must confess to a purely subjective urge. Someone very close to me died, too young. I don't accept this death. I am looking for some means to defend myself effectively against it. Searching, I write. The result is that I have to pin down this searching, as honestly, as exactly as possible" (IM 76).

17. The reviewers in East and West, in contrast—and in rare agreement with each other—, understood Christa T. as a failed person. Fritz J. Raddatz even goes so far as to read *Christa T.* as the "story of a suicide." Fritz J. Raddatz, "Mein Name sei Tonio K." *Der Spiegel* 23 (2 June 1969).

18. The thesis is part of the existing real material of the novel. Hans Mayer was acquainted not only with the fellow-student and friend of Christa Wolf who stands behind the literary figure; he also remembers her thesis on Theodor Storm. (Cf. note 5.)

19. Christa Wolf suggests something about this process, without, to be sure, revealing the salient point: "I suddenly faced myself. I had not foreseen this. The relations between 'us'- Christa T. and the narrator 'I'—shifted of themselves into the center. . . . If I were a mathematician I should probably speak of a 'function' —nothing tangible, visible, material, but extraordinarily effective" (IM 77).

20. The "German Writers' Convention" is the forum in which the authors of the GDR who belong to the "German Writers' Union" present themselves to each other and to the public. The aim, in lectures and discussions, is to determine the position and function of socialist literature in the respective phase of the GDR's social development. Tasks and goals are formulated, trends in current literature are approved or rejected, and special discussions are devoted to single works regarded as either positively or negatively exemplary. The language of the writers' convention expresses the "official" self-perception of writers in the GDR. The Sixth Writers' Convention met in Berlin, 28–30 May 1969. The September issue of *Neue deutsche Literatur*, together with a few supplementary articles in the following issue, extensively documents this convention in its synopsis of the most important materials.

21. [Editor's note: The reader is reminded that this article was first published in 1971. The climate surrounding this book in the GDR has changed significantly since that time.]

22. "For the time being" was the information given at the annual book fair in Leipzig in fall 1969. Cf. Wolfgang Werth, "Nachdenken aus einem stillen Deutschland," *Der Monat* 253 (October 1969). For further information, see also Jürgen Wallmann, "Nachdenken über Christa T.," *NdL* 124 (January 1970). The information regarding number of copies printed in the FRG, copies preordered from the Mitteldeutscher Verlag and the radio broadcast in the GDR is taken from Jürgen Beckelmann, "Der Versuch man selbst zu sein," *SZ* 26–27 July 1969.

23. The information about the details of publication and suppression is based more on speculations than on exact reports. The West German critics give highly varied information regarding the Mitteldeutscher Verlag's publishing run: the lowest estimate is 500, the highest is 4,000. The most frequently mentioned number is 800. The Mitteldeutscher Verlag did not respond to my request for authentic information. I am grateful to Roland Wiegenstein for the following information: A first draft of Christa Wolf's novel existed already in 1965. The revised version was printed in 1968 in an edition of 5,000 copies; of these, 800 were distributed. This means, however, that the majority was sent to selected critics, functionaries, and library officials; a smaller number arrived in the bookstores. This was followed by the definitive rejection of the book. The remaining 4,200 copies were sold by the *Mitteldeutscher Verlag* to Luchterhand. His copy,

incidentally, bears the following imprint: "Produced in the Karl-Marx-Werk, Pössneck (DDR)."

24. Heinz Adameck, director of GDR Television, explained: "There is evidently a lack of correlation between the ideological conception of these authors (Rudolf Bartsch, Günter Kunert, and Eduard Claudius were named in addition to Christa Wolf) and that of the readers and directors of the publishing house." Quoted in Jürgen Beckelmann, "Der Versuch man selbst zu sein," SZ 26–27 July 1969.

25. Heinz Sachs, "Verleger sein heisst ideologisch kämpfen," ND 14 May 1969.

26. We are not concerned here with the positive sections of the reviews. Generally praised are language and style, literary technique and differentiated psychology, probably most carefully in the interpretation by Horst Haase. We refer in this discussion to the following articles, which will be noted in the text henceforth only with authors' names in parentheses. Hermann Kähler, "Christa Wolf's Elegie," SuF 21, no. 1 (1969): 251–261. Horst Haase, "Nachdenken über ein Buch," NdL 4 (1969): 174–185. Elisabeth Simons, "'Das anders machen, von Grund auf.' Die Hauptrichtungen der jüngsten erzählenden DDR-Literatur." WB, Special Issue for the 20th Anniversary of the Founding of the German Democratic Republic (1969): 183–204. Werner Neubert, Sigrid Bock, Klaus Jarmatz, Eberhard Röhner, Elisabeth Simons, Frank Wagner, "Zu Errungenes und weiter zu Gewinnendes," NdL 9 (1969): 148–174; hereafter cited as Neubert et al. Max Walter Schulz, "Das Neue und das Bleibende in unserer Literatur," NdL 9 (1969): 24–51. From the contributions to the discussions at the Writers' Convention (all in NdL 9/1969), we refer to the following: Erik Neutsch, "Literatur als schöpferische Kollektivität," 52–57; Helmut Sakowski, "Die Wahrheit erkennen und gestalten," 57–61; Hermann Kant, "Poetisches Programm des Sozialismus," 61–68; Erich Reinholz, "Sozialistische Klassenposition unserer Literatur," 80–82; Martin Selber, "Leben und literarischer Stoff," 83–85; Wolfgang Joho, "Von den Schwierigkeiten des Schreibens," 85–90; Gerhard Bengsch, "Die Poesie im neuen Gegenstand," 91–94; Martin Viertel, "Das Schöne im neuen Menschen," 97–100; Fritz Selbmann, "Parteilichkeit—das Entscheidende!" 100–105; Ruth Kraft, "Die Neuheit menschlicher Beziehungen," 106–108; Horst Salomon, "Die Kraft des künstlerischen Vorbilds," 108–110; Jurij Brezan, "Weltgeschichte und Weltgeschichten," 112–115; Johannes Rech, "Jugend und Literatur," 115–116; Rosemarie Schuder, "Aktualität des historischen Romans," 116–117; Claus Hammel, "Das Eigene und das Andere," 117–118; Friedrich Plathe, "Erfahrungen schreibender Arbeiter," 118–121; Hans Koch "Vor neuen Schaffensproblemen," 121–126; Günther Deicke, "Wissen und Klarheit—Grundelemente des Talents," 129–132; Klaus Gysi, "Gültige Literatur der sozialistischen Menschengemeinschaft," 136–146.

27. "It is regrettable that the author's important contribution in her intensive comprehension of the manifold connections between the individual and society has not been expanded in Christa T. but rather has been radically reduced in a subjective direction. We must note a neglect, in the Brechtian sense, of the causality between the psyche and its environment. In her leitmotif-like evocation of Johannes R. Becher, Christa Wolf has not achieved an image of the complete socialist human being (of the sort that Becher strove for); the "coming-to-oneself" of the human being cannot be understood as an abstract development that takes place without reference to concrete social practice" (Neubert et al. 156). "It is not the right to happiness, but rather the possibility of finding genuine happiness in the productive involvement with community that creates the socialist character. In this respect, Christa Wolf's new book, Christa T., is not satisfying. . . . The conditions that define the essence of our human community, above all communal change, seem hardly to have touched Christa T. She lives with her view turned inward. . . . Christa T. demonstrates with her existence the 'attempt to be oneself,' or so it seems. But no individual, no inner values can succeed in self-activity outside the concrete social environment and the active mutual relation-

ship to it. Productivity and self-chosen isolation are incompatible" (Simons 200f.).

28. For Kähler, this is a "fatal sentence," which already judges Christa T.'s consciousness and her literary efforts. The narrator's comment, inserted at this point as a remark to a mutual former friend, annoys him even more: "You see, she was one-sided, of course she was" (172). "'One-sided' is, in the face of the burden of contemporary facts, at the very least a daring understatement or irresponsible transcription of the old '*poeta sum, ergo sum*'" (Kähler, 256f.).

29. Kähler defines the theme of the novel as follows: "An autonomous character without a social function is an illusion—in Christa T.'s case a tragic one." He describes the course of her life like this: "Christa T.—I cannot read the story any other way—did not only want to play a role in our workers' society, be it as teacher, as university instructor, as book reviewer; she did not want to bend to the somewhat standardized status of a profession—she wanted to retain the wealth of her own character—and with that she almost ended up in the smallest, least significant supporting role of 'wife,' whose heavens have their horizon just beyond the garden fence" (255f.).

30. "In general, the attitude of the narrator is defined by her admiration for Christa T. The noble picture of this character, unrecognized during her lifetime, is to be presented to posterity. There is therefore no real tension between the central character and the narrator-figure. Perhaps it is this lack of tension that denies the possibility of moving the book beyond a one-sided idealization and a certain resulting structural one-dimensionality" (Haase 180). "Shouldn't Christa Wolf have used more distance, superiority, filters for her Christa T.? Shouldn't one demand of her that she provide a more meaningful assessment when she creates a person who can barely come to terms with life?" (Kähler 260).

31. In *Christa T.*, according to Haase, "the real problem of power and violence is reduced to an ideal notion of sensitivity that reminds us in a dangerous way of certain sections of Marx's and Engels' criticism of Daumer's *Religion des neuen Weltalters*. The notion appears somewhat strange in its one-sidedness vis-à-vis such facts as the war in Viet Nam and the aggression of West German imperialism" (181).

32. The "poetic warmth" is emphatically praised. But Kähler then continues: "Warmth in literature ought to entail action as well as empathy; it should be Promethean as well as Epimethean, should involve dialogue as well as understanding" (259).

33. Cf. the Fritz Selbmann's speech, "Parteilichkeit—das Entscheidende," a general talk on the theme of party-mindedness that does not refer directly to Christa Wolf.

34. Haase notes: "Such abstractions of concrete historical events permit such multiple interpretation that they open gate and door to misappropriation in the ideological battles of our age" (183f.). At the Writers' Convention, Max Walter Schulz exemplified the danger of the book's misuse against the GDR as follows: "What use is a subjectively honest intention of good partisan will when the ambiguity of expression—both in the text and in the book's overall impression—is so clearly provocative that the other side only needs to choose what it wants for ammunition, only needs to read out of it what it would like to read. We socialists are, after all, not yet alone in the world. We do not let the enemy dictate our judgment. But the reactions of a man like Reich-Ranicki should give us something to think about. While he insulted and defiled Anna Seghers' great new novel in the most despicable manner (cf. Reich-Ranicki's review of Anna Seghers, *Das Vertrauen* (Trust) in *Die Zeit* 11, 14 March 1969), he simultaneously makes the following comment about *Christa T.*: 'Let's say it clearly: Christa T. dies from leukemia, but she suffers from the GDR'" (Schulz 47, 49). Hermann Kant also warns of the dangers of this perspective. "It can happen to someone who thought he was speaking of his own concerns that he generates a confused response. This calls for an examination, and I think it will be good for all of us,

for our socialist project and our literature of the socialist project, if we don't forget that something that doesn't please us does not for that reason have to please our enemies, or that it is intended for these enemies' pleasure" (Kant 65).

35. As examples for this, Haase cites the dialogue between Christa T. and her former student about morality and conformity and the New Year's question game (CT 110ff.; 172f.).

36. "This is the arena of science, that factor of human progress that has been essential for centuries. It is the arena of what has been the basis for meaningful activity since Marx and Engels—and this is equally applicable to the realm of human coexistence." The danger of the misuse of science and technology is admitted, but it is stressed that "socialism offers all the possible ways of avoiding it. . . . This art must appropriate the scientific and technological sphere, must master it aesthetically instead of rejecting it suspiciously. But it is just such suspicion that is heard as undertone in Christa Wolf's book." The wrong attitude toward science and technology is especially conspicuous for Haase in a scene of "symbolic content," that is, in the scene in which the characters wait in vain for the appearance of the Sputnik (CT 143–144). See Haase 181f.

37. See Schultz 47, 50. There is a contrast between the rejection of *Christa T.* by those responsible for literature and culture in the GDR and positive reception of the novel in the Soviet Union and Poland. The new book of the "well-known" author is announced and discussed with praise, if somewhat schematically, in the Moscow literary journal (*Literaturnaja Gazeta* 20, 14 May 1969). "The willingness to fight her way through, to move forward side by side with her homeland, does not leave the protagonist even in the most difficult situations. . . . Christa T. can serve as a moral example." More interesting is an article by Adam Krzeminski in the Warsaw weekly newspaper *Polityka* of 17 May 1969, titled "Rhythm of the Generation" (Rytm Pokoleniowy). In the subtitle he writes, "In Poland we don't know very much about the cultural life of the GDR." Krzeminski gives an overview in three thematic sections: theater, the younger generation, and specific works of literature. He finds little that is positive; he criticizes much and very sharply; the manner of his criticism betrays a disdain for his subject—in general his antipathy toward the GDR can barely be overlooked. For him the most dominant characteristic of cultural life in the GDR is provinciality, although he doesn't use this word. He finds sterile protection of tradition in two forms: reception of the bourgeois national cultural heritage in competition with the FRG and continuation of the socialist realist literature begun in the twenties and thirties. One produces *Minna von Barnhelm* or *Mutter Courage* and is, here as well as there, pleased with classicism and fearful of the present. He judges the younger authors quite negatively; only in Hermann Kant (*Die Aula*) and in Christa Wolf does he perceive serious confrontations with one's "own milieu" and "taking account" of history and the present. *Christa T.* is for him "the event of the year 1969."

38. Compare for instance the much sharper tone of the criticism of Rainer Kunze's volume of poems, *Sensible Wege* (Rowohlt, 1969) in the same speech by Max Walter Schulz in which he criticizes *Christa T.* Kunze is accused of "naked, irritated individualism—lusting for action despite all its sensitivity—that peers forth from this inner world and is already collaborating with anti-communism, with the malicious distortion of the image of the GDR. . . . When one reads the poems, one sees the fatal lyrical place between inner-wordly vision and anti-communism with increased clarity" (Schulz 46f.).

39. I am indebted to Roland Wiegenstein for his ready information concerning politics and personalities in the literary life of the GDR. Regarding this and following information, cf. also Hans Peter Klausenitzer, "Christa Wolf: Nachdenken über Christa T." *Publik* 40 (3 October 1969); Jürgen P. Wallmann, "Nachdenken über Christa T." *Neue deutsche Hefte* 124 (January 1970). Wolfgang Werth, "Nachricht aus einem stillen Deutschland," *Der Monat* 153 (October 1969).

40. Final sentence of Erwin Strittmatter's letter of greeting to the Sixth German Writers' Convention. *NdL* 9 (1969): 12.

41. Although literature can only become "potentially powerful" when the producer of literature has the possibility of creating in writing a connection to the "developed productive forces of the class . . . that determines historical progress" (Schulz 51). This means, for the present age, that literature can have potential power only in a society that is building toward socialism; concretely spoken, in the GDR but by no means in the FRG. Literature there is "necessarily" completely different and has a different social function, if it has one at all. The sharp and often polemically pointed rejection of all varieties of "convergence theory" and a "literature of the third way" must be understood from the vantage of this fundamentally dogmatic position. The confrontation with the contemporary literature of late capitalism is far more prickly for the GDR than it is for other socialist states—precisely because this "other" literature exists in the same language. This exceptional situation can promote multiplicity and experiment as much as it promotes defensive tendencies and withdrawal to what is supposedly "one's own"—to dogmatic immobility. The developments in general cultural politics and in specific literary politics in the GDR have gone through several different phases. The dominant tendency since 1965 has been one of encapsulation and of petty regulation and control of literary life. In the FRG there is no analogous, extraordinary situation engendered by the existence of the "other" literature in the same language, there the literature and literary life of the GDR still play an extremely minor role. German literary studies in the FRG have preferred more or less to ignore the unique situation of contemporary German literature. If I'm not mistaken, at the moment only one academic position exists for GDR literature in the FRG—at the Technical University in Hannover. This position is held by Fritz J. Raddatz (until 1958 editor-in-chief at the East German publishing house, *Volk und Welt*).

42. This corresponds to the fundamental position statement: "As long as we write socialist literature, as long as we are partisan in defense of it, we will not relinquish the common orientation toward the threefold faith in class, party, and the cause of socialism" (Schulz 24).

43. Heinrich Heine. *Französische Zustände*, Article VI (19 April 1832), in *Historisch-Kritische Gesamtausgabe der Werke*, ed. Manfred Windfuhr, vol. 12/1 (Hamburg: Hoffmann und Campe, 1980), 129–151. [I am indebted to Jeffrey Sammons for his assistance in locating this quotation.—Ed.]

44. "The meaning of history and of the stories, plays and poems we write lies in the nature of the solution, in the awareness of the necessity of a solution to the problems, contradictions and conflicts" (Schulz 30). In connection with the negative evaluation of *Christa T.*, Simons says: "The increased need for the artistic formulation of human problems in the socialist human community is directed above all at the models presented for the solution and overcoming of such conflicts. This does not by any means mean the rejection of 'open endings' or even the demand for a happy ending at any price; it has to do rather with the author's manifest partisan affirmation of the direction in which he expects to find a solution to such a conflict-constellation and which he recognizes in reality" (Simons 201).

45. This "pace-setting function" is demanded of literature in the letter of the Bitterfeld Chemical Concern to the Writers' Convention. *NdL* 9 (1969): 10.

46. Schulz reports the answer of collective farmers to an author's question concerning how they see themselves in the year 2000: "We'd like to learn that from you, Colleague Writer." Schulz continues: "Only one thing helps here: to do socialist communal work, to obtain solid ties to scientific collectives and to form scientific, creative collectives within the collective entity literature itself. We need a permanent school of creative science for our literature. Its schedule should conform to the seasons, and it should be administered locally as well as centrally; an executive committee would serve the exchange of experiences and to make decisions."

47. The social editor is supposed to be the pace setter for this integration. Cf. the above-cited article by Heinz Sachs in *Neues Deutschland*, 14 May 1969.

48. The "new left" is subjected to particularly strong condemnation—"bourgeois in Marx' clothing"—as is "leftist" literature in the Federal Republic —and in the GDR. Schulz speaks of "intellectualized pseudo-internationalism" and concludes: "The identification of writers who live in Germany today with one or another state . . . produces . . . two German literatures. A third German literature which disavows its identity with one or the other . . . is condemned to ineffectuality. . . . The bourgeois German writer . . . continues to be far closer to our socialist German literature than the literati of the third way. . . . Their so-called third way increasingly reveals itself as assuming a too-obliging position between 'inner world' and anti-communism" (Schulz 46f.).

49. The stylistic similarity of *Christa T.* with Uwe Johnson's works has often been noted. This seems correct to me, insofar as it concerns the style of his *Speculations about Jakob* in the remembering process that is conceived as a search for reality. Nothing in Johnson's work, however, corresponds to Wolf's transformation of remembered material into challenges and reminders, or to the active political and utopian element of *Christa T.* The title *Nachdenken über Christa T.* (Thoughts about Christa T.) is certainly intended to echo *Mutmassungen über Jakob* (*Speculations about Jakob*). The same could be said for the abbreviation, T., which suggests the figure K. in Kafka's *Castle*. Incidentally, Uwe Johnson, Christa Wolf, and the woman behind Wolf's literary figure Christa T. are all united by their common study of German literature in Leipzig under the aegis of Hans Mayer.

50. Christa Wolf writes in her "Interview with Myself": "I can only do my best in posing questions. I can only rely on the fact that my whole life, my experience gained through an intensive preoccupation with the development of our society will prompt me to ask questions and bring up problems that are also important—perhaps vital—to other people. But I cannot be sure of this.

Q. You believe literature to be vital?

A. If art did not produce something necessary and new to add to life I do not believe that humanity would for thousands of years have made its great efforts in what we call art, or that the forces needed for it would have been there in times of great material want. . . . Our scientific age will not be what it could and must be, if we are to avoid a terrible disaster, if art does not force itself to ask, does not refuse to be distracted from asking the great questions of contemporaries to whom it appeals. To encourage our age to be itself, that is, to constantly change, throughout life, change ourselves through creative work" (78–79).

51. Thus Christa Wolf in her answer to a questionnaire of the Moscow monthly journal, *Woprossy Literatury*, which devoted its December 1970 issue entirely to literature of the GDR. There, too, Christa Wolf stresses the task of "exploring reality"; she calls for the courage "to tell our own life-material unsparingly, always faithful to the truth" and concludes: "The socialist author, then, should not agree to any of the comfortable offers of capitulation, no matter who makes them, no matter how they are justified" (quoted in *NdL* 1 (1971): 70f.).

Traces of Ernst Bloch:
Reflections on Christa Wolf

Andreas Huyssen

I

    "But what are facts?"[1] Christa Wolf's novel *The Quest for Christa T.* gives the answer to Christa T.'s question: "Facts are the traces left in us by events" (172). This sentence has led to controversy.[2] Critics from the GDR accused the narrator of glorifying inwardness and the idyll, of reducing the relationship between individual and society to the merely private realm, of lacking an objectivizing and critical distance toward her character.[3] Christa Wolf's first novel, *Divided Heaven* (1963), had already drawn the criticism that some of its characters live and work too much according to their individual moral sensibilities and that the leading role of the party and the importance of class perspective had not been thoroughly enough developed.[4] In *The Quest for Christa T.*, however, the question of individual responsibility and of the role of the subject in the historical process is posed in a far more rigorous and, at the same time, more problematical way. Although a review of *Divided Heaven* could appear under the title "Tragic Experiences in an Optimistic Perspective,"[5] the discussion now concentrated on resignation and pessimism,[6] dubious exemplariness,[7] and questionable political aesthetics.[8] Christa T.'s failure was emphasized in the West as well, chiefly by Raddatz, who read the novel as the story of a suicide.[9] Numerous passages from the novel can be cited to support the pessimism

233

thesis, but if overemphasized this idea ultimately projects political wish-fulfillment on both sides. Critics in the GDR are extraordinarily sensitive to any sign of pessimism and resignation because they are reluctant to approach the problem of alienation in the GDR at all seriously. Western critics, on the other hand, either speak point-blank and gleefully of dissident literature, or they project theories of thaw and convergence[10] into their interpretations, which tend to neglect or falsify the historical conditions for Christa Wolf's novel.

Manfred Durzak provides an interesting suggestion for an alternative interpretation. He maintains that Christa Wolf's criticism of the social reality in the GDR fundamentally agrees with the literary doctrine of the second Bitterfeld Conference in 1964. Durzak quotes from Ulbricht's Bitterfeld speech, which mentions a "qualitative increase of the role of all subjective factors"[11] for the development of socialism. Durzak overlooks the fact, however, that Ulbricht is concerned with the effects of subjective factors on production under the new economic system, not with subjectivity per se. Such a distinction actually points to the significant difference regarding the role of subjectivity between *Divided Heaven* and *The Quest for Christa T.* While Rita Seidel's subjectivity develops in direct contact with the objectivity of the sphere of industrial production,[12] Christa T. is totally alienated from the production process. This suggests a change in the self-perception of the author Christa Wolf who, under the influence of the Bitterfeld Movement, worked like Rita Seidel in a factory brigade and is therefore well informed about the problems of artists and intellectuals in a socialist society. Christa Wolf's change is to be understood neither as a resigned withdrawal from the production process toward inwardness nor as the fulfillment of an allegedly altered doctrine of socialist realism. It is, rather, a matter of representing objective contradictions and pressing problems in the GDR's past and present. For Christa Wolf these contradictions can be solved only within the frame of socialist politics. Heinrich Mohr is therefore correct when he, in contrast to the West-East pessimism theory, terms *The Quest for Christa T.* a "future-addicted novel of remembrance"[13] and stresses the utopian dimension of the novel.

II

In the realm of contemporary Marxist philosophy, utopian thought is inseparably connected with the name of Ernst Bloch, and Christa Wolf indeed follows the lead of this thinker, who was professor of philosophy at the University of Leipzig from 1949 to 1957.[14]

Hans Mayer already suggests synchronous patterns of thinking when he likens Bloch's ideas to those expressed in the motto from J. R. Becher that precedes Wolf's novel.[15] We can also perceive traces of such synchronicity in two other central sentences of the novel that, while initially articulated by Christa T., are appropriated by the narrator to signal her own standpoint: first, the angry and challenging closing sentence of the novel, "When, if not now?" (185), impatiently demands the realization of a concrete utopia; and second, the key sentence of the whole novel, "The Big Hope, or The Difficulty of Saying 'I,'" alludes directly to Becher (169).[16] For Christa T. it is a question of self-realization in a socialist society: "What she wished for more intensely than anything, and I'm speaking now of Christa T., was the coming of our world; and she had precisely the kind of imagination one needs for a real understanding of it" (51). Precisely because Christa T. is a committed socialist, the difficulty of saying "I" leads her not into despair and nihilism—as so often happens in Western novels—but it is understood instead as "the big hope." Hope in the becoming-concrete (*Konkretwerden*) of utopia as a means to overcome alienation: this distinguishes Christa T. from her peers. Hope is the defining principle of her life. Thus, she removes from the wall of her rented room the framed motto that displeases her and puts it in front of her landlady's door. The motto reads: "Even if Hope's Last Anchor Breaks, Courage, Courage is What it Takes" (42). Ernst Bloch writes in the introduction to his major philosophical work, *The Principle of Hope*: "*Docta spes*—conceived hope—thus illuminates the concept of a principle in the world—a concept that remains there."[17] Where hope is principle there can be no last anchor that breaks.

The philosophy of hope is Marxism. "It is the practice of concrete utopia" (*PH* 16); it projects life on the horizon where hope is realized. The narrator and other friends of Christa T. make themselves unassailable, repress questions and doubts, less from fear than from insecurity (50–51). But Christa T. is profoundly conscious of the not-yet-realized (*Noch-Nicht-Gewordene*) in herself and in society. The narrator stresses that the reader will know as good as nothing about Christa T. "unless I can contrive to say the most important thing about her, which is this: Christa T. had a vision of herself" (117). This is meant in the sense not of unrealistic musings but rather of a daydream of the new human being, fully connected to reality. "Christa T. began, very early on, when one thinks about it today, to ask herself what change means. The new words? The new house? Machines, bigger fields? The new man, she heard people say; and she began to look inside herself" (56). The others, in contrast, say "scornfully": "The puny ego. . . . The old Adam, we've finished him off" (173). But Christa T. doubts that: "I really don't know. There must be some misunderstanding. All this trouble, just to make sure that every one of us gets to be different—and all so as to get rid of that difference in time too?" (173). Christa T. looks inside herself, but then she says "we," thus shifting her view from within herself toward the outside, to the others. She is never concerned only with herself: "She was all for reality, that's why she loved the time when real changes were being made. She loved to open up new senses for the sense of a new thing" (174). But the new human being whom the utopia requires does not arrive easily or quickly, not even in a socialist society. Early experiences of youth—the tomcat that was dashed against the stable wall by the tenant farmer—repeat themselves in the new society: the story of the toad. "Paradise can make itself scarce" (52); the old Adam is still the old Adam. Christa T. insists all the more on change, hopefully anticipates a future that extends beyond that which is already achieved, a future rewritten in Blochian language: "The future? The future is going to be Quite Different" (101).

This is Christa T.'s certainty, for something of this Quite Different-ness is in her, suspected in childhood—"child of a star, not a great gentleman's child" (17)—later consciously anticipated and recorded in her writing. We can see this, for instance, in the manuscript of the toad story, in which Christa T. makes the pupil Hammurabi— who had bitten the head off a toad on a bet—repent his deed, although he wouldn't think of repenting: "This conclusion—she must have wanted it badly. And we concur, deeply, with all who desire such conclusions all the more passionately the less often they come to pass" (110). Christa T. suffers from the fact that such conclusions still do not come to pass. This leads to "bitterness as the fruit of passion" (132)—as the narrator calls it at a later point, when Christa T. fails to convince a streetcar conductress, who is hospitalized after her third abortion, to change her life. The streetcar conductress will continue living with "her weary surrender to the sufferings inflicted on her by her husband" (131). But just these people, Hammurabi and the streetcar conductress, matter. Who can teach them, shake them awake? How can they learn that hope of which Bloch writes in the foreword to *The Principle of Hope*: "It is a matter of learning how to hope. Hope's work, in love with success rather than failure, does not resign. . . . The affect of hope leads beyond itself, it broadens human beings instead of constricting them" (*PH* 1).

Christa T.'s life is grounded in such consciousness, but she does not succeed in communicating to others, in involving others in her knowledge, her vision. She remains an outsider in her society, and it is thus only logical that she can "only cope with things by writing" (34). She is said to be "hungering for reality" (57); and with this hunger she pursues that which changes human beings, seeks the horizon, as Bloch would say, for instance in the farmers' experience with agrarian collectivization:

> As often as possible she drove about in the countryside with her husband. Her old greed for faces, the way they really look, receiving bad news or good, tensing, resolving, doubting, wavering, understanding, overcoming. She forgets herself when she sees the wild peasant faces. Justus has to go into their houses. What does the Herr Doktor honestly think about the cooperatives? Justus brings statistical charts: productions of milk, pork, cereals. The world record, compared with their own region. Christa T. saw that so much had never been asked of them before, an unprecedented step beyond their apparent maximum capacity. She risked a cautious word now and then, mostly among the women, with whom she'd be standing in the

kitchen, who'd be giving little Anna milk to drink and all the time
setting up their old lament, the usual complaint about their lives,
punctuated with violent accusations, and infrequently a quick question, with a glance at the door to the living room—just to make sure:
Who'll give a thought to us, ah, I don't believe a word of it, it's never
happened yet, that's news to us . . .

There are people, Christa T. would say, who are interested in
the news, and in new ideas, so you should do what you can about it.
(144–145)

She wants to present the life of these farmers in her stories "Around the
Lake." But her attempts at writing always break off at the beginning.
Again and again reality faces her "like a wall" (70)—in childhood as
during her stint as a teacher, at the university and later during her marriage. The time for the realization of her big hope seems not yet to have
arrived. This throws her into crises; for she ultimately sees herself always referred back to herself, having to cope alone, and for her, the socialist, this is insufficient for self-realization. The narrator understands
this contradiction in Christa T.'s life and displays mild criticism: "What
does the world need to become perfect? This and this alone was the
question which wrapped her up in herself; but more deeply still it was
the presumptuous hope that she, Christa T. herself, might be necessary
for the world's perfection" (53). And still further on we read again: "To
fuel her dangerous wish for a pure and terrible perfection. To say all or
nothing, and to hear, unmistakably, inside oneself the echo: nothing"
(147). And yet the narrator sees Christa T.'s strength in just this, even
during the weariness of her approaching death: "This much is certain:
what one does can never make one so tired as what one doesn't do or
cannot do. That was the case with her. That was her weakness and her
secret superiority" (140). But this secret superiority never becomes
really productive; Christa T. remains alone with it. In her writing attempts she never relinquishes the highest standards and therefore
rarely exceeds fragments.

In life, however, she admittedly enters into a compromise at the
very end: "Perhaps in life one can make certain cuts?" (144). But even
this compromise serves the goal of self-realization. *"To become oneself,
with all one's strength"* (149) we read at the beginning of chapter 17, in
which Christa T. speaks to her friends for the first time of her plans to
build a house. As usual she is not understood. Only later, during a visit
to the new house on the lake, does the narrator recognize "that this
house should be nothing but a sort of instrument that she meant to use
to link herself more intimately with life, a place with which she was
profoundly familiar because she had created it herself and on whose
territory she could take her stand against anything alien" (153). Conformity to reality, then—self-realization within the limits of that which
is possible for her. Christa T. is digging herself out, as she says—out of
fantasies and dreams:

> She knew quite well that this raw house with the wind whistling through it was further from completion than the dream house on the plans that happy evening at the seaside hotel, the white and beautiful house on the pieces of paper. But she'd also learned that real materials are more resistant than paper, and that, as long as things are still in the process of coming to be, one has to drive them tenaciously along. We saw that she no longer insisted on her sketches, but on these raw stones. (160)

Christa T.'s new experience can be interpreted in terms of Bloch's ideas on the "aporias of realization" as a "qualitative deficit in the *act of realization itself*" (PH 217).

The house construction should not be misunderstood as a retreat into a petit-bourgeois idyll, as a withdrawal into inwardness. Even life in the house on the lake has an element of the utopian, entirely in the sense of Ernst Bloch, who writes:

> Its aporias [the aporias of realization]—from the shortcomings of piecework, on the one hand, to the fact that even the best realization never fully corresponds to the envisioned image, on the other—can clearly not be considered at all separately from the utopia problem. This is all the less possible, *since so much of the utopian remains in that which is realized and reemerges after this realization, moving toward new goals.* (PH 221, my emphasis)[18]

The utopian elements that remain after Christa T.'s attempt at self-realization reemerge in Christa Wolf's novel and move toward new goals. This happens as a result of a meditative process, which admittedly comes too late for Christa T. In spite of Christa T.'s untimely death, however, we cannot speak of despair or resignation.

On the contrary, in her "Interview with Myself" Christa Wolf says: "I have discovered that she lived fully in the time vouchsafed her" (IM 78). This corresponds to Christa T.'s conviction: "I'm digging my way out" (151). This curious concept of digging out also plays a role in Bloch's work. In his chapter on the discovery of the not-yet-known he says: "The so-called essence of the universe is, therefore, in and of itself still inaccessible in the sense of not-yet-manifestation of its self; *its own nature, defined as permanent challenge, makes it difficult.* In order to eliminate this difficulty it is necessary to gain knowledge, not only in the sense of a digging out of that which was, but knowledge in the sense of defining a plan for that which will be" (PH 149).[19] The building of the house, this digging out of that which was and anticipating that which will be, is an individually realized hope, the subjective anticipation of that which Bloch calls *Heimat*, the goal of mankind.[20] The house is *Heimat* for Christa T., and she has thus reached the point at which knowledge has emerged from her presentiments. When Christa T. dies shortly after moving into the house on the lake, this death seems to refute an interpretation that understands the house as realizing *Heimat*. But even this contradiction can be interpreted. Let us not forget the "aporias of realization" that I have already mentioned in reference to Christa T.'s life. The house is indeed *Heimat* for Christa T. but again only for Christa T. *Heimat* in the Blochian sense, however, cannot be sought and reached individually; it must ultimately be a communal achievement. Herein lies an insoluble contradiction in Christa T.'s existence and in her relationship to her society, in which, she believes, the people have forgotten hope and restlessness and have forfeited *Heimat*—a society that denies to the individual human being and her concrete desires the role in the historical process accorded to her under the terms of Bloch's marxist philosophy.

Christa T.'s death, this "hardest counterpunch to utopia" (*PH* 15), however, is not only an end but also a beginning. She dies at time when the socialist reconstruction phase in the GDR is coming to a close, when hope and utopia are increasingly being bureaucratically controlled and thereby forgotten as irrevocable conditions for realizing a socialist *Heimat*. A "new world of people without imagination," of "up-and-doing people" (51) is making itself felt; in this, conformity is praised as the secret to good health (111). At just this time, however, the narrator begins to be preoccupied with Christa T.'s life. A second digging out takes place; this time, too, it is not only a digging out of that which was in the form of a novel of remembrance but also recognition in the sense of defining a plan for that which will be or ought to be. "Because it seems that we need her" (5), as the narrator resolutely says about Christa T. at the outset. This sentence illustrates that it is not a matter for Christa Wolf of sentimental recollection of a romantically transfigured past but rather of a remembrance aiming dialectically at the future. Bloch also makes this distinction: "The most progressive conscience does its work, when involved with memory and forgetfulness, not as in a space which is submerged and thus closed, but rather in an open space, in the space of process and its horizons" (*PH* 160f.). Things past are not to be rediscovered in this socialist novel of remembrance.

According to Bloch's marxist-utopian thought, no time can be entirely lost. Remembrance means in Christa Wolf's novel, not a confrontation with something past, but rather a meditation about something not-yet-become in the past that, precisely because it still desires to become, reaches into the present and points ahead to the future—not only in the work of art but also, significantly, in reality. Again Bloch's formulations parallel what Christa Wolf wants to show: "There exists in that which is present, indeed in that which is remembered, an incentive and an interruption, a brooding and an anticipation of the not-yet-become; and this double moment of interruption and incentive occurs not in the cellar of consciousness, but at its horizon" (*PH* 10).[21] In Christa Wolf's words: it is not memory as a form of forgetting (cf. 4) but rather remembering as "re-creation of the past" (*VI* 60) in which the past participates in the processes of the present. In her essay on the Soviet writer Vera Inber, Christa Wolf speaks of the difficulties of this undertaking and stresses that such a recreation of the past is possible precisely in that transient moment only, in which "the opaque present has retreated far enough into the past to be seen through, available to the narrator but still close enough for [the narrator] not to be 'through' with it" (VI 60). Ernst Bloch claims even the past can be illuminated only with the help of utopian consciousness. Wolf's novel is characterized by a dialectic interdependence of utopia and remembrance; Bloch writes of such interdependence: "The utopian consciousness wants to see very far, but ultimately only in order to penetrate the dark proximity of the just-lived moment, in which all being drifts and in which it remains hidden from itself. In other words: one needs the strongest telescope, that of the sharply cut utopian consciousness, just to be able to penetrate the closest proximity" (PH 11).[22]

III

But what is the aim of this penetration of the just-lived moment? What concrete significance does it have for Christa Wolf? The narrative technique provides a clue. As Hans Mayer has correctly pointed out, the novel presents each event as both lived event and artistic process. The use of modernist narrative techniques continually blurs the border between the narrating act and that which is narrated, between narrator and narrated figure, between present and past. Such techniques permit the emergence of questions and contradictions and provoke further reflection. They fully serve the content of the work and confirm Wolf's statement that she had to confront herself in the process of writing: "Later on, I noticed that the object of my story was not at all, or did not remain so clearly herself, Christa T. I suddenly faced myself. I had not foreseen this" (IM 76–77). Hans Mayer has concluded that the author-figures in Christa Wolf—applying to both subject and object of the narration—are involved in the process of a liberation through writing.[23] But Christa T. achieves this liberation not through writing but in constructing a house—and even then only partially. Christa Wolf, on the other hand, succeeds at a liberation through writing in the sense that she arrives at herself via her reflections about Christa T.; she becomes conscious of the not-yet-become in herself and recognizes Christa T.'s hope for the Quite Different as her own.

Because the narrator becomes aware of the meaning of Christa T.'s life only after her death, we may want to examine the reasons for this remarkable delay; the reasons are subjective as well as objective. In the title essay of the collection *The Reader and the Writer*, Wolf speaks of the noticeably delayed maturity of her generation, which for her is a result of a complete isolation from all major modernist literature during the Third Reich: "there is no doubt that it hindered us in growing up, in developing a critical understanding and reasonable feelings not maimed by the worst sorts of prejudices and resentments" (RW 187). The collection of essays also provides concrete evidence for this delayed maturation of critical acuity. In a short piece of 1966, "Brecht and Others," Wolf reports on the relationship of her generation to the playwright Brecht: "And there certainly was tension between us (who in the early 1950's thought we knew everything there was to know about wars, and especially the war that had befallen us) and the *Mother Courage* we saw on the stage. In possession of an all too well rounded knowledge, we adopted an impatiently condescending attitude to the play where patient reflection would have been more appropriate" (BO 58).[24] Patient reflection instead of impatient condescension, however, is a characteristic of the repeatedly inhibited and delayed development of Christa T., although admittedly her delayed development differs from Christa Wolf's. In contrast to Christa T., the narrator belongs to the inner circle of those students of German literature who are described in the novel in a manner that exactly parallels the process set forth in the Brecht essay: "The truth is: we had other things to do. We were fully occupied with making ourselves unassailable—perhaps the sense of that can be felt. Not only to admit into our minds nothing extraneous— and all sorts of things we considered extraneous; also to let nothing extraneous well up from inside ourselves, and if it did so—a doubt, a suspicion, observations, questions—then not to let it show" (50–51).

In the Brecht essay Wolf continues with her retrospective criticism of this kind of thinking and writes: "We repeated his ideas about 'the dawn of the scientific age' with enthusiasm and conviction, felt that he meant us when he said 'people of the scientific age will . . . ,' and did not and could not know that he was looking beyond us to what we might perhaps one day become after tremendous efforts—or even farther ahead to those who would come after us" (BO 58). Christa Wolf's path out of the fifties into the sixties could be described as one that moves from a certainty based on insecurity to a patiently questioning and doubting uncertainty based on security. Christa T. plays a decisive role in this process. She serves as the impulse for Christa Wolf to become conscious of and to question the past, which Wolf does with great effort in her novel.

But *The Quest for Christa T.* concerns itself not only with Wolf's attempt to defend herself in writing against the death of a woman who was close to her (cf. IM). Nor is it exclusively concerned with the delayed maturation process of the author. Christa Wolf herself justifies her entirely subjective impulse to write this novel by referring to objective developments in the GDR. In "Interview with Myself" she writes: "The years in which we were creating the foundations for individual self-realization by developing socialist conditions for production lie behind us. Our society is becoming more and more differentiated. And the questions people ask are also more differentiated, including questions concerning the form of art. People's willingness to accept complex answers has also developed" (IM 79).[25] The newly won political self-consciousness, articulated here and characteristic for the GDR of the sixties, is a precondition for a maturation of critical reason and a liberation through writing that should involve not only the writer but also the individual reader. Christa Wolf thinks that the novel, always read by a single reader, is especially suited as a medium for introducing the question of the role of the subject in socialist society. She argues for an "epic prose," "which undertakes to penetrate along paths not yet traveled into the innermost part of this individual, the reader of prose" (RW 201). Liberation, therefore, occurs not only through writing but also through reading. Christa Wolf accordingly regards her own writing as a means "to shift the future into the present" (RW 201).

Christa T. had run aground with her attempts to write during a time as yet unfavorable to undertakings of this nature. In retrospect, however, Christa T.'s life proves a heritage as important as it stands in contradiction to the further development of the GDR. Heinrich Mohr has already pointed out that her lack of strength is social and political rather than merely individual.[26] In Christa Wolf's opinion, reflecting about the contradictions in Christa T.'s life, which simultaneously suggest contradictions in the development of the GDR, can have entirely positive results.[27] About her fatal illness, Christa T. knows "that before long people won't still be dying of this disease" (182). Formulated as fact, this sentence sounds like a challenge to the future and points the reader toward the concrete and irrepressible hope that spontaneity and self-realization of the human being will find their *Heimat* in the GDR after the conditions have been created by the development of socialist means of production.

IV

But things are not quite so simple. Let us look back once again. At the beginning of the narrator's acquaintance with Christa T. there was Christa T.'s trumpet-blowing, a spontaneous cry of liberation that "for a fraction of a second lifted the sky up higher" (10). Here, in childhood, the narrator already suspected what made Christa T. so different: "suddenly I felt, with a sense of terror, that you'll come to a bad end if you suppress all the shouts prematurely; I had no time to lose. I wanted to share in a life that produced such shouts as her *hooohaahooo*, about which she must have knowledge" (11). But then come years of separation, years of living past each other, years of mutual misunderstanding. The shout, with which, incidentally, Bloch also begins *The Principle of Hope*, is suppressed after all. This childlike shout is revived in the narrator only with Christa T.'s death. In remembering she discovers, through writing, the not-yet-become in herself as a not-yet-become of socialist society; the novel of remembrance becomes a novel of the future.

Out of the subjective impulse to write about the friend who dies too young an objective challenge to society emerges. This becomes especially clear in the use of the word "people" in the last lines of the novel:

> One day people will want to know who she was and who it is
> that's been forgotten. They'll want to see her, and that's only natural.
> They'll wonder if that other figure really was there, the one we obsti-
> nately insist on when we mourn. Then people will have to produce
> her, create her, for once. So that the doubts may be silenced, so that
> she may be seen.
> When, if not now? (185)

Even if it appears that this refers only to recreating Christa T., which
Christa Wolf has indeed done with her novel, this creation also high-
lights that which characterized her life and still awaits fulfillment: the
hope for *Heimat*. Christa T.'s death—and this is the hope Christa Wolf
learned while writing the novel—ought to be a beginning rather than
an end. Once again we can point to a parallel with Bloch. With her
"when, if not now?" Christa Wolf suggests a projection of the abstract
ending of Bloch's *Principle of Hope* onto a concrete historical moment
in the development of socialist society in the GDR. The last lines in
Bloch read:

> The true genesis is not at the beginning, but at the end, and it only
> begins to commence when society and being become radical, that is,
> grasp themselves by the roots. But the root of history is the human
> being, who works, creates, redefines and overcomes the givens. If he
> has grasped himself and has grounded his essence, without loss or al-
> ienation, in genuine democracy, then there comes into being some-
> thing which appears to everyone during childhood and where no one
> has yet been: *Heimat*. (PH 1628)[28]

Just how the mediation is to be brought about between individual
self-realization and the becoming radical of society remains of course
an unanswered question—unanswered in both Ernst Bloch and Christa
Wolf. On just this problem Christa T. went aground. Christa Wolf
makes us conscious of this kind of failure as a problem of socialist development, but she seems unsure of how the utopia is to be realized.
Just this withholding of simple solutions from herself and her reader
supports the realism of her writing style. The author knows that the
conditions that will permit eliminating alienation and self-alienation
must be created in reality itself. But as long as this problem is
insufficiently mastered, a synchronicity with Bloch's philosophy of
hope must appear as plausible as it remains problematical. What does it
actually mean when Bloch's thought, emerging from entirely different
historical circumstances, finds its way, via allusion and inscription,
into a novel by Christa Wolf in the sixties? Can Christa Wolf, who was
a candidate for the Central Committee of the SED from 1963 to 1966,
believe that the contradictions and problems of socialist society in the
GDR can be solved with the principle of hope? Does she see that notions like Bloch's utopia, which even understands the dialectic of self-
realization in utopian terms,[29] are just not concrete enough to become
immediately practical under the conditions of the transitional socialist

society of the sixties and the seventies? With these questions we confront a methodological and historical problem.

With his major work, Bloch wanted to salvage and reword a discarded utopian tradition for Marxism. Thus he criticizes, as Habermas says, the myths, religions, and philosophies of the past as "Schein" (illusion), but he takes them seriously nonetheless as "*Vor-schein*" (preappearance) of something ultimately to be established.[30] This means nothing more than that utopian thinking in Bloch is always geared to practice. When Bloch places the greatest value on the practical, propelling power of human thought, it is necessary, before one criticizes it, to understand his thinking in terms of his frontal attack against the economism and reductionism of dialectical materialism. Bloch writes against those who thought that the basis-superstructure problem could be solved one-sidedly in terms of vulgar materialist determination. Habermas says: "Bloch wants to retain for socialism, which lives from the criticism of tradition, the tradition of that which is criticized."[31] Bloch even attempted to rescue a kernel of truth and authenticity in false consciousness. This task must have seemed all the more important to him because he took a position not only against the economism of dialectical materialism but also—at least in the first draft of *Principle of Hope*—against the falsification of bourgeois tradition by fascism. This historical constellation, from which Bloch's *Principle of Hope* cannot be severed, must be kept in mind if one wishes adequately to analyze the parallels between Christa Wolf's utopian ideas and Bloch's philosophy.

I do not believe that Wolf succumbs to illusions concerning an immediate realization of the utopia of *Heimat*. I suspect, rather, that her late reception of Blochian ideas is related to the delayed maturity of her generation. It is a belated maturity insofar as Christa Wolf comprehends only after Christa T.'s death just why precisely this woman's life, imprinted by the principle of hope, belongs to the socialist society of the GDR. The novel *The Quest for Christa T.* would thus preserve for the GDR a double heritage: the heritage of Christa T., who died too soon, and that of Ernst Bloch, who resettled from Leipzig in the GDR to Tübingen in the FRG. This heritage, however, must still be critically worked through in order to be made productive. The significance of *The Quest for Christa T.* lies in Wolf's apparent application to the present time of Bloch's implicit criticism of a past epoch's reductionist economic theory and practice and her development of this criticism in a narrative thematization of the not-yet-become of socialist society in the GDR. The closing question—"When, if not now?"—challenges both the future *and* the present. The commonality between Ernst Bloch and Christa Wolf rests in their shared concern for a not-yet-become of the past that must become "conscious-known" ("*bewusst-gewusst*") (PH 163) before it can be redeemed in practice: the principle of hope. The difference lies in the fact that Ernst Bloch had, as an exile, to wage his battle on two fronts—against fascism and against vulgar materialism; but Christa Wolf writes as the citizen of a country in which the conditions for the further development of socialism are given but in which at the same time Bloch's critical thought retains an undiminished explosive power.

Certainly one could reproach Christa Wolf, just as Bloch, for overstressing the propelling power of human thought. After all, the questions and contradictions raised in the novel remain real, especially in the societal reality of the GDR. But Christa Wolf's own interpretation of the principle of hope is entirely consistent with her definition of artistic prose and therefore with her own role as an author in a socialist state. In the last paragraph of "The Reader and the Writer" she writes, under the subtitle "Remembered Future": "Prose can push the frontiers of our knowledge about ourselves farther forward. It can keep awake in us the memory of the future that we must not abandon on pain of destruction. It helps mankind to become conscious subjects. It is revolutionary and realistic; it entices and encourages people to achieve the impossible" (RW 212). In the GDR today there are indications of an official recognition of the need for people to become conscious subjects. After six years of practically effective censorship, *The Quest for Christa T.* was reprinted in 1974 for the twenty-fifth anniversary of the GDR.

Notes

[This article first appeared in German in *Basis* 5, ed. Reinhold Grimm and Jost Hermand (Frankfurt/Main: Suhrkamp, 1975), 100–116. It has since been reprinted several times (see bibliography) but is here made available for the first time in English. Although published more than ten years ago, Huyssen's essay remains one of the seminal studies of *The Quest for Christa T.*; it is included here in a slightly revised version partly because it forms a referential basis for many other essays in this volume.

Huyssen borrows the title of Wolf's work to derive his own (in German, the second part is "Nachdenken über Christa Wolf," echoing Christa Wolf's *Nachdenken über Christa T.*). Unfortunately, the English translation of Wolf's title does not permit such a facile transfer, so the parallelism is lost in my translation of Huyssen's title.—Ed.]

1. *The Quest for Christa T.*, 172; hereafter references to this work will be cited with page numbers in the text.
2. See Hermann Kähler, "Christa Wolfs Elegie," *SuF* 21, no. 1 (1969): 251–261, especially 256ff.
3. See Horst Haase, "Nachdenken über ein Buch," *NDL* 4 (1969): 174–185; Hermann Kähler, 120; Heinz Sachs, "Verleger sein heisst ideologisch kämpfen," *ND*, 14 May 1969; Peter Gugisch, "Christa Wolf," in *Literatur der DDR in Einzeldarstellungen*, ed. Hans Jürgen Geerdts (Stuttgart: Kröner, 1972), 410.
4. See Martin Reso, ed., *"Der geteilte Himmel" und seine Kritiker* (Halle: Mitteldeutscher Verlag, 1965); Hans Georg Hölsken, "Zwei Romane: Christa Wolf *Der geteilte Himmel* und Hermann Kant *Die Aula*," *Deutschunterricht* 21, no. 5 (1969): 61–99.
5. Eduard Zak, "Tragische Erlebnisse in optimistischer Sicht," *Sonntag*, 19 May 1963.
6. See Horst Haase and Hermann Kähler.
7. Peter Gugisch, 410.
8. See Heinz Adameck's remarks at the Tenth Plenary Session of the Central Committee (May 1969). Quoted by Fritz J. Raddatz, *Traditionen und Tendenzen* (Frankfurt/Main: Suhrkamp, 1972), 386.

9. Fritz J. Raddatz, "Mein Name sei Tonio K.," *Spiegel* 23 (1969): 153–154.

10. See Wolfgang Werth, "Nachricht aus einem stillen Deutschland," *Monat* 21, no. 253 (1969): 90–94; Hans-Dietrich Sander, "Die Gesellschaft und Sie," *Deutschland-Archiv* 2, no. 6 (1969): 599–603.

11. Manfred Durzak, *Der deutsche Roman der Gegenwart*, 2d ed. (Stuttgart: Kohlhammer, 1973), 271ff.

12. On this point, see David Bathrick's talk, "Literature and the Industrial World: Christa Wolf's *The Divided Heaven*," presented at the annual conference of the M/MLA, St. Louis, Missouri, November 1974.

13. Heinrich Mohr, "Produktive Sehnsucht. Struktur, Thematik und politische Relevanz von Christa Wolfs *Nachdenken über Christa T.*," in *Basis. Jahrbuch für Gegenwartsliteratur* 2, ed. Reinhold Grimm and Jost Hermand (Frankfurt/Main: Athenäum, 1971), 233. [Translated in this volume as "Productive Longing." Further references to Mohr's article will be to this translation.—Ed.]

14. I assume, on the basis of Hans Mayer's hints (see note 15), that not only Christa Wolf but also Christa T. studied German language and literature in Leipzig. Quite probably both became familiar with Bloch's philosophy in the early 1950s in Leipzig, although the effect of Bloch's thinking on Christa Wolf most likely made its impact later.

I do not, however, want to be misunderstood as necessarily arguing that Christa Wolf had direct contact with Ernst Bloch and his works when she studied in Leipzig or when she wrote her novel. Even if she never read Bloch at the time, the philosopher's traces show up unmistakably in her text, perhaps only as testimony to their *Gleichzeitigkeit* (synchronicity), as Bloch might say, rather than as a result of a direct influence, however mediated it might be.—A. H., 1984.

15. Hans Mayer, "Christa Wolf: *Nachdenken über Christa T.*," *NR* 81, no. 1 (1970): 180–186. Mayer writes: "Becher, like Ernst Bloch, held fast to the 'principle of hope': the political powers in the GDR could only produce the conditions for the possibility of the 'coming-to-oneself' of the individual—that is, to bring about the dialectical abolishment of self-alienation" (Auch Becher hielt, wie Ernst Bloch, am 'Prinzip Hoffnung' fest: die politische Macht in der DDR durfte nur die Bedingungen für die Möglichkeit herstellen, den Menschen zu sich selber kommen zu lassen, den Zustand der Selbstentfremdung also dialektisch aufzuheben).

16. [The allusion is to Becher's journal of the early fifties, titled *Auf andere Art so grosse Hoffnung* (Berlin/Weimar: Aufbau, 1969). The citation in German quotes the last words of this title: "die grosse Hoffnung"—translated in English as "the big hope."—Ed.]

17. Ernst Bloch, *Das Prinzip Hoffnung* (Frankfurt/Main: Suhrkamp, 1959), 5; hereafter cited in text as *PH* .

18. [Ersichtlich sind deren Aporien (die Aporien der Verwirklichung)—vom Stückwerk bis zur noch vorhandenen Nichtdeckung auch der besten Verwirklichung mit dem Zielbild—ausserhalb des Utopieproblems überhaupt nicht behandelbar. Desto weniger sind sie das, *als ja Utopisches am Verwirklichten so mannigfach übrigbleibt und nach ihm, zu neuen Zielen, wieder hervortritt.*]

19. [Das sogenannte Wesen des Universums also ist noch an und für sich verschlossen im Sinne von: Noch-Nicht-Erscheinung seiner selbst; *diese seine eigene Aufgabe-Natur macht es schwierig.* Das Schwierige aufzuheben, dazu ist nicht nur Erkenntnis nötig im Sinne einer Ausgrabung dessen, was war, sondern Erkenntnis im Sinn einer Planbestimmung dessen, was wird.]

20. [The term *Heimat* (directly translated as "home"), central to Bloch's philosophy and to German thought in general, cannot be easily rendered into English or fully defined here. In broad terms, it means the individual's sense of a place of belonging and security, intuitively felt in childhood, but never (yet) truly experienced.—Ed.]

21. [Es gibt im Gegenwärtigen, ja im Erinnerten selber einen Auftrieb und eine Abgebrochenheit, ein Brüten und eine Vorwegnahme von Noch-Nicht-Gewordenem; und dieses Abgebrochen-Angebrochene geschieht nicht im Keller des Bewusstseins, sondern an seiner Front.]

22. [Das utopische Bewusstsein will weit hinaussehen, aber letzthin doch nur dazu, um das ganz nahe Dunkel des gerade gelebten Augenblicks zu durchdringen, worin alles Seiende so treibt wie sich verborgen ist. Mit andern Worten: man braucht das stärkste Fernrohr, das des geschliffenen utopischen Bewusstseins, um gerade die nächste Nähe zu durchdringen.

23. Mayer, 184.

24. Translation altered by author.

25. Translation altered by editor.

26. See Mohr, "Productive Longing."

27. "Gespräch mit Christa Wolf," in Joachim Walter, *Meinetwegen Schmetterlinge. Gespräche mit Schriftstellern* (Berlin: Buchverlag Der Morgen, 1973), 120.

28. [Die wirkliche Genesis ist nicht am Anfang, sondern am Ende, und sie beginnt erst anzufangen, wenn Gesellschaft und Dasein radikal werden, das heisst sich an der Wurzel fassen. Die Wurzel der Geschichte aber ist der arbeitende, schaffende, die Gegebenheiten umbildende und überholende Mensch. Hat er sich erfasst und das Seine ohne Entäusserung und Entfremdung in realer Demokratie begründet, so entsteht etwas, das allen in die Kindheit scheint und worin noch niemand war: Heimat.]

29. See Jürgen Habermas, "Eine marxistische Stellung," in *Über Ernst Bloch* (Frankfurt: Suhrkamp, 1968), 78.

30. Habermas, 62.

31. Ibid., 63.

The Writing on the Wall, or Beyond the Dialectic of Subjectivity (*The Quest for Christa T.*)

Rainer Nägele

S ubjectivity and its vicissitudes, its dialectic, constitute perhaps the most manifest theme of Christa Wolf's writing; and much has been written about it. For two reasons, I found it nevertheless worthwhile to pursue the problem once more. First, I think we still hardly know what we are talking about when we use words such as "subjectivity" and "dialectic"; second, I have been intrigued for some time by the symbolic machinery itself which links with relentless predictability signifier to signifier, name to name, name to concept, and so on, and creates what we call stereotypes.

With these two interests in mind, I started to reread *The Quest for Christa T.*, the novel that, so to speak, sets up the primal scene of the search for the self and for subjectivity. It certainly makes no secret of the message we are invited to ponder. A motto by Johannes R. Becher gives the keynote for the metaphysical tune: "This coming-to-oneself—what is it?" (n.p.).[1] And the first sentence, split into two parts, hammers it in with italicized emphasis: "The quest for her: in the thought of her. And of *the attempt to be oneself* " (3). The italics had the effect of a first stumbling block. Perhaps it was the somewhat paradoxical "oneself," which identifies the *self* as the nonidentifiable "one," implying an indefinite and exchangeable plurality. One could of course just pass over it as a mere figure of speech, a grammatical convention. But in a novel where the scene of subjectivity is so closely linked with writing and speech, figures of speech and grammatical conventions are not negligible quantities. And indeed by way of my attempt to map the scene of writing in the novel I stumbled onto something that pointed to a particular writing and a slightly displaced scene: the writing on the wall and a scene beyond the dialectic of subjectivity.

But before we are able to read or even to see that writing and the beyond it spells out, it is necessary to survey the field we transgress by going beyond—to read the writing manifestly offered us. That we are supposed to enter a scene of writing is made clear at the beginning. The italicized "attempt to be oneself" is a quote from Christa T.'s diaries, and the Quest of the novel is primarily an attempt to follow the traces of writing, which in turn lead to memory traces. But whose memory, whose traces, whose writing are we talking about? It soon becomes evident that the scene of writing is a scene of complex splittings, displacements, and transferences. An author by the name of Christa Wolf, born in 1929, invents a narrator born in 1929, who in turn writes about a woman by the name of Christa T., born in 1927. All three share the region of their birth, east of the river Oder, all three studied in Leipzig, all three are readers and writers, engaged in a web of projections and introjections on the scene of writing. In this entanglement of transference, identification, and distancing, the boundaries of each persona are blurred, and the scene of writing thus constitutes not so much a self-identical subject as destabilized self-identities. At the same time only through such displacements of identity from one persona to another can moments of subjectivity take shape and fade away.

So far, so dialectical, perhaps.

Very schematically, we can differentiate three forms in which a subject is traced on the scene of writing. First, implicit literary scenes are evoked by the author and/or narrator, as for example scenes of Fontane's *Effi Briest* and Flaubert's *Madame Bovary*. Although *Effi Briest* is not mentioned explicitly, the description of Christa T.'s move to a small provincial town in Mecklenburg (137), evokes very vividly scenes from Fontane's novel. *Madame Bovary* is explicitly mentioned twice: first the name occurs to the narrator spontaneously as a parallel to Christa T.'s situation, then she attempts to push it away: "'Madame Bovary' was missing the point" (156). Such literary allusions obviously only very tentatively and crudely approximate establishing some kind of identity through a process of repetition of the same and distancing from it.

Second, the most intensive and most explicit form is the process of writing itself, partly because all three personas are involved and are at stake in this process. But from the beginning on, writing is a very conflictual mode of finding one's self or finding anything whatsoever. Writing is conceived of as a form of "leaving traces" (33) and an attempt to discover the writing self in the written traces; but at the same time it is a covering up of traces, a disguise (33). The same ambivalence shapes the object-relations: writing is seen as a means of being able to "cope with things" (34), which can be read not only as overcoming things, but also as coming to terms with them. In this reading we could understand writing in the classical sense of Marxist aesthetics from Lukács and Ernst Bloch to Robert Weimann: writing as an appropriation of the world, as a mode of making oneself at home in its foreignness. But here, too, writing is at the same time a cover-up, a mode of exclusion, not only because of the incompatibility of 'saying things as they are' but also because of an active defense against them: "her supposed self-defense against the superior power of things" (34).

Third, I want to mention a mode explicitly stated in the text as a —or perhaps even *the*—function of writing, for "that's what writing means—to furnish examples" (44). The offering of examples might be a dangerous gift like the Trojan horse. Where there are examples, there are codes, rules, hierarchies, and most of all incorporations: the Greeks who penetrate the walls of Troy in the wooden horse are indeed in every example. Not by chance do pedagogy and authority love examples, and so do the Trojans, that is, those who are the objects of penetration by pedagogy and authority. Offering examples assumes a very specific sense in Christa Wolf's writing: it is immediately associated with the heroine Christa T., with "case" and with "model" (45). In other words, example here assumes the function of that which the contemporary psychojargon—indeed a Trojan horse full of repressive mentality in the disguise of emancipation—calls "role model." To be sure, the narrator has a sense of this and immediately tries to fend off dangerous implications by pointing out that Christa T. is not exemplary, not a "model." But of course, her very unexemplariness turns her into an example, a model. And thus, being a model, even of nonexemplariness, she confirms the rules of the game played through "examples." The reception of Christa Wolf's writing repeats the scene over and over again. The author herself has been turned into a figure for identification, into a role model, even into a kind of East German version of Ann Landers.

Christa Wolf might feel somewhat uneasy with this role, but her writing clearly stages and, to a certain degree, privileges an identificatory mode of writing and reading, which always implies a cover-up of the actual scene of writing, its literality. Not by chance does a major part of the novel deal with Christa T.'s reading and writing of and about nineteenth-century fiction: Raabe, Keller, Storm are her favorite reading matter, and the latter becomes the subject/object of her dissertation. In nineteenth-century fiction, the privileging of identificatory reading and writing, emerging in the eighteenth century, comes to a peak. Its tendency toward humoristic distancing does not contradict this diagnosis: identification always takes place between the narcissistic ego and the authoritative super-ego, which gives us a fatherly pat on the shoulder, so we don't take things too seriously, even if they are deadly. This is not the place to follow in detail the complex ambivalences of the identificatory processes. I would like to mention one indicative and symptomatic point because it seems crucial to me for all identification. Identification can never take place through the full other; its apparent completeness of presence is an imaginary fiction. To identify fully with another would imply to identify with all its/her/his conflictual ambivalences. But identification is precisely the means to avoid such conflictual ambivalences. Thus they have to be displaced from the scene of a conflictual interior that splits the fullness of the "figure" and "image" to a conflictual and separated exteriority. Thus Christa T. divides her ambivalence between the desire of security and simplicity (i.e., Raabe, Keller, and Storm), on the one hand, and her desire for "complicatedness, multisignificance, subtlety" (94) (i.e., Thomas Mann), on the other. And finally, the identificatory mode of reading is literally staged in an identification with the author/heroine of a novel of that century which, as I said before, initiated identification as a primary mode of reading. At the occasion of a rather tame and somewhat inhibited carnival party, Christa T. appears as the eighteenth-century author Sophie La Roche and also as her heroine Fräulein von Sternheim. The remarkable thing about this is that she does not appear in disguise, but as "herself," simply in the name of La Roche/Sternheim. This identity is not a matter of mask but of another persona incorporated. And the incorporation turns out to be deadly: the bodies incorporated take over. The leukemia of which Christa T. dies seems only the medical name for that which the foreign incorporated body is and does: the vampire that consumes the blood.

On this level, then, we seem to have arrived at a breakdown of the dialectic of subjectivity, at its point of failure. Of course, one could object to such an assessment by maintaining that there is another level, that of the narrator and the reader who are, in a certain sense, invited to turn the failure into a success: "When, if not now" (185) is the provocative last question. But as long as that remains within the boundaries of identification, the process we have read will simply be repeated.

However, as I mentioned at the beginning, there is another scene of writing in the text, one the narrator, and perhaps even the author, hardly reads but rather tries to ban. It is literally a writing on the wall, that is, a writing on the blackboard. And it occurs once and is then repeated in slightly modified form. The first time it can be read in the lecture room of the university where Christa T. and the narrator studied German literature: "On the blackboard in the large lecture hall stood a scanned line of verse: úns hât der wínter geschádet überál. No 'mene tekel,' this, no suggestion of a sign; and nothing in me was responding" (24).[2] A little later, exams are approaching; they have to face the writing on the wall again, by memorizing it, which in German is a process of externalization: auswendig lernen. "She . . . had herself tested on the metrics of the Merseburg Zaubersprüche [magical charms—Ed.]; obediently she declaimed Ik gihôrta d'at seggen" (36). There are several interesting and odd aspects about these two passages. First, they concern a literature very different from the nineteenth-century identificatory texts. And in a certain sense they are not read at all; they are quoted not to be read but to be rejected. Even the character of signs is denied them: "no suggestion of a sign." In the second passage the nonreading creates an odd mix-up. Christa T. is supposed to quote the *Merseburger Zaubersprüche*, but instead she quotes the first line of the *Hildebrandslied*. Because these texts are denied even the status of signs, it doesn't really matter. But precisely the fact that they are rejected as signs turns them into allegorical signs of indecipherable texts. They are allegories of pure alien otherness. They represent pedantic old philology, based on the "dead" letter, the schematism of metric syllable counts, in complicity with the bureaucracy of the state. Thus they radically oppose an ideology of signification based on understanding through direct access to subjectivity and interiority.

More than just the explicit rejection of the *Mene Tekel* by the narrator evokes the Book of Daniel in the Bible. It is worth briefly looking at that book, very much a text about writing, deciphering, and interpreting. The odd thing about the writing on the wall in that text is the fact that Daniel is not simply called to interpret the meaning of the words *Mene Tekel Upharsin*, but that he first has to decipher a writing unreadable to all the others. And this is the repetition of an earlier even odder occurrence, when Belteshazzar's father, Nebuchadnezzar, has a dream. And again, the king not only needs somebody to interpret the dream but also to tell it to him because he has forgotten it. Thus Daniel must first decipher a seemingly erased script before he can interpret it. In both cases, the subject, the all-powerful king himself, has no direct access to the text that directly concerns his own power.

In Christa Wolf's novel, there is no Daniel to decipher and read the writing on the wall, and if there were one—and actually there probably was one in the disguise of an old Germanic philologist—he was rejected by the demand of a subjectivity that acknowledges significance only in the immediacy of identificatory understanding. But what if we, the readers, assume the role of Daniel and actually read the writing on the wall and, like Daniel, apply it to those subjects who have rejected and forgotten it and therefore cannot read it? The results are surprising; I can here only briefly point them out. The first text, whose first line and metrical schema is written on the blackboard, is a two-stanza poem by Walter von der Vogelweide about the deadly and destructive force of winter and the desire and hope for a new spring.

Uns hât der winter geschat über al:
heide unde walt sint beide nû val,
dâ manic stimme vil suoze inne hal.
saehe ich die megde an der strâze den bal
werfen! sô kaeme uns der vogele schal.

Möhte ich verslâfen des winters zît!
wache ich die wîle, sô hân ich sîn nît,
daz sîn gewalt ist sô breit und sô wît.
weiz got er lât ouch dem meien den strît:

sô lise ich bluomen dâ rîfe nû lît.

(Winter has done us damage everywhere.
Heath and forest are pale where once one could
      hear so many sweet voices.
If I could see the girls again throwing the
      ball on the street: then the voices
      of the birds would come back.

If I could only sleep through the winter!
Being awake, I hate it, because its power
      reaches so far and wide.
But one day it will have to give in to May
Then I will gather flowers where frost now lies.)[3]

Given the context of the novel, which takes place in the early postwar years and has much to do with the "principle of hope,"[4] Walter's text reads like an allegory of the novel's present situation. The *Merseburger Zaubersprüche* seem more removed. But again, the two texts speak most eloquently to the situation at hand; one could even say that they, in condensed form, articulate the two motivating desires of the book: the first is a magical formula for liberation, the second a formula for unification.

First Merseburg magic formula:

Eiris sazun idisi, sazun hera, douder.
suma hapt heptidun, suma heri lezidun,
suma clubodun umbi cuoniouuidi:
insprinc haptbandun! inuar uigandun!

(Once women sat down, sat here and sat there.
Some knotted fetters, some kept the army away
Some untied the strings around:
Escape from the fetters! Escape from the enemy!)

Second formula:

Phol ende uuodan uuorun zi holza.
du uuart demo balderes uolon sin uuoz birenkit.
thu biguol en sinhtgunt, sunna, era suister;
thu biguol en friia, uolla, era suister;
thu biguol en uuodan, so he uuola conda:
ben zi bena, bluot zi bluoda,
lid zi geliden, sose gelimida sin!

(Phol and Wodan rode into a forest.
Baldur's colt sprained its ankle.
Then Sinhgunt spoke a charm, and so did Sunna, her sister;
Then Friia spoke a charm, and so did Volla, her sister;
Then Wodan spoke a charm, as well as he could:
Bone to bone, blood to blood,
Limb to limb, as if they were glued!)

Liberation and its difficulties on the individual as well as sociopolitical level permeate the novel; and only one paragraph after mentioning the *Merseburger Zaubersprüche*, the second one, never quoted, is articulated as a desire of Christa T.: "she was thinking out loud . . . about how one could make a whole life out of the bits one was presented with" (36). If, however, the magical formulas of liberation and unification are relevant both for the sociopolitical body of the newly founded state and for its individuals, the parallel desires are at the same time in conflict with each other: the liberation and unification of the political body restrains that of the individuals and demands their splitting as specialized functional members of the socioeconomic body.

As if to testify to that conflict in the parallel desire, Christa T. does not recite the magical formulas but the *Hildebrandslied*: the legendary deadly battle between father and son, in which the son, in all probability, dies before the father and through him. More than a decade after Christa Wolf's novel, a young author of the second generation of the GDR, Thomas Brasch, entitled one of his books *Vor den Vätern sterben die Söhne* (The Sons Die Before the Fathers),[5] and he is not the only writer of the GDR who inscribed a father-son struggle into the sociopolitical conflicts, not to reduce them to a generation conflict, but to point out a powerful dynamic intersecting with the political struggles.[6]

Our reading of the writing on the wall has uncovered a relationship to the text of the novel that that text not only does not acknowledge but also explicitly excludes and, in the sense of its narrative perspective, must exclude because it represents the uncanny scene of the dead letter through which the deadly laws of the father, the state, and the institution speak. Thus, they are silenced to nonsignificance. But the letters are insistent.

Most signs of the novel indicate that the authorial intention tends to side with the narrative perspective. But other traces give more play to the literality. There are the many explicit puns and literal uses of words and idioms (the title-word *Nachdenken* is the most prominent); and there are implicit puns, as in the slightly childish diary entry of the young girl Christa: "Ich möchte dichten und liebe auch Geschichten" (I would like to write poems and I like stories too [23]) where the wishing "ich" (I) succumbs to pure literal repetition and variation in mö**ch**te, di**ch**ten, Ges**ch**i**ch**ten. The literal inscription of the **ich** in di**ch**ten and Ges**ch**i**ch**ten not only testifies to the constitutive insistence of the letter without which no I could say "I," but it also reveals another aspect of the subject's desire to be a self-identical whole. *Dichten* throughout the novel is also a form of protection against a threatening other; in a literal pun it is also a kind of *abdichten*, insulating an interiority against an exteriority. Twice in this context the metaphor of building a dam occurs (123, 144). The *Ich* and the *Dichten* are engineers of exclusion: dams and walls. The *Ich*, in its desire for self-identity, totality, and wholeness, thus not only opposes and conflicts with the totalizing demand of the sociopolitical body, but also functions as that body's accomplice. If the two desires seem conflictual on one level, they are identical on another in their exclusionary politics that makes impossible the reading of the writing on the wall. Thus, they repeat indeed the scene of the *Hildebrandslied*, mechanically recited by Christa T., in which the deadly conflict between father and son arises from the identical desire to protect the integrity and honor of the self.

But is this not a classical scene of the dialectic of self-consciousness? What is beyond the dialectic of subjectivity? I think two moments point beyond, or at least indicate a rupture. The first concerns more specifically Christa Wolf's novel that questions the dialectic of subjectivity in such a way that the dialectic cannot be resolved on the level of the intersubjective struggle within the text but only through a reading of texts outside the novel. Unlike our experience of the dialectic of Hegel's *Phenomenology*, where the "we" that reads the developing dialectic of the spirit is a moment within the text and, at the same time, a moment toward which the text moves, our reading here had to remain strictly outside. In a certain sense, our reading is not so much the uncovering of a hidden relation between certain texts but rather an exclusion, although that exclusion concerns a cryptic interior of the excluding text. But one could argue on this level that if the text ultimately does not perform a dialectic of *subjectivity*, it could nevertheless point to a dialectical beyond, a dialectic beyond subjectivity.

Indeed, our conclusion makes that possible, but at the same time encounters another instance that ruptures the dialectic again. If we have, in our role as the prophet and decipherer Daniel, read into the text those texts it excludes, we also have read out of the text a literality to which significance is denied as much as to those texts we read: the combination of the letters i-c-h in "dichten" and "Geschichten" does not 'want' to be read as "ich." Reading them in such a way invests them with a foreign significance; we have read the "ich" into the text. But in doing that, we have actually done nothing but repeat the mode of reading presented us by the novel and its heroine and narrator. The identificatory reading they perform cannot do without the violence of narcissistic identification which incorporates the other. Nevertheless, the explicit exclusion of the writing on the wall differs from the literality of the text. Manifestly, the difference shows itself in the fact that literality does not need any explicit exclusion; it even can be played with in a certain limited and controlled way in the text. However, the exclusion has already taken place before any writing or reading could start. Learning how to write and how to read means learning to go beyond the spelling of the letters, in a certain sense, to forget them as letters, so we can read and write them as words and sentences. Only thus the non-sense of the letters can be turned into sense.

Yet the letters are insistent. In the puns, for example, they play with us more than we play with them. In the cryptonymic subtexts they spell underneath our speaking and writing, a phenomenon that has fascinated linguists such as Saussure[7] and Jakobson[8] as well as psychoanalysts such as Abraham and Torok,[9] who uncovered a whole English subtext in the Wolfman's narrative. The peculiarity of these subtexts is that in most cases they are inaccessible to the writing and speaking subject and incommensurable with the text 'itself.' (Of course, intentional, planned, and skillfully executed anagrams 'fit' into the text, but they already imitate a process that transforms the radical otherness of the letter into 'meaning.') Perhaps one should even ask whether it is correct to speak of a subtext, or whether one should not, in analogy to Freud's polemic against the word 'subconscious,' coin an analogical "untext" to Freud's "unconscious." Freud's argument against the term 'subconscious' is against the misleading notion that what appears in the psychoanalytical discourse is some kind of consciousness below our normal consciousness. But Freud's point is that what appears is a radical other of consciousness and should therefore only be named as its negation: the unconscious. Any story told about the unconscious already displaces that sphere that is radically inaccessible although or because it "is" nowhere but in and through those stories and texts.

In a similar way, the literality of the text is itself not a text but a nontext that appears nowhere but through the text it subverts and constitutes at the same time. And this otherness of the letter cannot be brought into any kind of dialectic.

Notes

1. Unless otherwise noted, all parenthetical notations refer to *The Quest for Christa T.*
2. Translation altered by editor.
3. Lachmann-edition 39, 1; author's translation.
4. On the parallels between Ernst Bloch's notion of "the principle of hope" and Christa Wolf's novel, cf. Andreas Huyssen, "Traces of Ernst Bloch: Reflections on Christa Wolf," in this volume.
5. Thomas Brasch, *Vor den Vätern sterben die Söhne* (Berlin: Rotbuch Verlag, 1977).
6. Thus, it is also a recurring motif of Wolf Biermann's songs.
7. On Saussure's anagrammatical studies see Jean Starobinski, *Words Upon Words: The Anagrams of Ferdinand de Saussure* (New Haven: Yale University Press, 1979).
8. See for example Jakobson's brilliant study on Hölderlin's anagrams: Roman Jakobson, *Hölderlin, Klee, Brecht. Zur Wortkunst dreier Gedichte* (Frankfurt/Main: Suhrkamp, 1976), 27–96.
9. Nicolas Abraham and Maria Torok, *Cryptonymie. Le verbier de l'homme aux loups* (Paris: Editions Aubier Flammarion, 1976).

I/She: The Female Dialogic in *The Quest for Christa T.*

Anne Herrmann

The *Quest for Christa T.* begins: "The quest for her: in the thought of her. And of *the attempt to be oneself.* She speaks of this in her diaries, which we have, on the loose manuscript pages that have been found, and between the lines of those letters of hers that are known to me" (3).[1] (Nachdenken, ihr nachdenken. Dem *Versuch, man selbst zu sein.* So steht es in ihren Tagebüchern, die uns geblieben sind, auf den losen Blättern der Manuskripte, die man aufgefunden hat, zwischen den Zeilen der Briefe, die ich kenne.) Thus, Christa T.'s presence makes its initial appearance through her writings, embedded in a story structured as intertextual dialogue. This passage interweaves three contrasting pronouns: "her" (*ihr*), "we" (*uns*), and "I/me" (*ich*), the first and third feminine, the second potentially so. They appear in opposition to the impersonal "one" (*man*), in German an abbreviated, lower-case rendition of the masculine noun meaning "man." The passage begins with the infinite possibility of the infinitive *nachdenken* and its semantic doubling, "to remember" and "to follow in thought," and ends with the verb *kennen* (to know). Conjugated in the first person, *kennen* signifies knowledge as the juncture between thought and memory, a form of intersubjectivity.[2] It is not Christa T., mentioned in the next phrase, whom the narrator knows, but her texts, specifically her diaries and letters: the most personal forms of literary production, meant for no audience, or an audience of one. Christa Wolf and Christa T. share the same name, but Christa T.'s patronym, abbreviated to the mere sign of one, lacks the authority required of patriarchal authorship.[3]

257

Anne Herrmann

Christa Wolf attempts to escape the inadequacy and dangers of language—which Christa T., leaving only fragments, already suspects —by rewriting the dichotomy between subject and object in terms of identity, as reflected in the specular image of an identical first name. Wolf, naming her protagonist Christa T., creates her own autobiographical fiction based on another woman's autobiography. The author, disinherited by the premature death of her friend, now inherits an unordered mass of unpublished writings and assumes the role of narrator to prolong a life only half-lived, by doubling it in years and by duplicating it as written text. Narrative emerges from excerpted manuscripts—with the aid of memory and invention—to fill the gaps between traces left by a woman who threatens to be not silent but invisible. Yet difference—that is, the ontological difference between the living (Christa Wolf) and the dead (Christa T.) and the structural difference between the narrator and the narrated—allows the narration to emerge as fiction. Christa T. fails to write because of an inability to postpone narration until narratable, by privileging presence over absence, as she reveals in her recurring interrogative: "When, if not now?" (185).[4] The narrator begins to write in the face of an absence, when the other threatens effacement and the only defense against her irretrievability is representation, even at the expense of falsification. Between silence, "It's as if she had to die all over again" (4), and domination, "I can do what I like with her" (4), the narrator chooses citation: "I can summon her up quite easily with a quotation, more than I could do for most living people" (4). By including the written fragments left by the deceased, the author mitigates the power endowed by authorship to encompass not only authority but also ambivalence toward language, literary history, and the novelistic heroine.

Naming as renaming, doubling rather than objectifying, finds its theoretical counterpart in the dialogic, a term that refers to double-voiced texts where competing discourses struggle for hegemonic ascendancy in a particular sociohistorical context.[5] Because any linguistic utterance as a form of social practice involves adopting as well as responding to prior speech, to enter the struggle between discourses means to engage in speech as citation. Dialogism finds its most explicit expression in the novel, where "extraliterary" genres such as the letter, the diary or the confession create an "intertextual" dialogue, between speech as created and as cited, between author and character, not as subject and object but as conflicting subjects. The texts of author and character collide, contradict each other and thereby limit each other's authorial power.

The dialogic relation between two subjects implies a relation between two social entities rather than two bodies, predicated on a structure, not a psychological or ethical content.[6] Until recently, the relation between author and character has been posited as ungendered and therefore masculine.[7] *The Quest for Christa T.* can be read as Wolf's gendering of the dialogic relation, not by filling the structure with a different psychological content (i.e., a "feminine" one), but by creating an intersubjectivity based on identity (the mirroring of the two Christa's) as well as difference (the difference between Christa T.'s fragments and Christa Wolf's novel). The other is both another subject, although the object of representation, and another representation of the self. The initial and most concrete enunciation of the relation between self and other can be found in the dialogic form of the epistolary.[8]

The first letter mentioned in the novel is the last letter the narrator writes to Christa T. Announced at the end of the prologue, it refers to their initial encounter and anticipates their ultimate departure. This letter, which the sender only now remembers, prefigures the end of the receiver's life as well as the narrative's beginning: "I don't know if she noticed this moment, or whenever else it was that I came into her life" (5). The letter that is never read by its addressee reappears when inserted chronologically into the narrative sequence and alludes to Christa T.'s original articulation: "Then she began to blow, or to shout, there's no proper word for it. It was this I reminded her of, or wanted to, in my last letter, but she wasn't reading any more letters, she was dying" (9). The author mentions the shout, a verbal disclosure emptied of its semantic content, to reinforce the insufficiency of linguistic signs. The sound for which there is no word makes Christa T. audible and visible but not necessarily comprehensible (or "knowable"). The lack of response requires that another text retrieve this dead letter by placing it within a narrative context.

This letter is mentioned a third time following the reunion of the narrator and Christa T. seven years later, after both have survived the war. The narrator remembers the letter to which she alluded earlier in the novel but which was written after the reunion that occurred first in the lecture hall, then in the department store of a wind-blown city. Here the narrator remembers a question that would have been appropriate to ask at the moment of their meeting, was obliquely suggested in her letter, and yet remains permanently withheld from the reader: "And this seemed the right moment to ask the question that occurred to me. But I didn't ask the question—either then or later; and only in my last letter, which she could no longer read, did I give a hint of it" (26). The request that could never be made verbally was written down but sent too late, embedded in a letter that never reached its destination. The response was never received, while the request can never be read, failing to enter the novel, the compendium of all texts. The letter likewise reminds the narrator of its inability both to defer death and to conceal her resentment at death's inevitability. The insurmountable loss of dialogue, "We never talked about it" (5), emphasizes the irretrievability of verbal articulation at the same time that it posits the possibility of a written text founded on the dialogic relation between actual literary fragments and the invention of possible scenes.

"She can talk to him as to herself" (62) captures Christa T.'s relationship to Kostia, the romantic poet, whose letter, written ten years after the incident it describes, becomes the narrator's. Christa T. would have read it shortly before her death as the reminder of a nearly forgotten chapter in her life. The narrator's retrospective reading reveals the content of the letter as a narrative, which in form adheres to the structure of an Aristotelian tragedy: "For it was, I now realize, a real short story, with introduction, main episode, climax, turning point, and rapid close, with a theme—*Love and Intrigue*" (65). "Love and Intrigue" (*Kabale und Liebe*) refers to Schiller's *Sturm and Drang* play, the text used to test Günter's ability to "demonstrate the superiority of social motives over personal ones" (66) as a school teacher, which he fails by falling prey to "subjectivism." Kostia, who takes "blond Inge" away from Günter, first in jest and then to marry her, reveals in this letter his wife's long-term infirmity, which prefigures Christa T.'s own illness and points to the parallel outcomes of two seemingly divergent life stories. Inge represents the woman as object of exchange, desirable because of her beauty, while Christa T. attempts to offer a different representation of the story in her diary. Finally the narrator offers her own interpretation: "But the events left different traces in each; the secret manipulations and evasions of memory are shown in different ways, in each the rapid and dangerous workings of oblivion take a different course. Accordingly, one can exaggerate the traces or fail to find any, depending on which source you trust" (64). The narrator edits these texts—neither of which is meant for her as reader—by constructing a third point of view, which suggests that all previous versions can only be construed as misreadings: "It didn't happen the way one can tell it" (64).

The narrator's own reading of the tragic romance plot focuses on the relationship between Kostia and Christa T., both poets, but differently gendered and therefore differently inscribed in literary discourse. The narrator begins by reconstructing that day "on the new artificial lake" during which Kostia refers to a Brecht poem, "The Ballad of Marie A.," in order to disclose his poetic, while disguising his romantic, identity.[9] By citing the poem he displays his privileged access to the models of male literary precursors who posit themselves as speaking subjects by consigning the feminine to silence. Christa T. interjects in her own defense as well as "Marie A's": "But she exists; she always exists in reality before she gets into a poem, and before you can admire her in peace" (63). By insisting on the literalness of the referent, Christa T. attempts to legitimize women's status as speaking subjects, even as they are disinherited by a literary tradition. Christa T. forces the issue by recasting the object of her discourse in the form of an audience, addressing Kostia as "you": "But you, she says, when you've forgotten my face, you'll know that you recited this poem to her, in a certain place, on a blue day in September. And the poet you thought of, long ago he slept with all your girls for you, with me too, ah Kostia" (63). For a male poet to "know" a woman restricts the meaning of *kennen* to its sexual sense, the very sense in which this particular poet will never know Christa T.

The difference between Christa T. as a speaking subject and Marie A. as the silenced feminine becomes elided in the sameness of their positions as products of the male imagination. This sameness can only be undermined by reestablishing a difference between the two referents. The transition from visual object to speaking subject occurs when Christa T. assumes the position of spectator.[10] By reversing her role in the spectacle, she succeeds in temporarily reversing gender roles, thus positioning herself as subject, rather than object, of desire.[11] As bearer of the look she continues to address Kostia in the second person: "Just sit still, beside me, let me look at you" (61). She immediately neutralizes this mandate through an insistence on reciprocity: "I won't force you. We'll go along facing in the same direction" (61). Before she has time to know her male counterpart, she is abandoned by him, knowing that the female ideal rests on an aesthetic idea: "The one and only girl you're saving yourself for, she doesn't exist. You have to invent her" (63).[12] "The one" turns out to be Inge, who takes the part of Kostia's wife, the role Christa T. eventually adopts in relation to Justus, the "right man."

Christa T. becomes a "veterinary surgeon's wife in a small Mecklenburg town" (137) via a costume ball, during which she plays the part of Sophie La Roche, the author of *Geschichte des Fräulein von Sternheim: von einer Freundin derselben aus Original-Papieren und anderen zuverlässigen Quellen gezogen* (The Story of Mademoiselle von Sternheim: Drawn from Original Papers and Other Reliable Sources by one of her [female] Friends [1771]),[13] and a probable literary model for *The Quest for Christa T.* The narrator compels her audience to transplant itself in history, "so that people may see her" (124), while Christa T. offers nothing to see when she arrives without a costume. Through renaming herself and disregarding her appearance, she avoids the role that would both relegate her to the object of the gaze and once again transform her into a male fiction. She eventually admits that the part she has adopted is not even the author's but her protagonist's, Fräulein von Sternheim; this disclosure elicits a horrified response from the narrator: "Seduction? Intrigues? A false marriage with this rogue Derby? A mournful country life in the English provinces? And, for God's sake, virtue?!" (119). Thus Christa T. portrays not an historical figure but a literary construct, legible only to the female reader acquainted with Sophie La Roche's epistolary novel. The narrator's sequence of interrogatives reveals her familiarity with a woman's text that lies outside the literary canon and questions the very components of a narrative structure that has governed the literary production for and by women and continues to govern their lives. At the very moment when Wolf's narrator can no longer prevent her heroine from entering the same plot, the reader is reminded that Christa T. has indeed chosen an appropriate role. Before the novel begins, Christa Wolf assures us that "Christa T. is a literary figure" (n.p.), who, like Sophie La Roche and Sophie von Sternheim, shares a name with her author. The scene's fictiveness, like its historical displacement, subsequently is replaced by an equally invented, yet seemingly less fantastic, encounter between the two future spouses on a Sunday afternoon in a small country town.

Christa T. reminds Justus "that every good love story comes to an end in marriage" (127–128). If marriage terminates the female romance plot governed by "virtue," Justus, like Kostia, initiates the plot by having access to prior forms of representation. These enable re-cognition of a woman as opposed to "cognition" in Wolf's understanding of the word *kennen*: "He remembers the picture on the wall in his parents' living room, the girl seen in profile, that's who she is, the picture cut from a calendar, portrait of an Egyptian queen" (114). By this point the representation of the feminine has evolved from poetic persona to a mass produced image. Kostia sees *through* Christa T. ("I've seen through you, he says one day, I can see your act" [62]); by recognizing the attempt she makes to play the female variation on the romantic poet—embodied by the roles of "Bettina [von Arnim, 1785–1859]" and "Annette [von Droste-Hülshoff, 1797–1848]"—he reads as anachronisms. Justus simply looks *at* her: "Justus was looking in her direction, his look was just as she wished it to be, he noticed everything: how long she'd stood before the mirror, that her hair was short" (122). In contrast to Kostia, who attempts to ridicule Christa T.'s identification with her Romantic literary precursors, Justus complicitously encourages her to accept the role of a wife. As bearer of the look, he fails to decode the message of her disguise at the costume ball (because there was "nothing to see") but succeeds in constituting her in the mirror. Christa T.'s literal mirroring allows her to exist as the construction of social, not literary, conventions. In contrast to the two sets of female friends whose identical first names produce a specular image based on identity, Justus privileges difference as the legitimized form of sexual difference. Betrayed by Kostia, who fails to reciprocate her look, Christa T. eventually betrays Justus by playing the part of Madame Bovary, the adulteress heroine of a nineteenth-century novel that ends not in marriage but suicide.

Christa T. finds another literary counterpart in the nineteenth century in the author Theodor Storm, this time as literary critic.[14] In contrast to the costume ball, which did not take place, Christa T.'s thesis exists as material object: "there it stands—a grayish springback folder with a green calf spine, number 1954/423—stored with hundreds of other theses which the decades have deposited; and only the dry dust of the institute shows any interest in them" (94–95). As her only piece of completed writing, it examines the closed forms of the lyric poem and the *Novelle*. The narrator, reading the thesis for the first time, expects to hear the literary critic's masterful discourse and instead hears Christa T.'s speaking voice: "She talks about the mental adventures of her poet, and it doesn't seem to disturb her that a relation is established between him and another person who remains unspecified but who is present" (95).[15] Once again an intertext mirrors the structure of the novel as a whole, based on the relation between two writers, one of whom functions as addressee. Like the narrator, Christa T. gradually relinquishes the impersonal "one" and the collective "we" to allow for the emergence of the first person: "And then, just when one has ceased to expect it, she does appear in person, undisguised, as 'I.' One can hardly believe one's ears" (97). Christa T. begins to write by inserting an autobiographical subject into the objective discourse of an academic thesis, written for an audience of one, her professor. She is able to complete this dialogue, an act never accomplished in her correspondence with the narrator, yet disowns the thesis's closure by failing to acknowledge its reception, "very good."

Christa T.'s resistance to closure and her need for an audience results in the commitment to an architectural rather than a literary project, the plan for a house that, although left unfinished, nevertheless outlives the death of its author. If "dichten" means "*condensare*, make dense, tighten" (16) and "writing means making things large" (168), then both terms imply a nonliterary structuring characterized by visibility and the stable image. The genesis of Christa T.'s house on the lake takes place on paper, not simply as a set of self-referential signifiers, but as sketches that prefigure an actual referent:

> She knew quite well that this raw house with the wind whistling through it was further from completion than the dream house on the plans that happy evening at the seaside hotel, the white and beautiful house on the pieces of paper. But she'd also learned that real materials are more resistant than paper, and that, as long as things are still in the process of coming to be, one has to drive them tenaciously along. (160)

Whereas writing recovers an ambiguous past through the arbitrary signifiers of language, the architectural sketch visualizes a future transformation of space by means of a material object. Christa T. moves from her relationship as reader of a text to the actual production of a rural, private sphere, as represented by such nineteenth-century realists as Storm. The house acquires a degree of closure never awarded her literary fragments, while at the same time it fails to succumb to the obscurity of her thesis.

Christa T.'s emergence as literary critic and submergence between the four walls of her domestic space offers a parallel plot to the transformation of the "I" into "she," which makes narration possible for the first-person narrator. The narrator constructs the other as fictional subject by displacing her own life story onto that of Christa T. By transforming the "I" into "she," the narrating subject is able to look at itself as the object of discourse. The third-person pronoun stands for the absent object, Christa T., and allows the subject to absent herself, to remain nameless as narrator. By writing about a third person rather than herself, the narrator indirectly introduces a "you," the addressee who appears not only as audience but also as the self disguised as "she." By providing her protagonist with the same name, the author avoids objectification, maintaining a specular relation between two women writers.

"One becomes acquainted through a (female) friend" (83) (Durch eine Freundin lernt man sich kennen),[16] the fortune teller tells Christa T., exploiting the ambiguity of the impersonal pronoun to suggest that Christa T. will make the acquaintance of either her future spouse or herself by means of a female friend. *Freundin*, as feminine form of "friend," represents the other woman writer who enables the narrator of this novel to begin: "If I were to have to invent her, I wouldn't change her. I'd let her live. . . . I'd let her sit at the desk, one morning in the twilight, noting the experiences into which the facts of real life had crystallized in her." (174). Because closure is both premature and ultimately impossible, the narrator continues: "If I'd been allowed to invent us, I'd have given us time to stay" (175). The conditional has been transformed from an obligation into a privilege, from the pronoun "she" into "we" characterized, not by difference based on domination, but by a dialogism that sustains the conflict arising from contradiction. The author knows that *kennen* involves giving her heroine the name she has withheld from her narrator, but even then the female "I" can only begin to know and narrate itself as "she."

Notes

1. Unless otherwise noted, all parenthetical notations refer to *The Quest for Christa T.*

2. "Through the intimacy which is knowledge, friendship becomes a vehicle of self-definition for women, clarifying identity through relation to an other who embodies and reflects an essential aspect of the self." Elizabeth Abel, "(E)merging Identities: The Dynamics of Female Friendship in Contemporary Fiction by Women," *Signs* 6 (1981): 416.

3. I use this term as analyzed by Sandra Gilbert and Susan Gubar in *The Madwoman in the Attic: The Woman Writer and the Nineteenth Century Literary Imagination* (New Haven: Yale University Press, 1979), part 1.

4. "Wolf is a presence in the text which constitutes itself in relation to the absence which is Christa T., and that process of self-constitution in intersubjective relationship is the coming-into-being of subjectivity free of domination. . . . This relationship provides a model for the sort of openness which makes possible intersubjectivity; but it also serves as a metaphor for a productive (i.e., non-reifying) appropriation of the past." Myra Love, "Christa Wolf and Feminism: Breaking the Patriarchal Connection," *NGC*, no. 16 (1979): 34.

5. For further elucidation of this term, see Mikhail Bakhtin, *Problems of Dostoevsky's Poetics*, ed. and trans. Caryl Emerson (Minneapolis: University of Minnesota Press, 1984), and *The Dialogic Imagination: Four Essays by M. M. Bakhtin*, ed. Michael Holquist, trans. Caryl Emerson and Michael Holquist (Austin: University of Texas Press, 1981).

6. See Tzvetan Todorow, *Mikhail Bakhtin: The Dialogical Principle* (Minneapolis: University of Minnesota Press, 1984), 39.

7. For a longer discussion of the gendering of the dialogic see my forthcoming book, *The Dialogic and Difference: "An/Other" Woman in Viriginia Woolf and Christa Wolf* (New York: Columbia University Press, 1988). For a reading of the dialogic as the dialogue between a female author and the male literary tradition,

see Patricia Yeager, "'Because Fire Was in My Head': Eudora Welty and the Dialogic Imagination," *PMLA* 99, no. 5 (October 1984): 995–973.

8. For the most recent and comprehensive discussion of the epistolary, see S. Linda Kaufmann, *Discourse of Desire: Gender, Genre, and Epistolary Fiction* (Ithaca: Cornell University Press, 1986).

9. It is interesting to note that the word left out of the first line of Brecht's poem as first quoted in the novel: "an einem Tag im schönen Mond September" ("on a day in the lovely month of September" [62]), is the word "blau" ("blue"), which can be read as an allusion to Anna Seghers's story "Das wirkliche Blau" and interpreted as the exclusion of the female author in the male mind, here specifically Wolf's own literary precursor. For further elucidation of literary allusions, see Alexander Stephan, *Christa Wolf* (Munich: Verlag C. H. Beck, 1979), 54–92

10. "In a world ordered by sexual imbalance, pleasure in looking has been split between active/male and passive/female. The determining male gaze projects its fantasy onto the female figure, which is styled accordingly. In their traditional exhibitionist role women are simultaneously looked at and displayed, with their appearance coded for strong visual and erotic impact so that they can be said to connote *to-be-looked-at-ness*." Laura Mulvey, "Visual Pleasure and Narrative Cinema," in *Woman and the Cinema: A Critical Anthology*, ed. Karyn Kay and Gerald Peary (New York: E. P. Dutton, 1977), 418.

11. For a theorizing of the female spectator, see Mary Ann Doane, "Film and the Masquerade: Theorising the Female Spectator," *Screen* 23, no. 3/4 (September/October, 1982): 74–87. See also Doane, *The Desire to Desire: The Woman's Film of the 1940's* (Bloomington: Indiana University Press, 1987).

12. Translation altered by editor.

13. Sophie von La Roche, *Geschichte des Fräuleins von Sternheim* (Munich: Winkler Verlag, 1976). For a discussion of this work, see Silvia Bovenschen, *Die imaginierte Weiblichkeit: Exemplarische Untersuchungen zu kulturgeschichtlichen und literarischen Präsentationsformen des Weiblichen* (Frankfurt/ Main: Suhrkamp, 1979), 190ff.

14. In his essay "Bürgerlichkeit und l'art pour l'art: Theodor Storm" in *Die Seele und die Formen* (Darmstadt: Luchterhand, 1971), 83, Georg Lukács likewise uses the metaphor of the mask to describe bourgeois, rather than female existence: "This bourgeois life-style is only a mask, behind which there hides itself the wild and fruitless agony of a failed, destroyed life—the agony of the romantic born too late."

15. Lukács identifies this as characteristic of Storm's own work: "For him, oral presentation established the criterion to discover whether the mood he wanted to capture had actually found expression in his works" (111).

16. Translation altered by editor.

A Guarded Iconoclasm: The Self as Deconstructing Counterpoint to Documentation

Sandra Frieden

T he recent critical discourse on autobiography offers us little access to Christa Wolf, although *Patterns of Childhood* was prominent among the autobiographies of the seventies. Nor do the categories and conventions associated with biography provide a comfortable framework for a book so unconventionally biographical as *No Place on Earth*. The genres have changed, but the critical discussions—at least for autobiography—have not kept pace. Theoretical commentary on autobiography has increasingly centered on the deconstructionist attacks that undermine the traditional definitions. I would like to confront this problem, first by focusing on autobiography, although many points apply to biography as well, and then by examining these two works by Christa Wolf from the perspective of my discussion.

Verifiability, autobiographical intent, and referential authority were once the mainstays of the definition of autobiography, but the force of these terms has considerably diminished, if not disappeared, under theoretical and philosophical assault. Once Roy Pascal[1] and his successors began to see autobiographical "truth" as tempered by imaginative (or even unconscious) design, autobiographical writings became subject in part—albeit a troublesome part—to statements regarding works of fiction, so that verifiability was relativized as a defining characteristic of autobiography. Wimsatt and Beardsley's[2] declaration of the indeterminacy and irrelevance of authorial intent for works of fiction had implications for autobiography as well, which were then pushed to

266

an ultimate extreme by Michel Foucault,[3] who dispenses with the author altogether as anything other than a function of textual dynamics. The coherent, historical identity behind autobiographical referential authority has exploded under deconstructionist and linguistic dynamiting: Jacques Derrida[4] questions the system in which referential authority functions as a term; and Emile Benveniste's[5] linguistic analyses posit the "I" of written discourse as an "empty form" constituted at any moment by the discourse in which it occurs. Michael Ryan[6] has followed this argumentation in his metacritical deconstruction of the concept of "self-evidence" as a basis for autobiographical identity; and Michael Sprinker,[7] with an eye to this controversy, has provocatively entitled his recent essay "Fictions of the Self: The End of Autobiography," a title that leads his editor, James Olney, to ponder whether indeed the demise of autobiographical discourse has occurred.[8]

Such dire predictions about the fate of autobiography have been made before—indeed, with regularity: Roy Pascal declared in 1960 that the time was "unpropitious to autobiography," dependent as this form was, in his eyes, upon the directing consciousness of a "whole person" who was necessarily an anachronism in this age.[9] Bernd Neumann made the same declaration in 1970, stating that the "outer-directed" citizen of this century could not possibly commit the inner-directed act of autobiography.[10] These forecasts, seemingly based upon reactions to social unrest, were in fact grounded in the limitations placed by the prognosticators on their category; for each espoused a severely restricted definition of autobiography contingent on prerequisites existing only in the past.

Indeed, it is perhaps more appropriate to say that autobiography has not come to an end, but rather our theories to explain how we write it, how we read it, and how we recognize it when we see it have ended. For we do recognize it, albeit more comfortably in some cases than in others. Although we thought we had managed, with our theories, to lay to rest any generic questions raised by Augustine, Rousseau, Goethe, and Proust, we find now that these questions were limited in the first place and that they somehow are inappropriate in our encounters with authors such as Christa Wolf or Peter Weiss.[11] The questions that no longer fit and explanations that no longer apply have apparently exhausted themselves in the attempt to keep pace with the generic and theoretical mutations of recent years, but the genre continues and evolves. As has been the case in the past when theorists declared the "end of autobiography," the need arises to shift from a line of argumentation that, though in itself challenging, does not adequately explore potential aspects of its topic, nor does it account for historical changes in the genre.

We find a more expansive model for our literary discussions within the communication context, which functions not according to concepts of philosophical validity but according to the pragmatics of discourse. "Truth" may well be illusory in the philosophical terms of some schools, but it is no less illusory nor elusive in spoken than in written discourse; and spoken discourse has always functioned according to a pragmatic acceptance of certain utterances as "truthful." Nor is the "truth" of spoken discourse easier to verify than that of written discourse, for the willingness of a speaker to elucidate on a statement never guaranteed veracity. We hear a "persona" of the sender in a spoken utterance, in much the same sense that literary communication displays to us the "implied author." Intent, truth, and identity may well be irretrievable in a philosophical context, but human discourse functions according to a set of rules that, in practice, disregards this lack of philosophical footing. It becomes a matter of curiosity to us that discourse functions in this way, and we may turn to other disciplines to explore how and why this is so. But we need not try to counter the principle of philosophical indeterminacy. We merely reject it as a theoretical basis for the functioning of the literary act.

What are the ramifications of this argument for our discussion of autobiography? By regarding a literary work as a text encoded by a sender/author and transmitted to a receiver/reader by means of a specific medium within a social context, we enlarge the discussion of autobiography to include both the dynamics of the genre as it functions and the historicization process inherent in the literary act. Although I focus chiefly on the text, it is obviously possible to explore each aspect of the communication process separately and in relation to the other aspects. The author will choose a medium for a particular message and, in so doing, commit to a set of dynamics specific to that medium; the potential ways of dealing with those dynamics are grounded in, but not bounded by, the historically changing codes or conventions for that type of message within that medium. The decision to tell a true account of one's own life by means of autobiography incurs certain problems, some of which are inherent in any written communication and some of which are specific to autobiography. Authors engaged in the encoding process must confront the basic problem of detachability of the written text: they will be absent from the transmission of the text, and, in the case of autobiography, they must inscribe themselves into the written work through signals that will "warrant" the referential reality of the message. The problem of risk is inherent in autobiography: personal revelations, although perhaps therapeutic in a psychological sense, may be threatening in terms of emotional, legal, or political consequences. And yet the written revelation may have differing effects—what for one author may be safety in distance, for another author, such as Michel Leiris, is insufficient risk: Leiris writes as "torero," revealing so much about himself that he feels he is "on the horns of the bull."[12] Another dynamic of the autobiographical text is the intensity of "otherness": a separation of self from self, both experienced in the attempt to recuperate one's own past and concretized in the detached text.

We deal with these, and many other discernable problems inherent in writing, in ways that change. Factors within the social context affect the distribution and reception of a particular medium; texts within a medium influence each other; and the signals used to encode the text, to make it recognizable as a type or a genre within a medium, are correspondingly affected. Thus, situating the literary act within the context of communication, we may deal with not only the dynamics of a particular genre but also the evolution of the genre at the hands of the author. This brings us back to Christa Wolf, who confronts the generic problems of autobiography and biography in the texts to be discussed here in ways that both extend the limits of these genres and reflect her own aesthetic and political positions.

Christa Wolf's "subjective authenticity"[13] is more than just her own version of Neue Subjektivität: she as author seeks the reflection of her own experience in literature and wishes to establish a relationship between herself and the text. By countering expected form, and by the example of her own "subjectification" (Subjektwerden),[14] she hopes to encourage a new awareness within the reader. Wolf has bannered her political commitment as well. While basically maintaining a positive vision of socialist society, she refuses to suppress her criticism, at times supporting writers out of favor with GDR officials[15] or speaking out in behalf of emancipating women from the confines of stultifying role-restrictions.[16] She exercises this criticism subtly, however, in a way that still allows her to remain within her own political system and with an ambiguity that renders her criticism applicable to any society. As an outgrowth of such commitment and of such a sense of literary responsibility, Wolf forges a style, not merely responsive to current writing trends, but challenging to present conventions and conventional thinking.

Wolf recalls in Patterns of Childhood the first sixteen years in the life of her narrator—from 1929 to 1945—a period dominated by the ideological indoctrination of the National Socialists. These recollections are occasioned by and inlaid into the account of the narrator's 1971 trip, in the company of her husband, her brother, and her teenaged daughter to the (now) Polish town in which she grew up. The description of this trip is, in turn, embedded in the almost diaristic account of the writing process, which extended from 1972 to 1975. Wolf problematizes each time level thematically in terms of its historical significance and structurally in terms of integrating past and present experience into both the recall-process and the act of writing. The autobiographically historical details are summoned from the childhood memories of the adult, act upon the adult retrieving them, and are commented upon by the reflecting writer, who views their significance within an ever-broadening spectrum of current events and moral values. This expansion of relevance from the specifically autobiographical to the general is rendered formally by the dissection of memory and its application to the present. In this way, Wolf lays bare the psychological and political ramifications of the socialization process by the example of her own life and work; and that which appears as content—the difficulty of breaking down and breaking through the layers of socialized consciousness—is mirrored in the dismantling of form.

Each time level has its own content: the most historically removed plane presents the dailiness of Nazi indoctrination in the life of a little girl, for whom the personal events of childhood interweave with the political influences of Fascist doctrine to create the texture of experience. Ordinary events—the hands of the minister at confirmation lessons (PC 254)—blend with the voice of Goebbels on the radio (PC 257); the child witnesses the embarrassing public punishment of a schoolmate and the interrogation of her mother by two men "in trench coats" (PC 166). Wolf's methodical detail not only provides historical data but also duplicates the insidious detail of the socialization process as it affects the vulnerable psyche of a child. On the next time level—that of the narrator returning to these scenes of her childhood for a forty-six hour period in July 1971—Wolf introduces a psychological context for the work as a whole. Whereas the remembered child of the past is presented in the immediacy of its experience, the remembering adult conjunctures the flood of memories and the awareness of implications, a filter of hindsight through which former deeds and values must now pass. The presentation at this level is the moment-to-moment recording of memory, thought, and response, the experience and knowledge of the remembering adult present as foreground, but without reflection, is instead reserved for the third level. This reflective third level provides a temporal and conceptual frame for the entire book, although all three levels are to be understood as merely heuristically separable from one another because the remembered, the remembering, and the reflective levels of consciousness are interwoven from the outset. The processes of remembering and of self-observation are now redoubled upon themselves as the narrating consciousness details its efforts to recall and to describe the remembering, to observe and to reflect upon the self in its own introspection. These new thematic elements yield historical and political parallels within the present, as well. World events that occur during the course of the writing become part of the internal context: the narrating consciousness, in its response to each event and in its recording of each response, relates the past directly to the present, bridging spatial and temporal expanses in order to bring together the elements of experience. On this level Wolf treats the question of whether insight gained from experience can be transmitted to another person (or generation), particularly through the act of writing; here, too, are implications of political and social criticism.

Patterns of Childhood has perplexed critics attempting to deal with the work within the confines of a fixed literary genre, and the designation "Novel" on the West German edition has only exacerbated the problem.[17] Most critics have regarded the work as autobiographical and have either verified or challenged Wolf's data, confirmed or disputed the accuracy of her portrayal of past time and her implications about the present.[18] In fact, the generic confusion that attends the reading of this book is an important feature: the dismantling of conventions within the discourse challenges the expectations of the reader, who must penetrate to increasingly deeper levels of perception in order to integrate anticipations with reality, memory with actuality, and—as Wolf would have us do—narration with experience. Wolf's encounter with the autobiographical problems of risk, otherness, and absence from the text is mediated by her aesthetics of subjective authenticity and by her political commitment to provoking reader awareness. The resulting text resists the current conventions for autobiography, overcomes their limitations, and presents an example of generic evolution.

The conventions against which *Patterns of Childhood* is written still dominate in the majority of currently published autobiographical works: the (more or less) linear narration of a chronologically structured life history, with a relatively clear separation of temporal levels; a claim to truth, often documented by "verifiable" data; and use of the pronoun "I" to represent both the past and the present writing self, though generally with nonreference to the act of writing. Although the use of these conventions does, of course, signal a comfortably recognizable generic format to the reader, it is precisely this comfort that Christa Wolf seeks to disrupt.

Wolf begins *Patterns of Childhood* with a carefully delineated temporal frame by which she on the first and last few pages enters into and then exits from the narrative: moving at the beginning of the work from the present-time of writing, back in time to her 1971 journey and then further into the years of her childhood, she reverses the series at the end in order to complete the frame. Once she establishes this frame, however, Wolf constantly juxtaposes levels, disrupts chronology, and creates a layer of self-reflexivity within the work that insistently interferes with the reader's conventional expectations. The constantly shifting temporal levels are perceivable, and they intrude into every attempt at linear narration. The difficulties of these temporal levels are paralleled and problematized thematically in the attempt to establish a historical continuum, the linearity of which is as elusive as that of temporality: the reader, forced to question temporal references, is encouraged to challenge historical and political continuities and discontinuities as well. In this way, the text, through disruption of convention, more nearly approximates the nonlinearity of perception and confronts historical and political assumptions with skeptical interrogation.

Wolf departs from the autobiographical convention of a claim to truth through a methodical relativizing of factual data and the objectivity that such data supposedly provide. Despite her account of the scrupulous gathering of proofs to demonstrate that each recounted incident may be "a documented fact" (PC 122), Wolf exposes the insubstantiality of her, or anyone's, claim to objectively ascertainable truth. In attempting to summon for the first time the image of herself as a child, for instance, she says: "But what about the child herself? No image. This is where forgery would set in" (*PC* 6). She does not conceal the fact that the conversations she presents are composites, and she questions the process of translating experience into literature. Her foreword to the book, in its ironic denial of external verifiability, does not conclusively cast the narrated figures as fictional or nonfictional:

> All characters in this book are the invention of the narrator. None is identical with any person living or dead. Neither do any of the described episodes coincide with actual events.
> Anyone believing that he detects a similarity between a character in the narrative and either himself or anyone else should consider the strange lack of individuality in the behavior of many contemporaries. Generally recognizable behavior patterns should be blamed on circumstances.
>
> C.W. (PC n.p.)

In this brief foreword, Wolf has not only parodied conventional novelistic disclaimers and the equally conventional autobiographical claim of truth; but she has also attacked conformity and established a parallel, a framework of comparison between "then" and "now"—and all, I might add, in her typically ambiguous way of *not* clarifying her point of reference. She may be, as critics in the West would say, lambasting a lost sense of individuality within the GDR; or she may be, as critics in the East would say, referring, in her humanistic vision, to a universal and dangerous tendency to conform to the demands of authority. (I would say at least both.)

Wolf's disruption of conventional pronoun reference is the most significant of her departures from expected form. Within our framework of communication, the literary text itself is narrated in a primary discourse between author as sender and reader as receiver. Embedded, or inscribed within the text is the secondary discourse: the persona of the narrator with the implied reader, conventionally an "I" and a "you," conversing about a she/he. The fictiveness of this she/he and the proximity of the "I/narrator" to the author are determined by the reader on the basis of text-external substantiation. Within this convention of pronoun reference, the I, the you, and the she/he are understood to be functional only within the secondary level of communication. Wolf deconstructs this system by not referring to herself as I until the final pages of the book: she addresses both her present writing self and the remembering self from 1971 as "you" and her childhood self as "she," and she gives the child a different name, Nelly. The use of "we" is, of course, ambiguous throughout the book; its reference is constituted variously as the "you" and others of her generation, "you" and the reader, and finally, people in general. Furthermore, the use of "you" more than substitutes for the conventional dichotomy of "narrating I" and "narrated I": Wolf's use of "you" for self-address startles and imposes itself upon the reader, suggesting a more pressing invitation to identify—with the writing self, with skeptical critics, and with humanity in general. Wolf's use of "you" opens the possibility for internal conversation, for response to the self as "other." And most significantly, Wolf's appropriation of the "you"-form for the functions of the narrating and narrated "I" leaves free the pronoun "I" to serve at a different level: as an approach for Wolf to the primary discourse, a point of entry for her into the text, it brings along the "you" as well for still another layer of significance, as point of entry for the reader.

How does this look in the text? Wolf problematizes reference at the outset, both thematically and structurally. The first sentences state her theme: "What is past is not dead; it is not even past. We cut ourselves off from it; we pretend to be strangers" (PC 3). This thought determines the course of the work, as Wolf separates herself from her still-living past, in the form of Nelly, and desperately seeks a voice in the midst of her dilemma: "to remain speechless, or else to live in the third person. The first is impossible, the second strange" (PC 3). The disruption of personal and historical continuity within her own consciousness takes on grammatical form: "The true reason for the disruption of language is revealed in the cross-examination of yourself: a perplexing sound-shift takes place between the monologue and the address, an awkward alteration of the grammatical references. I, you, she, merging together in thought, are to be estranged from each other in the pronounced sentence".[19] A number of times throughout the work, Wolf describes as a goal, "when the second and the third person were to meet again in the first or, better still, were to meet with the first person. When it would no longer have to be 'you' and 'she' but a candid, unreserved 'I'" (PC 349). Wolf seeks, through establishing a historical continuum for herself and through reclaiming her own severed past, the basis of a psychological, and grammatically represented, continuum as well. Her tenuous results appear at the end of the work in the form of the first-person singular:

> The child who was hidden in me—has she come forth? Or has she been scared into looking for a deeper, more inaccessible hiding place? Has memory done its duty? Or has it proven—by the act of misleading—that it's impossible to escape the mortal sin of our time: the desire not to come to grips with oneself?
>
> And the past, which can still split the first person into the second and the third—has its hegemony been broken? Will the voices be still?
>
> I don't know. (PC 406)

For Christa Wolf, the author and her own questioning process may and must enter into the text: "Because one acquires the rights to material of this kind by personally involving oneself in the game and by keeping the stakes sufficiently high" (PC 158). For Wolf, the self becomes the mediator for the text: that which is disrupted in the conventional expectations for the genre is a reference external to the self or

Sandra Frieden

falsely distanced from it. The flow of events, historical data, structures of self-reference are filtered through and structured by the author's subjectivity, which is itself presented not with a pretense of wholeness but in its inevitable diffusion. The historical function of autobiography to provide a sense of temporal continuity is maintained, for both individual and society, by acknowledging the gaps and the contradictions rather than trying to ignore them. Autobiography evolves in the hands of Christa Wolf: in a search conducted through literary form, she seeks the self and finds "other."

Wolf's 1979 prose text No *Place on Earth* describes an imagined meeting between Heinrich von Kleist and Karoline von Günderrode. Proceeding from an account in an early Kleist biography that the two might have met,[20] Wolf brings them together in the company of mutual friends for an afternoon of tea and conversation. Kleist—recuperating from nervous collapse in the care of his friend Dr. Wedekind, stretched too thin between his shattered ideals in Paris and his future as a bureaucrat in Prussia, and still seven years away from the resignation that would culminate in suicide—is the stuttering poet whose uneasiness threatens to pierce the artificiality of the afternoon. Günderrode—friend of the Brentano family, a published poet of little renown whose melancholy dominated her verse, and a woman two years away from the despair that would culminate in suicide—is the young "canoness" who moves as an outsider among her own friends. The company is small: Clemens Brentano, his sisters Bettina and Gunda, Gunda's husband the (later) Prussian justice minister Friedrich Carl von Savigny, the scientist Nees van Esenbeck, and several others constitute the changing conversational groupings. Kleist and Günderrode observe and overhear one another; they mingle in conversations. During an afternoon walk they converse alone and discover their mutual melancholia. The guests depart, moving on to their respective fates, and the work ends.

Published without a generic designation, the work is open to a perplexing variety of possible readings. As a "legend that suits us" (NP 4) it could qualify as historical fiction; but the scholarly research underlying the quotations that constitute the dialogues and the historical background suggest a biographical study. A utopian parable (or an antiutopian parable); a critique of patriarchal culture; a portrait of the artist; a masked autobiographical statement of Wolf's uneasiness as a writer in the GDR, her sense of being lost, as were Kleist and Günderrode, in an era of transition—each possibility has been suggested, and with each suggestion the complexity of the reader's task increases.[21] As is typical for Wolf's writings, the reception of the work has been dominated by political overtones and the work changes meaning as it crosses territorial boundaries. In the West, No *Place on Earth* describes Wolf's uneasiness as a writer in a land where she is not understood; in the East the work is a reclaiming of the once-repudiated Romantic era as

274

part of the cultural heritage and a warning against materialism; and on both sides, the stilted language is most often faulted for inaccessibility. Christa Wolf has herself directed some discussion through her publication in the same year of a biographical essay on Günderrode, "The Shadow of a Dream." The empathy Wolf feels for Günderrode permeates the essay, and critics are left to question whether empathy is the same as identification with so apparently tragic a figure as this nineteenth-century poet. Yet even here, Günderrode may be understood as embodying a utopian possibility that was characteristic of and also premature for the Romantic era. Günderrode indeed has found "a place, somewhere"; it is a place within her, a potential that must remain unrealized in the particular period in which she was born. Christa Wolf nurtures fervent humanist ideals, she believes in the potential of socialist society to foster these ideals, and she views women as better qualified to mediate between ideal and society; these convictions have stood out in her earlier writings and argue for an optimistic interpretation here. Wolf admits that the problems may be unsolvable—"No form can be found in which to cast an insoluble problem" (NP 112)—but continues to approach a solution through the act of writing and through her challenge to form.

Although No Place on Earth is not biographical in a traditional sense, it does exemplify the transgression of generic boundaries that has become so frequent in the seventies. Just as Wolf exploits the conventions of autobiography in Patterns of Childhood and thereby challenges readers to rejoin past with present and to restore the historical self to the framework of the present self, so too in No Place on Earth she thwarts our formal expectations and provides a bridge over a historical gap. Her use of form is presented as an answer to the questions of politics and history, of past and present, of ideal and reality, of self and other.

The option of conventional biography stood open to Christa Wolf; and indeed, she follows it rather closely in "Shadow of a Dream." Here, she presents the life of Günderrode through a linear narration of chronologically ordered life events, linked by episodes that lend significance to the life as a whole; information issues from documents —letters, works, eye-witness accounts; and the attitude of the narrating biographer, while hardly as objective as a scholarly historian might wish, is more or less non-self-referential. This form, however, was inadequate to absorb the content envisioned by Wolf in the Günderrode material, and in No Place on Earth she reshapes it—no longer according to traditional biographical format but rather in contradistinction to it.

Wolf subverts linear narration from the outset with a mixture of paradox and incantation: "The wicked spoor left in time's wake as it flees us," she begins, conjuring spirits from another dimension, "You precursors, feet bleeding. Gazes without eyes, words that stem from no mouth. Shapes without bodies. Descended heavenward, separated in remote graves, resurrected again from the dead, still forgiving those who trespass against us, the sorrowful patience of angels" (*NP* 3). She introduces the characters and dispenses (supposedly) with the question of fictionality—"The claim that they met: a legend that suits us" (*NP* 4) —stating time ("June 1804") and place ("Winkel, on the Rhine, we saw it ourselves. An appropriate spot" [*NP* 4]). After the question, "Who is speaking?" (*NP* 4), the dialogue begins; a dramatic tone has been set for conversations mediated ambiguously by an omniscient narrator—a perspective that is a prerogative of the epic form, here blended into the dramatic. Indeed, all that occurs does so within the dialogue, a back-and-forth exchange through which ideas and mutual understandings are generated. The dialogue thus serves as paradigm for reader response by presenting content in a form that preserves its dialectic nature and thereby engages the reader in the dynamics of that dialectic. Pronominal reference is not merely shifted, as in *Patterns of Childhood*, but it is actually blurred so that the reader cannot be readily certain which character is speaking or whether the speaker is in fact the narrator, speaking in the present. With virtually all the action occurring in the dialogues, the reader feels constrained to weigh each character's words all the more carefully and to measure each silence for possible significance. The present time that opens the work is taken up—or seems to be taken up—at the end. The players exit: "Now it is getting dark. The final glow on the river. Simply go on, they think. We know what is coming" (*NP* 119). A question posed earlier in the work—"Who is 'we'?" (*NP* 109)—applies here to the indeterminacy of the "we," which breaks through the linearity of conventional biographical narration by escaping fixed limits of time, reference, and generic expectation. "We know what is coming"; as spoken by Kleist or Günderrode, the line implies a resignation to the fate that awaits them both; or perhaps, but less arguable, that they sense the coming of a better time, though not within their lifespans. If, however, the "we" includes narrator and reader, the ambiguity is maintained, but the framework of the "legend" is exploded. The reader who has tried to treat the work as a story finds that it has transgressed the boundaries of fiction and moved into the realm of biography.

The conventional claim to biographical authenticity is not explicit in the work and sometimes seems to be denied: the setting is, after all, "no place." The work seems fictional because the illusion of reality is so frequently countered; the characters' innermost thoughts are revealed, the dialogues stylized into stiffness, and the time—marked by the parlor clock—barely passes within the hundred and fifty pages. On the other hand, the lines spoken by the characters are drawn from letters and poems written by their real-life counterparts; the book jacket quotes Christa Wolf's account of her visit to Winkel on the Rhine ("We saw it ourselves") and also the Kleist-biographer's reference to the meeting with Günderrode. The simultaneous publication of the Günderrode biography provides still more "factual" substantiation. Yet the documentation here, as in *Patterns of Childhood*, is used, not to authenticate, but to counterpoint the fiction—to contrast what is known to have happened with what is felt to have happened, all based on the same sources of information. Nor does the narrating consciousness oblige a biographical insistence on objectivity and invisibility: self-reference is implied by the montage of pronouns as the narrating self insists upon inclusion in the conversation. Whereas in *Patterns of Childhood* the narrating self must split into its component selves in order to concretize the autobiographical process, in *No Place on Earth* the narrating consciousness must blend with, must assimilate the characters it describes in order to approach them from a biographical perspective. In both cases, the task of the narrating self is to seek the "other" across boundaries of alienation. Here we find a boundary-crossing where the biographical and the autobiographical meet. For Christa Wolf, the self becomes the boundary, consciously extended and retrieved, the boundary against which conventions are measured. The self gives coherence to Christa Wolf's humanism as well as to her aesthetics: the ability of the self to approach the other gives hope; the capacity of the self to filter insight, experience, and values gives continuity; and the tendency of the self to absorb other boundaries extends the expressive possibilities of form.

Notes

This article was previously published in German in *Vom Anderen und Vom Selbst. Beiträge zu Fragen der Biographie und Autobiographie*, ed. Reinhold Grimm and Jost Hermand (Königstein: Athenäum, 1982), 153–166. It is published here in English for the first time, with permission of the author.

1. See Roy Pascal, *Design and Truth in Autobiography* (Cambridge: Harvard University Press, 1960).

2. See W. K. Wimsatt and Monroe Beardsley, "The Intentional Fallacy," *Sewanee Review* 54 (1946): 468–488.

3. See Michel Foucault, "What is an Author?" in *Language, Counter-Memory Practice*, trans. Donald F. Bouchard and Sherry Simon, ed. Donald F. Bouchard (New York: Cornell University Press, 1980), 113–138.

4. See Jacques Derrida, "Signature Event Context," *Glyph I* (Baltimore: Johns Hopkins University Press, 1977), 172–197; and "Limited Inc. abc," *Glyph II* (Baltimore: Johns Hopkins University Press, 1977), 162–254.

5. See Emile Benveniste, "Subjectivity in Language," in *Problems in General Linguistics*, trans. Mary E. Meek (Coral Gables, Fla.: University of Miami Press, 1971), 226.

6. See Michael Ryan, "Self-Evidence," *Diacritics* 10, no. 2 (1980):

7. See Michael Sprinker, "Fictions of the Self: The End of Autobiography," in *Autobiography: Essays Theoretical and Critical*, ed. James Olney (Princeton: Princeton University Press, 1980), 321–342.

8. See Olney's "Introduction," in *Autobiography*, 5ff.

9. Pascal, *Design and Truth*, 60ff.

10. See Bernd Neumann, *Identität und Rollenzwang: zur Theorie der Autobiographie* (Frankfurt/Main: Athenäum, 1970).

11. See, for example, Peter Weiss, *Ästhetik des Widerstands. Roman* (Frankfurt/Main: Suhrkamp, Vol. I, 1975; Vol. II, 1978; Vol. III, 1981).

12. See Michel Leiris, *L'Age d'Homme* (Paris: Gallimard, 1939); English, *Manhood*, trans. Richard Howard (New York: Grossman, 1963).

Sandra Frieden

13. See Christa Wolf, "Subjective Authenticity."

14. See Christa Wolf, "The Reader and the Writer," 181–185, 211–212.

15. See Wolfgang Müller, review of *Christa Wolf*, by Alexander Stephan, NGC, no. 10 (1977): 199–201; and Jürgen Nieraad, "Subjektivität als Thema und Methode realistischer Schreibweise," *Literaturwissenschaftliches Jahrbuch*, NS 19 (1978): 313.

16. See Christa Wolf, "Discussion with Christa Wolf," and "In Touch."

17. See Christa Wolf, *PC* and *DW*, for an example of the confusion that greeted partial publication of the work even before its completion.

18. For this type of criticism, see Alexander Stephan, review of *Kindheitsmuster*, NGC, no. 11 (1977): 178–182; Marcel Reich-Ranicki, "Christa Wolfs trauriger Zettelkasten," *FAZ*, 19 March 1977; Charles Linsmayer, "Die wiedergefundene Fähigkeit zu trauern," *NR* 88 (1977): 472–478; Hans Richter, "Moralität als poetische Energie," *SuF* 29 (1977): 678–681; Annemarie Auer, "Gegenerinnerung," *SuF* 29 (1977): 847–878; "Briefe zu Annemarie Auer," *SuF* 29 (1977): 1311–1322; Hans Mayer, "Der Mut zur Unaufrichtigkeit," *Der Spiegel*, 11 April 1977: 185–190; and Bernd Schick, "Brief eines Nachgeborenen," *SuF* 30 (1978): 422–426.

19. This passage is translated from the German version (*Kindheitsmuster*, [Berlin and Weimar: Aufbau, 1976], 9); it is a significant omission from the English translation.

20. See the reference to the biography by E. v. Bülow (1848) on the jacket of the German version (Darmstadt und Neuwied: Luchterhand, 1979) of *Kein Ort. Nirgends*.

21. See, for example, S. Wirsing, "Das Malheur zu allem Unglück," *FAZ*, 24 March 1979; W. Werth, "Für Unlösbares gibt es keine Form," *SZ*, 4 April 1979; S. and D. Schlenstedt, "*Kein Ort. Nirgends*," *Sonntag*, 12 August 1979; U. Püschel, "Zutrauen kein Unding, Liebe kein Phantom," *NdL* 7 (1979): 134–139; and H.-G. Werner, "Romantische Traditionen in epischen Werken der neueren DDR-Literatur. Franz Fühmann und Christa Wolf," *Zeitschrift für Germanistik* 1 (1980): 398–416.

Unter den Linden: Three Improbable Stories

Hans-Georg Werner

Among the works that are especially significant for the literary-historical context of Christa Wolf's volume of stories, *Unter den Linden*, is E. T. A. Hoffmann's *Kater Murr*[1]; Christa Wolf's title, "New Life and Opinions of a Tomcat," is an explicit allusion. But the recognition of such a connection bespeaks little. It raises the central question concerning whether, in fact, the explicit reference to Hoffmann does not signal a hidden connection to a broader web of appropriated heritage and whether certain intermediate works are relevant to the more obvious literary allusions. It asks what their function is, how and to what purpose Christa Wolf's writings correspond to those of E. T. A. Hoffmann and/or other authors, and finally from what traditions Wolf takes her cues.

Connections to tradition in the realm of art in no way represent a mechanical cause-and-effect relationship. Thus, an investigation that proceeds positivistically to determine such connections as a search for literary stimuli can do justice to neither the dialectics of the literary tradition nor their complicated function. It is, however, useful and necessary to determine what a literary work constitutes as *its* literary prehistory out of a confusing multiplicity of theoretically available traditional sources, to ask about the factors that have contributed to this appropriation and about its resulting social functions. Treated thus, an analysis of a work's allusions to tradition illuminates the uniqueness of the creative mentality that has produced that work. Accordingly, the following comments do not aim primarily to discover authorial intention; their object is, rather, a matter of poetic realization, of the ideological seen not as a characteristic of a person who writes but rather as a motive and function of writing.

An analysis of the connections to the literary heritage in *Unter den Linden*, undertaken in light of the above, can also help to describe Christa Wolf's creative development since *Christa T.* In 1966, Wolf responded to a question concerning her most significant aesthetic experiences with the names of Brecht, Gorky, Seghers, Thomas Mann, Wolfe, and Aragon (BO 59). She has also been deeply impressed by Goethe and the post-Romantics of the nineteenth century: Storm, Fontane, Keller, Stendhal, Flaubert, Tolstoy, and, probably later, Büchner and Dostoevsky (RW 188–189, 197–199, 203–206). Centrally important to their power to stimulate was, to quote Christa Wolf, the fact "that the structure of their works coincides in a very complicated, often totally indirect manner with the structure of their reality," with which these works "wage continual battle—evoking and effecting change" (BO 59). In this context, the appearance of E. T. A. Hoffmann's name may point to a new attitude on Wolf's part toward a new or differently seen reality.

At first glance, the three texts in *Unter den Linden* seem hardly comparable: the fantastic dream-narrative of a woman, the grotesque report of a tomcat, and then something like a piece of utopian literature. As the subtitle of the collection—*Three Improbable Stories*—would already suggest, however, all three prose pieces have one thing in common: they do not generate the illusion that they deal with probable events. The fantastic, the grotesque, the utopian, even the absurd are presented with such authority that they suggest an extreme reality. The organizing principle of the presentation is, in every case, a subject in search of himself/herself or that subject's grotesque negation: the writer-tomcat whose extremely arrogant narrative delivery is based in his presumptuous subjectivity. These shared traits produce formal similarities and technical correspondences and provide the basis for thematic connections among the narratives.

The story "Unter den Linden" is technically the most complicated and textually the most allusive in the volume. The title is multisignificant. Taken alone, it first brings to mind such things as the natural life, love, yearning, sorrow, poesy. The narrative, however, denotes it immediately as the name of the Berlin boulevard. And it becomes apparent with further reading that "Unter den Linden" describes a reality that cannot be reduced to the street that links the Brandenburg Gate with Marx-Engels Square; it is connected, instead, to a consciousness in which simple life, love, yearning, sorrow, and poesy have dominant functions. For the precise geographical descriptions and realistically detailed characterizations are fantastically estranged in the course of the narrative.

E. T. A. Hoffmann's attempt at a similar project constituted a first for German literature—in "Ritter Gluck," a narrative whose external events are, incidentally, fixed in the area between Berlin's Tiergarten, the Brandenburg Gate, and Friedrichstrasse.[2] Hoffmann guided the story that begins with a precise description of everyday situations toward a provocative and confusing conclusion in order to achieve a suggestive demonstration of the discrepancy between socially normal existence and the life—the "insanity"—of the artist. Christa Wolf approaches her topic with a view toward an ultimate resolution of the conflicts—more gently, but also, from the outset, in a more confusing and secretive manner. The author lets us know immediately, in the first sentences, that the narrative's project is personal. An "I" is introduced, and this "I" speaks comfortably and intimately with a "you" (du) about what it "likes" to do, what it "loves." There remains no doubt that we shall be dealing here with the most subjective of matters—a question of happiness. But this "most subjective" is important for things generally significant: the possibility of self-expression, the relationship to reality, the ability to communicate, the potential for credibility, and the inspiration to create poetry. This is indicated by sentences that, admittedly, suggest a certain direction rather than understanding of thought: the narrative "I," having been readmitted to the "League of the Happy Ones," considers it possible to pronounce: "Since I myself have been recently freed from doubt, I will be believed again. I am no longer chained to the facts. I can speak the truth freely. . . . For above all things, we treasure the desire to be known" (UL 7). These sentences, of which the last also alludes to the biblical sense of "being known" (SE 124), hint at the thematic frame of the narrative; it has to do with "coming to oneself," with the conditions of a fulfilled life and a fulfilled literary art.

The filling of this frame is accomplished by way of reporting a dream, for which the street, Unter den Linden, provides the scene. The presentation of dreams permits Christa Wolf to demonstrate the temporal expandability of the moment—that conflation in consciousness of present, past, and future—and to eliminate spatial fixedness together with the temporal. She seeks depth, about which she has written:

> If it's not a property of the material world, it must be the result of an experience, an ability gained through human beings living together over long periods of time that has not only survived, but also developed, because it was useful. So it is tied to us, subjects living in objective conditions. It is the result of unsatisfied needs, the resulting tensions, inconsistencies and tremendous efforts people make to grow beyond themselves or, perhaps, to reach up to themselves. This may be the meaning and task of depth of our consciousness; so we must not abandon it in favor of superficialities. (RW 180–181)

From the depths of the dream the narrator first realizes that her life is under the command of a higher authority. The narrative includes from the outset certain turns of phrase, unclarified at first, but obviously related to each other, that hint at a high command, at courts of law, trial, judgment: "then I dreamed that the day had come," "now I had been ordered to appear," "conspiracy," "that I made it so easy for them," "one is ordered to appear and must obey," "hour, place, and purpose of the hearing are not provided" (UL 8). To these correspond further narrative passages inserted at regular intervals: "to lie before judges' benches, lie down on the bare floor in front of the investigating commission, on the stone floor before the examining committees, lie quietly and, finally, refuse to make a statement" (UL 19); "I am certain that the tests seem to be easy in those precincts, but the penalties for minimal failure are heavy. The motto is: Everything or nothing!, and one is kept in the dark about the way one is supposed to adhere to it" (UL 21); "disposition," "authority" (UL 41–42); "criminals," "crime," "surrounded by witnesses," "proceedings," "piece of evidence," "statement," "court," "it is not their purpose to put me to shame; their job is simply to convict me," "judgment," "no appeal is permitted," "I had walked into the trap," "there must be some authority in this goddamned street with whom one can lodge a complaint: No, says someone next to me. You'd better not count on that" (UL 52–59).

Passages of this kind reflect the situation of a person who feels himself or herself to be at the mercy of a higher authority, an unknown court of law, oppressed by a secret guilt, pursued by imperceivable powers. These remind us of Kafka, above all of his *Trial*, but they do not suggest that Christa Wolf's project here is a literary renewal of a Kafkaesque situation of existential alienation. For while Kafka narrates toward a grotesque and irrevocable final situation, Christa Wolf's prose piece is designed such that the resolution of the reflected conflict is, on the one hand, anticipated without doubt from the outset—the first sentences of the text refer to the "readmission" of the narrator into the "League of the Happy Ones"—and, on the other, realized in the narrative process. At the end of the piece it becomes evident that the anonymous mandate, which had led the narrator to think that "the day had come" and which had caused her to dream of being propelled up and down the street, Unter den Linden, had had the aim of leading the narrator to herself. In the dream, the "I" sees a happy young woman and recognizes herself: "Now everything was explained at one blow. I was meant to find myself again—that was the meaning of the mandate. My body was filled, cell by cell, with a new joy. A whole set of inhibitions left me forever. No misfortune had pressed its mark onto my forehead once and for all. How could I have been so blind as to have submitted to a false verdict" (UL 74)?

Two aspects of this narrative conception are significant for the particular reception of tradition that occurs here. First, the law and the mandate are not of metaphysical origin; they come from the subject. Their ranking as "higher authority" is the necessary result of the fact that the consciously living human being is forced, by his/her own vital interests and by the interests of society, to seek answers to the question concerning which externally given maxims he/she chooses to follow in using his/her margin of freedom.

Second, the law does not remain unrecognized; self-alienation is abolished. The "I" finds herself. The "Kafkaesque" situation is thus alluded to only in order to be conquered. The reception of tradition consists in this case of the "quotation" of a narrative model that permits the concise introduction of a problem of life and narration. But this appropriation is undertaken on the basis of a broader self-understanding and consciousness of tradition, which relativize the quoted narrative model.

Kafka's trial and its related representation of human dependence on superior powers, of self-understanding that has been destroyed at its very foundations, of awareness of the frightening insecurity of the law, have a possible prehistory. Perhaps mediated by Dostoevsky, it reaches back, initially, to German Romanticism—Kleist, Hoffmann[3]—where, in contrast to Kafka, the prospect for a solution of the conflict is not entirely obstructed.

It is more important for understanding *Unter den Linden* to note that the demonstrated reference to Kafka is mediated by the writings of Ingeborg Bachmann. Almost all the motifs and key terms shown to exist in *Unter den Linden* are prefigured in Ingeborg Bachmann's early stories: life balance ("The Thirtieth Year," "A Wildermuth"), self-understanding, self-discovery, and a trial connected with a love affair ("A Step Toward Gomorrah," "Undine Goes," *Der gute Gott von Manhattan* [The Good God of Manhattan][4]). Search for identity,[5] "the day will come" (*TY* 55, 126–127), the relationship between truth and facts (*TY* 137, 143, 156), the problem of language (*TY* 50, 61ff., 101, 180 et passim), "the profit of new horizons against the loss of dreams" (*TY* 3), the authorities, or walking into a trap (*TY* 14, 102, 128).

Christa Wolf's theoretical writings make clear that Ingeborg Bachmann's early stories have confirmed and promoted her own understanding of prose to an extraordinary extent. They accord with Wolf's demand of writers that their work be "incorruptible in its insistence on the one and only experience" and give others "the courage of their own experiences" (RW 193). They were suited to strengthen her in her dislike of narrative clichés and in her sympathetic reception of fairy tales and dreams, and they were able to bring romantic elements closer to her, served her as an example that the "scope of narrative has four dimensions: the three fictive coordinates of the invented characters and the fourth, 'real' dimension of the narrator" (RW 198). And what she praised in Büchner's *Lenz*—"common sense and knowledge along with heightened sensibility," "a fantastic accuracy" (RW 199), Christa Wolf found as well in Ingeborg Bachmann. Above all, however, she prized in Ingeborg Bachmann's stories what she called "inner authenticity": "A voice speaking honestly about its own experience of things certain and uncertain. And, when the voice fails, an honest silence" (IB 83).

In spite of Christa Wolf's open confession of her affinity for the Austrian writer, it is still surprising how frequently and closely the stories of the two writers are connected to each other. Parts of *Unter den Linden* seem to constitute Christa Wolf's private answer to the peer and colleague who lives in another social world—in the connection to Ingeborg Bachmann's tale, "Undine Goes," for instance.

The tension-filled relationship of the human realm to the realm of elemental spirits was explored for German literature in multiple ways by the Romantics—among others by Tieck, Brentano, Arnim, Eichendorff, and Mörike. Fouqué wrote the fairly tale *Undine*, whose narrative core is the motif of the water nymph who yearns for human love and is betrayed by the beloved human. E. T. A. Hoffmann set to music a libretto based on Fouqué's story, with the intention of revealing especially "the mysterious spirit-realm of the Romantics."[6] The motif served Ingeborg Bachmann as a way to construct a poetic representation of the adversity of the spheres occupied by woman, for whom love and immediacy are necessary to existence, and man, forced into his "world of functional utility."[7] Undine's life in the water—"the just water" (TY 172)—is portrayed as a pure, transparent, indeterminate but also homeless and speechless existence; the surface of the water as the barrier that protects from the entanglements of society. Christa Wolf, who has referred emphatically to Bachmann's "daring"—"she does not retreat without a struggle, or fall silent without a word, nor does she abandon the field in resignation" (IB 83)—commented: "Weariness of civilization and doubts about progress are most strongly marked in 'Undine Goes': total alienation of man from himself and his like and romantic protest against it. Romantic not only in the adoption of Fouqué's motif, the figure of Undine, also romantic in attitude, the comparison of commonplace utility thinking with 'a spirit that is destined to no use.' That would have been destined to make a worthy use of itself, that would help to make 'time and death' understandable" (IB 92).

This commentary resounds with fascination and criticism, and these attitudes determine the way in which the Undine-motif is appropriated in "Unter den Linden." The dream-I climbs into the "blue-green tiled fountain" that is located in the interior courtyard of the municipal library: "I lie at the bottom of the fountain, just as I'd often imagined it: to lie before judges' benches, lie down on the bare floor in front of the investigating commission, on the stone floor before the examining committees, lie quietly and, finally, refuse to make a statement. . . . Now I understood that the problem until now had been my lack of heaviness, of specific weight. . . . It satisfied me that I had finally gotten to the bottom." The dreamlike transformation into a water spirit is, therefore, here as well a symbol of transposition into a higher form of existence—the acquisition of specific weight—and of the separation from those above the water's surface. "The faces that appeared over the edge of the pool to look at me did not concern me. The water line divided us. Curiosity and suspicion and malicious joy had no effect on me; and the pain passed, too." In contrast to Bachmann's Undine, Christa Wolf's dream-I does not remain in the cool element, which she describes, by the way, as "my element." Following a call, she emerges voluntarily, "to cast all old experiences to the winds, to go among people once again and to do damage to the taboos" (UL 18–19).

The difference is more significant than it appears at first glance. It marks the point at which Christa Wolf distances herself from Ingeborg Bachmann. In contrast to the writer surrounded by the "Bastille walls"[8] of capitalist reality, Christa Wolf recognizes that it is possible, in her country, to achieve the conditions that should exist. The contradiction between the poetic "I" and society is not, for Wolf, a result of the opposition of two irreconcilable life-spheres, although it may occasionally be comforting and necessary for the poetic "I" to maintain its awareness of its difference, its Melusine nature. Christa Wolf understands the poetic "I" as a productive element in her socialist society. Ingeborg Bachmann, too, was concerned with changing things, with educating with a view toward "new perception, new feeling, new consciousness": "When it grasps a new possibility, art gives us the chance to experience where we stand or where we ought to stand, how things are with us and how they ought to be."[9] Simultaneously, however, she is—deeply frightened—aware of the paradoxical situation of the human in a society that threatens to paralyze all efforts of the intellect: "Here inwardness and sense-connections, conscience and dream—there utilitarian functions, senselessness, phrases and speechless violence."[10] To be sure, she does not capitulate in the face of this paradox, but it does determine her boundaries.

Christa Wolf—inwardly touched by Bachmann's artistic purpose ("a moral one before all morality"[11])—does not need to accept these boundaries. Her efforts for change aim beyond the subjectivity of the individual at society as a whole, at the "creation of new structures of human relations in the present" (SA).

This intended social function of literature is built into the narrative structure of "Unter den Linden." It might thus be useful to give at least a sketchy reconstruction of the basic pattern of the text. The first-person narrator, a woman, speaks to a "you" (du), her lover: she "discovers" herself through the narration of a dream, in which she saw herself as a happy person on the boulevard, Unter den Linden. The narrator-I is thus speaking about her dream-I. Because the narrator-I provides continuous commentary on the dream, and the dream-I reflects, to an equal extent, the experiential realm of the narrator-I, the poetic "I" of the story embraces the narrator-figure and its dream form. The dominating position is assumed alternately by these two elements, although the narrator controls the narrative's beginning and end. This allows the narrative's clear orientation toward social reality.

The Romantic poets, again, were important participants in the literary tradition of discovering devices for the poetic coupling of real experiences with those of the dream world—one need think only of the prose works of Novalis, Tieck, and E. T. A. Hoffmann. These techniques allow Christa Wolf initially to produce a more fanciful, partially fabulous narrative about contemporary experiences. In addition to the use of the Undine-motif, stimulated by Ingeborg Bachmann, we might note, for example, her employment of the motif of the golden fish who accompanies the dream-I on Unter den Linden. Comparable to the little serpent—Serpentina—in "The Golden Pot,"[12] a fairy tale figure here makes everyday life strange; a subtle technique and poetic exploitation of processes of the conscience that can hardly be rationally controlled integrate the figure into the image of common everyday existence.

Above all, however, the combination of real and dream experiences of the poetic "I" allows the presentation of the relationship between the ideal and the real in a fairly brief and inclusive manner, at once subjective and universally valid, imaginary and concrete. In regard to the dream-I, the author has greater technical freedom to develop subjectivity. She can combine the most various elements of reality with far less strain than would be possible if she were limited by realistic description. The representational dream-medium therefore simplifies the figuration of the inner path of the poetic "I" to herself, a path whose expectations, attendant circumstances, implications, and functions are ultimately incommensurate.

At the start of this path, the dream-I experiences an episode of hysteria—an argument with a bus conductor. She seems not to adapt to her surroundings. This is followed by a commentary of the narrator-I on the further progress of the dream-I. Her mission is defined in an analogy to fairy tale: every child knows "that one should run off without a worry and confront everything in a friendly and unprejudiced way" (UL 9). The dream becomes a medium that allows establishing naiveté and uninhibitedness—attributes with which E. T. A. Hoffmann also endowed the heroes of his realistic fairy tales, such that they saw the blind utilitarian striving of their fellow human beings as reprehensible and recognized the poetry of the world.

The degree to which one's surroundings become strange when seen from this perspective is illustrated by the following grotesque dream sequence concerning the changing of the guard at the memorial monument on Unter den Linden: A customary ceremony becomes insignificant and absurd because one of its prevailing ritual steps is missing. (With this, too, "Unter den Linden" is linked to a tradition essentially developed by the Romantics—especially in Hoffmann's grotesque satire of the court in "Kater Murr" and in Arnim's presentation of the "Metamorphoses of Society" [Metamorphosen der Gesellschaft].) Nearly complementing this grotesque image of reality are the appearances of an "Indian with a ruby-red stone in his snow-white turban," of lithe black people "who move as though in a dance" (UL 10–11), of a happy couple, and then of a naively talkative teacher from Thuringia. The contrast among these phenomena points to the juxtaposition that defines the hypothetical construction of the narrative: a free and uninhibited existence opposed to one stiff and constrained.

Positioned among these episodic dream-descriptions, and designed to achieve such contrastive effects, are the first hints of those relics of traditional narratives contained in this prose piece. The narrator-I says: "the girl stepped into my dream. . . . Did I ever tell you about the girl? I probably kept quiet about it, but the story keeps following me like a theme that is repeatedly struck in me. It was held up to me as an example once, at a time when I wanted to hear absolutely nothing of it." The following is then narrated from the perspective of the dream-I: "Then I saw my old friend, Peter, coming out of the university" (*UL* 12). These sentences contain the beginnings of three stories. The story of the girl seems at first to be the most important—a student who loves her instructor, misses her lectures, is guilty of an impropriety as a result of which she is expelled, and now works in a light bulb factory.[13] To this is aligned the story of the "old friend, Peter," the university instructor who, having become an opportunist, has betrayed his wife, Marianne. Finally, the sentence "It was held up to me as an example once, at a time when I wanted to hear absolutely nothing about it" contains a barely perceptible allusion to the story of greatest significance to the narrator-I—the story of her love for a physician who shies away from the dangers of an imprisoning love relationship.

The dream situation allows Christa Wolf to merge these three stories. This happens by way of dreamlike identifications. The instructor whom the girl loves is brought into proximity with and finally subsumed by the figure of Peter. The girl becomes a kind of alter-ego for the poetic "I," for the physician demonstrates the social risks of a love between himself and that poetic "I" by holding up to her the story of the girl. Furthermore, the poetic "I" is forced by a vague feeling of guilt vis-à-vis the dominant moral norms to connect her own situation with that of the girl when she appears before the disciplinary commission herself. The dreamlike associative narrative method, by drawing the figures together, also blurs the boundaries between the different realms of experience, thus superimposing them, as it were. This is not primarily a matter of artistic effect. Christa Wolf's style in "Unter den Linden" is a result of her speculation about the presupposed functionality of literary techniques. In a different but comparable context, she explained: "You have to find writing techniques . . . that manage to free up those almost indissoluble bonds and constrictions that hold us in their grip, to unravel that vast range of elements that have become entwined during our development, so that patterns of behavior in which we thought we were firmly entrenched can be explained, and, where possible (and where necessary), still be changed" (SA). The result of such an effort is an extraordinary complication of the narrative method in "Unter den Linden." This is no stylistic phenomenon. The single text elements are, when taken by themselves, generally transparent and unproblematic. The complication is one of textual structure. The narrative levels intertwine in a manner that parallels the narrative interrelationship between the narrative-I and the dream-I. Furthermore, the "I" lacks self-confidence. Not only narrative-I and dream-I are interdependent; the dream-I alternates among different levels of comprehension of both self and world. The purpose as well as the result of this technique is that the reader—given his/her ability to follow the story—is drawn into the formative process of the subject's coming-to-itself. The dreamlike shifting among I, you, and it, virtually invites the reader to participate in the story with the help of his or her own imagination. The precise description of realistic details gives the contemporary reader the feeling of encountering the reality of his/her own life while penetrating into the story. The polyvalence of the poetic "I," which eludes any attempt to assign it unambivalent meaning; the gliding aspect of the narrative transitions; the alienation of the real, the density of the narrative material, the wealth of allusions—all create a figurative undertow. It is intended to lead the reader to understanding the social significance of subjectivity, to recognizing the connection between the most particular and the most general, and to realizing present circumstances as historically determined, that what is commonly taken for granted can be changed.

Christa Wolf's narrative project bears traces—multiply mediated and modified by a long history of tradition—of romantic origin. The subject encounters a world that is felt in at least certain regards to be alien and inimical, and she can prevail against that world only by disrupting social conventions. Christa Wolf's narrative even contains elements of the anxiety of civilization. The doctor, unprepared to risk love, is referred to as Mr. Everyman—an allusion to that dramatic figure who recognizes the meaninglessness of property and position only in the face of death. This occurs with a social emphasis borne by bitterness: "Mr. Everyman spends his money so that the people's economy might flourish, but he saves his feelings. Colleague Everyman becomes competitive. Comrade Everyman is successful" (UL 51).

The presentation of the relationship between subjectivity and society in "Unter den Linden" is nevertheless different from that found, for instance, in Hoffmann's tales. Subjectivity and humanity were preserved, for the writer of the "Golden Pot," only in art. The realms of art and society—in their bourgeois-capitalist forms as well as in their feudal-absolutist manifestations—appeared in his works as opposing worlds that, although they interconnect, have separate centers that are independent from, indeed in opposition to, each other. This world view provided the basis for the satirical exaggerations, the ironic refractions, the stupendous shocks, and fabulous transitions in Hoffmann's writings, which confronted their readers with the contradictions of social life. For Christa Wolf, the subjective human is a product of socialism— indicative are her repeated reminders of her subject's growth in socialist society and her energetic return again and again to the topic of betrayal—but that subject can, in her opinion, only exist by prevailing in (and occasionally against) that society, such that it contributes to its creation of new humanity and new subjectivity. Subjectivity as a product and as an object of society but, above all, as a factor in its change—this unsettling problem permeates "Unter den Linden."

Socialism has led the poetic "I" and her friend Peter to opt for a revolutionary attitude. Also under the influence of this society Peter becomes a traitor, while the poetic "I" remains true to herself. Nor is Mr. Everyman simply the legitimate result of socialist development. He represents a threatening trend. As a warning contrast figure, Christa Wolf creates the sympathetically drawn character of the old comrade Max, who has been made human and wise by the battle in the class struggle of his time. There is an alternative, then. And Christa Wolf's narrative method aims to make this alternative clear and to lead the reader to a choice—against Peter and for the poetic "I," against Comrade Everyman and for Comrade Max.

Finally, the subjective narrative approach offers a point of departure that allows the author, like the Romantic poets, to turn away from restrictive narrative models and thus to glimpse the possibility of achieving "inner authenticity" for her writing. A subjective condition for this is, for Christa Wolf, the willingness and the strength of the author "to express the living and thinking processes they are embroiled in directly in their work process" (SA). Authentic prose, in Christa Wolf's sense, must be based entirely on the inner realities of the author's life. The role played by truth in "Unter den Linden" thus becomes clear. It is touched upon already in the first sentences: "I am no longer chained to facts. I can speak the truth clearly." This initially puzzling antinomy hints at two things: facts are not unimportant for poetic speech, but they are secondary; our acquaintance with the narrative contents allows us to understand "facts" to mean events of social life insofar as these can be registered as unambiguous, noncontradictory, compact quantities. Truth seems, in comparison, profoundly subjective. In this category belong also, and especially, those experiences that cannot be verified—love, anxieties, images of dreams and fairy tales; facts, however, generally assumed to be taken for granted, from this perspective appear ambiguous and problematic. The contours of social reality become uncommon, sharper, more worthy of contemplation. A unique relationship is established between the fantastic and the true, again one is reminded of the idiosyncrasies of romantic narrative methods. The dream-I in Christa Wolf's story reflects this relationship: "on the day for which I'm waiting, because then there will no longer be anyone standing between me and those who want to believe me, not even I myself—on that distant day someone will tear the craziest inventions from my hands as pure truth and will force me, as a result, always to speak the truth, nothing but the pure, crazy truth" (UL 40–41).

In order to clarify what Christa Wolf means with statements of this sort, we must turn once again to Ingeborg Bachmann, whose stories —as becomes ever more evident—possess a downright definitive function in the allusive net of "Unter den Linden." Bachmann's story, "A Wildermuth," rigorously pursues the question of truth. The judge Wildermuth, raised from childhood to acknowledge truth—in this case to believe in the necessity and the possibility of the precise linguistic reproduction of external life events—this judge is profoundly disturbed by a trial he must conduct against an accused man of the same name. For he must recognize that the truth of the crime remains inaccessible to him, despite all the "'simple, hard facts that cannot be overlooked'" (TY 144); grotesquely, not even the truth about a button can be determined. The name equivalence with the accused finally forces the judge to question the truth of his own life. In the process, he arrives at various thoughts: "Yes, what then is the truth about myself, about anyone? The truth can be defined only in respect of point-like, minute moments of action, steps in the process of feeling, the most minute steps, about one drop after another out of the thought stream. But then it would no longer be possible to deduce that a person had such massive characteristics as 'thrifty,' 'good-natured,' 'cowardly,' 'thoughtless'" (TY 157).

Pursuing the truth of his life, he experiences, finally, his body's speechless agreement with the body of a waitress. The notion that truth can be captured in words becomes, for him, deeply suspect. He speaks about the fact that "we employ the most useful fag-end of the useful truth to put the noose around someone's neck"; he believes that truth can be grasped in words only "if one doesn't move, doesn't ask many questions, rests content with the crudest facts": "Then the result is a continual, cheap agreement between object and word, feeling and word, deed and word. . . . Indolent, apathetic word set on agreement at all costs" (TY 169). Truth seems to him, finally, only conceivable as a transcendental correspondence between subject and word: "A mute awareness compelling me to cry out, to shout out about all truths. . . . A truth of which no one dreams, which no one wants" (TY 170). The problem of truth thus becomes for Ingeborg Bachmann, a careful student of the linguistic philosophy of Ludwig Wittgenstein, at its root a problem of language.

It is this for Christa Wolf as well, although she attempts to resolve it in a different way. The withdrawal to a transcendental union between subject and world and the escape into silence contradict her awareness of social responsibility. However, she accepts Ingeborg Bachmann's thoughts regarding the difficult relationships between truth and word. The "bare, crazy truth" can, according to her, be formulated only in a language that does not set out to label humans and things, to reduce them to their utilitarian functions, to appropriate or destroy them, in other words, only in a language that validates the particular of every human being: his memories, his self-understanding, his vision of the future, his anxieties, his hopes. Bachmann's stories thus mediate connections to the sort of criticism practiced by Hoffmann in "Kater Murr" or Heine in his "Reisebilder," that is, directed at the strictly utilitarian language of the bourgeoisie.

Christa Wolf's thoughts on language theory also lead to the central theme of the tale: the right of the "I" to validate her own worth as well as her right to happiness and love. This is motivated not only by concern for the individual but also by social responsibility. Love includes a willingness to take a risk that is as dangerous to life as it is necessary. For Christa Wolf, neither political determination nor social understanding and human beauty are thinkable without this willingness. Love is first and foremost, however, the signal of a fulfilled individual experience and the magic word that fends off those external constraints that prohibit the individual from self-realization (coming to oneself).

Here Christa Wolf is again pursuing largely romantic intentions. This does not mean that she appropriates romantic ideas. But her writing shows an affinity with the romantic pursuit of the subject's self-assertion in the face of bourgeois demands for exploiting everything and everyone. Friedrich Schlegel's question—"What is the meaning of unconditional striving and progress if there is no pause, no center?"[14]—is also posed, accordingly, in "Unter den Linden." And Brentano's words about the fictive author of his novel, *Godwin*, points to a condition of life and literature that continues to unsettle Christa Wolf: "The meaning of his writing is clearly enough articulated—he had paid with his youth and his life for the fact that love in our age is imprisoned, that the circumstances of life are more highly valued than life itself, and that baseness can conquer enthusiasm. He employed his last strength to save others from this sacrifice. His fate was a battle with love; the battle for love was his profession."[15]

In "Unter den Linden," happiness and love are problems primarily in the life of woman; man, more strongly bound to the mechanics of the practical life, appears chiefly in the role of one who ranks love below his ambition, his pride, and his need for security. These views again come close to those of Ingeborg Bachmann. They further indicate once more the great extent to which Christa Wolf's writing is rooted in the intellectual world around and after 1800 that was influenced by the German Romantics. In Fouqué's work, Undine has more spiritual strength than the knight, who is dependent on social norms and thoroughly insecure. In "Die neue Melusine," which he counted among his "small, romantic tales,"[16] Goethe portrayed a man's relationship with a creature of the elements; he questioned the way in which socially determined motives—monetary greed, addiction to pleasure, self-love—lead to the man's faithlessness, his lack of respect for the Other, and lead the loving woman into a tragic situation. Friedrich Schlegel posed the question of woman's self-worth, her relationship to man, and the social implications of this relationship most decisively. Protesting against sex typology based on the opposition of platonic and physical love, according to which woman's greatest virtue was unconditional surrender to and complete assimilation with man, he analyzed in *Lucinde* the conditions of bourgeois marriage, in which the man loved "only the gender" in the woman, the woman, in turn, "only the degree of his natural qualities and of his bourgeois existence"[17] in the man.

Schlegel was strongly influenced in this work by his interest in the personality development of women. Revitalizing the old ideal of the androgyne, he advocated balancing out flamboyant femininity and exaggerated masculinity to achieve "full, complete humanness."[18] As the holiest of nature's wonders and the pure fire of noblest passion, he enthusiastically praised the sensual pleasure of lovers who have broken through the sex roles imposed on them by social restriction.

In keeping with the direction of Friedrich Schlegel's thoughts, Christa Wolf hones the problematic that underlies "Unter den Linden" sharply in her "improbable story," "Self-Experiment. Appendix to a Report." She describes stages of the experimental transformation of a woman into a man and analyses the experiences gathered in this process. The poetic construction that forms the external framework of the story's plot—the utopianlike metamorphosis of a woman—enables, by means of the grotesque alteration of the narrator's social role, an alienation of social relationships that aims at social criticism. If one seeks literary forebears for such a project, one will again find them—in the realm of German-language literature—primarily in the Romantic period. Hoffmann, for instance, provided in his "Nachricht von einem gebildeten jungen Mann" (Report on an educated young man) a very early example of the potential for exposing the social machine through representing such role-reversal; in Hoffmann an ape presents himself as a man of society.

Christa Wolf's "Self-Experiment" proceeds from a humorous concept: the experimental subject lets herself be transformed into a man because, paradoxically, she loves the man who has prepared and programmed this scientific experiment. The end, however, introduces an angry, sarcastic strain: the woman who has been transformed into a man has reconnoitered—like a spy—man's world from the inside and has discovered that this world, while kept in constant rotation by male ambition, is nonetheless a world without subjectivity, feeling, dreams, or imagination.

The theme of "Self-Experiment" is, then, the relationship of men to life—when judged from the perspective of woman. The basic notion is that men protect themselves from reality by means of their rationalism. The woman who writes the report accuses her professor of attempting to apprehend the world by means of a "net of numbers, diagrams, and calculations." "Like a criminal caught in the act with whom one need have no further dealings. From whom one can dissociate oneself—the cleverest way of doing so by reeling off endless facts, and then passing them off as scientific research" (SE 121).

The proximity of these formulations to Ingeborg Bachmann's discussions regarding the relationship of truth and facts is clear. Unmistakable, however, is again the kinship with elements of the romantic world view. One is reminded of Novalis's and Hoffmann's polemics—in "Klein Zaches" or "Meister Floh," for instance—against the rationalistic attempts of science to explain the world.

Christa Wolf's appropriation of romantic attitudes includes their transformation in this case as well. Novalis, Hoffmann, and several other Romantics turned against scientific methods of thinking because they, inadequate to the transcendental essence of the world, would therefore depoeticize it. In Christa Wolf's rejection of a scientifically based fact fanaticism, the aspect of cognitive theory plays no role. The socialist author warns against a blind faith in science by questioning the socially productive function of science. She does this not only in regard to the consequences of modern scientific discoveries and their possible endangerment of mankind but also in regard to the everyday role of the sciences in social life. She overlooks, in the process, the fact that the progressive elimination of nonquantifiable subjectivity from the sciences has released mighty powers of a destructive as well as and above all of a productive kind. She neglects the fact that the vital humanizing role of the sciences for humanity cannot be secured by retarding or even revoking its progress in the objective quantification of all natural and social processes. It can be secured, rather, only by society's determination of science's function. For Christa Wolf, it is simply important that those experiences, motives, subjective desires—the incomprehensibles of human life that reject every scientific analysis—be recognized in the order of social life. And in this regard it is for her, and here she encounters the Romantics once again, a matter of defending literature.

Accordingly, "Self-Experiment" presents for consideration not only the relationship between truth and facts but also the connection between truth and language. Turning to the professor, the report-writer states: "you . . . with your superstitious worship of measurable results, have made me suspicious of those words of my inner language which might now help me to contradict the unreal neutrality of this report by confronting it with my real remembrance" (SE 113). The connections between truth and inner, poetic language on the one hand and between fact fanaticism and the unreal neutrality of a scientifically normalized language on the other are here directly identified.

This problematic receives its specific turn in "Self Experiment" through allocating to woman's sphere the immediate experiences of reality, inner language, willingness to take risks, openness to present and future; the male sphere, in contrast, contains the worship of facts, coldness and distance, utilitarianism and ambition. The emphasis of the narrative reveals Christa Wolf's position with an unambiguity that is angrily melancholy, although not entirely hopeless. The woman writer of the report who threatened to become a man discovers the subjective motives for this experiment on her as a result of her metamorphosis. She wanted to get behind the mask of the beloved professor and achieves her goal. She finds out that he wanted to get rid of her, the loving woman, because he knows that he cannot love. The experimental subject's recognition of this motivates her decision to reverse the transformation: she wants to attempt to love.

293

This construction directs the reader's attention primarily to the recognition that women's emancipation cannot be simply a matter of integrating women into the traditional male world. Emancipation in the sense of social, professional, and legal equality of women is taken for granted in Christa Wolf's utopian sketch. The demand for emancipation that her writing makes goes beyond that. In response to a question regarding this, Christa Wolf explained: "Emancipation here [in the GDR—H.-G.W.], economic, social, material emancipation of women has come quite far. I've noticed this especially in comparison to other countries, the USA, for instance. . . . But we are now entering the phase in which one needs to ask questions about women's emancipation, I mean about the meaning, about the direction in which this emancipation will now develop after the resolution of very important basic questions. And that's what I'm concerned with in . . . 'Self-Experiment.'"[19]

The option of the report-writer in favor of her female individuality, of a woman's life, receives wide-ranging significance in the narrative: the task of human history is assigned to woman, to demonstrate the equal validity of her specific potential and ability, and more—to regenerate society with this potential, these abilities. For—as Christa Wolf has her report-author argue—the male privileges established over centuries have effected a social cleavage "that gives women the rights to sorrow, hysteria, and the vast majority of neuroses while granting them the pleasure of dealing with the outpourings of the soul . . . and with the vast, virtually inexhaustible sector of fine arts," while the men "hoist the world onto [their] shoulders" and devote themselves "unflinchingly to the realities . . . business, science, and world politics" (SE 128).

These ideas also connect to those of Ingeborg Bachmann, most directly to reflections on the role of women in "Undine Goes" and "A Step towards Gomorrah." In the latter story, the following describes the reaction of a woman to her thoughts about her husband's return: "Charlotte started, quickly memorized her duties: meet Franz at the station tomorrow morning, set the alarm, be fresh, rested, give the impression of being pleased" (TY 106–107). Similar to this is the narrator's description to the professor of his familial situation in "Self-Experiment": "Your mother's good mood, your wife's cheerfulness. Both those women have you surrounded by highly sensitive radar systems which transmit to them your every emotional impulse, no matter how slight. Your wife's face is ready to serve as a mirror, that's what it is. And the object for the mirror: you, always you" (SE 130). Both examples point to the fact that women do not live but are lived.

Ingeborg Bachmann, too, regards women's self-determination not only as an act of individual emancipation but also as an opportunity to create a new form of human relationships. In her story, "A Step towards Gomorrah," her main character reflects:

Her kingdom would come and when it came she would no longer be measurable, no longer estimable by an alien measure. In her kingdom a new measure was in force. Then it could no longer be said: she is like this, and like that, attractive, unattractive, sensible, silly, faithful, unfaithful, scrupulous or unscrupulous, unapproachable or consumed by adventures. She knew what it was possible to say and in what categories people thought, who was capable of saying this or that and why. She had always loathed this language, every imprint that was stamped upon her and that she had to stamp upon somebody —this attempted murder of reality. But when her kingdom came this language could no longer be valid, then this language would pass judgment on itself. (TY 126–127)

In regard to Mara, her friend, her creation, she plans the following: "But she would teach Mara to speak, slowly, exactly and not to permit any clouding by the common language. She would educate her, hold her to something which very early on, because she had found no better word, she had called loyalty. She insisted on this alien word because she could not yet insist on the most alien of all words. Love. Since no one knew how to translate it" (TY 127). Love—also Christa Wolf's seminal word—means change:

It was time for the change of shift, and now she could take over the world, name her companions, establish the rights and duties, invalidate the old pictures and design the first new ones. For it was the world of pictures that remained after everything had been swept away that had been condemned by the sexes and said of the sexes. The pictures remained when equality and inequality and all attempts to define their nature and their legal relationship had long become empty words and had been replaced by new empty words. . . . I wasn't born into any picture, thought Charlotte. That is why I feel like breaking off. That is why I want a counterpicture, and I want to construct it myself. No name yet. Not yet. . . . To hope for the kingdom. Not the kingdom of men and not that of women. . . . Not this, not that. (TY 130)

This taxing of the soul goes beyond all strength. The story ends with indications of total depression. However, at the conclusion of "Self-Experiment" the narrator opts for a new act of spiritual strength. "Now my experiment lies ahead: the attempt to love. Which incidentally can also lead to fantastic inventions—to the creation of the person one can love" (SE 131). This decisively different turn at the end is possible for Christa Wolf because, for her, the subject's demand for and right to self-realization do not have to be crushed by the mechanisms of social life; the subject has the chance, rather, to influence these mechanisms and thus to make her way through and against these structures.

As a result, the social-critical aspect in Christa Wolf's "Self-Experiment" is much more pronounced than in "A Step towards Gomorrah." Christa Wolf's opposition of a sensitive subject in the process of vital development with a society that unfeelingly reproduces itself has more in common with the hard confrontation of the ideal and the real as it is explored by the German Romantics and particularly by E. T. A. Hoffmann. More tenuous is its connection to Bachmann's insistence on subjectivity and directness and the related aggressive disclosure of the depravation and emptying of human beings who have subjected themselves to the bestial laws of capitalist reproduction.

It is significant that Christa Wolf's story most blatantly critical of social phenomena is also most directly connected to E. T. A. Hoffmann. The "New Life and Opinions of a Tomcat" refers already in the title to Hoffmann's "Life and Opinions of the Tomcat Murr." Christa Wolf revives Hoffmann's figure of the tomcat who bristles with vanity. As a result of his ability to conform unresistingly to the dominant norms of social life and of his talent for devouring and storing in his mind the raw material of "culture," the tomcat reacts like a human being who is at once thoroughly without substance and extremely arrogant. She uses this poetic model to create a satire of the rationalistic addiction that wants to program and to control all human events.

The tomcat lives in the home of a professor of applied psychology who is working with his colleagues on the development of a "system for the maximal health of body and soul," reduced to "SYMAHEBS," and to create thereby the conditions for "TOHUHA," that is, "total human happiness."

The comical radicality of the project leads to the absurd: for example, the characterization of the "soul" as a reactionary conceit (UL 83), the determination of woman's inferiority to man, belles lettres as an unproductive branch of the economy, and the reduction of truth to utility. In the interest of doing away with all "factors that inhibit achievement" (UL 84), it finally becomes necessary to program the human being as an "entity of reflexes" that, when managed from a single control center, responds to stimuli in a way that is precisely predictable, with a deviation of plus/minus zero (UL 110).

However, not only the intellectual results but also the surrounding circumstances carry the undertaking ad absurdum. The scientists are incapable of maintaining an awareness of their assumptions. They describe with "NH" the notion of the "normal human being," whose creative thinking has been amputated—together with faithfulness to convictions, daring, selflessness, mercy, imagination, aesthetic sensitivity, reason, and sexuality. This causes the tomcat, in his Bachmannian-Wolfian deliberations on the topic of "language and reality" to comment (with the help of Tallyrand) as follows: "At that moment I understood that human beings employ their language not only to make themselves understood, but also to hide from themselves that which has already been comprehended" (UL 114). Ultimately the events in the home of the professor, observed by the tomcat, refute the professor's basic scientific thesis that human happiness and achievement potential can be programmed. The professor's insistence on his theory not only results in an ulcer and makes him impotent in his marriage but allows him finally to get mixed up in a half-senile and vaguely malicious passion for an impertinent young girl.

Christa Wolf's satire refers at one level to a hypertrophic systemization of thought that hindered the development of scientific and social life in the GDR before 1970. On another level, however, it expands —not least because of the grotesque narrative situation and perspective —to a broader-ranging critique of civilization. But Christa Wolf's attack on "progress-bourgeois" (*UL* 109) is as lacking in opposition to progress *per se* as was Hoffmann's tomcat-satire in socially retrograde tendencies. E. T. A. Hoffmann used the tomcat Murr to make visible the dangers latent in the bourgeois way of life. The consequences of being corrupted by the desire for property and prestige could be demonstrated with extreme pointedness when exemplified by the tomcat; thus presented, they did not seem forced or exaggerated. Christa Wolf's appropriation of Hoffmann's novellistic figure is motivated by a similarly directed narrative intention. The attribution of "common sense" to a tomcat reveals this concept's modes of thought and argument to be completely useless. Marx and Engels repeatedly attacked this notion, that equates the simple with the just, the rationally thinkable with the possible, the middle road with the path of virtue; this concept considers itself infallible, and its total system of thought represents merely a specialized scientific form. Christa Wolf's ridicule of "common sense" corresponds to Ingeborg Bachmann's assertion: "Looked at from a distance, 'healthy human reason' shrinks and assumes a suspicious similarity to a grain of stupidity."[20] The grotesque is for Christa Wolf, therefore, also a means of giving a concise form to the socially average which, because of its nature, generally remains out of sight; in this way she enables a valuative grasp while simultaneously suggesting its general significance without representing it as something of socially definitive or future significance. Because the tomcat functions as the narrator-figure and because all the events in the professor's house are filtered through "the unusual—one could say distorted— world view" (*UL* 121) of the tomcat, the aesthetic dimensions of this figure determine also the satirical perspective of the world the tomcat presents.

It remains to ask about the general function of the allusions to tradition that dominate in *Unter den Linden*. First, we can ascertain that they have simplified the matter of coping in literature with the increasingly complicated dialectic of life under socialism. *Christa T.* had formulated experiences and problems similar to those in *Unter den Linden*. But because of its fixation on a poetic figure whose path toward life-fulfillment led, via her inner consistency, to a position at the edge of society, *Christa T.* had—despite the many narrative techniques erected as barriers against this danger—slipped occasionally into a precious sentimental mode.[21] Christa Wolf's attempt, underscored by references to Theodor Storm, to construct from an inner core an individual who, although vulnerable and wounded, was fundamentally healthy; the attempt at poetic sublimation of the process by which "the conflict between willing something and the inability to do it thrust[s] [the human being] into a corner of life" (CT 97)—these intentions elevated inwardness to a level at which it could not be artistically maintained, as indicated by the many built-in cliché elements of the book's last part. The references in *Unter den Linden* to narrative tradition originating in the Romantic period and strongly mediated by Ingeborg Bachmann made it possible to reach an uncompromised subjective narrative impulse. At the same time, they enabled the suggestion of multiple connections between subjectivity and society as well as sharpening the contours of the contradictions.

It is noteworthy as well that the project of these most recent writings of Christa Wolf pays much closer and more consistent attention to their function, that is, to prompt the reader's intellectual activity. Excited by the "question concerning change, . . . of the forms and possibilities of change, the obstacles confronting it" (D 71), Christa Wolf wants with her writings to assure that her readers do not react to what has been transmitted by society in a routine and opportunistic manner. For this reason she makes strange that which can be apparently taken for granted. She has taken the principle of alienation from Brecht; but forms and techniques—the fantastic, the representation of dreams, fairy tale elements, the socially critical grotesque, the absurd—derive to a great extent from a tradition that extends back to German Romanticism.

Christa Wolf's poetic conception does not set out to impose upon her public a complex of presentations and opinions in the most convincing way possible. The connection to tradition that she produces in her narratives implies the rejection of epic methods of representation that hide their subjective reality behind the appearance of objectivity. Christa Wolf's narratives aim, by insisting on experiences that are presented as subjective, to give the readers the courage of their personal experiences and, in this way, to let them discover the paths to themselves and to a social position firmly grounded in the subjective. In this connection, her narrative gesture leaves no doubt that her works are not addressed to a reader-collective of greater or smaller size but rather to individuals. The author explained: "Epic prose should be a genre which undertakes to penetrate along paths not yet traveled into the innermost parts of this individual, the reader of prose. Into the very inmost part, where the nucleus of the personality develops and consolidates" (RW 201).

The tradition to which Christa Wolf has turned confirms her assumption that the poetic strength necessary to achieve this depends on at least three conditions:

1. The poetic subject enters into the prose and thereby establishes the conditions for communicative contact between subject and subject;

2. In the process, the poetic subject places itself into the conflicts that it transfers to the hypothetical readers of its texts—the writings of Bachmann and Hoffmann (consider merely his figure of the "traveling enthusiast" or his Kapellmeister Kreisler) can function precisely in this regard as exemplary;

3. Writing is oriented equally in respect to subjective and to socially relevant problems that, if brought to consciousness, can initiate the self-motivation of individuals.

It is evident that Christa Wolf considers her own experience, her own life material, as the only appropriate subject matter for her prose. In this regard she is in accord once again with the German Romantics and with Ingeborg Bachmann, who—entirely surrounded, as it were, by an all-powerful tradition—could achieve the breakthrough to innovative and individualistic literature only by falling back on herself. But while the Romantics sought access to the world of poetry on the "inward path" and while Ingeborg Bachmann wanted to assure herself of the truth of her existence via the absolute directness of her poetry, for Christa Wolf it's a matter of releasing those internal powers that are captured in the innermost regions of the subject and of making their force, which she compares to "the energies bound up in the atom" (RW 201), useful for the development of socialist society.

In the process, she appropriates the Romantics' aversion to rationalism, achievement orientation, and material productivity without much criticism.[22] Social practice—work—seems to her in considering the contemporary social situation hardly a possible method of conquering the problems of social coexistence but rather almost exclusively a means of repressing the problems of subjective existence—a protection against the risk-filled self-realization of the individual through love. Now, no doubt the development and progress of socialist society assume the spiritual strength for love in as many of its numbers as possible. Nothing binds the human being more strongly to his/her surroundings than love. But if this connection is to become socially productive, it needs work—the basis of all relationships between human beings and their environment. Christa Wolf leaves this whole complex unacknowledged; this may be connected to the polemic, immanent in the stories, against an attitude that regards the success gained through work absolutely, as the only useful value of life; this may also be explained by Christa Wolf's conditions for her writing and the resulting subjective difficulties of configuration. Finally, however, it is the result of the fear "that technology and economy [we could add: science—H.-G. W.] will degenerate to ends in themselves and then adhere to their own destructive laws."[23] From this notion emerges a romantic image of the world, in which the laws of material production are opposed to those demands of humanity that rise from subjectivity.

The effects of this conception on Christa Wolf's writings do not have a lot to do with their presentation of society. The subjective narrative method relativizes the narrative perspective. The fantastic, gro-

tesque, absurd, fairy-tale-like, utopian forms of reflection presuppose—
and thereby also legitimatize—one-sidedness and exaggeration.

Not relativized is the notion of subjectivity that underpins the
narrative method. In 1964 Christa Wolf had announced: "We are just
beginning to write the first sentences of other stories . . . stories of people working hard, often to the limits of their endurance, of people who
have made up their minds to think of 'happiness' as being productive,
not as a chance to be indolent, and of 'unhappiness' as the loss of opportunity to be creative, not as the loss of possessions" (S 25). The concept
of the productive person that obtains here is reduced, in the stories in
Unter den Linden, to creative productivity. Definitive for the creative
power of subjectivity are mainly those human faculties, which—like
sensitivity, dream, conscience, imagination, and memory—guide the
inner life of an individual as well as faculties like observation, thinking, and speaking, insofar as these also have that primary function. This
perspective and the resulting formulative inclination have a socially
productive function. On the one hand, the poetic concern with the
differentiation, deepening, and stabilization of socialist subjectivity is
oriented toward the formation of humanity, self-confidence, solidarity,
and political faith. On the other hand, this conception makes it nearly
impossible to give a balanced presentation of the contradictory complexity of the system of reciprocal actions between individual and society. Above all, Unter den Linden makes evident that the technical devices of prose writing had to be strained beyond endurance in order to
do justice to all the necessary references to reality. And still, an important element remains almost incomprehensible: the practical possibilities of the individual to have a productive effect on her environment.
According to the project of the "improbable stories," the individual
only finds the way to himself/herself (and, thereby, also finds an end)
by means of an internal process. The "active link" of the subject "with
what is really going on in society" (IB 90)—recognized by Christa Wolf
as a historical necessity—is not the object of the stories in Unter den
Linden nor the target of their strategic effect. The poetic subject does
not call upon the subjectivity of the hypothetical reader as agent of material social change, or it does so only with considerable mediation.

Christa Wolf's stories thus harbor an affective contradiction.
They assume the unlimited perfectibility of socialist society, legitima-
tizing the great expectations for literature's effectiveness. But they treat
that factor that effects social progress—namely the productive and useful reciprocal activity between individuals and their society, mani-
fested in highly various forms of social coexistence and cooperation
and in social norms, institutions, and organizations—either not at all or
only marginally. In the stories, society is opposed to the individual as
an abstract entity that is, to be sure, specified in historical-political and
physical terms by means of a plethora of concrete details, but that remains unspecific in its connection to the individual because that connection is not established in terms of subjective social practice. Self-re-

alization thus does not appear as a process, as a theoretical-useful working-one's-way-up to an understanding of the present time and the resultant working-out of the individual's latent possibilities; instead, this self-realization appears as an event, as a *return* to the self that is possible only by resisting external demands. Because this self is not reflected in light of its historical determination and functionality and because it is comprehended in opposition to the dynamics of technical, economic, and scientific developments, it even faces the danger of being misunderstood and maltreated in the conservative sense.

Christa Wolf's concept of subjectivity is also grounded in the tradition to which the stories in *Unter den Linden* generally refer. Neither for E. T. A. Hoffmann, Friedrich Schlegel, Arnim, Brentano nor for Ingeborg Bachmann was work a means to productive integration into society. On the contrary, in their opinion work trapped the human being in a social cycle that not only reproduced but even increased the alienation of the human being. If, with Christa Wolf, one understands self-realization in the socialist sense, then this task involves everyone and thus also requires single individuals to cooperate in improving general conditions for their universal realization. The activity of the subject assumed necessary for the achievement of self-realization must thus be internal *and* external. The hoped-for productivity of creative writing would logically have to include the impulse for renewed, revised, increased practical activity.

But—this needs to be emphasized once again—the strategic effect of the stories treated here would be misunderstood if one were to take their object to be the "inner life" of a few single individuals. The presentation of the stories and the expressed intentions of Christa Wolf leave no doubt that the author is reaching out to all society via the single reader and hopes to achieve an objective universal effect by refraction through several singular subjects. In this regard, she is once again different from Ingeborg Bachmann, for whom the social isolation of the human subject was hopeless, and also from the Romantics, for whom the achievement of the human ideal seemed possible only in the realm of poetry, art, God, or in "simple" forms of life that were more or less outside society. Christa Wolf's conception of the effect of her prose, in contrast, demonstrates a certain kinship with the Classical idea of an "aesthetic education toward humanity." As a program for social change, this idea was utopian. As long as individual humanity opposed the social interests of the exploiting classes, the influence on social development by "aesthetic education" was of little note. Under the conditions of socialism, such a concept may perhaps again achieve socially useful significance. Just how it might be related to other notions of aesthetic effect, what specific possibilities it contains, and where it fails—these questions remain to be considered.

Notes

This essay was first published as "'Unter den Linden' von Christa Wolf," *Erworbene Tradition: Studien zu Werken der sozialistischen deutschen Literatur*, ed. Günter Hartung, Thomas Höhle, and Hans-Georg Werner (Berlin/Weimar: Aufbau, 1977), 256–298. That publication is a slightly modified version of Werner's earlier article, "Zum Traditionsbegriff der Erzählungen in Christa Wolfs 'Unter den Linden,'" *WB* 4 (1976): 36–64. It is reprinted here in translation with the permission of the author.

1. E. T. A. Hoffmann. *Lebensansichten des Katers Murr nebst fragmentarischer Biographie des Kapellmeisters Johannes Kreisler in zufälligen Makulaturblättern* (1820/22).

2. For a translation of this story, see *Tales of E. T. A. Hoffmann*, trans. and ed. Leonard J. Kent and Elizabeth C. Knight (Chicago and London: University of Chicago Press, 1969), 3–13; henceforth abbreviated Kent and Knight.

3. See Anna Seghers, *Über Kunstwerk und Wirklichkeit*, ed. and intro. Sigrid Bock, vol. 1 (Berlin/GDR: Akademie-Verlag, 1970), 150. See also Seghers, "Die Reisebegegnung," in *Sonderbare Begegnungen* (Berlin/Weimar: Aufbau, 1973), 109–148.

4. See Bachmann, *Der gute Gott von Manhattan, Die Zikaden, zwei Hörspiele* (Munich: Deutscher Taschenbuch Verlag, 1963).

5. Ingeborg Bachmann, *The Thirtieth Year*, trans. Michael Bullock (New York: Holmes and Meier, 1987); henceforth cited in text as TY. The connection to Bachmann has been noted already by Sigrid Damm and Jürgen Engler, "Notate des Zwiespalts und Allegorien der Vollendung." *WB* 7 (1975): 49f. See also Sara Lennox's essay, "Christa Wolf and Ingeborg Bachmann: Difficulties of Writing the Truth," in this volume.

6. E. T. A. Hoffmann to Friedrich Baron de la Motte Fouqué, 15 August 1812, in *E. T. A. Hoffmanns Briefwechsel*, collection and commentary by Hans Müller und Friedrich Schnapp, vol. 1 (Munich: Winkler, 1967–1969), 347.

7. Bachmann, "Frankfurter Vorlesungen," in *Bachmann: Eine Einführung* (Munich: Piper, 1963), 20.

8. Hoffmann to Fouqué, September 1816, in *Hoffmanns Briefwechsel*, vol. 3, 42.

9. Bachmann, "Frankfurter Vorlesungen," 17.

10. Ibid., 20.

11. Ibid., 14.

12. See Kent and Knight, 14–92.

13. Cf. "Diary," 71.

14. *Kritische Friedrich-Schlegel-Ausgabe*, ed. Ernst Behler et al., vol. 5, *Dichtungen* (Munich: F. Schönigh, 1962), 26.

15. Clemens Brentano, *Werke*, ed. Friedrich Kemp, vol. 2 (2d ed. Munich: Hanser, 1973), 453f.

16. Letter to Charlotte von Stein, 10 August 1807. Quoted from *Goethes Werke*, (Weimarer Ausgabe, Weimar 1887–1919), section IV, vol. 19, 386.

17. *Kritische Friedrich-Schlegel-Ausgabe*, 33.

18. Ibid., 13.

19. "Das wird man bei uns anders verstehen." UZ-Gespräch mit der bekannten DDR-Autorin Christa Wolf, *Unsere Zeit* (Düsseldorf), 2 November 1974.

20. *Der gute Gott von Manhattan*, 49.

21. See Horst Haase, "Nachdenken über ein Buch," *NdL* 4 (1969): 176; Hermann Kähler, "Christa Wolfs Elegie," *SuF* 1 (1969): 257.

22. See Haase, 182f.

23. Christa Wolf, in *NdL* 1 (1971): 70.

Dream, Fairy Tale, and the Literary Subtext of "Unter den Linden"

Brigitte Peucker

C hrista Wolf's "Unter den Linden" (1969) presents itself as the oral narration of a dream to an other—a "you" (du)—in a context reminiscent of the "tell me your dreams" situation of Freudian analysis.[1] In telling the story of her dream, the narrator refers to both the Freudian discourse and fairy tale elements; these constitute forms of both commentary and dream proper. I intend to examine briefly Wolf's use of dream and fairy tale and to ask what additional mode of hermeneutic engagement they encode. At every point in the closely woven texture of Wolf's narrative to pull at one thread—be it political, biographical, or literary—is to loosen the rest;[2] hence, when I speak of one of these meanings I do not intend to do so at the expense of the others.

Only after having had her dream about a walk down the boulevard Unter den Linden can the narrator finally speak, as she claims at the outset, about the street: "Now I can finally talk about it" (7). The fiction of the dream frees her from what she calls "the facts" and allows her, instead, to speak "the truth": "I am no longer chained to the facts. Now I am free to tell the truth" (7). With these words, "free to tell the truth," we are alerted to the kind of double-talk that Wolf will use repeatedly, and we sense that at stake in this project is something in addition to the "inner truth" revealed by dreams. At times opaque, seemingly hermetic, easily cast aside as private and lacking in general significance (it focuses on more than one adulterous love affair), the dream clearly allows Wolf a freedom of political commentary that might not otherwise be available to her. In her later essay on Bettina von Arnim (1980), "Yes indeed! But the next life starts today. A Letter about Bettina," Wolf will ascribe a similar strategy to Bettina's work, saying: "In troubled times there is a certain protection in not being taken seriously. . . . Who, I ask you, locks up a sibyl, a cobold, a pythia?" (BL 294). And, indeed, we find in this story a frequent crossing over from the psychoanalytic into the political domain—as, for instance, in the pointedly ambiguous references to the censor, that "dream censor" who charts the path of the dream, or to the "commission for conflicts" (60). Similarly in this regard, the course of the dream is shaped by the dreamer's sense of being questioned at the scene of the crime, Unter den Linden—the reference is to a "Lokaltermin" (14)—and her sense of being brought to trial before a high court.

Just as the reader's attention is frequently drawn to the psychoanalytic dimension of the dream, so the fairy tale elements come to the fore recurrently, in both structure and content of the story. The optimistic opening paragraph is rendered formulaic, in the fashion of fairy tales, by its repetition at the end. The dreamer's openness to dream experience and hence the dreamer herself are characterized with reference to the fairy tale: "Every child knows from fairy tales that you just have to run off without a worry and confront everything in a friendly and unprejudiced way" (9). And one central character of the dream, Peter, is compared with "Hans in Luck"[3] (15, 32). Perhaps of greatest importance to the fairy tale complex of images is the golden fish, "my magic fish" (32), which, after the fashion of dream images, simply joins the dreamer as she is walking along. Although in having recourse to this image—"this figure provisionally called 'fish'" (33)—Wolf probably draws on her knowledge that dreams are said to share pictorial representations with fairy tales and legends, the fairy tale content of her story, especially the golden fish, plainly does obtrude as an independent, rival hermeneutic.[4]

I have mentioned "Hans in Luck"; the golden fish evokes another Grimms' fairy tale, that of the fisherman and his wife (of which Günter Grass would make such extensive use in The Flounder, 1977). In Wolf's story, the fish is a symbol for the conjunction of imagination with social conscience; it is an emblem of the urge to utopia, the principle of wishing that dreams and fairy tales in fact share. Accompanying the dreamer, the fish frightens the would-be GDR consumers who guiltily move away from the display filled windows of the shops Unter den Linden: "Your appearance scares them, Fish. They run away, insulted and outraged, complaining that they hadn't reckoned with having to deal with you" (32). A little later on, the dreamer's barely veiled social criticism finds its target in the Linden Hotel, which is proudly proclaimed to render even more services than the American Hilton; with the help of the fish, the narrator says, she would be able to imagine, one by one, not only these services but also the customers inclined to use them.

Furthermore, it is said of Peter, "Peter in Luck," that at one time he often told stories about the fish—"about whom Peter, in his best days, knew how to tell incomparable tales" (30). The narrative implies that Peter no longer tells these stories, no longer projects dreams of a wished-for future laced with incisive criticisms of the present, because he has been coopted, convinced by the historians at the university to change the topic of his dissertation, a topic that might have uncovered politically embarrassing material.[5]

As I have been suggesting, insofar as the reader suspects that the coming-to-terms with previously repressed material involving her love affairs and the accompanying emergence of a self-aware and confident self—this being the function that the narrator virtually tells us that the dream serves—insofar as the reader suspects that this is not the sole concern of "Unter den Linden," he or she might be tempted to explain the evasiveness of the text, its allegorical references, and its detours and divagations as standing in the service of social commentary. And that is certainly present. One wonders, though, why such elaborate machinery is employed for such relatively minor criticism as that which we've noted, and we're led to ask whether something else lies behind the two allegorical fictions—dream and fairy tale—to which Wolf resorts in constructing her narrative. In the remainder of this paper I'd like to argue the point that the social meanings of "Unter den Linden," which are in some sense presented to the reader as *the* keys with which to unlock its allegories, function to an extent as decoys to divert us from other issues. The story is about sexual entanglements and the progress toward a sense of self; it *does* contain a veiled social critique, but it is also about something else. The submerged text is only in part social commentary; it also records the beginnings of Christa Wolf's literary involvement with Romantic women writers—Karoline von Günderrode, Bettina von Arnim, and Rahel Varnhagen—two of whom would attract the focus of Wolf's attention several years later.

As Hans-Georg Werner points out in his thought-provoking essay on "Unter den Linden," Wolf's story was originally published with two others in a collection entitled *Unter den Linden: Drei unwahrscheinliche Geschichten* (Three improbable stories).[6] After making brief reference to one of these other stories, "Neue Lebensansichten eines Katers," with its obvious connection to the E. T. A. Hoffmann text, Werner discusses "Unter den Linden" within the context of Romanticism, asserting repeatedly that "Christa Wolf's narrative impetus originates in Romanticism."[7] But Werner's assertion is not much documented, by Wolf's text or otherwise, and it appears founded almost exclusively on a perceived correspondence between Wolf's concerns in the story "Unter den Linden" and Ingeborg Bachmann's work, in particular "Undine Goes" of *The Thirtieth Year*. His contention, which I take to be correct as far as it goes, appears based on a statement of Wolf's concerning "Undine Goes," in which she says that the story is "romantic not only in the adoption of Fouqué's motif, the figure of Undine, also romantic in attitude, the comparison of commonplace utility thinking with 'a spirit that is destined to no use'" (IB 92). There is, no doubt, an allusion to Bachmann's Undine in "Unter den Linden."

But the connection with Romanticism occurs particularly through its women writers, and it is on another level of specificity altogether than that which Wolf indicates in connection with Bachmann's story. I share the opinion of Christiane Zehl Romero that Wolf came to this involvement primarily through the writings and friendship of Anna Seghers, who had repeatedly championed the cause of these women since the mid-1930s;[8] the preoccupation with fairy tale and dream in "Unter den Linden" is, in part at least, an homage to Seghers, who argued for their acceptability within socialist realism: "fantasy and dreams also belong to reality."[9] Thus, we begin to see a palimpsest emerge in the relation of these texts to one another: Günderrode's writings, Bettina's appropriation of them in her Günderrode novel, Seghers's references to both earlier writers, and Wolf's tribute to all three in "Unter den Linden." Despite Seghers's early and repeated attempts to rehabilitate certain Romantics for socialist German literature, efforts to recover the Romantic heritage were not officially sanctioned until 1972,[10] three years after the writing of "Unter den Linden." For which of these reasons, then, this literary subtext is suppressed—the political or the more personal and literary—I cannot say, but I suspect that both have their parts to play.[11]

One incident toward the beginning of the dream bears close scrutiny in this regard; it is framed by the ever self-conscious narrator with the language of psychoanalysis: "I had always suspected that this street leads to the depths" (18); she speaks of "finally getting to the bottom" (19). This moment of descent into the unconscious, into the past, is then represented by the dreamer's submersion in the fountain of the inner courtyard of the public library. By means of this episode critics have linked "Unter den Linden" with "Undine Goes," recognizing the common concerns—perhaps feminist concerns—of the two stories;[12] but this linkage is perceived as existing on the level of the narrative and its overt preoccupation with the relationship between men and women. It is my feeling, though, that this episode has broader implications, implications that also refer to the work of Ingeborg Bachmann. In the fountain's waters the dreamer feels herself to be in "my element" (19); after she emerges, the female gatekeeper (perhaps the guardian of a female literary tradition?) allows her to enter the library proper.[13] In "The Shadow of a Dream" (1978), her later essay on Günderrode, Wolf speaks of Günderrode's poetry as seeking "the path to the origins, to unformed chaos, to the underworld, to the mothers," and Bettina, she notes, eagerly adopted Günderrode's evocation of poetic powers that have their origin "in the womb" (SD 257, 258). For both Bettina and Karoline the womb is the place of dream; being within the womb is identical with the state of dreaming. In "Unter den Linden" the moment of submersion in water, the female element, and the conflation of unconscious

306

and womb that this moment entails—rendered parallel to the entry into a library—symbolizes a descent into a literary unconscious and a descent from a literary tradition that is at least in part female. A strong preoccupation of Wolf's first essay on Anna Seghers, "Faith in the Terrestrial" (1968), is the question of literary influence, or Seghers's relation to her sources: Wolf speaks of Seghers's "journey to the sources" and describes Seghers's idea of the writer in typically romantic terms as having "something of the idea of a diver or miner" (FT 121). The narrative of "Unter den Linden" explains the incident of the fountain within the context of a love affair whose details the dreamer has repressed, but what the fiction explains as being the object of the *dream's* repression is not, of course, identical with the object of the *fiction's* repression or suppression. The fiction is itself superimposed, or, if you will, representative of secondary elaboration.

Once we acknowledge the presence of these women in "Unter den Linden"—whose motto, taken from a letter of Rahel Varnhagen, already provides a clue to this presence—details that are otherwise puzzling or seem to lack a context may be accounted for.[14] For one thing, the story's sense of place, its setting Unter den Linden gains in significance. Hannah Arendt's book on Rahel Varnhagen quotes from a letter of Rahel in which she writes of a peculiar sense of "disconnectedness" that befell her one day while walking Unter den Linden: "yesterday Unter den Linden I was overcome by such a condition; strange, very strange."[15] It is possible that Wolf knew Arendt's book when she wrote "Unter den Linden"; the German edition appeared in 1958, and, in fact, Wolf's motto comes from one of the short selection of letters that Arendt appends.[16] But this detail is not actually necessary to my reading. We know that Berlin was Rahel's city, as it came to be Bettina's. Still more to the point, Bettina von Arnim lived at Unter den Linden 21, and Wolf takes care to mention this in her "Letter about Bettina" (BL 291).

In this same essay, Wolf call's Bettina's residence a "center for independent spirits" (BL 291), and this brings me back to my earlier contention that it is impossible to pull at one thread of this story without loosening them all. What I have been calling the literary subtext of "Unter den Linden" is not without its own political dimension. Interesting to me in this regard is the manner in which the political is channeled through literary history and biography. I quoted earlier a passage from the "Letter about Bettina" in order to make a point about the encoding function of dream, about its diversion into subjectivity by means of which dream masks the story's social implications. In Bettina's time (and, possibly, in her own?), Wolf argues in her "Letter," the conscience of society resided in its literature: "In times in which literature functions as the conscience of society because of a lack of political openness, it must anticipate sanctions that increase in strictness in proportion to the degree to which that literature can be understood by the people" (BL 297). Once again, the hermetic and allegorical literary text stands a better chance of evading the censors.

307

A major emphasis in Wolf's Bettina essay concerns Bettina's reaction to and involvement with the "Göttingen Professors" incident and with two of these professors in particular: the Brothers Grimm.[17] Bettina devoted so much of her time to their situation in 1839 that she put aside her Günderrode manuscript and was forced to delay its publication (BL 304). Wolf asserts that the Grimms' display of conscience in the face of autocratic power led Bettina to champion their cause. Obviously the point I am suggesting is that I see in the fairy tale motifs of "Unter den Linden" not only another means of encoding meaning, of making the text "incomprehensible," but also in some sense a tribute to Anna Seghers, who felt that even socialist literature should incorporate fairy tales, acknowledged her own literary indebtedness to them, and through whom Wolf was first introduced to the writings of Bettina.[18] Wolf writes of the pressure exerted by the *Zeitgeist* in the early 1800s— as though it were a matter of merely historical interest—"as though people and things had been touched by an evil spell. How could they avoid suspecting the worst and expressing this in evil, uncanny fairy tales?" (SD 246). I suspect that the episode of Peter and the professors in "Unter den Linden" is a subversive—and trivialized—adaptation to the present of the Göttingen incident, and I suspect also that the Grimms are honored by the presence in this story of the golden fish, and by the linkage of imagination with social conscience that the fish seems to symbolize for Christa Wolf.

I'd like to return now to the public library Unter den Linden, which touches on Wolf's story in yet another way. In "The Shadow of a Dream," Wolf quotes a Günderrode poem ("Der Kuss im Traume" [The Kiss in a Dream]) and adds, somewhat gratuitously at this juncture of the essay, separated off by dashes, the statement that "the manuscript [*das Blatt*=the page, leaf] is stored in the German Public Library Unter den Linden" (SD 250). This significant phrasing, if we use it as a gloss on "Unter den Linden"—"the [leaf] . . . Unter den Linden"—with its conjunction of leaf, poem, tree, and street, turns the scene of the dream into the scene of Günderrode's writing. And other concerns in "The Shadow of a Dream" lead me to believe that the figure of Günderrode already haunts "Unter den Linden." (The title of the essay itself, by the way, should probably count as evidence.) Günderrode, Wolf writes, was "a talented dreamer" (SD 260) and a talented interpreter of her dreams as well: "The dream appears to be allegorical; what is your opinion?" Wolf quotes from one of Günderrode's letters (SD 260). In fact, "dream" is one of Günderrode's *leitmotifs*—"key words," Wolf calls them (SD 250), a key to the poems as well as to the life.

Wolf reads the correspondence of Günderrode and Friedrich Carl von Savigny as the novel of an avoided love and thinks it a noteworthy touch that the authors of these texts should be their protagonists as well. She points out that the language of the letters themselves is continuously double-edged and contains a submerged text: "the inner plot, incidentally, is developed under cover" (SD 244). The existence of this submerged text makes the letters what Wolf calls "border disturbances between literature and life" (SD 244). As a matter of fact, the love story of Günderrode and Savigny, as Wolf portrays it in *No Place on Earth* (1979), shares certain features with the love stories from which the repressed material of the dream in "Unter den Linden" derives, and one wonders what kinds of "border disturbances" have occurred here. But the fact that "Unter den Linden" portrays two love triangles has, most likely, little to do with the love triangle in which Günderrode was involved with Savigny and Gunda Brentano. And the curious detail by means of which Wolf characterizes the relationship of the dreamer to "the unnamed one," her lover, in "Unter den Linden," is a detail she uses again later in writing of Günderrode and Savigny. Namely, in both relationships the man addresses the woman as "du" [thou], while the woman uses "Sie" [the formal "you"] until the very moment in which she realizes that he has lost his hold over her and switches in midconversation to the familiar "du"; this telling detail probably says more about Wolf's own life than about her reading (*UL* 67; *NP* 58). And, finally, the central desire that both the dreamer-narrator of "Unter den Linden" and the Günderrode of *No Place on Earth* feel so strongly—the driving, overarching desire to be *known*—is the central desire of all these women writers.

I mention these correspondences not because I think that they in any way "prove" what my other points are intended to argue—that Christa Wolf was already much involved with Romantic women writers while at work on "Unter den Linden" and that the story both internalizes and suppresses this involvement. I mention them as further examples of boundary crossings, "border disturbances," and as seeming evidence that boundary crossings of this kind have much to do with women's writing: to exclude biography from a discussion of women's literature seems futile. Wolf herself subscribes to this view; she stresses it in her essays on all of these women writers, including Seghers and Bachmann; Undine speaks, she says, with the barely disguised voice of Ingeborg Bachmann (*IB* 93). In "The Shadow of a Dream" she formulates this idea as follows: "Women lived for years without writing; then they wrote—if the expression is permitted—with their lives and for their lives. They're doing that still—or again—in our time" (SD 225). But women, like men, also write about their reading. In fact, trapped within Wolf's formulation, with its originary proclamation of an impressionistic, personal judgment—"if the expression is permitted" —is an echo from yet another letter of Rahel Varnhagen: "our language is our lived life."[19] Perhaps another point of correspondence, the casual references to Goethe's *Sufferings of Young Werther* that can be found in both "Unter den Linden" and *No Place on Earth* (*UL* 63; *NP* 47), is a signal that these boundary crossings are sometimes committed by male writers as well.

I'd like to return at last to the topic of dreaming. In "Unter den Linden" Wolf locates herself among the women whose dreams, recorded in their letters, she also sees as literary texts; she sets out to demonstrate that she, too, is "a talented dreamer." But the narrator of "Unter den Linden" and, we infer, Wolf refuse to lead a dream *life*—either in the sense of Günderrode, whose poem "Kiss in a Dream" contains the line "And so I live, forever observing dreams" or in the sense of Rahel Varnhagen, whose recurrent dreams pursued her in her waking life. Hannah Arendt even speaks of "the dreams that dim daytime brightness with sharply-outlined silhouettes."[20] Indeed, it is important for the dreamer-narrator of "Unter den Linden" to distance herself from any such ambiguous interpenetration. Her running commentary, with its references to the interpretability of dreams and to the usual analytical machinery of the Freudian *Interpretation of Dreams* controls the dream and establishes a relation between day and night, to use Arendt's terminology, that does not allow night to dominate day.

But who is the "you" to whom the narrative of "Unter den Linden" is addressed, for it is not simply the reader. The remarks made to this "you" are expressive of intimacy, but they vary in their stance: some have a tone of complicity, some nearly of self-abasement; there are moments when Wolf's "you" seems to function as a super-ego. But we know that it is male; at one point he is addressed as "Lieber" (dear man) (19). An old friend, we might conclude, or a cast-off lover—but why, in a narrative about attaining self-awareness and self-sufficiency, does the character to whom it is related stand in a position of authority toward the narrator? I've implied before that this relation resembles that of patient to analyst, but the narrator does not take her dream to this other for interpretation; insofar as she is interested in interpretation, she has accomplished it herself. Furthermore, something about the nature of their intimacy is not compatible with the attachment of patient to analyst, even in the transference. Perhaps we can turn to Karoline von Günderrode to gloss even this problem in "Unter den Linden," for in *No Place on Earth* Wolf says of this poet: "She dismembers herself, making herself into three people, one of them a man" (*NP* 117). Not only does Christa Wolf assert rhetorical control over dream and, in a Romantic context, over the imagination itself through the Freudian discourse, but she rewrites the analytical situation by presenting the dream to the "you" as in some sense already interpreted.[21] When she goes even further than this by expressing the relation of dreamer-narrator and the silent other—the "you"—of the analytical situation as a relation between selves ("one of them a man"), as I'd like to suggest, Wolf's authority over her dream, her story, and its submerged literary subtext is complete.

Notes

1. Christa Wolf, *Unter den Linden* (Darmstadt: Luchterhand, 1977); henceforth cited parenthetically.

2. After having completed this section of my paper I discovered that Wolf used just this image in writing of Anna Seghers's literary criticism—"Every

thread that she carefully draws out of the fabric draws others with it" (FT 131)—
and I admit to feeling that if Wolf had written in this way about her mentor I
must be on the right track about her own work.

3. [A figure from the Grimms' fairy tale that bears the same name: "Hans im
Glück"/"Hans in Luck." See *Grimms' Tales for Young and Old. The Complete
Stories,* trans. Ralph Mannheim (Garden City/New York: Doubleday, 1983), 287–
291.—Ed.]

4. Sigmund Freud, *The Interpretation of Dreams* (New York: Avon, 1965), 381.

5. Brigitte Bradley refers to Peter's opportunism in an interesting essay that
examines Wolf's story from a perspective very different from my own. Brigitte
Bradley, "Christa Wolfs Erzählung *Unter den Linden:* Unerwünschtes und erwünschtes 'Glück,' " *GQ* 57, no. 2 (Spring 1984): 240.

6. See Hans-Georg Werner, "*Unter den Linden: Three Improbable Stories,*" in
this volume.

7. See Werner.

8. Christiane Zehl Romero, "The Rediscovery of Romanticism in the GDR: A
Note on Anna Seghers' Role," in *Studies in GDR Culture and Society 2; Proceed-
ings of the Seventh International Symposium on the GDR,* ed. Margy Gerber et al.
(Washington, D.C.: University Press of America, 1982), 19–28.

9. Ibid., 21.

10. Ibid., 20.

11. Bradley points out that Wolf's *The Quest for Christa T.,* "which revealed
her deviation from the programmed literature with its system-stabilizing heroes,
was held back for two years before its publication was permitted in the GDR in
1968" (245). Wolf would have been reluctant, one supposes, to be put in this position again.

12. Bradley, 239; and Werner.

13. Different though it is, one is reminded of Virginia Woolf's visit to the Brit-
ish Museum in order to do research for her paper on the topic of women and
fiction in *A Room of One's Own.*

14. "Ich bin überzeugt, dass es mit zum Erdenleben gehört, dass jeder in dem
gekränkt werde, was ihm das Empfindlichste, das Unleidlichste ist: Wie er da
herauskommt, ist das Wesentliche" (Suffering insult to one's greatest sensitivi-
ties, and to the greatest degree bearable, is, I am convinced, a part of every person's life. The important thing is how one gets past this).

15. Hannah Arendt, *Rahel Varnhagen. Lebensgeschichte einer deutschen Jüdin
aus der Romantik* (Munich: Ullstein, 1975), 159.

16. Arendt, 283. Letter of February 8, 1831.

17. Patricia Herminghouse connects Wolf's interest in this incident with
"Wolf's own tribulations as a signer of the Biermann petition of November 17,
1976." Herminghouse, "The Rediscovery of Romanticism: Revisions and Reevaluations," in *Studies in GDR Culture and Society 2,* ed. Margy Gerber et al. (Washington, D.C.: University Press of America, 1982), 14.

18. Zehl Romero, 21–22; Wolf, "Fortgesetzter Versuch," in *Lesen und Schreiben. Neue Sammlung,* 154: "Once I went to Winkel on the Rhine and looked for
and found Günderrode's grave at the cemetery: I had encountered her name
again and again in the essays and letters of Anna Seghers."

19. Arendt, 218.

20. Ibid., 130.

21. Steven Marcus offers an interesting interpretation of Freud's Dora, who interrupted her analysis with Freud, as someone who "refused to be a character in
the story that Freud was composing for her, and wanted to finish it herself."
Marcus, "Freud and Dora: Story, History, Case History," in *Representations: Essays on Literature and Society* (New York: Random House, 1975), 306.

Twilight Zones: Myth, Fairy Tale, and Utopia in *No Place on Earth* and *Cassandra*

Judith Ryan

W hat does it mean, to change?" asks Christa Wolf in her novel *Patterns of Childhood*. The question comes at a point when her (autobiographical) narrator is most forcibly struck by the difference between the East German and the American views of the self and its development. While on a visit to the United States, the narrator watches a television program in which a well-known psychologist expresses his opinion that the personality is determined in the first three years of life. This conception of human development puzzles the visitor from the GDR because the entire social and political theory of her country is based on the idea that radical change is possible, even in adults. The problem raised by this incident is one that underlies all of Christa Wolf's fiction. It is a decisive factor in the conflict of *Divided Heaven*, with its concern for a young woman's need to choose between the two Germanies, and an even more problematical issue in *The Quest for Christa T.*, with its exploration of the dialectics of individualism and conformity. Wolf's unwillingness to espouse a simplistic view of the East German theory of change in the individual determines even the narrative form of *Christa T.* and *Patterns of Childhood*, where the self is presented—can only be presented—through a division into two. In varying ways, *No Place on Earth* and *Cassandra* continue this probing of the self in its dual aspect of constancy and changeability, but they shift the problem to a different arena: the question of the individual's power to change the world around him or her.

No Place on Earth *and* Cassandra

In effect, Wolf's two most recent novels expand her concerns for the self, history, and writing through a set of imaginative projections that go beyond autobiography and the problems of contemporary Germany.[1] While *Christa T.* and *Patterns of Childhood* (and, though only by implication, *Divided Heaven*) had depended structurally and thematically on a problematic relationship between past and present, the past depicted in each case is a relatively recent one still connected with the experience of the narrating, that is, present self (or in the case of *Divided Heaven*, the protagonist). In *No Place on Earth* and *Cassandra* Wolf moves back in time, first into the nineteenth century and then into mythical Greece. The present day no longer figures explicitly in these novels, though the underlying gesture of self-identification with personages from the past suggests its existence as a point of reference. Despite this apparent shift from the present to the past as the locus of narration, the basic issues remain unchanged. Wolf's interest in the problem of the individual self in a time of historical transition, a concern of paramount importance in the development of the East German state, has simply been transferred to two other historical epochs that she perceives as parallel periods of transition. The poet Karoline von Günderrode, her male equivalent Heinrich von Kleist, and the Trojan prophetess Cassandra become analogs for the problems of the present-day writer, specifically Wolf herself. But oddly enough, the narrative problem that had consisted in the earlier novels in an attempt to come to terms with the past, has been transformed into a conflict concerning present and future. Thus, tempting though it may be to read *No Place on Earth* and *Cassandra* as fairly simplistic allegories, a dimension remains inaccessible on this level. In the last analysis, the two novels go beyond the naive parallel in which Christa Wolf is the misunderstood poet-prophet of her time.

We can best address this problem by asking what role the two novels assign the writer as a mediator between epochs. In *Christa T.* and *Patterns of Childhood*, writing had been presented as a way of preserving potential from the past that would otherwise be lost to us in the present: it survives in a transformed state, as the memory-traces of Christa T. or the metamorphosing dream at the conclusion of *Patterns of Childhood*. Narration is a form of consciousness-raising that aims to reintegrate the past into a new understanding of the present. Simultaneously part of the past and separated from it, the narrating self is the crucible in which this process begins, though Wolf is careful not to resolve the problem too glibly at the end. But in *No Place on Earth* and *Cassandra* the gap between the narrative point of view and that of the reader has increased dramatically: it is simply harder for us to identify completely with a figure from the nineteenth century or, worse still, from the Trojan War. Here past and present are less easily mediated. "The time between epochs is a twilight zone"—the central experience of the poets in *No Place on Earth*—is a formulation that can be applied equally well to *Cassandra*. This more pronounced separation between reader and narrator permits Wolf to begin exploring areas left relatively untouched by her other forays into the domain of fiction and history: the role of myth, fairy tale, and utopia[2] in shaping our awareness of time and self. What relation do these three self-contained modes bear to history and our view of it? Apart from the theme of poetry, this is the single issue the two novels have in common; *No Place on Earth* is concerned with the interplay of fairy tale and utopian vision, *Cassandra* with that of myth and utopia. Nonetheless, the shift of emphasis from the earlier novels is less extreme than it might at first appear. In fact, the two most recent novels take up in a more explicit form the problem of codified views of history, schemata of perception that determine, sometimes for the worse, our understanding of the events we experience.

"Who am I?"[3] Christa Wolf asks in "The Reader and the Writer." One possible answer is a list of books read: "For without books I am not I" (RW 190). This idea that the self is in part determined by literary schemata also applies to one's understanding of external phenomena. In her *Conditions of a Narrative*, Wolf explains that *Cassandra* was motivated by "a process which has changed my lens on the world" (C 142). And the question she sets about answering is one that suggests that there is some way, perhaps, of escaping preexistent schemata, of getting to the truth that lies behind them: "Who was Cassandra before anyone wrote about her?" (C 273). Yet even as she asks this question, she knows that there is, in fact, no other accessible reality than the Cassandra of fiction, and even the act of making Cassandra "speak" is akin to that other literary model, the coming to life of Helen in *Faust* II (cf. C 227–228, 297–298). In taking as the subject of *No Place on Earth* and *Cassandra* two writers and one figure known only through literary tradition, Wolf draws attention to the problematic relationship between history and literature.

Although myth and fairy tale belong in a sense to the past, and utopia to the future, they nonetheless have something in common. All three subsist in a realm outside historical time and space. Fairy tale and utopia share a basically optimistic view of the outcome of things.[4] In other respects, there are radical differences. Myth and fairy tale suggest an inherent patterning or an archetypal basis in events; utopia presupposes the possibility of change. The mechanisms by which myth and fairy tale on the one hand and utopia on the other function are also at odds with each other. Fairy tale and myth are magical or ritualistic in nature; utopia is essentially rational. The two wicked stepsisters scrape their feet bloody in their vain attempts to fit into the glass slipper; but this has no causal connection with the success of the seemingly unremarkable Cinderella. By contrast, utopian narrative functions dialectically: its imagined resolutions are intended as a critique of existing social and political structures. Utopian fiction has an activating effect, fairy tale a protective one. In combining utopia and fairy tale in *No*

Place on Earth and utopia and myth in *Cassandra* Wolf sets up questions that are by no means easy to answer.

No Place on Earth opens with a direct reference to fairy tale. "You precursors, feet bleeding" (*NP* 3) is how she addresses her two predecessors, Heinrich von Kleist and Karoline von Günderrode. Unfortunately, the English translation, "feet bleeding," obscures the fairy tale allusion. What Wolf actually wrote was "blood in the shoes," a phrase that is a recurring motif in the Grimms' version of the tale "Cinderella." As the handsome prince searches for the owner of the glass slipper, many try it on in vain; Cinderella's two stepsisters, in a particularly desperate attempt to make it fit them, end up with bloodied feet. Only when Cinderella herself tries it on is there "no blood in the shoe." Now if the two Romantic writers, Kleist and Günderrode, are the stepsisters who try in vain to squash their feet into the glass slipper, then Wolf, one assumes, must be the Cinderella whom it fits. But why would she associate her precursors with the wicked stepsisters and herself, apparently so immodestly, with Cinderella's ultimate success? I suggest that she is less concerned with the wickedness of the stepsisters than with the motif of the slipper that does not fit, that becomes a metaphor for Kleist's and Günderrode's painful perception of themselves as misfits in their own age. Wolf is embarrassed and distressed by her own present success in contrast to Kleist, whose work was undervalued during his lifetime, and Günderrode, whose work was known only to a small circle during hers. "We know what is coming" (*NP* 119) seems to refer to the fact that the two Romantics ended their lives by suicide. Yet Cinderella, as we also know, lived happily ever after. What at first seems to be an act of self-identification with her predecessors thus turns out, on one level at least, to be a deliberate contrast. But there is surely another level as well. By evoking Kleist and Günderrode in an imaginary scenario that allows the two misfits to see that they are not alone, Wolf attempts to undo the damage done to them by the age in which they lived. In the end, her narrative strategy transposes the primitive alignments of her two characters with the fairy tale figures suggested at the beginning: posthumously, Kleist and Günderrode themselves become transformed Cinderellas. Identification is again possible. What can Christa Wolf mean by this complex harmony and counterpoint?

From the outset, Wolf connects the Cinderella story with the theme of language, comparing verbal and material poverty in the phrase, "ashen taste of words" (*NP* 3). In the context of the Grimms' fairy tale, ashes suggest Cinderella (her name is *Aschenputtel* in German). But for anyone writing in the German language after World War II, ashes must also conjure up the Nazi extermination camps. Wolf is thus performing the work of mourning (*Trauerarbeit*) on several levels at once: she is mourning the fate of her Romantic precursors in their own age and revalorizing them for our own; she is evoking, as she had done in *Christa T.*, potential writers blotted out by Nazism; and she is asking whether words—writing—have the power to transform these tragedies of historical reality, as the fairy godmother did Cinderella, into something new and positive.

What is the relationship of the actual world to words, images, and dreams? Do ideas have consequences? Are ideals translatable into reality? The novel suggests repeatedly that words are instruments that, by substituting for reality, in a sense "kill" it: "To exorcise it, indeed to kill it, by calling it a name" (*NP* 103), thinks Günderrode. By the same token, the poet who lives in words is metaphorically dead: "To give birth to what slays me" (*NP* 97) is her description of poetic activity. The idea of suicide is thus not merely an expression of the poets' suffering within the confines of their world but a necessary consequence of their choice to work with words. It is not accidental that both poets, Kleist and Günderrode, secretly share the same view of Goethe, whose play *Torquato Tasso* they explicitly mention. Both despise what they regard as Goethe's dependence on dualisms—in this case, the antinomy of poet and society. Within the context of their particular understanding of language, they are distressed, affronted almost, by Goethe's consoling conclusion, in which the poet Tasso, to the last unable to validate his claim to importance in the scheme of things, finds a desperate relief in the fact that he can put his suffering into words: "The gift of a god—to speak whereof I suffer." For Kleist and Günderrode, continued existence is not made possible for the poet through the expression of suffering; on the contrary, expression obliterates the very substance of their existence.

When Kleist describes the Rhine banks between Mainz and Koblenz as "a sort of poet's dream" (*NP* 52), he is not, as one might think, resorting to a familiar cliché but illustrating the novel's central principle, the problem of translating reality into dream and vice versa. If a geographical location can appear as the poet's dream, can the poet's dream be turned into reality? The novel's time frame, the Romantic era, is depicted as an epoch of fluidity and transition, a no-man's-land between historical periods. "Between one time and another," Günderrode thinks, "is a twilit region" (*NP* 118). But it is not merely a historical "twilight zone." The historical transition experienced by Kleist and Günderrode only brings out more clearly the ambiguous status of writing itself. The "twilight zone" becomes an image for the realm of the poet. Is this realm just a delusion, or is it capable of affecting the progress of history?

No Place on Earth constantly explores the interaction between poetry and reality. The title itself identifies the problem. The German words, "kein Ort; nirgends," are essentially dictionary definitions of the word "utopia"—literally, "no place." The title refers simultaneously to the nonplace of utopian (poetic) vision and the nonplace of fairy tale, and the development of these ideas in the novel suggests that we should examine more closely the value of such nonplaces in our conception of reality.[5]

By making her novel dependent upon the primitive layer of fairy tale and the future-directed component of utopia, Wolf gives it its own special dynamics. The novel speaks simultaneously to the problem of determinism versus changeability and to the question of the difference (if any) between masculine and feminine views of the world. By having the two Romantic poets meet in a social setting—a literary salon—, Wolf brings to the forefront the essential difference between the role of the male poet and that of the female poet in the nineteenth century. But in the last analysis, what counts for the two of them, in the "twilight zone" of their dreamlike meeting, is the sense of a shared vision. They seem to stand aside from the buzz of chatter that sustains the others and to move, as if in slow motion, toward the discovery of this underlying identity. At the same time, however, they wish to move beyond the "twilight zone," to translate their dream-discovery into the world of reality.

How is this to be accomplished? Theoretically, all the two poets can do is transform the world of things into a world of language. But the world around them is also, in a sense, unreal. The conversation-happy age in which they live seems to drain the world of substance: "Kleist has a vision of an age founded on empty talk rather than actions" (*NP* 78). What we see of their contemporaries consists almost entirely of conversation. For the two poets this means that their own language must take on another quality. Their interior monologues, which make up the greater part of the novel, form a silent dialogue that moves as if by telepathy, a harmonious duet of thought that constitutes the substratum of *No Place on Earth*. Through this duet we come to see the poets' counterimage of reality. Neither believes, for example, in the kind of utopia projected by nineteenth-century science. Both reject the belief in historical progress shared by the others, the more so because it appears to stress logic at the expense of imagination: "Our modern-day civilization is steadily expanding the sphere of the intellect, steadily restricting that of imagination" (*NP* 79), comments Kleist in a debate on scientific progress. His words are not very original, and he knows this; but this is a function of his conception of the poet's role as a kind of protective mechanism in society: "The poet's charge is the administration of our illusions" (*NP* 80), he says, with rather savage irony. He suggests, indeed, that the poets are more conscious than others of the fact that we live by illusions. He is annoyed when Savigny accuses poets of being divorced from reality ("the equivocal, challengeable aspects of the poet's existence" [*NP* 82], is how Savigny puts it). "Of all the people here, perhaps there is none more intimately bound to the real world than I am" (*NP* 82), Kleist reflects. To his mind, the popular notion of progress is a greater and more misleading deception than the illusions of poetry.

One question that concerns the two Romantics[6] is how they can profit, not merely suffer, from the transitional nature of their age. Here their discussion of Goethe is especially revealing. They see the privy councilor as too eager to reap the benefits of modern science and they regard his writing as wrongly valorizing deeds over words. *Tasso*, with its central conflict between the man of action and the poet resolved essentially in favor of the former, is a prime example. But Kleist's and Günderrode's opinion of Goethe also recalls the general Romantic disgust with Goethe's activity-filled world—as exemplified, for instance, in Novalis's contention that Goethe's *Wilhelm Meister* was a "Candide against poetry." To avoid involvement with deeds, which they regard as illusory ways of confirming one's existence, Kleist and Günderrode take a drastic position: they claim they would rather be dead than alive. Words, as opposed to deeds, are for them associated with dream and sleep, not with rationality and consciousness. Günderrode's strange conversation with Savigny is described by the narrative voice, presumably in empathy with Kleist's observation of the scene, as a dreamlike event: "It is thus that we speak when we are dreaming, or when we have leave to utter our final words on this earth" (NP 48). And she is suddenly glad when she catches herself thinking of herself in the past tense, as if she were no longer alive (NP 58). Similarly, when Kleist recounts an anecdote about a dog caught between the conflicting orders of two masters, he reflects wistfully: "If only one could sleep one's whole life away" (NP 62).

Both of them would like to be removed from temporality. Günderrode, though at first said to be "unassailed by the transitory" (NP 4), is terrified by thoughts that come to her about another young woman's aging: "Change is unrelenting, and I . . . would prefer not to have to go through it" (NP 72). When Savigny suggests that "the abysm of time" is like "the crater of a volcano" (NP 82), she is delighted with the image. We have the feeling that she might throw herself into it, like Hölderlin's Empedokles. And Kleist, who sees himself as a machine running at high revs, would really prefer, like the baffled dog of his anecdote, to sleep away time (NP 88).

Dream thus becomes for the two poets a new way of relating self and world. In keeping with this privileging of dream over reality, the two dreams recounted in the novel have a special significance. Their symmetry is obvious. Günderrode dreams that she is a deer shot by Savigny's arrow, yet subsequently magically cured by his hand (NP 6-7); Kleist dreams of shooting a wild boar that dies convulsively before his eyes (NP 28). Both dreams are evidently sexual in nature, as Kleist's fiancée guesses, but more importantly they concern the two poets' death wishes. Kleist's analysis of his dream suggests that it represents his divided nature: he feels that he has the choice of killing off that part of himself that is dissatisfied with reality or giving this dissatisfaction free rein and being destroyed by it (NP 29). Similarly, Günderrode connects the dream with her suicide plans, wondering why the wound in the dream should be on her neck when she has planned to kill herself by a dagger blow to the heart (NP 7). As she comes to reflect on the dream, she realizes for the first time what Savigny means to her: he offers her, she says, "the shadow of a dream" (*NP* 7). It will not escape anyone familiar with the work of Christa Wolf that this is the title Wolf gave to her edition of Karoline von Günderrode. The suggestive phrase is never actually interpreted in *No Place on Earth*. But Günderrode's ruminations imply that the dream has given her an idea of what it would be like to really let herself go, to stop compromising with the conventional world around her: "The danger is that she might get carried away, slacken the reins, and charge full speed ahead, and that then, at a wild gallop, she might collide with that opposition which others call reality" (*NP* 8). The dream has become a premonition of an alternative mode of existing.

While Kleist and Günderrode see this new mode of being as another form of death, they also suspect that it can be seen as something that might be realized in the future. The spark of understanding that flies between them separates them from their own age but connects them to a possible future one. "To think that we may be understood by beings who have not yet been born" (*NP* 110). This future perspective is the kernel of their utopian idealism: it expresses the sense in which, after all, ideas can have consequences (*NP* 113). As their conversation fades into silence ("What are they talking about now, or are they thinking?" [*NP* 119]), they come to regard themselves as provisional projections of something yet to come: "To understand that we are a rough sketch—perhaps meant to be thrown away, perhaps to be taken up again: we have no control over that. . . . Signed and signing. Assigned to perform a work which remains open, open like a wound" (*NP* 118). The fact that they are rejected by their own age gives them, as they see it, a certain freedom to project utopian visions that will be understood by a later age.

Their status as precursors—projections of the future—gives them a kind of prophetic insight. The conclusion of *No Place on Earth* indicates that they have attained a depth of vision beyond that of their contemporaries. "We know too much. People will think we are raving mad" (*NP* 119), they reflect, in the strange union of minds that mingles with the silence of nature at the end. Knowledge and madness are of course characteristics of the seers of antiquity, with whom the Romantic poets tended to identify themselves.

In a remarkable fashion, the very last line of the novel fulfills their poetic prophecy: "We know what is coming" (*NP* 119). On one level, the "we" of this sentence refers to the two characters of whose interior monologue it is part. On another level, it refers to the narrator and to us, as readers. The coincidence of past and present, in which the poets' knowledge is transferred, as it were, to us, seems at first glance to be a sort of resolution. But it would be misleading to regard it as the final meeting of the parallel lines in infinity—the Romantic image for the projected end to the eternal progression. Not only can this meeting point by definition never be reached, but the knowledge of the poets is quite different from the knowledge of the text's modern readers. The

319

sentence gains its effectiveness from the reverberations of this unresolved ambiguity.

Where are we to situate this ending—in history, in fairy tale, or in
utopia? It seems to step out of the dreamlike sequence of wordless gestures that proceeds as if in a kind of slow motion. It leaves the novel
open, like the open wound referred to several paragraphs before. At
once painfully and reassuringly, it leads us out of a re-vision of the past
into our own age. In so doing, it reenacts the essential function of literature by revealing it to be the transition point in the dialectical interplay
of ideas and reality. The "twilight zone" is revealed as the peculiar
arena of fiction as mediator between utopia, fairy tale, and history. We
know what happened in the past: Kleist and Günderrode committed suicide; the Romantic age was followed by an age of realism. But what do
we know of the future? The ending of *No Place on Earth* is as unsettling
in its ambiguity as the endings of fairy tales are reassuring in their predictability.[7] Cinderella's dreamlike transformation into the beautiful
lady at the royal ball evaporated only temporarily; in the end her
dream—marriage to the prince—became reality. *No Place on Earth*
works with the categories of the fairy tale and questions them: under
what conditions, by what mechanisms, it asks, can such a transference
of wishes into reality take place? Are utopian ideals sustaining or
destructive?

Cassandra takes up some of these issues again in a different way.
Here, too, the situation is transitional. Captive before the gates of Mycenae, Cassandra reflects in an extended interior monologue upon the
events that have led to her predicament. Her monologue is the product
of a "twilight zone"—the few hours she still has to live—but she also
comes to see that her whole life has taken place, as it were, in a
"twilight zone." As the prophetess whose words no one believed, she
has lived in the agonizing simultaneity of present and future, unable to
have any influence on events as they take place. In rewriting the story
of the Trojan War from Cassandra's point of view, Wolf challenges us to
rethink the relationship between myth and history. But Wolf is not just
reworking something from the past. She herself describes *Cassandra* as
a *roman à clef*—a designation perhaps not quite literally meant, in the
sense that one can assign to each character a corresponding personage
in "reality"—but certainly the tale has present significance on a number of levels. Seen through the filter of the Romantic vision presented
in her preceding novel, *Cassandra* becomes another exploration of the
role of the poet in society, questioning the Romantic tenets that the
poet is also a prophet and that the function of poetry is to construct
projections of the future.

In her *Frankfurt Lectures on Poetics*, essentially a commentary on
the genesis and meaning of *Cassandra*, Wolf gives an account of her
motivation in rewriting Homer. "My interest in the Cassandra figure: to
retrace the path out of the myth, into its (supposed) social and historical
coordinates" (C 256). The parenthetical word "supposed" makes clear

that it is not a simple question of contrasting myth and history: even history, insofar as it has to be reconstructed from incomplete and imperfect evidence, has an element of the imaginary. As with *No Place on Earth*, *Cassandra* also takes issue with socialist realist notions of development and change.[8] "Why should the brain be able to 'retain' a linear narrative better than a narrative network, given that the brain itself is often compared with a network? What other way is there for an author to tackle the custom . . . of remembering history as the story of heroes?" (C 262). In developing Cassandra's story as a nonlinear structure, she presents a counterimage to the cliché of history as a continuous progression. Cassandra's prophetic gift is, in essence, another form of this opposition to linear history: her existence in a "twilight zone" untouched by conventional ways of thought enables her to "see" present, past, and future at one and the same time. In this context, Wolf comments on the external form of her novel in terms of closedness and openness: "Narrative techniques, which in their closedness or openness also transmit thought patterns. I experience the closed form of the Cassandra narrative as a contradiction to the fragmentary structure from which (for me) it is actually composed" (C 266). In fact, however, *Cassandra* is only "closed" with respect to plot: we know from the outset that Cassandra is to die at the end; we know from the outset the precise course the Trojan War will take. We have here a more pronounced version of the premises upon which *No Place on Earth* had been based: "We know what is coming." But as with *No Place on Earth*, the apparent closed structure is in fact an open one—open because it asks the reader to rethink, with Cassandra, the seeming inevitability of the events it recounts.

Wolf takes pains in *Cassandra* to identify her prophetess with the motif of writing, to make it clear that Cassandra is in some sense a stand-in for herself. "Keeping step with the narration, I make my way into death" (C 3),[9] she announces at the very beginning. She continues, "Here I end my days, helpless, and nothing, nothing I could have done or not done, willed or thought, could have led me to a different goal" (C 3). Yet despite her powerlessness to change history, she decides, even in these last hours, that her visionary gifts are worthwhile: "I . . . lived on in order to see" (C 4). The question is, why? If she cannot change her own fate and that of her loved ones, is there some other power her "tale" can exert? One answer may be the new patterns of thought that her way of seeing brings with it, the utopian impetus that outlives the prophetess herself. The novel sets out to show us that stories, words, can indeed be powerful.

This raises, as did *No Place on Earth*, the question of the relative valency of poetry and reality. Through Cassandra's narrative we come to see that the Trojan War itself lacks substance: it is a war "waged for a phantom" (C 69), because Helena is not with Paris, as everyone believes, but in reality with the King of Egypt. What counts is not reality, however, but people's view of it: "People's heads were turned by the thought that the beautiful Helen was inside the palace of their king" (C 67). A fabrication has set in motion the entire Trojan War, and its perpetuation—Cassandra is forbidden to speak of what she knows—ensures that the war will continue. Cassandra's dreams, discounted by all around her as the ravings of a madwoman, turn out to be closer to reality than the views of her countrymen; similarly, the "narrative" of her interior monologue, the novel, forms a counterreality to the fiction of Homer. The conventional relation of fiction and reality is turned inside out.

Wolf is not just trying here to transform Homeric myth back into an imagined counterreality, however. She is also attempting to reconstitute the reality of myth by restoring to it one element that myth, almost by definition, does not have: the psychological dimension. In discussing this experiment in the *Frankfurt Lectures*, Wolf adduces some remarks by Thomas Mann, who had claimed that the way to restore myth from its misuse by the fascists was to psychologize it and thus to restore its original humane potential. Wolf's comment on Mann's idea is central to her intentions in *Cassandra*: she calls it "the embryo outline of a utopia" (C 248). Restructuring myth to reveal its psychological underpinnings is to transform it from a primitive, archetypal version of what history presents in a more complex guise into a forward-looking model for an eventual rethinking of history. What was myth becomes utopia.

As I suggested at the beginning of this essay, the crux of this paradox lies in the contrary presuppositions of myth and utopia with regard to change: myth implies inevitability; utopia is rooted in the belief that the world can be changed. "What is supposed to happen, happens. We are not here to prevent it" (C 108), says one character in *Cassandra*. But though Cassandra cannot change what happens, she can change how we see it.

The form of the novel is an explicit alternative to the tradition of heroic epic: hence the first-person narration, the nonlinear time, and the lack of a hero in the conventional sense. In a neat allusion to Brecht, Wolf says, through Cassandra's voice: "we have no chance against a time that needs heroes" (C 138).[10] Yet the novel itself, with its powerful conjuration of an alternative vision, provides proof that indeed something can be done to counteract the age's need for heroes. Wolf calls this alternative narration the moment when the imaginary comes to life, when a phantom begins to speak. Although Helena is absent from the action of *Cassandra*, she lives in a different form in the prophetess herself. This Helena is less the figure from the myth of Troy, however, than the character from Goethe's *Faust* II. The Helena-Act in Goethe's poetic drama is one of his most clearly developed explorations of the curious interplay between poetry and reality. Having existed hitherto as a mere idea, a product of the imagination (the word used for it in *Faust* is "*Idol*," [shade]),[11] Helena is brought to life by the magic art of Mephisto and is taught by Faust to speak in rhymed verses characteristic of his age, not hers. In her commentary on *Cassandra*, Wolf infuses this motif with the spirit of feminism: "Do people suspect, do *we* suspect, how difficult and in fact dangerous it can be when life is restored to an 'object'? When the idol begins to feel again? When 'it' finds speech again? When it has to say 'I,' as a woman?" (C 298) *Cassandra* is an extended exercise in restoring life to the phantom, making the female view the subject, rather than the object, of history. It deconstructs heroic myth by showing how the myth arose and helping us both to see through it and to reconstitute it by restoring to it its humanistic basis.

Both *Cassandra* and *No Place on Earth* transform those most primitive elements of our storytelling, myth and fairy tale, into new modes with utopian implications. Literature itself is seen as a "twilight zone" whose intermediary nature, far from disqualifying it as a form of "reality," in fact enables it to become the crucible in which new views of reality, and hence new realities, can be created. The conception of past, present, and future in their relation to one another is extremely complex. "To learn to read myth is a special kind of adventure. An art that presupposes a gradual, peculiar transformation; a readiness to give oneself to the seemingly frivolous nexus of fantastic facts, of traditions, desires, and hopes, experiences and techniques of magic adapted to the needs of a particular group—in short, to another sense of the concept 'reality'" (C 196). *Cassandra* is more than just an attempt to give expression to the other "reality" of myth, however. In "returning myth to its (imagined) social and historical coordinates," Wolf has not so much made it more historical as she has made it more future-directed. In particular, she stresses the capacity of fiction to forge new ideologies: "It was not my birth that made me a Trojan," says Cassandra, "it was the stories told in the inner courts" (C 33), but the experience of telling her own story moves her beyond this primary identification with Troy. At the end she sees that the most important thing is not to remain caught up in static categories of thought. Of her lover, Aeneas, she says that she wants to see neither his transformation into a monument nor his permanent classification as a "hero" (C 138). The counterimage to this dreaded immutability of myth (or history) is contained in the novel's final sentences: "Here is the place. These stone lions looked at her. They seem to move in the shifting light" (C 138). The narrative voice, now, as in the very first paragraph of the novel, a voice not identical with Cassandra, has made several important adjustments to its original observations: the past tense has become the present; the movement of the stone lions is clearly assigned to the realm of perception. That the lions are headless need no longer be mentioned: we have entered a sphere where the imaginary and the real coincide; the headless can see, and stone can (at least appear to) move. The new way of seeing has been completed. We are in the "twilight zone" where fiction, that essential unreality, can nonetheless be recognized as a genuinely transforming influence upon the real.

If we take the two novels, *No Place on Earth* and *Cassandra*, as a literary sequence,[12] we can see that the second points to the fulfillment that was left tantalizingly open in the first. Kleist, Günderrode, and Cassandra, though all powerless to change the course of history during their own lifetimes, share the belief that narration does have the potential to alter things to come. The darkness that ends both novels ("Now it is getting dark" [*NP* 119]; "The light went out. Is going out" [*C* 138]) gives way in *Cassandra* to a new vision that takes us beyond the disillusionment of the central character, suggesting, more subtly than the traditional utopian novel, a world-view that has not yet (quite) come into being. Wolf's return in these two works to myth and fairy tale presupposes the hope that there will eventually be a time when Cinderella fits the glass slipper, when Cassandra's prophecies will be heard. The mismatch between reality and the imagination—the "feet bleeding" motif of *No Place on Earth*—will cease to exist as the reader comes to identify with the hidden utopian dynamics of the two novels.

Notes

1. The problem of Christa Wolf's identification with her characters is treated more fully in Sigrun D. Leonhard, "Strategie der Annäherung: zur Erzähltechnik in Christa Wolfs *Kein Ort. Nirgends*," *GR* 60 (1985): 99–106, and from the East German point of view by Siegfried Streller in "Christa Wolf: *Kein Ort. Nirgends*," *WB* 29 (1983): 359–362.

2. For a discussion of myth and history in *Cassandra* against the background of GDR literary policies, see Rudolf G. Wagner, "On Christa Wolf's *Cassandra*," to appear in *Five on Five*, ed. M. Birnbaum. On the question of utopia, see Barbara Gentikow and Kirsten Søholm, "Christa Wolfs *Kein Ort. Nirgends* und *Kassandra* oder Lebensbedingungen des Utopischen in der Literatur und ästhetischer Theorie der DDR," *Text und Kontext* 12 (1984): 387–409; and Klaus Wille, "'Welch ein Trost, dass man nicht leben muss.' Zum utopischen Aspekt der Erzählung *Kein Ort. Nirgends* von Christa Wolf," *Doitsu Bungaku* 67 (1981): 32–39.

3. Against the background of contemporary feminist theory, Helen Fehervary gives an account of the problems of constituting the self in her essay, "The Gender of Authorship: Heiner Müller and Christa Wolf," *STCL* 5, no. 1 (1980): 41–58. Barbara Lersch also treats the question of subjectivity in her article on Christa Wolf's "anti-poetics": "'Hervorbringen müssen, was einen vernichten wird.' Mimik als poetisches Prinzip in Christa Wolfs Erzählung *Kassandra*," *DVjs* (1985): 145–166.

4. Christa Wolf once again links fairy tale and utopia in her meditation on the nuclear accident at Chernobyl, *Störfall. Nachrichten eines Tages* (Darmstadt/ Neuwied: Luchterhand, 1987).

5. Gentikow and Søholm trace the history of the term "utopia" in the GDR. They demonstrate that its usage was mainly negative in the fifties and sixties and that despite a more positive turning since the early seventies the *Kleines Wörterbuch der marxistisch-leninistischen Philosophie* (4th ed. 1979) still describes the concept as anachronistic and reactionary.

6. An excellent account of Christa Wolf's place in the reception of Romanticism in the GDR can be found in Monika Totten, "Zur Aktualität der Romantik in der DDR. Christa Wolf und ihre Vorläufer(innen)," *ZfdPh* 101 (1982): 244–262.

7. Selina Ganguli says quite appositely that "while putting down the book one cannot help feeling that the search for utopia has only just begun" ("Looking for utopia. Christa Wolf's story *Kein Ort. Nirgends*," *German Studies in India* 5 [1981]: 94).

8. The eight passages removed from the GDR edition of Christa Wolf's Frankfurt lectures testify to the ways in which she takes issue with socialist theory; see Peter Graves, "Christa Wolf's *Kassandra*. The censoring of the GDR edition," *MLR* 81 (1986): 944–956.

9. Translation modified by editor.

10. The reference here is to Brecht's *Life of Galileo* and the concluding exchange between its protagonist and Andrea: "Unhappy the land that has no heroes!"—"Unhappy the land where heroes are needed." In Brecht, *Plays, Poetry and Prose*, ed. John Willett and Ralph Mannheim, vol. 5, part 1: *The Collected Plays* (London: Eyre Methuen, 1980), 98.

11. Johann Wolfgang von Goethe, *Faust I & II*, trans. Stuart Atkins (Boston: Suhrkamp/Insel, 1984), 224. Helen Fehervary points out the political implications of the attack on classicism in *No Place on Earth* (Fehervary 144–145).

12. Gentikow and Søholm also appear to regard the two texts as a related pair.

Quotation as Authentication: *No Place on Earth*

Ute Brandes

No *Place on Earth*, which appeared simultaneously in Weimar (GDR) and Darmstadt
(FRG) in 1979, integrates authentic literary, biographical, and historical
material into a fictive presentation.[1] All figures in the narrative are historically known personalities from the early Romantic period. Merten,
a wealthy merchant, has extended an invitation to tea at his country es-
tate on the Rhine; his guests include the poets Heinrich von Kleist, Karoline von Günderrode, Clemens von Brentano, his sister Bettina,
Kleist's doctor Privy Councilor Wedekind, the lawyer Carl von Savigny, the scientist Christian Nees von Esenbeck, his wife Lisette, and
others. Kleist and Günderrode feel like outsiders in this circle of successful burghers, scholars, and artists. Christa Wolf first directs attention to the changing conversations of the entire assembly, which frequently regroups. Thereafter, the focus of the narrative narrows. The
two young poets leave the others and continue their conversation during a walk.

Although the narrative gives precise references to time, place, authentic personalities, and historical details, it is not intended as an historically realistic report about an important gathering. The narrator describes such a meeting as "a legend that suits us" (4). Furthermore, a
quotation on the book jacket specifically draws attention to the fact that
a personal acquaintance between Kleist and Günderrode is in no way
historically documented. But Christa Wolf chooses to draw on a casual
remark of the Kleist biographer Eduard von Bülow, whose conjectured

326

meeting of the poets was written more than forty years after this June day in 1804:

> On his way home [from Paris], Kleist was overcome in Mainz by a severe illness, from which he recovered under the care of Privy Councilor Wedekind only after six months. In the meantime, his friends had no notion of his whereabouts.
> During this time he is said to have made the acquaintance of Günderrode and to have enjoyed a tender relationship with the daughter of a pastor who lived near Wiesbaden. (Eduard von Bülow, 1848)[2]

As Christa Wolf interprets it, the quite speculative meeting of the two young poets is based on the deep inner truth of their affinity. Both feel alienated from their times and their society. A few years later and independently of each other, both will voluntarily take their own lives. The twenty-six-year-old Kleist finds himself in a grave spiritual crisis. In a moment of deepest despair he has just destroyed his most ambitious work, *Robert Guiscard*. The impoverished Fräulein Günderrode secretly publishes her works under a pseudonym. As woman and artist, she fails to fill any possible roles appropriate for a twenty-four-year-old noble canoness in the society of her day. Both artists are aloof, and both have accepted the invitation to this tea unwillingly.

With sparse external action, the narrative traces the slowly developing mutual acquaintance of the two main figures from its tentative, groping beginnings to the eventual profound concern each feels for the intellectual world of the other—a process that can overcome, for brief moments, their feeling of alienation. It is a case of neither a love relationship, however, nor even a passing attraction, but rather it is a case of unexpected mutual recognition of spiritual equals struggling with similarly difficult circumstances. In its immediacy, their frank conversation "closely resembles a sensual intoxication" (118). These few minutes of understanding admittedly change very little. At the end of the narrative Kleist and Günderrode part as easily as they have become acquainted and retreat to their separate worlds.

The construction of the work plays on the artful tension between the poles of intentional blurring and extreme precision. Introduced by a quotation from each poet, the voice of the narrator uses the "we"-form to suggest its own involvement and to invoke the two as fellow victims, long since marked ("You precursors, feet bleeding" [5]). It wakes them from their old graves, as it were, asks itself and them "who is speaking?" and reveals Kleist as the first articulator of their mutual problems only after three pages. Similarly blurred transitions, from narrative voice to inner monologue to *erlebte Rede* to conversations between the two poets, recur throughout the narrative. At the climax of their understanding, Kleist and Günderrode overcome the isolation of their "I"-voices and are united in a "we." Thereafter, the respective "we"-speakers can no longer be distinguished from the narrator's commentary.

The actual conversations between the characters stand in marked contrast to this narrative technique of fluid transitions, which intentionally produces confusion and thus continual reflection in the reader. Not only Kleist and Günderrode, but also Bettina and Clemens Brentano, Savigny, and others converse with extreme precision and refinement of expression. The aphoristic quality of many of their discussions points to literal quotation as the core of many conversations:

> He feels strangely moved by the comment which wafts in his direction from Günderrode, who has sat down beside Bettina on a window seat: Poems are a balm laid upon everything in life that is unappeasable. Remarkable the way, even when this woman is speaking to other people, what she says appears to be intended for him, and that she seems to him the only person who is truly real in a horde of specters.
>
> Then Brentano says in a grave tone which disposes Kleist in his favor: You're right, Kleist. In our times it's impossible to write poetry. One can only try to do something for poetry. The poet lives, as it were, in a wilderness, prey to the attack of wild beasts, for not all of them can be tamed by Orphic song; and those who follow dancing in his wake are apes.
>
> Kleist, also very earnest, replies without thinking: life is growing increasingly more complicated, and trust becoming ever more difficult.
>
> A pause ensues, involving no feeling of embarrassment. Kleist perceives that Günderrode has been listening to them. (64)

At least three authentic literary-biographical quotations are hidden in this excerpt from the narrative.[3] Although even the casual reader may recognize from their half-hidden, sententious form that they are probably preformed external material, Christa Wolf has worked them so smoothly into the progressing narrative context that they have become part of the dialogue. Admittedly, a certain stylistic remoteness is apparent, but there is no break between the core quotation, the surrounding words of the speaker, and the transitional commentary of the narrative voice. I have succeeded thus far in discovering the sources for more than ninety passages in Wolf's narrative. Undoubtedly, even more quotations are hidden in the work.

These conversational kernels are brief images and maxims that in each case transmit a conviction, a situation, or an intellectual attribute of the times in greatly abbreviated form. They continually introduce new hints at or explicit references to biographical and intellectual-historical material that achieves full significance only if the reader is already well-informed about both the respective speakers and the time around 1800. Adhering faithfully to the original texts, Christa Wolf has enriched her narrative with authentic details, literal quotations, and actual biographical traits. All of these come from the letters and works of the speakers, and most can be located in the years from 1800 to 1804.

Why is this fantastic precision coupled with the simultaneous blurring of the boundaries between the characters and the narrator? Why is Christa Wolf not satisfied with description and simple narrative progression? Nearly all the critics of this work have pointed to the high stylistic demands it makes on the reader. Silvia and Dieter Schlenstedt value the obvious artistry of the story but lament its extreme narrative intensity and condensation, for "the actual circumstances of the characters are given no definitive outline. . . . The narrative thus possesses a certain exclusivity, is for the initiated."[4] Patricia Herminghouse warns of the "extreme demands that Christa Wolf's narrative style makes even on those readers familiar with her earlier works and essays."[5] Jürgen Engler sees "dangers" in the technique of having the poets speak in a high style, for "the author herself is ultimately forced, even in those passages in which her characters with 'elective affinities' do not speak, to remain on the stylistic level she has chosen."[6] Hans-Georg Werner, in contrast, finds an apt image for Christa Wolf's style, even if he does not pursue the function of these structures: "In many passages, the verbal skin of poetry is distended from within through the use of conversational material distinguishable as quotations, and is occasionally stretched to the point of tearing."[7]

I intend to show in this essay that the narrative's high stylistic level, criticized above, is a precondition of Christa Wolf's particular technique of quotation. After a closer look at the form and the function of this external material, we will be able to recognize to what extent the structure of citation underlying the text functions to connect the spirit of the early Romantic epoch with the *Zeitgeist* in the GDR. The temporal depth thus acquired releases in the author a process of self-realization, which, finally, should also have a productive effect on the reader through the provocation of the narrative's title.

An overview of the authentic material in the narrative may help to clarify terminology. Not all nonfictional references and literary facts are quotations. I employ the designation, rather, to understand "quotation" in the sense of Herman Meyer's definition: "the content of literary passages [is] referred to and to a certain extent faithfully reproduced."[8] The quotations used in *No Place on Earth* are taken from biographical and literary sources. Acording to their particular form and function, they can be divided into three groups: general quotation, identified quotation, and unidentified self-quotation.

General Quotation

A slightly altered quotation sets the tone at the very beginning of the narrative: "Kleist . . . flees on the pretext of excuses he does not dare to see for what they are. Aimlessly, it seems, he sketches with his eccentric footprints the lacerated map of Europe. Happiness is the place where I am not" (4). The cryptic quotation in the last sentence comes from the song "The Wanderer," which became famous in Schubert's setting.[9] Only slightly altered ("there, where you are not, is happiness"), it stands as a cipher for the restlessly searching Romantic, a wanderer who roams the countryside full of yearning for a spiritual homeland and a sense of connection. This quotation establishes the theme for the narrative. Individual motifs like loneliness and despair about the present condition already resound fully here; already we see the yearning for the "land which speaks my language"—a topic lent much significance later in the narrative. Further references to the motif of the wanderer can be found in not only the text but also its title. The citation of the wanderer therefore possesses a revelatory function for the motif structure of the narrative.

Other quotations characterize the figures. For instance, in Privy Councilor Wedekind's stream of thought the Schiller-quotation appears: "Dem Manne kann geholfen werden" (Easy to help the man) (18). This unidentified phrase, which has become an unreflected part of Wedekind's speech repertoire, indicates that Kleist's doctor belongs to the educated reading public. But the extraneous element simultaneously reflects the limitations of the speaker. This same physician—who has handled Kleist very competently as a medical man, who, full of human sympathy, helps to hide his patient's attacks of weakness from the others gathered for tea, who is obviously well-read and intellectually involved—insists a short while later on the necessary boundaries between literature and life, on the separation of ideal and reality; that is precisely the division that destroys a genius like Kleist, who strives for totality. The quotation here becomes an important building block in indirectly characterizing the doctor: although the words of a poet have become part of his own inner world, Wedekind cannot truly comprehend them. He is an educated philistine who decks out his conversations with familiar quotations the meaning of which, however, he is incapable of penetrating.

Identified Quotations

In contrast to the above quotation from Schiller, which functions more or less anonymously, those citations that are explicitly identified in the narrative are doubly significant: the name of their author functions like a signal, to provoke certain reactions from the speakers, and the name itself plays as great a role as the contents of the quotation.

The most important name calling forth discussions in this manner is that of Goethe. No one is impartial to him. The breadth of emotions ranges from the deepest regard to jealous love and the ambitious desire to surpass him. Scattered throughout the narrative are explicit and cryptic references to classical balance, "harmony, moderation, extenuation" (12), to the classical as the healthy, the Romantic as sick or insane, to Goethe as one self-possessed because he "is out of touch with real life" (99), and to Kleist's ambition to surpass the king of poets. Günderrode unknowingly formulates Kleist's profoundest social agony —that chasm, accepted by others, between art and life, art and power, which tears him asunder—with the help of a quotation from *Tasso*: "I feel as if all my bones were shattered deep inside me, and I am alive simply in order to feel this" (83). This Goethe citation simultaneously leads to discussing the differences between Kleist and his famous rival in Weimar. In Kleist's opinion, Goethe "believes that those contrary forces which are active in the world can be divided into two branches of reason—he calls them good and evil—both of which, ultimately, make an essential contribution to the progress of mankind" (83–84). Kleist, in contrast, is incapable of viewing the world's "tendency to crack" (*Gebrechlichkeit der Welt*) (50) from a similarly self-possessed standpoint. For him, the laceration not only exists in the external world but also reaches into the innermost regions of his soul; he is torn apart by this and destroys himself, like Tasso. He, however, perceives the injustice not as something he construes for himself but rather as an injustice inflicted on him by the world.

Other quotations with a similar function, which are explicitly identified and which contribute to clarifying a particular perspective, come from Shakespeare, Günderrode, and Brentano. In every case they initiate a discussion that alters the course of the general conversation. In this way they fulfill a structural function in the narrative, characterize the speakers, and transmit historical insight into the intellectual climate around 1800.

Unidentified Self-Quotations

The most important and frequent use of quotation, however, involves words and phrases from the poet-figures' own letters and journals. Christa Wolf weaves this authentic material into the fictive conversations of each speaker in such a way that it does not interrupt the flow of action. Thus, the 180-year-old elements merge smoothly into their modern surroundings and the narrative maintains a balanced stylistic level. Occasionally the reader may notice a certain stylistic intensification, but the fact that most conversations are structured around a core quotation becomes evident only when one consults the works and letters of Kleist, Günderrode, the Brentanos, and other contemporaries.

Obviously these unidentified quotations are hardly to be regarded as tacit plagiarisms, but their very authenticity functions as an important structural component of the work. Christa Wolf has suggested this insight herself, for she has provided her readers access to a source study of the originals. Her edition of the writings of Karoline von Günderrode, *The Shadow of a Dream* (1979), to which she provided an introductory essay, appeared simultaneously with *No Place on Earth*.[10] In these writings, but particularly in the works and letters of Günderrode and in the letters of her correspondents, which are also included, one can find many literary passages utilized in the narrative in their original context. Kleist's works, in contrast, are easily accessible.[11] It seems almost like a literary anecdote that Christa Wolf has here simply followed Kleist's own habit when she allows the fictive Kleist of her work to repeat his own striking formulations, "for without thinking twice about it he uses the very same turns of phrase in letters to all sorts of other people" (17). This biographically verifiable practice is confirmed by Curt Hohoff: "Kleist not only used certain images and letters, often employing the same words, several times; identical descriptions also appear in his letters to different people. In letters and stories there are parallel passages and concepts which can not only be explained by his good memory but which must, in each case, have been copied. The source for these reproductions was the *Ideenmagazin*, which is perhaps identical with the journal."[12]

Christa Wolf, then, has based the structure of her own citation method on a biographical fact. Kleist was especially proud of those passages he repeated several times; for him they represented a felicitous combination of content and expression.[13] Christa Wolf has used this trait. She has selected from the biographical-literary material of the writings and letters of both Kleist and Günderrode those ideas and figures that could serve her particularly well in the expression of the most important concerns of the early Romantic era. In transmitting the history of ideas, each person in the narrative's ensemble of figures plays one or more roles, roles that are expressed in abbreviated form in the quotation-core of their conversations. These fictive-authentic figures, who function to transmit the ideas of their times and who speak in words that they themselves considered important, thus also assume documentary character.

Let us now examine this quotation technique of poetic authentication with the help of some examples. First, consider the form of the citations: most borrowed passages are compact, already constituting in the context of the original text the core of a discussion, so that Wolf has integrated them into her novella unchanged, or with slight syntactical alteration. Kleist's letter of October 10, 1801 to Wilhelmine von Zenge can serve as an example. In this letter Kleist reports his desire to find a suitable profession, and he laments the fact that civil service is out of the question, as his inner convictions make it impossible for him to accommodate himself to a public career: "I bear an inner precept inscribed in my heart, compared to which all external maxims, were they sanctioned by a king himself, are of no value whatever." He wishes therefore to withdraw to a practical activity of some sort and begs Wilhelmine to follow him.[14] In the context of the narrative this passage appears as a quotation. But it is now embedded in a far-reaching discussion that oversteps and radicalizes the original sense of the letter. First, should the individual accommodate himself to the state and repress his own convictions for the welfare of society? And second, according to which "inner precepts" should the state guide itself?

If only it [the state] could convince me that it does in fact satisfy the needs of the farmer and the merchant: that it does not compel all of us to subjugate our higher aims to its interests. The crowd, it's called. Am I fraudulently to transform my aims and views to accord with theirs? And above all the question remains: What would really benefit this crowd in the first place? But no one poses this question. Not in Prussia.

Kleist, my good man! cries Savigny. What deep waters are you heading for?

Yes, it's true, says Kleist. Many things which people consider worthy of veneration are not so to me. Much of what to them appears contemptible is not so to me. I bear an inner precept inscribed in my heart, compared to which all external maxims, were they sanctioned by a king himself, are of no value whatever.

My God, man! Savigny exclaims. . . . Aren't you afraid? Do you really feel no fear? (67–68).

The original sense of the letter passage was that the personal value system of its author prohibited him from accommodating himself to the external demands of a public office in Prussia. No discussion in the letter concerns either the sense or senselessness of the laws of the state or whether these would be worthy of personal sacrifice in the service of public welfare. The fictive Kleist in Wolf's narrative, however, goes a step further. He doubts the value of voluntary conformity because it is not at all clear that the goals of the state correspond to the commonweal. Wolf has broadened the historical Kleist's very personal statement to his fiancée into a political argument, whose radicalness is emphasized by the fearful and resisting exclamations of lawyer and later Prussian Minister of Justice Savigny.

In addition to such compact quotations, whose form and original contents are merged completely into the fictive text but whose meaning is expanded and sharpened by their new context, there are montage quotations. In the full context of the original sources these are occasionally pages long; in the reworking they are poetically condensed, their contents are abbreviated, and they thereby assume clearer meaning. Such an intensification can be seen in the narrative in a dreamlike conversation between Günderrode and Savigny. Here, for the first time, the poet is able to take a decisive stand for her talent and her art. In doing so, she simultaneously attempts to break out of the destructive conventions of the time, which understand a female artist to be hybrid or hermaphroditic in nature: "She writes poetry? Disastrous. Is she compelled to do so? Does she know no better way to pass the time, to dispel boredom?" (19). Just how self-destructive was her confinement to the conventional role of a woman who defines herself exclusively through her relationship to a man has become clear in the course of her unhappy relationship to Savigny. The dangerous game with her feelings, which she has been playing for years—as a third party in a love relationship—consists of skirmishing and flattery on the part of the man, who has meanwhile married Gunda Brentano, and of a strong attraction on her part, which she can hide only with painful effort.

The historical Günderrode did not arrive at such a decisive avowal of her art as that presented here. In the original words of the letter the stress lies in the woman's loving consideration for the man who, as she knows, is bound to convention. The art of poetry is the deeper, constantly recurring topic in the letters as well. But the remarks about her poems and dramas, her reading, and her intellectual interests are scattered among several letter passages, and as fragmented avowals they are unequivocal. Occasionally, when her "unfemale" traits as an artist become too obvious, the historical Günderrode takes back what she has just said. In the letter of February 26, 1804, for instance, she admits that she is so involved with her new drama that her "own life is becoming alien" to her. Immediately thereafter, however, she accuses herself of feminine inconsistency: "I think my life is uncertain, full of fleeting apparitions which alternately come and go, and without continuing sincere warmth. Even so, I beg of you, please forgive me my innate badness."[15]

In Christa Wolf's interpretation, the fictive character Günderrode has become more definite and consistent, and she assumes a decisive position, opposing the current standards of the times. From the beginning, the poet is simultaneously outsider to and secretly admired by those gathered at the tea party. She does not hesitate to take a conscious stand in her own interest, and she is also able to master the confusion of her feelings. The following passage is constructed from four authentic quotations that originally functioned much less decisively when scattered among various letters:

> I'm quite serious, dear friend. My heart has turned away from you. It has just occurred to me that this is what I have been trying to tell you all this time, and you can see for yourself that I don't shrink from saying it. I lead a very active life, Savigny. I'm having Müller's history of Switzerland read aloud to me, I'm applying myself with great diligence to the study of Schelling, and—I feel like a fool to tell you—I am writing a drama, and my whole being is wrapped up in it. I project myself so vividly into the drama, I become so much at home within it, that my own life is becoming alien to me. Do you understand, Savigny, I know of no better life for me than this. Gunda says that it's foolish to let oneself be dominated to this degree by such minor artistry as mine. But I love this flaw in me, if indeed it is a flaw. Often it makes up to me for everything else. And it helps me to believe in the necessity of all things, even that of my own nature, imperfect as it may be. (60)

The characteristically tender, intimate tone of the letters is still maintained here, made manifest in the repetition of Savigny's name (and, in the German, in the playful alternation between the proper "Sie" and the more intimate "Du"—an authentic trait from the letters). But the montage quotation surpasses the original texts, for it has now become a coherent acknowledgment of writing as a life commitment. The joining of heretofore separately recorded individual remarks signifies not only the temporal compression of years into this one afternoon. It intensifies the particular life of Günderrode into a paradigm. With her proud insistence on her work and her talent, the poet not only characterizes herself, but sketches as well a budding self-awareness of woman as she begins for the first time to define herself in terms of her own intellectual involvement. The individual self-confidence of the woman and the female artist, that is admittedly still fragmented in the original letters of Günderrode, but can nevertheless be authentically documented, has become so condensed in Wolf's presentation that it assumes a symbolic position at the beginning of a new development.

In her essays Christa Wolf confirms this function of Günderrode as a model for a rising new feminist consciousness. In the intellectual circle of early Romantic poets around Brentano there emerged among the women a new, utopian manner of thought that postulates the highest ideals in a materialistically oriented and reactionary bourgeois world:

> I became ever more interested, and this also found its way into the narrative and into my essay about Günderrode, in discovering the roots of the conflicts experienced by women today—the dissatisfaction with life. This can be observed well in the early Romantic period, in the time around 1800: when society, tailored to think in terms of the division of labor, has no use for a particular type of human being who seeks totality, who demands a universal happiness. That's where the roots lie. (WS 61)

I will briefly consider quotations in a third form. In addition to the already discussed compact passages and to the montage quotations, significant single words or quotation fragments throw sudden new light onto a certain character trait or the relationship between two conversants. Kleist's despairing phrase concerning the "tendency to crack" becomes, in the mouth of the successful Savigny, who has come to terms with the condition of the world, the formula of the "law of laws . . . on which rest all our human institutions with their inevitable flaws, their tendency to crack" (49). The speaker here is an established person who is not bothered by the fact that there exists in society a deep chasm between humanistic ideals (acknowledged by all) and reality (determined by profit-oriented thinking). Savigny's remark causes a reaction of amazement in Kleist and Günderrode, and they are thus marked as idealists in contrast to the successful burghers present at the gathering. A second example is a passage from a letter that is merged unaltered into the narrative as a short quotation, characterizing the relationship between Savigny and Karoline: "Your letter made me so happy, so truly happy, deep down" (47).[16] Just how unfulfilling this love is, however, becomes clear in another passage: playfully, but with distinct self-abasement, she calls herself "that horrid little Günderrode-my-pet, your dear little duck" (45); an authentic signature from a letter of June 28, 1804, clearly showing the humiliation that Karoline, with Savigny's help, brings upon herself as the third party in a love relationship.[17] Although such short quotations do not influence the structure of the work, they do abbreviate important motifs and allow them to stand out briefly in condensed form.

The three variations of quotation in this larger group of citations, which function as authentic cores of a poetic statement, can be summarized as follows: The unaltered complete quotations have their own compact point that, however, is modified in every case according to the specific intent of the new context. The montage passages are presented in such a way as to give concentrated significance to heretofore scattered single remarks. The quotation fragments function to recapitulate the circumstances in a brief moment of illumination. These three groups, despite their different forms, are the chief transmitters of ideas in the discussion and, in every case, the core of the conversation. At the same time they provide the narrative with its underlying foundation of documented reality. Through them, the authentic aspects of the early Romantic period are so merged into the fiction of the modern narrative that these aspects, although their original characteristics may still be evident, have been in every case assimilated into Christa Wolf's own poetic statement.

This condensation and poeticization of the citation material thus always takes place on two levels. Because the narrated time of the work embraces only one afternoon and the quoted material from approximately four years is tacitly condensed and abbreviated to fit into these few hours, the time of the action ought to be regarded as a fictitious frame. Intended here is not a definite June day of the year 1804 but rather a typical moment in the time around 1800. This condensation of an epoch becomes even more meaningful when one reduces the contents of the conversations of the various participants in the tea party to their central themes. The narrative then shows us a spectrum of concerns of the times, not only clarifying life around 1800 and typifying the speakers but also touching the narrator so immediately that the latter's identity often disappears in the "we" of complete agreement with the figures. The second, indirect level is therefore the current epoch, the narrative time, and its concerns are seen as analogous to the problems of the early Romantic period.

Such a connection between the two time periods extends far beyond the theme of woman. Every time the narrator joins with Kleist and Günderrode in the use of "we," their sufferings are extended to the present day. In this way, the problems presented reveal a remarkable ambiguity. The quotations point beyond themselves and connect times and political systems in a suspended and unresolved comparison. The present is seen through the medium of the past, and the past epoch is examined with today's standards. In her essay on Günderrode, Christa Wolf has discussed more specifically the attitude of contemporary GDR intellectuals motivating her to such a daring literary experiment:

Fascinated by relationship and proximity while aware of the times and events which lie between us and them: one full revolution of the "wheel of history"; and we, pulled along body and soul by its motion, just now having caught our breath, come to our senses, to circumspection—we look around, motivated by the no-longer-deniable need to understand ourselves: our role in history, our hopes and their limitations, our accomplishments and our failures, our possibilities and their conditions. And, if it is possible, the reasons for all of this. (SD 226)

These modern successors have long acquiesced to the precepts of a literary canon. They experienced the unjust devaluation of many artists by "teachers and professors," including "the weighty verdict pronounced by Georg Lukács against Kleist, against the Romantics" (SD 226). Now, with newly found resolution, they search for their own standards. As socialists they base their sense of crisis on the fear and suspicion that the promised ideals of a free socialism may not be realized. Their sensitivity protests against the dull rationalism of their environment, against the postrevolutionary society that is consolidating its power. Such a self-conscious, searching position is advocated in the narrative by Kleist and Günderrode and therefore also by the narrator as "successor." They are not afraid of defending their own principles and, in doing so, they maneuver themselves ever further into a remote position in society. Christa Wolf's critique of the present can easily be recognized in the topics discussed by the two poets in her narrative.

The fictive conversations revolve around ideal and reality, the responsibility of the artist in a materialistically oriented society, and the deeply rooted conventions that separate both man and woman from the essence of being human. Both poets are deeply disappointed with Germany, which was unable to renew itself with a revolution, and with France around 1800, given the reactionary outcome of the French revolution. They are still inwardly guided by the humanistic challenge of the Enlightenment and thus become outsiders in their restorative society. In the new century, the old ideals serve at best as topics for conversation among the educated bourgeoisie, while mercantile profit, the growth of technology, and the division of labor define real life. Now the people of action, those rigorously prepared to divide ideal from reality, are successful. These are represented, among those present at Merten's tea party, by the scientist Esenbeck, the merchant Merten, the lawyer Savigny, and the doctor Wedekind; all agree that "it is a beneficent arrangement to keep the realm of thoughts neatly cordoned off from the realm of action" (48–49).

In this society and in this epoch, the poets have a clearly defined function: they nurture illusionism and the old idealism as though it, too, defined reality; they give new nourishment to the realm of freedom of thought. At one point, Kleist notes bitterly: "The poet's charge is the administration of our illusions" (80). Without intending it, Goethe, as portrayed in the narrative, fills such a function. In the conflict between ideals and reality, he has taken the side of the ideal, and he disregards anything that does not fit his conception. Brentano, the third artist-figure present in Christa Wolf's work, admittedly shares the insight of Kleist and Günderrode into the discrepancies of the times. But he is presented as a charming aesthete who loves writing more than people. He thus avoids open conflict and, in doing so, willingly permits himself to be used de facto for the larger goals of society.

But there are also differences between Kleist and Günderrode. While they define their outsider positions in a shared idealistic opposition to their age, their sufferings have individual and role-specific traits. Kleist's essence as poet exists in the destructive division between a burning "male" ambition and a concomitant profound doubt about his talent. He unconsciously shares the generally held prejudices, which he regards as laws of nature. He thus contributes to strengthening these structures. Like the other men in the narrative, he has firm convictions about the duties expected from men and women. Women should be docile and "remain inconspicuously in the background" (15); the art of writing is reserved for men. Günderrode, on the other hand, lives her convictions and, in her absoluteness, fits no role whatsoever. She protests against being forced into a certain convention contrary to her nature. For her, writing is necessary to life: in poetry she collects herself as if in a mirror, supersedes herself, and then hides her inner truth in the poems. For her, there is a "place" where she can exist: her verses and dramas, published under a male pseudonym, are her spiritual home in which she can find release, for poetry is a place where no one suspects truth but rather mere convention.

But the intellectual and spiritual half must be connected to life. And here Christa Wolf gives women (more than men) at least the hope of a possibility of breaking out of convention into a personal free space. Society orders the male to fulfill himself through his work, through his profession. The female is supposed to do this through love. But it might be possible for a "youth-maiden" like Günderrode to attain the ideal of an individually defined self-fulfillment if she insists quite definitively on her own demands. She could combine the poles in her life—writing and being human, embracing the roles of man and woman—in a private compromise with a beloved man. But the tragic disunion of the epoch also makes this solution unlikely: "because the men for whom we might care are themselves entangled in inextricable dilemmas. The constant round of responsibilities you men must deal with cut you into pieces which scarcely bear any relation to each other. We women are looking for a whole human being, and we cannot find him" (93). Günderrode will therefore have to augment herself in a fantasy love; she will love an ideal man "whom she will create for herself" (117).

The profound crisis of the period presented here, extending from the most private realm into that of the state's business and aggravating the sensitivity of the artist figures in the narrative, is directly reflected in language.[18] Kleist and Günderrode, these two masters of expression

338

for whom a pure feeling finds immediate crystallization in the poetic word, are helpless and speechless when confronted by the lack of understanding and the superficiality of the people surrounding them. Other guests at the tea party are not so strongly affected. The "chatter" of the people, expressing nothing, their "talk, talk," is a socially accepted masquerade and gesture of politeness (45, 82). Their animated conversation veils inner alienation and serves the status quo of human distance among the guests. Günderrode reacts to the empty conventional expressions with inner discomfort. She wishes that the thoughts of the others might suddenly become audible; at the same time she knows that that would be considered a "licentious desire" in the eyes of the world (45).

The struggle for words attains, of course, central significance for the two poets. For Günderrode, the roots of her creativity lie in her conscious resistance to the conventions opposing the expression of her inner world. Writing poetry is her command: "For me it is an established fact that I must write. There is a longing in me to express my life in enduring form" (23). Thus bound to her talent, she no longer fits a woman's role. She may express her individual sense of life only in the language of poetry, and she hides her truth in her poems. She overcomes occasional writing difficulties by writing. Her subject matter itself urges her to resolve externally imposed tensions. The crisis of language and the struggle for pure expression are located for her not in the insufficient possibilities of formulation but in the restrictive rules of society.

Kleist's relationship to language, however, is far more profound and destructive. His acute personal crisis expresses an inner despair, the fear that his talent is insufficient to present validly the deep contradictions of the times. As long as he can find no suitable word for a problem, he cannot rid himself of it. His physical collapse in Mainz is the result of the inner agony suffered during his creative crisis in Paris, when he burned his *Robert Guiscard* in almost insane, nihilistic joy. But the narrative does not make a personal inability responsible for his apparent failure as an artist: the drama could not have been completed. The heroic material Kleist chose to treat belongs in a past or future more ideal time; the present can create no form for such an undertaking: "The subject of the play is colossal, to fail at it no disgrace" (116).

Wedekind recognizes that Kleist's speechlessness is the most significant aspect of his suffering. The poet has been under his care for months, and the privy councilor attempts to heal the spiritual crisis by having Kleist express the conditions of his *angst*. Kleist becomes somewhat more contained when he is finally able to verbalize his inner agony: "he had fallen into the grinding mechanism of a mill, which was breaking each of his bones one by one, and at the same time tearing him to shreds" (38). The insufficiency of his words causes him physical agony, moaning, distortions, the feeling of being tortured. "Since that time Kleist has known that words are incapable of depicting the soul, and he believes that he will never be permitted to write again" (38). At the same time he senses an inner command to formulate his spiritual torture. He perceives the sense of his life in discovering a name for his *angst*. After recognizing this, he "abandoned his hope for an earthly existence in any way corresponding to his needs" (108). "His work is the only point at which he can become one with himself" (117).

But Kleist's speechlessness does not always express his inner torture. Occasionally he remains silent while the most animated inner voices are speaking within him. His silence then also protects him from the world. Those passages that deal directly with either denying speech or courageously articulating current problems make it quite clear just how thin the skin can be between Kleist's Berlin around 1800 and Christa Wolf 's Berlin after 1976.[19] At times a mechanical block, a stutter, manifests itself in Kleist, as though an inner voice were preventing him from saying more than he should. In these instances, his overzealousness checks itself. But this restraint disappears entirely when consonance of opinion allows him free expression. At times, and more obviously than this subjective psychological control mechanism, political wisdom demands silence. When conversations concerning politics, art, and state in Prussia lead to consternation, Kleist breaks them off, and he recommends this strategy to others. Although he knows that only the courageous articulation of problems will further the world, as someone who is in political danger he must adapt to circumstances. The narrator hints at the inner burdens Kleist will have to bear as a civil servant in Prussia because of his self-censorship. And once again the restriction of the spirit is reflected in his physical condition: "Sometimes . . . he will be seized by a wicked desire to shriek. He will grit his teeth, clench his fists, suppress the impulse and after a moment dry the sweat from his forehead" (110).

In the narrative, then, there are two causes of speechlessness: first, verbal expression is limited when it has to describe openly a questionable condition in the world; and second, the individual protects himself through the denial of speech if he is in political danger. Such a situation makes necessary the search for nonverbal agreement. Spontaneous insight into people and nature, the sensitive comprehension of phenomena not understood earlier, and silent observation offer at times an unexpected insight into a totality that cannot be exactly described by words.

Nature offers such a freedom not yet destroyed by social chatter. While wandering through France in aimless despair, Kleist at one point senses quite unexpectedly an intense release from his inner compulsion to name all things. One night he feels spirited nature around him; the hills lay

> about him like the backs of great warm animals, he saw them breathing; he stood still and felt the heart of the earth beating under the soles of his feet, and he gathered his strength in order to endure the

sight of the heavens. For the stars . . . in their glittering enormous corporeality were threatening to cascade down upon him. He forgot himself . . . he ran for a long time. . . . He knocked at a door, a woman
opened it, her face seemed beautiful to him in the candlelight, she let
him in, mutely placed a bowl of milk before him on the rough table,
and showed him to a bed of straw. He stretched out and experienced
in body and limbs what freedom is, without a word even once entering his mind. (98)

When the human being is part of nature, artistic officious elo-
quence becomes superfluous. Everything has its innate sense, and
Kleist feels that he has found the way back to himself. But society
around 1800 no longer took Rousseau's ideas seriously. Conventions
and manners have caused the natural impulses in man to atrophy. The
language of the body is repressed, tamed by the "military uniform and
the religious habit" (98). Vital joy in life is regarded as inappropriate or
insane: "One must first be beside oneself in order to know the longing
to tear off one's clothing and roll around in this meadow" (98).

But the spontaneous, nonverbal impulses in the narrative stem
often from despair. Romantic *Weltschmerz* haunts the work in the form
of an unnerving "hellish laughter." The text begins and ends with this
"centuries-old laughter." It causes an "echo, monstrous, bouncing off
innumerable barriers. And the suspicion that nothing more will happen
but this reverberation" (3–4). This same bitter laughter, which arises
from despairing sadness and hopelessness, can nonetheless produce
affinity between those who think alike: "For no reason she suddenly
begins to laugh, first softly, then loudly and heartily. The laughter is
infectious, and Kleist laughs, too. They have to hold on to each other in
order not to fall down laughing. They will never be closer than they are
at this moment" (118). Such laughter is located at the edge of the abyss,
for it originates in the insight that the ultimate act of freedom, the decision regarding whether to live or to die, belongs to each person alone.
This wild feeling eliminates all constraints, and it exists in the free
space beyond language.

In one passage in the book, language is not just circumvented, it is
made completely powerless. In a utopian moment Kleist and Günderrode recognize each other in their innermost selves. All worldly exter-
nalities fall from them, like the useless words that refer not to essence
but to disguise. This existential moment begins with the "they" of isolation, develops to the "you" of a conversation, and ends with the "we" of
a newfound unity. This new "we"-voice speaks from a position beyond
convention and prejudice. It defines community in the recognition of
limitations. But it opens at the same time a utopian perspective in
which the narrator, as successor to the two poets, also participates:

They stop and turn toward each other. Each of them sees the sky behind the other's head. The pale blue of late afternoon, little proces-
sions of clouds. They examine each other candidly, without reserve.
Naked gazes. Self-abandonment, a tentative experiment. Smiles, first

341

hers, then his, ironical. Let's pretend it's a game even if it's deadly earnest. You know it, I know it too. Don't come too close. Don't stay too far away. Conceal yourself. Reveal yourself. Forget what you know. Remember it. Masks fall away, superincrustations, scabs, varnish. The bare skin. Undisguised features. So that's my face. This is yours. Different down to the ground, alike from the ground up. Woman. Man. Untenable words. We two, each imprisoned in his sex. That touching we desire so infinitely does not exist. It was killed along with us. We should have to invent it. (108)

In this passage all the threads of the narrative come together in a knot. The close connection of the motif of the language crisis with the technique of quotations and with the utopian hope of new contact is evident here in the hint at the possibility of a new unity, a "we." We have already seen that, through adherence to original texts and through temporal condensation, the characters' authentic self-quotations underscore themes in the narrative. The literal quotations thus battle with utmost seriousness against the observed linguistic crisis and the self-censorship of the characters and the narrator. In spite of the limits of language, through their self-quotations Christa Wolf wrests more from Kleist and Günderrode than just their personal problems. In its mediation through the narrator, what is said continually reflects back onto the current level. Because of this linkage, the quotation as both biographical and mediated document perhaps becomes the most important structural element of the narrative.

These authentic passages, although already poetic expression, are nonetheless themselves the result of speech in a crisis. There is no quotation hidden in the staccato of voices in the passage above. In the demasking of encrusted concepts, in the search for substance overwhelmed by convention, it becomes clear that the familiar, the already formulated, cannot be repeated again. An entirely innovative search for truth is necessary for human beings to be united once again. This utopian demand becomes a provocation, especially when one recalls the title *No Place on Earth.* But the total pessimism suggested in the title applies only to the speaker of these words, Kleist (108). Death awaits both him and Günderrode, as every reader knows. Even in the final remaining minutes of their mutual walk the two poets can find no new beginning other than their spontaneous "hellish laughter," no way out of their situation. In correspondence with the logic of the narrative structure, their further conversation is therefore once again dotted with quotations.

The function of Kleist and Günderrode is to express "yearning": "Time seems to be trying to bring about a new order of things, and we will experience no part of it except the overthrow of the old" (108–109). This yearning for a new time is admittedly quite vague, and we hear the articulation of strong doubts about the mere possibility of a new "ideal state": "Often I think: What if the primal, ideal state created by nature, which we were compelled to destroy, could never lead to that second ideal state we envisage, via that organization which we have created for ourselves?" (117). But the doubts must vanish, for hope is necessary to life: "If we cease to hope, then that which we fear will surely come" (117).

The inner gesture of the narrative thus becomes clear: the "precursors" Kleist and Günderrode express Christa Wolf's own passionate concerns about the times: the existential loneliness of the thinking person in a state that does not permit open discussion of its goals; the lofty revolutionary ideals that have been overtaken by reality and summarily declared to be realized; the beginning doubts in the possibility of improving the condition of the world; the conviction that science and technology alone do not determine progress and that, instead of humanizing the world, they will merely accelerate the specialization and alienation of human beings. Finally, Christa Wolf's central concern: the "becoming human" (*Menschwerdung*) of man and woman.[20]

While the characters Kleist and Günderrode cannot yet find a new beginning to escape their misery, Christa Wolf now has time on her side. Kleist's statement that he can find no spiritual homeland makes him into a restless wanderer in his times. But this statement is not to be regarded as analogous to the current time level. Certainly all the earlier signs are there again: depression, regret over missed opportunities and possibilities, alienation. But the historical overview is new, as is the hope that the historical parallels might prove productive: "The narrative is meant to be understood as a model," Christa Wolf confirmed in 1979.[21]

The text wants to provoke the reader to his own reaction. It demonstrates how the desire for open discussion can loosen the web of restrictions, even if initially only for moments. With the motif of physical sufferings representing spiritual ones, Christa Wolf shows Kleist's attacks of *angst* and weakness, Günderrode's shortness of breath and migraines. After their passionate conversation we observe their relief: Günderrode has no headache and has enough air to breathe; Kleist is free of his attack of *angst*. The narrative is a model because it demonstrates the freedom and the healing that can ensue from frank conversations as well as the pessimism and human loss caused by silence. The expression of problems is the first step to a new beginning: "People who are not deceived about themselves will extract something fresh out of the foment of every age, simply by lending it expression. I feel that the world could not go on if this were not done" (82).

It is obvious that the communication demonstrated and demanded anew in this narrative cannot merely be renewed chatter. In view of this demand in *No Place*, it becomes clear that the work itself can be understood as a new beginning, as the first realization of that synthesis of art and life demanded in it. The macrostructure of the narrative expands into an easily perceived image: The work, in the form of a broadly conceived authorial monologue, is presented as if it were the private nightmare of the author in which she considers her situation as artist and woman in the GDR of "really existing socialism," in a state that has postulated itself as an ideal while banishing its well-meaning critics into exile. Her thoughts return to the period of the beginning bourgeois age, where she finds many roots for current problems, for the fruitful beginnings at that time were also pushed aside and deadened by society. Because all the figures, including the connecting and organizing voice of the narrator, emerge from the dream-consciousness of the author, the boundaries between them are often unclear. As though reminding himself of his function, the narrator occasionally asks, "Who is speaking?" This points to the inner gesture of the story, which does not intend to be a careful reproduction of historical figures and facts but centers rather on the problems themselves in a dreamlike poetic manner.

This dream-mood becomes quite evident at the beginning of the narrative. With entreaties suggestive of myth, the narrative voice raises the two poet-figures from their graves, speaks about them separately, and then explains time and place of the action:

> The claim that they met: a legend that suits us. The town of Winkel, on the Rhine, we saw it ourselves. An appropriate spot.
> June 1804.
> Who is speaking?
> White knuckles, hands which hurt, so they are mine. So I recognize you and command you to let go of what you cling to. What is it? Wood, a beautiful arc, the back of a chair. The gleaming seat cover of an indeterminate color, silvery blue. The shining mosaic of the parquet floor on which I am standing. People informally distributed over the space of the room, like the chairs, in decorative groupings. They understand the social graces, one must give them that. Unlike us Prussians. More sumptuous, more refined. Good taste, good taste. They call it civilization, I call it luxury. Be polite and keep quiet, it will be over soon.
>
> It's settled, Kleist thinks, I'll go back this month. (4)

The narrative perspective shifts from the "we" of the narrator to a figure at first not identified, who, as if awakening from deep sleep, must recognize itself through the beginning sensations in its hands. The "I" on which the focus falls discovers first itself and then the world around it: its own hands, the chair, the floor, the people in the room, the tasteful surroundings. This person is certain of his own identity from the beginning—he knows he comes from Prussia—he is Kleist.

One of Christa Wolf's artistic devices consists in retrieving long-dead characters from their graves and investing them with new life, "resurrected . . . from the dead" (3), and then sounding out the present through these examples. The inner eye of the dreamer, which can penetrate to the thoughts of the characters she has thus conjured forth, moves from one to the other and examines their thoughts and words. This dream cannot be recreated from the perspective of an omniscient narrator. Although the narrator stands very close to the author, he still remains only the organizer for this work. The narrator is occasionally overtaken by the dynamics of the events here set in motion ("Who is speaking?"). In the memory of the well-read dreamer, the preexisting material—quotations, significant formulations, biographical facts—rise into contemplative consciousness, and this raw material helps to illuminate the essence of particular details, problems, and personalities. That which is known is recalled to memory, and the narrator is the mediating voice and bridge between the quoted and remembered sections and the specific narrative situation.

In this process of the author's self-disclosure, the quotations attain a dual importance: as biographical evidence from the lives of the poets they make these historical figures (more often than their literary products) points of reference for comparisons between the two historical periods. This method of quotation as an impulse for recollection is practiced by Kleist in the text itself: "That was eleven years ago and happened in another lifetime. The memory of it would have vanished utterly had he not enclosed it in a fortress of words, which now enables him to conjure up the experience as often as he chooses" (16–17).

In addition to this function as a biographical, extremely precise frame for the contemplations of the author, the quotations also have an aesthetic significance that goes far beyond the limits of this work. They are related to the tradition of Romantic "mixed forms" and continue a manner of writing practiced by Bettina von Arnim. Christa Wolf has drawn attention to important stylistic traits in Bettina's book about Günderrode: "Bettina has been criticized for the free manipulation of her material—abridging letters, borrowing sections from other correspondences, inventing some things" (SD 255). Christa Wolf proudly places her own work in this tradition through her technique of quotation in *No Place on Earth*. Although she has developed her own new form in *No Place*, her words about Bettina's technique present important suggestions about her own aesthetics as expressed in the narrative. She welcomes the open form, the letters and short sections in which the personality can present itself in all its contradictory traits. A closed form would have had to reduce, smooth, and level off the material. As Wolf says about Bettina: "What should be most noticeable in this book is also what is most easily overlooked, because it is not formulated: the statement inherent in the structure of the book—namely, its refusal to conform to an aesthetic canon" (BL 309–310).

As a successor to the Romantics, Christa Wolf's narrative thus belongs within the revived tradition attempting to eliminate the boundaries between art and life. "No place on earth" stands for the Greek concept of "utopia" that, in spite of everything, still poses a noble challenge to East and West. It remains to be seen whether Wolf's vision will be more than an aesthetic statement.

Notes

The German version of this essay appears as a chapter in Brandes's book, *Zitat und Montage in der neueren DDR-Prosa* (Frankfurt/Main: Lang, 1984), 61–100. It is reprinted here by permission of the publisher and the author.

1. Unless otherwise noted, all parenthetical references are to *No Place on Earth*.

2. Wolf, *Kein Ort. Nirgends* (Darmstadt: Luchterhand, 1979), book jacket. See also Curt Hohoff, *Heinrich von Kleist* (Hamburg: Rowohlt, 1958), 60f.

3. "Poems are a balm laid upon everything in life that is unappeasable," Karoline von Günderrode to Bettina Brentano. From Bettina von Arnim's epistolary novel *Die Günderode*. Quoted in Karoline von Günderrode, *Der Schatten eines Traumes*, ed. Christa Wolf (Darmstadt: Luchterhand, 1979), 244f. "The poet lives, as it were, in a wilderness, prey to the attack of wild beasts, for not all of them can be tamed by Orphic song; and those who follow dancing in his wake are apes," Clemens Brentano's letter to Achim von Arnim, April 2, 1804. Quoted by Renate Knoll, "Das 'innerste Innere.' Christa Wolf und die Tradition des 18. Jahrhunderts. Eine phänomenologische Skizze," *TuK* 7, no. 1 (1979): 148. "Life is growing increasingly more complicated, and trust becoming ever more difficult," Heinrich von Kleist to Adolphine von Werdeck, November 29, 1801. Heinrich von Kleist, *Briefe 1793–1804. Sämtliche Werke und Briefe in sieben Bänden*, vol. 6, ed. Helmut Sembder (Munich: Deutscher Taschenbuch Verlag, 1964), 228.

4. Silvia and Dieter Schlenstedt, "Elegische Provokation," *Sonntag* 32 (1979). Reprinted in *Kritik 79: Rezensionen zur DDR Literatur*, ed. Eberhard Günther et al. (Leipzig: Mitteldeutscher Verlag, 1979), 235–240.

5. Patricia Herminghouse, "Die Wiederentdeckung der Romantik: Zur Funktion der Dichterfiguren in der neueren DDR-Literatur," in *DDR-Roman und Literaturgesellschaft*, ed. Jos Hoogeveen and Gerd Labroisse, *Amsterdamer Beiträge zur Neueren Germanistik* 11/12 (1981): 243.

6. Jürgen Engler, "Herrschaft der Analogie," *NdL* 7 (1979); reprinted in *Kritik 79*, 227–234.

7. Hans-Georg Werner, "Romantische Traditionen in epischen Werken der neueren DDR-Literatur: Franz Fühmann und Christa Wolf," *Zeitschrift für Germanistik* (Leipzig), 1 (1980): 407.

8. Herman Meyer, *The Poetics of Quotation in the European Novel*, trans. Theodore and Yetta Ziolkowski (Princeton: Princeton University Press, 1968), 10.

9. "Der Wanderer." Text by Georg Philipp Schmidt von Lübek.

> Ich komme vom Gebirge her,
> Es dampft das Tal, es braust das Meer.
> Ich wandle still, bin wenig froh,
> Und immer fragt der Seufzer: wo?
> Die Sonne dünkt mich hier so kalt,
> Die Blüte welk, das Leben alt,
> Und was sie reden, leerer Schall,
> Ich bin ein Fremdling überall.
>
> Wo bist du, mein geliebtes Land?
> Gesucht, geahnt, und nie gekannt!
> Das Land, das Land so hoffnungsgrün,
> Das Land, wo meine Rosen blühn,
> Wo meine Freunde wandelnd gehn,
> Wo meine Toten auferstehn,
> Das Land, das meine Sprache spricht,
> O Land, wo bist du?

Ich wandle still, bin wenig froh,
Und immer fragt der Seufzer: wo?
Im Geisterhauch tönt's mir zurück:
"Dort, wo du nicht bist, dort ist das Glück!"

(I come from the mountains,
The valley steams, the ocean roars.
I wander quietly, am seldom glad,
And always the sigh asks: where?
The sun seems so cold to me here,
The blossoms wilted, life old,
And their speech empty noise,
I am a stranger everywhere.

Where are you, my beloved land?
Sought, imagined, and never known!
The land, the land so ripe with hope,
The land where my roses bloom,
Where my friends wander,
Where my dead are resurrected,
The land that speaks my language,
Oh land, where art thou?

I wander quietly, am seldom glad,
And always the sigh asks: where?
The spirit's voice comes back to me:
"There, where you are not, is happiness!")

10. Karoline von Günderrode, *Der Schatten eines Traumes: Gedichte, Prosa, Briefe, Zeugnisse von Zeitgenossen*, ed. and with an essay by Christa Wolf (Berlin/GDR: Buchverlag der Morgen; and Darmstadt: Luchterhand, 1979).

11. Heinrich von Kleist, *Sämtliche Werke und Briefe in sieben Bänden*, ed. Helmut Sembder (Munich: Carl Hanser Verlag, 1961); unabridged and unedited paperback edition (Munich: Deutscher Taschenbuch Verlag, 1964).

12. Curt Hohoff, *Heinrich von Kleist in Selbstzeugnissen und Bilddokumenten* (Hamburg: Rowohlt, 1958), 14; emphasis is Hohoff's.

13. In his edition of the letters, Helmut Sembder has attempted to reconstruct the contents of the *Ideenmagazin* by using boldface type for those frequent passages from Kleist's letters that are repeated verbatim. Heinrich von Kleist, *Geschichte meiner Seele, Ideenmagazin, das Lebenszeugnis der Briefe*, ed. Helmut Sembder, Sammlung Dieterich, 233 (Bremen: Schünemann, 1959).

14. Kleist, *Werke und Briefe*, vol. 6, 217.

15. Günderrode, *Schatten*, 206.

16. Ibid., 197.

17. Ibid., 212.

18. Manfred Jäger has traced the concern with language in the work of Christa Wolf from the beginnings up to *Patterns of Childhood* and has determined an ascending curve of language skepticism. The less the ideological healing of a figure takes place in a given work, the stronger the gap between thing and word. Manfred Jäger, "Die Grenzen des Sagbaren," in *Christa Wolf Materialienbuch*, ed. Klaus Sauer (Darmstadt/Neuwied: Luchterhand, 1979), 130–145.

19. Both here and in the essay on Bettina one can locate hidden references to Wolf Biermann's expulsion from the GDR in November 1976. A Biermann quotation is worked into Kleist's words when he notes "that his native land looked much better to him the farther away from it he got" (65). Patricia Herminghouse has drawn attention to Wolf's relation of an historical affair of state to political problems of the present: In the essay on Bettina, Wolf reminds us of the Göttin-

gen professors around Wilhelm Grimm (the "Göttingen Seven"), who submissively petitioned the Prussian king that he might observe the constitution. Wolf dates this episode November 18—the date of the protest petition of GDR intellectuals and artists against the Biermann expulsion. Patricia Herminghouse, "Die Wiederentdeckung der Romantik," 247.

20. Sara Lennox maintains: "Christa Wolf brings to developments in both East and West the most radical feminist critique of any woman writing in Germany today." Lennox considers the motif of "touching"—so important in the utopian recognition scene in *No Place* and in Christa Wolf's foreword to Maxie Wander's *Guten Morgen, du Schöne* (Good Morning, Thou Pretty One)—to be Wolf's key concept for a female attitude "which regards its object with sympathy and understanding." Sara Lennox, "Trends in Literary Theory: The Female Aesthetic and German Women's Writing," *GQ* 1 (1981): 71.

21. At the end of a reading session on 8 May 1979 in Münster, Westphalia, Wolf emphasized this meaning of the narrative. Reported by Renate Knoll, "Das innerste Innere," 161.

Cassandra: Creating a Female Voice

Heidi Gilpin

Although Cassandra is mentioned in many works of classical literature, she figures most prominently in two Greek tragedies: Aeschylus' *Agamemnon* and Euripides' *Women of Troy*.[1] Aeschylus presents a frenzied Cassandra who prophesies the bloody future of the house of Atreus and the death of Agamemnon after she refuses to follow him into the palace. The citizens who welcome Agamemnon home listen compassionately, convinced that her sufferings have driven her mad, but they make no effort to go to Agamemnon's assistance. Aware of her own imminent death, Cassandra appeals to the gods to make it swift and enters the palace, whereupon Clytemnestra kills her.[2]

Euripides presents Cassandra among the Trojan women before they are taken away by their captors at the end of the war. Having heard that she is to be Agamemnon's concubine, Cassandra bears torches and invites the women to dance and "wildly whirl and turn in purest ecstasy" in mad celebration of her "marriage."[3] She beseeches her mother Hecuba not to mourn for her lost virginity because she foresees her own death and that of their enemy Agamemnon and thus will avenge his violation of her chastity.[4]

Christa Wolf's version of the Cassandra legend does not adhere consistently to these classical portrayals. Although generally it remains similar to documented accounts, Wolf's narrative incorporates details and episodes that never appear in classical texts. Wolf admits: "I am really trying to present a new interpretation of the Cassandra story and

349

of the story of the Trojan war."[5] Wolf recreates history from the point of view of this mythical woman and gives her a voice with which to speak of her own experience: she thereby creates an experimental and unprecedented interpretation.

The narrative *Cassandra* is Wolf's exploration of a previously suppressed female voice.[6] Written in the first person singular, Cassandra's retrospective inner monologue reveals her memories and thoughts and recreates a life of multiple episodes. These episodes are unified by the narrator Cassandra, who has her own unique and independent view of the world. Her voice conveys a distinct impression of Trojan life before and during the long war from the perspective of a woman who is simultaneously inside and outside her culture and who knows that she will be destroyed because of her participation in it.

The narrative takes place within the few seconds or minutes before Cassandra's death: she is sitting on a wagon in front of the palace of Mycenae with her servant Marpessa and her two sons. She "sees" that Clytemnestra will kill Agamemnon within minutes and knows that her own death must follow. According to Wolf, Cassandra understands Clytemnestra. She realizes that the queen must kill both her and her sons in order to fulfill her vengeance for Agamemnon. Painful as this is to accept, Cassandra does not lament away her last seconds of life in either begging for mercy or in self-pitying condemnation of her past mistakes.[7] In her final lucid moments she reflects on the course of her life and the process whereby she was blinded to the truth: "There is no more time left, and so self-reproach is not enough. I must ask myself what it was that made me blind. The humiliating thing is, I could have sworn I already had the answer, did have for a long time" (C 77).

Cassandra's interior monologue examines how people ignore the truth; it accordingly illustrates a marked progression from peace to war and from her involvement in Trojan affairs to her eventual disassociation from them. The narrative begins with a portrayal of Cassandra's profound love for her father Priam, for her city, and for the Trojan people. With a keen awareness of political developments in Troy she observes the growing conflict between Greeks and Trojans. But when she prophesies the war that will end in Troy's destruction, neither Priam nor the Trojans believe her, and consequently they ignore her. Later Priam imprisons her to prevent her interference in his political decisions. In the course of the years that follow, Cassandra observes the changes that lead the Trojans toward a more warlike mentality. She and her mother Hecuba are excluded from the city council, and their advice is ignored through the rationale that war is not woman's business.[8] Cassandra notices that many women become objects of political decisions and that men begin to play increasingly dominant roles in public affairs by excluding women.

In the lectures that comprise the first four-fifths of the *Cassandra* piece, Wolf examines the causes of self-destruction and draws important and specific parallels to our present-day situation. The first and second lectures describe her trip to Greece in 1980 when she first became interested in ancient Greek culture. Her ideas about the Cassandra theme are inspired by Crete and the ruins of the mysterious Minoan culture, in which women apparently played a significant political role. In these two lectures it becomes obvious that Wolf's image of Cassandra is rooted in the mythology of matriarchy. The third lecture takes the form of working papers that most explicitly point out the analogies between ancient Troy and modern times: they focus specifically on the significance of the Cassandra theme today with regard to the search for peace. In the fourth lecture Wolf explores the historical reality of the Cassandra figure and discusses writing from a female point of view. Her new, very personal approach to Greek mythology (her "viewing lens" [Seh-Raster]) focuses on the role of women in society and culture; it presents a distinct contrast to the traditional interpretation of ancient women in the literature of the last three thousand years. Her discovery of mythological female voices, which began for Wolf with her research on Cassandra, now assumes such an overwhelming importance in her thinking that she significantly compares it to her initial exposure to Marxist theory and attitudes thirty years earlier (C 278).

This study of both the *Cassandra* narrative and the accompanying lectures will address the central issues in thematic structure and examine aspects of form with regard to history and language. Special emphasis will be placed on Wolf's conscious development of a female voice and her recent exploration of a feminine aesthetic. Although references will be made to material in the lectures where it pertains to the story, the primary focus of this study is the narrative itself.

Thematically, this narrative presents a distinct progression of thought, firmly supported by material in the lectures. According to Wolf, male-dominated "rational" thinking leads directly to war. She depicts Troy as a society based on hierarchical structures. It pursues its heroic goals in the name of the *polis* while losing its former awareness of the larger issues of human dignity, equality, and peaceful development. Its focus on such values as "honor" and the conquest of other polities closely resembles modern societies in their potentially self-destructive drive to domination. This kind of thinking led to the Trojan war, and it still exists today, promoting the nuclear arms race that similarly threatens the survival of mankind. Women's perceptions of events are different from men's, however. Potentially, women can affect the aggressive patriarchal tendency by searching for alternatives to it in thinking and living. If women are permitted to influence and contribute to politics and culture, there will be hope for a more peaceful society based no longer on hierarchy but on egalitarian respect and cooperation.

According to this argument, Wolf thematically structures her narrative by illustrating in her characters various possible modes of human behavior. Close examination of these characters reveals not only distinct parallels between women and men but also explicit representations of peaceful and warlike thinking. It also elucidates Wolf's purpose in *Cassandra*: to reflect modern society in the reinterpretation of myth.

In her examination of society and the causes of self-destruction, Wolf thus demonstrates an entire spectrum of human behavior in her characters. At one end of this scale the reader finds characters who exemplify warlike characteristics such as pure aggression, anger, and cruelty. These characters see absolutely no alternative to war and total conquest, and they have no choice but to kill or be killed. The two most prominent examples of such behavior are the Amazon leader Penthesilea and the Greek warrior Achilles. Penthesilea exemplifies the true warrior: she believes so firmly in her cause that she is willing to die and have others die for it. Achilles, the most fundamentally evil character in the narrative, likewise embodies an almost demonic lust for total war and domination.

Other characters, such as Polyxena, Briseis, and Hector, sustain the egalitarianism of Wolf's message: both men *and* women can conform to inhumanity and narrow national pursuits without recognizing the inherent depravity of such action in human terms. The avoidance of a larger truth is a nearly universal characteristic that leads people toward an increasingly hopeless future; for they refuse to see that alternate ways of thinking and acting are possible. Polyxena could refuse to marry Achilles if she were to disagree with the councilmen's tactics to use her as a pawn. She does not realize that her involvement in such political affairs only debases herself and prolongs war.

Arisbe and Anchises, at the other extreme, leave Trojan society altogether. They cannot justify life in a society of deceit and war and remain firmly committed to shaping their alternative culture on Mount Ida. In contrast to Trojan society, the significant characteristics of this peaceful community are the absence of fear and the strong desire to learn.

It is important to note that both sexes can potentially exhibit such characteristics. Both Anchises and Aeneas have consciously stepped out of their bellicose society in their desire to overcome the disastrous confinements of "male rationality." Their social and moral values closely resemble those of the women on the mountain. It becomes apparent, then, that Wolf bases her feminist assertions on cultural, not biological, differences between the sexes. Although Anchises and Aeneas are anomalies when compared to the policy-shaping men of Troy, they are just as nurturing, explorative, loving, and supportive in a personal context as the women on the mountain.

The mountain community, with its honest and fearless acceptance of life as well as its explorative and creative way of thinking, represents a marked contrast to the attitudes of the Trojans whose "rational" thinking either consciously or unconsciously begins and prolongs war. Cassandra's description of life in this ideal society takes on a utopian dimension: "Who would believe us, Marpessa, if we told them that in the middle of the war we used to meet regularly outside the fortress on paths known to no one but us initiates? That we, far better informed than any other group in Troy, used to discuss the situation, confer about measures (and carry them out, too); but also to cook, eat, drink, laugh together, sing, play games, learn?" (C 52).

Such a society is only shown as an alternative, however; the possibility that it could influence Trojan events never exists in the narrative. This communal living system is no longer based on the heroic pursuits of the ruling class but on the solidarity of its members who are committed to common peaceful goals. In its remoteness it retains its visionary nature for the future only. The mountain community as a whole, then, becomes the most peaceful "figure" on Wolf's spectrum of human behavior. This collective character represents the active people who reject the corruption they see in traditional political rule and depart from Troy in order to create their own functioning culture. For Wolf, this collective character is predominantly female because its membership, except for Anchises and Aeneas, consists only of women. Wolf suggests that women's way of thinking incorporates contradictions into a web of reality, while men's way of thinking (as exemplified by Priam and his councilmen) prefers to avoid or ignore conflicting views on the basis of ideology.[9]

Significantly, even the two men, Anchises and Aeneas, loyal and active in the mountain community during the war, return to their traditional roles after the fall of Troy. When Aeneas is offered the chance to lead a group of "heroes" to a new country, he accepts it without any hesitation and fails to realize that he will perpetrate the same kind of hierarchical system from which he fled earlier. In the last passages of the narrative Cassandra not only recognizes that Aeneas will continue to recreate a similar corrupt traditional mentality in future societies; she sees this as inevitable. Time is simply not ripe for the radical changes that the ideals of the mountain community propose:

> The new masters would dictate their law to all the survivors. The earth was not large enough to escape them. You, Aeneas, had no choice: You had to snatch a couple of hundred people from death. You were their leader. "Soon, very soon, you will have to become a hero."
>
> "Yes!" you cried. "And so?" I saw by your eyes that you had understood me. I cannot love a hero. . . . We have no chance against a time that needs heroes. (C 138)

In this context, Clytemnestra and Aeneas have much in common. Like Aeneas, Clytemnestra also represents a shift backward on Wolf's scale toward traditional, albeit corrupt thinking. Conscious of the inherent depravity in her motivations, Clytemnestra still chooses to act according to the rules of her society and fulfills her vengeance on Agamemnon. Although aware of the alternative not to kill Cassandra and her two sons, Clytemnestra realizes that she must murder them if she is to maintain her authority and adhere to the rational thinking she has adopted from men. Again Cassandra perceives the situation as inevitable: "She was doing what she had to do" (*C* 41). And again Wolf suggests that time is the significant factor that prevents Clytemnestra from both recognizing the profound flaws in her own way of thinking and acting differently: "In different times nothing would have prevented us from calling each other sister. That is what I read in my adversary's face" (*C* 41).

Due to civilized society's unreadiness to accept and implement social and political alternatives in their time, both Clytemnestra and Aeneas choose to maintain traditional societal rules and values despite their awareness of alternate possibilities. The inevitability of the status quo produces exactly the opposite effect in Cassandra, however. She refuses to compromise her beliefs for a culture that rejects them and thus chooses to step out of society completely: when Aeneas departs to found a new Troy, Cassandra leaves to die.[10]

In this ultimate rejection, Cassandra is alone on Wolf's spectrum of human behavior. Unlike the other characters in the narrative, Cassandra has no male counterpart who reflects her commitment to social responsibility.[11] Cassandra can neither ignore nor abandon the problems of her people. This socially responsible attitude proves very difficult in practice, as the harsh treatment she receives for sharing her visions illustrates. Cassandra acknowledges the difficulty when she intersperses her monologue with the all too relevant question: "Why did I want the gift of prophecy, come what may?" (*C* 4, 9). And her response exhibits a principle aim of the narrative: "To speak with my voice: the ultimate. I did not want anything more, anything different" (*C* 4).

Distinct from the other characters, Cassandra wavers between Troy and the mountain community, finally to be outside both. Her desire to participate actively in a society that determines the future initially causes her to remain in Troy despite the hardships she must endure. Although aware of the women on Mount Ida and respectful of their peaceful attitude, Cassandra realizes that this alternative society has no influence on Trojan affairs and therefore refuses to join it until Trojan reality becomes unbearable. Even amidst the women's warmth and supportive goodwill, Cassandra cannot remain: her strong commitment to influence Trojan affairs in a positive way continually brings her back to Troy. As Wolf observes: "Cassandra . . . must have loved Troy more than herself" (BP 331). Her prophecies, based on objective observations, are motivated only by her desire to serve as an equal member of society. Cassandra reminds herself: "Well, my desire to exercise influence over people; how else could a woman hold a position of power?" (*C* 26).

Though Cassandra is extremely conscious of the fundamental cultural difference between women and men, especially of woman's role as peacemaker in society, she realizes that women will only be capable of peacefully influencing society if they trust their own perceptions, remain true to their own values, and acknowledge their cultural difference from men. This realization is illustrated in the central Penthesilea episode.

Penthesilea, similar to today's militant feminists, argues that the only way for women to stop men's destruction is to fight men on their terms. Cassandra and others disagree with her because such fighting denies the significant difference between the sexes and the constructive peaceful influence of women. Furthermore, the self-destructive nature of mankind is turning against *people*, not just women, as Arisbe argues: "That part of the inhabited world which we knew had turned against us ever more cruelly, ever more swiftly. 'Against us women,' said Penthesilea. 'Against us people,' Arisbe replied" (C 118). When Penthesilea retorts that women *must* fight men, Arisbe points to the primary flaw in Penthesilea's thinking, namely, that by fighting men women would deny their difference: "We should do what they do in order to show that we are different?" (C 118).

Cassandra, as a mythological figure who actively explores the possible ways in which people could peacefully influence the social and political development of civilization, continues to challenge modern society with many ideas for reflection. Wolf suggests that this was also Cassandra's intention; she was predominantly concerned with the future of mankind and the transmission of knowledge from one generation to the next. As a prophetess and priestess of high rank in her society, Cassandra knows that her name will remain in legends for future generations: "Your name will go on," she is told (C 11). But this does not satisfy her: she wants her vision and her knowledge to remain in order to discover the roots of the self-destructive tendency in human nature. This is also the most urgent concern of the women in the mountain community when they actively search for ways to transfer information about their experience to later societies, in order to avoid a repetition of history: "But more than anything else we talked about those who would come after us. What they would be like. Whether they would still know who we were. Whether they would repair our omissions, rectify our mistakes. We racked our brains trying to think of a way we could leave them a message, but did not know any script to write in" (C 132–133).

Full of frustration and lacking a more effective means, these women leave their fingerprints in the clay walls of their caves: "We pressed our hands side by side into the soft clay. We called that immortalizing our memory, and laughed" (C 133). Cassandra realizes that, as a famous prophetess and legendary figure, she can transmit the ideas and thoughts of the mountain community more clearly and effectively than this, but she can only do so by dying. According to Wolf, Cassandra's death is a clear statement of her fervent desire to be discovered by subsequent peoples. Her conscious decision to die rather than help Aeneas in continuing their race will alert later generations to the serious problems of her society and time. No one would notice conflict if she joined

Aeneas and died a natural death. But Cassandra's death is the unnatural result of her deliberate consideration: its aim is to provoke thought and discussion.[12] More than anything, she wants to leave behind her voice to be rediscovered by others. Although Cassandra sees that at this point in history her last wish is in vain, her final urgent words before death call for a writer who could retell her experience and perpetuate her visions:

> "Clytemnestra, lock me up forever in your darkest dungeon. Give me barely enough to live on. But I implore you: Send me a scribe, or better yet a young slave woman with a keen memory and a powerful voice. Ordain that she may repeat to her daughter what she hears from me. That the daughter in turn may pass it on to her daughter, and so on. So that alongside the river of heroic songs this tiny rivulet, too, may reach those faraway, perhaps happier people who will live in times to come." (C 81)

With *Cassandra*, Wolf shows her readers that Cassandra's wish was not in vain. Three thousand years later, she has unearthed this mythical voice from which all members of modern society can learn. This contemporary author recreates Cassandra's voice and involves her readers in the process of thought that Cassandra hoped to pass on to later generations. How she accomplishes this is central to the following examination of the formal elements of *Cassandra*. For Wolf is extremely conscious of her process of both rediscovering the Cassandra figure and of drawing her readers into the process:

> It is my wish that the reader will rebel—as I did while writing—against this death of more than three thousand years ago, will refuse to accept it. [Cassandra] cannot see it that way, although she understands everything—it has to be seen by the reader. For this reason I attempt to harm the figure as little as possible, to avoid making it into an object. I wrote sixty pages in the third person before I noticed that that did not achieve what I was after. I then wrote the whole thing as a monologue, and this allowed a greater intensity and stronger identification with the figure, which may transfer itself to the reader. (DO 108)

Wolf chooses a form of writing that enables her and her readers to participate actively in the themes and questions raised. She encourages her reading audience to develop the protagonist further by presenting the Cassandra figure in an open-ended, nondidactic manner. This style urges the reader to argue and converse with the ideas Wolf presents, thereby discovering her/his own ideas. Helen Fehervary, a friend and critic of Wolf, comments on this phenomenon: "What interests me is . . . that I participate in this process that you are going through. I rediscover myself in the process, I cooperate, I attempt to think along. Actually it is a conversation" (DO 99).

Wolf characterizes her work on *Cassandra* as an unfinished process. The description of her work in the introduction to her lectures does not pretend to assume authority: "this fabric which I want to display to you now did not turn out completely tidy, is not surveyable at one glance. Many of its motifs are not followed up, many of its threads are tangled. There are wefts which stand out like foreign bodies, repetitions, material that has not been worked out to its conclusion" (C 142). Rather than presenting her work as a conclusive series of thoughts, Wolf emphasizes its constant development. She insists that she in fact never reaches a final perspective:

> I have the impression that I am at the beginning. This is not false modesty, for I really believe that I still have to formulate my central concern. Whenever I've formulated anything I have the feeling: now I have formulated a specific part of my development. And I know then for certain that, in a short while, I will experience this like a foreign skin, and that it will be torn away from within and without. With all this I only wanted to say: it's tentative. (DO 103)

Wolf illustrates this process of continual development in the formal structure of *Cassandra*. Although various combinations of essays and narrative prose are not new to twentieth-century literature, Wolf's ongoing search for answers to universal problems is exemplified in a new narrative technique that surpasses the traditional boundaries of the interior monologue. In *Cassandra* this technique gains a uniquely new dimension, superseding its traditional counterparts.

In addition to recording the unspoken thought processes of an agitated mind just minutes before death, Wolf also actively engages the reader's consciousness in these highly charged issues. In a remarkable technique of establishing a blurred ambiguity of speakers at the beginning and conclusion, Wolf supersedes the heretofore established limits of traditional interior monologue. Her recreation of the Cassandra myth in light of present-day problems is carefully anchored in the mind of the reader, who cannot but assume the role of an active participant.[13]

Cassandra speaks alone in a direct interior monologue in all but the first and last passages of the narrative. What would otherwise seem to be a detached and private soliloquy becomes a unified collective process through a few carefully worded sentences at these two points. The author bridges time here; she invites the reader to join her voyage into the time and thoughts of Cassandra at the beginning of the narrative, and leads the reader back to the present day at its conclusion. This technique invites the analogy that Wolf emphasizes between the ancient experiences and perceptions of Cassandra and the reader's situation in modern society.

The author begins in twentieth-century Greece. Yet as she stands before the gates of Mycenae where Cassandra once stood, she does not speak alone. Rather, both author *and* reader join to speak in the unified voice of a modern third-person narrator who attempts to reach into the past, to recreate Cassandra's experience: "It was here. This is where she stood. These stone lions looked at her; now they no longer have heads" (C 3).

Author and reader stand in the present and look into the past in these first lines of observant description. But in one sentence the distance between present and past, between author/reader and Cassandra, vanishes. All become one as they stand in the same place: "Keeping step with the narration, I make my way into death" (C 3).[14] This transitional sentence is remarkable in its suspended ambiguity of speakers and meaning. "Narration" from the point of view of the author is the literary product before us. For Cassandra, the protagonist, it is her private recollective process about to begin; for the reader, it is the tale about to be related. When author, protagonist, and reader are thus united in one collective narrator, "narration" assumes, in addition, the heretofore unheard feminine voice retrieved from a historical and legendary past. Now for the first time it is ready to speak about ancient and modern issues in a communal voice.

Furthermore, this transitional sentence departs on a voyage: there is *movement* here, as indicated by the verbal construction, "make my way" (in German more directly *gehen*—to go). Cassandra's short process of reflection before she takes her last step toward death is a journey of exploration for author and reader into the past, toward an uncharted realm of a woman's voice. At this point the direction of this voyage into death remains a certainty only for Cassandra, the seer. Her example, however, imparts an intense urgency of purpose to the remaining collective voice of the narrator/reader, namely, *not* to follow the protagonist into death. The communal narrator now finds herself/himself urgently and subjectively involved in all utterances of the interior monologue. Although technically only Cassandra's voice is heard in the main body of the narrative, the reader remains an active participant in what is now a collective search for truth.

Because author and reader are incorporated into the "I" with which Cassandra speaks throughout her monologue, then, this introduction to the tale proposes that Cassandra does not speak alone. With the inclusion of the reading audience into one subject, Cassandra's experience becomes analogous to our own. When we read of the moment in which Cassandra decides to stay behind and die, these participating and observing voices are brought to a shared understanding: life in an antagonistic role that contradicts all one's innermost convictions is not valuable; one must effect change for the future.

"I am staying behind" (C 138), the collective voice says. And then the return toward the present day begins in reverse order, just as the entrance into the past began: author and reader separate from Cassandra and describe the place where she stood. Only now, finally, what began as a foreign experience of observance in the past tense has become a shared perception in the present: "Here *is* the place. These stone lions looked at her" (C 138, emphasis mine).

This unusual narrative technique fulfills Wolf's intent to rediscover a female voice while it subjectively incorporates the reader in the process. Far from imposing authority, this technique consciously dismantles the hierarchical boundaries between author and reader and invites participation in what Wolf hopes will be an active, collective effort to search for answers to the universal questions of human nature, the role of women, and modern prewar society.

Wolf's specific use of language—of style and of syntax—likewise challenges the reader to become actively involved. In her lectures, the author employs a range of stylistic modes and genres: travel accounts, journal entries, letters, and narrative. This variety suggests a work in progress, an unfinished process. The tone of the narrative is particularly interesting in this respect. Wolf develops a discontinuous prose that shuns the continuous linearity of traditional realistic narration. Yet her technique does not seek to reproduce a style of modernist writing. Instead of developing yet another structure of fragmentation, it strives for "subjective authenticity."[15]

In her monologue Cassandra speaks in a personal and almost colloquial style. Her language conveys thoughts, remembered and re-created scenes, as well as conversations with people. Cassandra's inner thoughts flow in the natural sequence of spoken language with all its inherent breaks, shifts, and dialectical emphases. By characterizing the protagonist through such a highly realistic, almost contemporary conversational tone, Wolf avoids any hierarchical difference between speaker and reader. Wolf's writing transcends the boundaries between spoken and written language in an attempt to reach her reader on a more personal, equal level. As such it contradicts the traditional modes of literary and stylized language that were established in much earlier writing by a narrating voice. In 1953, Roland Barthes defined such hierarchical boundaries between narration and oral communication: "All modes of writing have in common the fact of being 'closed' and thus different from spoken language. Writing is in no way an instrument for communication, it is not an open route through which there passes only the intention to speak. . . . Writing is an anti-communication, it is intimidating."[16]

In contrast, Wolf's writing *is* communication; its central aim is to converse with the reader on friendly terms of shared interest, not on antagonistic terms of difference. Myra Love elucidates this point in relation to *Christa T.* when she suggests that Wolf's prose expresses the intention to speak while not denying that it is writing.[17]

By subverting the opposition of speech and writing, of communication and literature, Wolf bridges the gap between experience and "high" culture. As Love suggests, "She demystifies authorship by removing it from its traditional position of depersonalized authority and returning it to its function as a means of social communication."[18] That Wolf employs similar methods in *Cassandra* illustrates her experimental, if not radical attempt to deconstruct the often hierarchical oppositions so well established in "learned" literary prose. Conscious of a different form of writing that resembles a netting or fabric of thoughts rather than the traditional linear point-by-point progression of ideas toward a conclusion, Wolf argues for the validity of such an "open" form.[19]

Wolf acknowledges that open-ended writing best suits her way of thinking. Yet an "open" form is impossible in terms of the formal limitations of an interior monologue related by a protagonist who knowingly walks to her death. Although Wolf's ideas on the Cassandra-theme are fragmentary in nature, she cannot express them as such in her protagonist's voice. For Cassandra's life as a famous prophetess was built on certainty of vision, whereas life in modern society rests on uncertainty. There are no fragments in Cassandra's life as her monologue defines it: she is about to die, reflects on the course of her life, and dies. The logic of this interior monologue prevents its expression in a more open form, as Wolf admits: "Narrative techniques, which in their closedness or openness also transmit thought patterns. I experienced the closed form of the Cassandra narrative as a contradiction to the fragmentary structure from which (for me) it is actually composed. The contradiction cannot be resolved, only named" (C 266).[20]

Although this contradiction remains in the narrative as Wolf attempts to recreate Cassandra's own voice, it disappears when read in the formal context of the lectures. By combining narrative with a personal and fragmentary form of essayism, Wolf reconciles this contradiction of form. She wished to incorporate the narrative and the lectures into one volume, thus establishing a contemporary voice. Attempts to publish the five lectures separately in disregard of Wolf's personal requests therefore do injustice to the work as a whole.[21]

Wolf's treatment of history in *Cassandra* closely resembles her deliberate use of literary forms and thus invites attention within this formal analysis. Both form and historical reinterpretation are motivated by the desire to break down barriers of opposition and to present a female voice of past *and* present. Although the author does not do injustice to the core of the legendary figure, and the narrative, when read by itself, could well be understood as yet another version of the myth, such a reading would be superficial. The work, when seen as a whole, achieves a unity in its overriding attempt to create a communal female voice. Cassandra's monologue, as introduced by the collective narrator; her language, as it strives to break down barriers between ancient legend and present-day reality; and finally Wolf's placement of the tale as yet another part in an open literary form—all these aspects establish the protagonist also as a vivid contemporary woman with whom the reader can easily identify. Cassandra is thus not an ancient mythical figure far removed from modern life. Sara Lennox confirms that Wolf's use of history is not historicist but dialectical: "to learn from the victories and defeats of the past their meaning for us in order to shape the future more carefully."[22]

In her dialectical use of history, Wolf chooses to incorporate certain historical and literary legends in her narrative while omitting others. Most strikingly, she recreates the story of the Trojan war with a rare version of the Helen myth. According to most accounts, the Trojan war was fought over Helen.[23] But Wolf's account portrays the Trojans and Greeks fighting over an illusion: "No one can win a war waged for a phantom" (C 69).[24] Similarly, while Herodotus writes that Helen never returned to Troy with Paris and that the Trojans honestly told the Greeks of her absence, Wolf reinterprets this uncommon myth to emphasize the dishonesty involved in warlike thinking.[25] In *Cassandra*, the Trojans lie about Helen's absence and pretend that she returned to Troy with Paris just to maintain their honor. This version of the Helen myth does not appear in mythological texts. Wolf's adaptation clearly supports the argument that the Trojans do not want to face the truth: they would rather create an illusion than honestly defend their position.

Wolf also reinterprets Clytemnestra in a way distinct from traditional legends in order to rediscover her and change her image: "I did not want to present this figure the way she has survived in myth—as the bad old lady, the bloodthirsty woman of whom one must be afraid" (DO 110). Her purpose in recreating Clytemnestra is consciously to voice those fractions of society that have formerly never been heard.

Wolf's new conception of Clytemnestra is striking due to the two women's implied relationship, radically different from previous legends. In the narrative, Cassandra and the queen share a special understanding: "we looked at each other, agreed as only women agree" (C 104). Wolf comments further: "They share a brief smile, a brief contact: too bad, we cannot become friends. We are on opposing sides, that's the way it turned out. I, Clytemnestra, cannot leave my side and allow you to live—that would mean that I would have to give up everything for which I've worked for the last ten years: power" (DO 110). Wolf retells Cassandra's and Clytemnestra's relationship, consciously opposed to traditional versions recorded by men. Her research illuminated the distinct prejudice of male authors toward potentially powerful women: "In my view . . . Aeschylus reveals his prejudice in the detestation which the two women, Cassandra and Clytemnestra, show for each other. . . . That is how the male poet chooses to see these women: vindictive, jealous, petty toward each other—as women can be when they are driven out of public life, chased back to home and hearth" (C 179). It is Wolf's conviction that more sympathetic and egalitarian versions of mythological female figures should be included in the wealth of biased classical legends of male authorship. This inspires her original interpretations of Cassandra, Clytemnestra, and other figures in *Cassandra*. Her striking version of pious Aeneas as Cassandra's lover, for example, never appears in mythological texts; but as a character of egalitarian nature, this Aeneas significantly balances the narrative.[26] Cassandra often mentions their profound understanding of each other: "not just that I understood Aeneas; that I *knew* him. As if I were he" (C 5). That Aeneas accepts Cassandra's twin sons as his own despite the ambiguity of their conception also suggests that Aeneas is much less egotistical than the average Trojan male.

Here again, Wolf recreates mythology to point toward future possibilities for human qualities in both men and women. According to traditional legend, the father of Cassandra's twins is Agamemnon.[27] But Wolf tells the story so that the potential father is either Aeneas or Eurypylos, Cassandra's short-lived husband.[28] The ambiguity remains for the reader to interpret. But if Eurypylos were the true father and Aeneas knew this and still accepted the twins as his own, he would represent a glimpse of hope among the heroic men who perpetrate the corruption of their traditional system. At least as far as his relationship with Cassandra is concerned, he would have demonstrated the nurturing qualities and humanist tendencies crucial for a survival of the human species.

By interpreting these legends of classical mythology in her own personal way, Wolf illustrates what she calls her "viewing lens," her new individual approach to mythology. Because mythological legend is by nature fictionalized, Wolf is actually only contributing another fictionalized interpretation. Yet this practice meets with great criticism. In an article in the important GDR journal *Sinn und Form*, its chief editor Wilhelm Girnus accuses Wolf of falsifying well-established scholarly accounts: "Christa Wolf's treatment of Greek mythology sounds poetic, to be sure, but it betrays evidence of idiosyncratic arbitrariness and of a disregard for proven results of research."[29]

Furthermore, Girnus criticizes Wolf's historical representation of women's role in society: "The picture she gives of woman's historical role (based on the poet Sappho) is not a true image."[30] He fails to recognize that the "true image" he finds in literary and historical texts is necessarily created by other, prior interpretations mostly written by men, not women, and that what was true for men was not automatically true for women. The male mythological tradition has resulted in the certainty of the contemporary critic that myths can neither change nor take on interpretations that disagree with earlier interpretations. But why modern myth should be categorically wrong or whether it is particularly a problem of modern woman's reinterpretation of myth are questions that remain unanswered. Unconscious of the bias in his own image of a historical figure, Girnus sees only the bias in Wolf's representation. Wolf, however, is aware of the translation through which mythical figures appear to contemporary readers. In this respect she suggests that Cassandra is actually a poetic invention: "Who was Cassandra before people wrote about her? (For she is a creation of the poets, she speaks only through them, we have only their view of her)" (C 287).

In her own interpretation of Cassandra, then, Wolf mainly intended to portray Cassandra and other figures as exactly and with as little prejudice as possible: "I wanted to reveal the psychological and social tendencies in this figure as precisely and as carefully as possible. I wanted to refrain from judgment, that is, not to say: this is right, or: there she should have behaved in an entirely different manner" (DO

108). But Girnus disputes this; from his traditional Marxist perspective he argues that Wolf overemphasizes the repression of women throughout history and the cultural differences between the sexes:

> From the fact that Christa Wolf further implicitly connects the problem of oppressed women—in a manner incomprehensible to me—with the "murderous who-whom," the impression is suggested to the reader—possibly unintentionally—that history is at bottom not the struggle between exploiters and exploited, but rather between men and women—indeed, even more grotesquely: between "male" and "female" thinking, between causal and acausal, between rational and emotional behavior, so to speak. It simply cannot be true that such obvious nonsense gets published in a socialist country.[31]

Girnus's polemical statement is an important document: in addition to refuting any emotional, cultural, and historical differences between women and men, it confirms Wolf's accomplished break with the officially proclaimed Marxist ideology of the GDR. Wolf now goes her own way. Instead of continuing to see the modern world crisis in the orthodox light of class antagonisms, as Wilhelm Girnus does, Wolf introduces her own feminist thinking to the issue.

Wolf's new, independent thinking, however, is not anti-Marxist. In refuting the validity of present-day GDR ideology, she rather confirms basic historical assumptions. By reinterpreting history from a female perspective, she returns to the fundamental problem of the origin of all exploitation. This was explored by Friedrich Engels in *The Origin of the Family, Private Property, and the State*: "The first class law to appear in history coincides with the development of the antagonism between man and woman in monogamous marriage, and the first class oppression with that of the female sex by the male."[32]

From this fundamental tenet of Engels's theory, Wolf has developed her own process of exploration, her own way of seeing which clearly acknowledges the differences between women and men. *Cassandra* illustrates this process. In its thematic and formal structure, Wolf's work acknowledges an autonomous female experience and demonstrates the search for new forms in which to express and interpret it authentically.

Notes

1. Cassandra appears and is cited in the following works of Greek literature: Euripides, *Andromache*, 293–300; Homer, *Iliad*, 13.361–382, and *Odyssey*, 11.421–423; Apollodorus 3.12.5, "epitome" 5.17, 5.22–23; *Cypria* 1; *Sack of Ilium* 1; Pausanias 2.16.6–7, 3.19.6, 3.26.5, 10.27.1. She is also mentioned in Roman literature: Virgil, *Aeneid*, 2.341; and Ovid, *Metamorphoses*, 13.411. For an extensive scholarly discussion of Cassandra's role in these works, see W. H. Roscher, *Ausführliches Lexikon der griechischen und römischen Mythologie* (Leipzig: B. G. Teubner, 1890–1894).

2. *The New Century Classical Handbook*, ed. Catherine B. Avery (New York: Appleton-Century Crofts, 1962), 259.

3. Euripides, *The Women of Troy* in *The Bacchae and Other Plays*, trans. Philip Vellacott (1954; rpt. New York: Penguin Books, 1981), 101.

4. Euripides, *The Women of Troy*, 103.

5. "A Dialogue with Christa Wolf," trans. Christine Friedlander. *PEN American Center Newsletter*, 53 (Winter 1984): 12.

6. In the longer version of this essay, the notion of what Wolf also calls a "female voice" emerged through specific treatment of a historical and theoretical development represented in the works of Maxie Wander, Irmtraud Morgner, and Christa Wolf, as well as upon reference to continental feminist theory. Due to space limitations, these historical and theoretical aspects could not be included here.

7. "I feel no more sorry for myself than for others" (C 8).

8. "We want to spare you," Hector explains. "The things we have to talk about in the council, now in wartime, are no longer the concern of women" (C 92).

9. Wolf introduces her entire work on the Cassandra theme as a web, a netting, a fabric of thoughts (C 141–142). Similarly, the American feminist poet Adrienne Rich also writes of thinking in this way when she defines "truth": "There is no 'the truth,' 'a truth'—truth is not one thing or even a system. It is an increasing complexity. The pattern of the carpet is a surface. When we look closely, when we become weavers, we learn of the tiny multiple threads unseen in the overall pattern, the knots on the underside of the carpet." Adrienne Rich, *Women and Honor: Some Notes on Lying* (Pittsburgh: Motherroot Publications, 1977), unnumbered pages. Wolf also writes of "truth" in this fashion. She criticizes the reductionist use of the word, which diminishes rather than expands complexity: "A word came up, as if newly invented: truth. We kept repeating it, truth, truth, and believed the word was more closely than ever our concern, truth, as if it were some animal with small eyes which lives in the dark and is timid but which one can surprise and catch, to possess it for all time. Just as we'd possessed our earlier truths. Then we checked ourselves. Nothing is so difficult as turning one's attention to things as they really are, to events as they really occur" (CT 133–134).

10. Sigrid Weigel similarly describes Cassandra's decision as a conscious stepping out of history: "It is Cassandra's decision to deny history, to step out of a (hi)story that will continue to promote and sharpen the delineated connection between hero cults, war, and the subjugation of the female/women, out of a history of progressive patriarchalization" (Es ist Kassandras Entscheidung zur Geschichtsverweigerung, zum Austritt aus einer Geschichte, die den beschriebenen Zusammenhang von Heldenkult, Krieg und Verdrängung des Weiblichen/der Frauen weiter vorantreiben und zuspitzen wird, aus einer Geschichte fortschreitender Patriarchalisierung). Because history has actually taken this course, and myth recounts it thus, Weigel suggests that death is Cassandra's only alternative: a tragic downfall replete with meaning. Cf. Sigrid Weigel, "Vom Sehen zur Seherin: Christa Wolfs Umdeutung des Mythos und die Spur der Bachmann-Rezeption in ihrer Literatur," in *Text und Kritik*, 46, ed. Heinz Ludwig Arnold (3d rev. and expanded ed.; Munich: Verlag C. H. Beck and Verlag edition text + kritik, 1985), 69.

11. Although Aeneas represents an emotional counterpart to Cassandra, he does not embody her social consciousness.

12. Its aim is to alert readers to the issue of rewriting history from a female perspective. In her excellent study of *Cassandra*, Sigrid Weigel describes the message Cassandra's death conveys: "While the death of a mythological figure appears as unavoidable tragic fate, Cassandra's death in Christa Wolf's story gains meaning via a remembering-process that contributes a history. The revision of the myth thus creates a new meaning that simultaneously denies and contributes history; the withdrawal from male history is compensated by the sketch of a female one" (Während der Tod einer Figur im Mythos als unabwend-

bares tragisches Schicksal erscheint, erhält der Tod Kassandras in Christa Wolfs Erzählung durch (eine) geschichtsstiftende Erinnerungsarbeit Bedeutung. Die Umdeutung des Mythos begründet so einen geschichtsverweigernden und geschichtsstiftenden Sinn zugleich, der Austritt aus der männlichen Geschichte wird durch den Entwurf einer weiblichen entgolten) (70–71).

13. In her novels since *The Quest for Christa T.*, Wolf has increasingly expanded on this extraordinary technique of establishing a blurred ambiguity of speakers and incorporating the reader into a communal voice of "we." The narrator in the first passages of *CT*, for example, incorporates the reader into the writer's experience: "But must we give her up for lost?" (*CT* 3). And likewise in the initial lines of *NP*: "And we, still greedy for the ashen taste of words" (*NP* 3).

14. Translation modified slightly by editor. [This seminal sentence is extremely difficult to render into English, owing to the ambiguity of voice and the meaning of the German word, *Erzählung*, which can mean story, narrative, narration, telling, tale: it refers, in other words, simultaneously to the finished object of narration as well as to the act of narration itself. In order to transmit this multiplicity of meaning in the English translation, one would have to render it approximately thus: "With this telling/tale I go toward my death."—Ed.]

15. Wolf first coined this term in her conversation with Hans Kaufmann to describe the poetic principle she sees as central to her prose and essay-work. For a fuller assessment of this principle, see Alexander Stephan, "Die subjektive Authentizität des Autors: Zur ästhetischen Position von Christa Wolf," in *Text und Kritik* 46, ed. Heinz Ludwig Arnold (2d rev. and expanded edition, 1976; rpt. Munich: Verlag C. H. Beck and Verlag edition text + kritik, 1979), Chapter 1: "Subjektive Authentizität: Biographie und Zeitgenossenschaft," 7–22. See also Myra Love, "Christa Wolf and Feminism: Breaking the Patriarchal Connection," *NGC*, no. 16 (Winter 1979): 45.

16. Roland Barthes, *Writing Degree Zero*, preface Susan Sontag, trans. Annette Lavers and Colin Smith (1953; rpt. New York: Hill and Wang, 1983), 12–20. More recently Helene Cixous argues that throughout history, thought has worked by opposition: "Speech/Writing, High/Low." See Cixous, "Sorties," in *New French Feminisms: An Anthology*, ed. Elaine Marks and Isabelle de Courtivron (New York: Schocken, 1981), 90ff.

17. See Love, 33.

18. Ibid., 34.

19. See *C* 262: "What kind of memory does the prose of Virginia Woolf require and endorse? Why should the brain be able to 'retain' a linear narrative better than a narrative network?"

20. There seems to be a progression on this idea in Wolf's work, for in *No Place on Earth* Wolf could find no form to express contradictions. As Günderrode tells Kleist: "No form can be found in which to cast an insoluable problem" (*NP* 112).

21. Although the West German edition remains in two parts, the East German version was published as one volume, as was the English translation. See "A Dialogue with Christa Wolf," 10. The publication of the Cassandra works was also intended to be simultaneous in the GDR and the FRG, but the GDR edition met with complications apparently in part due to censorship. According to a notice in *Die Zeit* (9 March 1984), some sixty lines were omitted in the GDR version. The following passage from the third lecture, found on pp. 229–230 of the English translation, is among those omitted: "Armed with nothing but the intractable desire to allow my children and grandchildren to live, I conclude that the sensible course may be the one that holds out absolutely no hope: unilateral disarmament. [I hesitate: in spite of the Reagan Administration? Yes, since I see no other way out: in spite of it!] By choosing this course, we place the other side under the moral pressure of the world public." Wolf has similarly incorporated two essays in her most recent edition of *No Place on Earth* for the same reasons. Her introduction to this volume explicitly addresses this question of formal con-

tradictions between essayism and fiction. See Wolf, *Kein Ort. Nirgends.* / *Der Schatten eines Traumes—Ein Entwurf* (Darmstadt/Neuwied: Luchterhand, 1981).

22. Sara Lennox, "Christa Wolf and the Women Romantics," in *Studies in GDR Culture and Society* 2, ed. Margy Gerber et al. (Washington, D.C.: University Press of America, 1982), 40.

23. For further discussion of dates and details, see Richard Lattimore's introduction in his translation, *The Iliad of Homer* (Chicago: University of Chicago Press, 1951), 12.

24. The extraordinary tale that Helen never went to Troy at all is ostensibly the invention of the Himerian poet Stesichorus. It became familiar and formed the basis of Euripides' *Helen*. In this romantic comedy, the heroine explains that Hera, angry at Paris for judging in favor of Aphrodite, gave him a phantom Helen made of cloud, while Zeus arranged that Hermes should transport the real Helen to Egypt where King Proteus took charge of her. In *Electra* Euripides lays the blame for creating the phantom Helen on Zeus, who sent her to Troy solely for the purpose of provoking war. See Edward Tripp, *The Meridian Handbook of Classical Mythology* (New York: Meridian Books, 1970), 265.

25. Herodotus writes that Helen was kept by Proteus and Paris sent home when they landed on Greek shores during their journey to Troy. See Herodotus, *The Histories*, trans. Aubrey de Selincourt, rev. with introd. A. R. Burn (1954; rpt. New York: Penguin Books, 1981), 173f.

26. This is probably the most extraordinary reinterpretation of the figures of Aeneas and Cassandra possible. According to mythological sources, Cassandra is a priestess, a virgin until she is violated by Ajax at the end of the war, and Aeneas is a pious, straightlaced man who would never dream of sleeping with a priestess. There is never even mention of them befriending one another. See Tripp, *The Meridian Handbook of Classical Mythology*, or Roscher, *Ausführliches Lexikon der griechischen und römischen Mythologie.*

27. See Tripp and Roscher.

28. Cassandra tells the story with tongue-in-cheek irony: "Eurypylos arrived: there were worse men than he. He was killed the day after his first night with me. . . . I went back to the Scamander again; no one mentioned my brief time away. During the last year of the war there was hardly one pregnant woman in Troy. Many looked enviously, compassionately, sadly at my belly. When the twins were born . . . they had many mothers. And Aeneas was their father" (*C* 133–134). The ambiguity of paternity arises later, when Cassandra expresses her surprise at Aeneas' assumption that the children are his: "I should take our children—he said that: our children!—and leave the city" (*C* 137).

29. Wilhelm Girnus, "Wer baute das siebentorige Theben? Kritische Bemerkungen zu Christa Wolfs Beitrag in Sinn und Form 1/83," *Sinn und Form* 35, no. 2/3 (1983): 442. It should be noted that Girnus was basing his criticism on the earlier publication, in *Sinn und Form* (35, no. 1 [1983]: 38–62), of the fourth of the five *Cassandra*-lectures ("A Letter, About Unequivocal and Ambiguous Meaning, Definiteness and Indefiniteness; About Ancient Conditions and New View-Scopes; About Objectivity"), and addresses this material so specifically that we can assume that he was not yet familiar with the entire work. His criticism in a later article, however, bears similar prejudice. Cf. "Kein 'Wenn und Aber' und das poetische Licht Sapphos: Noch einmal zu Christa Wolf," *Sinn und Form* 35, no. 5 (1983): 1096–1105.

30. Girnus, "Wer baute das siebentorige Theben?," 442.

31. Ibid. [My translation attempts to retain some of the clumsiness in Girnus's phrasing—his use of the passive voice and his complex syntactic formulation—in order to give a sense of the "tone" in which he speaks here.—Ed.]

32. Friedrich Engels, *Der Ursprung der Familie, des Privateigentums und des Staats.* Wolf quotes this in her response to Girnus: "Zur Information. Siehe Wilhelm Girnus: Wer baute das siebentorige Theben? Sinn und Form 2/83," *Sinn und Form* 35, no. 4 (1983): 865; editor's translation.

Killa's Tertium: Christa Wolf and Cassandra

Laurie Melissa Vogelsang

In *Cassandra*,[1] Christa Wolf expands upon more than a decade of experimentation with fiction that reaches all the way down to the level of syntax and grammar. Whereas earlier works, such as *The Quest for Christa T.*, concentrated on the expressive aspect of language (how to speak truthfully), *Cassandra* deals with the *influence* of language on and within society. Literature does not merely mimic experience and cognition: it affects and carries consequences. Language *affects* because of the inextricable interrelationship between linguistic structures and sociopolitical systems. As a socially and ethically responsive and responsible writer, Christa Wolf searches for nonconventional linguistic expressions that will make a new and positive impression upon her readership.

In connection with *The Quest for Christa T.*, Myra Love has observed that Wolf's fiction is responsive to the social structures (or "system") inherent in a patriarchal culture.[2] This observation arises

> within a specific experiential and conceptual framework. Out of this framework comes the notion that *the identification of subjectivity and domination lies at the heart of patriarchy*. This identification has at least two interrelated manifestations. Both depend on the division of reality into a system of dichotomous and mutually exclusive opposites. . . .
> One can and should read *The Quest for Christa T.* as a process which breaks down the system of dichotomous oppositions compromising the patriarchal world of perception and discourse.[3]

367

The structure of Wolf's novel merits the distinction, "feminist," in this argument not because Wolf propounds feminist ideology, but rather because she consciously strives to become postmale, that is, not traditionally patriarchal in her style. This postpatriarchal style that, for lack of a better term, I too shall call feminist, is at issue here.[4]

In order to address the incipient feminism of Christa Wolf's style, Myra Love utilizes methodologies made available through Derridian or deconstructive criticism. There are some obvious reasons why deconstruction lends itself to Christa Wolf. Coming from a Hegelian/Marxist heritage, Wolf has conceptualized her earlier fiction on the model of opposite pairs out of which a third term evolves.[5] Deconstruction likewise employs a triadic model. However, there are two important distinctions between the Hegelian/Marxist and deconstructive triads. Whereas thesis and antithesis are equally opposed forces, pairs of "binary opposites" are necessarily ranked hierarchically. The second difference concerns the third term. The Hegelian/Marxist synthesis evolves out of the initial opposition. There is an aspect of neutralization (*Aufhebung*). The Derridian "re-inscribed" term is outside and other. As a result, the deconstructive model is better equipped to address the utopian implications in *Cassandra*. For one final reason, aspects of deconstructive criticism lend themselves to a discussion of *Cassandra*: Wolf's language skepticism, which has sociopolitical roots that reach back to her childhood and the unavoidable recognition of verbal manipulation, is nonetheless akin to the language skepticism that is fundamental to deconstruction.

Of course Christa Wolf is a far cry from a deconstructionist. Whereas the deconstructionist is skeptical of language per se, Wolf attempts to break down the specific, if unfortunately pre*dominant* language of modern, patriarchal society. Wolf's specific criticism must not be mistaken for a blanket rejection of the word. On the contrary, *Cassandra* expresses Wolf's fundamental faith in the power of language. From the outset, in her first lecture Wolf asserts: "The centering around the Logos, the word as fetish—perhaps the deepest superstition of the West, or at least the one of which I am a fervent devotee" (162). Wolf professes precisely the logocentricism that deconstructionists repudiate. Yet despite this logocentricism and her ultimate goal of reestablishing the integrity of the word, Wolf first undertakes in *Cassandra* a deconstruction of the traditional language (and thereby of the corresponding social structures) behind the politically pernicious mystifications of her day. *Cassandra* attempts to realize the potential for utopian thinking (and writing) that is outside the contemporary political language of deception and hierarchical power struggles.

Although I do not wish to deconstruct *Cassandra*, certain aspects of Derrida's critical language *will* be useful in illuminating it. The fundamental assumption of deconstructive philosophy is the recognition that Western, metaphysical thinking arises out of a system of binary oppositions; for example, subject-object, closed-open, male-female, speech-writing, presence-absence, or spirit-nature. Derrida insists that necessarily these pairs are ranked hierarchically, that is, that one term in each pair always dominates the other. One must first "invert" or "overturn" the binary opposites. In *Positions*, Derrida explains:

> We must traverse a phase of *overturning*. To do justice to this necessity is to recognize that in a classical philosophical opposition we are not dealing with the peaceful coexistence of a *vis-à-vis*, but rather with a violent hierarchy. One of the two terms governs the other (axiologically, logically, etc.), or has the upper hand. To deconstruct the opposition, first of all, is to overturn the hierarchy at a given moment. To overlook this phase of overturning is to forget the conflictual and subordinating structure of opposition.[6]

The relationship between the opposites is one of conflict and domination. The first step in undermining this relationship is to "invert" or "overturn" the hierarchy. To invert the terms does not mean simply to establish a new hierarchy in which the formerly subordinate term now dominates. In "overturning" the binary opposition unacknowledged affinities between the two terms are revealed. A third, "re-inscribed" term emerges. It is essential to stress that deconstruction is a two-fold process. First, the opposition is inverted or undermined; then a new, re-inscribed term emerges as alternative in the face of a void. Derrida explains: "By means of this double, and precisely stratified, dislodged and dislodging, writing, we must also mark the interval between inversion, which brings low what was high, and the irruptive emergence of a new 'concept,' a concept that can no longer be, and never could be, included in the previous regime."[7] The new, re-inscribed term is to the previous hierarchical linguistic structure as *Cassandra's* matriarchal utopian vision is to the contemporary patriarchal social structures. That re-inscribed vision would be a feminism, not as a derivative of patriarchy, but rather as an alternative "that can no longer be, and never could be, included in the previous regime."

In *Cassandra* Wolf confronts the king-pin dichotomy fundamental to all Western discourse, namely that of subject over object. She has moved from a concern with interpersonal (and intrapersonal) relationships in the earlier works to a more theoretical concern with language structures: those structures that precede and influence human relationships. Wolf asks herself how, or whether it is at all possible to produce a literary object that is not necessarily dominated by and therefore alienated from a subject-author. Is it possible to have a literary object-subject? Or are subject and object necessarily at odds with one another? Our current language and social structures would seem to bear out the latter. Is it possible to render powerless this language of domination and lies? Is it possible thereby or simultaneously to dismantle the concurrent social structures? Wolf wonders in her "Work Diary," "Is it 'realistic' to try to neutralize the hierarchical male reality principle?" (257).

The utopian cast of Wolf's thinking is conveyed by a grammar of ambiguity. She strives in *Cassandra* for a certain polysemy. Her remarks in the fourth lecture concerning a poem by Ingeborg Bachmann draw attention to the logic that informs Wolf's own praxis: "the poem itself gives an example of the most precise indefiniteness, the clearest ambiguity. Things are this way and no other way, it says; and at the same time (this cannot be thought logically) things are that way, a different way. You are I, I am he, it cannot be explained. The grammar of manifold simultaneous relations" (276).

Wolf's own style in all five lectures similarly resists the logic and thought patterns of Western, political, patriarchal language, which has gone the way of "segregation, of the renunciation of the manifoldness of phenomena, in favor of dualism and monism, in favor of closed systems and pictures of the world; of the renunciation of subjectivity in favor of a sealed 'objectivity'" (287).

Consider here in detail several examples of Wolf's own "grammar of manifold relations." Notice particularly how in her syntax Wolf plays at inverting subject and object. The first example is from her introductory remarks: "The first and second essays . . . attest to how the figure of Cassandra takes possession of me and experiences her first, provisional incarnation."[8] In the first phrase, the Cassandra-figure seizes possession of the narrative voice.[9] The word "possession" rings of bourgeois materialism, domination, and the reification of a human being. Yet within this same sentence, the powerful figure-subject becomes shaped. That is, the Cassandra-figure is treated as an object. Due to the passive aspect of the verb "experiences," the subject becomes in effect the object of the clause. The implied subject—the one doing the shaping—is the narrative voice.

Several pages later Wolf writes: "Cassandra. I saw her at once. She, the captive, took me captive; herself made an object by others, she took possession of me" (144). The oscillation is beautiful. We begin with "Cassandra," moving immediately and paratactically to the narrative voice. The narrative voice enters as the subject, "I." The fictive character becomes the (direct) object. In the third sentence their roles are reversed. However, the appositions, "the captive" and "herself made object by others," prevent the reader from forgetting that this subject is an object as well.

Finally, consider this third example: "I seem to know more about her than I can prove. She seems to look at me, to affect me, more keenly than I would wish" (148). "I," the acting subject-narrator, knows about her, the passive object-Cassandra, because she, Cassandra-object-now-acting-subject, appears to stare sharply at the narrator-subject-now-passive-object. What we have here is an object—the figure of Cassandra —capable of possessing, controlling, seeing. Christa Wolf discovers and demonstrates in the object these characteristics, which one traditionally associates with the subject and through which the subject reigns superior over the object. Conversely, the author-subject is affected, shaped, and changed by her encounter with the material for a story. Rather than dominating, the subjective author, Christa Wolf, depends on the object for self-definition. The subject reveals herself as object-like. The object commands new respect. By inverting the binary opposition, Wolf undermines the traditional conception of subject and object. She thereby nullifies the basis for the hierarchy. We now need a new, nonhierarchical or re-inscribed term to express the collective field of the former subject-object binary opposition. This tertium proffered to us by Wolf is the seer-poet, Cassandra, who tells her story. Cassandra is the subjective author *and simultaneously* object of the fifth lecture. (Just as Christa Wolf is author and object of the first four lectures.)

The plot of the narrative (the fifth lecture) echoes the story enacted in the syntax of the individual sentences just quoted. *Cassandra*, the narrative or fifth lecture, is the story of one figure located within a hierarchical system of dominating subjects and fungible objects. Wolf explains in the third lecture: "Assumption: Cassandra is one of the first women figures handed down to us whose fate prefigures what was to be the fate of women for three thousand years: to be turned into an object" (227). Cassandra suffers the inception of reductive, dualistic thinking. For her (and three thousand years of women following her) patriarchal domination is reality. Recall, by way of contrast, Killa's obliviousness and hence immunity to these thought patterns. With childlike innocence and naiveté, Killa tries to win the "man-killing warrior woman" (7), Penthesilea, over to the thought patterns of the women in "the caves along the Scamander." She pleads to Penthesilea:

> "Come join us." "Join you? What does that mean?" "Come to the mountains. The forest. The caves along the Scamander. Between killing and dying there is a third alternative: living." (118)

Killa has not yet been indoctrinated into the "Western thought . . . in favor of dualism" (287). It is still possible for her to believe in a life free and distinct from the reductive binary opposition of "kill or be killed." She is simply unaware of the impending patriarchy.

But Cassandra actively seeks, through her use of language, a (utopian) alternative to the system. Is it possible for Cassandra to enter consciously into this dualistic age, but preserve Killa's utopian consciousness? Can Cassandra, herself treated as an object, defy the pernicious, self-perpetuating spiral of alienation? That is, can Cassandra, who is treated by the politicians around her as an object, avoid being impaled on one horn or the other of this subject-object dilemma? Is such utopian thinking/language possible in the modern age? These are the questions the plot of the narrative addresses. In the third lecture, the narrator offers us this insight into the figure of Cassandra: "No self-pity; she lives her life even in the war. Tries to lift the decree that has been pronounced over her: that she is to be turned into a object" (239). There is a suggestion that it is indeed possible to retain life and the integrity of Killa's tertium in the midst of domineering power struggles such as war. Yet to what extent can an individual determine her/his own life and to what extent is she/he the object of external (social, economic, linguistic) forces, that is, structures?

The response proffered by *Cassandra* is not simple. The figure Cassandra tells us how she *lived* her life. The author Wolf recounts her own experience of "reading" the Cassandra myth. There would seem to be alternatives and life in the very processes of reading and of narrative. At the conclusion of Cassandra's narrative (and it must end) comes her death. Yet the story can be retold and reread and hence revived. Like the author Wolf, we as readers are not tied to any final interpretations, we can always reread.

To further complicate the paradox of the vital while staid nature of narrative, particularly of written narrative, Cassandra's tale is replete with poignant vignettes depicting the reification of human beings, especially women. In spite of the curse that her prophecies and her insights are fated for oblivion, that her narrative will be reduced to an object, and that people will correspondingly be reduced to objects, Cassandra persists in seeing and saying that human beings are being reified. The character Arisbe helps Cassandra to continue seeing, despite the apparent futility and impending doom.

The first character in the narrative to be dealt with as an object (toward the end of someone else's personal gain) is Paris.[10] We learn about Paris's childhood very indirectly. Cassandra has just recalled her first encounter with Agamemnon. This prompts her to recall a much earlier exchange with Arisbe, regarding Iphigenia and then Paris:

> Long ago, after my first encounter with this man of ill omen, I told Arisbe: "No priest could have gotten Priam to make such a sacrifice." Arisbe stared at me wide-eyed; then I thought of Paris. Was it the same thing? Was it really the same thing: to have an infant child killed secretly, or to butcher a grown girl in public? And did I fail to see that it was the same thing because not I the daughter was affected but Paris the son? "You're slow on the uptake, my dear," said Arisbe. (53)

"Arisbe stared at me wide-eyed." Arisbe *sees*. She is the first person to see the signifiers on the wall. Cassandra, who thought she was being so perspicacious by pointing the finger at Agamemnon for sacrificing Iphigenia, has her eyes opened. Arisbe helps Cassandra develop her own capacity to see, such that Cassandra succeeds in becoming conscious of and then moving outside patriarchal language and thought patterns of reification. The implication is that utopian vision is less a "gift" and more a skill (or attitude) that can be acquired. With the figure of Arisbe, Wolf tenders an affirmative response to the question: "Is it realistic to try to neutralize the hierarchical male reality principle?" (257).

The story of Paris is something of an exception in the narrative. Above all, *Cassandra* is the story of *women* being made into objects. Paris wants to possess Helen. Cassandra gets married off in a political bargain. Perhaps the most poignant scenario is when Cassandra's sister, Polyxena, is used as bait to lure Achilles, who has long since reduced Polyxena to the object of his desires, into a death trap. In vain Cassandra attempts to reawaken her father and his minister Eumelos to what they are saying and planning. Her admonitions are in vain, for these 'politicians' can no longer see. Cassandra begins:

> "That means you're using Polyxena as a decoy. . . . You are using her."
> "Using whom?"
> "Polyxena."
> "But aren't you capable of getting the point? It's not she we're concerned with. We're concerned with Achilles."
> "That's exactly what I'm saying." (125–126)

Achilles carries the degeneration and depravity in interpersonal relations so extremely far that everyone (but especially the women) sees, that is, experiences or *feels*, the significance of what is happening. Achilles' rape of the slain Penthesilea is a hyperbole that is both shocking and compelling.

> Achilles the Greek hero desecrates the dead woman. The man, incapable of loving the living woman, hurls himself on the dead victim so that he can go on killing her. And I moan. Why? She did not feel it. We felt it, all of us women. What will become of us if that spreads? The men, weak, whipped up into victors, need us as victims in order not to stop feeling altogether. Where is that leading? (120)

Like Cassandra before them in her conversation with Arisbe, "all of us women" are made to see. They awaken to a new feeling of self and come face to face with the desperate urgency of their plight. Their incipient critical consciousnesses reject exhausted assumptions and superannuated attitudes: the women are thinking in "re-inscribed" terms. The Greek men are appalled as well but fail to see themselves implicated in Achilles' crime. The dominators continue to be governed by the established patterns of belligerency. Not only do they miss the opportunity for an alternative thought, they go on to affirm and preserve the logic that gave rise to the hideous act. Continuing where the quote above leaves off, the narrator tells us: "Even the Greeks felt that Achilles had gone too far. So they went further in order to punish him: Had horses drag the dead woman across the field—he wept for her now —and threw her into the river. Flay the woman in order to strike at the man" (120). In order to generate self-definition, Achilles and the "men" must become the oppressors of somebody else: "The men, . . . whipped up into victors, need us as victims in order not to stop feeling altogether." The only feeling of self of which Achilles is capable is that of dominating subject in conflict with an object. Achilles is the antithesis of the seer-poet.

The dominating subject, Achilles, is incapable of seeing; he is incapable of empathy or sympathy: he is incapable of love. In order to achieve a sense of self-affirmation, Achilles feels driven to dominate Penthesilea. In her "Büchner-Prize Acceptance Speech," by contrast, Wolf attributes to Cassandra precisely the capacity to love (someone else, even more than herself). Wolf writes:

> I imagine Cassandra must have loved Troy more than herself when she dared to prophesy to her compatriots the downfall of their city. Have these two countries, I ask myself, perhaps not been loved enough by their inhabitants and tend—like an unloved person who therefore cannot love—to destroy themselves and others? I ask this so that I may refute myself sharply, and to prove the contrary, as absurd as it may seem, I point to literature. (BP 11)

Literature as an expression of love! The vexed word "love" makes us all nervous without helping (initially) to clarify the relationship between literature and alternative thought patterns. Nor does Wolf pause to explain her seemingly idiosyncratic association of *caritas* with the seer-poet, Cassandra. I find a passage written by the English philosopher and novelist, Iris Murdoch, very helpful here. Murdoch similarly associates loving with the capacity to see and be free. In *The Sovereignty of Good*, Murdoch writes:

> It is in the capacity to love, that is to *see*, that the liberation of the soul from fantasy consists. . . . Freedom is not strictly the exercise of the will, but rather the experience of accurate vision, which, when this becomes appropriate, occasions action. It is what lies behind and in between actions and prompts them that is important, and it is this area which should be purified. By the time the moment of choice has arrived the quality of attention has probably determined the nature of the act.[11]

Clear-sighted attention converges with loving and with liberation. Conversely, blindness and self-deception converge with alienation, domination, reification, and ultimate downfall or death. The freedom of which Murdoch speaks is the freedom from either self-centered fantasies or language that dominates and mystifies. Freedom is an exercise in perception or an "experience of accurate vision." Murdoch and Wolf feel confident that if one (motivated by *caritas*) hones one's perception, then benevolent action or political and social engagement will follow on their own. Critical insight undermines stagnant thinking and the retrogressive actions that issue from it. Such a critical consciousness consists in and of "re-inscribed," utopian terms. In other words, it is realized by and is indeed accurate vision and alternative language: literature.

In the third lecture we are told that if Cassandra's tale is to be utopian rather than historical it must recount her process of becoming separated (liberated) from extant beliefs and thought patterns.

> What would that imply about the conflicts which might have confronted Cassandra, particularly with respect to religion and the cults which must have co-existed? To take a utopian rather than a historical view, might she not in the end have freed herself inwardly from *all* faith, including—indeed primarily!—from her own; for her story would have to be a process of liberation? (231–232)

Must Cassandra remain the object of external forces and structures? If yes, then Wolf 's[12] representation of her must be historical. Or can *Cassandra* become a literary, utopian projection? Can Wolf locate Cassandra—the figure and the "literary object"—outside the subject-object opposition?

To what extent is Wolf, as author, external to her contemporary social and linguistic structures? She is, for instance, as much the object of the first four-fifths of the piece as Cassandra is the object of the final fifth, the narrative. I have discussed thus far Wolf 's resistance to "making objects" on the levels of syntax and plot line. Wolf 's role and the overall organization of the piece remain to be considered.

The fact that the piece defies any genre categorization further supports Wolf 's goal of freeing herself from established patterns. Furthermore, the first four lectures are integral and essential to understanding the last: these are Wolf 's (and the reader's) process of seeing/ reading Cassandra anew. They force the reader to retrace Wolf 's revision of an old tale. In the second lecture Wolf explains the importance of learning to read (to perceive) "myth": "To learn to read myth is a special kind of adventure. An art that presupposes a gradual, peculiar transformation; a readiness to give oneself to the seemingly frivolous nexus of fantastic facts, of traditions, desires, and hopes, experiences and techniques of magic adapted to the needs of a particular group—in short, to another sense of the concept 'reality'" (196). The reader (Wolf in this case) forfeits control. She/he is prepared to change and to surrender herself/himself to unfamiliar concepts ("another sense of the concept 'reality'"). The seer/poet/reader/person does not dominate, nor does she/he reduce the archetype to an object. She/he interacts and grows with the story.

The first and second lectures document the transformations in Wolf as a direct result of her preoccupation with the story of Cassandra. As one of the numerous examples, consider the following comment in the second lecture: "But I [Wolf] cannot change the fact that . . . my notion of the sea Cassandra looks at is formed here [in Crete]" (202). The material for the story seems to have taken control of its author. "Cassandra. I saw her at once. She, the captive, took me captive; herself made an object by others, she took possession of me" (144).

In other instances Wolf asserts her own subjective imagination. Consider her attitude toward the character Aeneas. When his name arises Wolf considers—with no apologies—the possibility of conjecturing a love relationship between him and Cassandra. In the beginning of the second lecture she writes: "Quick as a flash Aeneas sprang up before my inner eye, and Cassandra had known him. Merely known him? What was there about him that might have touched her more deeply? Consideration, coupled with strength? So, I was transferring a contemporary ideal to a mythological figure who cannot possibly have been that kind of person? Of course. What else?" (184). With this remark Wolf acknowledges that an author inevitably shapes and controls her/his art object.

Ultimately Wolf cannot write a poetics that totally eludes reification. Cassandra acknowledges this fact when she states in her first paragraph: "With the story I go to my death."[13] Yet even if the product of a poetics is stagnant and lifeless, Wolf sees the potential for vital, progressive thinking in the *process* of perception and narration. Wolf's revision of the Cassandra myth, her "experience of accurate vision" to borrow Murdoch's words, "lies behind and in between" *Cassandra*. She entreats her readers likewise to be open to alternative thought patterns, to forfeit control of the material, to read attentively, to see accurately, and to revise their received notions. "To learn to read myth is a special kind of adventure" (196).

Notes

1. Throughout this paper I refer to Wolf's five Frankfurt lectures as a unified work under the collective title, *Cassandra*. References to this work are noted parenthetically in the text. [The reader should note that the West German publication consisted of two distinct volumes: *Kassandra: Erzählung* and *Voraussetzungen einer Erzählung: Kassandra*, published simultaneously by Luchterhand in 1983. The English translation of this work combines those two volumes but in the reverse order from that intended by Wolf, i.e., the "story" precedes the four theoretical lectures on Cassandra, whereas in the original presentation it was the other way around. The translation of Wolf's introductory remarks to the lectures (the translator calls them "essays") reads: "The first and second essays—a two-part *record of a trip to Greece*—attest to how the figure of Cassandra takes possession of me and takes on her first, provisional incarnation. The third essay has the form of a *work diary* that tries to trace the vise grip between life and subject matter. In the fourth essay, *a letter*, I ask questions about the historical reality of the Cassandra figure and conditions for the woman writer past and present" (142). These sentences are followed, in the German version, by: "The *fifth lecture* is a narrative entitled *Cassandra*" (*Voraussetzungen einer Erzählung: Kassandra*, p. 8).—Ed.]

2. Myra Love, "Christa Wolf and Feminism: Breaking the Patriarchal Connection," *NGC*, no. 16 (Winter 1979): 31–53.

3. Love, 32; her emphasis.

4. With respect to *Christa T.* Love is careful to qualify that "it would be very questionable to assert that Christa Wolf was writing an intentionally anti-patriarchal work. However, since patriarchal conditions become a focus for her later works, though but one of many, it would not be pure fancy to recognize in *The Quest for Christa T.* anti-patriarchal and even germinally feminist insights"

(32). With *Cassandra*, Wolf's postpatriarchal style has become central to the work.

5. For example, Wolf concludes her essay, "The Reader and the Writer," by referring to the book as a third reality. This third derives from a "merging" of "subject matter" and "author." "The merging of 'subject matter' and 'author' could not be more profound, more uncanny. The third, the new reality of the book, first emerges out of this" (RW 205).

6. "J'insiste beucoup et sans cesse sur la nécessité de cette phase de renversement qu'on a peut-être trop vite cherché à discréditer. Faire droit à cette nécessité, c'est reconnaître que, dans une opposition philosophique classique, nous n'avons pas affaire à la coexistence pacifique d'un *vis-à-vis*, mais à une hiérarchie violente. Un des deux termes commande l'autre (axiologiquement, logiquement, etc.), occupe la hauteur. Déconstruire l'opposition, c'est d'abord, à un moment donné, renverser la hiérarchie. Négliger cette phase de renversement, c'est oublier la structure conflictuelle et subordonnante de l'opposition." Jacques Derrida, *Positions* (Paris: Les Editions de Minuit, 1972), 56–57; trans. Alan Bass (Chicago: University of Chicago Press, 1981), 41.

7. "Aussi faut-il, par cette écriture double, justement, stratifiée, décalée et décalante, marquer l'écart entre l'inversion qui met bas la hauteur, . . . et l'émergence irruptive d'un nouveau 'concept', concept de ce qui ne se laisse plus, ne s'est jamais laissé comprendre dans le régime antérieur." Derrida, 57; Bass, 42.

8. 142. Translation altered slightly by editor.

9. [It should be noted that the characters in Christa Wolf's narrative are not to be considered identical to those of Greek myth. In order to avoid confusion, however, we have used the familiar spellings also used in the translation of Wolf's work.—Ed.]

10. Is it so surprising, considering his childhood, that Paris strives as an adolescent to *possess* Helen?

11. Iris Murdoch, *The Sovereignty of Good* (London: Routledge & Kegen Paul, 1970), 66–67.

12. In the closing paragraphs I refer to the author/narrator of the first four lectures as Christa Wolf. The fact that these lectures were actually presented in Frankfurt might justify the direct, biographical reference. Conversely, the fact that the lectures are published as fiction justifies distinguishing between Wolf and her narrator. The distinction is not ultimately important to my argument. My choice to refer to Wolf directly reflects nothing more significant than convenience.

13. Translation altered by editor.

Resisting Aesthetics:
The Cassandra Motif in
Christa Wolf and Aeschylus

James I. Porter

And how & by what paths I have been brought
  To this dread pass, methinks even thou mayst guess;
Why this should be my mind can compass not;

  Whither the conqueror hurries me still less.
But follow thou, & from spectator turn
  Actor or victim in this wretchedness

—Shelley, *"The Triumph of Life"*

Christa Wolf is a notoriously difficult writer, not least because she writes directly in the face of the difficulties of writing, at the very limits (impasses) of knowledge, utterance, history, and truth that would define an "archaeology," or discursive probing, of these traces. The metaphor, although borrowed, is nonetheless apt. "Archaeology," as Wolf is well aware, suggests the unearthing *and* the loosening of foundations and presents unlimited opportunities for broaching further, unimaginable limits. "The archaeology of the last hundred years," Wolf notes drily, "offers an opportunity to observe the manufacturing process of a so-called historical truth."[1] Writing at the limits of thought, Wolf causes one to think the unthinkable, or more precisely, to think these limits in their irreducible discursive substance, *without* the defense mechanisms of aesthetics, and without the surreptitious—because imaginary—assurances of a realm "intact" and beyond, as though such a realm were waiting to be discovered in some far-off state of pure unimaginability. The following meditation on the meaning of annihilation illustrates, in an oblique way, this suspicion of Wolf's toward the notion and implications of the "unrepresentable," here applied to what in the West has recently fallen under the dubious heading of the "nuclear sublime": "Several times a day, if only for a few second, I try to picture what annihilation would 'look like,' how it would feel—how it *will* feel. Why only for a few seconds? Because the inner images are unbearable? That's one reason. But above all, because a deep-rooted dread prohibits me from 'bringing on' the misfortune by imagining it too intensively, too exactly. By the way: Cassandra's 'guilt' is precisely this" (254).

This is a case of neither atavistic superstition nor regressive fears about the powers of sympathetic magic (a *nomen omen* complex, say) but a recognition of the powers and horrors of representation, in the widest possible sense of the term. If there is no transgressing beyond language to an image or even beyond (beyond representability), this, Wolf suggests, is because language always has a way of "catching up," from the opposite corner. At such a point as that described by Wolf here, actor and victim are joined in a disquieting solidarity, by virtue of a common imaginary (for to create the possibilities for destruction one must first imagine destruction) and a common reality—"all the things that . . . make us into *accomplices* of self-destruction; and that enable . . . us to *resist* it" (253, emphases mine). As it goes in thought and action, so too in poetics. The complicities and resistances of writing—of a writing conceived of as *critical* affirmation—encourage a meditation on this same relation between limits and their nontransgressibility that writing inevitably reproduces in its self-resistant substance. As if to test the rigor of her criterion of the limit, Wolf poses to herself the further challenge: the threat to grammatical relation that her writing's own "grammar," "the grammar of manifold simultaneous relations," embodies (276). The result is, inevitably, a constant challenge for the reader and the critic, whose responses to the demands set by Wolf can take one of two forms: either an insistence upon the rigid demarcation and retrenchment of limits of all kinds (grammatical, generic, historical, institutional) or a more active response to the conditions that engender and displace those limits. A full appreciation of Wolf's project, in particular the *Cassandra* project, requires, I feel, the latter kind of response, although this has not always been the kind of reception her work has met.

Two early responses, coming from two classically trained scholars around the publication date of *Cassandra*, first in German and then one year later in translation, were of the former kind. The issues that these criticisms raise in regard to Wolf's work merit a brief, if critical, reflection. Ideological questions aside, the two critiques, one by the East German academicist Wilhelm Girnus, which prompted a flurry of debates in the journal *Sinn und Form*, and the other by the American classicist Mary Lefkowitz, in a review article that appeared in *The New York Times Book Review*, are marked by the standards of philological precision, or rather fidelity, that they bring to bear against Wolf's work.[2] Wolf naturally invites comparison with her classical sources, particularly with an author like Aeschylus, who supplies the dramatic model for the inaugural, threshold scene of *Cassandra*. As is also natural, comparisons readily breed suspicions of shortcomings. In the following pages I will try to correct this comparative bias. My more immediate purpose, however, will be to show, briefly, that the two responses and their guiding assumptions—the predominantly philological presuppositions of Wilhelm Girnus, and the predominantly literary assumptions of Mary Lefkowitz—miss some essential qualities of Wolf's work. By naming these two kinds of presupposition separately I do not by any means wish to suggest that the categories or activities of philology and literary criticism (even philologically informed literary criticism) have to be thought separately. Nor, I will venture to say, would Wolf. It is therefore imperative that, even before turning to *Cassandra*, we consider the nature of the presuppositions at work in Wolf—Wolf's own philology, in other words, and her own criticism of literature.

Christa Wolf is, beyond any doubt, eminently aware of the intrinsic strengths and risks of presuppositional activity. In the fourth companion essay to *Cassandra*, an emphatically philological and literary critical essay ("A Letter about Unequivocal and Ambiguous Meaning, Definiteness and Indefiniteness; About Ancient Conditions and New View-Scopes [*Seh-Raster*]; About Objectivity"), Wolf discusses Schiller's own literary version of Cassandra and notes the following: *"Schiller changes the (pre)suppositions [Voraussetzungen] in order to set Cassandra in opposition to the general mood"* (289, italics mine). We might consider what led Wolf to this rather candid observation about the restiveness of literary tradition and then to her subsequent critique of Schiller's literary failure—not, be it noted, his failure to adhere to the classically received and canonically fixed Cassandra, but his failure to give this oppositionality (*Gegensatz*) a sufficient edge of complexity. Absent from Schiller's Cassandra, Wolf writes, is the sense of "a long, contradictory (*widersprüchliche*) historical development" (290), which is to say, a sense of the palimpsestic quality of Cassandra (or the Cassandra tradition) that defined her as a literary or mythological figure from her first appearances in narrative. The title Wolf gave to her companion volume of essays takes some of its meaning from this statement about Schiller: "*Voraussetzungen einer Erzählung*," not just "Conditions of a Narrative," as the English translation renders it, but "*Presuppositions of a Narrative*." Perhaps we should consider whether there might not be, in Wolf's mind, a stronger (more complex) connection between presupposition, opposition, and self-contradiction than a less charitable reading of her treatment of the discursive formations of the past might lead one to believe. Appreciating some of this manifold complexity will be the aim of what follows. For reasons of brevity, I will limit myself to those kinds of tension that best summarize, and as it were localize, the historical layering deeply imbedded in Wolf's work.

I

Girnus's insistent adoption of an etymologizing critique, that is, a critique that seeks to establish the *etymon*, the original radical of truth, in a *logos*, Wolf answers with a decisive counterresponse: she is not interested in etymologies but rather in the appropriation of a word's radical into mythology—"die Übernahme eines Wort-Stammes in die Mythologie" (*SuF* 35, 863). Etymology gives way to mythology. The way from the one to the other is not a passive transit but an "appropriation" (*Übernahme*), an active assumption that, the sequel shows, is also a transumption (a metaleptic crossing, from one figure to another). Tracing the effects of this action, through what Wolf in her lectures and her narrative emphatically labels "historical analysis," is a means of assessing the pathology of linguistic action; it requires analysis of both the forces exerted upon linguistic and semantic change and the violences wrought in the process. And lest we wonder whether any given word harbors a specifically semantic origin in its pristine radical, we should consider the following qualification of "root" (*"Wurzel"*) that Wolf gives in the next sentence: "It is rather the case that the two meanings of the word [the word in question is *Moirai*, the spinners of fate, derived from lot, share] are related in a common economic root (hängen . . . in ihrer ökonomischen Wurzel zusammen)." At the root of this word, as of all other words, lies an economic *relation*, not a hypostatic meaning. Tracing out such economies (of sense, and of material conditions) and their violent evolution (their successive mythologizings)—such is what I take to be the radical philology of Wolf's writing practice. Aeschylus shared a similar view of the inheritance (genealogy) of verbal and conceptual violences. One can find parallels, at a certain level, in Marx (for instance, in Part I of *The German Ideology*) and later in Nietzsche. One example from Marx is particularly germane, and I would simply draw your attention to his critique of "sensuousness":

> The sensuous world around [us] is not a thing given direct from eternity, remaining ever the same, but the product of industry and of the state of society; and, indeed, in the sense that it is an historical product, the result of the activity of a whole succession of generations, each standing on the shoulders of the preceding one, developing its industry and its intercourse, and modifying its social system according to the changed needs. Even the objects of the simplest "sensuous certainty" are only given [us] through social development, industry and commercial intercourse. [Because he lacks this approach], Feuerbach sees [in Manchester] only factories and machines, where a hundred years ago only spinning-wheels and weaving-looms [modern avatars of the Moirai?—J.P.] were to be seen, or in the Campagna of Rome he finds only pasture lands and swamps, where in the time of Augustus he would have found nothing but the vineyards and villas of Roman capitalists.[3]

Wolf explicitly affiliates herself with Marx's analysis, though her commitment to the senses, to the materialism of experience and of writing, takes a decidedly different direction, as we shall see or rather glimpse later on. But to return to the issue of Wolf's radical philology: Girnus's blindness to this possibility (i.e., the possibility of Wolf's taking philology at its word) also rendered him blind to the fact that, for Wolf, the word "etymology" and the concept it represents are themselves forms of mythology, the very mythology that is the object of Wolf's critique. This in turn opens up the further paradox that is also inescapable: is not Wolf herself guilty of proliferating mythologies? Is not her critique of mythology vulnerable to itself? It indeed is, and no one is more aware of this consequence, or more willing to confront it, than is Wolf. The fruits of this self-critique will be visible in a moment.

Professor Lefkowitz operates under assumptions not wholly dissimilar from those held by Girnus. Her lack of appreciation for *Cassandra* stems in part, I suspect, from her judging it by the canons of the "historical novel." The *etymon* that controls her criticism is governed by three criteria: laws of imitation, a preconception of the "historical," and a schema of genres (which, notably, fails to include "reality" as one genre type; cf. *Cassandra*, p. 300), here instanced by either "the novel" or the ideal fit of a novel to its "original," a tragedy. We have already seen how, in Wolf's eyes, historical analysis is indissociable from a genealogy of forces. We shall soon see that what on one view constitutes the unproblematic conjunction of history and fiction, the very possibility of their conjointment and of the legislation of norms for their reception, is for Wolf the source of unending questioning and searching. Furthermore, the "novel" as such belongs to the categories of a classical and post-Romantic aesthetics, which Wolf repugns, for reasons that we must consider in a moment. History and the novel that would claim to represent it are both mythical constructs—delusive "back-formations," in both the linguistic and psychoanalytic senses of the word. "To show how the historical Cassandra ('die historische Kassandra'), whom I take as my basis, and her historical surroundings are guided by ritual, cult, faith and myth; whereas for us the material is 'mythic' *in its entirety* (während für uns das *gesamte* Material 'mythisch' ist)" (264).

This quotation from Wolf's third lecture only superficially contradicts what I have just said: here she is attacking, in elliptical language, a simplified and, as it were, undialectical construction of the idea of "myth." Important for our purposes, however, is the allowance that is made to the coexistence of the historical and the mythical, as well as the rigorous insistence by Wolf upon the material specificities that ultimately absorb both categories. Later we shall see how Wolf explicitly deconstructs the opposition she is here subtly unsettling (myth/history).

Rather than dwell on the two critiques from which we set out, it would be more profitable to ask ourselves what is absent from them both. The answer would seem self-evident: an appreciation of the aesthetic thrust of Wolf's writing. Such a response, however, ought to be characterized not so much as a failed aesthetic response but as a *resis-*

tance to an aesthetic response.[4] Just what is it that triggers such a resistance to Wolf's writing? Before suggesting an answer, let me pose another question. Would we be more at ease if critics were to respond willingly and consentingly to an *irresistible Cassandra*; if they only remarked at its aesthetic character and pronounced it "good," despite its philological errors and erroneous reconstructions because it is, after all, a piece of fiction, and writers are mad or compulsive liars or only writers, and anyway they are to be tolerated in this republic of ours? To respond in this way is to judge Wolf by the canons of "true" and "false" (*logos* and *mythos*) and to dismiss a portion of her writing as aberrant confusion or misinformation that is nonetheless acceptable because emarginable, as such. What if, however, Wolf's aberrancies are calculated and integral to her work (which I think is, with slight qualification, the case)? And what if Wolf has herself anticipated, even provoked, the resistance to aesthetics that is legible only in the diminished aesthetic response that is so conspicuous in readings like those mentioned here, or in the lines of resistance that a more accommodating reading, such as the one I just hypothesized, would be obliged to inscribe ineradicably and uncritically into the failed structure of *Cassandra* itself (*Cassandra* and its shadow, its *etymon*-other)? This possibility is, I think, the case, without any qualification whatsoever. But even as I say this, I do not believe it; I resist it, or else I sense in the knowledge of it a resistance to a belief in it. Inasmuch as knowledge is determinable only as the resistance to knowledge, one cannot believe what one knows. For Wolf, this impossibility makes knowing what one knows or believes—even a knowledge of one's own belief—literally speaking, incredible. "I notice that I cannot believe what I know" (78). Cassandra stands under the ban of her own curse, but her curse is shared in the measure that it is not believed. For it is not the case that Wolf's critics, when they read Wolf and when they fail to respond aesthetically (critically) to her work, are resisting aesthetics as such. In Wolf they are resisting not aesthetics, but a resistance to aesthetics—Wolf's own resistance to aesthetics. And it would be wrong to end here without adding: to her *own* aesthetics—a resistance that Wolf, out of consistency and rigor, not weakness, resists herself, and which she positively names in passing, as a future conditional, "the aesthetic of *resistance*" ["die Ästhetik des Widerstandes"] (236). To this complex of resistance and aesthetics we should next turn.[5]

II

Although the lectures, which Wolf delivered to a West German audience in 1982, evidently bore as their title "Poetikvorlesungen" ("Lectures on Poetics," the fifth of these being the narrative, *Cassandra*), they are ostensibly Wolf's attempt to account for the reasons why she has no poetics of her own. The contrast between title and objective is what unifies the five, highly individuated lectures, which open with the following words of preface:

Ladies and Gentlemen:
This enterprise bears the title "Lectures on Poetics," but I will tell you at once, I cannot offer you a poetics. (141)

The knowledge that Wolf has no poetics is, however, irreducibly the belief or suspicion ("*Verdacht*") that she has none. "This has only struck me in the last couple of years, and so it may be (und so *kann* es sein; my emphasis) that, incidentally, these essays will also treat a question that I have never put to myself (die gar nicht gestellte Frage): the question of why I do *not* have a poetics (warum ich *keine* Poetik habe)" (141).[6] The sequel is equally circumspect in tone, and I will quote a little more of it at length:

> Many or most, maybe the most important things will go unsaid (*ungesagt*); indeed, probably they are unknown (*ungewusst*) to me as well. I want to set a fabric (*Gewebe*) before you. It is an aesthetic structure (*ästhetisches Gebilde*), and as such it would lie at the center of my poetics *if* I had one. But this fabric which I want to display to you now did not turn out completely tidy, is not surveyable at one glance. Many of its motifs are not followed up, many of its threads are tangled. There are wefts which stand out like foreign bodies (*Fremdkörper*), repetitions, material that has not been worked out to its conclusion. This is not always intentional . . . (141–142)

Poetics, and the aesthetic structure that would occupy its center more in the form of a texture (*Gewebe*) than a structure (*Gebilde*), like the "story" (*Erzählung*) and its "untold subjects" (*ungezählte Subjekte*) (142),[7] or the "question" (*Frage*) and its being wholly unposed (*gar nicht gestellt*)—all these couplings, constituted by a fragile line of demarcation, are hopelessly at odds with one another whenever art threatens to objectify itself into an "art object," which means virtually whenever there are works of art and other products of alienation from, and within, a culture (142). The fragility of these oppositions lies in their elements' being simultaneously co-determining (collaborating) and reciprocal negations (co-existing). Thus it comes about that poetics, narration, and question, existing as they do on a single plane, can be exchanged analogically for one another, can form a textual unity (*Gewebe*) out of their very non-relation to *Gewebe*, and can build a structure through their arrangement of gaps—a structure that is never even constructed (*gestellt*), a subject that prevents itself from being viewed as an object or simply *prevents itself*, by extending itself through a narration of its own going into view, its own coming into extinction. This *relation by virtue of non-relation* determines the "structure" of the *Cassandra*-project as a whole: the lectures, the narration, and the non-narration of a non-aesthetics that the whole collectively resists. "It was here. This is where she stood. These stone lions looked at her; now they no longer have heads. This fortress—once impregnable, now a pile of stones—was the last thing she saw" (3).

The narratorial presence, evoked but unnamed by the indexical references in these, the first lines of the narrative, assumes and disavows its name in a moment of fade-out, by way of the pivotal and equivocal "I" introduced in the sentence that reads, "Keeping step with the story, I make my way into death" (3)—literally: "With the story, I go into death." With this sentence, the narrator describes or narrates the figurative death, or suspension, of the narrator function. The hiatus created by the hint of impossibility (the tension between the literal and the figural possibilities) is filled by the rhythm of an indecision, which not even the next sentence, in more ways than one a new para-graph, can resolve: "here I end." Such para-cidal para-graphisms will constitute the actual text of the narrative that follows, not its moments of delusory fullness, but the chain of depletions—formal, logical, material, tropic—that hinge and unhinge the narrative sequence. Above, I said "describes or narrates," but there is of course a crucial difference between these alternatives. One can describe a narration (as here) or narrate a description (likewise, as here), or one can wish to perform either or both of these, and in fact perform neither, as is also the case here: for to the extent that Cassandra succeeds in the one narrative act she has failed in the other. Consider Wolf's remark in the fourth lecture: "My professional interest is wide-awake and aims precisely at description, but it must hold back, withdraw, and it has had to learn to want and to bring about its own defeat" (278). Must we add, along with Wolf, that narration is the resistance to narration? The *Cassandra* narrative only corroborates this suspicion:

> Now everything inside me is in revolt. I will beg that terrible woman for my life. I will throw myself at her feet. "Clytemnestra, lock me up forever in your darkest dungeon. Give me barely enough to live on. But I implore you: Send me a scribe, or better yet a young slave woman with a keen memory and a powerful voice. Ordain that she may repeat to her daughter what she hears from me. That the daughter in turn may pass it on to her daughter, and so on. So that alongside the river of heroic songs this tiny rivulet, too, may reach those faraway, perhaps happier people who will live in times to come." (81)

To which she directly adds, in shocked disbelief,

> And I could believe that, even for one day?
> Slay me, Clytemnestra. Kill me. Hurry. (81)

("I notice that I cannot believe what I know.")

The refrain of this lament, comprising the three final imperatives, is indecisive between being a description (of Cassandra's imaginary dialogue) and a narration (in *erlebte Rede*, or free indirect discourse); its content, however, destroys the distinction and the very possibility of either of the two modalities. Here, as earlier, the language repudiates much more than the lucid coherence of epic structures ("remembering history as the story of heroes," as Wolf writes in a lecture [262]): it is in-

trinsically self-defiant, self-resistant language, the echo of its own negation. Hence the grim paradox, in the context of this passage, that the
death that can complete (undo) language can nonetheless exist only as
a linguistic referent (as the ultimate deixis), is achievable only through
a narrative speech-act (as the ultimate performative) and must take
place well in advance of Cassandra's actual death. It is, accordingly,
highly problematic. Wolf's remark on "narrative techniques" and narrative closure is relevant here: "I experience the closed form of the Cassandra narrative as a contradiction to the fragmentary structure from
which (for me) it is actually composed. The contradiction cannot be resolved, only named" (266). Cassandra's language does not achieve its
sought-for terminus but rather resists *and* affirms it (names it). One can
illustrate this linguistic death (which is the death of narrative—impossible, because uncontainable) by putting it in a different form: resistance is *not* a form of negation. With this last sentence I have not expressed a negation, I have thrown up a resistance to the logical
predication that the sentence simultaneously expresses. Whenever the
resistance to language-effects takes the form of a death-wish for language, inasmuch as this wish can only be wished in and through language, there will be a resistance to resistance (a linguistic death). Hence
the fact that Cassandra's discourse, at its moment of utterance and in
positing no end beyond itself, is irretrievably a *posthumous*, not an
apocalyptic, discourse.

III

One could, at this point, document and examine the varieties of
"negation" (*Verneinung*) that run through the text at its critical sutures,
that wound its body, mark it not with actual pain but with "phantom"
pain (*Phantom-Schmerz*), not just the pain of a phantom limb but the
memory of a nonexperience, "for limbs that have not yet been formed,
not developed; for unlived feelings, unfulfilled longing" (232; cf. 6).
Such rememorative moments typically coincide with moments of ab-
sorption in unsurpassed beauty, with highly charged aesthetic impressions: "Europe, if you watch it decline, see it as declining, can at many
moments look as beautiful as Atlantis" (232). One could give a pathology of *Cassandra*, note its points of congestion and condensation
around such phantom members with their phantom pain and memory,
those points at which the narrative, clotted with negation, contracts
with the response of a nervous system to a "foreign body," achieves
density, consistency, resistance, but also resists textual collaboration as
well. For "Panthous [Cassandra's "Widerpart"—"fencing partner" (21)
—literally, and ambivalently: her "resistance"] drew my attention to
the fact that words have physical effects. 'No' had a contracting, 'yes' a
relaxing, effect" (114).

The text, read through the filter of all such negations, has a
rhythm of its own, intersecting with the narrative path that it refuses to

travel: "'Come on, stay!' I looked at Arisbe, Anchises. Yes, I had to go. Hecuba led me straight to the council. No. Wrong. To the hall where the council used to be held. Where conspirators crouched together now, led by King Priam. They refused to let us in" (125). To this counterrhythm, which insinuates itself into every event, every meaning, all readings respond, with their no or yes. One of these moments of disjunctive coincidence, one of these "gaps in time" (124), would be the figure of Helen (85)—the "phantom" (69), "rigidified into an idol" (297), that is "real like Helen," part "texture," part "structure"—, which would occupy the center of the narrative, and any possible poetics of this narrative, as its "aesthetic" kernel, if one could ever—phantasmatically—locate such a center. There will always be differences of opinion, territorial disputes, lines drawn and redrawn, centers claimed and forsaken, criticisms and incriminations. The war waged in the name of this phantom, if not person, will always be a war of aesthetics. "A people who are fighting for beauty!" (68), Cassandra exclaims at one point, to herself, not to her "people." Behind her veils, the beauty of Helen-the-aesthetic is promiscuously active behind every scene, imposing herself on every landscape, every vision, image, and shape, with a force that goes beyond all comprehension, and all credibility—she is "unbelievably beautiful" (124). Not only in spite of but also because of her illusory presence it must be said, for instance, "that we were speaking in metaphors" (134). Helen, this aesthetic *force de choses*, touches all language, all words, every mouth, including Cassandra's own; Cassandra is, after all, herself just a "word," a "heading" ("For the past two years I have been tracking a key word (*Stichwort*): 'Cassandra,'" [141]), a word that is also the object of disbelief, an uncertain word, a sound-shape, not quite image, not quite word, a contra/diction in terms: "the time as a priestess, a white block; father back: the girl—here I am caught by the very word 'girl,' and caught all the more by her[/its] form. By the beautiful image. I have always been caught by images more than by words. Probably that is strange, and incompatible [more literally, '*in contradiction*'] with my vocation; but I can no longer pursue my vocation" (21).[8] The phrase "her[/its] form" ("*seiner Gestalt*") never frees itself entirely from the grammatical and contextual possibility that the "form" in question is not a pure image but the material "form" of a word (its "physical effect"), a "beautiful image" that stands simultaneously, vocally, in "contradiction" to the calling of words. The materiality of a resistance. Cassandra is nowhere more complicit with Helen than in her avoidance of her here: the phenomenality of the aesthetic, the spectral source of all vision and of the voicing of words, is also the death of spectacle, the voiding of meaning, the "naked, meaningless shape of events" (42), a voidance/avoidance without which no meaning and no vision could exist. The battle fought over this sensuous phenomenon, and everything it comes to represent, may be won, or lost. The only question is whether the victory one wins is to be chalked up "in reality" (*in Wirklichkeit*) or "metaphorically" (*im Gleichnis*).

Had I not sat one year before with the other girls in the temple grounds of Athena just after I bled for the first time—hadn't I been forced to sit there? I thought as I had at the time, and the skin of my scalp crawled with dreadful shame. . . . Even now I could point out (bezeichnen) the cypress tree under which I sat, provided that the Greeks did not set fire to it; I could describe (beschreiben) the shape (die Form) of the loose row of clouds from the Hellespont. "Loose row" ("Lockerem Zug"). Absurd, ridiculous words: I cannot waste any more time on them. (16)

Resisting the aesthetic, "overtaxed by the gift of sight" (27), Cassandra embodies a repudiation of sight, in her repudiation of the vocation to clairvoyance. "I saw nothing" (27). To accept the premises of vision is to live by appearance ("scheinhaft wie nie"), to give oneself over to appearances ("Erscheinungen"). Appearance and a de-realized reality (86) cross over in a chiasmus that denies all the possibilities and allurements of visual pleasure. "Seeing" ("Schauen") is deflated and replaced by "seeing through" ("durchschauen");[9] prophecy, by political diagnosis (no longer an exclusive gift); madness, by the sanity of intimate, corporeal self-awareness ("the quaking inside me intensified. Like everyone's, my body gave me signs; but unlike others, I was not able to ignore them" [58]).

IV

It is at this moment that Wolf, in resisting aesthetics, rejoins her classical sources, to an extent that may have exceeded even Wolf's expectations. The denial of the visual in the face of man-made destruction—this resisting, on the one hand, the aesthetic, and on the other, emptying it out of all content—is perfectly in keeping, I would argue, with classical Greek sensibilities, certainly, at any rate, with Aeschylean sensibilities.[10] The optical model on which the Agamemnon and even the Oresteia as a whole are based is not, as consensus among classicists would have it, that of a progressive movement from obscurity to clarity, but rather one of an excessive, painful clarity, from start to finish. Let me speak just briefly about the Agamemnon, the play that Wolf as it were turns around and views from a reverse optic, without, however, changing the lens. This drastic reversal of perspective—in Aeschylus Cassandra occupies the stage for only a portion, though a dramatically considerable portion of the play—will continue to make Wolf's Cassandra so fascinating to classicists, regardless of their critical persuasions. The motto of Agamemnon might well be two words spoken by the Chorus to Cassandra toward the play's end: toron agan, "all too clear, too painfully clear," in response, curiously enough, to Cassandra's dark threat that she is about to hold forth in prophetic discourse. The full context runs like this:

Ca: O the marriage of Paris, deadly to those he loved!
O my native stream of Scamander!

There I was reared and grew about your banks, ah me!
But about[12] the shores of Cocytus and of Acheron
I am likely soon to prophesy.

Ch: Why have you voiced this saying, all too clear?
A child might hear and understand. And I am struck once more by a
deadly pang (peplēgmai), etc. (1156–1164)

After a few more words by the Chorus, Cassandra bursts out, *iō ponoi ponoi*, "O pains, sorrows!"—sorrows of her city, although the implications for Argos are almost self-evident—which lacked all *akos*, all remedy. This shrill-voiced exchange occurs in the so-called epirrhematic sequence before both parties have modulated back into iambics. Some sixty lines later (1214), Cassandra breaks out into another cry, *iôu iôu, ō ō kaka*, "Ah ah, oh misery!" and then mentions further *ponos*, further pain, that is, now, *visual* pain. "Once more the dread pain [*ponos*] of true prophecy whirls me round, / troubling me with sinister preludes. / Do you see here sitting near the house these young ones, like to the shapes we see in dreams? Children slain, as it were, by the hands of their kindred." The vision, or preview, depending upon how you are disposed, is of a genealogical image of the crimes of the House of Atreus. Further on, lamenting her own imminent fate but in words that will reappear, uncannily, for the last time in Agamemnon's mouth, upon his death-cry (1343, 1345), *epeuxomai de kairias plēgēs tuchein*, "I pray I may receive a mortal stroke," Cassandra states her final, consummate wish, *hōs . . . omma sumbalō tode*, "that I may close these eyes of mine" (1292).

Cassandra is not the only character in the play who has difficulties keeping her eyes open. In a sense, the Chorus has been struggling with a repressed vision and knowledge from the start, beginning with the repression of the sorrows of the House of Atreus, about which we learn for the first time, here at the end of the play, that "the whole city is crying them aloud [*boāi*]" (1105f.). This statement is calculated to arrive as a shock. It roundly and "loudly" contradicts the opening speech of the play, uttered by the Watchman (*phulax*), whose function, as his name implies, is to watch for the beacon-signals from Troy (*kai nun phulassō lampados to sumbolon*, 8). The Watchman's final words are famously enigmatic: "But for the rest I am silent; a great ox stands upon my tongue [*boun epi glōssēi*]; but the house itself, if it could find a voice, could tell the tale most truly; for I of my choice speak to those who know; but for those who do not know I forget." The contrast between the dark sayings of the Watchman and Cassandra's final unriddling of her prophecies is false. The ox that weighs so heavily upon the Watchman's tongue bespeaks the sacrificial beast to which Agamemnon, Cassandra, and the other victims of this extended tragedy will be likened and have been likened since Homer sang of the way in which Agamemnon was slaughtered "like an ox at his manger," *hōs boun epi phatnēi* (*Odyssey* 4.535). The Watchman does more than perform his appointed task. He resists it. Like Lynkeus in Goethe's *Faust*, "the keeper on the watchtower of the palace, singing," he is "To seeing born, / To scanning called," he is a visual emblem of the visual, or rather of the union of vision and song (here: tragic vision and song). Unlike Lynkeus, who can continue in all his blithe naivité, "To the watchtower sworn, / I relish the world," and conclude, "All . . . / was so lovely to me!" (*Es ward doch so schön*),[13] Aeschylus' Watchman resists the aesthetics of his own visual labors, which could never end soon enough: *his* prologue begins on quite a different note, "To the gods I beg deliverance from these toils" (*apallagē ponōn*), namely from the *burden* of spectacle, a labor (*ponos*) that is less divided than it is shared with Cassandra. He begins his prologue:

> From the gods I beg deliverance from these toils (*apallagē ponōn*),
> From my watch a year long, through which, sleeping
> upon the house of the Atreidae, like a dog,
> I have learned to know the assembly of the stars at night
> and those who bring winter and summer to mortals,
> the bright potentates, shining in the sky
> the stars, when they set and at their rising.
> And now I am watching for the signal of the torch
> . . . .
>
> And when I keep my couch that sends me wandering
>   by night, my couch wet with dew,
> this couch of mine that no dreams visit—
> for Fear instead of Sleep stands by it,
> so that I may not close my eyes fast in sleep—
> and when I have a mind to sing or hum
> incising this remedy of song against sleep,
> then I weep, lamenting the misfortune of this house,
> not now, as in time past, excellently kept in order.
> But now may there come a happy deliverance from toil
>   (*apallagē ponōn*),
> as the fire that brings good news shines through the darkness!
>   (vv. 1–8, 11–20)

The wished-for negation of spectacle expressed twice by the Watchman ("To the gods I beg deliverance from these toils" [*apallagē ponōn*, vv. 1, 19]), yields something of a visual paradox. Thematically, it tends to bracket and annul the content of the watchman's vision; formally, it resists the very grounds on which an interpretation of the wish can be made by the viewer: it is the equivalent of Cassandra's death-wish for narrative ("With the story, I go into death"). A further contrast: unlike Lynkeus', the Watchman's song, the song he sings to accompany his lonely vigils, is a an *antimolpon*, a song that brings tears, in place of and "against" sleep. ("Their singers will pass on none of this." [*Cassandra*, 107].) The sole purpose of the Watchman's song is to prevent him from achieving the one thing he wishes most to do: to shut his eyes, *blephara sumbalein* (15), the very same expression Cassandra uses to express the self-same wish ("that I may close these eyes of mine," *hōs . . . omma sumbalō tode*)—the wish for the death of spectacle (his and her cure, *akos*: the medical term occurs in line 17, as it did in 1169, the first-quoted speech by Cassandra). The act of spectating is demeaning (he is crouched "like a dog," *kunos dikēn* 3). Cassandra will be said by the Chorus to have a keen scent, like a dog (*kunos dikēn*, 1093).

Song is here the resistance to the visual medium and its contents: as anti-song, it is antidote to spectacle, to the painful clarity of vision, that is, to the pain of recognition; for the Watchman's vision is a discriminating, diacritical vision, a discerning and deciphering gaze (4–7). But song as anti-song is also an antidote to the pain of song. The song he sings, tautologously, is the song he is currently singing about ("*this antimolpon*"), the prologue to the play we are being forced, demeaningly, to watch this very moment (or is it, this "anti-moment"?: *antimolpon* may be Aeschylus' way of encoding this self-reflexive inversion); the coordination suggests identity: "and *when* I have a mind to sing or hum, incising this remedy of song against sleep, *then* I weep, lamenting the misfortune of this house" (18). "But now may there come a happy deliverance from toil" (*apallagē ponōn*). A fresh song, or the termination of all visual constraints (all vision)? "The misfortune of this house" is the song that is reluctant to vision as well as this very reluctant vision which it resists; it is the tragic spectacle that Aeschylus denies under the label *Agamemnon*, and Wolf under that of *Cassandra*.[14] Such is the labor of textual resistance.

V

It would be wrong to conclude this discussion without concluding in the way that Wolf does (though not Aeschylus, for reasons too complex to go into here). I will be excessively brief. For, leaving things as we have, one might conclude that, when "strategies of deterrence" have superseded all "strategies of the real" (to cite Baudrillard), when simulacra have replaced resistances, when the nuclear—that vast "delusional thinking" (226, etc.)—has become "the apotheosis of simulation" (to quote, now, Wolf), the place of the aesthetic—the congener of simulation—has become doubtful indeed. When the resistance to aesthetics is locked in a stalemate with the aesthetics of resistance, Wolf is likely to respond to this summary of things and to her own response: "false alternatives" (267). In the face of numbing alternatives no different from a progressive anaesthesia, a revitalization of the senses, a coming to one's senses, is in order and vitally imperative—an oppositional practice that is dictated, though nearly precluded, by circumstances never entirely beyond one's imagination, not to say one's control. Wolf recommends marshaling into practice a "living word," "a subversive, carefree, penetrant" word that "could help to create a posterity again, perhaps even a future. This word would no longer produce stories of heroes, or of antiheroes, either [for these are, again, 'false alternatives']. Instead, it would be inconspicuous and would seek to name the inconspicuous, the precious everyday, the concrete. Perhaps it would greet with a smile the wrath of Achilles, the conflict of Hamlet, the false alternatives of Faust" (270–271). Most important, it would be a word that does not resist its perishability or material contingency. "It would have to work its way up to its material, in every sense, 'from below,'" and be "viewed anew through a different lens" if it is to "reveal hitherto unrecognized possibilities" (271).[15] "Knowledge which has not passed through the senses can produce none but destructive truth." This is not Wolf but Wolf citing da Vinci (268). Such a sensation and such a knowledge would be a *granular*, specific sensing and knowing. No shame before lowly origins, no *pudenda origo* here. No terror before the senses, nor before their innate capacity for delusion, once one allows that the resistance to aesthetics *is* nothing other than an aesthetics of, which is to say an aesthetics constituted in, resistance.

Cassandra's voice goes out when her captors come. "They are coming" (138). "We know what is coming," is the unexpressed next thought, which we must supply from the end of Wolf's earlier work, *No Place on Earth* (119).

Her captors come, not Aeneas the hero. "I cannot love a hero," Wolf has Cassandra admit, simultaneously renouncing the epic and tragic premises of her approaching end—to which she adds, "I do not want to see you being transformed into a *statue*" (138, my emphasis). Cassandra was raped by Ajax at the temple of Apollo (or Minerva: the confusion is symptomatic). Clasped in her hands, the statue of the god-(dess) came toppling down with her in her fall (226).

The narrative resists, however, and persists beyond its death, as if borne by the momentum of a possible notion, even if only through a slight, minimal, delusive shift in perspective capable of stirring and articulating granitic matter (stony figures), and if need be, of shattering it. "Here is the place. These stone lions looked at her. They *seem* to move in the shifting light" (138, my emphasis). In words that recall even as they modify those of Marx from the passage of *The German Ideology* cited earlier, these appearances are not *given* "direct from eternity," but on the contrary, they are *hard-won* from experience, being not a copy but the complication of appearance (an apparent appearance). They derive from nothing less than a granularization—or refiguration —of a material, penetrant vision "from below," a demanding, specifying vision that resists the premises on which any possible narrative about Cassandra would have to be staked. Only so can Wolf's *Cassandra* be faithful, in the end, to the presuppositions from which it departs.

Notes

This paper was originally presented as a talk for the German Colloquium Series at the University of Michigan, Ann Arbor. I would like to express my thanks to Marilyn Fries for her invitation to speak on that occasion and for general encouragement before and after the event. The text remains substantially unchanged from the orally delivered version.

Resisting Aesthetics

1. *Cassandra*, 261. All further references to this title will be given in the body of my text. Wolf's formulation and her practice in general recall, perhaps not fortuitously, Michel Foucault's emphasis on the *discursive* nature of limits and especially his emphasis on the impossibility of their "transgression" to a "beyond" (which they also define and inhabit). See, in particular, *L'archéologie du savoir* (Paris: Gallimard, 1969).

2. Wilhelm Girnus's response to the fourth essay in *Voraussetzungen einer Erzählung* [*Conditions of a Narrative*, published as a separate volume in West Germany, but included with *Cassandra* in the English translation] was presented in *Sinn und Form* 35, no. 2 (1983): 439–447. Wolf's reply appeared in the next issue, pp. 863–866. The debate continued without any further contribution from Wolf, first with a series of responses to Girnus (*SuF* 35, no. 5 [1983]: 1087–1096), and then with a response and restatements by Girnus (35, no. 5: 1096–1105). The quality of the debate degenerates after Wolf's withdrawal (the nadir being a sentence like Girnus's: "Mit 'Wolfgestalt' kämen wir der Sache schon näher" [1099, "We might get a better angle on the matter with the notion of the 'figure of a wolf.'"]. The review by Mary Lefkowitz appeared in *The New York Times Book Review* 89, 9 September 1984: 20. I thank Marilyn Fries and Cathy Hutchison for making these materials available to me.

3. The citation is taken from Gayatri Chakravorty Spivak, *In Other Worlds: Essays in Cultural Politics* (London: Methuen, 1987), 59. The supplements are hers.

4. Compare the following concluding remark from the review by Lefkowitz: "Mrs. Wolf's Cassandra, brooding about her past in a disjunctive stream of consciousness, stirs up not such much reflection as revulsion; we are asked to react, not think."

5. With this phrase, Wolf may be alluding to Peter Weiss's three-volume novel, *Die Ästhetik des Widerstandes* (1975–1981). If so, then the futurity of the statement and its highly contingent status ("The aesthetics of *resistance* to it all has yet to be developed") would suggest a comment, perhaps, on the incompleteness of the project (or its intrinsic incompletability)—another instance of Wolf's resistance to aesthetics, here, characteristically, to an aesthetics of resistance. Weiss's novel is dealt with at length by Andreas Huyssen, in *After the Great Divide: Modernism, Mass Culture, Postmodernism* (Bloomington and Indianapolis: Indiana University Press, 1986), 115–138; and by Judith Ryan, *The Uncompleted Past: Postwar German Novels and the Third Reich* (Detroit: Wayne State University Press, 1983). For a laudable expansion of "aesthetics" into the sensory realm and a more restrictive reading of "resistance" as oppositional *écriture féminine*, see Sonja Hilzinger, "Weibliches Schreiben als eine Ästhetik des Widerstands: Über Christa Wolfs *Kassandra*-Projekt," *NR* 96, no. 1 (1985): 85–101. Without entering into this wider arena, I will simply say that Wolf's writing appears to mark a complication of feminism: hers is a feminism resistant to feminism. The focus of the present essay will be not so much on the meaning of "the aesthetics of resistance" as on the resistance to aesthetics (even to any possible aesthetics of resistance) exhibited in and by Wolf's work. The position of resistance to be examined here, rather than approximating the surface meaning of the "aesthetics of resistance," stands somewhat closer to the Nietzschean concept behind de Man's closing statement in his essay, "The Resistance to Theory": "Nothing can overcome the resistance to theory since theory is itself this resistance" (*Yale French Studies* 63 [1982]: 20).

6. Translation modified by author.

7. Translation modified by author.

8. A colleague pointed out to me how singularly indefinite the German original of this last sentence is ("Ich habe immer mehr an Bildern gehangen als an Worten, es ist wohl merkwürdig und ein Widerspruch in meinem Beruf, aber dem kann ich nicht mehr nachgehen" [K 26]): the antecedent to the final relative clause is ambiguous ("dem") and could well refer to "Widerspruch" (contradic-

393

tion), not "Beruf" (vocation)—in which case the translation should read, "but I can no longer pursue [or go into] that incompatibility." Considering that Cassandra's vocation was to contradiction, I find it difficult to decide between these two alternatives. "Dem" could also refer to the thought contained in "*es ist merkwürdig*," "*it is strange* (but I cannot go into that strangeness)."

9. Analogously, Wolf: "The character continually changes as I occupy myself with the material; the deadly seriousness, and everything heroic and tragic, is disappearing; accordingly, compassion and unilateral bias in her favor are disappearing, too. I view her more soberly, even with irony and humor. I see through her (*Durchschaue sie*)" (264).

10. I argue along these lines, but in considerably greater detail, in "Patterns of Perception in Aeschylus" (forthcoming, in *Cabinet of the Muses: Essays on Classical and Comparative Literature in Honour of Thomas G. Rosenmeyer*, ed. Mark Griffith and Donald J. Mastronarde [Scholars Press, 1990]).

11. Aeschylus, *Oresteia, Agamemnon*, tr. Hugh Lloyd-Jones (London: Duckworth, 1979).

12. *Amphi* ("about") is ambiguous; it can be spatial, as well as delimit the verb and furnish a topic.

13. Johann Wolfgang von Goethe, *Faust: A Tragedy*, trans. Walter Arndt, ed. Cyrus Hamlin (New York/London: Norton, 1976), 286–287.

14. "I can no longer view Cassandra as a tragic figure" (C 230).

15. Translation modified by editor.

Bibliography

I. Primary References

A. English translations (with original, most accessible reference, and date of first publication).

Accident/A Day's News. Trans. Heike Schwarzbauer and Rick Takvorian. New York: Farrar Straus Giroux, 1989. (Original publication: *Störfall. Nachrichten eines Tages*. Berlin: Aufbau, 1987.)

"An Afternoon in June." Trans. Eva Wulff. In *Cross-Section*, ed. Wieland Herzfelde and Günther Cwojdrak, 256–272. Leipzig: Edition Leipzig, 1970. (Anthology of the PEN Centre German Democratic Republic). (Original publication: "Juninachmittag." *Neue Texte 6. Almanach für deutsche Literatur*, 166–184. Berlin/Weimar: Aufbau, 1967.)

Cassandra. A Novel and Four Essays. Trans. Jan van Heurck. New York: Farrar Straus Giroux, 1984. (Original publications: *Kassandra. Erzählung* and *Voraussetzungen einer Erzählung: Kassandra*, Darmstadt/Neuwied: Luchterhand, 1983; *Kassandra. Vier Vorlesungen und eine Erzählung*, Berlin/Weimar: Aufbau, 1983.)

"Change of Perspective." Trans. A. Leslie Willson. *Dimension* (Special Issue 1973), 180–201. Reprinted in *German Woman Writers of the Twentieth Century*, ed. Elizabeth Rütschi Herrmann and Edna Huttenmaier Spitz, 94–100. Oxford: Pergamon Press, 1978. Also translated by Dagmar Stern. *Semiotexte: The German Issue* 4, no. 2 (1982): 18–34, and as "Changing Viewpoint" by Joan Becker. In *The Reader and the Writer*, 35–49. (Original publication: "Blickwechsel." *NdL* 5 [1970]: 34–45.)

"Culture is What You Experience—An Interview with Christa Wolf." Trans. Jeanette Clausen. *NGC*, no. 27 (Fall 1982): 89–100. (Original publication: Frauke Meyer-Gosau. "Kultur ist, was gelebt wird. Ein Interview mit Christa Wolf." *Alternative* 144/45 [1982]: 118–27. Also as "Projektsraum Romantik," in *DA*, 878–895.)

Divided Heaven. Trans. Joan Becker. Berlin/GDR: Seven Seas Books, 1965. (New York: Adler's Foreign Books, 1981). (Original publication: *Der geteilte Himmel. Erzählung*. Halle: Mitteldeutscher Verlag, 1963.)

"In Touch." Trans. Jeannette Clausen. In *German Feminism. Readings in Politics and Literature*, ed. Edith Hoshino Altbach et al., 161–169. Albany: SUNY Press, 1984. (Original publication: "Berührung." Foreword to Maxie Wander. *Guten Morgen, du Schöne*. Darmstadt: Luchterhand, 1978. Also in *NdL* 2 [1978], *LS.NS*, 209–221, and *DA*, 196–209.)

Bibliography

The Fourth Dimension: Interviews with Christa Wolf. Trans. Hilary Pilkington, intro. Karin McPherson. London: Verso, 1988. (Translated from interviews
collected in *DA*.)
Patterns of Childhood (formerly *A Model Childhood*). Trans. Ursule Molinaro
and Hedwig Rappolt. New York: Farrar Straus Giroux, 1980, 1984. (Original publication: *Kindheitsmuster.* Berlin: Aufbau, 1976.)
No Place on Earth. Trans. Jan van Heurck. New York: Farrar Straus Giroux,
1982. (Original publication: *Kein Ort. Nirgends.* Berlin: Aufbau, 1979.)
The Quest for Christa T. Trans. Christopher Middleton. New York: Farrar Straus
Giroux, 1970. (Original publication: *Nachdenken über Christa T.* Halle:
Mitteldeutscher Verlag, 1968.)
The Reader and the Writer: Essays, Sketches, Memories. Trans. Joan Becker. Ber-
lin/GDR: Seven Seas Books, 1977. (Original publication: *Lesen und Schrei-
ben. Aufsätze und Betrachtungen.* Berlin: Aufbau, 1972.)
"Self-Experiment: Appendix to a Report." Trans. Jeanette Clausen. *NGC*, no. 13
(Winter 1978): 109–131. (Original publication: "Selbstversuch. Traktat zu
einem Protokoll." *SuF* 2 [1973]: 301–323. Most accessible in *UL*, 123–168,
Darmstadt: Luchterhand, 1974; and in *GE*, 192–226, Darmstadt/Neuwied,
1974, 1980.)
"'Shall I Garnish a Metaphor with an Almond Blossom?': Büchner-Prize Acceptance Speech." Trans. Henry J. Schmidt. *NGC*, no. 23 (Spring/Summer
1981): 3–11. (Original publication: "Rosetta unter ihren vielen Namen." *SZ*
18/19 October 1980. Most accessible under "Büchner-Preis-Rede" in *LS.
NS*, 319–332, 2d enl. ed., Darmstadt/Neuwied: Luchterhand, 1981, and as
"Von Büchner sprechen. *Darmstädter Rede*," in *DA*, 611–625. Speech delivered in September 1980.)

B.   Selected list of Wolf's untranslated works (Emphasis is given here to Wolf's
fictional works, major theoretical statements, and those works referred to in the
essays of this volume. Wolf's early critical reviews, edited collections, film
scripts, and several later publications in newspapers, journals, and multiple-au-
thor volumes are not listed. See bibliographies listed at the beginning of section
II for further information on Wolf's extensive production.)

Autoren-Werkstatt. "Christa Wolf. Gespräch mit Joachim Walter." *Die Welt-
bühne* 9, 1 (1973): 51–55. Reprinted as "Unruhe und Betroffenheit," in *DA*,
751–772.
"Beispiel ohne Nutzanwendung. Beitrag zum PEN-Kongress Stockholm." *Mod-
erna Sprak* (Stockholm) 3 (1978). Reprinted in *LS.NS*, 106–112, and in *DA*,
504–510.
"Christa Wolf spricht mit Anna Seghers." *NdL* 6 (1965): 7–18. Reprinted as "Ein
Gespräch mit Anna Seghers," in *DA*, 279–292.
"Das starke Gefühl, gebraucht zu werden. Gespräch mit Christa Wolf zum Er-
scheinen ihres Buches *Kassandra*." *Wochenpost* 31, 10 February 1984: 15.
Reprinted as "Zum Erscheinen des Buches *Kassandra*," in *DA*, 929–940.
"Die Besten springen in den Riss der Zeit" (Schiller-Prize Acceptance Speech
1983). *Stuttgarter Zeitung*, 18 November 1983. Reprinted as "Rede auf
Schiller," in *DA*, 677–691.
*Die Dimension des Autors. Essays und Aufsätze, Reden und Gespräche 1959–
1985.* Berlin: Aufbau, 1986; Darmstadt/Neuwied: Luchterhand, 1987.
"Dienstag, der 27. September 1960." *NdL* 7 (1974): 11–22. Reprinted in *GE*, 24–40.
"Diskussion mit Christa Wolf." *SuF* 4 (1976): 861–888. Reprinted in *CWM*, 33–48,
and as "Erfahrungsmuster: Diskussion zu *Kindheitsmuster*," in *DA*, 806–
843.
"Documentation: Christa Wolf" (includes "Eine Diskussion über *Kindheitsmus-
ter*," "Ein Gespräch mit Christa und Gerhard Wolf," "Ein Gespräch über
Kassandra"). *GQ* 57, 1 (Winter 1984): 91–115. Revised version reprinted

Bibliography

under "Aus einer Diskussion an der Ohio State University," in *DA*, 896–911.

"Ein Brief." *Mut zur Angst. Schriftsteller für den Frieden*, ed. Ingrid Krüger. Darmstadt: Luchterhand, 1982. 153–154.

"Ein Satz. Rede nach dem Empfang des Bremer Literaturpreises 1977." *SZ*, 11/12 February 1978. Reprinted in *LS.NS*, 100–105, and in *DA*, 54–60.

Erzählungen. Berlin/Weimar: Aufbau, 1985.

"Fortgesetzter Versuch." In *Über Anna Seghers. Ein Almanach zum 75. Geburtstag*, ed. Kurt Batt. Berlin: Aufbau, 1975. 19–25. Reprinted in *LS.NS*, 151–157, and in *DA*, 339–345.

Fortgesetzter Versuch. Aufsätze Gespräche Essays. Leipzig: Reclam, 1979, 1982.

Gesammelte Erzählungen. Darmstadt/Neuwied: Luchterhand, 1974, 1980.

Hans Kaufmann: "Gespräch mit Christa Wolf." *WB* 6 (1974): 90–112. Reprinted as "Die Dimension des Autors." *LS.NS*, 68–99 and as "Subjektive Authentizität" in *DA*, 773–805.

"'Ich bin schon für eine gewisse Masslosigkeit': Christa Wolf im Gespräch mit Wilfried F. Schoeller." *SZ*, March 10/11, 1979. Revised version in *CWM*, 53–63, reprinted in *DA*, 865–877.

"Kleiner Ausflug nach H." *GE*, 151–191.

"'Komm! ins Offene, Freund!': Können wir den Frieden retten?" *SZ*, 42 (February 20/21, 1982): 100.

"Land in dem wir Leben. Die deutsche Frage in dem Roman 'Die Entscheidung' von Anna Seghers." *NdL* 9, 5 (1961): 49–65.

Lesen und Schreiben. Aufsätze und Prosastücke. Darmstadt and Neuwied: Luchterhand, 1972.

Lesen und Schreiben. Neue Sammlung. Darmstadt/Neuwied: Luchterhand, 1980; enl. ed. 1981.

"Max Frisch, beim Wiederlesen oder: Vom Schreiben in Ich-Form." *TuK* 47/48 (1975): 7–12. Reprinted in *LS.NS*, 200–208, and in *DA*, 166–174.

Moskauer Novelle. Halle: Mitteldeutscher Verlag, 1961.

"Nachwort." In Ingeborg Bachmann. *Undine geht*. Leipzig: Reclam, 1973.

"Neue Lebensansichten eines Katers." *GE*, 118–150, and *UL*, 79–121.

"Notwendiges Streitgespräch. Bemerkungen zu einem internationalen Kolloquium." Ed. Wolfgang Joho. *NdL* 3 (March 1965): 100–101. Also in *DA*, 399–408.

"Nun ja! Das nächste Leben geht aber heute an. Ein Brief über die Bettine." Afterword to Bettina von Arnim. *Die Günderode*. Leipzig: Insel, 1981, first in *SuF* 2 (1980): 342–418. Reprinted in *LS.NS*, 284–318, and in *DA*, 572–610.

"Der Schatten eines Traumes. Karoline von Günderrode—Ein Entwurf." Foreword to Karoline von Günderrode. *Der Schatten eines Traumes. Gedichte, Prosa, Briefe, Zeugnisse von Zeitgenossen*, ed. Christa Wolf. Berlin: Buchverlag Der Morgen: 1979; Darmstadt/Neuwied: Luchterhand, 1970. Reprinted in *LS.NS*, 225–283, and in *DA*, 511–571.

"Sinnwandel (zu Thomas Mann)." In *Thomas Mann—Wirkung und Gegenwart*. Frankfurt/Main: Fischer, 1975. Reprinted in *LS.NS*, 198–199, and in *DA*, 164–165.

Till Eulenspiegel. Erzählung für den Film. (with Gerhard Wolf) Berlin: Aufbau, 1972; Darmstadt: Luchterhand, 1973, 1974; Frankfurt/Main: Fischer, 1976.

"Über Sinn und Unsinn von Naivität." In *Eröffnungen. Schriftsteller über ihr Erstlingswerk*, ed. Gerhard Schneider. Berlin/Weimar: Aufbau, 1974. 164–174. Reprinted in *LS.NS*, 56–67, and in *DA*, 42–53.

"Unter den Linden." *UL*, 7–75, and *GE*, 65–117.

Unter den Linden. Drei unwahrscheinliche Geschichten. Berlin: Aufbau, 1974; Darmstadt: Luchterhand, 1974.

"Zur Information. Siehe Wilhelm Girnus: Wer baute das siebentorige Theben? Sinn und Form 2/83." *SuF* 35, 4 (1983): 863–866.

II. Secondary References

NOTE: For additional information on the wealth of material available in German on Christa Wolf, readers are referred to the bibliographies in the following books:

Arnold, Heinz Ludwig, ed. *Christa Wolf. TuK* 46. 3d. rev. and enl. ed. Munich: edition text + kritik, 1985. 113–133.

Bock, Hans Michael. "Bibliographie zu Christa Wolf." *Kritisches Lexikon zur deutschsprachigen Gegenwartsliteratur,* ed. Heinz Ludwig Arnold. Vol. 5. Munich: edition text + kritik, 1978–.

Hilzinger, Sonja. *Christa Wolf.* Sammlung Metzler, Vol. 224. Stuttgart: Metzler, 1986. 148–187.

Sauer, Klaus, ed. *Christa Wolf Materialienbuch.* Darmstadt/ Neuwied: Luchterhand, 1979. 146–170.

Stephan, Alexander. *Christa Wolf.* Munich: Beck, 1979. 163–167.

Wolf, Christa. *Divided Heaven.* Intro. and bibliography by Jack Zipes. New York: Adler, 1981. 215–228.

A. Articles and books in English on Christa Wolf

Abel, Elizabeth. "(E)Merging Identities: The Dynamics of Female Friendship in Contemporary Fiction by Women." *Signs* 6, 3 (Spring 1981): 413–435.

Buehler, G. *The Death of Socialist Realism in the Novels of Christa Wolf.* New York and Frankfurt/Main: Lang, 1984.

Caute, David. "Divided Hearts at the Wall." *The Nation,* 13 February 1967: 215–216.

Cicora, Mary. "Language, Identity, and the Woman in *Nachdenken über Christa T.*: A Post-Structuralist Approach." *GR* 57, 1 (Winter 1982): 16–22.

Clausen, Jeanette. "The Difficulty of Saying 'I' as Theme and Narrative Technique in the Works of Christa Wolf." *Amsterdamer Beiträge zur Neueren Germanistik* 10: 319–333.

Crick, Joyce. "Dichtung und Wahrheit: Aspects of Christa Wolf's *Kindheitsmuster.*" *London German Studies II.* University of London, Institute of Germanic Studies, 1983. 168–183.

Ezergailis, Inta. *Women Writers. The Divided Self: Analysis of Novels by Christa Wolf, Ingeborg Bachmann, Doris Lessing and Others.* Bonn: Bouvier, 1982.

Fehervary, Helen. "The Gender of Authorship: Heiner Müller and Christa Wolf." *STCL* 5, 1 (Fall 1980): 41–58.

Fehervary, Helen, and Sara Lennox. Intro. to "'Self-Experiment': Appendix to a Report." *NGC* 13 (1978): 109–112.

Frieden, Sandra. "'In eigener Sache': Christa Wolf's *Kindheitsmuster.*" *GQ* 54, 4 (November 1981): 473–487.

Fries, Marilyn Sibley. "Christa Wolf's Use of Image and Vision in the Narrative Structuring of Experience." In *Studies in GDR Culture and Society 2,* ed. Margy Gerber et al., 59–74. Washington, D.C.: University Press of America, 1982.

Hill, Linda. "Loyalism in Christa Wolf's *Nachdenken über Christa T.*" *Michigan Germanic Studies* 2 (1981): 249–261.

Hollis, Andrew. "Timelessness and the Game: Christa Wolf's 'Juninachmittag' and Joachim Walther's 'Wochenende im Grünen'." *NGS* 7: 145–167.

Huebener, Theodore. "Christa Wolf." In *The Literature of East Germany,* 112–115. New York: Ungar, 1970.

Jackson, Neil, and Barbara Saunders. "Christa Wolf's *Kindheitsmuster*: An East German Experiment in Political Autobiography." *GLL* 33, 4 (1980): 319–329.

Bibliography

Joyce, Steven. "The Politics of Love: Ideology and Romance in Christa Wolf's *Der geteilte Himmel. NGS* 13, 1 (Spring 1985): 31–41.

Koerner, Charlotte W. "*Divided Heaven* by Christa Wolf? A Sacrifice of Message and Meaning in Translation." *GQ* 57, 2 (Spring 1984): 213–230.

Kuhn, Anna K. *Christa Wolf's Utopian Vision: From Marxism to Feminism.* Cambridge: Cambridge University Press, 1988.

Lamse, Mary Jane. "*Kindheitsmuster* in Context: The Achievement of Christa Wolf." *University of Dayton Review* 15, 1 (Spring 1981): 49–55.

Lennox, Sara. "Christa Wolf and the Women Romantics." In *Studies in GDR Culture and Society 2,* ed. Margy Gerber et al., 31–44.

——. "Trends in Literary Theory: The Female Aesthetic and German Women's Writing." *GQ* 54, 1 (1981): 63–75.

Liddell, Peter G. "Christa Wolf, Goethe, and the Dictionary." *Proceedings of the Pacific Northwest Conference on Foreign Languages* 30, 1/2: 60–63.

Love, Myra. "Christa Wolf and Feminism: Breaking the Patriarchal Connection." *NGC,* no. 16 (Winter 1979): 31–53.

McPherson, Karin. "Christa Wolf in Edinburgh. An Interview." *GDR Monitor* 1 (Summer 1979): 1–12.

——. "Christa Wolf" (*Kindheitsmuster*). In *The Writer and Society in the GDR.* Tayport: Hutton Press, 1983.

——. "Christa Wolf—An Introduction." *The Fourth Dimension: Interviews with Christa Wolf.* Trans. Hilary Pilkington. London: Verso, 1988. vii–xxvii.

——. "In Search of the New Prose: Christa Wolf's Reflections on Writing and the Writer in the 1960s and 1970s. *NGS* 9, 1 (Spring 1981): 1–13.

Parkes, K. S. "An All-German Dilemma: Some Notes on the Presentation of the Theme of the Individual and Society in Martin Walser's *Halbzeit* and Christa Wolf's *Nachdenken über Christa T. GLL* 28 (1974–1975): 58–64.

Pickle, Linda S. "'Unreserved Subjectivity' as a Force for Social Change: Christa Wolf and Maxie Wander's *Guten Morgen, du Schöne.*" In *Studies in GDR Culture and Society 2,* ed. Margy Gerber et al., 217–230.

Robert, Louis. "Novel Form in Apulaius and Christa Wolf." *Classical and Modern Literature: A Quarterly* 3, 3 (Spring 1983): 125–138.

Romero, Christiane Zehl. "'Weibliches' Schreiben—Christa Wolf's *Kassandra.*" In *Studies in GDR Culture and Society 4,* ed. Margy Gerber et al., 15–29. Lanham, Md.: University Press of America, 1984.

Ryan, Judith. *The Uncompleted Past. Postwar German Novels and The Third Reich.* Detroit: Wayne State University Press, 1983.

Sevin, Dieter. "Christa Wolf: Georg Büchner Preis and Büchner Reception." In *Studies in GDR Culture and Society 4,* ed. Margy Gerber et al. 31–44.

——. "The Plea for Artistic Freedom in Christa Wolf's 'Lesen und Schreiben' and *Nachdenken über Christa T.*: Essay and Fiction as Mutually Supportive Genre Forms." In *Studies in GDR Culture and Society 2,* ed. Margy Gerber et al. 45–58.

Smith, R. C. Y. "Socialist Realism and Christa Wolf's *Der geteilte Himmel.*" *Bradford Occasional Papers* (University of Bradford) 1: 74–125.

Stern, Dagmar Cäcilia. "From the Mouths of GDR Babes." *Publications of the Arkansas Philological Association* 6, 2: 86–96.

Wendt-Hildebrandt, Susan. "*Kindheitsmuster*: Christa Wolf's 'Probestück.'" *Seminar* 17, 2 (May 1981): 164–176.

Zipes, Jack. "Growing Pains in the Contemporary German Novel - East and West." *Mosaic* 5, 3 (1972): 1–17.

——. "Christa Wolf: Moralist as Marxist." Introduction to *Divided Heaven.* Trans. Joan Becker. New York: Adler's Foreign Books, 1981. v–xxxvii.

B.   Review articles in English on Wolf's works

Cassandra

Booklist 80, 15 June 1984: 1432.
Bestsellers 44 (October 1984): 253.
Kirkus Reviews 52, 1 June 1984: 530.
Los Angeles Times Book Review, 29 July 1984: 1.
Library Journal, 109 (July 1984): 1328 (Anna K. Kuhn).
New York Times 133, 31 July 1984: 21.
NYTBR 89, 9 September 1984: 20 (Mary Lefkowitz).
New Republic 191, 30 July 1984: 40 (Michael Naumann).
Publishers' Weekly 225, 18 May 1984: 144.

Divided Heaven

Booklist 74, 1 September 1977: 26.
Nation 204, 13 February 1967: 215.
NYTBR 12 September 1965: 18 (Rudolf Walter Leonhardt).

Gesammelte Erzählungen

TLS 3 October 1980: 1108 (Joyce Crick).
World Literature Today 55 (Spring 1981): 310.

Kassandra

World Literature Today 57 (Autumn 1983): 629.

Kein Ort. Nirgends

TLS 3 October 1980: 1108 (Joyce Crick).
World Literature Today 53 (Autumn 1979): 671.

Kindheitsmuster

TLS 7 April 1978: 396.
World Literature Today 51 (Autumn 1977): 611.

A Model Childhood (later published as *Patterns of Childhood*)

Atlantic Monthly 246 (September 1980): 108 (P.-L. Adams).
Booklist 76 (15 June 1980): 1465.
Books of the Times 3 (September 1980): 451.
Best Sellers 40 (September 1980): 216.
Kirkus Reviews 48, 15 June 1980: 830.
Library Journal 105 (August 1980): 1664 (M. R. Yerburgh).
Listener 107, 15 April 1982: 23 (H. Maccoby).

Bibliography

London Review of Books 4 (April 1982): 15.
New Statesman 103, 16 April 1982: 20 (A. Shearer).
New Statesman 104, 17 December 1982: 40.
Nation 231, 6 December 1980: 613 (Thomas Flanagan).
NYTBR 29 July 1980 (J. Leonard).
NYTBR 85, 12 October 1980: 11.
NYTBR 12 October 1982 (Stephen Spender).
NYRB 28, 5 March 1981: 28–30 (Neal Acherson).
Observer (London) 25 April 1982: 30.
Publishers' Weekly 217, 20 June 1980: 72.
SR 7 (August 1980): 62 (Carole Cook).
Times Educational Supplement 10 June 1983: 26.
Times Literary Supplement 4 June 1982: 608 (M. McHaffie).

No Place on Earth

Kirkus Reviews 50, 15 June 1982: 700.
Library Journal 107, 1 September 1982: 1678 (Inge Judd).
Listener 110, 14 July 1983: 24.
London Review of Books 5, 21 April 1983: 22.
New Statesman 105, 25 March 1983: 26 (Angela McRobbie).
New Statesman 106, 16 December 1983: 40.
New York Times 131, 6 September 1982: 13.
NYTBR 87, 10 October 1982 (Marilyn French).
New Republic 188, 4 April 1983: 38 (Amity Shales).
Observer (London) 20 March 1983: 32.
Publishers' Weekly 221, 25 June 1982: 102.
San Fransisco Review of Books 7 (November 1982): 15.
TLS (May 1983): 498 (Margaret McHaffie).

The Quest for Christa T.

Booklist 67, 15 April 1971: 686.
Best Sellers 30, 1 February 1971: 481 (L. G. Crane).
Best Sellers 32, 1 May 1972: 71.
Book World 5, 11 April 1971: 7 (Paul West).
Christian Science Monitor 63, 4 March 1971: 7 (Sarah Begley).
Choice 8 (July 1971): 680.
Guardian Weekly 104, 5 June 1971: 17.
Kirkus Reviews 38, 15 November 1970: 1266.
Library Journal 95, 1 December 1970: 4195 (Karen Horny).
Listener 85, 3 June 1971: 719 (P. N. Furbank).
London Magazine, October/November 1971: 149 (I. Wedde).
New Leader 54, 31 May 1971: 21.
New Statesman 103, 16 April 1982: 20 (A. Shearer).
NYRB 17, 2 September 1971: 21 (John Willett).
NYTBR, 31 January 1971: 7 (Ernst Pawel).
Observer (London) 16 May 1971: 32.
Observer (London) 25 April 1982: 30.
Publishers' Weekly 198, 9 November 1970: 58.
SR 54, 8 May 1971: 31–32 (Peter Moscoso-Gongora).
TLS 24 July 1969.
TLS 13 August 1971: 961.
TLS 4 June 1982: 608 (M. McHaffie).
Virginia Quarterly Review 48 (Winter 1972): R 19.

Bibliography

The Reader and the Writer

Choice 15 (October 1978): 1058.
GQ 51 (November 1978): 578.
TLS 6 April 1973: 396.

Unter den Linden

TLS 10 October 1975: 1208 (Rex Last).

Voraussetzungen einer Erzählung: Kassandra

World Literature Today 57 (Autumn 1983): 629.

C. Works cited in this volume

Abel, Elizabeth. "(E)merging Identities: The Dynamics of Female Friendship in Contemporary Fiction by Women." *Signs* 6 (Spring 1981): 413–435.
Abraham, Nicolas, and Maria Torok. *Cryptonymie. Le verbier del'homme aux loups.* Paris: Editions Aubier Flammarion, 1976.
Adorno, Theodor. *Prismen: Kulturkritik und Gesellschaft.* Berlin and Frankfurt/Main: Suhrkamp, 1955.
Aeschylus. *Oresteia. Agamemnon.* Tr. Hugh Lloyd-Jones. London: Duckworth, 1979.
Annan, Noel. *Leslie Stephen: His Thought and Character in Relation to his Time.* London: McGibbon and Kee, 1951.
Arendt, Hannah. *Eichmann in Jerusalem. A Report on the Banality of Evil.* New York: Viking, 1963.
———. *Rahel Varnhagen: Lebensgeschichte einer deutschen Jüdin aus der Romantik.* Munich: Piper, 1959; Ullstein, 1975.
Arnold, Heinz Ludwig, ed. *Christa Wolf. Text und Kritik.* Vol. 46. Munich: Beck, 1975; 2d ed. 1979; 3d ed. 1985.
Auer, Annemarie. "Gegenerinnerung." *SuF* 29 (1977): 847–878.
Autorenkollektive. *Geschichte der deutschen Literatur.* Collectives headed by Hans Kaufmann and Silvia Schlenstedt. Vol. 9. Berlin/GDR: Volk und Wissen, 1974.
Avery, Catherine B., ed. *The New Century Classical Handbook.* New York: Appleton-Century Crofts, 1962.
Bachmann, Ingeborg. "Frankfurter Vorlesungen." *Bachmann: Eine Einführung.* Munich: Piper, 1963.
———. *Der Gute Gott von Manhattan, Die Zikaden: Zwei Hörspiele.* Munich: Deutscher Taschenbuch Verlag, 1963.
———. *The Thirtieth Year.* Trans. Michael Bullock. New York: Holmes and Meier, 1987.
———. *Werke.* Ed. Christine Koschel, Inge von Weidenbaum, and Clemens Münster. Munich: Piper, 1978.
Bakhtin, Mikhail. *Problems of Dostoevsky's Poetics.* Ed. and trans. Caryl Emerson. Minneapolis: University of Minnesota Press, 1984.
———. *The Dialogic Imagination: Four Essays by M. M. Bakhtin.* Ed. Michael Holquist, trans. Caryl Emerson and Michael Holquist. Austin: University of Texas Press, 1981.
Barthes, Roland. *Writing Degree Zero.* Preface Susan Sontag, trans. Annette Lavers and Colin Smith. 1953; rpt. New York: Hill and Wang, 1983.

Bibliography

Bathrick, David. "Literature and the Industrial World: Christa Wolf's *Divided Heaven*." A paper presented at the annual conference of the M/MLA, St. Louis, Missouri, November 1974.

Batt, Kurt, ed. *Über Anna Seghers. Almanach zum 75. Geburtstag.* Berlin/Weimar: Aufbau, 1975.

Beckelmann, Jürgen. "Der Versuch, man selbst zu sein." SZ, 26–27 July, 1969.

Beicken, Peter. "Nachfolge, nicht Nachahmung: Zur Beziehung Anna Seghers—Christa Wolf." In *Deutsche Exilliteratur. Literatur der Nachkriegszeit*, ed. Wolfgang Elfe et al., 114–132. Bern, Frankfurt/Main, Las Vegas: Lang, 1981.

Beicken, Peter, and Rolf J. Goebel. "Erzählerische Selbstverständigung. Christa Wolf zwischen Tradition und Moderne." *Monatshefte* 74, 1 (Spring 1982): 59–71.

Bengsch, Gerhard. "Die Poesie im neuen Gegenstand." *NdL* 9 (1969): 91–94.

Benjamin, Jessica. "Authority and the Family Revisited: or A World without Fathers." *NGC* 13 (Winter 1978): 35–57.

Benjamin, Walter. "The Author as Producer." In his *Reflections: Essays, Aphorisms, Autobiographical Writings*, ed. Peter Demetz, trans. Edmond Jephcott, 220–238. New York: Harcourt Brace Jovanovich, 1978.

———. "Theses on the Philosophy of History." In his *Illuminations*, ed. Hannah Arendt, trans. Harry Zohn, 253–264. New York: Schocken, 1969.

Benveniste, Emile. "Subjectivity in Language." *Problems in General Linguistics.* Trans. Mary E. Meek. Coral Gables, Fla.: University of Miami Press, 1971.

Bettelheim, Bruno. *The Uses of Enchantment: The Meaning and Importance of Fairy Tales.* New York: Knopf, 1976.

Bilke, Jörg B. "Die Wirklichkeit ist anders. Kritik und Pessimismus in drei neuen DDR-Romanen." *Der rheinische Merkur*, 10 October 1969.

Bloch, Ernst. "Nonsynchronism and the Obligation to Its Dialectics." Trans. Mark Ritter. *NGC*, no. 11 (Spring 1977): 22–38.

———. *Das Prinzip Hoffnung.* Frankfurt/Main: Suhrkamp, 1959.

Bloom, Harold. *The Anxiety of Influence.* New York: Oxford University Press, 1973.

Bovenschen, Silvia. *Die imaginierte Weiblichkeit: Exemplarische Untersuchungen zu kulturgeschichtlichen und literarischen Präsentationsformen des Weiblichen.* Frankfurt/Main: Suhrkamp, 1979.

Bradley, Brigitte. "Christa Wolfs Erzählung 'Unter den Linden': Unerwünschtes und erwünschtes 'Glück.'" *GQ* 57, 2 (Spring 1984): 231–249.

Brasch, Thomas. *Vor den Vätern sterben die Söhne.* Berlin: Rotbuch Verlag, 1977.

Brecht, Bertolt. *Life of Galileo.* In *Plays, Poetry and Prose*, ed. John Willett and Ralph Mannheim, vol. 5, part 1: *The Collected Plays*, 98. London: Eyre Methuen, 1980.

———. "To Posterity." In *German Poetry, 1910–1975*, ed. and trans. Michael Hamburger, 169–173. New York: Urizen, n.d.

———. "Writing the Truth: Five Difficulties." Trans. Richard Winston. In Brecht, *Galileo*, trans. Charles Laughton, 131–150. New York: Grove, 1966.

Brentano, Clemens. *Werke.* Ed. Friedrich Kemp. 2d ed. Vol. 2. Munich: Hanser, 1973.

Brettschneider, Werner. *Zwischen literarischer Autonomie und Staatsdienst. Die Literatur der DDR.* Berlin: Erich Schmidt, 1972; 3d ed. 1980.

Brezan, Jurij. "Weltgeschichte und Weltgeschichten." *NdL* 9 (1969): 112–115.

"Briefe zu Annemarie Auer." *SuF* 29 (1977): 1311–1322.

Brückner, Peter. *Ulrike Marie Meinhof und die deutschen Verhältnisse.* West Berlin: Verlag Klaus Wagenbach, 1976.

Büchner, Georg. *Lenz.* In his *Werke und Briefe.* Leipzig: Insel, 1952.

Cixous, Helene. "Sorties." In *New French Feminisms: An Anthology*, ed. Elaine Marks and Isabelle de Courtivron. New York: Schocken, 1981.

Bibliography

Damm, Sigrid, and Jürgen Engler. "Notate des Zwiespalts und Allegorien der Vollendung." *WB* 7 (1975): 37–69.

de Beauvoir, Simone. *The Second Sex.* Trans. and ed. H. M. Parshley. New York: Vintage, 1974.

de Bruyn, Günter. "Fragment eines Frauenporträts." In *Liebes- und andere Erklärungen: Schriftsteller über Schriftsteller,* ed. Annie Voigtländer, 410–416. 2d ed. Berlin/Weimar: Aufbau, 1974.

———. "Rita und die Freiheit. Nach Christa Wolf." In *Das Lasterkabinett. Deutsche Literatur von Auerbach bis Zweig in der Parodie.* Leipzig: Reclam, 1970.

de Lauretis, Teresa, et al., eds. *The Technological Imagination: Theories and Fictions.* Madison, Wis.: Coda Press, 1980.

de Man, Paul. "The Resistance to Theory." *Yale French Studies* 63 (1982): 3–20.

de Salvo, Louise A. *Virginia Woolf's First Voyage: a Novel in the Making.* London: Macmillan, 1980.

Deicke, Günther. "Wissen und Klarheit—Grundelemente des Talents." *NdL* 9 (1969): 129–132.

Dennis, Michael. "Women and Work in the GDR." In *The GDR under Honecker, 1971–81,* ed. Ian Wallace. *GDR Monitor,* Special Series, No. 1.

Derrida, Jacques. "Limited Inc. abc." *Glyph II.* Baltimore: Johns Hopkins University Press, 1977. 162–254.

———. *Positions.* Paris: Les Editions de Minuit, 1972. Trans. Alan Bass. Chicago: University of Chicago Press, 1981.

———. "Signature Event Context." *Glyph I.* Baltimore: Johns Hopkins University Press, 1977. 172–197.

"Documentation: Christa Wolf." *GQ* 57, 1 (Winter 1984): 91–115.

Durzak, Manfred. "Ein exemplarisches Gegenbeispiel. Die Romane von Christa Wolf." In *Der deutsche Roman der Gegenwart,* 270–293. 2d ed. Stuttgart: Kohlhammer, 1973.

Ellis, John M. *One Fairy Story Too Many: The Brothers Grimm and Their Tales.* Chicago: University of Chicago Press, 1983.

Engler, Jürgen. "Herrschaft der Analogie." *NdL* 7 (1979). Reprinted in Günther et al., eds. *Kritik 79:* 227–234.

Euripides. *The Women of Troy. The Bacchae and Other Plays.* Trans. Philip Vellacott. 1954; rpt. New York: Penguin Books, 1981.

Fehervary, Helen. "The Gender of Authorship: Heiner Müller and Christa Wolf." *STCL* 5, 1 (1980): 41–58.

———. "History and Aesthetics in Bertolt Brecht and Heiner Müller." *NGC,* no. 8 (Spring 1976): 80–109.

Foucault, Michel. *L'Archéologie du Savoir.* Paris: Gallimard, 1969.

———. "What is an Author?" In *Language, Counter-Memory, Practice,* trans. Donald F. Bouchard and Sherry Simon, ed. Donald F. Bouchard, 113–138. Ithaca: Cornell University Press, 1980.

Freud, Sigmund. "Female Sexuality." In *Standard Edition of the Complete Psychological Works of Sigmund Freud,* ed. James Strachey, 21. London: The Hogarth Press and the Institute of Psycho-Analysis, 1964.

———. *The Interpretation of Dreams.* New York: Avon, 1965.

Fürnberg, Louis. *Ein Leben für unsere Zeit,* ed. Hans Böhm. Berlin/Weimar: Aufbau. 1963.

Ganguli, Selina. "Looking for Utopia. Christa Wolf's Story *Kein Ort. Nirgends.*" *German Studies in India* 5 (1981): 94.

Gentikow, Barbara, and Kirsten Søholm. "Christa Wolfs *Kein Ort. Nirgends* und *Kassandra* oder Lebensbedingungen des Utopischen in der Literatur und ästhetischer Theorie der DDR." *Text und Kontext* 12 (1984): 387–409.

Gilbert, Sandra, and Susan Gubar. *The Madwoman in the Attic: The Woman Writer and the Nineteenth Century Literary Imagination.* New Haven: Yale University Press, 1979.

Bibliography

Girnus, Wilhelm. "Wer baute das siebentorige Theben? Kritische Bemerkungen zu Christa Wolfs Beitrag in Sinn und Form 1/83." *SuF* 35, 2/3 (1983): 439–447.

———. "Kein 'Wenn und Aber' und das poetische Licht Sapphos: Noch einmal zu Christa Wolf." *SuF* 35, 5 (1983): 1096–1105.

Goethe, Johann Wolfgang von. *Dichtung und Wahrheit*. Werke, vol. 9. Hamburg: Christian Wegner Verlag, 1955.

———. *Faust: A Tragedy*. Trans. Walter Arndt, ed. Cyrus Hamlin. New York/London: Norton, 1976.

———. *Faust I & II*. Trans. Stuart Atkins. Boston: Suhrkamp/Insel, 1984.

———. *Werke*. Edition commissioned by Grossherzogin Sopie von Sachsen (Weimar Ed.). Weimar, 1887–1919.

Graves, Peter. "Christa Wolf's *Kassandra*. The censoring of the GDR edition." *MLR* 81 (1986): 944–956.

Graves, Robert. *The Greek Myths*. Vol. 1. Harmondsworth: Penguin, 1960.

Grimm, Reinhold, and Jost Hermand, eds. *Arbeit als Thema in der deutschen Literatur vom Mittelalter bis zur Gegenwart*. Königstein/Ts.: Athenäum, 1979.

Gugisch, Peter. "Christa Wolf." In *Literatur der DDR in Einzeldarstellungen*, ed. Hans Jürgen Geerdts. Stuttgart: Kroner, 1972; Berlin/GDR: Volk und Wissen, 1976.

Gysi, Klaus. "Gültige Literatur der sozialistischen Menschengemeinschaft." *NdL* 9 (1969): 136–146.

Haas, Erika. "Der männliche Blick der Anna Seghers." In *Notizbuch 2*, ed. Friederike J. Hassauer-Roos and Peter Roos, 134–149. Berlin: Wölk und Schmid, 1980.

Haase, Horst. "Nachdenken über ein Buch." *NdL* 4 (1969): 174–185.

Habermas, Jürgen. "Eine marxistische Stellung." In *Über Ernst Bloch*. Frankfurt/Main: Suhrkamp, 1968.

———. *Legitimation Crisis*. Trans. Thomas McCarthy. Boston: Beacon Press, 1975.

Hammel, Claus. "Das Eigene und das Andere." *NdL* 9 (1969): 117–118.

Heine, Heinrich. *Französische Zustände*. In *Historisch-Kritische Gesamtausgabe der Werke*, ed. Manfred Windfuhr, vol. 12/1. Hamburg: Hoffmann und Campe, 1980.

Heller, Agnes. "Enlightenment Against Fundamentalism: The Example of Lessing." Trans. David Caldwell. *NGC*, no. 23 (Spring/Summer 1981): 13–26.

Herminghouse, Patricia. "The Rediscovery of Romanticism: Revisions and Reevaluations." In *Studies in GDR Culture and Society 2*, ed. Margy Gerber et al., 1–17. Washington, D.C.: University Press of America, 1982.

———. "Die Wiederentdeckung der Romantik: Zur Funktion der Dichterfiguren in der neueren DDR-Literatur." In *Roman in der Literaturgesellschaft*, ed. Jos Hoogeveen and Gerd Labroisse. *Amsterdamer Beiträge zur Neueren Germanistik*, 11/12, 217–248. Amsterdam: Rodopi, 1981.

Herodotus. *The Histories*. Trans. Aubrey de Selincourt; rev. with introd. A. R. Burn. 1954; rpt. New York: Penguin Books, 1981.

Das Hildebrandslied. Lachmann-edition 39, 1.

Hilzinger, Sonja. "Weibliches Schreiben als eine Ästhetik des Widerstands: Über Christa Wolfs *Kassandra*-Projekt." *NR* 96, 1 (1985): 85–101.

Hoffmann, E. T. A. *E. T. A. Hoffmanns Briefwechsel*. Collection and commentary by Hans Müller and Friedrich Schnapp. Vol. 1. Munich: Winkler, 1967–1969.

———. *Lebensansichten des Katers Murr nebst fragmentarischer Biographie des Kapellmeisters Johannes Kreisler in zufälligen Makulaturblättern*. Leipzig: Reclam, 18—.

———. *Tales of E. T. A. Hoffmann*. Trans. and ed. Leonard J. Kent and Elizabeth C. Knight. Chicago/London: University of Chicago Press, 1969.

Bibliography

Hofmannsthal, Hugo von. "Ein Brief." In *Gesammelte Werke*, ed. Bernd Schoeller. Vol. 7. Frankfurt/Main: Fischer, 1979.

Hohoff, Curt. *Heinrich von Kleist in Selbstzeugnissen und Bilddokumenten*. Hamburg: Rowohlt, 1958.

Hölsken, Hans Georg. "Zwei Romane: Christa Wolf *Der geteilte Himmel* und Hermann Kant *Die Aula*." Deutschunterricht 21, 5 (1969): 61–99.

Homer. *The Iliad*. Trans. and preface Richard Lattimore. Chicago: University of Chicago Press, 1951.

Horkheimer, Max, and Theodor Adorno. "The Concept of Enlightenment." In *Dialectic of Enlightenment*, trans. John Cumming, 3–42. New York: Herder and Herder, 1972.

Huyssen, Andreas. *After the Great Divide: Modernism, Mass Culture, Postmodernism*. Bloomington/Indianapolis: Indiana University Press, 1986.

———. "Auf den Spuren Ernst Blochs. *Nachdenken über Christa Wolf*." In *Basis* 5 (1975), ed. Reinhold Grimm and Jost Hermand, 100–116. Frankfurt/Main: Suhrkamp, 1975. Rpt. in *Wirkungsgeschichte von Christa Wolfs "Nachdenken über Christa T.,"* ed. Manfred Behn, 147–155. Königstein: Athenäum, 1978.

Jakobs, Karl-Heinz. "Wir werden ihre Schnauzen nicht vergessen." *Der Spiegel* 48 (1981): 86–108.

Jakobson, Roman. *Hölderlin, Klee, Brecht. Zur Wortkunst dreier Gedichte*. Frankfurt/Main: Suhrkamp, 1976.

Jäger, Manfred. "Auf dem langen Weg zur Wahrheit. Fragen, Antworten und neue Fragen in den Erzählungen, Aufsätzen und Reden Christa Wolfs." In *Sozialliteraten. Funktion und Selbstverständnis der Schriftsteller in der DDR*, 11–101. Düsseldorf: Bertelsmann, 1973.

———. "Die Grenzen des Sagbaren." In *CWM*, ed. Klaus Sauer, 130–145.

———. "Die Literaturkritikerin Christa Wolf." In *Christa Wolf. Text und Kritik* 46, ed. Heinz-Ludwig Arnold, 42–49. Munich: Beck and edition text + kritik, 1979.

Johnson, Uwe. *Mutmassungen über Jakob*. Frankfurt/Main: Suhrkamp, 1959.

Joho, Wolfgang. "Von den Schwierigkeiten des Schreibens." NdL 9 (1969): 85–90.

Kähler, Hermann. "Christa Wolfs Elegie." SuF 21, 1 (1969): 251–261.

Kant, Hermann. "Poetisches Programm des Sozialismus." NdL 9 (1969): 61–68.

Kaufmann, Eva, and Hans Kaufmann. *Erwartung und Angebot: Studien zum gegenwärtigen Verhältnis von Literatur und Gesellschaft in der DDR*. Berlin: Akademie-Verlag, 1976.

Klausenitzer, Peter. "Christa Wolf: Nachdenken über Christa T." *Publik* 40, 3 October 1969.

Kleist, Heinrich von. *Briefe 1793–1804. Sämtliche Werke und Briefe in sieben Bänden*, ed. Helmut Sembder. Vol. 6. Munich: Deutscher Taschenbuch Verlag, 1964.

———. *Geschichte meiner Seele, Ideenmagazin, das Lebenszeugnis der Briefe*, ed. Helmut Sembder. Sammlung Dieterich, 233. Bremen: Schünemann, 1959.

Koch, Hans. "Vor neuen Schaffensproblemen." NdL 9 (1969): 121–126.

Koerner, Charlotte. "*Divided Heaven* by Christa Wolf? A Sacrifice of Message and Meaning in Translation." GQ 57, 2 (Spring 1984): 213–230.

Kraft, Ruth. "Die Neuheit menschlicher Beziehungen." NdL 9 (1969): 106–108.

Kroll, Renate. "Das 'innerste Innere.' Christa Wolf und die Tradition des 18. Jahrhunderts. Eine phänomenologische Skizze." *Text und Kontext* 7, 1 (1979): 146–165.

Krzeminski, Adam. "Rytm Pokoleniowy." *Polityka*. 17 May 1969.

Kunert, Joachim, director. *Die Toten bleiben jung* (Film Script), 1968. Script: Christa Wolf, Joachim Kunert, Gerhard Helwig, Günter Haubold, Ree von Dahlen.

La Roche, Sophie von. *Geschichte des Fräuleins von Sternheim*. Munich: Winkler Verlag, 1976.

Bibliography

Lefkowitz, Mary. "Can't Fool Her." *NYTRB* 89, 9 September 1984: 20.

Leiris, Michel. *L'Age d'Homme*. Paris: Gallimard, 1939. English: *Manhood*. Trans. Richard Howard. New York: Grossman, 1963.

Lennox, Sara. "Christa Wolf and the Women Romantics." In *Studies in GDR Culture and Society 2*, ed. Margy Gerber et al., 31–43. Washington, D.C.: University Press of America, 1982.

———. "In the Cemetery of the Murdered Daughters: Ingeborg Bachmann's *Malina*." *STCL* 5, 1 (Fall 1980): 75–105.

———. "Trends in Literary Theory: The Female Aesthetic and German Women's Writing." *GQ* 1 (1981): 63–75.

Leonhard, Sigrun D. "Strategie der Annäherung: zur Erzähltechnik in Christa Wolfs *Kein Ort. Nirgends*." *GR* 60 (1985): 99–106.

Linsmayer, Charles. "Die wiedergefundene Fähigkeit zu trauern." *NR* 88 (1977): 472–478.

Love, Myra. "Christa Wolf and Feminism: Breaking the Patriarchal Connection." *NGC*, no. 16 (Winter 1979): 31–53.

Lukács, Georg. "Bürgerlichkeit und l'art pour l'art: Theodor Storm." In *Die Seele und die Formen*, 82–116. Darmstadt: Luchterhand, 1971.

McPherson, Karin. "In search of the new prose: Christa Wolf's Reflections on Writing and the Writer in the 1960s and 1970s." *NGS* 9, 1 (Spring 1981): 1–13.

Marder, Herbert. *Feminism and Art: A Study of Virginia Woolf*. Chicago and London: Chicago University Press, 1968.

Mayer, Hans. "Christa Wolf: Nachdenken über Christa T." *NR* 81, 1 (1970): 180–86.

———. "Der Mut zur Unaufrichtigkeit." *Der Spiegel* 11 (April 1977): 185–190.

Marcus, Steven. "Freud and Dora: Story, History, Case History." In his *Representations: Essays on Literature and Society*, 247–310. New York: Random House, 1975.

Marx, Karl, and Friedrich Engels. *Basic Works on Politics and Philosophy*. Ed. Lewis S. Feuer. Garden City, N.Y.: Doubleday, 1959.

Meyer, Herman. *The Poetics of Quotation in the European Novel*. Trans. Theodore and Yetta Ziolkowski. Princeton: Princeton University Press, 1968.

Mitscherlich, Alexander, and Margarete Mitscherlich. *The Inability to Mourn: Principles of Collective Behavior*. Trans. Beverly R. Placzek. New York: Grove Press, 1975.

Mitscherlich, Margarete. "Die Frage der Selbstdarstellung: Überlegungen zu den Autobiographien von Helene Deutsch, Margaret Mead und Christa Wolf." *NR* 91 (1980): 291–316.

Mohr, Heinrich. "Produktive Sehnsucht: Struktur, Thematik und politische Relevanz in Christa Wolfs *Nachdenken über Christa T*." In *Basis. Jahrbuch für Gegenwartsliteratur 2*, ed. R. Grimm and J. Hermand, 191–233. Frankfurt/Main: Athenäum, 1971.

Morgner, Irmtraud. "Sündhafte Beteuerung." In *Liebes- und andere Erklärungen: Schriftsteller über Schriftsteller*, ed. Annie Voigtländer, 13–16. Berlin/Weimar: Aufbau, 1974.

Müller, Heiner. "Der glücklose Engel." In his *Theater-Arbeit*. West Berlin: Rotbuch, 1975.

———. "The Walls of History." *Semiotexte* 4, 2 (1982): 38–76.

Müller, Wolfgang. Review of *Christa Wolf* by Alexander Stephan. *NGC*, no. 10 (1977): 199–201.

Mulvey, Laura. "Visual Pleasure and Narrative Cinema." In *Woman and the Cinema: A Critical Anthology*, ed. Karyn Kay and Gerald Peary. New York: E. P. Dutton, 1977.

Murdoch, Iris. *The Sovereignty of Good*. London: Routledge & Kegan Paul, 1970.

Naumann, Manfred et al., eds. *Gesellschaft - Literatur - Lesen. Literaturrezeption in theoretischer Sicht*. Berlin/Weimar: Aufbau, 1973.

Bibliography

Neubert, Werner, Sigrid Bock, Klaus Jarmatz, Eberhard Röhner, Elisabeth Simons, and Frank Wagner. "Zu Errungenes und weiter zu Gewinnendes." *NdL* 9 (1969): 148–174.

Neumann, Bernd. *Identität und Rollenzwang: zur Theorie der Autobiographie.* Frankfurt/Main: Athenäum, 1970.

Neutsch, Erik. "Literatur als schöpferische Kollektivität." *NdL* 9 (1969): 52–57.

Nieraad, Jürgen. "Subjektivität als Thema und Methode realistischer Schreibweise." *Literaturwissenschaftliches Jahrbuch,* NS 19 (1978).

Pascal, Roy. *Design and Truth in Autobiography.* Cambridge: Harvard University Press, 1960.

Plathe, Friedrich. "Erfahrungen schreibender Arbeiter." *NdL* 9 (1969): 118–121.

Plavius, Heinz. "Mutmassungsmut." *NdL* 22, 10 (1974): 154–158.

Püschel, U. "Zutrauen kein Unding, Liebe kein Phantom." *NdL* 7 (1979): 134–139.

Raddatz, Fritz J., ed. *Marxismus und Literatur: Eine Dokumentation in 3 Bänden.* Reinbek: Rowohlt, 1969.

————. "Mein Name sei Tonio K." *Der Spiegel* 23 (1969): 153–154.

————. *Traditionen und Tendenzen.* Frankfurt/Main: Suhrkamp, 1972.

Rech, Johannes. "Jugend und Literatur." *NdL* 9 (1969): 115–116.

Reich-Ranicki, Marcel. "Bankrott einer Erzählerin: Anna Seghers' Roman *Das Vertrauen.*" *Die Zeit* 11 (14 March 1969): 12.

————. "Christa Wolfs trauriger Zettelkasten." *FAZ,* 19 March 1977.

————. "Christa Wolfs unruhige Elegie." *Die Zeit* 21 (23 May 1969): 21.

Reinholz, Erich. "Sozialistische Klassenposition unserer Literatur." *NdL* 9 (1969): 80–82.

Renolder, Klemens. "Im ungeistigen Raum unserer traurigen Länder: Zu Utopie und Geschichte bei Christa Wolf und Ingeborg Bachmann." In *Der dunkle Schatten, dem ich schon seit Anfang folge: Ingeborg Bachmann—Vorschläge zu einer neuen Lektüre des Werks,* ed. Hans Höller, 185–198. Vienna: Löcker Verlag, 1982.

Reso, Martin. *"Der geteilte Himmel" und seine Kritiker.* Halle: Mitteldeutscher Verlag, 1965.

Rich, Adrienne. *Women and Honor: Some Notes on Lying.* Pittsburgh: Motherroot Publications, 1977.

Richter, Hans. "Moralität als poetische Energie." *SuF* 29 (1977): 678–681.

Romero, Christiane. "The Rediscovery of Romanticism in the GDR: A Note on Anna Seghers' Role." In *Studies in GDR Culture and Society* 2, ed. Margy Gerber et al., 19–29. Washington, D.C.: University Press of America, 1982.

————. "Vertreibung aus dem Paradies. Zur neuen Frauenliteratur aus der DDR." In *Studies in GDR Culture and Society* 3, ed. Margy Gerber et al., 71–85. Washington, D.C.: University Press of America, 1983.

Roos, Peter, and Friederike Hassauer-Roos, eds. *Anna Seghers Materialienbuch.* Darmstadt/Neuwied: Luchterhand, 1977.

Roscher, W. H. *Ausführliches Lexikon der griechischen und römischen Mythologie.* Leipzig: B. G. Teubner, 1890–1894.

Ryan, Judith. *The Uncompleted Past: Postwar German Novels and the Third Reich.* Detroit: Wayne State University Press, 1983.

Ryan, Michael. "Self-Evidence." *Diacritics* 10, 2 (Summer 1980): 2–16.

Sachs, Heinz. "Verleger sein heisst ideologisch kämpfen." *ND,* 14 May 1969.

Sander, Hans-Dietrich. "Die Gesellschaft und Sie." *Deutschland-Archiv* 2, 6 (1969): 599–603.

Sakowski, Helmut. "Die Wahrheit erkennen und gestalten." *NdL* 9 (1969): 57–61.

Salomon, Horst. "Die Kraft des künstlerischen Vorbilds." *NdL* 9 (1969): 108–110.

Sauer, Klaus, ed. *Christa Wolf Materialienbuch.* Darmstadt/Neuwied: Luchterhand, 1979.

Schick, Bernd. "Brief eines Nachgeborenen." *SuF* 30 (1978): 422–426.

Bibliography

Schlegel, Friedrich von. *Kritische Friedrich-Schlegel-Ausgabe.* Ed. Ernst Behler, Jean Jacques Anstett, and Hans Eichner. Vol. 5, *Dichtungen.* Munich: F. Schöningh, 1962.

Schlenstedt, Dieter. "Motive und Symbole in Christa Wolfs Erzählung *Der geteilte Himmel.*" *WB* 10, 1 (1964): 77–78.

Schlenstedt, Silvia, and Dieter Schlenstedt. "Elegische Provokation." *Sonntag* 32 (1979). Reprinted in *Kritik 79.* Ed. Eberhard Günther et al., 235–240.

———. "Kein Ort. Nirgends." *Sonntag,* 12 August 1979.

Schuder, Rosemarie. "Aktualität des historischen Romans." *NdL* 9 (1969): 116–117.

Schwab, Gustav. "Der Reiter und der Bodensee." In *Deutsche Balladen,* ed. Hans Fromm. Munich/Vienna, 1981.

Seghers, Anna. *Aufsätze, Ansprachen, Essays 1927–1953.* Berlin/ Weimar: Aufbau, 1980.

———. *Aufsätze, Ansprachen, Essays 1954–1979.* Berlin/Weimar: Aufbau, 1980.

———. "Christa Wolf spricht mit Anna Seghers." In *Aufsätze, Ansprachen, Essays, 1954–1979,* 410–423. (First published in *NdL* 13, 6 [1965]: 7–18.)

———. "Für Christa Wolf." *Aufsätze, Ansprachen, Essays, 1954–1979,* 393–395. (First published in *SuF* 31, 2 [March/ April 1979]: 282–283.)

———. *Glauben an Irdisches.* Ed. Christa Wolf. Leipzig: Reclam, 1969.

———. "Die Reisebegegnung." In *Sonderbare Begegnungen.* Berlin/Weimar: Aufbau, 1973.

———. *Das siebte Kreuz.* Berlin/Weimar: Aufbau, 1964.

———. *Über Kunst und Wirklichkeit.* Ed. and introd. by Sigrid Bock. Vol. 1. Berlin: Akademie-Verlag, 1970.

———. *Das wirkliche Blau.* Berlin/Weimar: Aufbau, 1967.

Selber, Martin. "Leben und literarischer Stoff." *NdL* 9 (1969): 83–85.

Selbmann, Fritz. "Parteilichkeit—das Entscheidende!" *NdL* 9 (1969): 100–105.

Spivak, Gayatri Chakravorty. *In Other Worlds: Essays in Cultural Politics.* London: Methuen, 1987.

Sprinker, Michael. "Fictions of the Self: The End of Autobiography." In *Autobiography: Essays Theoretical and Critical,* ed. James Olney, 321–342. Princeton: Princeton University Press, 1980.

Starobinski, Jean. *Words Upon Words. The Anagrams of Ferdinand de Saussure.* New Haven: Yale University Press, 1979.

Stefan, Verena. "Shedding." Excerpt trans. by Johanna Moore and Beth Weckmueller. *NGC,* no. 13 (Winter 1978): 133–152.

Stein, Gertrude. *The Autobiography of Alice B. Toklas.* New York: Harcourt Brace, 1933.

———. *Three Lives.* London: Pushkin Press, 1945.

Stephan, Alexander. *Christa Wolf.* Munich: Verlag C. H. Beck, 1979.

———. Review of *Kindheitsmuster* by Christa Wolf. *NGC,* no. 11 (1977): 178–182.

———. "Die subjektive Authentizität des Authors: Zur ästhetischen Position von Christa Wolf." In *Text und Kritik* 46, ed. Heinz-Ludwig Arnold, 7–22. 2d rev. and enl. ed., 1976; rpt. Munich: C. H. Beck and edition text + kritik, 1979.

Streller, Siegfried. "Christa Wolf: *Kein Ort. Nirgends.*" *WB* 29 (1983): 359–362.

Symons, Alphonse James Albert. *The Quest for Corvo: An Experiment in Biography.* New York: Macmillan, 1934.

Temple, Ruth Z. "Never Say 'I': *To the Lighthouse* as Vision and Confession." In *Virginia Woolf,* ed. Claire Sprague. Englewood Cliffs, N.J.: Prentice Hall, 1971.

Tetzner, Gerti, and Christa Wolf, correspondence. In *Was zählt die Wahrheit. Briefe von Schriftstellern der DDR,* 9–33. Halle: Mitteldeutscher Verlag, 1975.

Theweleit, Klaus. *Männerphatasien.* Frankfurt/Main: Verlag Roter Stern, Vol. 1, 1977; Vol. 2, 1978.

Bibliography

Totten, Monika. "Zur Aktualität der Romantik in der DDR. Christa Wolf und ihre Vorläufer(innen)." *ZfdPh* 101 (1982): 244–262.

Tripp, Edward. *The Meridian Handbook of Classical Mythology*. New York: Meridian Books, 1970.

Trommler, Frank. *Sozialistische Literatur in Deutschland*. Stuttgart: Kröner, 1976.

Viertel, Martin. "Das Schöne im neuen Menschen." *NdL* 9 (1969): 97–100.

Wagner, Rudolf G. "On Christa Wolf's *Cassandra*." Forthcoming in *Five on Five*, ed. M. Birnbaum.

Wallmann, Jürgen. "Nachdenken über Christa T." *NdH* 124 (1969): 149–155.

Walther, Joachim, ed. *"Meinetwegen Schmetterlinge." Gespräche mit Schriftstellern*. Berlin: Buchverlag Der Morgen, 1973.

Weigel, Sigrid. "Vom Sehen zur Seherin: Christa Wolfs Umdeutung des Mythos und die Spur der Bachmann-Rezeption in ihrer Literatur." *Text und Kritik* 46, ed. Heinz-Ludwig Arnold, 67–92. 3d rev. and enl. ed. Munich: C. H. Beck and edition text + kritik, 1985.

Weiss, Peter. *Die Äesthetik des Widerstands. Roman*. Frankfurt/Main: Suhrkamp, Vol. I, 1975; Vol. II, 1978; Vol. III, 1981.

Werner, Hans-Georg. "Romantische Traditionen in epischen Werken der neueren DDR-Literatur. Franz Fühmann und Christa Wolf." *Zeitschrift für Germanistik* 1 (1980): 398–416.

———. "Zum Traditionsbezug der Erzählung in Christa Wolfs *Unter den Linden*." *WB* 22, 2 (1976): 36–64.

Werth, W. "Nachricht aus einem stillen Deutschland." *Monat* 21, 253 (1969): 90–94.

———. "Für Unlösbares gibt es keine Form." *SZ*, 4 April 1979.

Wille, Klaus. "'Welch ein Trost, dass man nicht leben muss.' Zum utopischen Aspekt der Erzählung *Kein Ort. Nirgends* von Christa Wolf." *Doitsu Bungaku* 67 (1981): 32–39.

Wimsatt, W. K., and Monroe Beardsley. "The Intentional Fallacy." *Sewanee Review* 54 (1946): 468–488.

Wirsing, S. "Das Malheur zu allem Unglück," *FAZ* 71 (24 March 1979).

Witte, Bernd. "Ingeborg Bachmann." In *Neue Literatur der Frauen: Deutschsprachige Autorinnen der Gegenwart*, ed. Heinz Puknus, 33–43. Munich: Verlag C. H. Beck, 1980.

Wittgenstein, Ludwig. *Tractatus logico-philosophicus. Logisch-philosophische Abhandlung*. Frankfurt/Main: Suhrkamp, 1963.

Wolf, Gerhard. "An einem kleinen Nachmittag: Brecht liest Bachmann." In *Der dunkle Schatten, dem ich schon seit Anfang folge: Ingeborg Bachmann—Vorschläge zu einer neuen Lektüre des Werks*, ed. Hans Höller, 173–182. Vienna: Löcker, 1982.

Wood, Michael. *In Search of the Trojan War*. New York and Oxford: Facts on File Publications, 1985.

Woolf, Leonard. *An Autobiography*. Oxford: Oxford University Press, 1980. Vol. II, 1911–1969.

Woolf, Virginia. "Defoe." In *CE*. London: Methuen, 1966–1969, I.

———. *Jacob's Room*. London: Triad/Panther, 1981.

———. "Memories of a Working Women's Guild." In *The Captain's Deathbed*, 207–224. London: Hogarth, 1950.

———. *Moments of Being*. Ed. J. Schulkind. London: University of Sussex Press, 1976.

———. "Mr. Bennett and Mrs. Brown." In *The Captain's Deathbed*, 90–111.

———. "Professions for Women." In *The Death of the Moth and Other Essays*, 149–154. London: Hogarth, 1947.

———. *A Room of One's Own*. New York and London: Harcourt Brace Jovanovich, 1981.

———. "Thoughts on Peace in an Air Raid." In *The Death of the Moth*, 154–157.

———. *Three Guineas*. Harmondsworth: Penguin, 1982.

———. *To the Lighthouse*. New York and London: Harcourt Brace Jovanovich, 1981.

———. *The Waves*. New York: Harcourt Brace, 1931.

———. *A Writer's Diary*. Ed. Leonard Woolf. New York: Harcourt Brace, 1953, 1954.

Woolf, Virginia, and S. S. Koteliansky, trans. *Stavrogin's Confession*. London: Hogarth, 1922.

Zak, Eduard. "Tragische Erlebnisse in optimistischer Sicht." *Sonntag*, 19 May 1963.

Zipes, Jack. *Breaking the Magic Spell. Radical Theories of Folk and Fairy Tales*. London: Heinemann, 1979.

Index

413

The manuscript was edited by Lisa Novak Jerry. The book was designed by Don Ross. The typeface for the text is Melior. The display face is Melior. The book is printed on 50 lb Glatfelter and is bound in Joanna Arrestox B grade cloth.

Manufactured in the United States of America.